The Ordeal of the Reunion

The Littlefield History of the Civil War Era

Gary W. Gallagher and T. Michael Parrish, editors

Supported by the Littlefield Fund for Southern History,

University of Texas Libraries

This landmark sixteen-volume series, featuring books by some of today's most respected Civil War historians, surveys the conflict from the earliest rumblings of disunion through the Reconstruction era. A joint project of UNC Press and the Littlefield Fund for Southern History, University of Texas Libraries, the series offers an unparalleled comprehensive narrative of this defining era in United States history.

The Ordeal of the Reunion

A NEW HISTORY

OF RECONSTRUCTION

MARK WAHLGREN SUMMERS

THE UNIVERSITY OF NORTH CAROLINA PRESS Chapel Hill

All rights reserved. Manufactured in the United States of America.
Set in Charter and Glytus by codeMantra. The paper in this book meets
the guidelines for permanence and durability of the Committee on
Production Guidelines for Book Longevity of the Council on Library
Resources. The University of North Carolina Press has been a member
of the Green Press Initiative since 2003.

Library of Congress Cataloging-in-Publication Data
Summers, Mark W. (Mark Wahlgren), 1951–
The ordeal of the reunion : a new history of Reconstruction / by Mark Wahlgren Summers.
pages cm. — (The Littlefield history of the Civil War era)
Includes bibliographical references and index.
ISBN 978-1-4696-1757-2 (cloth : alkaline paper) — ISBN 978-1-4696-1758-9 (e-book)
1. Reconstruction (U.S. history, 1865–1877) 2. United States—Politics and
government—1865–1900. 3. Southern States—Politics and government—1865–1950. I. Title.
E668.S943 2014
973.8—dc23
2014012355

18 17 16 15 14   5 4 3 2 1

Contents

Illustrations

Acknowledgments

A book forty-six years in the making incurs debts so long that acknowledging them all would take a second volume. Librarians and curators at the Library of Congress rolled out carts of boxes in infinite array, and sometimes, on my regular reappearance at the desk, rolled their eyes as well. But nowhere, from the Historical Society of Pennsylvania to the Southern Historical Collection at Chapel Hill to the staff of the Austin Public Library, did I find a single staff member slow to provide material or advice, when asked. A number of them, particularly at the Alabama Department of Archives and History and the Illinois State Historical Society, asked as many good questions as they answered.

My colleagues, faculty and graduate, at the University of Kentucky made thoughtful comments on parts of the manuscript at brown-bag lunch seminars. I am tremendously grateful to those who agreed to read the whole thing; indeed, I have adopted every single suggestion they made. Jane Calvert asked provocative questions, and between Tracy Campbell, David Hamilton, and Paul Chamberlain, it is impossible to say which one had more of an effect on the final version. But nobody did more, line by line, word by word, and foolish error by foolish error, than my good friend Michael Fitzgerald at St. Olaf College. Doubtless he could have written a better book; in fact he *has*—at least three of them. At the University of North Carolina Press, Mary Caviness, invaluably keen of eye and tactful of admonition, made the right call in every aspect but one: I remain convinced that there is such a word as "slurge," or if not, ought to be. My family, particularly my wife, the incomparable Susan Liddle, endured sheaves of notes sprinkled around countless floors, books laid on top of stove-burners, daylong hikes in the Sierras devoted to explaining just what distinguished the "conquered provinces" from the "state suicide" theory, and occasional fits of rage at how badly Charles Sumner had been treated. Finally, my parents. Evelyn W. Summers, as always, read through the manuscript with a clear eye for the incomprehensible and was always right. May she continue to be right, on the next book and the next! Clyde W. Summers listened to my ideas and gave the very best help he had in him—as he always did with any friend, colleague, or student with whom he dealt. That listening began with the first raw ideas voiced in high school and continued for a lifetime. If this narrative of Reconstruction was built with the patient, deliberate speed and persistent devotion that he gave to the stone walls he raised from the earth, then his labors are its inspiration. I can hardly hope that it will endure so long.

Introduction

J ust after the battle at Williamsburg in Virginia in May 1862, Charles Sumner rose in the Senate to make trouble. General George McClellan, reporting victory over retreating Confederate forces, had asked the War Department's advice on whether to inscribe the triumph on the army's banners. Sumner now tendered a resolution, barring anything of the kind. A radical Republican, impatient with McClellan's conservatism and sure that blows against slavery alone could bring a triumph worth having, Sumner did not mean to do the general any favors, but spite did not explain his resolution at all. He wanted to make the point that this was no war against a foreign power; it was a struggle among a people who should have remained united and must become so again. Sumner was looking to peace and to reconstruction in its most basic sense, the reintegration of a country torn apart. Three years later, he offered an amendment that the paintings of America's national history in the Capitol include none of victories won over "our fellow-citizens."[1]

That did not make him any less the champion of universal freedom and equal rights. Sumner believed that the two went together—must go together. Until slavery and the racial prejudice that went with it were removed, no peace, no reunion, could last. But the desire for a reconciliation with white southerners, the sense that they still were and must again be fellow countrymen, was every bit as genuine and heartfelt. It was something he never forgot. Nor did his colleagues, conservative as well as radical, even if they refused to act on his resolution and the War Department gave regiments permission to place the names of battles on their flags. Nor is it something that historians should forget today.

This book makes no pretensions to being *the* history of Reconstruction, for two reasons: first, because such a thing cannot possibly exist, and second, because it already does. As to the first point, every scholar will view the time differently, and from a different perspective. The dreadfully entertaining and entertainingly dreadful story that Claude G. Bowers told

"Let Us Have Complete Restoration, While You Are About It." Thomas Nast, *Harper's Weekly*, December 18, 1872. Charles Sumner's proposal to keep the record of Civil War battles off U.S. regimental flags caused no stir in 1862. Ten years later, his effort to remove those names led to his legislature censuring him.

of a white South put to the torture has nothing in common with Jackson Lears's *Rebirth of America* except a sense of outrage based on an extremely selective use of sources and a talent to amuse. Heather Cox Richardson's integration of West and South, like that of Richard Slotkin, is as keen a recasting of the period as Richard Henry Bensel's analysis of the postwar political economy or Leon F. Litwack's epic of emancipation, but only a reader already in the know would recognize what might seem like separate islands as once parts of a single continent.[2] As to the second point, no survey in the last two generations, or, very likely, the next two, will surpass Eric Foner's *Reconstruction*. In placing the struggle for equality and a meaningful freedom at its center, in blending social with political history, in its theme of the ambiguities and transformation of free labor, and most of all in its inexhaustible mining of sources, it has created a narrative utterly compelling and convincing.[3]

Part of the reason is because in its main interest, it speaks so well to our time. Yet I am not altogether sure that it speaks quite as well to *their* time: to those coming out of a terrible conflict and seeking to reconstruct not just society but a Union, or, on the losing side, coming to terms with a new, more consolidated nation.

This book's perspective is, in essence, different from others, and that difference is defined in part by its place in a series devoted to the Civil War. Recognizing that in many respects Reconstruction was indeed a beginning, an "unfinished revolution," it chooses to lay greater stress on its other character, as an end, a postscript to the war and the age of bitter sectional conflict. "Reconstruction," as most popular accounts use the term, generally means "the Reconstruction of the South." Often, this rendering is shorthand for "The Reconstruction of Southern Society with a particular emphasis on Southern Race Relations." There is a good case for streamlining one's approach to the postwar years. So much of the Union's destiny depended on what happened to slavery, to those held in slavery, and to those who were degraded in order to make slavery work. But it seems to me that to most Americans in 1865, "the Reconstruction of the Union" was more important. That priority may offer a strong clue, indeed, to why and how black civil rights were so speedily furthered just after the war and why they were so readily abandoned in the 1870s. With some justice, antislavery advocates once gibed that Mr. Lincoln would *like* to have God on his side, but he *must* have Kentucky. Very possibly, the same could be said of those on the Union side as the fighting ended. They would have *liked* to see justice done; but they *must* have security—a settlement that would stick, assuring that there would be no new war, no new wounds. Like Sumner, a majority of them came to feel that ending slavery worked for both ends, justice and security. But what if the two goals parted company?[4]

In the end, the search for security helped justice go far beyond what most observers in 1865 expected. Freedom was just the first installment in a broadening of rights. The Constitution's basis would endow the nation with a broad authority to break the patterns that slavery and prejudice had set on American society. It may have opened the way to a second American revolution. But it is important to recognize that most white Americans had not been looking for a revolution, and a near majority of them probably would have been content with a modified restoration. If we make the mistake of defining Reconstruction's exclusive end as remaking the South on the basis of equal rights and democracy in a truer sense of the word than its inhabitants had ever known, then we can't help calling Reconstruction at best a failure—though that failure seemed less clear, unambiguous, and complete in 1877 than in retrospect. But if we see Reconstruction's purpose as making sure that the main goals of the war would be fulfilled, of a Union held together forever, of a North and South able to work together, of slavery extirpated, and sectional rivalries confined, of a permanent banishment of the fear of vaunting appeals to state sovereignty, backed by armed force, then Reconstruction looks like what in that respect it was, a lasting and unappreciated success.

Make no mistake: that success had fatal consequences for the freedpeople and their white allies down south—quite literally. This book will neither belittle nor conceal the price in blood for tens of thousands, paid because a nation weary of war and wary of advancing too near to a wholly egalitarian society would not raise the men or the means to give them protection. While it lasted, the reconstruction of the South was downright revolutionary, radical by any standard Americans had experienced. No country emancipating serfs or slaves moved so quickly to do so much for so many. But Reconstruction's primary purpose may give one more clue to why that revolution would be unfinished and why the North let the gains be rolled back. The defense of equal rights depended not on a sense of justice alone but on a sense of urgency, the need for protection for the Union. By 1875, it was plain that the Union would not be undone. However much they prided themselves on their southernness, white southerners would never go out of the Union, would never seek a new war. When the press began to speak of outrages against blacks instead of "loyalists" or "Union men," when it adopted the term "bloody shirt" to belittle the mention of outrages against Republicans, mostly black, in the South, as if it were typical partisan claptrap, it showed that Reconstruction could no longer depend on one of its most powerful driving forces.

No account can cover everything. Some things this book deals with more briefly than others have, among them emancipation and the economics of tenancy. Readers will understand why: no coverage, either in sources or sophistication, could surpass Michael Fitzgerald's survey of southern Reconstruction, or Steven Hahn's work on black solidarity and aspiration in slavery and freedom. Labor's story gets terrific coverage in David Montgomery's books and the writings of both Philip and Eric Foner. I could not better their findings; this book would become Little Sir Echo. In place of that, this account has rather more to say about the travails of balancing reconciliation and national security. It lays less emphasis on the forces of racism and class privilege, both undeniable, in undermining the North's commitment to equal rights, and more on the reasons why so many Americans had had mixed feelings about the extraordinary uses of government power in peacetime, and how far the Reconstruction process itself added to the very reasonable feeling that something had gone badly wrong somewhere. This book also makes side trips into the West and stands with those looking beyond the water's edge. Both subjects owed much to the legacy of the war—its traumas and its triumphalism; both played their part in making southern Reconstruction turn out the way it did. So did a whole range of actions that, on their face, seem to have nothing to do with the South at all: among them, the Woman's Crusade against liquor, the hope and hubris of activist government, and a gang of grafters in New York.

The Reconstruction years saw the nation transformed, and, outside of what went on in politics, Americans might even have felt they had some right to bask in the glow of self-appreciation. Reconstruction, seen in terms of the war, meant a rebuilding of relations between white and black but also of a whole society gone to wrack: buildings, farms, levees, personal lives, and underlying preconceptions and principles. It meant returning America to a peacetime footing—re-creating the many bonds that made one nation instead of two—strengthening and devising new connections, and at all hazards, making a nation made to last. In the postwar generation, the descendants of immigrants filled a vast open domain beyond the Missouri River. Their government brought real Indian wars to an end and helped railroads create a dynamic market economy. The national flag spread into the South Pacific and to the Bering Straits. Freedom became so ingrained that even the old masters swore that they would not revive slavery, even if they could—and nobody thought they could. Never had any country been so generous in restoring the rights and lands of those who, with rifle and sword, had tried to undo it. There would be no conquered provinces, no wholesale hangings, no abandonment of constitutional safeguards for the sake of the country's security. The federal system, where states had large responsibilities, weathered the war and reinvigorated itself in peace. In policy, at our best, we were, as one visitor called us, "the great transatlantic workshop."

All these accomplishments belong in the fuller story of the age. Yet readers may not find in them comfort enough; at least I hope not. Every one of them also had a part to play in undoing the South's experimental move toward greater economic and political democracy. Against all those forces, the courage and resourcefulness of those who fought to make their freedom real would not be enough to hold on to all their gains. Well before the first state was "redeemed," the tide was turning. From that point on, readers will not mistake the book's meaning if they come away hearing the

> long, withdrawing roar,
> Retreating, to the breath
> Of the night-wind, down the vast edges drear
> And naked shingles of the world.[5]

CHAPTER ONE

The Great Unfinished Task Remaining before Us

On January 31, 1865, that new birth of freedom that Abraham Lincoln had evoked in his Gettysburg Address found its fulfillment. After a long and often doubtful struggle, the Thirteenth Amendment to the Constitution, ending slavery sea to sea, came to a final vote in the House. Under the hammer-blows of war, the "peculiar institution" had been perishing for some years. Not the least came on New Year's Day, 1863, when Lincoln's Emancipation Proclamation ended slavery in Confederate-held territories. In loyal states, Union recruiters enrolled slaves as volunteers, no questions asked. Every battle in which black soldiers died—before the entrenchments at Fort Wagner and Port Hudson, under the black flag of "no quarter" that General Nathan Bedford Forrest's men bore in the taking of Fort Pillow—hardened the North's commitment to repay loyalty with freedom. One by one, what critics would describe as Mr. Lincoln's bayonet-backed state governments, from Missouri, West Virginia, and Maryland in the Border South to Tennessee, Arkansas, and Louisiana in the cotton kingdom, had amended their fundamental laws to end slavery forever. With hundreds of thousands of signatures gathered by northern women, the Senate had moved to clear away any legal doubt about whether the government could abolish slavery by a constitutional amendment. Narrowly defeated in the House the previous June, Republicans united to reconsider the resolution.[1]

Democrats represented four northerners out of ten and with white southerners included very likely a majority of American voters. United, they could deny the majority of the two-thirds vote needed, and they could make a plausible case against action at that time. They could protest that the amendment process had unspoken limits (a premise that even some Republicans admitted). Any change strengthening the central government's power at the expense of the state, or destroying the one institution that had most defined southern society, subverted the people's charter that the Founders had intended. They pronounced slavery so obviously dying that it needed no constitutional executioner. Several pointed out that no constitutional majority could pass the amendment because with twenty-two southern senators and eleven states' representatives absent, Congress had no such majority. Many voices reminded the nation that making emancipation irreversible might prolong the war and reinvigorate Confederates' will to fight. A dwindling few even tried to show that slavery was natural, right, and necessary, when two incompatible races had to live together.[2]

The president made personal solicitations. His most conservative friends, like recently dismissed Postmaster General Montgomery Blair, made pragmatic appeals. A shadowy lobby that Secretary of State William Seward assembled offered more tangible rewards. Still, the opposition's ranks nearly held. Nearly was not good enough. The resolution passed 119 to 56, thanks to ten Democratic converts and eight more conveniently absent. A "perfect snow-storm" of white handkerchiefs waved in the galleries as the final vote was announced, and the hall exploded into cheering. "Some embraced one another, others wept like children," wrote the austere congressman and lifetime abolitionist George W. Julian of Indiana. "I have felt, ever since the vote, as if I were in a new country." The Thirteenth Amendment won a speedy ratification. Within a fortnight, fifteen states had rushed it through, generally with lopsided majorities. Just three Union states held back in the end. "Liberty is the law of the land," the *Chicago Tribune* summed up. "Liberty will end what loyalty began."[3]

Those words need emphasis, taking the amendment as a culmination of rather than the first step in a journey toward full equality. Democrats, of course, saw differently. One great change, they had warned, would require others. An amendment stripping the states of their power over a defining domestic institution would breed others, a whole nest-full of cockatrice's eggs. The public must expect to have "Sambo for breakfast, Sambo for dinner, and Sambo for supper, through a course of years," one editor wrote. Republicans would fiddle with the Constitution to give southern blacks the vote or to force Chinamen, Malays, and South Sea islanders into the electorate—or far, far worse: "Immediately behind the negro . . . stands the woman," the *Cincinnati Enquirer* warned.[4]

On the opposite extreme, radical Republicans and abolitionists hoped for more than a bare freedom in law. In the amendment's second provision, giving Congress the power to pass appropriate legislation, they saw the authority to end the myriad discriminations that the law placed on free blacks, and not just in the slave South. In Julian's own Indiana, the law forbade blacks' entry into the state and barred them from juries and public schools. Outside of New England, they could nowhere vote on the same terms as whites. In fact, not counting those meeting New York's property qualification, they could not vote at all. Northern law had none of the comprehensiveness or severity of even the most lenient southern code, and abolitionists and black petitioners had helped wipe out some of the worst restrictions before the war. With emancipation, the pace of change had quickened. Thanks to the Lincoln administration, America had recognized the black nations of Haiti and Liberia and repealed the Fugitive Slave Law. For the first time, a nonwhite attorney had been admitted to practice before the Supreme Court. Thanks in part to the earnest endeavors of Senator Charles Sumner of Massachusetts, one of the earliest members of an antislavery party to come to the Senate, Lincoln had appointed as chief justice one that had arrived there earlier still. Former secretary of the Treasury Salmon P. Chase now wore the robes that once had draped the sagging shoulders of Roger Brooke Taney, the jurist who in the 1857 *Dred Scott* decision had denied that any black could become a U.S. citizen. In words that Pennsylvania's radical congressman Thaddeus Stevens said would doom him to everlasting fame "and, I fear, everlasting fire," he opined that the country's history taught that the black man had no rights that the white man was bound to respect.[5] It had never been wholly true, but even now, it remained truer than the Sumners and Julians, the fieldworkers against discrimination like the orator Wendell Phillips, the former slave Frederick Douglass, or woman's rights activist Elizabeth Cady Stanton would like. Blackface minstrel shows delighted audiences with lustful "negresses" and strutting overdressed darkies (white actors, mostly, behind the burnt-cork makeup and underneath the outlandish white gloves) and comforting songs of gay times on the old plantation. Currier and Ives lithographs of "darktown" antics or of slaves capering by their rose-decked cabin door, showed what popular assumptions the struggle for equal rights had to overcome. For all Sumner's efforts, the law still limited post office jobs to white men. Until the year before, it had paid black soldiers less than white ones.[6] Black groups and white allies already were mounting campaigns to open Washington and Philadelphia's streetcar lines to those of all races, others to remove racial restrictions from the witness box, the school laws, and, in Minnesota and Connecticut, the ballot. When Lincoln's own state wiped out its infamous "Black Laws" that winter, it made a down payment on a debt to equality long since due. "The foundations of the Republic are to be laid anew," wrote New Hampshire senator Aaron Cragin. "These foundations must be laid broad and deep in the eternal principles of truth. This done, we may look for the favor and blessings of God."[7]

Later history remembers the radical few, who spoke to what proved to be America's future; it forgets the conservative many, whose influence and power would confine how far any movement toward equal rights had any chance to go. Too easily, all their constitutional scruples, their unfulfilled fears can get distilled into a code for racism—as it often was. But the real surprise may come among those, hostile to slavery and advocating the amendment, who saw its chief purpose as related to the present, more than to the future. For them, ending slavery would remove the one great cause that had made this terrible conflict and, left alone, might make another. Abolition dealt a final blow to disunion. With its enactment, a Union triumph would usher in "a blessed and enduring peace," the *Kennebec Journal* predicted.[8]

The musket had yet to win that peace when thawing winter set General Ulysses S. Grant's armies in motion again against the Army of Northern Virginia outside Petersburg, but only the blind could fail to glimpse the end in sight. Every day the Army of the Potomac's strength grew, while Robert E. Lee's defenders in the trenches dwindled. As both sides waited, General William Tecumseh Sherman's forces carried the fight northward from Savannah, a swath of ruin across South Carolina, of lone chimneys where houses had been ("Sherman's sentinels," some called them) and rails heated, bent and twisted around trees or telegraph poles ("Sherman's hairpins"). With cities "daily tumbling like ripe apples," no Rebel force could even slow them. They took Columbia; 1,300 houses perished in a torrent of flame. Barnwell became "Burn-well." Wherever the "bummers" marched, slavery dissolved. So did every other institution in the Palmetto State. Lawlessness, anarchy, and roving bands of plunderers, some still clad in Confederate grey, spread into the low rice country along the coasts. Union enclaves along the Atlantic coast widened. Wilmington fell, the last consequential port in enemy hands. Soon Sherman's army would reach Virginia, and with it, Lee might find himself pinned between two hosts, each greater and better-fed than his own. Then, if not before, would come the end. No half-made, barely implemented plans from Richmond to enlist slaves under the Rebel flag, no negotiated settlement, could long delay the outcome. At Hampton Roads, Lincoln told emissaries from Richmond, his old congressional colleague, vice president Alexander Stephens, among them, that the United States would accept no terms but a complete submission to the laws of the United States. The Confederacy was dying hard, but dying.[9]

It died that the republic that the Founders had made might live: not simply the Union and not a new, consolidated, centralized nation unrecognizable to those white southerners who claimed to have left it four winters since. At first, this assertion sounds like a truism sucked dry of truth. So much had changed, partly because those southern lawmakers that had barred the way could no longer impede the majority will. To pay for the war, a northern-dominated Congress had raised import duties to their highest point ever. The Morrill "War Tariff" in essence would survive the next half century. A national banking system had given some coherence in place of the hodgepodge of private and state institutions from before the war. Their banknotes passed as good anywhere in the land. A flood of nationally issued paper money, greenbacks, circulated, too, unmoored from their value in gold. Not until 1879 would the United States "resume" exchanging a dollar in gold for a dollar in paper. Excise duties on distilled liquor and tobacco, a federal income tax, and countless small exactions added to the revenue that U.S. bond sales handled through Jay Cooke & Company's banking house had raised. Across the West, two railroad companies surveyed a route and began grading a line between Council Bluffs, on the Missouri River, and Sacramento. Public money and land grants paid the cost; other transcontinental lines would join them at the Treasury door. The Morrill Land-Grant College Act had applied the national domain to the founding of agricultural schools that would in time become great state universities, open to the poorest, woman or man. The Homestead Act sent an open invitation to would-be farmers of what had once been known as the Great American Desert. If they would settle on 160 acres of public land for five years, it would be theirs, for a ten dollar filing fee. Together, all these measures could have fulfilled the ideals of Jefferson's republic, with every man an independent landholder, beholden only to nature and the vagaries of season for his livelihood. But they also fostered a more industrial America, rousing itself in commercial might to match its rivals in the markets of the world.[10] Wartime necessity had brought to fulfillment those dreams cherished by Whigs since Henry Clay's time, of a government committed to make Americans better-off, not just better, and the Jacksonian Democratic commitment to the fullest of opportunity for nature's noblemen, the producing classes; and both ideals had become finely woven into the Republican Party, that evolving coalition that came out of the 1864 election with a two-thirds majority in both Houses, a president and a Supreme Court leaning its way, and most of the statehouses from Augusta to Sacramento.

For many conservatives, the "farmers' republic," the "great white republic" had passed away forever. Lincoln dragged "the bleeding Constitution of the United States behind his chariot as Achilles dragged the dead body of Hector around the walls of Troy." Democrats pointed to the "densely populated bastilles" that the secretary of state, by a mere tap on a bell, could order to furnish lodging for some unwilling critic of "Abraham Africanus I." They had seen Union mobs wreck Peace Democratic ("Copperhead") presses and strew the type in the street, the military arrests in Kentucky and Maryland, the soldiery crowding close to the polls in slave-state elections, the strident pamphleteering of the Union Leagues and other patriotic societies, defining acquiescence as the first duty of a citizen in wartime. Conspirators gathering arms for an uprising against the Republican governments of the Midwest now languished under death sentences, after a military commission had judged their guilt. How could bringing blacks into the free labor force do anything but degrade free white workingmen? How could a government doling its favors out to privileged economic interests do anything but speed democracy's evolution into a place of elites and commoners? Adapting the fears for free governments' fragility that every party had used since Sam Adams's day, they saw in Lincoln a Caesar, in the Julians and Thaddeus Stevenses the Marats of a coming reign of terror, in the freed slaves the savages that impaled white babies and raped their mothers in Santo Domingo some seventy years before. They would turn "a *bouillion* of babies" into "the fashionable breakfast dish in every household," or even convert to Mormonism. A few even prayed for a Brutus, and slightly fewer on April 15th rejoiced in secret when the news broke that John Wilkes Booth, who saw himself as exactly that, had killed Abraham Lincoln at Ford's Theatre the night before and escaped, crying, "Sic semper tyrannis"—thus be it ever with tyrants.[11]

Beyond the Confederate picket lines, the nightmares held an even stronger grip. In their anxious moments, white southerners supped full on the potential horrors of a Union reforged. Slavery would go, but not with any mere, formal freedom to follow. Nature made it impossible that two races could live together as equals. One must perish or one must dominate. The North, having taken the African American's side, would put that race on top. The gallows' shadow fell across every southern leader. Where true Unionists came into their own, mass reprisals would begin. Negro uprisings, wholesale land confiscation, military rule, the erasing of state boundaries: any and all seemed possible, as possible as the rumored French fleet, steaming to the Confederacy's rescue and raining shell down on New York and Washington. The nation would live, but any meaningful republic die. White southerners would be serfs, subjects, slaves before the proud bidding of the North.[12]

Those conjuring these grave new worlds let their dreads father the thought. The Union's defenders were battling for those things that had made the old republic worth dying for: a nation of laws, not decrees; a country in which the people chose their servants and rulers ruled always by the limits of the Constitution, a central authority supreme in national matters but confined or shut out of those that states could handle on their own; a federation of states equal in rights and privileges and the better for lacking that uniformity in law or custom that consolidated realms imposed. "A republic so vast must have joints," the Reverend Henry Ward Beecher explained; "if unjointed like a turtle's back, its weight will break it; if jointed like a lady's bracelet, it will coil around the wrist of Liberty without danger of breaking." States' rights, the great antislavery orator Wendell Phillips agreed, was "the corner-stone of individual liberty." Scholars had propounded a new idea, that in wartime, necessity allowed a more generous reading of the central government's constitutional power than in peacetime, but that was just the point: after the combatants had laid down their arms, the Constitution would revert to its normal condition. After America had been reconstructed, the states would resume their just powers. Even South Carolina, the worst offender, would stand in relation to its northern counterparts pretty much as it had stood before.[13]

That desire to return to the way things had been went to the heart of white northerners' ideal of "Reconstruction." To reconstruct meant to build again, for some to build anew, but for many others to raise an edifice, with more solid foundations, perhaps, but a distinct resemblance to the structure that had stood before the war. The place of blacks in the new order of things must change, but the essence of a republic, federal and not consolidated, must not. Finally, there was a point so obvious that later generations could overlook it. The one indisputable aim of the war had been to bring the Union together again and, the issue of slavery aside, a Union recognizably like the one left behind, based on the consent of the governed and the widest possible latitude for state power and personal freedom consistent with rule by law and a supreme national authority.[14]

Reunion would take reconciliation if it was to win over those whose allegiance had been lost. Any settlement that was going to last must come by mutual agreement, and the harsher the terms set on the Confederate states, the less prospect that the settlement would last very long. Northern

Republicans saw the South as a different society, perverted from what democratic, dynamic society ought to be by its reliance on slave labor and its commitment to a caste system, but not even they could quite see white southerners as a different people. They shared too many traits to be anything but a variant strain of American, and the language of the southern states as wayward "sisters" or southern men as "brothers" in arms never wholly died out. If those in the thick of the fight saw the fallen Confederates at Gettysburg as nothing more than dead Rebels, the reporter John Trowbridge gazed on the killing field with a more sympathetic eye. Though "altogether in the wrong, and their cause infernal," the Confederates had been "brave men; and, under different circumstances, with no better hearts than they had, they might have been lying in honored graves up yonder, instead of being buried in heaps, like dead cattle, down here." The moral for Trowbridge came naturally: "Is there not a better future for these men also?" The Union, then, was not meant to destroy the South so much as to save it, against its will. Few northerners could match Chief Justice Chase's record in opposing the so-called Slave Power. But touring the South just after the war, Chase went out of his way to stress his goodwill. Never in the history of the world had a nation suppressing rebels waged it "with so little rancor or vindictiveness," he wrote in a letter clearly meant for public view. Now the vital need was that those who had gone into rebellion feel that "the first wish of the loyal people" was to reestablish "fraternal sentiments."[15]

So while some strident voices spoke of hangings and reprisals and hard-drinking Senator Zachariah Chandler of Michigan thrilled crowds by declaring that the Rebel had only "the constitutional right to be hanged, and the eternal right to be damned," the hangman only used the rope once, on Captain Henry Wirz, and that not for treason but for his responsibility as commandant for the inhuman treatment of prisoners of war at Andersonville camp. By the time Robert E. Lee surrendered the Army of Northern Virginia on Palm Sunday, 1865, and Union soldiers kept the peace in Richmond, the song "We'll Hang Jeff Davis to a Sour Apple Tree" had become as distant a memory as Bull Run. Davis and his cabinet were in flight already, and Lincoln would have been just as happy seeing him escape the country.[16]

When, on Good Friday, Booth and his fellow conspirators slew Lincoln and nearly cut Seward's throat as he lay helpless in bed, Northerners had good reason to suspect that that top Confederates shared in the conspiracy. It fit their side's methods too well: the murder and enslavement of prisoners of war, the efforts to spread yellow fever through the North, bank

"Pardon. 'Shall I Trust These Men–'" Thomas Nast, *Harper's Weekly*, August 5, 1865. Columbia ponders those suing for amnesty, among them Generals Robert E. Lee, Richard Ewell, and John Bell Hood; Confederate vice president Alexander Stephens; and former Georgia senator Robert Toombs. A preferred symbol of the national will, Nast's Columbia was modeled on his wife.

robbery, arson in New York City hotels, and perhaps the explosion on the steamboat *Sultana* that slaughtered hundreds of soldiers returning from the war a few weeks later. Cries of vengeance flew from the pulpits. Congressmen like Julian, shocked at Lincoln's death though they were, saw it as a godsend, removing the leading voice for an overly trusting, too forbearing peace. Captured in flight that May, Davis himself was lodged in Fortress Monroe, awaiting trial for treason. For a while, fetters shackled his legs. But the passion for revenge scarcely outlasted Booth's death in a barn and the hanging of his feckless and often misled accomplices. None of the Confederate generals faced the noose or filled a cell. When Unionist authorities issued an indictment of Lee, and Andrew Johnson, Lincoln's successor, intimated that he might bring him and other officers to trial for treason, General Grant himself kept the plan from going any further. He had given his word, as one officer and gentleman to another, that Confederate soldiers would be allowed to go home safe and unhindered. In the end, only those officials suspected of some complicity in Lincoln's assassination found themselves imprisoned for long, and "long" was measured in weeks or months, not years.[17]

In most cases, a gentleman's parole sufficed. Those that, at war's end, had not lost their property suffered from the fear that the U.S. government would confiscate their estates rather than the reality of it. Most of them whose property had passed into Union hands eventually got it back; the biggest exception was General Lee's family's estate at Arlington, turned into a burial site for soldiers who died putting down the rebellion that he had helped wage. Lee himself became president of Washington College, unhindered. Even Davis won his freedom on bail two years after his capture, and northern Republicans—*Tribune* editor Horace Greeley leading the way—raised the sum. Unable to find a jury in Virginia likely to convict him of treason, unwilling to stretch the Constitution to try even the "archtraitor" outside of the venue where his crimes were rated as having taken place or by military commission in peacetime, the government abandoned any effort to prosecute.[18]

Many northerners, from the start, had believed that most white southerners had wanted no part in secession or disunion. Either they had been herded into it by a small band of wicked traitors, their power magnified by the undemocratic nature of the southern political system, or they had been grossly misled. Their love for the Union, at heart, was still there, waiting to be touched again by the better angels of their nature. Four years of war had dimmed, not destroyed that faith. The war for southern soil had ended; the war for southern hearts had yet to be won. Cruel and bloody punishments were the surest way to lose them for good. Fortunately, white southerners having learned their lesson in four hard years of war, conversion would not take all that long.

Generals could impose unconditional surrender, but the nature of the republic put constraints on just what winners could do. The Constitution had been stretched in wartime; everyone admitted it. The war powers that the federal government took on were an abnormality, brought on by the necessities of war. They provided no guideline for what in peace the Constitution was capable of, and certainly not of what it should do. Many northerners felt considerably alarmed about the way that executive decree and military law, mob violence and patriotic cant, had unbalanced the system as they had known it till now. The sooner all of that was done away with, the sooner the whole nation could recover its unique balance of liberties and separate spheres of authority. Returning to normalcy, then, must happen soon. The process must begin at once. There could be no long transition period, in which the South was held outside of normal political processes, or as Congressman Thaddeus Stevens argued, as a subject province, until a new generation, trained to appreciate republican values, could replace the old. The army to impose the federal will was dissolving day by day—a good thing. The powers that the federal government had brought to its rescue were dissolving with the war itself—a better thing. Whatever solution would be imposed must be done within the Constitution, amended in the particular of slavery but not necessarily in any other ways, and with most of the transformation of the South handled by southerners themselves. And that, whether northerners admitted it to themselves or not, meant something very different from what the term "unconditional surrender" conveyed. Any process requiring southern cooperation had to accept the reality that southerners would have some say in how far those peace terms could go.[19]

That is where the problems came in: what did the Constitution permit? And what did the North want, in a peace settlement? The two questions intertwined, for beyond the one basic requirement, the laying down of arms, the Confederate South would cooperate only as far as it was pushed. But how much authority did the national government have to do the pushing?

Between Democratic conservatism based on constitutional rigidity and Republican radicalism where everything was constitutionally permissible within the spirit of the Declaration of Independence's assertion that all men were created equal, lay a wide spectrum of opinion; within the Republican

Party alone one could find whole worlds of difference.[20] Still, if common ground could have been found among most people in the free states, it would have rested on a Reconstruction that guaranteed a lasting peace, a lasting Union, and a last reunion, where the free exchange of people and ideas would know none of the barriers that the slaveholding states had set up before the war. In practical terms, that did not mean liquidating the master class, the so-called Slave Power of planters and nabobs that characterized the plantation South, politically as well as socially. What the North needed were tokens of a change of heart and intention in the former Confederacy. Northerners and Unionists should be as free to come south to live or make a living as southerners were to open a law office in New York, as hot-blooded former Virginia congressman Roger A. Pryor did, or as did Confederate officer John Q. Fellows, who eventually became New York district attorney. For those, white and black, who stood by the flag in wartime, peace should bring no punishment for their patriotism. Indeed, the South could give no better proof of good behavior than by giving Union men the preference over Rebels as their postwar guides and leaders. The former Confederate states must reject treason forever, by admitting not just that they had lost but that their idea of a right to revolution through secession had been wrong to begin with. Traitors must not prosper: not those who led them into this war or those holding fistfuls of Confederate bonds and IOUs worthless now unless state governments made those debts good. The flag must be respected and honored again, and so must the wartime commitment to freedom for four million enslaved Americans.[21]

For radical Republicans like Julian, Sumner, and Stevens, the guarantees needed to go further. Fearful that without economic independence the freedpeople would remain at the mercy of their former masters, Stevens and Julian favored confiscating traitors' estates to parcel out in farms for black families to work. They and others had no faith that those who fought the Union would find a ready change of heart anytime soon. Till that distant day, there must be northern supervision over the former Confederate states, with sufficient armed force to see that justice was done, and if civil courts could not provide it, then military courts must. Deeply distrustful of all but the most tested and truest of Union men in the South, they wanted every potential wielder of power to go through a filtering process, the kind enshrined in the "ironclad" test oath, where an applicant for office swore that he had never given aid or comfort of any kind to the Confederate cause. Finally, they argued that neither equal rights nor the Union itself had any sure protection unless the most loyal class of all shared in power—unless

"Franchise. 'And Not This Man?'" Thomas Nast, *Harper's Weekly*, August 5, 1865. The cartoonist's point was clearly that amnesty and suffrage must go together, but note that it goes no further than to endorse giving black Union soldiers the right to vote.

southern black men had political rights as well as civil: the right to sit on a jury, the right to vote.[22]

Democrats would score Republicans as hypocrites for wanting to give blacks the vote in the South but not in their own states. "To every Southern village shall Negro suffrage come / But not to fair New England—for that's far too close to home" was a taunt that went over better among crowds unaware that in five of the six New England states blacks *did* vote, and their failure to do so in Connecticut, not to mention New York, Ohio, Pennsylvania, Wisconsin, Minnesota, and Iowa was not Republican voters' fault: they had overwhelmingly voted in its favor.[23] But Republicans also could argue that special conditions made the South a special case. In no northern state could it be claimed that democracy was materially lessened by denying the franchise to a tiny minority of the population. In Alabama, where 45 percent of adult males were black, or in Louisiana and Mississippi, where the proportion was a little more than half, or in South Carolina, where it came near 60 percent, an exclusively white suffrage was a serious affront to government by consent of the governed. No northern counties had black majorities. But counties in just about every southern state did, and there, the injustice was far more palpable. What made the injury of national concern was that southern states, unlike northern ones, owed their power to the millions they shut out of the political process. Blacks might not vote, but they counted for apportioning representatives and presidential electors. With slavery ended, they would count more than ever, not as three-fifths of a man, but as five-fifths. Finally, and for some Republicans most conclusively, loyalty could not rule when only white loyalists were entitled to go to the ballot box. Why Michigan should not be required to do what Mississippi did was perfectly simple: Michigan had not threatened the life of the nation, and nobody had any suspicion that it would do so in the future. With all their flaws, northern laws and courts gave African Americans more of a fair chance than ones run by yesterday's masters would. Nowhere north of the Ohio would black men in chains be whipped for showing grief at Lincoln's assassination, as happened in Louisville. To make freedom real, Senator Henry Wilson of Massachusetts pointed out, "we must hold the rebels in subjugation for years with the bayonet, or we must put the ballot into the hands of the colored men of the South." Which would harm republican institutions less?[24]

The prominence of black suffrage as a condition, or, for that matter, any serious discussion of how far ending slavery entailed a commitment to equal rights at all, came only in the last days of the war, because Reconstruction's conditions were changing as one of its original purposes, of restoring national authority, lost its pressing importance.

In the Border South, indeed, the reconstructing had begun as a bulwark against a disloyal minority coming into power in the first place. West Virginia, Maryland, and Missouri were largely self-reconstructed, all of them under different conditions. In Maryland, the Confederates never had a chance of bringing the state out of the Union. In Missouri, loyalists took control early and, with federal troops, managed to defeat Rebel armies but never quite suppress a partisan insurgency that ravaged the southern and western counties. West of the Blue Ridge Mountains, nonslaveholding farmers and enterprisers looked toward the Ohio rather than the Potomac. Ever restive under Richmond's control, they called a convention of their own, to disown disunion. Federal soldiers helped them clear the area of Confederates and allowed them to pose, for a time, as the real Virginia, one that never went out of the Union. In 1863, those counties plus others with heavily Confederate sympathies became the new state of West Virginia under a constitution abolishing slavery. In Maryland and Missouri, the more radical Unionists split with their conservative allies to battle for constitutional conventions that would end slavery there, too, and write into law restrictions on voting by any but the indisputably loyal.[25]

Farther south, Reconstruction required prodding from outside, and that began almost as soon as Union forces found secure footholds on Confederate soil. In each case, they held authority by decree, required loyalty oaths, and arrested those who by word or deed expressed support for the Confederacy. But all of them relied for day-to-day governing on what civilians they could find, and these exclusively among those whose loyalty to the Union entitled them to trust. And in all, the question came uppermost: how to put normal state governments into operation again? With Confederate officials fled and having by their renunciation of allegiance to the U.S. government lost their legitimacy, the mechanism for creating a new political order must come from outside, either initiated by military authority, by the president, or by Congress. Always, the administration hoped to create a nucleus around which white southerners would gather, draining away support from the rival Confederate state government. So Lincoln invited civil governments to begin in North Carolina and Florida, where state officers may have outnumbered its loyal constituents, and even recognized a conclave in an enclave as the official government of Virginia.[26]

Tennessee proved a showcase for what might be possible. Soon after federal troops entered Nashville in the winter of 1862, Lincoln appointed as military governor one of the most prominent civilians in the state and Unionist to the backbone, Senator Andrew Johnson. The new executive arrested the mayor of Nashville for talking treason, fired the city council, shut down newspapers, and imposed oaths on whole classes of people to get his way, ministers included (five of whom ended up behind bars for refusing to swear). When the first Emancipation Proclamation was issued, the slaveholding governor lobbied to make sure that Tennessee would not be covered by the final version's provisions but gave it strong support as a war measure everywhere else. "Damn the negroes!" he shouted. "I am fighting those traitorous aristocrats, their masters!" He freed his own slaves, and in early 1865 when a constitutional convention debated whether to end slavery in Tennessee, Johnson's influence threw his influence to the abolitionist side. He may even have tipped the scales against any explicit provision limiting the vote to white men only. "Settle the nigger question," he advised delegates. "Leave franchise out of the question; . . . if you want a certain class disqualified as voters, say so; but do not put it in your Constitution." When in 1864 he promised a crowd of freedpeople that he would be "their Moses," very likely he meant it. When Republicans needed a Democrat to balance Lincoln on the newly christened "National Union" ticket in 1864, Johnson seemed an inspired choice, a southern patriot who had grown to meet the temper of the time and carried his state with it.[27]

The Deep South had no Johnsons to initiate Reconstruction, and by late 1863, the administration was ready to replace its state-by-state improvisations with a template for what self-reconstruction should look like: the so-called 10 percent plan. By executive order, under his war powers, the president proposed to remake southern states by appointing a military governor who would call a constitutional convention. The process would begin after 10 percent of the white voters from 1860 had sworn loyalty hereafter to the U.S. government. With so much territory in each state beyond federal authority, Lincoln's scheme fell woefully short of majority rule. At the same time, it did make clear that the process of Reconstruction, begun and enforced by military personnel, must involve constitutional conventions, chosen at free elections and ratified by what electorate the military permitted. Congress was also brought into participation; only its recognition of these new-made states would allow their admission to representation in either house and a restoration of their full rights within the Union. Military decrees must give way to law; the states that were to be readmitted would come in with all the rights and privileges of any other state—and, except for Virginia, the same boundaries as in 1860. Those citizens who had given passive support to the Confederacy and belated converts to the Union could share in the reconstructing process. In most respects, then, Lincoln's reconstruction looked very like a restoration—under Unionist management. The one exception, though, was huge and carried with it a tremendous social and political transformation. Those new states, Lincoln made clear, must come in clear of slavery. As they covered great swaths of territory that the Emancipation Proclamation had not covered, that meant a permanent broadening of freedom's domain.[28]

In each case, the gainers from the 10 percent plan were not just slaves but yeoman whites that Republicans hoped might discover themselves liberated from the oligarchy. In June 1864, Maryland held a constitutional convention, with delegates voting for the immediate, unconditional end of slavery by nearly two to one. They also did away with a representation skewed heavily toward slaveholding counties at Baltimore's expense and apportioned delegates on the basis of the white population alone. No longer would governors be chosen by rotation, with each of the three sections of Maryland given a turn. Delegates established a new public school system. Democratic efforts to keep blacks from coming into Maryland and explicitly to deny them any share in the education fund were beaten; so was a proposal to allow them to be imprisoned for debt.[29] In Virginia, Governor Francis Pierpont also arranged for a constitutional convention to assemble. The political advantage that planters enjoyed under the 1851 constitution was diminished considerably. In place of viva voce voting, with its possibilities for intimidation of the poorer sort, Virginia adopted the paper ballot. All property now would be taxed according to its assessed value. The legislature was given authority to set up a public school system. To make sure that Union men controlled the courts, the new constitution made judgeships appointive. To allow recently arrived northerners and Unionist refugees to vote, residency requirements were trimmed. Any white male who had given up allegiance to the Confederacy by the start of 1864 could vote. Most momentously, the delegates abolished slavery.[30]

Under the guidance of General Nathaniel P. Banks, with nudges from Lincoln, Louisiana carried the process furthest. When its constitutional convention met in April 1864, in what had been newly christened "Liberty Hall" in New Orleans, it was no assemblage of radicals, Yankees, or working-class Louisianans. It was largely middle class, with a generous scattering of shopkeepers, schoolteachers, and professionals. Many had been Treasury agents or tax collectors, postmasters or sheriffs. Nearly all of them were Louisiana residents of long standing. That personnel in itself seemed revolutionary; bankers, planters, and too-long-experienced statesmen had no place here. This was a gathering committed to creating a very different Louisiana, one open to development and prepared to find its prosperity through free labor. After five days of debate, it did end slavery; the main sticking point came on giving the owners compensation. No language in the new constitution restricted the militia to whites only. Equality before the law was mandated. There would be a public school system, with facilities for blacks as well as whites and paid for out of the general tax revenues; in effect, that meant that white taxpayers would be shouldering most of the cost for African American schools. Even the new apportionment in the legislature based seating on the number of eligible voters rather than on whites only.[31]

Yet even as the "Free State" convention wound up its debates, Lincoln's Reconstruction plan ran into serious trouble. At first, nearly all Republicans welcomed it, relieved that the president's peace terms found no place for slavery continuing. But the grumbles on Capitol Hill grew over the months that followed. Radical Republicans wanted to commit the new states to more than a mere freedom: protections for essential civil rights and even, perhaps, steps to open the vote to blacks qualified to vote. Occupation commanders seemed bent on pushing freedpeople into a form of labor closer to slavery than freedom. Moderates disliked the whole concept of initiating new governments by military fiat and with so miniscule an electoral basis. With emancipation based on nothing more than presidential decree and satraps created by executive proclamation, judges upholding the supremacy of civil law could overthrow the governments they set up and abolish abolition itself. To pass constitutional muster, any Reconstruction must be rooted in law, lawmakers insisted; Congress must share in the process, and had an inalienable right to do so, under the constitutional clause guaranteeing every state a republican form of government. When senators and congressmen from the refurbished states of Arkansas and Louisiana trooped to Washington, Congress refused them admittance.[32] Instead it came up with a Reconstruction plan of its own.

The Wade-Davis bill was shaped by leading radicals, the brilliant Congressman Henry Winter Davis of Maryland and bluff Ohio senator Benjamin Wade, but Republicans in both houses gave it near-unanimous backing. The president would select a provisional governor, subject to Senate confirmation, not a military overlord. Reconstructing must wait till peace and order were secure, though slavery and unequal punishments for black and white would end at once, and federal courts would widen their scope.

The governor would direct the enrollment of all white male U.S. citizens on the voter lists. Once a majority of the electorate had sworn future loyalty, he could call a constitutional convention, but delegates to it must take the ironclad oath, affirming unbroken past devotion to the Union. The new constitutions would abolish slavery and repudiate the war debt. They would disfranchise Confederates of the higher military or civil ranks as well. Then the voters must pass on the conventions' work. Any new civil government required their consent.

Between the presidential approach and that of Congress, there were no really irreconcilable differences, except in two respects: the idea that slavery could be abolished by mere law, and the 50 percent requirement, a condition that would almost certainly delayed self-reconstruction until the war's end. In Louisiana and Arkansas, the new constitutions would have to be set aside and authorities would have to begin again—if by the remotest prospect they could scrape together an electorate, half of which would swear to future loyalty. To Republicans' general astonishment and Wade and Davis's fury, Lincoln pocket vetoed the bill, largely because he thought his plan more workable.[33]

Lincoln had won a round, but Congress would have the final say. The following winter, it found itself wrangling over admitting the Free State representatives for Louisiana. By now, radicals had come to see it as everything wrong about the president's approach. "This whole civil reorganization in Louisiana is a cheat and a swindle and everybody knows it," Treasury employee George Denison wrote to Chase. The legislature was the mere creature of martial law. The people "have not pleased to reorganize," the black-owned New Orleans Tribune insisted; "a very large portion of them is still in actual rebellion, and they hated, and despise and vilify the National Government." That left Louisiana neither a state nor a territory.[34] The vote to call a convention, some 6,000 in all, had been disturbingly small for a document made to last. The vote to ratify was not quite 9,000. Was this a fundamental law passed by the will of the people?

And who were the people? Louisiana brought into sharp focus the issue of whether any government based on an electorate limited even to half of its adult white males qualified as republican at all. The state's large black population constituted nearly half the inhabitants. In the Union-occupied parishes, it outnumbered whites, loyal and disloyal. New Orleans contained one of the largest free black communities in the lower South. Many of its members were well educated and property owners. A few were rich. A much larger number paid taxes. Cultured, cultivated, many of them lighter-skinned than the field hands in the countryside, the *gens de couleur*, as euphemism dubbed the Francophones among them, had built cultural institutions. Some of them could have passed for white, and quite a few preferred to call themselves Creoles. The free blacks had their own newspapers, their own schools, and their own experienced and articulate spokesmen. Of all the groups in New Orleans, none had a firmer loyalty to the Union. Of all African Americans in the occupied South, none seemed fitter for sharing power.[35]

Radical beyond most Louisianans' imagination until recently, the Free State constitution dismayed the *gens de couleur* in particular and free blacks in general; by 1864 they had hoped for so much more. "Freedom without equality before the law and at the ballot box is impossible," the *New Orleans Tribune* protested. Without additional pressure from General Banks, who was off refreshing his reputation for military incompetence, lawmakers tossed aside every bill that spread the franchise beyond the white community and showed no interest in any step to enforce equality before the law, much less to give even the lightest-skinned and most propertied Creoles the vote. When the state "extends to negroes the right of suffrage," a lawmaker vowed, "I shall leave it forthwith and go live in China." Protesters looked to Washington and found a warm ally in Charles Sumner, whose eloquence could carry the case beyond the Senate chamber. To him, the reconstructed government was "an oligarchy of the skin," "a mere seven month's abortion, begotten by the bayonet in criminal conjunction with the spirit of caste, and born before its time, rickety, unformed, unfinished—whose continued existence will be a burden, a reproach, and a wrong." Sumner did not have the votes to prevent Senate recognition of the Free State government, but he filibustered to death any step in that direction. By then, he and other radicals were coming to see impartial male suffrage, without any racial restriction, as a necessary condition for Reconstruction; nine months hence, they hoped, Congress itself might see things the same way.[36]

Lincoln's Reconstruction experiment did survive him. His last public address, on April 11th, showed that he had moved far himself. He was open to the possibility now that some black southerners might be allowed to vote. When he defended his southern governments, he emphasized that they were experiments that needed more time to work, and that radical critics had not yet made a good enough case for him to change his mind. The president had Louisiana in mind particularly.[37] From a broader perspective, though, Lincoln's Reconstruction, and that of Unionists elsewhere, were in very deep trouble. In North Carolina and Florida, they had petered out long since. Elsewhere, they were about to meet their most challenging test, and almost certainly doomed to fail. For the governments erected were premised on the belief that a substantial body of the population was either Unionist or ready to be so. If that premise was wrong, then those new governments must violate the first essential rule on which any lasting Reconstruction must be based, governments of and by the people.

Unionism certainly did exist. Even in Confederate Mississippi, true believers provided men for the Union army, though most such recruits came from the upper South. Some 42,000 white Tennesseans donned the blue, with Virginia and West Virginia enlisting 30,000, Arkansas 10,000, North Carolina 5,000. Alabama did better than most of the cotton South, with 2,500 white volunteers—about the same number as those from Georgia, Florida, and Mississippi combined. All the same, crucial as many of those soldiers would be in the formation of a white Republican Party later, those figures did not amount to much. In Virginia, 80 to 90 percent of all eligible white males served in the Confederate army, and while it was true that 12,000 deserted, two-thirds of them would reenter the ranks. Even in Unionist areas, there had been outright Confederate service. In eastern Tennessee, whites volunteered; among their officers, about the same majority owned no slaves as was the case with Tennessee Unionists. Young men who came of age there in the 1850s more readily embraced the slaveholders' revolution than did their elders. Their attachment to the Union was less for having been raised in a time of fierce sectionalism. They were likelier to be Democrats, even in Andrew Johnson's eastern Tennessee.[38]

Unionist sentiment, much of it at least, perished with secession and war. Local loyalties and allegiance to the states in which southerners lived were genuine and often ran deep. So did family ties, and once members rallied to the Bonnie Blue Flag, their kin found it hard not to give them support.[39] Prejudices against northerners went further than Confederate sympathies did, and did not take actual injuries to be incited. One Virginia woman hated the profiteering prices she had to pay all the more because it only proved how far Yankee notions had infected southerners. But anyone wanting to count up injuries found them in plenty. The loss of life at northern hands, the ravaging of the landscape, were powerful forces in rousing anti-northern feelings and strengthening them. A war of soldiers against soldiers was one thing, but especially in the upper South, it had been a war on civilians, too, even without the more thorough methods that General Sherman would eventually adopt. Fences, cattle, chickens all vanished as the armies passed. So did slaves, and owners blamed Yankees for having "stolen" the one piece of their property hardest to replace. Stories spread of women violated (occasionally) and insulted or their personal space invaded (commonly). Virginians could bear witness to the way the enemy shelled churches or bombarded towns. "No victory of the war has ever done me so much good," a soldier wrote in December 1862. "I hate them worse than ever in the first place, and then their destruction of poor old Fredericksburg! It seems to me that I don't do anything from morning to night but hate them worse & worse." So at the war's end, many Confederates accepted surrender because they felt worn down, rather than because they had decided that the government they had made was unworthy of their allegiance. "I wept four years ago when I saw the old flag hauled down," a Richmond Unionist told a journalist, "and I tell you the truth, I wept a great deal harder the other day when I saw it go up again."[40] Often Union occupation did just the opposite of what the North expected. Far from galvanizing latent, silent, Union sentiment, it gave the inhabitants reasons to resent federal authority and took away their sense of grievance against the Confederate administration.

Wherever national authority prevailed, the government's commitment to emancipation put intolerable strains on the Unionist coalition. Maryland's ratification of the constitution had been closer than proponents had expected and without the soldier vote would have failed outright. Thousands of Unionists stayed home; Baltimore, where a projected 10,000 majority was expected, fell 3,000 short of it, and in the fourteen slaveholding counties, the constitution lost by four to one (poorer whites, the New York Tribune alleging, showing their "serfdom" under the slaveholders rather than their "untrammeled convictions"). Turnout there climbed more steeply than anywhere else, a grim omen of what would happen when more than 10,000 Confederate soldiers trooped home at the war's end to resume their political duties. The slavery issue also shattered what Unionist support Tennessee had. When the 1864 elections came, proslavery Unionists stayed home, assuring a very small turnout. Those who had turned against the Lincoln administration called their own convention, hoping to separate eastern Tennessee from the rest of the state. They endorsed General McClellan's presidential candidacy.[41]

In the border states, as a result, a lasting Unionist success only came by making sure that there would be fewer, if better, voters—35,000 to 50,000 fewer in Missouri alone. There were good reasons, beyond political ones, for disfranchisements; courts, sheriffs, and juries stacked with Rebels quickly gave plenty of examples of how the law could be used to persecute and impoverish loyalists, given the chance. Maryland's constitution required every voter to swear to past loyalty; so must lawyers and schoolteachers. Any aid or support to men in arms against the Union would deprive a freeman of his right to vote. Liberal in many ways, its new constitution went before an electorate culled by proscriptive loyalty oaths, supervised by federal troops at the polls, and supplemented by returns from army camps, where voting Democratic was a particularly daunting experience—assuming that the commanders passed along those returns at all. One northern newspaper thought that, handled correctly, the restrictions should have barred two-thirds of the white males in several counties from the polls and shut out half of those in five more. "The Rebels have a large and well-oiled swallow for oaths, but this one rather choked them," the *Tribune* commented. On October 12th, Marylanders went to the polls and narrowly ratified the new constitution. (One vote against it went uncast: Chief Justice Roger Brooke Taney, Maryland's most powerful defender of slavery, died on Election Day.)[42]

To break up the power of local enemies, West Virginia's legislature shifted county seats from pro-Confederate towns and put them in secure areas. They moved cases from the courts in less certain Unionist counties to reliable ones farther north and west. The Wheeling conventions had put through an ordinance to arrest and banish "suspicious persons"—which meant sympathizers with secession and came very close to covering any opponent of the conventions themselves. Delegates had seen to it that every southern sympathizer could be removed from state and local office and all aspirants of that sentiment be disqualified in future. Captious editors found their newspapers suppressed or cooled their ardor in jail. In war, Brigadier General Robert Milroy explained, "no newspaper or party should be tolerated which disseminates error and cultivates hostility to the government."[43] In such a climate, the overwhelming majorities that radical Unionists amassed at the polls gave an illusory sense of the public will.

Conditions in the Confederate South were even more fraught. By border state standards, Virginia's franchise was liberal, but it still shut out the vast majority of people in the state, most of whom would have voted down the constitution, given a chance. The constitution was not submitted for ratification. It was simply announced as in force.[44] One might see how weak Louisiana, Arkansas, Tennessee, and Virginia were, not simply by counting their supporters, but by measuring what a tiny fraction of the white electorate they made for sending representatives to the legislature or for ratifying their new constitutions, and what an immense proportion of counties had no polls opened at all. In terms of enforceable authority, the "restored State" of Virginia was more like an archipelago. Its writ ran only in specks and spots of territory held by the Union along the coastline and riverbanks, Norfolk included. Beyond New Orleans's limits, Louisiana's Free State authority all but vanished. Which Lincoln government could have survived a week, even within its confines, without federal military backing and full administration support? Which of them so much as tried? And how long could any of them last when that outside backing fell away? No Lincoln governments could be described as really republican, or able to pass muster once the war was over. All were, in that respect, halfway houses toward real restoration—and all open to challenge on any legal basis.[45]

The controversy over emancipation assured that any self-reconstruction above the cotton South would be impermanent and politically vulnerable. But doing *nothing*, the Reconstruction governments were also at risk of their coalition fracturing; every month, the emergency measures on which those governments had been founded lost supporters, convinced that the emergency had passed and that measures that could be justified only in those terms were no longer justifiable. Week by week, hour by hour, the coalitions that put the unconditional Unionists into power grew smaller, weaker, and more isolated. Every step toward freedom drove away allies; every step toward civil rights beyond freedom cost even more. For governments so much based on minority power already, this was sure to shrink a base already far too narrow, and, to keep them in power, compel further disfranchisements. Every step toward equality led away from political democracy and created more of a rump state than before.

This is clearly not what Lincoln had hoped. He had had visions of governments that would gather strength and support as they continued—the untainted tenth, as it were, in the 10 percent plan, augmented at every election. But the opposite seemed to be occurring. The problems with the president's wartime expedient had already surfaced before his death—problems that he did not yet consider fatal. No government could survive much longer without the support, at least the acquiescence of its wartime enemies, the former Confederates, the conservatives with property and authority, the true representatives of much, if not most of, the white population. And if they were to be won over, Lincoln's Reconstruction must veer in a more conservative direction than it had done and accept much that most northern Republicans would find unacceptable.

But could the former Confederates be won over on any terms? That assumed at least a certain amount of acquiescence in the new order, a readiness to accept the federally constructed governments as a legitimate basis for making a new political beginning, or even that the United States had had any right to wage war at all. None of these assumptions held true.

Confederates readily allowed that they had been beaten on the field. That secession was not a legitimate constitutional right, they were not so quick to allow. Ready to return to allegiance to a fundamental law as they had always interpreted it, they still thought the Constitution a compact made not by the whole people but by sovereign states. As sovereign states they left the Union and so they meant to come back, as if the choice lay with them. After Lee and General Joseph Johnston surrendered their forces in April, governors in the Deep South called legislatures back to the capital for special sessions. Emissaries from Alabama came to Washington to beg the president to allow the old legislature to reassemble to take steps returning the state to the Union. In Georgia, Joseph E. Brown did so, but eleven days before the body could meet, he was put under military arrest. The session was canceled. Mississippi's legislature did meet on May 18th, though only on the understanding with the military that it acted as "a committee of safety," and without legislative authority. Its sessions had barely begun before the army closed it down and arrested the governor. Other Confederate governors were under arrest by that time, all except Henry Watkins Allen of Louisiana, who had fled to Mexico. The point could not be missed: the national government would not recognize any state government existing under the Confederacy as having any legal power to initiate the process.[46]

Whatever Confederate forces had surrendered, the Confederate mind had given up nothing. Force would make it drop certain doctrines like the right of secession and state sovereignty but not to admit itself in the wrong. Yankee decrees could wipe out slavery but not Nature's law giving whites the right and duty to rule every other race. Those protesting that they would "comply with every reasonable demand that the Government might make" defined just what would be "reasonable."[47] A Cincinnati reporter stopped overnight in southern Alabama with a returned Confederate private. His only fortune was a large family of children and two hound dogs, his hospitality no more than a hoecake. He alone in the household had seen an American flag or a northern newspaper, which, perhaps, nobody in the household could have read. Yet this man, never a slaveholder, swore that the peculiar institution was divinely inspired. Utterly defeated, he invoked what he termed "our rights."[48]

So no sooner did they regain power than former Confederates allied themselves with Republicans' conservative critics and worked to wrest the states from them. They aimed at as close to a restoration of the old political order as they could manage. In Kentucky and Delaware, unconditional Unionists were crushed at the polls even before the war ended. In Arkansas, Governor Isaac Murphy did all he could to propitiate returning Confederates, and only found himself isolated, because the new electorate did not accept any of the wartime Reconstruction experiments as legitimate, his own included.[49]

In Virginia, the dissolving of the Confederate state government spread wartime governor Francis Pierpont's authority across the Blue Ridge Mountains. Naturally, the Alexandria legislature could not pretend to administer so wide a domain on its own. In early May, an executive order transferred state authority to Richmond. Two weeks later, local elections were held in all the counties unrepresented in the old government. The results dismayed Union men. Confederate sympathizers turned out in force. When the old "restored" legislature met in June, it started dismantling the disfranchisement provisions in the 1864 constitution, amending them to let in the multitudes that had stood with the Confederacy till the war's end. Any white man could cast a ballot who declared himself willing to take the oath of future loyalty mandated in the president's amnesty proclamation, including the larger property holders that the presidential amnesty did not cover. The officeholding bans were kept in place, but voters were allowed to empower the next legislature to remove them.[50] That October, the enlarged electorate did just that and elected a new legislature, even further from Unionist orthodoxy than before.

Conservatives had given the governor their personal assurances that those who had done the most to take the Old Dominion out of the Union would not be allowed to direct its courses now. Hundreds of onetime Rebels needed presidential pardons, and a friendly word from Pierpont could make clemency certain. In return, he would find the newly loyal as cooperative as he could wish.[51] Pierpont backed applicants generously. He consulted with former Confederates and appointed men of questionable loyalty to county offices. There simply were not enough true Union men to form a government, he explained to one journalist. "In many counties you will not find one." He called for removal of the constitution's disabling clause.

By December, the governor was finding how hollow the promises really were. Old Whigs, not secessionists, filled the general assembly, but they were the antithesis of radicalism, and unsympathetic to any transformation of the Old Dominion along newer, more Yankee lines. On the second day of the session, they repealed the 1862 act consenting to West Virginia's creation. A later act handing West Virginia two other counties was repealed as well. The Board of Works was cleared out, and less unconditionally Unionist officers filled the vacancies. The school system went unbuilt, unfunded. By resolution, the legislature asked the president to release Jefferson Davis; by constitutional amendment, it proposed to remove the loyalty oath from officeholding requirements. A Black Code with a wide-ranging vagrancy law passed soon after. By winter, it was clear that in local and legislative affairs, Confederate sympathizers were back in charge. Grand juries were stocked with citizens unable to take any oath and loath to indict ex-Rebels accused of killing or assaulting Union men. The commonwealth attorney in one county had served in the Confederate army and denounced all supporters of Reconstruction as the true disloyalists. "Secession was never so intolerant, so ripe, so rampant, as it is here at this time," a Virginian complained.[52]

In Maryland, the story played out even worse, with the governor himself going over to the other side. There, Unionists felt their support crumbling even before they carried a new constitution. Basing their action on the premise that Rebels had forfeited the right to vote and perhaps the assumption of the *Tribune* that at least half of those who had sworn loyalty and voted against the new constitution were "Rebels at heart," and aware that loyalty oaths might no longer be enough, Unionist lawmakers pushed through a registration law that gave officials the power to pick and choose a loyal electorate as they liked. That meant Confederates everywhere, conservative Unionists in some places, and prewar Democrats of any stripe in others. In one election district in Anne Arundel County, only ninety out of more than three hundred applicants were permitted to register.[53] Those laws only strengthened as the prospect grew that many former Confederate Marylanders would be coming home and assembling a majority that Henry Winter Davis's forces might not be able to match.

Elected in 1864, Thomas Swann soon realized that his political survival depended on his adapting to changing conditions. By the time he took office in December of the following year, the Thirteenth Amendment had become fixed fact. So had a new and winning coalition between Democrats and Conservative Unionists, committed to holding black freedom to the narrowest possible confines. With the governor's help, their victory would be assured, and the governor gave it. By his appointments, he gutted the registry law so that any Confederate could perjure himself and vote. In November 1866, Democrats swept Maryland's legislature. The first thing that the party of "Dixie, Davis, and the devil" did was to call for a constitutional convention. Arguing that a fundamental law imposed by federal bayonets and rigged voting had no legitimacy, Democrats promised to wipe out proscription and, perhaps, compensate slave owners for their losses.[54]

The only alternative was what Tennessee, Missouri, and West Virginia did: to keep culling the electorate of voters that might vote against the Unionists in charge. Postwar lawmakers refined their disfranchising laws. In West Virginia, they denied seats to elected representatives with Confederate war records. Every county was given a board of registration, able to administer loyalty oaths and bar voters of dubious loyalty; attorneys had to swear a loyalty oath (though suitors in court no longer had to do so). But time stood with the conservatives. As the Unionists sundered, it would take stiffer and stiffer restrictions on who could vote to refine West Virginians to an electorate that could be relied on. Each attempt to refine them only brought on the parting of the ways for more loyalists. For many of them, the defining test for voting no longer seemed to be wartime allegiance but radical views. "If they do not like you they strike you off their register," cried Benjamin H. Smith, the Democratic nominee for governor, "but . . . if you will say 'I vote with you' the registrar never inquires what has been your past history." In 1866 when a disfranchisement amendment went before the voters and showed how fractured the Union coalition was becoming, the governor worried that it might fail. As the governor conceded, wartime Republicans deserted in droves. "We have all the wealth *nearly* & a great part of the talent against us," he wrote. Without the registration law, the amendment would not have passed; as it was, it became part of the constitution by almost 7,000 votes.[55]

Farther south, the war's end only guaranteed that any state-managed Reconstruction would come on terms very different from those that most northerners considered the minimum requirements for peace. For all the southern whites with nightmares of a consolidated empire dominating them, others hugged delusions of a very different sort. Wartime Unionists saw no vengeful, savage North, and beyond being trusted to lead a remade South, did not expect much to change. Those who gave the Confederacy only a guarded backing were sure that whoever might suffer, they might come out unscathed. Still others spoke of a peace restored "upon terms . . . honorable and satisfactory to every portion of it."[56] That implied give-and-take from both sides and the assumption that the South, either as a whole or each state separately or together with northern delegates in a national convention, would set certain conditions for its reentry into the Union: delusional, but no more so than the story going the rounds after Lee's surrender, of a French fleet, guns blazing, come to rescue the Lost Cause.

And what would those terms be? Quite a few hoped that slavery would get some lingering reprieve, a transition period, say, during which new limits could be built for a race quite unfit for its fresh-found freedom. Or perhaps emancipation would only cover active Rebels; or the government would compensate loyal owners for their losses. So, too, the Constitution's whole premise of state and national authorities sharing power meant that southern state governments could set and define the terms of Reconstruction. Reconciliation could not happen without the acquiescence of the South, and acquiescence implied consent. That consent, white southern leaders felt, must not come too cheaply—not when, as they still believed, they alone grasped the right reading of liberty, republicanism, and the Constitution. Two months before the war closed, a mass meeting in North Carolina promised to go along with any amendment that a national convention proposed, if "compatible with civil liberty and tending to promote the general welfare." A copy of the resolutions went to all the governors, north and south, on the apparent assumption that northern states were prepared to negotiate on equal terms with their southern counterparts. "The simple truth is, they stand ready to claim everything, if permitted, and to accept anything, if required," a journalist concluded that summer.[57]

With such differences in viewpoint, what peace between North and South could come? Indeed, what peace could come to the South at all? Bands of deserters and draft evaders lived off the land. Any civilian was fair game. In suppressing resisters and bushwhackers alike, the vigilantes and patrollers could be equally lawless. The war was over in most places by April's end; the killing and raiding went on. southern soldiers in Union blue, Confederates returning to Unionist communities, loyalist refugees returning home, and most of all, former slaves found themselves in deadly peril. What, then, were the prospects for this new birth of freedom having a safe delivery?[58]

CHAPTER TWO

When This Cruel Peace Is Over

L
ate in May, the armies of the republic put on one last show of force: the two-day Grand Review down Pennsylvania Avenue. Schools closed. Business suspended. Two thousand schoolgirls strewed flowers before the legions on streets "radiant with bunting." Onlookers shinnied up lamp posts and jammed terraces and porticos for the best views. They even perched on rooftops. Zouave and engineer, western bummer and ambulance corps, Irish brigadier with green sprig in his cap: past president and cabinet they marched. Then it was over, and they passed into history. The crowds had not come just to hail them but to make a farewell, for the saviors of the Union were nearly all state regiments, heading home to disband forever and, in the *New York Tribune*'s words, to exist thereafter "only in name."[1]

Nothing, perhaps, so became that assemblage as the disbanding of it. All the apparatus of war—the requisitioning of supplies, the restrictions of trade with the South, the enlistment and draft boards—dissolved, leaving not a wrack behind. At the start of the month, the Union had over a million volunteers in uniform. Three months later, over 600,000 had gone home, with another 200,000 departing by Thanksgiving. If the regulars stayed on, three times as many as served just before the war, their numbers were dwindling, too. By late 1866, Congress set the army's new limit at 75,000 men. Weeks before the fighting closed, the navy also had begun dismantling its forces. Within two years, five-sixths of its fleet had gone out of commission.[2] Whatever the war had done to America, it had not turned it into a garrison state, its citizens moving henceforth to a military cadence.

Even so rapid a demobilization came too slowly for soldiers and sailors. Those held into summer groused when other regiments mustered out before their own. They had saved their country. Why should they do guard duty when every man among the foe had returned to office or plow? "A little guard duty in camp; no drill, no picket, no war," a New Hampshire recruit grumbled; "the most onerous duty that falls to us is to eat our army rations, of which we are thoroughly tired. . . . We are prisoners of war." Mustering out came with easy informality and "not much parade about it." Many impatient enlistees parted without waiting for official orders.[3]

That dissolving view testified to the enduring quality of those republican values for which both sides fought. Here were multitudes discharged from military service in a matter of weeks and passing to their homes "at will, without guard or escort, without violence or jar, and all as quietly as if their immediate four years of tremendous war were but a natural and commonplace incident of an American citizen's life," a soldier wrote. "Of such another scene history is dumb." By July the warriors of six months before were "cradling wheat in Illinois, plowing corn in Iowa, chopping pine in Wisconsin, and gathering fruit in Missouri," an editor boasted. Not just the military array but the fiscal state that supported it would be unmade. Americans had no intention of shouldering guns, the moment peace came, nor the tax burdens that war had required. The revenue system would need to produce more than before the war for their lifetimes and those of their children: to save the Union, the government had borrowed heavily. That debt must be serviced and in time redeemed. The states' outlay in the national defense needed disbursement from Washington, and the funds helped pay for Kentucky's new state capitol and a veterans' memorial in Topeka. (In the 1990s, California was still litigating for a share.) The soldiers must be remembered, too, and over the next thirty years Congress set up fifteen homes for disabled veterans, as well as passing private pension bills by the thousand. The five billion spent on pensions by 1915 would surpass what war itself cost the Union.[4] But as far as impositions could be removed, Americans meant to remove them, by liquidating as much of the extraordinary government functions as possible.

At least Union soldiers had homes to return to. Not every Confederate was so lucky. The news that a postwar army of reporters sent from the South was of ash, anarchy, and tribulation. When retiring soldiers torched Richmond in the last days of the war, they only added it to the list of devastated cities. "A city of ruins," was how a visitor described Charleston, "of desolation, of vacated houses, of widowed women, of rotting wharves, of deserted warehouses, of weed-wild houses, of miles of grass-grown streets, of acres of pitiful and voiceful barrenness." "Shall we go first to the statue of Calhoun?" one apocryphal tourist inquired of another. "It is scarcely necessary," his companion replied, gesturing around him at the wreckage—"here is his monument."[5]

Military depredations were not wholly to blame for the conditions that travelers saw. The necessities of total war had forced many sacrifices and created serious shortages. Lacking firewood, the people of Mobile had torn up their wharves. The loss made little difference: the Union blockade had closed all coastal ports in the end. Charleston's piers of palmetto logs stood, only to rot. Wagons that might have been used to carry goods and further facilitate commerce were commandeered for the army. So were draft animals; Arkansas lost half its mares and horses and nearly that many of its cows. Businessmen furnishing the Confederate forces now had worthless IOUs to show for their supplies.[6]

If an invader's success is to be judged by the damage wrought on the enemy's productive power, then the Union army had succeeded famously east of the Appalachians. Northern commanders had tried to preserve houses in Georgia and North Carolina, but they viewed gristmills, waterwheels, and cotton gins differently. These devices served the southern economy and furthered the war-making ability of the Confederate government, and the federal troops wrecked them whenever possible. To a much lesser extent, clashing forces had wrought damage to farms in the Mississippi Valley and Tennessee lowlands. Soldiers tore up the fences for firewood and, as one Virginian commented, solved the problem of sheep in the meadow and cows in the corn by removing the livestock, too.[7]

More important, because it was more widespread, was the simple decay that war inevitably created in the rural areas. Enlistment and conscription drained the Confederacy of its white manpower needed to till the soil and supervise slaves. A plantation required ceaseless attention, and without the master's presence, nor, indeed, his whole slave force, everything could go to wrack. Shortages made it hard for owners to find the supplies for repairs. Weeds choked the rice fields in the Carolinas, already near exhaustion and barely breaking even for any but the largest planters. As dikes broke, salt water flooded many paddies, reverting them to wild marsh. Neglected for lack of resources or government attention, levees along the Mississippi had breached. Thousands of acres of prime cotton and sugar land lay under standing water. One Mississippi owner had to row by dugout to reach the corners of his property. Rich farmland lay open and untilled, prey to waist-high cocklebur and thicket. In vain a traveler scanned the landscape between Jackson and Meridian, Mississippi, for a cotton patch. "Whites and negroes alike seem to have fallen into a stupor, from which starvation alone will rouse them," he wrote.[8]

The southern transportation system had all but collapsed, the roads all muck and mudhole, the railways fragmentary: bridges gone; rails torn up, commandeered, or twisted; boxcars nearly impossible to find; warehouses and depots reduced to ember and ash. Even where no armies had trod, simple wear and tear had made engines and iron rail alike unusable; and in war, the Confederacy had neither time nor means to do upkeep. Rusty engines leaking steam from their boilers limped along at ten miles an hour.[9]

Never possessing the abundant money supply that the free states had enjoyed, the seceding states staked all on a currency issued by a government that had gone with the wind. Financial institutions used Confederate bonds for their security and took Confederate paper for their deposits. When that money lost all value, most banks closed down.[10] Monetary stringency affected everyone: the railroad seeking a loan to rebuild and re-equip, the planter required to pay a workforce no longer working from fear of the whip, the farmer needing supplies or seed for the coming season, the storekeeper hoping to stock the shelves for sale to those who, for the next year at least, must buy on credit.

Only luck, magnificent harvests, and premium prices could save those dependent on the South's cash crop economy, and this in a countryside where the labor system was being revolutionized. Small wonder some whites despaired or sold out, placing their plantations on the market for a song. Alabamans offered estates for one-tenth their previous value, or simply for the cost of the buildings on them—and found no takers. Want, even penury, seemed inevitable for a generation to come. Just in the ten counties around Atlanta, 30,000 pounds of meat and 800 bushels of corn were needed each day to fend off mass starvation that spring. "The wealthiest people with us are now the poorest," a Virginian lamented, "with hundreds of acres they can't raise a dollar."[11] There were loungers at every crossroad, and folk who accepted charity without a twinge of mortification.

Clear-eyed reporters agreed: the South was ruined, and its people lacked the will or the wallet to save it. Yet when Sidney Andrews, a Boston reporter, reached Atlanta late in 1865, he could not believe his eyes: "From all this ruin and devastation a new city is springing up with marvelous rapidity. The narrow and irregular and numerous streets are alive from morning till night with drays and carts and hand-barrows, and wagons,—with hauling teams and shouting men,—with loads of lumber and loads of brick and loads of sand,—with mortar-makers and hod-carriers,—with carpenters and masons, . . . with a never-ending throng of pushing and crowding and scrambling and eager and excited and enterprising men, all bent on building and grading and swift fortune-making." Atlanta's revival stood alone, but other commercial centers also made swifter recoveries than feared.[12] Indeed, the South seemed ready to rise again and, more important, with very much the same economic elite calling the shots. Why so swift a change?

Several reasons stand out. First, defeated southerners possessed greater advantages and greater resources than they recognized in their hour of defeat. Fences and barns vanished, but the soil remained, some of it the richest and most productive in the world. War had not devastated all parts of the interior South in equal measure. A visitor found nothing but undespoiled land as he approached Roanoke, North Carolina. All the fences stood in good repair, "herds are grazing in the meadows, the workmen in the fields guide the plow, chickens and turkeys fill the barn yards." Cotton growers could recover much faster than sugar planters, whose losses in sugar-house machinery were devastating: an industry worth $200 million to Louisiana before the war had lost $190 million of its property. Cities that supplied the hinterland like Atlanta had customers enough to make a fresh start at once. Second, impoverished southern businessmen still had an edge over most outsiders in the friendships that they had made in their communities, the support possible from an extended network of kin and clientele, and the respect in which they were held, an asset from good times that did not dissolve wholly in bad ones. A merchant might lack specie. He might find himself short on provisions for his shelves, but he knew he could count on customers to come and buy when the goods were to be found, and northern financial backers knew it, too. The same advantage of familiarity with the ways of slave society helped the established planter. He may not have had the same labor system as he had enjoyed before the war, but unlike newcomers, he had some idea of what his workers could do, if no clear idea of how to get them to do it. Finally, the fact that so many people were poor and so much needed doing must have enhanced the opportunities of those with limited personal wealth, wealth that before the war would have been considered insignificant.

Even more important, the South's speedy recovery was a national priority. Even leaving out compassion and the desire to erase all visible reminders of the damage from a war in which the American people had made war on themselves, the North had its own economic self-interest to think of. Before the war, it had been one of the essential driving forces for the country's prosperity. That had not changed: an impoverished section held in thrall at taxpayer expense would put heavy burdens on the economy and stoke the kind of discontent and disorder out of which new civil tumults might come. Northern factories were crying for cotton. Yankee financiers were eager to resume ties with their former clientele, and creditors had every reason to extend deadlines for repayment on debts long past due, lest money owed them be lost for good. Steamboat traffic along the Mississippi revived under federal control. Northern philanthropists joined their efforts with those of the Freedmen's Bureau and the army to bring food and medical supplies to poor southerners of all races. A Southern Relief Fair in Baltimore collected over $100,000. Californians sent $45,000, and New England churches sent both physical and spiritual comforts southward.[13]

From the federal government came help for the railroads, to speed their return to normal operations. The Union army needed railroad service. So did a national economy. The War Department helped make those repairs. In wartime, national authorities had seized many privately owned roads and kept them in good condition for transporting men and materials. Soon after the fighting ended, the army returned those roads to their original owners and sold military property, including rolling stock and machinery, to private parties on generous terms. Engines and cars worth $7 million, brought from the North for military purposes, now passed into southern companies' hands at once, even before payment was made; indeed, most of it was never paid for. With outside help, the railroad networks made a quick recovery. Just about all of them were running, or limping along, on the mend, within the year. By June, "branch lines, like spiders' webs covering the Atlantic coast in every direction," had restored some semblance of linkage between north and south, ports and hinterland. Already, the army had restrung telegraph wires, restoring a direct connection between New York and New Orleans, so efficiently that one reporter suggested that the government ought to assign them the job of successfully laying the not-yet-operational Atlantic Cable.[14]

Contrary to some planters' fears, King Cotton quickly restored itself. The pent-up demand from the war sent the price skyrocketing briefly and set off a scramble to get it by any means possible, including the illegal trade in the national government's supply. "Cotton *fever awful*," wrote a southerner in New York City to his friend, an Augusta cotton factor; "hold on to your Cotton don't let any one frighten or swindle you or your friends out of it." A host of newcomers, anticipating bargains in ruined estates, hustled south to buy up property and see whether they could prosper better on free labor than the old masters had on slave (much to their eventual disappointment, in most cases: workers out of bondage saw no reason to labor as long or for as poor a remuneration as they had under the lash). With buyers fanning across the South looking for stock privately held, owners found northern customers eager to advance the money to revitalize the trade. To their surprise, merchants from Charleston and Augusta came back from northeastern cities with news that good terms and extensions on their debts were easily arranged. They found themselves "treated like gentlemen everywhere." In late September, New York City financiers helped create the American Cotton Planters' Association to facilitate growing with five-year loans to planters.[15]

They could not have been too disappointed at the results—in the long term. Over 210,000 bales made their way north over the first postwar season, over 350,000 four years later, and by 1880, a good million. Still more made it overseas from the southern ports, a growing proportion as railroad connections eased delivery to Mobile, Savannah, and Norfolk. "In the American Quarter, during certain hours of the day," traveling correspondent Edward King observed from New Orleans in 1873, "cotton is the only subject spoken of; the pavements of all the principal avenues in the vicinity of the Exchange are crowded with smartly-dressed gentlemen, who eagerly discuss crops and values, and who have a perfect mania for preparing and comparing the estimates at the basis of all speculations in the favorite staple." By that time, New Orleans had created its own cotton exchange to handle the traffic, and, wrote King, "merchants and planters were alike surprised that they had not thought its advantages necessary before."[16]

A very different kind of northern intervention created the stability without which recovery would have been impossible, though it got little thanks from former Confederates: the military occupation force stationed in every city of consequence. Until legal governments could be set up and civil courts reopened, the U.S. army kept order, opened military hospitals, hauled away the debris, and in some places took a census of living residents. They reopened those few public schools that the South had, as well. Charleston, Sidney Andrews noticed, bore "thorough military rule; but the iron hand rests very lightly. Soldiers do police duty, and there is some nine-o'clock regulation; but so far as I can learn, anybody goes anywhere at all hours of the night without molestation. 'There never was such good order here before,' said an old colored man to me. The main street is swept twice a week, and all garbage is removed at sunrise. 'If the Yankees was to stay here always and keep the city so clean, I don't reckon we'd have "yellow jack" here any more,' was a remark I heard on the street. 'Now is de fust time sence I can 'mem'er when brack men was safe in de street af'er nightfall,' stated the negro tailor in whose shop I sat an hour yesterday." In Arkansas, commanders arrested those who swore in public; in Mobile, they required all prostitutes to register with the provost marshal, and everywhere, they set up interim agencies to find homes, jobs, or missing family members among the newly freed population. Union officers also set about restoring confiscated properties to their original owners and dispensed army rations to the women, elderly, and destitute in general. In Petersburg, many a former Confederate ate "the bread of loyalty with a relish of satisfaction, if not with thanks." So did many others in the occupied states—29,000 a day in Virginia and over 215,000 in North Carolina. If civilians could get along without Yankees spreading lime in noisome alleys and whitewashing trees, they could not get along without some armed force; the roads and back-country teemed with discharged soldiers turned desperado, bushwhacker, and horse thief. Broadcloth authorities must decide how the South's civil governments would be put back into operation, but in the meantime, blue-coats made the pragmatic choice that creating a functioning authority mattered more than having the army handle day-to-day administration. Using their discretion, they left matters as far as they could to those who knew the business best, and did not probe too deeply into what they had done during the war.[17]

Northern action, then, played a crucial role in restoring the Confederate states to a peacetime condition, but repairing damage could not restore the world that the Slave Power had lost. Nor, indeed, did all southerners have that in mind. However deep the section's trauma of defeat, its vision of sectional greatness revived even as widows and orphans mourned their losses. New voices had begun to rise, and over the next few years, they would grow stronger and more confident, calling not just for a recovery but a rebirth. Few called it a "New South" yet; the term was not in common use, but the most fervent opinion-makers meant nothing less.[18]

Always, the Old South that planters had eulogized had been less a reality than an ideal. The name conjures pictures of a stable, placid, agricultural paradise, where large plantations and genteel ideals throve, where honor counted for more than thrift. Hustle, bustling, and bargaining—these were "Yankee notions." In fact, the South had been far from the Arcadia that its most enthusiastic spokesmen made it out to be. Mines, tobacco-processing plants, iron mines, and even some textile mills and ironworks had found a place below the Potomac, though they took firmest hold in the border and upper South. Even as whites mourned the loss of the Old South, leading conservative figures among them now softened their grief with hopes for the future. No place had richer soil than the cotton states, promoters argued. The Appalachians only waited for miners to unlock their stores of coal and iron; the Gulf coast was America's potential Italy, as fit for tropical fruits or wine as for wool and wheat. From all directions an Arkansas journalist heard the shouts, "Build! build!" Little Rock could "smelt iron, run ingots, mould pigs, spin thread, weave cloth, make wooden ware,—all but nutmegs."[19]

With industrialization, a few southerners foresaw an end to the dominant part that the plantation system had played. Some editors called for subdividing the great tracts of land and replacing them with "small farms in a constant state of improvement." Advocates of a regenerate South urged that white immigrants be invited to make their homes there. Newcomers would infuse the section with principles of industry, morality, and religion, said Governor Isaac Murphy of Arkansas, and his state sorely needed such values. Editors suggested that landholders would gladly part with pieces of their unused acreage to outsiders of the right kind. *DeBow's Review* continued its prewar campaign to have farmers diversify, and former governor Henry Wise of Virginia called for an entirely new labor system.[20]

Proponents often saw this New South not as a replacement for the plantation economy but as a complement to it. Railroad connections would open new lands for cotton-growing and cut the cost and unreliability of transport. The former Confederacy would do all that it had before, and much that the North had done for it. Its sponsors envisioned a section not so much merged into a national economy as capable of standing on its own. White southerners resented the fact that it was they who made the raw materials and then had to pay outsiders to process them and export their finished products. It stung their pride and drained off their wealth to rely on nonsoutherners for food for their families, hay for their livestock, clothing made from their own cotton, and manufactured goods of all kinds. A self-sufficient South would be an independent one, or at least one worthy of the respect of the money-changers, mudsills, and moralists of Yankeedom.

Planters wanted out, or some despaired early and claimed they did. Yet the plantation world did better than just survive. After the first two terrible years, much of the elite recovered. The complaints of impoverishment, so powerful in the 1860s, diminished over time, partly because the affluence was restored. Even in the Carolina rice country, where yields per acre fell and foreign markets shrank steadily, more than forty-two million pounds went on the market at century's end. Many planters went on to invest in railroads or textile mills and to foster the making of the new industrial order of the New South. Sugar planters in many cases had substantial estates to bequeath to the next generation, and some of those fortunes lasted well past century's end.[21]

The search for a New South may have awakened from whites' despair about making any satisfactory replacement for the one institution that had defined both the economy and society before the war: slavery itself had gone for good. The issue involved more than economics. With little faith in blacks' adjustment to free labor and a long polemical history of scorn for what free labor meant in the degradation of white people up north, slave owners found it hard to imagine any revival without controls to hem black freedom in as closely as possible. As summer came on, they discovered just how challenging any such task would be.

The full story of what freedom meant to four million Americans of African descent has been told too fully and well to need full repetition here. The emancipation process had begun in the first days of the war, as slaves set themselves free by running to Union lines. By the time Lee surrendered, there were not just many thousand gone, but hundreds of thousands. As the army pressed into the Confederate South, more became free, ready to take employment growing cotton or toiling on the estates of masters who had fled before the invader. Where the Union army occupied country, slavery eventually perished. Yet most slaves remained still in bondage when peace came, with auctioneers advertising their wares into early May. Full emancipation took months longer. Union military authority remained crucial in forcing masters to unbind their human property. "The dark dissolving, disquieting wave of emancipation has broken over this sequestered region," a minister wrote in late August. "It has been like the iceberg, withering and deadening the best sensibilities of master and servant, and fast sundering the domestic ties of years."[22]

Many owners tried to conceal the news of emancipation from their slaves. In the more remote places, they may not have known for sure themselves. In the Virginia backcountry, freedpeople unaware that their status had changed worked months beyond the close of the war, and in Texas as long as three years. One Mississippi boy found out only when his brother rode onto the property and scooped him up to carry him off. When action could not be put off, planters might assemble all their slaves to tell them the news and to offer to keep them going on what, to their minds, were generous terms. Others put a gloss on freedom that would allow them to get all the work possible at the lowest cost. "When freedom come Dr. Guidry . . . come 'roun' and tell 'em de slaves free," Agatha Babino remembered. "But dey have to sign up to work for money with dey marster for a year, and if dey want to go to work for somebody else, he couldn't take 'em in 'till he find out dey was sent off by de Old Marster."[23]

If the way in which freedpeople found freedom varied, so did their readiness to accept it. Some chose to stay on the old place, for lack of better alternatives, or because a bond of kinship or common experience made them prefer it to the alternatives. Others left over the next few weeks or months, or when the crop was in. Those employers known as the most cruel or unfair, and those who had broken their word, were likelier to lose not just a few but all of their servants. But many employers who had thought highly of their own generosity woke to find that those they lorded over had not felt the same way. Masters and mistresses who had told themselves that their slaves thought themselves members of the family sometimes discovered that their slaves, for all their professions of goodwill, had been shamming the whole time. House servants, more than field hands, produced the greatest shock, with personal interaction having been the closest and the sense of betrayal strongest when they left "without bidding any of us an affectionate adieu."[24]

Some freedpeople who left assured their former masters that their leave-taking had nothing to do with ill-treatment. Freedom could never feel complete as long as one worked for those whose discipline and demands had been the servant's every care. Only with another employer could a former slave feel as if he or she had become an independent agent. Some went for a season and then returned. Others stayed for the first season, until they could measure their freedom fully, and then left for better opportunities elsewhere. Some moved many times, in one freedperson's words, like "bees trying to find a setting place." Children without parents were likeliest to stay, at least till they reached their majority. They were also easiest to coerce into remaining by local courts forcibly "apprenticing" them to the former master. Mothers put off their departure when told that they must leave their children behind.[25] Still others never left, or parted only when their former owner died. Farmers may have found it easier keeping their former slaves than planters did. One journalist thought that relations hardly changed "in the back country . . . on the little cracker plantations." Those who worked in the fields found a parting the hardest, especially with the crop unharvested. To leave at once was to lose any pay for work already put in. The army offered at least the promise of requiring landowners to make some kind of division of the crop at season's end. Many who left took employment down the road with a neighbor, or in a nearby town. Not all felt that they had bettered their condition. Some would ask to be taken back; others returned after they had proved their point, that they could get along without the old master and that remaining was an explicit choice on their own part. In some cases, workers came back even when their employer had decided that he could do without them, because they considered the plantation their home and resisted anybody's right to separate them from it. "Local attachment, you know, has always been a ruling passion with the agricultural classes of our people," a South Carolina official explained—a more generous appreciation than a Freedmen's Bureau agent's conclusion that older freedpeople "had the bump of locality like old cats."[26]

Slavery's end, then, was a drawn-out, untidy, often traumatic process. A few owners furnished their former slaves with a mule or cow to start life with, and others with land that they could work, but without legal title. A very few furnished money, many more gave well-meant advice. Some masters wept as they told their slaves that they were free, either from the tension of a dramatic moment or because they now separated from people who in some distant way had been family or, at least, property with sentimental value. Told that "Jinny" was free along with the others on one farm, the "missus" found it the worst blow. "'My ma gimme Jinny w'en I was sixteen year' ol,'" she burst out. "An' she start cry." Commonly, white accounts expressed a sense of resentment, tendering liberty to an ungrateful people, with no understanding of what they had been given—and, more to the point, what they had lost. "Our nurse Susan took herself off this morning leaving us *niggerless* indeed," a Georgian noted in his diary. "The more I see of these *beings* the more certain I feel that they have very small souls—if any!"[27]

For freedpeople, freedom was frightening, baffling, and exhilarating. "We was glad to be set free," a Texan commented later. "It was just like opening the door and lettin' the bird fly out. He might starve, or freeze, or be killed pretty soon but he just felt good because he was free." Freedom meant choosing one's own name, in some cases not the one that the master had picked, which occasionally had the whimsy appropriate to pets—naming quadruplets for railroad destinations, for example. For some planters, their surname denoted their possession of a piece of human property. Those that they held in special esteem might be given leave to choose a last name of their own, but that decision only underlined the fact that this was a privilege that the master could confer or not. On plantation books, slaves had no surnames, but sometimes they had chosen what they called "titles" for themselves. Now these became formal last names. Blacks who had fled to Union lines often chose to drop their master-given surname, but those emancipated after the war were rather more willing to adopt it, if only because it was the name by which they and their parents always had identified themselves. Now and then wives in slave marriages had kept their master's last name. In freedom, they took their husband's.[28]

So many activities that whites took for granted, the trivial small change of freedom, had inestimable value to those so lately in bondage: the right to travel without a pass, to visit friends and kin on neighboring plantations, to ride a horse or mule or even in a carriage, to decline to yield their place on the sidewalk when a white came the other way. It meant the right to dress like ladies or carry canes like gentlemen. "Negro women dressed in the most outré style, all with veils and parasols for which they have an especial fancy," one white wrote disgustedly. "Riding on horseback with negro soldiers and in carriages."[29] Those privileges did not just mark freedom but, to whites' view, an assertion of racial equality. Canes were not just for display. Symbolically, they were weapons. Only ladies bore parasols or wore veils, and a black woman, by definition, could not be a "lady." Persons of the lower class vaulted above their presumed station in fancying "gold watches, and chains, bracelets, and *blue veils* and silk dresses," as one plantation's servants did. Going hunting, owning a gun, or for that matter a dog—these were the master's privilege, and in freedpeople, seen as an affront, if not an outright threat. "The Master he says we are all free, but it don't mean we is white," George G. King of South Carolina commented. "And it don't mean we is equal. Just equal for to work and earn our own living and not depend on him for no more meats and clothes."[30]

As freedom spread, a growing stream of black southerners took to the roads, not out of restlessness so much as to return to their homes. Planters had removed slaves from the most vulnerable areas, close to the Yankee lines. Now the emancipated multitudes were trying to find their way back, or to a country that required the kind of farming that they knew: corn did not take the same skills as rice. As late as December, "parties of hungry, ill-clad Negroes" were trudging toward the coasts. Other freedpeople were looking to rebuild their families. Mothers whose children had been sold away from them, children whose parents had been auctioned off, husbands seeking their wives, wives seeking their husbands, went looking for them. Many never found their lost ones. A few found freedom an easy way to loose themselves of family bonds, of a daughter they did not want to take care of, a common-law wife they had tired of living with, a baby who hindered their going. Others found those they had lost remarried or changed.[31]

Freedom did not mean simply the reuniting of families but the formalizing of ties. Slave law did not recognize bondspeoples' relationships as binding, but ex-slaves did. They applied to civil authorities and to the army for marriage certificates. Those owned by different masters were particularly determined that their matrimony receive formal acknowledgment. The practice was not universal. Some freedpeople welcomed the chance to get out of an affinity that had turned out badly. Those in a loveless marriage used the opportunity not to legitimate a relationship that had not been on their initiative in the first place. Others kept to the common-law relationship already in place. Many former slaves, since their parting with one wife or husband, had been forced by the master to take another. For them, at least, the end of slavery brought a painful, gradual adjustment, as it did for children, torn between the custody demands of their natural and adoptive parents.[32]

If former masters had had their way, that adjustment would have been a return to the work patterns of slavery time, beyond their wildest hopes. "Intelligent and thinking men" in South Carolina all agreed that free labor could not possibly work and advised the North to prepare for the consequences of that failure. "These people really believe that, in submitting to the emancipation of the slaves, they have virtually saddled themselves with an equal number of idle paupers," a reporter marveled. Much of it was built into the rationale for slavery, that without compulsion, African Americans would never work. Indolence was "a feature in the character of the African for which he should be no more held responsible than the leopard is for his spots," Governor Jonathan Worth of North Carolina admonished. "It is his nature." Even some northerners worried that blacks would unlearn their good habits by mixing with the lazy and idle slackers that lounged all over the South: their white neighbors! As long as the life of leisure was the mark of a southern gent, a business agent commented, freedpeople could hardly help thinking that this was what equality meant.[33]

Planters that first summer certainly saw disheartening evidence of the old discipline broken down. "At Fairntosh and Stagville [two plantations]," the landowner complained, "all are going to the devil or dogs as fast as they can—wont work—and destroying stock—out houses, enclosures!" For a few blacks, freedom did mean the chance to do "absolutely nothing," though not many of them felt that they could indulge in it, beyond a much-deserved vacation after years of toil. A South Carolina planter quoted one of his former slave's lament that she had seen no freedom yet: "She had to work just as hard now as ever. And that was the feeling of a great many of them." On one set of terms or another, most of them agreed to work through the season and did so. Reporter John Richard Dennett was struck by the unanimity with which white Virginians told him that blacks would not work—and then allowed that in their own particular neighborhood, the freedpeople were doing most of the field labor and tolerably well. "I have worked negroes all my life, and prefer them in my business to any other class of laborers," a Yankee entrepreneur in Richmond agreed. "Treat a negro like a man, and you make a man of him."[34]

Complaints crested just at year's end, when new contracts were to be signed. Even the freedpeople who stayed through the first season after the war made clear that, come the New Year, they intended to leave or better themselves somehow. They proved very reluctant to sign articles for 1866. As 1865 closed, a feeling of panic set in among prospective employers. Christmas Day was the worst point of all. On many plantations, all the workers were gone to celebrate the holidays, with no guarantee that any of them would come back. Alarming stories spread that the freedpeople, deluded into thinking the master's lands theirs by right, intended a bloody insurrection. Most blacks hoped for land and thought it their due, nothing less. "Didn't dem large cities in de North grow up on de cotton and de sugars and de rice we made?" one asked. They knew how crucial property that they could call their own was to their independence. Rightly they could wonder, as one freedman did, what use it was in "giving us freedom if we can't stay where we were raised and own our houses where we were born?" Blacks took over abandoned estates in rice country and armed to resist any authority coming to take it away; on some islands they apportioned the land, wrote up constitutions and laws to govern themselves, and drove off the previous owners when they tried to reclaim the property. Based on the allotments that the army had given them on the Carolina Sea Islands and Georgia coast, freedpeople there had reason for thinking that the government might allow them some stake in the soil that their labor had made bountiful, but it never happened. The president worked overtime to return property to its original owners, without any conditions protecting workers' right to compensation for improvements made. Freedpeople protested, petitioned—and submitted, even those in rice country. But after contracts had been arranged, expressions of white discontent faded. They could still be found. At midsummer 1866, planters around Sumter, South Carolina, contended that their employees were only half-working, "and that in a very careless and unsatisfactory manner," with serious injury to the final crop. But more often it was agreed that freedmen behaved quietly and stuck to their jobs as resolutely as workers anywhere in the country. In Arkansas, the planters' leading grievance was not that blacks refused to work but that their fellow planters were outbidding them and enticing last year's labor away. Far from wishing they were rid of African American hands, landowners could not get enough of them and had to draw on Georgia's labor supply to meet their needs.[35]

Work, in fact, was the one means by which the freedpeople could be independent of white control. Nothing afforded independence as well as money earned and saved. "Slavery means shirk and liberty means work, and to work for yourself," the black lawyer John Mercer Langston reminded a congregation. Where the difference lay was in what labor meant. The problem was not so much getting labor from blacks but getting "persistent labor," as New England manufacturer Edward Atkinson commented. Freedpeople did not toil as hard without the lash at their backs, nor in the same long, unbroken stints. They insisted on time off to grow food for themselves and their family, and expected a garden plot from the owner's property to do it on. Women hired to work the field no longer performed double duty once the harvest was in, making clothing and butchering meat for their employers as in slavery days—not without pay for it. Where freedpeople had the chance, they quit the rice fields and sugarcane plantations. Many of them resented the poor return that came their way in the cotton patches. "If ole massa want to grow cotton, let him plant it himself," a Georgian burst out. "I'se work for him dese twenty year and done got nothin' but food and clothes, and dem mighty mean now."[36]

Those who did plantation work were not willing to be worked in the same old way, in gang labor. They rebelled against having any driver, whip in hand over them. While those in lowland South Carolina were willing to have a black driver over them as supervisor, and did good work, A. Warren Kelsey reported, they would not hear of him being *called* an overseer. That name had too much the connotation of servitude. Nor were they willing to work seven days a week, or even always for six. It sometimes also involved taking women and children out of the workforce, or setting clear limits on what services they should be expected to perform. No longer were they to be contracted for in the husband's terms of employment. The adjustment of women's labor conditions might not be dictated simply by the husband on her behalf but on his own; part of the way the man felt his freedom clearest came in being able to do what slavery never fully permitted and be the undisputed head of the household. "When I married my wife, I married her to wait on me," a Tennessean told his employer, "and she has got all she can do right here for me and the children." But women also made the choice to limit when and where and define how they would work, the more so when their labor put them at risk of white employers' abuse or assault. Most, in fact, simply exchanged one form of toil for another: tending the family garden and caring for the family.[37]

What freedpeople got in the first season varied. Many landowners were cash-poor and paid in corn or meat. Blacks around Beaufort, South Carolina, were told that "for the present year as much as they could reasonably expect from their former masters would be their victuals & clothes." A Mississippi slave remembered the promises of payment if they worked to the end of the year. But the hands got nothing. What they had eaten, they learned, was worth more than what they had produced. This treatment was all the less punishable because so often the agreements were verbal, and the terms were left as vague as the North Carolina planter's promise, "We pay youse what's right."[38] Cotton country saw the beginning of the share-wage arrangement. Some workers contracted for a fourth of the year's crop, others for a third, a half, even two-thirds. Elsewhere, the owner promised cash wages, and in the sugar fields, where gang labor, rather than individual initiative, was the only way to bring in the cane during its brief season of ripeness, share-wage arrangements never caught on.[39]

"The white man down here has learned to *lean* on the negro for support and they can't do without him, *and the negro knows it*," A. Warren Kelsey wrote from Montgomery. His statement fit with other predictions that white dependence on black labor would solve the race problem itself. Planters needed blacks so badly that it would protect their hands from abuse.[40] This was fantasy. Whatever power farm labor had could not match the power that money, guns, and white-run courts gave to employers. On cotton plantations, working conditions looked much like slavery days, with laborers toiling in gangs and living together in the old slave cabins, under the landowner's suspicious eye. Contracts stipulated that workers be "obedient and faithful," forbade them to entertain visitors or go in for "frolicking": without leave. "Sun-up to sun-down" work hours had any number of add-ons that employees had to complete before or after leaving the fields. Even the rations were the same: a peck and a half of cornmeal and four pounds of bacon or pork a week for each adult. When the crop was in, the worker lost all control. He could be driven off the land without pay on various pretexts or forced to stay on the plantation, not by good conditions being offered but by threats and violence. The "demand for labor" meant little, as long as white owners banded together, which, at year's end, happened regularly.[41] Freedom, then, came hard-contested. How far that freedom would have meaning depended on how hard former slaves pushed for their rights and how much outside help they had.

On the first point, northerners who had come south had few doubts. They found a freedpeople eager for more than a bare freedom and a bare subsistence. What money and time they had went into self-improvement and into the creation of communities. Schooling, the ability to read and write, opened to them the Bible, not just the white preacher's rendering but all of it from Jonah delivered from the belly of a great fish to the liberation of the children of Israel from Egyptian bondage. Unlettered, they stood at the mercy of those drawing up contracts for the coming year and confined in their rise beyond the field hands' toil. Within a year of the war's end, makeshift schools could be found in every city and dotting the countryside: in wagon and cotton-gin houses, corn cribs, barn lofts, church basements; and in Savannah, in the auction room and jail cell of a former slave market. The sites might be unplastered rooms, drafty in cold weather and over-crowded, and the supply of teachers could never keep up with the demand. In some places, the children went by day and plantation hands went by night. Where no outside instructors were available, the freedpeople's community might hire the best-lettered among their number; in some towns they levied a tax on the black community to support schooling. The "thirst after knowledge," one missionary wrote, had no parallel "in the history of any people or nation."[42]

Freedpeople also wanted churches of their own, the most vital of institutions, after the family, for creating a black community able to define its own standards of conduct and morality. As with marriage, making a black church often simply gave formal shape to what had existed beforehand; the emergence into the open of religious communities on plantations that in slavery days had met clandestinely in the dark of night away from the master's surveillance. With emancipation, they could break with the white churches in which they had been seated, forming congregations of their own. Not all took this step immediately. They sometimes sought some greater recognition within the white churches. Church leaders sometimes obliged, though rarely as far as freedpeople wanted. They had good reason to want to keep black congregants. As in slavery, white ministers and the disciplinary machinery of the church could train them in temperance, obedience, honesty, and subservience, the moral values that would replace the control of the master. Failure to do so meant growth of the black churches instead. As all hope of a lasting accommodation between the races on white terms faded, the pace picked up. Inviting parishioners to cast off "the slave-yoke of Southern Methodism," the African Methodist Episcopal Church from the North made the greatest gains, but as early as November, a visitor could attend any of six black churches of three denominations, all but one still draped in mourning for Lincoln.[43]

There were other ways that community showed itself: the creation of black newspapers, most of them initiated by whites to begin with, and nearly all short-lived, the gathering in cities for parades and celebrations of Emancipation Day, the Fourth of July, and commemorations of those Union dead whose sacrifice had helped buy their freedom—the first forms of what the North soon turned into Decoration Day. By fall 1865, freed-people were assembling in state conventions to petition the legislature and then Congress for expanded rights. If their requests began diffidently and the reforms they asked for were moderate ones, they found fuller voice by 1866, and the tone grew more insistent that without the power to protect themselves with the vote, they would be remanded to a half-slavery. "It may be that we are so ignorant we don't know what the word 'Constitution' means," a barber told one gathering, "but none of us are so ignorant that we don't know what the principle of justice means!"[44]

But if the freedpeople's own actions helped push the outer bounds on that freedom that the white South was prepared to offer them, they could not have done it on their own. Just as the economic revival of the South, the restoration of order, and the ending of slavery took direct northern involvement, so, too, emancipation owed its scope to influences out of New York, Philadelphia, and Washington. From the first, the Protestant churches and antislavery societies of the North provided the 3,000 or so schoolteachers and much of the funding to open black schools in the South—and to rebuild them regularly, after arsonists burned them down. "School marms" handed out clothing from northern benevolent associations and spread what they considered uniquely Protestant Yankee values: hygiene and hard work, regular mealtimes and marriages, savings accounts and scrub brushes.[45] The money and personnel to build a black church in the South came out of the North. In every southern city where Union troops were still stationed that winter, the black soldiers served as a reminder and an example to freedpeople of what liberty meant—examples, white communities protested, in "insolence" and the free use of firearms and liquor.[46] Finally, the former slaves depended on the guidance of the greatest social welfare agency created by the national government up to that time. Shot through with prejudices and misimpressions, stunted in its development, it provided a symbolic reminder to white southerners of what the victors expected of those that they had defeated, and to black southerners of a commitment to make the end of slavery a palpable, substantive freedom.

Created just at the end of the 38th Congress in March 1865, the Bureau of Refugees, Freedmen, and Abandoned Lands, known as the Freedmen's Bureau, was intended as a temporary agency—until one year after the war's end—in one freedwoman's words, "to get things going smooth after the war." Handled by the War Department and staffed by army officers overseen by General Oliver O. Howard, it provided food, clothing, and fuel for the destitute of both races, and in many places far more whites than blacks applied. It helped reunite former slave families. It set up freedpeople's schools, night schools, Sunday schools, industrial schools, and a few colleges for training blacks to act as instructors themselves, all with the help of antislavery and religious societies in the North, and helped bring teachers there. Agents appointed at the county level fielded complaints from former slaves and opened tribunals at which black testimony could be taken. They encouraged the negotiation of fixed, written labor contracts with planters and farmers, with wages carefully specified, and had clear ideas of what those wages ought to be. Hospitals and clinics were erected for freedpeople, as well.[47]

Among the bureau's key duties was to adjust and instruct white and black toward free labor. The assumptions were northern ones, in what family life should look like and domesticity. Its founders wanted to teach the right personal habits: initiative, hard work, self-discipline, frugality. With full opportunity, the freedpeople could make themselves independent, but they could also learn individual responsibility, their bad habits inculcated in slavery no longer hampering their ability to adjust to a world where market forces ruled. Instead of providing the freedpeople with land, it would be better to have them earn money to buy it themselves. So the bureau busied itself discouraging drinking or hiring lecturers to encourage temperance or teach the duties of citizenship, and encouraging marriage, even going so far as to have the agents punish adultery. They forbade hunting and fishing on Saturdays and founded branches of the Freedman's Savings Bank to instill thrift and create a cushion against risk.[48]

To create free labor systems, the bureau turned to various ways established by the army in wartime. But along with the imposition of labor on freedpeople, the bureau also had to deal with some of the most obvious components of free labor that, to the white employers (or, indeed, some bureau agents), were not so obvious: the right of the former slaves to a lien on the crop for their work, freedom from whipping or physical abuse, the right not to have to pledge their family's labor along with their own as a condition of service, and the freedom of the laborer from coercion into signing contracts for the new year from the employer in the old, or, indeed, contracts lasting more than a year. It had to defend employees' right to bear arms and to encourage planters to put provision in their contracts providing medical care to their employees. It also occasionally had to counter sugar planters' insistence on Sunday labor. Agents enforced the regulations making sure that freedmen had garden plots of their own, with full right to grow whatever suited them and contract stipulations letting them use their employers' horses and mules or farm tools; they also guaranteed their right to raise animals of their own, to be permitted to cut or haul wood from the owner's land, even to gather Spanish moss for their own use. All these supplemented freedmen's wages.[49]

The bureau had deep limitations. It never had money enough, nor personnel enough, to make a full enforcement of freedpeople's rights. Some 2,441 men served as agents, but never more than 900 at any one time. Their service had to be supplemented by making civil magistrates into ex officio agents—men almost never prepared to pay attention to the freedpeople's point of view and often reluctant to permit black testimony in disputes over the labor contracts' fulfillment. Living alone and working on their own locally, with less military resources to call upon as time went on, military agents struggled to have their orders enforced; and the caseloads on them were often insupportable. Family disputes, discussions of the terms of contracts, and the heavy stream of paperwork, the monthly reports to the assistant commissioner for their state, imposed enormous burdens on their time. Some fell ill. Many wore out. "I virtually become a 'pack horse' for the whole county," one wrote. Many quit when the exhaustion and strain grew too great; few outlasted a two-year stretch. Charles Sumner's efforts to give the bureau an independent, permanent existence at cabinet rank failed. For funding, the bureau had to depend on private contributions and an annual appropriation from Congress. Presidential authority constricted its power, with any of its officers subject to dismissal.[50]

Many of its officers had limited sympathy for blacks, a patronizing quality that assumed them incapable of negotiating on their own and swollen with outlandish expectations for what freedom would mean. They felt bemusement, if not amusement, at their ignorance and cultural values. For some agents, their black charges were curiosities, and for some, very much a nuisance, "promiscuous," "trifling and indolent," at risk of falling back "into those heathenish customs and rules" practiced in Africa. "I cannot help remarking that these people as a general thing are both shiftless and lazy, preferring rather to beg subsistence from the government than earn it by honest toil," an Arkansas agent commented. Not unexpectedly, agents with that outlook took the masters' side in disputes and others felt that their chief responsibility was to see to it that freedpeople worked and that the bureau applied the force to make sure that they did so, whatever the terms. That meant putting the whip back in masters' hands. Yet without the change, free labor would have been far less free, with owners combining to force their workers into virtual serfdom.[51]

"The fact is that while we are debate what amount of capacity the black man possesses he has gone beyond the anticipations of his warmest friends," A. Warren Kelsey wrote from Charleston, "—he not only realizes that he is free, but he is not at all disposed to accept any restrictions on his perfect freedom."[52] But would he have any choice but to accept them? The North's contribution to the remaking of the South had carried the revolution some distance, indeed, by the end of 1865. But if the pressure should slacken? Left unsupervised, how far could the white South accommodate itself to the new order of things? The prospects that winter were dark ones, indeed. The armies of the North had disbanded, but the forces of the Slave Power were still under arms. The old patrols, the state militia were reconstituting themselves and raiding black communities to forestall the "Christmas uprising" that rumor told them was sure to happen—and that everybody but the freedpeople expected. The organized power of a subdued Confederacy was turning to the destruction of any prospect of a continuing, evolving change, carrying the postwar South away from the society and customs which it had known.

CHAPTER THREE

Restoration, 1865–1866

"**N**ow, the question comes, what that victory means, and what reconstruction on that victory means?" Wendell Phillips told one audience. "If it means any thing, it does not mean dragging South Carolina to the feet of Massachusetts and chaining her with clamps of iron. It means that North making over the South in its likeness, till South Carolina gravitates by natural tendency to New England. [Applause.] . . . Reconstruction begins when the South yields up her idea of civilization, and allows the North to permeate her channels and make her over."[1]

Here and there, southerners talked of renewing the war. North Carolinians would only allow that they "supposed" they were whipped but claimed that the Lost Cause had not had "a fair 'showin,'" and expected the conflict to reopen whenever the United States "gits into a brile with foreign nations." But those who talked loudest for war were least likely to have got close enough to smell gunpowder—rather like Kentucky, where, so the joke went, the state only joined the Confederacy after there no longer was one. As a northerner concluded, the South had "supped full of horrors. The habilments of mourning . . . will cast their dark shadow upon any future attempt at secession." The truth was, "we have had the devil whipped out of us," a Virginia colonel told an interviewer. "I fought you with all my might, until we got whipped; then I gave it up as a bad job; and now there's not a more loyal man in the United States than I am." Even in South Carolina, one Unionist predicted, "a barrel of cider never ferments twice."[2]

There was much talk, too, of how readily white southerners would accommodate themselves to any terms proffered. "We are lying down for the wave to wash over us," a Virginian explained; "all we ask is that we will not be allowed to be washed entirely away, and submerged in the great deep forever." Yet the North underestimated how deeply commitment to the Confederacy spread, or how widely. "We have for breakfast salt-fish, fried potatoes, and treason," a lodger at a Virginia boardinghouse wrote. "Fried potatoes, treason, and salt-fish for dinner. At supper the fare is slightly varied, and we have treason, salt-fish, fried potatoes, and a little more treason." In Raleigh, lawmakers could give the American flag nothing more than the "Irish hoist," one reporter wrote. But Confederate flags waved everywhere. They decorated playing cards, with Rebel mottoes along the sides. In Arkansas, the Stars and Bars flew at the head of the Fourth of July parade to a picnic ground, with marchers flinging insults at every Union man they passed. (This kind of event was rare: most white communities refused to celebrate Independence Day at all.) The military in South Carolina forbade anyone to wear Confederate military buttons, but in the upcountry many new articles of clothing flaunted the buttons, more as a political statement than otherwise. In other towns, young men obeyed the military order defiantly, wearing their coats with no buttons on them at all.[3]

"They've left me one inestimable privilege—to hate 'em," a North Carolina hotel keeper snarled. "I git up at half-past four in the morning, and sit up till twelve at night, to hate 'em. . . . I'm like a whipped cur; I have to cave in; but that don't say I shall love 'em." That vehemence was strongest (and safest to express) among elite women. Fiercely, a Virginian wrote her sister, "Had I sons, this is the religion that I would inculcate from the time they could lisp: *Fear God, love the South, and avenge her!*'" Northerners found themselves frozen out with glacial stares and snubs. A young Union officer seated at a hotel table tried to pass a plate to a lady in black. He met only indignation and scorn. "So you think a Southern woman will take a dish of pickles from a hand that is dripping with the blood of her countrymen?" she exclaimed, and flounced out of the room.[4]

That fervor was by no means unanimous, nor whole-hearted, not even in the Palmetto State, neither before the war nor during it. Confederate vice president Alexander Stephens made no secret of his defeatism. Former senator Henry S. Foote of Mississippi, in applying for a pardon after the war, pleaded that by making himself such a pest in the Confederate Congress, he had hindered the Rebellion more than some armies did— which was very likely so. As an uplander explained, many who swore loyalty to the Confederacy did so "only from the teeth out." Many white southerners refused allegiance on any terms. They were beyond the spread of the plantation economy, or in northern Alabama counties where, as a Union soldier put it, the folks were "poorer than skim piss," but their hostility came from more than economic resentment. Disaffection spread as the war continued. "Some of the hottest secesh, too, got to be right good Union before the wa' was over," a farmer told one Northerner, "—they found the Yankees treated 'em so much better'n they expected and the Rebs so much wuss."[5]

Tentative and conditional Confederate loyalties withered away under the shortages and impositions of war. The more centralized the Rebel government became, the more resentment built among those whose first loyalty had been to their state or their community. Nobody liked taxes, and those who paid the most were the nonslaveholding farmers, some of whom felt that the planters, with more to fight for, should have carried a heavier load. With profiteering and shortages at home and bread riots in Virginia and Georgia, desertions mounted. Conscription set off furies. Talk of a "rich man's war and a poor man's fight" intensified as the draft provided exemptions for planters with more than twenty slaves. If the Confederacy had survived, there "would have been no chance for white labor," a Confederate soldier told one visitor. "Every rich man would have owned his nigger mason, his nigger carpenter, his nigger blacksmith; and the white mechanic, as well as the white farm-laborer, would have been crushed out."[6]

Unionism had been strongest among three groups of southern whites, and among them there was a serious disparity as to what Unionism meant and why they were for the Union: northern-born inhabitants, old Whigs, and the small farmers and yeomen of the upcountry. Some opponents of the Confederacy crossed fighting lines to enlist in the Federal army—no small number at that. More came from Tennessee than all the cotton South combined. Counted with recruits from the Union South, Missouri especially, the volunteers may have approached half a million in all. To be an implacable Unionist in some places was to put one's life at serious risk. Confederate commanders began by hunting down the dissidents' ringleaders, thinking that a few arrests would quell the others, and focused their attentions on those who put unfriendly words into action but widened their scope as the resistance in the hill country went on. Unionists in southwestern Arkansas claimed that under one military judge, hundreds of draft resisters were tried and shot, without the executions being entered on the books. The home guard in three North Carolina counties arrested scores of women for internment, with shocking results, a Unionist protested. "Women have been frightened into abortions almost under the eyes of their terrifiers." For many of those who waged the lonely fight on Rebellion from within, the traumas of war flung them outside the political order for good. They could not forget their injuries, nor that their losses had been in the country's service. "During the war if we could have collected all the mules in Christendom and have shod them rough shod and have made them kick rebs to death *we would have done it*," an eastern Tennessean wrote his senator in 1866. "Or if we could have mustered all the venomous serpents to sting rebs to death we would have done *that*."[7]

Yet, just as Confederate devotion fluctuated over the conflict and had different intensities, so, too, Unionism was a protean thing. It flared or guttered, or made a great show of smoke and went out, often in the same individual. A person could go from disaffection to disloyalty and then back to mere disaffection again. North Carolina governor Zebulon Vance's opposition to secession had been genuine, but by the time he ran for reelection in 1864, he reportedly swore that the South would fight the Union till Hell froze over and then finish the war on skates. Some Union men gave in. Others decided that they had been wrong all along. He had always been true to his country, a former candidate for governor protested, "but one day a wheezy old sidewheel steamer labeled Secession came puffing along and hove up to the wharf. As everyone else was jumping aboard, I jumped too; and all hands went to hell together." Some Unionism was passive, some active—some no more than a vague longing. In some cases it was based on self-interest and faded when the comparative advantages and disadvantages shifted.[8]

In other cases, it represented a nostalgia for a past America that, as it became clearer could never be restored, changed into a state loyalty. And that opposition to disunion based on the fear that a disruption of the established order would jeopardize slavery became a fiercer Confederate sympathy when that nation became the likelier hope for slavery's survival. Much of Unionism remained to the end of the war, a conditional Unionism, the kind best calculated to protect the essential interests of the South. Such a Unionism could live very well with slavery, and was, indeed, Unionist precisely because it was proslavery. Among eastern Tennesseans and countless other Unionists, there was no choice offered to begin with between saving the Union and preserving slavery. If that choice had been made, many would have shifted to the Confederate side.[9]

Unionism based on a profound conservatism, hostile to innovations that undermined the prevailing social order, was not about to overturn that order when the war was over. Unionists would insist on the reassertion of authority to cope with the stealing and pillage and disorder that plagued the South.

For many, indeed for most of the disaffected whites in wartime, and for the conditional or Cooperationist Unionists who were permitted the chance to hold office after the war, the experience of power only gave them the chance to rebuild the connections with those from whom they had been estranged for the past four years. They were all the more eager to find reconciliation with the rest of the white community by breaking with diehard Unionists or finding the excuse to do so; but the demands that the emancipation of the slaves put upon them proved more than excuse enough.[10]

So Unionism, however widespread it might seem in its many variants, could not shape itself into a unified party. It responded to different stimuli, reacted in different ways. It longed to go back to the way things used to be—and was determined to change society so that things could never be that way again. It included Unionists who kept their foot in the other camp and were ready to make terms with former Confederates. It was a coalition of outsiders who did not want to be outsiders, and for whom any association with former slaves would provide no solace, cultural or spiritual—nothing but a sense of their own personal social isolation.

Their vindication depended on one of their own. Andrew Johnson's birth in a log cabin gave him a lifelong sense that he was one of the people and represented their thoughts in ways no better-born adversary could. Taught to read by his wife as he worked on a tailor's bench, his lack of a formal education gave him contempt, perhaps flavored with envy, of the well-read and pampered aristocracy, intellectual as well as landed. In all, one critic hit near the mark in his gibe that Johnson had the pride of no pride, and, he might have added, the self-satisfaction of an insecure man. As a Jacksonian Democrat, resentful of the banks and broad-acred estates, disdainful of the self-proclaimed natural leaders of society who favored the Whig Party, he saw himself as the people's champion against an endless succession of conspiracies: political cliques, anti-Catholic Know-Nothings, abolitionists, and disunionists. Democracy for Johnson meant cheaper government and cheaper lands for those who wanted them, free homesteads in the West, and a free public school system in Tennessee. As with his political idol, Andrew Jackson, it also meant a polity committed to the broadest states' rights within an unbreakable Union.[11]

None of those values carried Johnson far from his mountain constituency. His talent as a stump speaker, as well as his courage and pugnacity in a fight, helped lift him from Greenville alderman to Congress, the governorship, and finally the Senate. But the higher he rose, the more he exposed his limitations. Always a loner, unable to confide in others and unwilling to take their counsel, he had no social graces to help him get along, and none of the self-effacing humor, the tact, or the readiness to compromise that made Lincoln so formidable a political player. The late president's skill to stay on excellent terms with the Copperhead congressman Dan Voorhees, "Tall Sycamore of the Wabash," and the radical Charles Sumner, much less Edwin M. Stanton, the bullying, hot-tempered secretary of war, showed a gift that Johnson would need badly. Schools came to Tennessee, and a Homestead Act went on the books, but not by Johnson's doing.[12]

Slavery had nothing to fear from Johnson. The runaway apprentice grew up to become a master himself. For him, the glory day of democracy would come when every family had its own slaves, just as he did. Affluence did nothing to remove Johnson's resentment of black people, who, he was sure, looked down on poor whites like himself. Nor did it erase his conviction that freed slaves, permitted to aspire to equality, would set off a war of races, one sure to end in their extermination. Between these beliefs and a firm commitment to the Union there was no contradiction. When Tennessee secessionists tried to stampede the state into the Confederacy, Johnson would have no part of it. He crossed the state, bringing the message that Democracy and Union had been, and must be, one. Behind the Confederate regalia he glimpsed the same privileged classes for whom personal and pecuniary advantage had always their first and deepest loyalty. Heading back to the Senate, he continued to speak for a Tennessee that, in his view, had never left the Union legally, and for a war to bring it back to a proper allegiance. As Lincoln's military governor, whatever strict construction of the Constitution Johnson maintained up to the beginning of the conflict, he proved a vigorous believer in a broader set of war powers once the fighting started. He arrested without warrant and jailed without cause. Yet it was because he remained an unapologetic Democrat and a man of southern sympathies that Republicans put him on their presidential ticket. Doing so, they sent the Confederate states the message that when they came back purged of their treason, it need not be as political outcasts within the Union.[13]

Elected largely by Republican votes, replacing a well-liked and increasingly respected chief executive, the vice president would have found it no easy task keeping the party's goodwill. The drunken spectacle he had made of himself at Lincoln's inaugural, where the secretary of state had to pull him back into his seat by his coattails, added to those doubts. Johnson remained, as he had been, a political and personal outsider, with a few close friends among former Democrats and not much beyond that. Radical Republicans hoped for the best, but even a few of them were alarmed at how bloodthirsty the new president sounded in his first weeks in office. His emphasis on the punishment of traitors might be well enough in its way, but radicalism had never been as much about bloodletting as it was about re-making the South somewhat more in the North's image, with men of tested loyalty holding the offices, slavery's legacy eradicated completely, and new governments formed by Unionists black as well as white.[14]

Andrew Johnson let them down from the first. After having given friendly hints, he gave the lie to them with his program to reorganize the seceded states. In a series of proclamations that spring and summer, he created provisional governments that would call constitutional conventions to ratify what to Johnson were the essential requirements for a restored, reconstructed Union. Only those covered by Johnson's Amnesty Proclamation could vote for delegates, but, having dictated who could not share in the franchise, the president pleaded that states' rights did not allow him to dictate who could. As before the war, only white men could vote. Once the conventions had made the recommended changes, the provisional governors could call elections for legislatures and state governments, again on an exclusively white basis, and, after the legislatures were called into session, they could adopt the Thirteenth Amendment, abolishing slavery. Discarding the diehard secessionist politicians, the reconstructed states would pick men who had either stood by the Union in wartime or stood aside. With the normal machinery in operation, the provisional governors would be relieved and replaced. "The government of the State will be provisional only until the civil authorities shall be restored, with the approval of Congress," Secretary of State William Seward explained in July; by that he meant that in the end, Congress would have to pass on the president's work, and, finding it good, would readmit the southern delegations to Congress.[15] But that Congress would find it good, neither Seward nor the president doubted— at least, at first—if the South did its part in good faith to accept the terms of peace.

Those terms were not stated outright. Clearly they involved renouncing secession, reassuming a loyalty to the Union, and clear recognition that slavery was gone, not to be revived. It meant an acknowledgment of defeat. But Johnson did not want to be too explicit, and he did not give detailed instructions to most of his provisional governors. As the summer went on, the terms grew a little clearer. To the governor of Mississippi, Johnson suggested that it might disarm critics in the North if at least some blacks, those able to read and write, or those able to pay taxes on real estate of $250 value, might be allowed the vote. (The advice was ignored, and the president dropped the subject. As he would explain, blacks, if enfranchised probably would ally to planters against yeoman whites like himself.) He also advised that the state ratify the Thirteenth Amendment. When the North Carolina convention met, a new requirement arose about which Johnson had not thought much at all: repudiation of the Confederate war debt.[16]

As became clear from the start, the proper penitent spirit would have to be guided. The least intrusive ways would be by a generous policy of pardons, evoking a generous, or at least grateful, response in return. The other would be that the president could make suggestions, often very intensely repeated ones, to steer the voluntary process in the South to where he meant it to end. He wanted the concessions to seem as if they came from the states themselves, as if there were no actual coercion. The more openly the president manipulated the conventions or intervened in the process, the more doubtful that loyalty would look. Visibly coerced cooperation would never reassure the North that Confederates were sincere in making amends. A hidden-hand Reconstruction had the best chance of working without offending states' rights sensibilities and giving the southerners who complied an excuse to repudiate their pledges once their states were equal partners in the Union again. There was every good reason why former Confederates would enter the process, cooperating as far as they could. If they wanted representation in Congress, or removal of the Freedmen's Bureau, they must heed Johnson's wishes, which was the very least that the North would expect of them. The press helped fix the picture indelibly, of a president and of a deeply divided North, with the people on one side and "Northern fanaticism" shouting for "blood & confiscation" on the other. It also made southerners assume that Johnson had the power to protect them, that his political support built a bulwark against their enemies. Satisfy him, and their toils would be lifted. Southern conservatives therefore chose not to consult with Republican leaders or to learn the will of the Congress. Their neglect would cost them dearly.[17]

Some ex-Confederates expected the worst after reading the Amnesty Proclamation's exceptions. Lincoln with his six classes of excepted people had been more generous than Johnson with his dozen, some of them charged. "It is harsh & unrelenting, & foreshadows his revengeful policy against our people," South Carolinian Henry William Ravenel feared. In fact, the list of exceptions did not so much rule a select group out of mercy as require their pardons to come by personal solicitation for a presidential dispensation. Most white southerners quickly discovered that the one concrete act that the conquerors expected of them was only to take an oath of allegiance. Ministers had to swear it if they wanted to preach. For those with property or a wish to do business, this oath was vital if they were to protect themselves from confiscation—or so they thought; in spite of the warnings that those who did not take the oath would be turned out of doors and all their possessions destroyed, no such dire consequences followed. The oath did not require a renunciation of past or present belief. It simply acknowledged a renewed commitment to the Union and the Constitution, "without mental reservation or secret evasion." Long lines stood before the provost marshal's offices in Georgia waiting to take the "D'am nasty oath," well before the officer in charge could find the necessary blanks. Planters traveled thirty miles to take the oath, only to find themselves in the wrong county, outside the proper jurisdiction.[18]

The pardoning policy had real possibilities, but only if handled rigorously. There lay one of the problems. The government had no agency, no extended bureaucracy, to go into the cases of so many applicants over the summer. It would have taken years. But Presidential Reconstruction had no more than a season to get under way. The restoration of order in the South required legitimized state and local governments quickly. American traditions pushed for an end of military supervision as soon as possible, and in any case, there was less and less army to handle the job every day, and that army ever more disproportionately black. Together, those forces threw most of the responsibility on the president himself.[19]

Johnson did not act entirely on his own. A practice developed where an applicant's chances would be improved by character references from undoubted Unionists. These were easier to get than northerners might have imagined. Quite a number of Confederates had kept up their relationships with Unionist neighbors, sometimes offering them protection from persecution, or refuge and succor from those who had done them harm. In any case, they could find Unionist sponsors, and Unionist sponsors' word went far toward guaranteeing a pardon. That was most true of the provisional governors' word. The president seems to have decided to lay the responsibility on the governors as a way of shifting an impossible burden off himself. No request would receive consideration unless it had a governor's backing, and in a circular letter, Johnson gave the governors some tips on who would be worthiest of approval. But once he had made this arrangement, the president had virtually obliged himself to defer to their judgments. In doing so, Johnson ran the risk of giving away the whole game. The governors were even less able to hold the line on applicants than he was. They needed support locally. Political eminence and influence went together, and the one way to win over the men of influence was to extend them the benefit of the doubt in their petitions for pardon and to hope that by recommending clemency, their help in Presidential Reconstruction could be obtained.[20]

In its original form, Johnson's pardoning policy promised to give him the political cover necessary to reassure Republicans that his Reconstruction would remake the South and the muscle to see that southern leaders followed his directives for a "voluntary" adoption of a program that the president was, in reality, forcing upon them. Until August, the president had given no pardons at all to anyone schooled at West Point or Annapolis, any officer in the Rebel army or navy, any antebellum congressman or member of the Confederate government. But such a policy could work only if it were the president, and not the white southerners, who decided how far and how fast the pardoning process was to advance. By September, the administration found itself compelled to issue pardons simply to keep its Presidential Reconstruction working, including ones belatedly given to officials elected while still ineligible. Pardon-broking soon became a thriving trade. In all, by the end of August, there were reportedly 50,000 pardon applications on file in Washington, and 400 more coming in every day. Several hundred people showed up at the White House daily, the sweat and fume of "abominably filthy" bodies mingling with the stench of tobacco juice, aimed but not always hitting the spittoon in the room. As pardons went, the *Cincinnati Gazette* grumbled, "the greater the traitor the greater the grace."[21]

In choosing provisional governors, Johnson could not have drawn from the first rank of politicians, even if he had wanted to. Necessarily, the candidate must have opposed secession; what came after that was not as rigid. The vital thing was to find someone able to induce ex-Confederates back into the Union, a resident of the state well within the political mainstream and having much in common with the traditional economic and social leadership. These requirements all but ruled out diehard Unionists or the firebrands favoring radical social transformation. Any outspoken enemy of slavery, much less a believer in what a Charleston paper would call "the antiquated, abstract theories of Thomas Jefferson" about human equality, could not inspire the cooperation that his limited powers obligated him to rely upon.[22]

The provisional governors were not masters of their own fate. At least on paper, they had powers no civil governor exercised, "greater than ever were claimed for an English monarch since 1688," in one North Carolinian's words. From the first, they risked being considered as alien figures imposed on the southern states. Survival required building their own power base. That could be done best by using pardons and patronage to draw the wealthiest and most influential men behind them. In making policy, from the first they had had to look to Washington. Every appointment a governor made would only last until the state held elections, and the officeholders knew it. At the same time, the provisional governors had unique limitations on their authority, made so by the presence of the U.S. army keeping authority on their soil. The provisional government could not administer the amnesty oath; that was the army's doing. The governors could not fight the president. But they could fight the army and in some states did so whenever an opportunity arose.[23]

For the provisional governors, the first problem came in trying to fill all the offices—in North Carolina, 3,000 town officials and justices of the peace over two months. The executives had to move fast because the administration set deadlines for the self-reconstructing process, but also because of a well-founded fear of disorder. County courts had not opened in months in some places, and in one Mississippi court, not for the past three years. Business before it was piling up. In state after state, that meant putting the incumbents back into office, whether they could take the iron-clad oath or not, and making a rare removal only when proofs of disloyalty became too plain to ignore. Given the option, of course, governors would choose conservatives over original secessionists, those who opposed disunion at first and gave the Confederacy little beyond lip service in wartime, but they often had no ready pool of applicants to choose from, and certainly not among the men holding pardons. In South Carolina, the president's complaint that Union men were being denied a fair share of the government was even met with South Carolina governor Benjamin F. Perry's brusque answer that the state had no true Union men, never had, and that anyone claiming to be one was lying to get into office. At most, appointees there were "original Union men," meaning that they had changed their allegiance once secession took place.[24]

The one area in which none of the provisional governors showed much interest was advancing civil rights for the freedpeople beyond a bare freedom. Their legitimacy rested on making clear that their racial ideas reflected southern, not northern, white attitudes. Governor James Johnson's silence only excited Georgians to accuse him of being wobbly on the color line. As it was, most provisional governors grouched about the presence of black troops on their soil and carped about the Freedmen's Bureau. Their dissatisfaction was not lost on a white electorate. In his proclamation announcing his accession to office, North Carolina governor William W.

Holden lectured blacks on their obligation to work hard, save their money, and remain temperate. "I will be your friend as long as you are true to yourselves," he announced. But that friendship did not entail any commitment to have public schools funded for them—only a recognition of their right to learn to read, if they took the trouble. As one of their self-proclaimed best friends, Florida governor William Marvin cautioned them, "You must not think because you are as free as white people, that you are their equal, because you are not."[25]

The moment when a Unionist South might have come into being could have been that summer when the Confederate states chose delegates to constitutional conventions. The Unionists held most of the advantages. Most of the big-name Confederate officers and the planter class still went unpardoned. They could not take part in politics, and none of them did so. Those elected in turnouts ranging from slim to nearly nothing were opponents of secession in 1861 by two to one, and were for the most part ex-Whigs. But this was no unconditional Unionist set of gatherings. They were not the bottom rail, by any means, nor the struggling yeomen. Lawyers, businessmen and well-to-do farmers outnumbered all the others, men, one delegate commented, of very moderate ability alongside "a good many chuckle heads." In most gatherings, the number of strong wartime Unionists was small indeed: one in South Carolina, six in Georgia.[26]

In several cases, the conventions moved tentatively toward a more democratic politics. South Carolina's parish system was ended by seventy-eight to thirty; Charleston's twenty representatives were reduced to no more than a dozen. For the first time, South Carolinians could vote for a president and governor. The property qualification for serving in the legislature was done away with. Alabama changed the apportionment from the "federal ratio" that counted slaves as three-fifths of a person in allotting representation to a system based on white people exclusively. Georgia counted total population, adding to the advantage that the white minority in Black Belt counties enjoyed.[27]

With no commitment to black southerners beyond a reassurance that they would not be remanded to slavery, Johnson expected far less from the conventions than what the North considered an absolute minimum and nothing more than an acceptance of realities. Even these came with ill grace. Delegates did the basics expected from them—nothing more and, where possible, just a little bit less. South Carolina, Mississippi, Georgia, and Florida were prepared to repeal their secession ordinances, not to declare them null and void. Practically, it amounted to the same thing, but symbolically, the difference was key. The one act implied that an act, once done, had been lawful, and that the states voluntarily decided that in this case, they had mistakenly exercised a state's sovereign right. The other implied that secession had never been a legitimate right in the first place, and that the states acknowledged that fact, and acknowledged that the Union's war had been made on just grounds. To nullify the secession ordinance, opponents contended, fastened the label of traitor on every person who abided by the state's action, on their own "fathers, brothers and sons who had died in battle." In South Carolina, the difference between repeal and annulment never came up, but a northern reporter noted the "suggestive silence" in contrast to the "salvos of artillery and clanging of glad bells" when the state had passed the secession ordinance in the first place. North Carolina ended up annulling the secession ordinance overwhelmingly, Florida and Mississippi more narrowly. Georgia joined South Carolina in passing a simple repeal motion. In Alabama and Texas, the majority pronounced secession null and void, but only from now on—not in the past.[28]

As for slavery, the state conventions agreed that it had been abolished, but it took some struggling on Johnson's part to make them do so, and the restlessness was what the northern press picked up the most. In Mississippi, opponents offered a preamble to the abolition amendment, making clear that slavery's end was strictly the federal government's doing and that the convention only recognized a distasteful reality. Diehards responded that the ordinance made southerners accomplices in bringing that reality about. Members still thought that it could be salvaged. The Thirteenth Amendment might fail, for lack of enough states ratifying it; negotiations for compensated emancipation might get under way, particularly if the North felt that it had no other alternative. "We seem to forget where we stand," a bewildered James L. Orr chided his colleagues; "we forget that we made the war and have been beaten; we forget that our conquerors have the right to dictate terms to us. And I tell you, it is to the good favor of Andrew Johnson that our terms are no worse,—nay, are so liberal. He is the dike between us and the waves of Northern fanaticism."[29]

Nor, throughout the proceedings, did delegates mislead anyone into believing that their change of policy carried with it a change of heart. Well aware that their new governments were on probation before northern policymakers, they were doing what they did on compulsion. They did not welcome slavery's end. They did not regret secession. It may have been meant to soothe their pride and to get right with their constituents that they made these points so clear. But they went against the whole idea of a real change of mind in the South that Johnson's program counted on. Some of them argued that even meeting at all was "humiliation enough to satisfy any reasonable man." "We are living under a tyrannical military despotism," one of them stormed; "our hands are tied; we have no free will of our own." To push an antislavery ordinance through South Carolina's body, Orr had to portray a North even more frightening than the one pressing them now. "There have been cases in which whole peoples were swept from the face of the earth," he warned; "is that what we covet?"[30]

On one issue all the conventions agreed, and their agreement made clear that they felt that no demands from Washington imposed any obligation on them in this respect: there would be no steps toward race-neutral voting or even full equality of rights. Allowing that slavery was "dead forever," Governor Perry inveighed against black soldiers and quoted the 1857 *Dred Scott* decision to show that blacks could never become American citizens. Governor William G. Sharkey, in spite of the president's hints that a measure of black enfranchisement would be politically expedient, did not even bring up the issue, and no Mississippi delegates did, either. But, then, not even the few unconditional Unionists were keen on the idea. Delegates freely declared that "the negro is an animal," and the convention treated him as a thing "whose presence is endured but is no way desirable." The worst of it was, a reporter commented, their opinions were probably more enlightened than those of their constituents: they represented "the best intelligence of their respective districts." The worst intelligence expressed views more concretely. To knock a freedperson down with a club "or tie one of them up and horsewhip him, seems to be regarded as only a pleasant pastime," a traveler noted. As a bureau officer in North Carolina explained, "A great many of these people, if a negro says anything or does anything they don't like," would put a bullet in him. The talk around the hotels showed one listener that killing a former slave was "held to be an evidence of smartness, rather than otherwise." Whites generally agreed that the freed race would die out anyway, and many frankly hoped for it. "D—n their black souls, they're the things that caused the best blood of our sons to flow," a Mississippian raged. "The infernal sassy niggers had better look out," another warned, "or they'll all get their throats cut yet."[31]

What was done on compulsion was work that stood every chance of being undone, and both sides knew it. "The convention has adjourned & has made almost a new constitution instead of correcting the section only, as required by our lords & masters in Washington," wrote South Carolina's William Huger. "I hope one of these days to see it altered again to suit ourselves." That may have been one reason why no Deep South convention trusted its work to the voters. In Alabama and Mississippi, resolutions to do so were offered, and in both places they were beaten by wide margins.[32]

The fall elections showed how wise they had been. As the returns came in, northern observers thought they saw the same old host of enemies, "dagger in hand ready to strike down the Goddess of Liberty," as the *Cleveland Leader* put it. Ten Confederate generals and five lesser officers, nine members of the Confederate Congress, and sixteen minor officeholders under the Rebel government had been chosen. As for new legislatures, many resembled that in Arkansas, where a visitor found "Colonels and captains . . . thick as bees." Most places, Whigs from before the war won—and men whose support for the Confederacy had come late or had been lukewarm, as close to Union men as a largely Rebel constituency was prepared to tolerate. That, to them, seemed a good-faith effort to show that they were abiding by the president's requirements.[33]

In the upper South, of the twenty-five men elected to Congress, five were Union veterans. Just about all of them could take the ironclad oath, if need be—and the two exceptions in Virginia's delegation had been the most reluctant and belated of Confederates. In the cotton South, by contrast, most of the winners had to have some kind of Confederate war record at the least. "I hope every district in the State will elect a man for Congress who can't take that d—d test oath," a Georgian exploded; "I want to see the Yankees try it on; if Georgia isn't a free sovereign State, I think, by G-d, it's time we knew it!"[34] Among those who won office were those whose war record not only made their rejection from Congress certain but left them unpardoned. Certainly they went a very short way toward putting the small yeoman farmers and wartime Unionists of Johnson's own kind in charge.[35]

So poorly did the conventions do that Johnson by late October had begun to harden in his demands, expecting more. Now it was the legislatures that must take remedial action: ratification of the Thirteenth Amendment, the admission of black testimony, and laws "passed for the protection of freedmen in person and property, as justice and equity demand." But in the end, the president did not dictate; he bargained, assuring the governors that the second section of the amendment was merely verbiage, not meant to expand federal powers. Mississippi and Alabama accepted the amendment with resolutions hitched on as provisos. Mississippi's view was that slavery ended only in those states adopting the amendment but not in the others.[36]

One issue dominated the sessions from the start: the control of the freedpeople. "Without regular, systematic, and reliable labor," a South Carolina correspondent predicted, "this fine country becomes a wilderness." For that reason, the law must compel that labor. Beyond that, the *Jackson (Miss.) News* caught the purpose exactly when it declared that lawmakers must enact a code that would keep blacks "in the position which God almighty intended them to occupy: *a position inferior to the white man.*"[37]

The model lay closely at hand. In most cases, all that needed to be done was to stretch the antebellum laws covering free blacks to take in the large freed population, and Arkansas simply left those laws operational. But even before Presidential Reconstruction had begun, northerners could see what the Black Codes would look like. They had to look no further than the "loyal" South: Virginia and Tennessee, where vagrancy and labor contract laws had gone through just at the war's end. In Tennessee, all blacks had to register with the county clerk, and punishments for violation of the law included sale of the defendant for a term of forced service. Vagrancy was deliberately left so vague a term that it could sweep up any and every freedperson where convenient. No black testimony in cases involving whites was allowed, an invitation, as one newspaper charged, for whites "to outrage blacks with impunity." Rape was a capital offense—but only for black defendants.[38]

Later defenders of the law would make the case that, in effect, the Black Codes expanded black rights considerably, including those of free blacks. The old laws forbidding them from entering certain occupations, requiring them to have a permit before moving from one place to another, or learning to read and write were taken off the books. Former slaves now could sue and be sued in court. They had the right to hold, buy, and sell property. They could plead in any court of law or equity. Except in Texas, they could marry legally, and those already cohabiting in Mississippi were considered lawfully espoused, even without their acquiring a license; the children of ex-slaves were declared legitimate. The code defining laborers' duties included their rights: not to work in snow, sleet, or rain, for example. Landlords could not throw homeless or aged ex-slaves off their land in South Carolina, and in a few states, antivigilante laws gave some paper protection against white thugs assembled "for the purpose of injuring persons of color in their persons or property, whether under pretense of punishing crime or otherwise." Four states guaranteed a worker first lien on an employer's property for unpaid wages.[39]

By any standard understood outside the South, that mildness showed itself neither in the debates nor in the final provisions. Lawmakers were quite frank in making clear that they acted not to emancipate former slaves but to bind them in. No one had kindlier feelings toward "that unfortunate race" than one former slaveholder, but, he went on, he would never give equal rights in court to a people "influenced more by stomach than intellect—to whom the proffer of a hogjowl was an irresistible argument." Such an ugly stir did the South Carolina code make that most of the other states hastened to avoid its mistakes by leaving specific mention of race out of the statutes and by enacting penalties that at least from the wording of the laws applied to black and white alike.[40]

Work was reinforced with severe vagrancy laws. The breadth of the laws depended on their definition. Alabama defined a vagrant as "any runaway, stubborn servant or child," and any laborer "who loiters away his time" or failed to obey the terms of a contract—or, in the frank words of one apologist for the law, to any "not quite industrious" worker. Vagrancy applied in Louisiana to any black who had not signed up in a new contract by early in the year.[41] Under the law, judges could hire out vagrants for their labor. There were no provisions for jury trial.

On their face, the apprenticeship laws seemed a means for training orphans to gainful employment. As many as 30 percent of all black children in Texas may have qualified—though most of them had lost their parents in a different sense: one or both had been sold away to places unknown in slavery days. Under the new statutes, courts could apprentice children up to age twenty-one (and, in South Carolina, down to the age of two), and if they were over fourteen, that action must come with their consent. But it did not just apply to orphans; the law also covered any children whose parents the court thought unable to support them, and in some states no parental consent was necessary. The new master must post bond, promise to clothe and feed his charges, give them humane treatment with "such moderate corporal chastisement as a father or guardian is allowed to inflict on his child or ward at common law," and instruct them in reading and writing. But whether the law said so or not, the apprenticeship system was aimed almost exclusively at black children, not white ones. Black parents in North Carolina could lose their children if the county court ruled that they did "not habitually employ their time in some honest, industrious occupation." No such requirement fell on white parents. Children whose mothers were capable of supporting them were taken away on the oath of the person bent on obtaining their labor. In Alabama, a nineteen-year-old, well dressed and with a character witness, was haled into county court as a minor, taken from his mother, and bound to work for ten years as an apprentice at no pay.[42]

Plantation workers could get by with less fieldwork, as long as they could live off the game in unfenced property. "A man could go out and kill a dozen squirrels, they was that thick," a former slave recalled. For the planters, this hunting deprived them of game that they deemed theirs by right as much as "our chickens and turkeys." Close the hunting grounds to blacks, and they would be more closely confined and unable to supplement their diets by hunting. Georgia forbade hunting on Sunday, but only in the heavily black plantation counties. Georgia law also forbade taking anything "of any value whatever" from private property, which discouraged berry-gathering or collecting fuel for fires. In several coastal counties, special laws taxed hunting dogs, guns, and muskets on every plantation—in practice, those of the owner's workforce, and not the planter himself; the planter was given power to enforce the tax. The legislatures also put through more severe laws dealing with larceny. A very real problem did exist. For many former slaves, stealing or poaching had a certain legitimacy. Employers who paid too little had a good chance of seeing their cattle and hogs disappear, in an informal augmenting of compensation. Stock-raising in South Carolina would end, planters predicted, because "the negroes have shot and stolen them all."[43]

In most states, two movements went together: the rebuilding of white militia to keep order and hold the freedpeople in awe, and the disarming of the black population. South Carolina restricted blacks to fowling pieces only, and Mississippi's blacks were allowed firearms only after they obtained a special license from the county board of police. Kentucky law permitted any white to confiscate any deadly weapon, "powder, or shot" in blacks' possession and, with the court's consent, make it his own property.[44]

In all states, interracial marriage was forbidden. North Carolina inflicted the death penalty for blacks attempting the rape of a white woman, fine and prison for a white man committing the same offense, but did not cover assaults on black women at all. Florida's code had four death penalty offenses, one of which was rape—but only if the victim was white and the accused perpetrator black.[45]

Blacks could testify in court, but only with serious restriction, in most states only when they were interested parties to a case. "Why, no nigger can believed whether he is under oath or not," a Mississippian blurted out. "No one that knows a nigger will ever think of believing him if it's for his interest to lie." What accommodation lawmakers made, they did under force. As one state senator expressed it, Negro testimony was ransom paid to occupation authorities for the right to control freedpeople in other ways—with vagrancy laws, for instance. In Mississippi, it took the governor's best efforts and a telegram from the president to bring lawmakers around. Under duress, the governor of Texas opened the witness box to blacks, though he grumbled that it would lead "to perfect social and political equality." Kentucky would not permit black testimony on any terms.[46]

All of these laws had had some northern counterpart. Alabama and Louisiana's vagrancy laws took that of Massachusetts for their model. But they were harsher in penalty and provisions, and unlike northern laws, actually enforced—and on one race exclusively. No northern state deemed a person caught cohabiting with someone of another race a vagrant, or people gathered in unlawful assembly, "common railers," fortune-tellers, play-actors, circus performers, and those exhibiting waxworks without a license. While the Freedmen's Bureau had issued circulars on apprenticeship and vagrancy, it meant them as nothing more than a temporary expedient. None was as harsh or allowed so little consent from the parties involved as state law mandated.[47]

Furthermore, even where the laws did not mention race or color, they were enforced that way. Prosecutions under the enticement laws showed that clearly: rare was the white kept from taking up a better offer. "As the drayman ordinance practically operates, in the main, against colored draymen alone; as the chain gang is composed entirely of colored convicts, so the apprentice law will practically operate principally upon colored minors," the *Mobile Nationalist* warned, and on every one of them that the statute's wording could be poked and pulled into covering. The provision that gave masters preference in being assigned freedpeople's children only made the Alabama law's intentions explicit.[48]

Penalties were even more specifically biased on the basis of race. In most cases, the difference lay in the application of the pillory or whipping post for freedpeople's offenses. In Florida, those punishments went with a broad range of crimes: selling leaf tobacco or cotton without proof of ownership, setting fire to fences or buildings, hunting with a firearm on someone else's property, cutting a boat loose, or extinguishing street lamps. Distinctions in punishment, Florida's select committee explained, were "founded upon the soundest principles of State policy. . . . To degrade a white man by punishment, is to make a bad member of society and a dangerous political agent. To fine and imprison a colored man . . . is to punish the State instead of the individual."[49]

The codes were enforced rigorously—except the provisions penalizing white men for cohabiting with black women, which stirred ire only when

"'Slavery is Dead'?" Thomas Nast, *Harper's Weekly*, January 12, 1867. Nast's cartoon draws on the punishments meted out to blacks under southern Black Codes. A Copperhead snake writhes around the states' rights skeleton.

northerners did it or when sanctified by marriage. Blacks in many communities found themselves disarmed and their homes invaded. In Kentucky, discharged Union veterans were fined for bringing their muskets back from the war. They lost the guns, too. The apprenticeship and vagrancy laws brought out the creative impulse everywhere. The mayor of Aberdeen, Mississippi, declared hundreds of blacks vagrants without formal proceedings and gave all defendants a few hours to select an employer for the following year or have one chosen for them. In one county, white planters found themselves short on field hands; blacks earned more in the turpentine forests elsewhere. They solved it by inducing the local court to have several hundred of their former slaves classed as orphans and bound out to them.[50]

Those northerners who had imagined that with defeat, southerners would turn with fury on the leaders who had ruined and beggared them found just the reverse. Men who had denounced Jefferson Davis's handling of the war were unanimous in expressing sympathy with him as a prisoner. All their indignation turned on his jailors. General Robert E. Lee was positively revered, his Confederate service lauded as turning away "all the kingdoms of the earth" for "the agony and bloody sweat of Gethsemane."[51] Far from feeling vindicated, Unionists found themselves taken into court, assaulted, and driven from their homes by those they had helped defeat. On the Tennessee & Alabama line, all the Union men were dismissed and replaced with their Confederate neighbors. In Richmond, Union men were tabooed generally, and it was widely agreed that any jury daring to convict Jefferson Davis of treason would be mobbed and killed. Even businessmen who stuck to their trade found the prejudice cutting into their custom. "I never hated a Johnny, you know," a Union officer fumed, "and I guess all our fellows felt the same way. But, by Jupiter, I wish now that they'd leave off singing the 'Bonnie Blue Flag' and damning us poor devils. . . . I want 'em to get up another war, you know, and then I want a cavalry command. Won't I raid through Georgia! There shan't be anything left behind me."[52]

The "Free State" Louisiana government that General Nathaniel P. Banks had made in 1864 and that he and Governor Michael Hahn had left behind was in the hands of Governor J. Madison Wells. "A political trickster," General Phil Sheridan called him. "His conduct has been as sinuous as . . . a snake." Some twists back, it had been the course of a true Union man. A cotton planter from the Red River who had refused to join a war on his country and gone into hiding for two years, Wells had fled to New Orleans after the Federal army moved in, bringing thirty of his slaves with him—which he freed. In 1864, he had become running mate on the Free State ticket, a perfect symbol that their movement represented the whole state, Rebel-held parishes included. When Hahn resigned as governor in March 1865, Wells changed his colors, or, perhaps, lowered them. Calculating that with the war's end the Confederate part of Louisiana would shift the electorate sharply away from General Banks's Republicanism, he set out to win friends and build a political machine of his own. Quite possibly he grasped at that glimmering hope that he could revitalize the state's Whig Party, at least in spirit.[53]

Out went the "Banks oligarchy," and in came the archconservatives and former Confederates who had opposed the Free State constitution. When the general tried to protect his friends, Wells appealed to the president, who relieved Banks of his command. With jurisdiction over the state for the first time after Lee's surrender, the governor had a whole state's worth of offices to staff, from police jurors to sheriffs and recorders. He chose people with influence or influential backers, because only they could count on having their will respected. Not many of them could have taken the ironclad loyalty oath without a smirk. "The best recommendation that an applicant for office can bring the Governor and party is that he was in the Rebel army," an Ohioan warned his congressman, "while a Yankee brought here by the war or the result thereof, is a barbarian to be discouraged and driven from the State." By June, the city press expressed Confederate sympathies and denounced Lincoln openly. Local Black Codes, General Carl Schurz informed the president that September, "study, not how to build up and develop a true system of free labor, but how to avoid it." True Union men felt betrayed, afraid. With the courts and constables on their enemies' side, they could not expect protection if attacked, and the attacks had begun.[54]

Governor Wells, to all appearances, was riding high. Democrats, heavily weighted with former Confederates and "quite a Superior class of men generally," nominated him for governor in his own right in the fall election. Conservative Unionists did so, too. The only opposition he faced came from the unauthorized candidacy of wartime governor Henry W. Allen, unpardoned, in exile, and unlikely to return; behind Allen stood the most unregenerate Democrats, those who argued that the Free State constitution was illegal and null, and that the 1852 fundamental law still was operative. But the National Democracy that endorsed Wells was not much less extreme. It declared the Free State constitution a fraud, though it agreed to abide by it, and came close to putting through a platform affirming secession as a legitimate state's right. Wells won hands down. Arguing that the Free State constitution was illegal and casting ballots for a "territorial delegate" to go to Congress, Republicans got no more than 2,500 of 20,000 votes polled in the state; if the blacks casting ballots in the city's eleven wards in the "voluntary election" had been counted, the number would have risen to 18,840, very nearly half the total.[55]

Any prospect of a moderate alternative to the Rebel Democracy vanished as a thoroughly Democratic legislature came in with its own agenda. One item was to call a new constitutional convention, vacating every office in the state, Wells's included, so that former Confederates could make a clean sweep. By year's end, executive and legislature had drawn daggers over a bill deferring state taxes for the war years, but only to the Confederate end of the state. The president's failure to back up the governor on appointments exposed his vulnerability; without his patron, he could count on nobody's respect and certainly nobody's fear.[56]

Unconditional loyalists had long since despaired of either the governor or government. For months, they had been reporting that in many parishes, a loyal man could not live so much as a day. There, some masters still worked their hands as slaves, threatening to kill those who left. In the interior, a "kind of aimless lawlessness" made it impossible for the American Missionary Association to send missionaries. Without contracts or prospects, Low Country blacks still refused to go up the Red River, telling recruiters, "They is killed too many black folks in that country." One visitor saw a picture gallery in New Orleans showing Lincoln and John Wilkes Booth's portraits side by side and above them both, "a large, handsomely finished portrait of Robert E. Lee!" Removing military forces from Louisiana would be "an act of madness," radical lawyer Thomas J. Durant wrote onetime occupation commander Benjamin Butler. "Those who have occupied advanced positions here in favor of the suffrage of the colored man would be slain or driven from the state, if they did not resort to flight."[57]

As with Louisiana, so it was everywhere. By 1866, the evidence was mounting that conservatives saw their every concession as tactical and temporary until they got the federal government off their back. Far from serving as a way-station on the road to full equality, the Black Codes, it became very clear, were the absolute most that southern states were prepared to concede and only as long as they had to. In Texas, J. W. Throckmorton, soon to be elected governor, had no welcome for newcomers, not "greedy, psalm singing, lying, windling Yankees & sour krouts & blackguard Irish." Bring them in, he protested, and children would marry "these d-m-d negro worshipping skunks and Southern blood is tainted & spoiled forever." Returning confiscated property to its former owners did not just close off the possibilities for black landownership. It brought about the eviction of Freedmen's Bureau hospitals, asylums, and schools that had occupied many of the buildings. The white community refused to rent alternative space. Boardinghouses closed their doors to northern schoolteachers more resolutely than ever. Without a federal presence, the Black Codes' protections for freedpeople's rights would be ignored, while the restrictions would be given unofficial enhancement. Given the chance, representatives from the white counties tried to repeal whatever black testimony laws graced the books, though not successfully. "Just so soon as civil power is fully restored," Mississippians boasted, "there shall be an end to Nigger schools & the presence of Nigger teachers." Cotton merchants in Georgia had more comprehensive hopes. From "the hour the military are withdrawn, and the 'Nigger Bureau' removed," they told a reporter, "darkey blood will run in Macon's gutters, and . . . a hundred negroes per night must perish." Quarrel with each other though they might, every shade of Unionist now looked to Congress to act. "Strike hard and do justice," Louisiana judge Edward H. Durell wrote Banks.[58]

CHAPTER FOUR

Reconstruction at Last, 1865–1867

P residential Reconstruction worked nearly as well as Johnson hoped. However grudgingly, the conventions and legislatures did accept the president's terms. Slavery was ended, ordinances of secession repealed, and if many of the first crop of elected officials paraded their Confederate credentials, most of them had given the Rebellion only half-hearted support, if any. If the fall elections showed anything, they proved that Connecticut, Minnesota, and Wisconsin were not ready for impartial suffrage—at least for themselves—and that elsewhere Republicans found their winning issue in their having won the war. But the Johnson "experiment" appalled radicals and left moderates in varying degrees of unease. The unconditional Unionists were hopelessly beaten for office. Though the restrictions on southern blacks scarcely troubled Andrew Johnson, they were far from what most Republicans thought a fair settlement.[1]

They were also increasingly disturbed by how this reconstructing had taken place. Nearly all of them believed in states' rights, and all but the radicals among them believed that the national government had no authority to set voting requirements. They, too, had felt uneasy with the expanse of presidential power in wartime. Far from lusting for a powerful nation-state driven by an all-supreme Congress, most Republicans longed for a return to a federal government as the Founders had meant it to be, with presidents administering the law and fulfilling executive duties, Congress fashioning policy, the Supreme Court keeping both within their constitutional confines, and the states remaining the real arena of policymaking. In reconstructing the South, nearly all Republicans would have agreed that any settlement, to pass muster with the courts, must be made by law, not by executive decree. They were well aware that the further from the war the country came, the more those "war powers" that presidents had declared for themselves would become suspect. Yet by the time the gavel fell in the House that December, southern reconstruction seemed nearly completed, and all of it outside of the law.[2]

As the advance guard of the party, radical Republicans saw the president's policy as having fallen fatally short, in its refusal not only to protect freedpeople's civil rights but to give them the vote, the one power by which they could most protect themselves. Most had come to the antislavery cause early. Quite a few had been outright abolitionists, not content simply to fence the peculiar institution out of the territories. Others' views had intensified in wartime, when it became clear that without a fatal blow against slavery, the rebellion might yet live. Where the abolitionist Liberty Party had made a showing in the 1840s, in upper New England and on the northern rim of the country generally, radicalism flourished. Cleveland had more radicals than Cincinnati, Chicago more than Cairo, and the Protestant churchgoing farming communities more than either. The less rural and the farther south in the Union states one traveled, the more radicalism became exceptional. Wherever cotton-spinning and the southern trade made compromise a paying proposition, radicalism had to struggle for a hearing. The new Midwest, areas settled in the 1840s and 1850s, produced a heavy crop of radicals; those areas had just about no southern emigrants to provide a second opinion on slavery. In every case, though, the political flavor after the war reflected the pungent quality of Republican politics before it. Military service, while it may have stamped love of country deeper into northern recruits and forged an indissoluble link between Union and emancipation, did not become a nursery for radicalism. With a few exceptions, radical leaders formed their beliefs and began their careers in the 1830s and 1840s; Thaddeus Stevens had been taking fugitive slaves' cases pro bono since the 1820s. They might even be called, as England's future prime minister William Ewart Gladstone was, old men in a hurry.[3]

Later historians would describe the radicals as vindictives, warped by hatred for the South into harpies of vengeance. Cruel war bred bitterness everywhere in the North, and Republican doctrine from the party's beginning had played to resentments of a South with too much power, too much pride, and no good reason to deserve either. Republicans of all stripes pointed with alarm at the "Slave Power," the conspiracy of southern elite to force their institutions on free people everywhere, and if anything, those partisans who cared the least for the slave shouted about the "Slave Power" the loudest, turning a struggle over slavery and freedom into one of South against North. Those who had seen slavery in operation or remembered the vaunting and bullying congressmen from the slave South may have had more reason to feel unforgiving than others. A few of them talked harshly. But talk was cheap, and when it came to action, radicals seemed much less keen on punishing white southerners than in lifting up black ones and in affirming a stronger, more comprehensive and active nationality. "You cannot kill off all the white men who cherish a hatred toward democratic institutions," Wendell Phillips cried. "You can only flank them, as Grant flanked Lee—flank them by democratic elements—Yankee commerce, black suffrage, divided lands."[4]

Radicalism also carried a later infamy as the vanguard of industrial capitalism, and some scholars hinted that their philanthropic talk was a pose, a moral front for selfish interests behind. In fact, the same case could have been made against the whole Republican Party, if a belief in free labor's superiority over that of slaves was the defining principle. Republicans had argued from the first that slavery did not simply oppress blacks; it impoverished the South and bore hard on nonslaveholding farmers forced to compete against their planter neighbors. The institution held back economic development and gave a positive discouragement to investment in industry, all of which, Republicans contended, made a South ill-clad, ill-fed, ill-housed, and ill-served. True to the Whig tradition out of which so many Republicans came, radicals and moderates alike thought that the government could spur development by working out a partnership with banks and railroads, and by providing protection to American industry against foreign competition. Protected interests, makers of woolen and cotton cloth included, had strong reasons to be beholden to the Republicans in general. But well-propertied classes did not always vote their pocketbooks. For many of them—especially those in overseas trade and those supplying southern planters—the radical Republicans did nothing but harm when they turned their attentions southward. Any businessman who resented soaring tax rates or thought that sectional antagonisms would cripple the economy had good reason for opposing the Republicans, radicals particularly. The "cotton Whigs" and commercial classes in every big northern city applied their money on conservatives' behalf instead.[5]

The grey eminences of centrist politics lacked the gaudy coloring that would make so many radicals the stage villains or heroes in later histories. "Cold as an iron wedge," General William Tecumseh Sherman's brother John, the Ohio senator heading the Finance Committee, would hold high office until the turn of the century, the statute book loaded with major legislation carrying his name, among them an antitrust act and a silver purchase act. But there was nothing exciting about Sherman. One reporter spotted him "standing up like an Indian in the dry goods trade, the polite, the practical and the ambitious rolled into the long sapling of him." In vain one looks for quotes about Illinois senator Lyman Trumbull like Ben Wade's coarse remark before the war that the difference between his friends and the Slave Power's was lands for the landless and "niggers for the niggerless." The peevishness and dyspepsia of Maine's senator William Pitt Fessenden could never make the good copy of Thaddeus Stevens's clubfoot, chestnut-colored wig, and presumed mistress. Stevens's well-cultivated reputation for cynicism and his deftness at parliamentary law and vituperation made him one of the most perilous and picturesque figures in the House, so much so that one might miss how regularly he ended up losing a war after winning a battle. The polished oratory of Senator Charles Sumner gave him a national following to reckon with but irked his colleagues almost as much as his pompous self-righteousness and contemptuous dismissal of the half-loaves that Stevens would accept every time, rather than lose all. But it was with the moderates that the real power lay and, as far as Congress heeded, the more convincing arguments.[6]

Radicals and moderates agreed on certain essentials. Almost all Republicans outside the most conservative edge believed that mere freedom would not be enough and favored equal rights under the law. The vast majority felt that race should not be grounds for denying any man the vote, though moderates doubted that former slaves were fit yet to exercise the privilege. They were prepared to extend the vote to blacks in the District of Columbia—as they finally did in early 1867—and some were prepared to require impartial suffrage in the territories. As the winter went on, many moderates' early hope that the Johnson governments would be steered more in the right direction faded. Along with radicals, they had refused to admit the southern representatives to Congress, until a joint committee on Reconstruction headed by Fessenden had investigated conditions; differing in their grounds, they nonetheless argued that Congress had the right to decide whether the Johnson governments met the basic qualifications for republican forms of government—a natural doubt of authorities created by presidential fiat and exercising power on the basis of unratified constitutions. In laying a lasting settlement, they welcomed Johnson as a partner but not as the last word in what the North expected of the former Confederacy.[7]

But the differences between radical and moderate were crucial. Moderates placed a higher value than radicals on restoring the good feeling between the sections that a permanent Union would need and on making sure that any postwar settlement had a firm constitutional basis. The war had been fought on the argument that states had no right to secede and could not leave the Union, even if they would—the very grounds on which southern conservatives argued that, once the fighting ended, southern states still kept their sovereign rights and could reconstruct themselves as they and only they saw fit. On the opposite extreme, Stevens argued that the disunion crisis, uncontemplated by the Founders, put its settlement outside of the Constitution. Legally, states could not create a separate nation—but they had. The glint of their bayonets on the field proved that well enough. They had been conquered and, as "conquered provinces," stood outside of any of the guarantees for states that the Constitution had set up. The government could not try Rebels for treason any more than it could enemy combatants of any other foreign power. But Congress could confiscate property—say, from 70,000 planters—redraw boundaries, mandate school systems, or hold the South under military rule for as long as it chose.[8]

Sumner's "state suicide" theory did not go as far. As one of his supporters put it, there was no way of removing a state from the Union "except by unhinging creation and transferring the soil to some other planet." All the same, by seceding, the states had forfeited their political character. To argue otherwise would be to admit that Confederate governor Isham Harris had been the proper authority in Tennessee in 1862 and Andrew Johnson a usurper. "They say a State cannot be killed," Senator Timothy O. Howe told a Wisconsin audience. "I might be made to believe it, if I had not seen it done." That did not make the inhabitants any less part of the United States or unfit them for civil government—quite the reverse. Congress, not the president, must furnish it, by remanding the states to territorial status. Covered by the Constitution's protections, inhabitants might even be permitted their own legislature, but the government could use all those powers it had over territories, including defining who could vote and the process for achieving statehood.[9]

Moderates' theory (and Johnson's as well) resembled Sumner's in recognizing that national authority alone could set the states on the road to full reconstruction, but where Sumner saw in the Constitution's power to guarantee a republican form of government the permanent oversight to preserve justice, the centrists looked to the speedy return of southern states to Congress, with the same rights as those that had never left. The nation's power to change conditions lasted only while it held those states in what legal scholar Charles Henry Dana called the "grasp of war"—a matter of a few months or years at most. Congress could decide whether the Johnson governments met minimal standards for republican government. It could require the states to go to work to meet those standards. Beyond that, under the Constitution, it could not go. The Shermans and Trumbulls had none of Wendell Phillips's confidence "that if I give a black man a ballot to-day and forty acres of land to-morrow, the best Democrat in South Carolina will ask him to ride the day after," and understood well enough that the *Nation's* insistence that America was willing "to maintain an army of two hundred thousand for twenty years . . . to garrison the rebel States and enforce the national laws" simply did not fit the impatient cries from all members' constituents to trim forces and funds for them to the bone.[10]

Moderates told themselves that the president had only acted until Congress could make his work legal, either by accepting it or by offering modifications to it. In this they had Johnson's own encouragement, and Johnson continued to mislead them off well into the new year. Perhaps hope was father to the thought. Nobody wanted a bruising confrontation. The political risks of deadlock were far too great, and, at the back of some northerners' minds there may have lingered the fear that a divided North might inspire a surrendered South to try a new rebellion. Even radicals who had lost all faith in Johnson stressed how far his words and their beliefs merged— Sumner included, though he already had learned better after a testy interview at the White House during which the president used the senator's hat as a spittoon. Every day that went by, it was true, southern authorities entrenched themselves more deeply. Overturning them now seemed impossible, and no centrist in Congress talked seriously about doing so. Pretending that Johnson considered the new governments as merely experimental rather than a fixed permanency seemed equally fabulous. But moderates' hopes were fed by visits to the White House, where the president seemed quite reasonable, listened to their suggestions politely, and seemed to be very nearly in full accord with their plans for legislation to amend the wrongs laid on black southerners.[11]

On December 19th, Lyman Trumbull announced his intention to introduce a bill continuing the Freedmen's Bureau and enlarging its powers to "protect every individual in the full rights of person and property and furnish them with means for their vindication."[12] His offering, in fact, became two bills introduced early in the new year: S.60, relating to the Freedmen's Bureau and S.61, a civil rights bill.

Under S.60, designed with the bureau commissioner's input, the agency was not simply continued indefinitely. It got expanded powers. Two sections defined the deprivation to blacks of any civil rights that whites enjoyed— among them the right to bear arms—as a misdemeanor and gave the bureau's military courts jurisdiction until a state resumed its normal relations in the Union. It also allowed the agency, for the first time, to hire civilian agents to replace the dwindling supply of military officers in any county with significant numbers of blacks. As an added provision, the bill gave the War Department authority to distribute food, medicine, clothing, and fuel for "destitute and suffering refugees and freedmen."[13]

Necessarily, the bureau bill's main focus was on the insurrectionary states. Proponents could invoke the extraordinary war powers that the emergency had conferred on Congress as their justification. But if Republicans could make that argument, they did not feel wholly comfortable making it the sole basis for action, particularly since the bill's provisions covered Union states, too. For the bureau, which was meant as a temporary agency, helping along the transition between slavery and freedom, the appeal to war powers had more force than one for a permanent agency. The further from the conflict the country went, the more its authority weakened. The connection to the Thirteenth Amendment provided a complementary rationale. Section 2 of the amendment had given Congress "appropriate powers" to end slavery, which, in a liberal reading, included slavery's effects and the confusion surrounding slavery's end. For a peacetime measure like S. 61, however, the section held even greater importance.

Democrats questioned the whole premise for Congress acting. Civil rights had always been a state concern, they insisted; the Bill of Rights applied to national government action exclusively. The Thirteenth Amendment had not changed that at all. It had abolished slavery, yes. But it had conferred no new powers on the national government at the expense of the states, beyond those of seeing that one person did not hold another in involuntary servitude. Republicans took no such view. To take the master's power away and leave him "at the mercy of the State to be deprived of his civil rights" would make the promised freedom "a delusion." Abolishing slavery, Congress had meant to abolish slave codes. Under the Thirteenth Amendment, the government had the power "to educate, improve, enlighten, and Christianize the negro; to make him an independent man; to teach him to think and to reason; to improve that principle which the great Author of all has implanted in every human breast, which is susceptible of the highest cultivation, and destined to go on enlarging and expanding through the endless ages of eternity." None of that would be done by legislation "for freedmen" per se. Radicals themselves knew that remedy would be inconsistent with "a republican form of gov't." But seeing that all laws applied alike to every race was different. "Give equal rights to whites & blacks," Assistant Commissioner Eliphalet Whittlesey wrote Oliver O. Howard; "impose the same taxes, the same duties, the same penalties for crime, and then execute the laws with simple justice; and the result will be peace, safety, prosperity."[14]

The civil rights bill was a monumental step forward, from its first words, redefining U.S. citizenship to cover "all persons born in the United States and not subject to any foreign power." It guaranteed to all citizens the same rights "to make and enforce contracts, to sue, be parties and give evidence, to inherit, purchase, lease, sell, hold, and convey real and personal property, and to full and equal benefit of all laws and proceedings for the security of person and property, as is enjoyed by white citizens," with the same punishments for infraction of the law. Federal courts for the first time got jurisdiction over cases in which civil rights were denied, and the bill's supporters meant the remedies to cover more than southern statutes. Democrats were right to see it as radical, however far moderates shaped it. At the same time, the civil rights bill conferred no right to vote, hold office, or sit on juries. These, Republicans contended, were political rights, involving as they did the exercise of power. Nor did it overturn laws like Indiana's that forbade interracial marriage, as long as the punishment on white and black for violation was the same. Nor did all of the bill's supporters think that it covered private acts of discrimination.[15]

By late January, though, insiders must have felt much more uneasy than they let on. From the White House came no statement to show that Johnson would welcome congressional intervention to fix the drawbacks in his southern policy, or even that he thought any drawbacks existed. About the attacks on loyalists and the injustices in the Black Codes the administration was mum. From Democrats and southern conservatives, though, words came in endless litany, claiming Andrew Johnson for one of their own. They appealed to him as their bulwark against the radicals, and built him up as the forceful man who would use his executive powers to cleanse the Capitol of its usurpers and fanatics. Republicans became less sure of Johnson's goodwill and by February 1866 knew that he had lost whatever faint willingness he might have had for giving blacks the vote. But those who had written the Freedmen's Bureau bill were sure that the president would accept it. The authors of the civil rights bill, undoing most of the restrictions in the Black Codes, were equally confident.[16]

Their faith was shattered on February 19th, when Johnson returned the Freedmen's Bureau bill with a veto. Some of his arguments found ready sympathizers among Republicans—the objection to the military courts adjudicating in peacetime, for example—but the whole tone of the presidential message was brutally frank that no bill, however modified, would find favor. Under the original law, the agency would continue for some time thereafter—not, Johnson admitted, that freedmen needed protection. Equating bureau agents with slave overseers, the president denounced the bill as wholly unconstitutional. The agency had been created for "the military destruction" of slavery and to "suppress a formidable rebellion." Slavery was gone. The Rebellion plainly was "at an end." Not only did a government program funding schools and asylums break precedent; it was more than had been done for toiling white people. And, the president indicated, as long as southern states were not yet readmitted to their seats, Congress acted presumptuously in legislating at all.[17]

Even for some radicals, the veto outdid their worse expectations. Johnson had "begun the war," James A. Garfield wrote, "—has opened fire on the Sumpter of our civil liberty." Across the South, whites took the veto as a sign that the bureau would close down soon and all lands in freedpeople's hands be returned immediately. Officers worried that the veto would let owners think that they had license to cheat and exploit their workers while it would make freedmen wonder whether the government would leave them in possession of sequestered lands long enough to reap the next harvest. Without martial law, a commissioner warned, "we can do nothing. It will be impossible to try any criminal by military commission."[18] Yet with all their indignation, Senate Republicans could not quite muster the unity to override the veto.

On February 22nd, when a Democratic club came serenading, the president responded in a speech that proved an even worse shock than the veto message. Comparing himself to Jesus Christ, referring to himself more than 200 times, charging an "irresponsible central directory" with seizing "nearly all the powers of government," accusing radicals of plotting to assassinate him as they had Lincoln and of intending the annihilation of eight million southerners, he singled out enemies of the Union as dangerous as Jefferson Davis: Thaddeus Stevens, Charles Sumner, and Wendell Phillips.[19]

Fearful of a party split and of the president's ability to use patronage to widen it, Republicans struggled to find some common ground. Moderates convinced themselves that Johnson might join them there by accepting the civil rights bill. On military tribunals and open-ended commitments to the bureau they could give ground, but not on guaranteeing equality before the law. Perhaps the president hove closer to the Republican position than his veto message implied. With a little encouragement, he might be made perfectly tractable. If Republicans had known that the president remained convinced that Congress meant to vacate his office unless he did as it wanted, they would have seen that all talk of a meeting of minds was fantasy. Their illusions shattered late in March when the president vetoed the civil rights bill in more implacable terms than ever. Far from denying that discrimination on a racial basis existed in the South, Johnson justified it as right and proper. If Congress could interfere this way, he warned, nothing could keep it from ending laws that kept blacks from marrying whites. Under Section 1, the president warned, Congress made citizens of the Chinese! of Gypsies! of Indians! Most of all, the president treated civil rights legislation as an invasion of the rights reserved to the states and discrimination "in favor of the colored against the white race."[20]

To the end, the two-thirds vote needed in the Senate remained uncertain. Indeed, only six bills had ever passed over a presidential veto, the last of them in Franklin Pierce's administration. When two conservative Republicans called at the White House to see what compromise could be worked out, they discovered that Johnson would accept no civil rights bill on any terms. Sadly, they trooped back to Capitol Hill, resolved to override the veto. It carried, just barely. "And then you ought to have heard the galleries," Senator Timothy Howe wrote home. "They sprang to their feet clapping hands, stamping, shouting, yelling, waving handkerchiefs." On April 9th, the House overrode the veto by 122 to 41. A "glorious day," wrote Speaker Schuyler Colfax, a "day of days." Later in the session, Congress enacted a new, more limited Freedmen's Bureau bill. This time they had no difficulty overriding a veto.[21]

Already, both houses were at work on a new constitutional amendment, intended as a settlement of one of the loose ends left by slavery's destruction: an adjustment of the South's representation in the House. The three-fifths clause in the Constitution no longer functioned, but the alternative was, to northern minds, still worse: a large black population, shut from power, but now counted fully in apportioning House seats, thus giving the southern delegations more weight in legislation than before the war. Twenty-eight extra seats from the South, twenty-eight more electoral votes cast on behalf of men held unfit to testify in court or sit on juries, and all to strengthen those who once had betrayed the government: no Republican found that tolerable. Fairness decreed that if four million people were unworthy to share in the governing of a country, they should not swell the power of those that *did* govern.[22] But what kind of amendment could erase that advantage and still have any chance of three-fourths of the states ratifying it? If those three-fourths included the eleven former Confederate states, success would require not only a unanimous North but unanimous states in the upper South as well.

That consideration ruled out the most obvious solution from the first. Radicals would have liked to see some or all black southern men given the right to vote. But quite a few Northerners would not relish a larger southern contingent in the House, no matter how legitimately deserved. They also worried that blacks dependent on white planters for their livelihood might vote as directed. Most Republicans also had misgivings about taking away the states' power to decide who should vote and who should not. To shift this decision to the national government would be a revolutionary step toward centralization—and few people in either party wanted that to happen. A more feasible remedy based representation on the number of qualified voters. Cutting blacks out of the apportionment, it would reduce southern delegations to well below their antebellum numbers while offering an implied and incremental reward for states enfranchising the freedpeople. Then New Englanders calculated the costs and realized that with their literacy and naturalization requirements and the highest ratio of women to men in the nation, they stood to lose seats by the change. The joint committee took up an alternative leaving the basis for representation and direct taxes as the Constitution had set it, based on population, but with a proviso that when race or color led to the denial or abridgment of the right to vote, all members of that race would be taken out of the count.[23]

After several false starts and dead-end alternatives, the committee took up the proposed amendment in April and got a nudge from former Indiana congressman and utopian reformer Robert Dale Owen. Owen suggested not a bunch of amendments but a single omnibus, handling representation, the validity of the Union's war debt, the restriction of former Confederates' rights, and a constitutional definition of citizenship that would put the civil rights law's provisions beyond court challenge and for the first time effectively secure most of the freedoms in the Bill of Rights against states' abridgment. As his plan stood, it would cut many Confederates out of the vote and bestow it on southern blacks in 1876, giving the South time to educate and fit them for the suffrage. Radicals and moderates agreed on Owen's general framework, but they kept their eyes as clearly as ever on the necessity for something with near-certain support of every northern state and a decent prospect of success in at least a few southern ones.[24] There any plan with Negro suffrage would fall short.

On April 30th, the committee reported a five-part amendment with a broad guarantee for equal protection of the laws, a proportional reduction in representation, based on the extent of male disfranchisement, and removal of the vote in national elections from "all persons who voluntarily adhered to the late insurrection, giving it aid and comfort." The restriction did let former Rebels vote in state and local elections, however, and it restored full voting rights on July 4, 1870. For Thaddeus Stevens, the disfranchisement section was the one saving grace. "Without that, it amounts to nothing," he told other members. "Give us, therefore, the third section, or give us nothing." Party ranks held firm, driving the measure through the House by more than three to one. The Senate responded more skeptically. No matter how just the joint committee's program might be in itself, it stood scant chance of winning a single state south of the Ohio River. Without that, the amendment's adoption looked impossible, and if an amendment must embody a settlement of the war's issues, then Congress was no nearer a solution than ever. Waiting for the inevitable rejections would take months; the readmission of southern congressmen would be postponed for years, with all the economic uncertainty and government expense that entailed. Impatient voters might accept Democratic alternatives as better than no reconstruction at all. How safe would even the most minimal civil rights be then? Anything beyond what the public security absolutely demanded, any provision that an impartial northern mind might deem unjust, must go.[25]

In plain English, that meant Section 3. Southern Unionists were alarmed because many of the most loyal would be deprived of the vote. Those who had evaded military service by taking county and local offices, those drafted into the ranks, would also fall within its provisions. Beyond question, disfranchisement would embitter white southerners, including many of those not directly affected by it, and, if that proved the case, at the end of four years, the newly enfranchised would be raring for vengeance. Section 3 would take a large military presence for its enforcement or, if it fell to local officials, would be as good as a dead letter.[26] It was not so much as punishment as a safeguard for the future that northerners saw Section 3, and for that purpose, simply keeping traitors out of positions of power would satisfy the Union's most pressing need. Loyal men could stand to let Rebels vote, one paper summed up, but to hold office—never. So replacing disfranchisement of the many with disqualification of the few was not only more enforceable; it was a fall-back position almost certain to be made.

As the final version of the amendment passed the Senate, alterations defined national and state citizenship in the first section to include "all persons born in the United States, and subject to the jurisdiction thereof," cleared out the disfranchisement portion, and put in a third section disqualifying from office those Confederates who had broken an oath taken before the war to uphold the Constitution—a small proportion of the whole. The restriction was not meant as a permanent punishment. An escape clause was added: by a two-thirds vote of Congress, any disqualification could be removed. Section 4 was expanded to include a positive guarantee for the federal debt. Democrats later contended that the terms were designed to assure their rejection: that no southern state would adopt the amendment, even in its revised form. In fact, the changes were made based on the very real hope of just the reverse. Republicans talked confidently of Tennessee and Arkansas ratifying and even thought the chances good in Louisiana and Virginia.[27]

Radicals could grumble but dared not stray from party ranks. Some clung to the faint hope that Section 2 would bring black suffrage. Southern states might prefer a wider franchise, just to keep a larger presence in the House. All the same, the choice would remain where it always had been, with individual state legislatures and not with policymakers in Washington. Representing North Carolina's interests, B. S. Hedrick wrote home that in essence, the proposed amendment demanded two things that would have been unavoidable in any case: a deprivation of the South's right to claim representation for blacks without bringing them into the body politic and a ban on the Confederacy's civil and military officers holding office. Beyond its provisions, the so-called Howard Amendment gave the party a unifying, winning platform for the fall. No terms were imposed on the former Confederate states; they could accept or reject as they pleased. The amendment, Congress hinted very strongly, would be treated as a final settlement of the issues raised by the war. Any southern state adopting the amendment would give weighty (but not necessarily conclusive) proofs that it had reconstructed enough to deserve representation in Congress. Just in case the hint was not taken, Congress before it adjourned had admitted Tennessee— the first former Confederate state strong-arming the amendment through and, as it turned out that fall and winter, the last. From the conservative South came an almost universal chorus of execration and defiance.[28]

Moderates' faint hopes that the president would accept the amendment as a fair settlement were dashed almost immediately. Within days, Johnson took steps sure to unite all but the most conservative Republicans against him. He threw his weight behind efforts to form a new National Union Party, merging his Republican backers with Democrats. Accepting slavery's end and wrapping their cause in the American flag, the new organization might carry the 1866 elections up north and ready the way for readmission of the southern states without making the Howard Amendment a condition. For some participants like Secretary of State William Seward, the new organization would serve as a more moderate version of the Republican Party and drive radicals from control; for Democrats, the door opened outward, not inward, allowing moderates to join their organization instead, while Johnson seems to have looked to a new party entirely, one able to elect him president in his own right two years hence.[29]

With such a conflict of purposes, the National Union movement began to sputter right away. Three cabinet officers resigned rather than endorse the movement. Fearful of leaving Johnson in undisputed control of the army, Secretary of War Stanton clung on but made no secret of his opposition. Seward's friends might think that the amendment, modified, might serve as a settlement with the South; Democrats denied that Congress had the right to impose any terms on the South at all. Neither group offered any welcome to Union men who thought that restoration ought to set conditions beyond those that the president had solicited the year before. A movement for what Thaddeus Stevens called "universal amnesty and universal Andy Johnsonism" hemmed itself in pretty closely. To have much draw among northern Republicans, the movement had to cleave to a definition of Unionism not so wide open that any soldier in grey or Copperhead in butternut was allowed entry. As a consequence, any movement in which ex-Rebels from the South played an active role would rouse suspicions in the North. Southerners clearly expected that the convention would include all Democrats, especially the "immortal band, which, throughout the long struggle of the last five years, forbore not, in season and out of season, to raise their voices in behalf of the muniments of liberty"—meaning the most extreme Copperheads. The South wanted to make room not only for its most offensive characters but for its even more offensive doctrines. The *Montgomery Mail* did not conceal its own distaste at the initiating call's "unrepublican language" declaring the union of the states "indissoluble and perpetual" and its "formal denial of the corner-stone of our political system" the right to abolish any government "subversive to the just ends of its institution." If its support ranked as Unionism, what kind of support did not? Confederates had tried visiting Philadelphia before, the *Newark (Ohio) Courier* joked—in 1863. Then they made it no further than Gettysburg. Now the same parties would be on hand, their trip completed.[30]

That was how it looked, as the delegates were chosen. There was no question of sending delegations that had stood by the Union in wartime. Leaders of the convention movement who assumed to distinguish between "Secessionists and Unionists," the *Memphis Appeal* asserted, or instructed the South on whom to send were being dictatorial and impertinent. Doubtless the 140 Confederate officers sent felt the same way. No southern delegation could possibly agree to anything that would recognize, even implicitly, the loyalty test oath or the provision declaring the Union of the states "in every case indissoluble and . . . perpetual." As for requiring any concessions in return for readmission, that was out of the question.[31]

When the National Union Convention met on a sopping August day, it put on a good spectacle. Fifteen thousand attendees assembled before a flag-festooned speaker's platform. Behind the podium hung a canvas backdrop, with an arch of thirty-six stones painted on it and the motto "1776–1866: United We Stand, Divided We Fall." Below it was suspended a rather damp stuffed eagle. (Significantly, the assembly, a supposed continuation of the forces that had elected the Great Emancipator, was wholly Lincoln-free: no portraits, banners, mottoed flags with his name, and no reference to him in any of the prepared remarks.) The band played "Rally Round the Flag Boys," then "Dixie," then "The Star-Spangled Banner." The master of ceremonies banged a gavel carved from the timbers of the USS *Constitution*. The high point, the best-rehearsed moment as well, came as the delegates from South Carolina and Massachusetts entered arm in arm: massive Governor James Orr and wee Union general Darius Couch leading the way. The crowds roared, cheered, and wept. They continued to cheer as cut-and-dried resolutions went through, denouncing the congressional amendment and the unlawfulness of a Congress legislating in the absence of eleven states' delegations. So tight a control was kept on any spontaneous fits of honest opinion from the floor that cheering was nearly all that they could do. But by the time an official delegation had brought news of their doings to the president, who responded by referring in passing to the legislative branch as a body hanging on the edge of government *claiming* to be a Congress, the National Union movement's power to affect politics had been blighted beyond repair.[32]

Events in New Orleans had wrecked it a fortnight since. With Governor Wells fending off a Democratic legislature's efforts to undo his government, Free State leaders embarked on a bold comeback attempt. Using the technicality that the 1864 constitutional convention had not formally adjourned, they proposed to call it back into session. Conceivably that body might narrow the vote to loyal whites or broaden it to blacks, or both. Delegates could then submit their amended constitution to Louisianans of either race. Winning, as in any full turnout they surely would, Unionists would control the state and could brandish a fundamental law so radical that the very congressmen who had fought hardest to keep Louisiana out would welcome it back in.[33]

The idea was too clever by half and crazy twice over. Governor Wells disliked the idea of blacks voting as much as he did Rebels ruling. Many Unionists drew back from the proposal. Black leaders and the original Republicans of the state, with much better lines of communication to Capitol Hill, wanted nothing to do with the scheme. The convention would need to call elections in all the parishes unrepresented in 1864, and with an all-white electorate, it was sure to be packed with delegates bitterly hostile to the Unionist remnant. Appalled by the whole idea, Judge Edward Durell, the presiding officer, refused to call the convention. Some forty of his old associates had to depose him and choose a new president who would. A month passed before the governor called a special election for delegates on September 3rd and issued writs of election for the unrepresented parishes. One thing only needed to be done; the fragment of the 1864 convention could take no action without a quorum, but it must meet on July 30th to count the vacancies among the old membership. Some had died, some resigned, and many, it was clear, had no intention of showing up. Only with an authoritative list of no-shows could the governor put out special writs of election for their seats.[34]

The delegates met, but before they had discovered themselves too few to do business at all, white mob violence, helped along by the city's police and firemen, attacked a parade of black and white supporters of the convention. Murder, atrocity, and mutilation followed. There had been race riots already. One in Memphis that May had gone on for three days, with forty-six blacks and two whites killed and unnumbered black women raped. "Laborers quietly returning to their homes . . . were shot down like dogs," an investigator wrote, "—defenceless old men and women were butchered in the streets and their own houses. Dwellings were burned by the dozen, and in one instance a young woman dying was thrown into the flames of a burning house and consumed." Churches, schools, and stores in the black community went up in flames. But the political implications put the New Orleans massacre on a different order of magnitude. Former governor Michael Hahn was shot in the back of the head; he survived his wounds. Former state treasurer Anthony P. Dostie did not. Shot five times, stabbed with penknives and a sword, and trampled on, he died six days later. Rioters butchered the wounded and invaded the hall, shooting unarmed men waving a white flag. "The floor was covered with blood," one victim remembered, "and in walking downstairs the blood splashed under the soles of my boots." Well over forty blacks were killed and over one hundred wounded. Later, the local court made arrests—of delegates and other victims. None of the riot's perpetrators were brought to justice. The *New Orleans Times* advised radicals to strip Dostie's skin and sell it to Barnum to defray the expenses of "negro newspapers." His body "will make good soap," it added. "Let him be boiled down, preparatory to being distributed in bars to Yankee 'school marms.' Delicious will be the kisses by those angular females from ebony cheeks, late lathered with sweet scented Dostie."[35] Andrew Johnson's response alienated those Republicans still wavering between his side and that of Congress. Not only did he berate and order the governor around as if Louisiana were a provisional state under his direction rather than the sovereign commonwealth that he had claimed all the former Confederates to be; he laid all the blame for the violence on radicals, who fomented the violence for political effect, and on a conspiracy directed from Congress.[36]

Late in August, Johnson sealed his doom by heading to Chicago to dedicate the tomb of Stephen A. Douglas. Making speeches all along the way on what came to be called the "Swing Around the Circle," the president used the occasion to defend his policies and blackguard Congress as radical-dominated, fanatical, and bloodthirsty. Campaigning was considered utterly unpresidential. Anything beyond bland generalities would have brought Johnson into bad repute, but he worsened it by celebrating every step in his career and exchanging insults with hecklers that began speckling his crowds. Comparing himself to Christ and the Freedmen's Bureau to slave masters did not help his case, and one onlooker hoped he would be suspended from office until it could be proved that he had not uttered the word "alderman" for three months. "If all of Mr. Johnson's I's were suffused with tears, what would be the depth of salt water in the streets of Washington?" one newspaper wondered. Public reactions grew so ugly that General Grant, taken along as a showpiece of the president's patriotic credentials, went off on a binge and found excuses to quit the journey. At some stops, the engineer started the train before Johnson could finish speaking to crowds ready to shout him down. By the time he returned from "Andy's Adventures in Blunderland," as one diarist called them, even his press spokesmen were trying to distance themselves from him.[37]

Uniting on the Fourteenth Amendment as reasonable, even generous terms of peace, Republicans radical and moderate turned the midterm elections into a referendum on the Union, beset again by traitors and risked by renewed civil war. Audiences did not have to take their word for it; southern loyalists like "Parson" Brownlow of Tennessee and Andrew J. Hamilton, the president's own provisional governor for Texas fanned across the North giving expert testimony that Rebels had taken charge across the ex-Confederacy. Democrats' appeal for the Union "as it was" and the Constitution "as it is" meant a return to a past of civil strife and injustice. Hamilton would have none of it: "I want the Union as it wasn't and the Constitution as it isn't." Republicans could make a good case that the Democrats who denied Congress's legality might well use any gain in House seats to create a House of their own, admitting the excluded southern representatives and counting on Johnson to put the army on their side, even if it meant dispersing the Republican House at bayonet point. When a newspaper published the story that the president had asked his attorney general whether Congress was a constitutional body, it took several days before readers realized it for the fake that it was. The president's own public statements made it seem completely plausible. So worried about a possible coup was General Grant that when Johnson invited him to head a mission to Mexico, he half suspected that the president's real purpose was to get him out of town so that the army could be placed in more dutiful hands. Secretary of War Edwin M. Stanton was equally upset. After the election, the two worked together to reduce future risks by having Congress require all presidential orders to go to the army through Grant, as general in chief.[38]

On the Democratic side, orators roused listeners against "Congress with all its nigger" and "the negro-equality constitutional amendment." Radicals meant to make "negro legislators and negro judges" of a race that worshipped reptiles as gods and built temples of human skulls, one Union general charged. The amendment only would prolong stalemate, as Democrats saw it. There was no prospect of its being ratified by the South, nor any intention on Republicans' part that the South do so. They wanted the southern states excluded from all power, at least through the next election. That would give them more time to force Negro suffrage on the nation, suspend or eject the president, dissolve state lines, and make the South into a "Poland" held down by 200,000 soldiers. Their "secret and rich" Union Leagues, the paramilitary forces banded in the newly formed Grand Army of the Republic, planned to overthrow the republic. "It is threatening to shake down the pillows [sic] of constitutional government," said the *Portland Eastern Argus*, a little infelicitously. "There is no whoa to this aggressive spirit. Its very nature renders it impossible to halt. Death is its only goal."[39]

Northern voters could not be convinced. In every state, Republicans carried the governorship and most of the legislatures. They won more than two-thirds of the House seats as well. The next Congress promised to be even more radical than the Thirty-Ninth. More than that, the returns sent a message that moderates were sure the South could not miss: Johnson's claims to the contrary, the amendment had robust northern support. Its terms were the very least that the South could expect to concede. Having been undeceived about the president's representing public opinion, the southern states would surely adopt it immediately. Even Johnson might bow to the inevitable.[40]

Instead, down south, the elections changed nothing. Even before the November returns, conservatives had persuaded themselves that taking the entire country as a unit, the white vote stood with them and against Congress. All that a Republican landslide proved was that a minority had lied and gerrymandered itself into control of the House and Senate. The real test of public opinion lay two years hence in the presidential race. Freed from any sense that the people had spoken against them, unwilling to believe even that the elections spoke for the North as a whole, well aware that the president was on their side, white southerners indulged in no second thoughts about ratifying the Howard Amendment. It disqualified statesmen from office and undermined local elites' control of their counties. It enhanced national power over matters belonging to the states, like civil rights. It deprived the South of its full share of representatives in the House. Accept the amendment, the *Selma Times* warned, and the South fastened the test oath on the Constitution. "The Southern States cannot, without degradation and dishonor, ratify an amendment which inflicts the disgrace of disfranchisement on a large number of their own citizens."[41]

Disgrace, degradation, dishonor: the language of southern conservatism had taken a truculent edge. A year before, they had advised expediency; now they breathed defiance, reminiscent of secession days. "If I have to eat [dirt]," one Georgian stormed, "I want to be compelled to do it, not to be hospitably invited to it as a desirable meal." Contemptuously, North Carolina's governor proposed using the Freedmen's Bureau funds to send the blacks north, where radicals seemed to love them so much. The wrath was real, but broadcast north, it could only confirm what radicals had been saying all along, that opinion-makers in the South had learned nothing and changed nothing since 1861 in the way they had treated the North. They would come into the Union on Andrew Johnson's terms or none at all. Indeed, southerners were now declaring that even the terms acceptable to them a year ago, the president's own plan for admitting loyal members only, were more than southern honor would accept. Texas governor J. W. Throckmorton not only called on legislators to reject the Fourteenth Amendment; he gave them liberty to reject the Thirteenth, the offspring of "a parcel of experimenting, humbugging, rascally, fanatical hounds of hell, who have served the devil all their lives," as he put it.[42]

Equally disturbing, the violence against loyalists of both colors increased. "Go home and establish good schools at every county town," Freedmen's Bureau assistant commissioner Clinton B. Fisk advised an African American convention. "Such schools will catch like cholera." They caught, in fact, like kindling: white arsonists saw to that—sixteen in Tennessee in just one year. Replacements were built. They burned, too. For teachers, there were death threats, knifings, and corrosive abuse. "School marms" were treated either as unsexed fanatics or "strumpets . . . in quest of negro husbands." Sent to upstate Louisiana to open a school for freedpeople, George T. Ruby was hauled from bed in the dark of the night. A gang of whites knocked him about and dragged him to the creek. "S'pose you thought the United States government would protect you, did you?" one shouted. "D—n the United States, we don't care for it." The "d—d nigger school teacher" was driven out of town on pain of death; compared to others of his race, he got off lightly. Landowners attacked their black hands with pistols, hatchets, bricks, and chains, particularly as harvest season came on. A freedperson could lose his life for trying to leave one employer for another, for reporting an incident to the local bureau officer, for not surrendering his whiskey flask, for failing to take off his hat, for defending his wife from outrage, or just because rowdies wanted to "thin out niggers a little." Itinerant black ministers were set upon, stabbed, and mobbed; one was assaulted until, in a fellow evangelical's words, he looked "like a lump of curdled blood." Freedmen's Bureau files were filled with heartrending appeals from mothers whose children had been seized without warning and "apprenticed" without due process. The bureau courts had been dismantled once state courts permitted Negro testimony, but that testimony did not ensure justice. When a Maryland judge invited prosecutors to skip a trial and simply have the black defendant taken out and hanged, when crimes against blacks were dismissed or shrugged off with nominal fines, when penniless freedmen found their only recourse against landowners' violations of contract in mounting expensive court challenges before white juries refusing to believe a word any black witness said, justice was a farce. Disguised "regulators" terrorized black communities. They killed at least thirty freedpeople in a single Texas county in less than a year. The perpetrators were well known, but no indictments were found. If war broke out again, an Austin Unionist predicted, his kind "would stand but a poor show for their lives."[43]

For the wartime Unionists in the Deep South, conservative recalcitrance gave them the real hope that Congress would go further than it had the spring before. They knew now that the amendment fell far short of what was needed. The more spirited the legislators' rejection of it the better, so that Congress could make improvements. From New Orleans, an Ohio congressman found the universal desire for a new provisional government and an electorate defined by wartime loyalty and not by race. Congress should not deceive itself, wrote Texas loyalist Edmund J. Davis. A "very qualified suffrage for the negroes will not be of much service to them or us." Freedpeople's conventions made the same point. "If we are free, we want the right to protect that freedom," one speaker pleaded. "Give us that, and we will show the nation that we are no broken-legged, or patched-up Unionists. . . . Give us the ballot, and we ask protection from no man or class of men."[44]

So while the winter session held back on Reconstruction legislation, it had other ways of showing radical tendencies. The District suffrage bill was one, a bill admitting Nebraska to statehood another. Moderates were of two minds, not one. They all agreed that the amendment must be ratified by the southern states, and that nothing else would be adequate as the conditions for readmitting their representatives to Congress. But while for some a swift ratification would be sufficient, others emphasized that unless action came, and came soon, they would set other conditions. Tennessee's readmission had been not simply because it agreed to the amendment but because that ratification fit into a pattern of steps to prove its regeneration into a loyal state. (Those steps were continuing. With any new white support outside his reach, Governor William G. Brownlow convinced fellow Unionists to give blacks the vote and muster a state guard to protect them from white violence.) And in all Republicans, the conviction was hardening that whatever the state governments' standing in law, their ability or willingness to protect loyal men's property and lives was failing to meet the most elementary tests. Amendment or no amendment, something must be done about that, and if need be, the national government would have to step in with all the power at its command—and soon. In the *Milligan* case, the Supreme Court had just overturned a military court's conviction of an Indiana Copperhead, declaring such tribunals illegal in the absence of war or invasion. "The Constitution . . . is a law for rulers and people, equally in war and peace, and covers with the shield of its protection all classes of men, at all times, and under all circumstances," Justice David Davis declared. How long, then, could military courts or even Freedmen's Bureau courts pass muster down south if judges ruled the wartime emergency past or the southern governments legal?[45]

By New Year's, Republicans could see that every southern state that had not rejected the Howard Amendment so far was sure to do so. What was more, the president encouraged them to resist. Democratic editors assured the South that if they killed the amendment, Congress would not dare try any policy more drastic. With Johnson's veto power and a faltering majority in either house, the worst to expect would be deadlock. Never was there worse advice. Early in January, Thaddeus Stevens offered a bill replacing the Johnson state governments with provisional authorities and requiring elections to new constitutional conventions. Southerners had the chance to vote for or against holding a convention and for or against ratification of the new constitutions that would guarantee impartial laws without regard to race, language, or previous condition. Any adult male over twenty-one and with a certain period of residency could vote—any, that is, except those over twenty-one when Lincoln was inaugurated president who swore allegiance to the Confederacy or held any office under it. They would lose their citizenship for the next five years and could regain it only then by filing naturalization papers and taking a new oath of fealty to the United States. Once the states had written suitable constitutions, they could present the documents to Congress, and if Congress approved of them, the states would be fully restored to their old places in the Union. The wording made a guarantee of sorts, that southern compliance might lead to readmission to Congress, but left open the possibility that new conditions might be imposed later on. "Its revolutionary purpose is as clear as the sun-light," a Wisconsin congressman warned. It simply would "get rid of the Constitution or some provision of it."[46]

The bill did not make it out of the House, but in the Senate another measure keeping the former Confederate states under military supervision created some means of protecting loyal peoples' lives. Members were prepared to accept it, but they wanted to give southerners some route back toward civil government and a normal condition of political affairs that would resume in the near future—at any rate, before the next presidential election. They found that sign in an amendment that Congressman James G. Blaine of Maine offered. Under its terms, after the Howard Amendment had become the law of the land, and once the southern states had ratified that amendment, enacted suffrage requirements that were color-blind on their face, and put through new constitutions by a popular vote, they would be entitled to representation in Congress.[47]

Blaine's amendment was framed deliberately to appeal across the party. It would put the House on record as declaring the amendment ratified when three-fourths of the states represented in Congress adopted it and excluding the ten former Confederate states from the count. It committed Congress to manhood suffrage in the South and made an official declaration that the Johnson governments had no legal standing beyond what Congress permitted. Unlike Thomas D. Eliot's bill covering Louisiana, it applied to all ten states, not just the one. Radicals wanted more. With no provision for disfranchising a single former Confederate and no machinery to create a provisional government, Blaine's change could well allow the conservative civil governments to go on existing, checked by military power. Without violating any of the terms of the Blaine amendment, former Confederates could control the South's political affairs indefinitely. They could call constitutional conventions with an exclusively white electorate; there was nothing to require Negro suffrage before the end of the Reconstruction process, and even then Blaine's plan opened the possibility of *impartial*, not universal, suffrage. While that may not have been moderates' intention, by Section 5's terms, loyal men might well find constitutions drawn up by their enemies with a mere handful of blacks eligible to cast ballots, and then would have the bitter choice between voting for the documents, unjust and discriminatory though they might be in most respects, or voting it down and leaving the states unreconstructed and in Rebel hands, perhaps forever.[48]

With Democratic help, radicals beat the Blaine amendment, only to find it resurrected in the Senate. Moderate and conservative alike knew that military rule of any kind skirted the edges of what their constituents thought constitutionally acceptable. They worried about weakening republican institutions. At the very least, the military bill needed some escape clause pointing the way toward civil government. In its final revision, the Sherman Military Reconstruction Act required constitutional conventions chosen by white and black males alike, except for those Confederates disqualified from office under the pending amendment. When color-blind constitutions had been framed and ratified and the new government chosen under them ratified the Howard Amendment, then only would Congress readmit their delegations.[49]

Conservative Republicans could feel thankful that matters had not ended worse. As they pointed out, on most points, the measure was a considerable advance toward the radical demands. It made wartime treason a disqualification for office, required universal, not just impartial, suffrage, and made guarantees for equal rights. In all respects, it demanded more from the South than the Howard Amendment had and combined it with the military protection that loyal men needed. It also made the amendment's adoption almost a sure thing. Trumbull felt as most moderates did that matters in the South were so desperate that they had no choice. "It is the last thing to put the rebel states under military rule," he wrote one of his lieutenants in Illinois, "but the People there behave so badly there seems to be no other way of protecting loyal men."[50]

The bill that passed undoubtedly was more radical than what moderates wanted and a far cry from the possible settlement at the session's beginning. But that did not make the measure a conservative triumph. In any case, Republicans agreed that they had no time to do more. Consequently, the closer the session's close came, the more ready Republicans of all ideological stripes were to work out some kind of deal, so that something—anything—would pass. The bill was voted through by 105 to 55. With less than ten working days left of the session, Johnson had enough time to make a pocket veto, and a few moderates hoped he would let it pass without his signature. Instead, a searing veto message went in. Congress wasted no time in overriding it.[51]

What had Congress wrought? From the South came an almost unbroken chorus of editorial opinion that the republic had received its death blow. "Impeachment of the President—Reorganization of the Supreme Court—Reduction of late Confederate States to a Territorial Condition—these are the leading measures now occupying their attention," a South Carolinian fumed. "We have only to look on as passive spectators of the destruction of civil liberty & the constitution of the country." Northern Democratic newspapers made the same cry.[52] And by any standards up to the Civil War, Congress had indeed taken unheard of steps away from the old republic. Even a few Republicans thought so. From the vantage point of 1867, the picture did not look anywhere as momentous. Congress had not imposed military rule on the South so much as continued it. It had left the president with the power to appoint commanders over the five military districts and to remove them. It had come close to overturning southern state governments, but however far their forms resembled authorities before the war, they rested on the much shakier basis of presidential proclamations founded in powers that no president before Lincoln would have dreamed of claiming. Enacted without being submitted even to white voters, their state constitutions did not approach the most basic standard of republicanism.[53] For Congress to have done nothing would itself have set a revolutionary precedent, which

"We Accept the Situation." Thomas Nast, *Harper's Weekly*, April 13, 1867. Taking the commonplace uttered by so many ex-Confederates, Nast celebrates passage of the first Reconstruction Act. Note the African American's military cap, linking wartime service with his deserving the right to vote. Note also the contrast between a thriving black home and family in the background on the left and the unrepaired ruins on the right—indicating which group of southerners had put the postwar years to good account.

in the long run would have been as destructive to the states. To interfere in the South to restore order was radical, but so was the level of violence, unchecked and unpunished. It had no match in antebellum times. Even in determining who should vote at the South, Congress could point to the precedent set by Andrew Johnson's own proclamations, which had done the same thing. Between presidential ukase and law, which came closer to meeting constitutional requirements?

Lost in the fume of Democratic rhetoric, too, may have been the Sherman Act's most important quality. Treating military oversight as a temporary expedient, it had committed Congress to restoring states to their places as equal partners with equal rights and privileges. Instead of mandating new constitutions, it gave southern voters white and black the opportunity to draw up these constitutions themselves. There would be no confiscation, no wholesale disfranchisement, not even a limit on whites' right to bear arms—only to assemble as state militias. Congress would nudge—nudge hard, perhaps—but these new southern commonwealths must be self-created and self-sustaining. Equality before the law mattered, but to Congress's thinking, assuring a loyal South, ready to stand by the Union permanently, mattered more.[54] For all but the radical minority of Republicans, the Sherman Act was much closer to the end of the national government's role in reconstructing the Union than the beginning.

CHAPTER FIVE

Bottom Rail on Top, 1867

T wo months' work went into the Sherman Military Reconstruction Act, but it took scarcely two days for the holes to show. The Thirty-Ninth Congress had pointed out the ultimate goal but not set up the machinery for reaching it. Who would call the conventions? Who would supervise the registration and police the polls on Election Day? How soon would the process begin? Would the members of the "provisional" governments disqualified under the Howard Amendment be dismissed, and who would choose their replacements?[1]

Radicals may have feared that conservatives, left to themselves, would take the lead, limiting Reconstruction to the barest minimum: a few tweaks to the existing fundamental law, with sitting governors setting the time for and conditions on which elections would be called, giving black and white Unionists no chance to mobilize their forces. Within a week of the Fortieth Congress assembling, however, informed observers saw two equally troubling alternatives. Preferring military rule and the status quo to a biracial polity, southern leaders might not start reconstructing at all. They would wait it out until 1868 when, with luck, the Democrats would return to power and make a deal more to their satisfaction. In the meantime, the oppression and random killings would continue. Alternatively, the authorities would call one set of elections, native Radicals another, with each side boycotting the polls set up by the other. At best, two constitutional conventions would write two fundamental laws. Two sets of returns would be sent to Washington, each claiming the exclusive right to be recognized. At worst, the process would bring on bloodletting: another New Orleans massacre in every state—or every county. The threat was real. Within a few weeks, the most radical Unionists already had started organizing, preparing to call constitutional conventions on their own. What was "everybody's business was nobody's business," as one Republican explained, in supporting a supplemental Reconstruction bill. It "must be placed in the power of somebody to begin this work, somebody to go forward in it."[2]

At the same time, just about everybody agreed that whatever new order Reconstruction created must have greater legitimacy than congressional recognition could bestow. New constitutions had to earn the consent of the governed. The conventions and the constitutions that came out of them must be accepted not just by a majority of those voting but by something more indisputably reflective of the public will, in elections attended by a majority of all registered adult males.

A year later, observers rubbed their eyes wondering how Republicans could have acted so foolishly. White conservatives could register en masse and then boycott the polls. Every absence, willful or from illness, would count as much as a vote against. But Republicans acted with eyes wide open. Radicals did not want the states returned with former Rebels sitting passively at home, ready to overturn the new governments the moment Congress had readmitted their states, and some of them even indicated that this was one reason why they inclined to as few disfranchisements as possible. Any fundamental law imposed by the convention's fiat, as the Johnson constitutions had been, or adopted by a small, heavily black minority of the state's citizens would bring immediate tumult and swift overthrow to the whole Reconstruction process.[3]

Far from wanting to impose a solution on the South, Congress was eager for the South's cooperation and tokens of its consent; and that consent must be given without delay. The longer government remained unsettled and the violence and disorders went on, the harder it would be to defend the drastic policies that Congress had adopted. Like other Republicans of all stripes, Charles Sumner felt uneasy about letting generals oversee politics. That was why he tried to place registration and election oversight in civilian hands in his bill. Other members had started worrying that the instability and destitution in the South were not simply linked; they were dragging down the whole national economy, which, by early 1867, was entering a slump. If the delay in Reconstruction did not cause it, Democrats could still make a convincing case that it did. With the presidential election approaching, time no longer seemed on Republicans' side. At all costs, they must restore the Union and complete the reconstructing before the campaign began. But the price for this was a full stop to new initiatives and advances. That included anything that might be seen as a new condition, whether it was Missouri senator Charles D. Drake's amendment requiring a secret ballot in place of the viva voce system or Sumner's provision requiring that the Reconstructed states erect school systems. Newly elected Senator Oliver Morton of Indiana spoke for senators in general when he warned, "The condition of things down there is abnormal. We must hasten to make it normal, to bring these States into harmonious relations with this Government as soon as it can be done consistently with liberty, with safety to all, and with equal rights to all."[4]

Congress stayed in session barely long enough to pass the Supplementary Reconstruction Act, but it had time enough to drive home the message that what the North did to the South came from its need for guarantees, not from a desire for oppression, humiliation, or revenge. Underlining the point, Senator John Sherman sponsored a bill removing the political disabilities from former Georgia governor Joseph E. Brown. Brown had not joined the Republicans, but he had won national attention by advising his fellow southerners to cooperate in reconstructing on Congress's terms. Never brought to a vote, the bill nonetheless sent the message that some Republicans, at least, had no desire for lasting punishments; all they wanted were tokens of good faith from former Confederates before welcoming them back as full partners. A few days later, the point was underlined when Congress considered a generous appropriation to relieve distress among the destitute down south. The measure passed the Senate, one opponent fretted, "with about as little concern as you would light your cigar." (It did not make it through the House; but massive aid through the Freedmen's Bureau served the same purpose.) On March 19th, Thaddeus Stevens gave a lengthy speech, setting forth his plan for confiscating 70,000 ex-Confederates' property and restoring southern public lands to the national government. Not one of his usual allies rose to endorse the bill, which never saw the light of day again.[5]

Until Reconstruction was completed, ten states remained under military overlordship. Military rule was, on the whole, pretty mild stuff, not far removed from what had come before it; the troops had been on duty since the war's end and, most of the time, responded when called on by the civil authorities as an extra support to law enforcement. Even conservatives recognized that civil authorities could use help in suppressing disturbances or nabbing horse thieves. Far from heaping them with execrations, residents in some villages felt relief to have troops on hand—blacks because they expected more protection from white attacks, and whites because they held the lingering fear of black insurrection and race war. The post band might even be offered on loan for public functions or even weddings, and the offer accepted. Many of the enlisted men had no particular fondness for blacks, and sometimes an open contempt. In many states, the commanders treated the possibility of Negro uprising seriously and acted quickly against it. In Florida, reports that blacks were holding night meetings and arming spurred General John Pope to outlaw gatherings after dark. From Mississippi, General Edward O. C. Ord sent back alarming reports of impending race war just in time for Christmas, "of burning Cotton Gins—and armed bands plundering." His solution, which superiors did not agree to, was the wholesale disarming of freedpeople and the transfer of troops to protect white people in the river counties.[6]

Not all the commanders had been partisan on Republicans' behalf, though most of them favored Congressional Reconstruction, at least to some extent. All of them protested that they did nothing more than their orders required. General Alvan C. Gillem spoke for them all when he disassociated himself from national politics. A soldier's "only rule of action should be . . . 'Fidelity to his country and the laws,'" he insisted. Many officers were Democrats, and most Republicans probably stood closer to the conservative end of the party. General John Schofield of Virginia had made clear his disapproval of the Howard Amendment, though he had urged the state legislature to ratify it as the best deal possible. He was known to oppose disfranchisement of former Confederates and universal suffrage for blacks, few of whom he felt qualified for the ballot.[7]

General Daniel Sickles, military commander for the Department of the Carolinas, represented one extreme. He was, to be sure, no radical. A prewar Democrat with a hot temper, he would have been happier if Congress had adopted a policy of universal amnesty along with universal suffrage. But he was not one to shrink from using his authority when nothing else could right a wrong, and from his perspective as head of the Second Military District, the wrongs abounded. Then that same impulsiveness burst out that brought him to kill his wife's lover before the war and carried him into the peach orchard on the second day at Gettysburg to retrieve a situation that was only worsened by his intervention (as well as costing him a leg, later put on display in a museum). Now Sickles lost no time in letting civil authorities know that their government was merely provisional. He could override it where his responsibilities dictated, or replace any official among its members. In one general order he quarantined Carolina ports to keep out infectious disease. In another, he banned the manufacture of grain alcohol to keep down the soaring cost of grain. Even more sweepingly, his General Order No. 10 ended the collection of debts contracted in wartime and suspended the process for debts from before it, as well as mortgage foreclosures. Under his decrees, branding, whipping, maiming, corporal punishment for crimes, and imprisonment for debt stopped. The death penalty for burglary and larceny was abolished. Carolinians were forbidden to carry deadly weapons.[8]

Edward O. C. Ord, commanding the Fourth Military District at the start of Congressional Reconstruction, stood at the opposite extreme. At best apolitical and at worst making Republicans complain that "his counsels would seem to have been directed by the rebel governor at Jackson," he was quick to issue orders advising blacks of their duty to work and discouraging them from attending political meetings. Never holding any faith in universal suffrage, he also held views common to the military, that civil authority must handle the process. That obliged him to carry out the duties that the law imposed upon him but to read them to give white conservatives as much of the benefit of the doubt as possible. His order to registrars to give no instruction to voters beyond the strictest letter of the law—that by registering, the applicant was entitled to vote—seemed reasonable on the face of it, but, as Republicans pointed out, conservatives had been misinforming blacks that the real purpose of the process was to impose a poll tax and find out who had been slaves, the better to reenslave them later. Ord's registrars could not correct those misimpressions. That fall, he all but ordered the Union Leagues to disband. His words had to be countermanded from Washington, and Ord retired, elated to be quit of a job that he had loathed from the start.[9] His replacement, Alvan C. Gillem, shared his distaste for politicians in general and Republican ones in particular. In Louisiana, General Winfield Scott Hancock, much less radical than the generals he succeeded, sacked Republican-leaning city officials and rescinded the military order making blacks eligible for jury service. New Orleans conservatives saw Hancock as epitomizing the president's views, "the dew and the gentle rain that have revivified the weeds cut down by the sword," as a reporter commented. When he entered the theater, minstrel-show performers recited doggerel in his praise.[10]

But even at their most meddling or, in Pope and Phil Sheridan's case, the most radical, commanders acknowledged limits to their authority. More than ideological and professional bias explains their restraint. They knew that they could be removed by the president with or without cause—as the most Republican three, Sheridan, Sickles, and Pope would be—and how little actual power they possessed. They also knew that without cooperation from those they had been sent to oversee, Reconstruction would founder. That cooperation would come more reluctantly every day. Whatever goodwill they began with among white southerners would dissipate. With mounting attacks, the army's reputation was sure to suffer—and this in an America where the professional soldier remained a figure of suspicion, if not contempt. Committed as he was to a thorough change along the lines that congressional moderates intended, Grant himself wanted Reconstruction completed as quickly as possible, the sooner to end the generals' authority. However "temperate" commanders were in using their power, he wrote, a prolonged military rule brought with it "great danger of a reaction against the Army." That must be avoided at all costs. Without firm support at the capital for the officers' performing their duties, one of them wrote, every federal law bearing on the South would "prove but a dead letter."[11]

For that reason, too, district commanders preferred to stay on decent terms with conservative administrations. They consulted them, met their patronage requests when they could, and obliged them however they might. Governor Robert M. Patton in Alabama took pride in the close official and personal relations that he had with General Wager Swayne and had nothing but praise to transmit to his superiors. "I have devoted my utmost exertions in favor of placing this State in harmony with the ruling power of the Federal government," he wrote General Grant. "Gen. Swayne has earnestly labored for the same thing. I believe he has accomplished much good, and given as much satisfaction as any officer could have done in his situation."[12]

In theory, at least, they could have made a clean sweep of every office that conservatives held and appoint army officers or unconditional Union men. That certainly is what Unionists pleaded, petitioned, and prayed for, not simply out of greed, but for their own safety against marauders, assassins, and legal harassment. The right of removal itself was vital, but even one of the generals most radical and most energetic in using it, General Phil Sheridan, understood that it would be most effectively used when used sparingly and that the right was vital precisely because there were too few soldiers to handle administering by themselves. "The very moment that the civil authorities know that they are beyond the power of the Military Commander; that moment they will defy him and impede the law," he explained to General Grant.[13]

What removals from office the army made only gave greater evidence of the military's weakness. With so many responsibilities and so small a force at their command, district commanders found themselves helpless when civil authorities refused to cooperate. Only by removals could they get things done, simply because so many duties had to be handled by the civil authorities still serving; one or two exemplary firings, an appointment to one of the key positions, might have a salutary effect on the rest. A salutary effect was what was needed, because army removals obscured the fact that, based on the Howard Amendment's disqualifications, many more civil officials could have been removed at once, and perhaps should have been. But the army found itself hard put to find competent replacements, and for the most part, commanders preferred experienced administrators to the obscure set recommended by the newfound Republican Party. Military personnel could be relied on to obey their superiors' orders, but too many of them lacked civil experience and there were not enough of them to attend to the tasks that the army had been given as it was.

So conservative governments elected in most of the South, even once their terms of office had expired, hung on, unless they engaged in open obstruction of the Reconstruction Acts. Louisiana proved to be a serious exception, in large part because its officials were offensive not only to the commanding general but to many of the white citizens. No conservative newspaper complained about the quarrelsome, shifty, Republican-leaning Governor Wells's removal. They were much less happy when the general sacked twenty-two New Orleans city councilmen and appointed several blacks to the new government.[14]

Most vacancies in offices that the military filled were due to reasons other than removal, but when commanders did make appointments, they preferred natives to newcomers, civilians to soldiers, and whites to blacks. In Florida, where there were no more than fifteen removals, most vacancies were filled with people that the governor or other civil officers had proposed. "We in Florida have been fortunate in military appointments," the *St. Augustine Recorder* admitted, "and if we live under a military despotism, we have scarcely felt its iron heel." Radical views, if anything, worked against a potential administrator's chances. Even in Alabama, where General Wager Swayne had an undisguised interest in Reconstruction's success (and, potentially, a Senate seat for himself), Unionists complained that the general allowed secessionists to hold bureau jobs and serve as sheriff. Many appointees, a Mississippi Republican charged, "had to have the oath greased to make it go down easy." But there was not much else that commanders could have done. As some of them complained, a rigid application of the test oath would have left them unable to find manpower qualified to fill the offices.[15] With conspicuous exceptions, therefore, nearly all the permanent offices remained in white hands. In General Pope's district, the military actively discouraged Republicans from forwarding black names for appointments because of the possible repercussions in the North. (Appointments for registrars for the coming convention elections proved the exception there and elsewhere. Pope saw to it that one in three came from the freedmen.)[16]

Generals showed real caution about when they involved themselves in civil law enforcement. General Thomas J. Wood, commanding in the District of Mississippi, insisted that whenever the military was called in, the civil authorities must give them detailed instructions in writing, a copy of which must be sent to him. Where civil courts could do the job, officers were almost eager to let them handle matters. That was all, really, that would have been possible. The forces at the army's command were too small to cope with local needs. Louisiana's commander had 2,400 officers and enlistees—not quite half the force that he had had the year before Congressional Reconstruction passed. Pleas for reinforcements got nowhere. Only two states had more: Virginia and Texas. At the height of Congressional Reconstruction, the commander in Mississippi could staff fifteen posts, usually in cities and major towns. Even with two detachments of cavalry, he complained that he could not meet the crime wave. That same limitation in power applied to the Freedmen's Bureau in the state, where only eleven counties out of sixty had an agent in residence. Military orders outlawing the carrying of concealed weapons and forbidding armed men to gather, however necessary they may have been, could scarcely get more than a symbolic enforcement.[17]

The circuit courts met on schedule and held their customary sessions. State courts handled the vast majority of cases. They rarely had to worry about military orders countermanding their sentences. North Carolina's military generally only took on cases where they foresaw a strong chance of convicting. Even then, one scholar has concluded, they left the civil courts to deal with nineteen cases out of twenty. About one arrest in eight was the military's doing; usually officers turned the arrested party over to civil authorities almost at once. What generals like Daniel Sickles insisted on was the right to oversee decisions and, in extreme cases, to refer them to military tribunals. Where civil authorities failed to arrest suspects, post commanders might be directed to do so. On rare occasions they haled them before military commissions. In the whole Third Military District, General Pope held just thirty-two military trials, meting out fifteen convictions. Protection for blacks came far less often than attacks on them might have required. If, as General Gillem told his superiors, reports of assaults had fallen off sharply, it may have been because freedmen had become used to the military doing nothing about it.[18]

A conservative white press had most of the leeway it needed to fulminate against military tyranny. For the most part, newspapers were allowed to publish as suited them, and generals did not interfere. No speakers were arrested, no pamphleteers jailed, and very few conservatives harassed or threatened by military force. When "the spitfire Editor" William H. McCardle of the *Vicksburg Times* issued a fiery editorial against the district commanders as "infamous, cowardly, and abandoned villains," fitter to "have their heads shaved, their ears cropped, their foreheads branded, and their precious persons lodged in a penitentiary," it cost him his liberty for a time, but no military trial followed. Soon McCardle emerged on bail to fulminate as fiercely as before, and the charges were dropped.[19] Suppression, if it came at all, came in a more indirect way. In General Pope's district, the military mandated public printing for papers that did not openly oppose Congressional Reconstruction. Doing so meant survival for struggling Republican newspapers just starting up and denied advertising from white merchants in town—a "bonus of from $1500 to $3000 per annum to a loyal press in each county," as one Alabaman calculated. It also dealt a serious financial blow to conservative presses that depended on the revenue from publishing town council proceedings and ordinances and notices of sheriff's sales and tax orders, indirectly as well as directly: to get crucial information, many subscribers would have no choice but to take the Republican paper over the conservative one.[20]

All of these cautions do not make the military into enemies of Reconstruction. On the contrary, without the army's presence and the active intervention of the commanders, no substantial Reconstruction would have happened at all. In most states, generals saw their job as expanding the middle ground. They must discourage the diehard Confederates while tamping down the unconditional Unionists and radicals. Conditions could have been far worse without the military protection that Republicans got, however patchy it was. Congress acted sensibly in "inaugurating a Government of bayonets" for the South, a Union officer wrote. It offered the possibility, at least, of showing "that killing negroes is rather an expensive luxury." Most white southerners would never see reason on "the nigger question," he concluded. "They are like children on this subject and must be made to hold still and take the dose however unpleasant it may be."[21]

Haltingly, inconsistently, the military presence nonetheless intervened to make sure that the minimal requirements of the Civil Rights Act were met. Black testimony in court was upheld and the excesses of the vagrancy and apprenticeship laws checked. Ahead of other officers, General Sickles issued an order ending discrimination against blacks in public conveyances. In some states, commanders ended the white monopoly on jury service as well, though the change was more symbolic than substantive.

In Mississippi, the boards of registration had former Union officers, where they could be found, along with two citizens, one conservative and one allegedly radical. Most of the boards of registration had recently-discharged army officers presiding in Virginia, with local white Unionists given second priority and nonresidents appointed as a last resort.[22]

The use of military power, then, provides two important points about the success and failure of Radical Reconstruction. On the one hand, the relative restraint that the commanders showed reflected their awareness that most Americans, northern Republicans included, distrusted authoritarian means, even to so good an end as restoring and reconstructing the Union. The more the military intervened, the more it discredited the whole process and made a mockery of the ultimate consent of southerners in their own reformation. On the other hand, the army was taking on tasks that would be unheard of in peacetime and that only a sense of emergency could justify, and to serve one party's agenda—in some cases, pretty blatantly. From the Rio Grande to the Potomac, the congressional majority had established "a military despotism more absolute than any other in any civilized country within the last two hundred years," Wisconsin senator James R. Doolittle told one crowd. Carl Schurz, the Missouri radical, knew tyranny well. He had fled Germany for his life after the collapse of the revolution of 1848. If Senator Doolittle had bothered to talk with "some little German boy" on his recent European tour, Schurz suggested, he might have come back wiser. He would have learned how the Hungarian revolution of the 1840s ended, with long rows of gallows rising, all liberally used. If the North had done like the czars and emperors, Confederate generals would have become carrion long ago rather than teaching school, promoting railroad enterprises—and helping write the Democratic national platform in New York.[23] But Schurz was missing the point: he knew too much. By Old World standards, nothing so contrasted with tyranny than the South's treatment. By the standards of freeborn Americans' past, nothing resembled it so closely.

No sooner had the Reconstruction Acts passed than southern politics stirred to life. Discovering too late the fix that northern Democrats had put

(opposite) "All the Difference in the World." Thomas Nast, *Harper's Weekly*, September 30, 1868. Disgusted northern politicians and Irish lowlife hold their nose at the Republican freedperson, who is associated with the schools and churches he belonged to. By contrast, the African Americans voting Democratic, done up in the most extreme of racist stereotype, are blessed by Virginia's former governor Henry Wise, are given friendly advice by Klan leader Nathan Bedford Forrest, and have Confederate general Wade Hampton to shine their shoes.

ALL THE DIFFERENCE IN THE WORLD.

"BUT—"

117

them into, conservatives sued for terms. Those most ready to cooperate included members of the wealthiest class in the South, ready to call all their paternalistic good deeds done in slavery times into play and fearful that a biracial working-class party might actually become viable. Conservative reconstructionists came in many forms. At the far end were those prepared to join Republicans, and moderate their counsels. Others were willing to meet Republican moderates on undisputed ground, to propose a party of the center, where every white could vote and none need fear to see his estate confiscated. In either case, cooperationists meant to hold radicalism to its sharpest confines, not just racially, but economically. No change of heart underlay the change of base. As General Wade Hampton explained, the only choice left to white southerners was "whether they will be horse or rider."[24]

Soon there were mixed gatherings elsewhere. Even in Mississippi, eminent secessionists like former senator Albert G. Brown and ex-Confederate congressman Ethelbert Barksdale argued for cooperation. In some states, Alabama among them, talk of cooperation got no further than that. In Louisiana and Mississippi, where the possibilities of a heavily black Republican Party were nearly 100 percent, conservatives had every reason to take the first step to form a non-Republican alternative. Editors organized with their mouths. But the machinery of local parties, the kind of concentration on nuts and bolts that the Union Leagues had been doing all through the spring and summer, simply never made a show until close to election time, when it was far too late.[25] The catch was that the more the cooperationists succeeded, or thought they succeeded, the stronger the pressure from northern Republicans grew to push their southern brethren in moderate directions. Conservative Reconstructionists did not build a party of the middle in Virginia; they simply helped Republican leaders force their rank and file centerward.

Cooperationism hardly drew the black vote at all, but it put a new fracture in the white response to Reconstruction. Without full support from the white conservative electorate, cooperationism really had no chance. That support never was there. Many whites would not lift a hand on a coalition's behalf. Some lacked the heart to do so; some felt sure that, whatever they did, Congress would alter the terms to enthrone whom it liked—and it certainly would not like them. And many more could not abide the whole idea of clasping hands with the Negro. The worse the prospects of drawing the black vote grew, the wider the conviction spread that any cooperation would just be a sellout. Hopes had been strongest when the prospect of a heavy white registration shone most brightly. By late June, those hopes were dimming. The Third Reconstruction Act that July, with its broad discretion for military officers to rule out white former Confederate applicants to vote, only made certain that in certain states no solid white vote could be mustered and that in others the disfranchisements would be so extensive that it would require an even greater share of the black electorate for conservatives to prevail. That would take even more humiliating advances and even greater concessions, and every concession stirred a deep distaste.[26]

By June, the resistance had found its voice, and that voice grew louder as the tallies came in from registration. The white South was under no obligation to steer the revolution, opponents argued—not when it could stop it completely by registering heavily and then staying home, or they could show up and vote "No Convention."[27]

The worst that could happen, diehards argued, would be that the states would not be readmitted to Congress before the next presidential election. They would stay under military rule. But every day showed that, whatever the language of Caesarism and satrapy, military government bore pretty lightly on the white South. In any case, there was every hope that in 1868 the Democrats might come into their own. A Democratic president would lift the white South out of its toils, and all without the humiliation of accepting the terms of an unconstitutional law or the consequences of what might be reversible revolution. "We are overpowered, but not conquered," Georgia's former governor Herschel V. Johnson wrote in a public letter. "They can rob us of *freedom*, but never let us *agree* to be *slaves*." Recalcitrance was made firmer by conservatives' conviction that they had other options available. A court appeal would save them. So would the North, once it was roused. Moderation in Reconstruction might pass muster among northern voters, but, unleash radicalism, and many a northern voter would realize how right the Democrats had been after all, and at the elections would rush to the rescue. "A change at the North is our only hope for civil liberty in this country," a North Carolinian wrote the governor; "and I am quite willing the Radicals should make themselves blacker and blacker, until they become in the sight of all men . . . *black and all black*!" Under the circumstances, every step to mitigate Reconstruction's evils was a step to impose Reconstruction of one sort or another permanently on a white South that wanted it in no form, moderate or otherwise.[28]

The strategy, though, did not work as well in practice as conservatives had hoped. Virginia, Georgia, Arkansas, Texas, and North Carolina all had white majorities on the registration books. In Florida and Mississippi, white abstentions, combined with black absences, would have denied the conventions the majorities they needed. In Louisiana, Alabama, and South Carolina, it would have taken a very heavy white registration to have swollen the rolls far enough for the abstainers to have forestalled a convention, but it was at least possible. But white conservatives split. Many had chosen not to register, probably many times more than those who applied and were turned away. Some went, determined to vote "No Convention," and others refused to attend the polls at all.[29]

No such uncertainty developed on the other side. Before Congressional Reconstruction began, blacks had begun organizing in the cities and larger towns. Where a free black elite had built institutions and a forum for public expression before the war, the job of political mobilization came easiest. Gang labor in the Louisiana sugar parishes allowed the close communication and the sense of hierarchy and discipline that organized politics needed much faster than the sharecropping system in the cotton fields, where potential voters worked and lived at some distance from one another; but in every village, they came together wherever they could find space all their own, to talk politics and learn the mechanics of registering and voting. As the social center of many communities and the necessary adjunct of family life, the churches opened their doors for political speakers and raised funds for spreading the word. There, especially, political events embraced women and children as well as men.[30]

In the cities, Charleston and New Orleans particularly, the free black community before the war had raised a class of well-educated, propertied men whose professional careers entitled them to respect in the white community. Veterans of the black Union regiments could point to their sacrifices and their wider experience in a greater world to compare themselves to blacks who remained behind. But most important were the ministers and preachers. Outside the cities, they often were the best-read, and certainly the most experienced at public speaking. In Georgia, the Reverend Henry M. Turner, freeborn, had come to Macon before the war. Serving as chaplain with the First United States Colored Troops, mustered out to work for the Freedmen's Bureau, he already was preaching politics and braving down mobs a year after the fighting ended. Indeed, he claimed to have "put more men in the field, made more speeches, organized more Union Leagues, Political Associations, Clubs, and . . . written more campaign documents that received larger circulation than any other man in the state."[31]

Many more blacks made their political awakening through the Union Leagues, whose very secrecy made them into mythological monsters.

Whites swore under oath to their incendiary teachings, though what precisely these were, beyond the right of black males to vote or hold office, they had difficulty describing, never having attended a league meeting or met anyone that had. In fact, the Union Leagues had a respectable history. They had begun in the North during the war as a means of spreading the ideology of nationalism, with a Loyal Publication Society assigned to broadcast tracts explaining the war's purposes. Chapters in Philadelphia and New York City would become Union League Clubs, pillars of well-propertied Republicanism, in time the one society that any gentleman with the right politics would belong to, but working-class patriots had their own societies. Before the war ended, they had begun pushing their organization south to bolster and solidify Unionist sentiments there. Union soldiers stationed in the South or looking for like-minded neighbors found the league a rock in a wary land. By April 1865, Union Leagues had sprung up in Wilmington, North Carolina, and two of them marched in a memorial procession honoring Lincoln. Alabama's State Council claimed 18,000 white members by mid-1866. By early 1867, the numbers may have approached 30,000.[32]

Where there had once been wartime Unionist societies like the Red Strings and a patriotic underground, the leagues became a forum for people who, in peacetime, found them as beleaguered as before, if not more so. In some cases, it gave them the chance to arm in their own defense. With Congressional Reconstruction, Republican organizers made the leagues into a school in the elementary political education that they were thought to lack and a counter to the version of events that former masters were likely to give. The leagues were also meant to channel their radical sentiments in more partisan and less agrarian directions; the league's top administrators inclined to the moderate side.[33]

Some leagues remained white, though they accepted more readily the logic of cooperation with their black neighbors. Churches helped with the recruiting, and the *Mobile Nationalist*, a black-owned newspaper, helped spread the message and sent its promotional agents through Mississippi and Alabama. In the countryside, a council might have as few as fifty or as many as five hundred participants, mostly men. The better-organized would meet every week, usually on Saturday nights after the week's work was completed. Always there was secrecy; armed sentries would guard the meeting place, or scouts to spread the alarm if white patrols were on their way. But blacks, coming into the Union League, were not bewitched by mumbo jumbo and daunted into remaining by dire oaths, as conservatives later contended. They knew what they were getting and stayed because they were getting it. They were no more prisoners of the organization than parishioners of a church were vassals to the minister. For many of them, these gatherings were their first chance to make speeches or even to hear them; for most of them, the league meetings provided an introduction to parliamentary procedure and debating. They also found protection and solidarity.[34]

That protection included arming for self-defense. Black military companies were not created by the leagues, but they grew up alongside and worked with them. Across the white South by the summer of 1867 conservatives had heard stories of ex-slaves drilling, or going to league meetings well armed. This may not have been what the league's national officials desired. Many of them worried about the growing risk of a clash and the long-predicted war of races. Where they could, white northern supporters encouraged blacks to leave their guns at home. But they found that their influence did not go very far. In that respect, certainly, the new "masters" over the freedpeople had no stronger power than persuasion. As time went on, the Union Leagues became less the white leaders' organizations and more the instruments of their members, with different agendas, including protection for their rights as workers and under labor contracts. One white South Carolinian noticed that those who came to listen soon learned to participate. Indeed, freedmen turned into "the most irrepressible democrats it is possible to conceive." They were very far from passive vessels into which the true word was poured. Where black leadership could be found, white leadership sometimes gave way, or had to struggle simply to hold on. The leagues also became a power in local Republican politics. Their recommendation for appointments, their endorsement for nomination, carried particular weight.[35]

The white sponsors for the Union Leagues generally came from the North, just as much of the money to set up the societies did, and they shared a common infamy with all those other northerners settling in the South after the war and holding to their Republican beliefs. The so-called carpetbaggers already had a bad reputation even before they had a name—which, seemingly, was not attached until sometime in mid-1868.[36] They were by definition northerners who voted Republican, but many of them had not come south to enter politics, and most appeared long before there had been any serious prospect of universal suffrage. Some had arrived at the war's end, Union soldiers who thought to make the South another West, where they could settle, develop the resources, and make themselves rich by building up the country. A few tried to go into planting. Some went broke, some struggled along, and quite a number quit and went north before Congressional Reconstruction began.[37]

Those likeliest to come were those who had shaken loose home ties already before the war, in a country on the move. Many of them had gone west first, and come south afterward, seeing no harm in either. The war itself had snapped ties for hundreds of thousands more, soldiers who, having left home, discovered a world of new possibilities. Those stationed in the South had the best opportunity to go into private business. They were also especially well positioned to take government jobs, among a population where the loyalty oaths disqualified the bulk of propertied, educated, and politically experienced residents. Freedmen's Bureau agents built on their army experience and extended their acquaintanceship. Registrars in bankruptcy, collectors of internal revenue and customhouse employees all had reasons to stay south and take advantage of its opportunities. Then there were the others, sent south as part of the missionary impulse that emancipation had fired, some as schoolteachers and others as ministers. "The whole West is peopled by a race of our carpet-baggers," General Daniel Sickles snorted. "William Penn was a carpet-bagger of the right sort. Daniel Boone of Kentucky, [Senator] Lewis Cass of Michigan, [Senator] Stephen A. Douglas of Illinois—they were all 'carpet-baggers.'"[38] So, he might have added, were Lincoln and Jefferson Davis.

Even more important, they shared the free labor ideals universally held in the North, that slavery had held back southern economic development, and that with its replacement, the South would prosper more speedily than anywhere else, if only because it had so much catching up to do. Convinced that the South's resources made it ideal for industry and commerce, they saw the section not so much as a feeder of northern manufacturing but as a diversified economy capable of supplying itself.[39]

Those connected to the national government found a poor welcome in white society. Those with Republican sentiments learned that speaking up could be a killing matter, and for many of them, that was a politicizing discovery, one that reminded them again of how alien southern society was from the one that they had left behind. For them, a new social order, a revolution, would be necessary before the South could function as a free and liberal state. They were far from being abolitionists or fanatics, but seeing blacks as inferior to some extent did not mean that they believed them incapable of improvement or learning, or so benighted that a share in politics would be beyond them not just for the moment but forever. They were prepared to do something about it, if they could.[40]

Carpetbaggers by themselves could not make up a particularly large electorate, and it is probable that northerners who voted Democratic or stayed out of politics entirely outnumbered the Republican ones in the South. But their numbers were crucial. In states with the heaviest black vote, and particularly Mississippi, Louisiana, and South Carolina, all of which had black majorities, white Republican leaders were hardest to find, because associating with so overwhelmingly a black rank and file guaranteed abuse and ostracism as it would nowhere that a "respectable" number of whites voted Republican. Where native white leadership failed to develop, blacks were eager for northern leaders, those more experienced and knowledgeable about national politics than they.[41]

The third group in the Republican coalition came from southern whites themselves. In the most heavily black states, their numbers were comparatively small, but in the upper South in particular, and in the hill country from the Ozarks to the Blue Ridge Mountains, many more could be found. In certain areas, they constituted a majority of the voting population, and in a few, a heavy majority of it. They were likelier to come from the antebellum outs than the ins. Douglas Democrats and Whigs, the likeliest to resist secession, had the most compelling reasons for being Republican, though for many Whigs, the Republican economic program, with its commitment to government promotion of the economy through aid to internal improvements, a centralized banking system, and a protective tariff, was one more reason for finding a common ground—and these planks always had appealed not just to forward-looking merchants, bankers, and industrialists in the cities but to many artisans. Long habits of battling against the Democratic leadership were a good training ground for challenging that leadership after the war, and those who had fought the Democratic elites came not just from the old Whig Party but from the areas on the outskirts of the plantation economy, in the less productive or more rugged lands, including those in the Appalachians. Many of them were Unionists in wartime and persecuted afterward. They had seen how little the ex-Confederates gave and how little they could expect.[42]

The scalawags included some of the poorest whites, many of the middling sort, and a scattering of big landholders. All the same, their leaders were less likely to come from the top ranks of society from before the war or to have had education beyond the elementary school level. Those who were planters held smaller estates, and the slaveholders among them were likely to have owned fewer slaves. Indeed, most "scalawags" owned no slaves at all. Their leaders were by no means unlettered, and perhaps two in five had held some state, local, or national office before the war. But they represented people of less property and social prestige than the Democrats, and it showed. If they had no deep hostility to slavery, many had had a much stronger resentment of the political and social privileges of the big slaveholders.[43]

The former Confederates among them had varied reasons for supporting the Republican cause. Conservatives believed that a revolution with the potential to be agrarian and hostile to property needed to be guided into safer directions. General James Longstreet, South Carolina–born and Georgia-raised, came to New Orleans after the war to set up selling insurance and marketing cotton. His Confederate credentials matched those of anybody. But in the spring of 1867 he came out in public letters for accepting Reconstruction in good faith. His goals were anything but radical, for he was no believer in black suffrage. What he wanted was to keep the peace and uphold the law in a society short on both. Others wanted to be sure that if the South was remade, it was in the South's interest and not in the North's. Well aware that many blacks might follow northern white leadership if given no alternative, they were prepared to intervene for that purpose. But others favored Reconstruction as the only way to create a South not fettered to the plantation economy and ready to modernize on terms that the North had set. If factories and investment were to come, then the party that could promise those things should be put in charge, and that happened to be the Republican Party.[44]

Few white southerners committed themselves to racial equality as good in itself. Some tried to show that African Americans were fit to vote but not fit to rule. Most of their fellow workers were prepared to go further. They recognized that change could only come through black votes and that if white Unionists wanted protection, they could only get it with freedpeople's help. They understood, too, that the very least that the North would accept in Reconstruction would be equality before the law and a political system that gave the right to vote and sit on juries to whites and blacks alike. To believe in the inequality of the races and in equality before the law was quite consistent. For Judge Hugh Lennox Bond of Maryland, racial inferiority was a given. But it did not carry with it the presupposition that African Americans should be denied the advantages of education. "If a man can beat another in a race, why insist on tying a weight to the legs of his competitor?" he asked.[45]

Obviously, the "scalawag" constituency tugged in different directions. Businessmen who thought they saw some good in Republicanism after all had no real interest in enshrining loyalty or disfranchising former

Confederates. For upcountry Unionists, disfranchisement loomed far larger. Propertied creditors might support a policy friendly to development, but they balked at debtor relief and stay laws; yeoman farmers and a few planters who owed more than they could afford to pay liked no part of the Republican platform so much.

A new party assembled from such disparate elements could not hold together on a single issue, not even the two most palpable, the need to create an egalitarian society and to create a South with reliable and enduring loyalty to the Union. The Republican Party took as its premise that the two were indissolubly linked, that only with a color-blind suffrage could the kind of loyalty on which a united nation depended come into its own. The strongest white Unionists would stand by the colors, and among the freedpeople, the promise of equal rights and the experience of the half-slavery to which white leaders had consigned them just after the war were more than grounds enough to vote for the party of Lincoln. But outside of South Carolina, Louisiana, and Mississippi, the party would need more than a fistful of white votes to create a lasting majority, unless it was prepared to disfranchise thousands of former Confederates forever. It must win over the most influential class of whites, the professionals, businessmen, and even the planters, that could give a largely lower-class party the respectability on which its members' physical safety depended. The Republican appeal would need to be supplemented with other, more material promises, a gospel of prosperity.

Universal misery presented a ready-made issue. In Georgia, at least one sheriff sold property at auction in breach of a miserably inadequate bankruptcy law, and land went from seven cents to two dollars an acre. The suffering, Republicans insisted, was all the more deplorable because it need not have happened, not with innovative leadership. "The real issue is not over a 'white-man's party,' but the *poor-man's party*, and of equal rights to all," a Vicksburg editor contended. Equal rights meant protection from seizure for the farmer's property with a homestead exemption and from distraint on the craftsman's tools. Stay laws would keep the courts from foreclosing on debtors in their direst need or, for that matter, planters just getting under way again. Radical Reconstruction meant taxpayer-supported public school system open to children of all races, and tax policies that shifted the burden of sustaining the state from the artisan's personal property to the landholder's property. It also meant a government prepared to develop a more commercial and diversified southern economy, with public aid helping to build railroads and repair the levees along the Mississippi, incentives for immigrants, and less dependence on the plantation economy. Alabama had mountains of iron, one partisan argued. Experts declared that from a single vein they could build a furnace every 400 yards and still make a profit: "A few furnaces send up a pillar of cloud by day and of fire by night— the harbingers and guides to our coming deliverance."[46]

Without an increased labor supply, industrial employment would empty the cotton fields, and southern Republicans had no intention of going so far. They wanted new blood in the South as well as new investments. But where conservatives wanted workers to replace freedpeople in the field, Republicans argued that the section needed fewer field hands, not more. Yeoman farmers and men with capital were the section's chief need. Once implemented, the gospel of prosperity would open more opportunities to all. It would give states and men a chance to prosper—such was the substance of the Republican appeal. The party cast it in a distinctly evangelical argot, that of salvation. The sword of Gideon would prevail at last, W. S. Furay told a crowd, "and the government of our fathers, purified by the fiery ordeal through which it has passed, will shine again resplendent as the sun in heaven."[47]

In addition, Republicans could make the pitch that without northern help, no New South could evolve. The federal government could help with subsidies and appropriations, but only after the states' readmission to Congress, where their votes and influence made them worth heeding. Thousands were starving and needed national help, but how could they get it, former Texas provisional governor Andrew J. Hamilton asked, if they refused to reconstruct? What held true for the national government held for private investment as well. As Republicans noted, capital and immigration shunned places where lawlessness and illegitimate governments made life, liberty, and property insecure. Reconstruct Arkansas, General Mason Brayman promised, and he could find all the money he needed to build a trunk line across the state. Till then, as the *Little Rock Republican* cautioned, no one could borrow a dollar in New York, even on approved security.[48]

North and south, conservatives would counter the appeal by talking up the supposed radical desire to confiscate the big estates. What investor would venture south if hot-eyed agrarians toppled the pillars of property? The problem came in finding any responsible Republican leader who actually promised any such thing; fearmongers almost never heard it said themselves—not outright.[49] Undoubtedly some radicals were keen for some redistribution of lands, for two good reasons: to break the political and economic power of the Democratic elite and to give some economic independence to the freedpeople. Former slaves felt that their sweat had given them some right to the acreage that they had plowed and improved for generations. "Our wives, our children, our husbands, has been sold over and over again to purchase the lands we now locate upon," one Virginia black argued; "for that reason we have a divine right to the land." Many poor whites, too, wanted a homestead. True, public land stood open to settlement in every state. Yet even the small payment required was too much for most freedmen; the lands often were of poor quality, and land officers kept the location of property secret from African Americans. On the other side was Republicans' commitment to the rights of private property. Black ministers argued that land was something to be earned, not given, if labor was to deserve its rewards. When confiscatory policies came up in Republican state conventions, those favoring a takeover of estates got nowhere. The more the party reached out for upper-class white support, the more of a nonstarter any commitment to confiscation became, and some of its original friends ate their words or issued clarifications to explain their meanings away.[50]

At the same time, Republicans never slammed the door on land redistribution in some form. They appreciated how deep the desire among their members went. With blacks, they gave tantalizing signals. They attacked the large landholders' monopoly of the good lands and vowed to break the planters' power. By levying a property tax on every acre, Republicans aimed to make the biggest land-hoarders throw their untilled acreage into the market. Darkly, moderates warned that men more extreme than themselves—Thad Stevens, say—had more drastic remedies in reserve; the confiscators could be held back, for now. But what if white conservatives blocked Reconstruction by voting against the conventions? Then Congress would set new terms: new, radical civil governments, disfranchisement for every ex-Confederate—or wholesale confiscation. Those fears certainly made Democrats think twice about organizing to defeat the conventions and gave white supporters of the process a rationale that their conservative neighbors might accept.[51]

No election would pass without intimidation. Conservative newspapers blamed the Union Leagues for browbeating blacks and warning out white Republican defectors, but the mass of unpublished complaints pointed at white employers using their economic clout to keep dependents home. The continued sporadic, almost casual violence against field hands and domestics failing to live up to their employers' notion of faithful servants gave a chilling reminder of where most of the physical power would lie once the military was withdrawn. Even so, Radicals got the conventions they wanted, by overwhelming votes. For all the predictions and in spite of the fact that in South Carolina and Louisiana, blacks went in force, "some with guns," the elections proved peaceful and unusually sober (perhaps because, as one newspaper theorized, the conservatives did not vote).[52] White foes stayed home. If they hoped to deprive the convention of its required supermajority by registering and failing to attend, their strategy failed everywhere. Rather, it made sure that in most places, the conventions would have a paltry conservative presence. Blacks, by contrast, turned out en masse and almost unanimously cast ballots for Reconstruction. But the Republicans' greatest successes exposed grave weaknesses. Even with the army to protect them and a disorganized opposition, they could not muster their full strength. In most of western and southwestern Alabama's counties, one black in four did not show up to vote for Reconstruction, some because of threats, some because of a deliberate misinformation campaign that the election had been postponed.[53] That meant trouble next time around, when the conservatives mobilized, as Radicals were pretty sure they would.

There was one more weakness, not so apparent. Throughout, this new radical party had come about with northern help, northern money, northern encouragement. All too easily painted by its foes as an alien force, unrepresentative of the real South, it lacked the financial or military means to sustain itself. What, then, would the harvest be when northern Republicans turned their funds and faces elsewhere? Whatever its majorities, how could a party so conceived and so dedicated long endure?

CHAPTER SIX

The Critical Year: 1868

As the constitutional conventions met, conservatives expected the worst. Sure enough, they saw "in wide-awake reality, such a mixture of the grotesque and terrible as a man might dream, who had supped on blood-pudding and laughing gas," as one reporter put it.[1]

The truth was nowhere near so horrifying. The black-and-tan conventions, as they were called, were not all that black and tan. More than half the members were southern whites. In seven of the ten assemblies, they held an outright majority. There were 268 black delegates, with 164 white nonsoutherners. The overall figures conceal the disparities. Seventy-six percent of the delegates in Texas were white southerners, in South Carolina barely 28 percent. There and in Louisiana, black delegates outnumbered white ones, but those two states contained nearly half of all the blacks in all conventions. In Texas, they amounted to barely one in nine—but one of them was George T. Ruby, the Louisiana schoolteacher come to Galveston and master-spirit of the state's Union League. Among the 200 delegates assembled in Atlanta, an onlooker might spot "some of the most dignified gentlemen of the state," including judges, doctors, and lawyers. The three dozen African American delegates, who, from press reports, would have been expected to show up "in dirt and rags," appeared "as finely attired as broad cloth and kid boots can make them." In every state, a majority of blacks could read and write. Many held property, especially the freeborn delegates from New Orleans and Charleston. They were likelier than their constituents to be lighter-skinned and urban. Those that were had the most confidence about sharing in the debate.[2]

Democrats had predicted wholesale disfranchisements from the conventions, going well beyond the disqualified classes in the Howard Amendment. If upcountry scalawags had had their way in some states, that might have happened. Rightly, a conservative predicted "more difficulty with the southern Republicans than the Northern—& the whites are more vindictive than the blacks." Delegates did not need to wonder what Republicans in Washington wanted. Alarmed at setbacks in the 1867 state elections, prominent northern Republican editors condemned Alabama's restrictive provisions and even hinted that Congress might not readmit any state where so large a proportion of whites was denied a say in the government. Emissaries came to Richmond and Raleigh to see to it that they made no such mistake. "Impose no disfranchisements in your Constitution," a New York congressman told North Carolina's Republican caucus. "The Republican party wants the moral influence of a conciliated loyal South." Even some self-confessed radicals worried that "the policy of heavy disfranchisements" would injure poor people, white and black alike. In Georgia, Florida, and Texas, white Republicans dropped the idea quickly. South Carolina's large black majorities made disfranchisements needless, while North Carolina had enough white Republicans to make disfranchisement less a must.[3]

Removing the color qualification from voting, and, by implication, from jury service and officeholding, was an unquestionably radical step, and everywhere, Republicans united to write it into fundamental law. But scalawag delegates were not ready supporters of anything beyond the essentials on civil rights issues. Georgia's natives could not even agree on an explicit commitment to blacks' right to hold office. The final provision could be read either way. Most blacks did not make a priority of furthering what critics branded as "social equality," a term including everything from intermarriage to opening schools and public accommodations to all races. Even if they had, the scalawags would have held back. The most the Georgia Constitution would do was to declare that the "social status of the citizens shall never be the subject of legislation."[4] The conventions had much less difficulty writing provisions to establish taxpayer-supported public school systems. Some instituted a poll tax to pay for it. A few constitutions declared all citizens entitled to schooling; South Carolina made attendance mandatory and decreed a six-month school session. Virginia gave counties a deadline for getting schools started.[5]

From the moment the conventions opened, delegates were on the floor offering relief measures. Unless private debts were annulled, or at least judgments against debtors stayed for a time, the courts would "force our people en masse into bankruptcy," one delegate warned. The debtors' property would pass over to "a few note-holders, capitalists and lawyers, and not one-half of their present indebtedness satisfied." Relief cut deeper than conscience—straight to political common sense. As Robert C. DeLarge reminded his South Carolina colleagues, a constitution without such provisions would fail at the polls. So Republicans just about everywhere accepted debtor relief in some form. Stay laws put all debts made in wartime outside the jurisdiction of the courts and voided all contracts in which either party meant the agreement to advance the Confederate cause. Exceptions were made for suits over debts due for mechanical or manual labor, suits against corporations, and suits instituted by charitable or literary institutions. Nine conventions passed provisions guaranteeing married women's property rights, less a blow for gender equality than a protection against the husband's debts picking the family clean. The conventions also declared a certain amount of land and personal property as a homestead exemption permanently beyond the reach of the law—with conditions.[6]

Helping those with land keep it was one thing. Giving land to those without it was quite another. For all their talk of the virtues of a society in which every man rested under his own vine and fig tree, the delegates did not do much to increase the number of freeholders in the South. Just about no convention gave serious consideration to measures that would break up the estates directly. In Louisiana, one delegate offered a resolution to give the legislature the right at its first session to provide the landless with homesteads, but the proposal never came to a vote. Another radical presented an ordinance to make the tax on uncultivated land double that on cultivated land. Such a measure might have forced unused property onto the market and lowered the price. It died in committee. Constitutional provisions changing the tax structure to make real property pay more heavily and personalty pay less did add to landowners' burdens, but for freedmen, this raised only faint hopes. Higher assessments might cause property to change hands, but mostly to those who already had land and money, not those without means to buy. In setting up a Land Commission, able to take over lands forfeited for taxes and parcel it out in homesteads, South Carolina did more for the landless than any other state, though less than radicals had hoped.[7]

Reconstruction meant more than relief. Delegates of all parties hoped that Congress would embark on an ambitious system of internal improvements. The states along the Mississippi wanted a national program of levee construction and maintenance, and every state hoped for river and harbor improvements. The conventions showed an equally keen interest in railroads and to use their own states' money to speed on development. Five ordinances with a total of $2.15 million in aid went to North Carolina railroads. One enterprise got not just $1.2 million in state bonds but the state's interest in the Cape Fear and Deep River Navigation Company. All but two of the new constitutions permitted state support for internal improvements of all kinds; Texas did not permit land grants, while Mississippi forbade any pledge of the public credit on behalf of a private corporation.

When the conventions completed their work, their members had good reason for pride in their handiwork. Georgia's constitution was surprisingly conservative, compared to the prophecies. Having sneered from the start at "the Oderiferous concern" in Atlanta, Noel Burton Knight found its finished work "a most admirable constitution" that resembled the conservative document of 1865. Except for the political provisions, the Reconstruction constitutions everywhere were ones that business interests could live with and, across the rest of the country, had been living with for years. The provisions taxing lands and establishing schools resembled those in northern constitutions, and the support for internal improvements only furthered trends already visible in the postwar South. Four states for the first time put a specific right to bear arms into their Bills of Rights: Georgia, Louisiana, South Carolina, and Virginia. In the others, the whites-only restriction was removed. Even so, some radicals expressed disappointment at how little had changed. They charged the majority with selling out party ideals. Moderates had won out on political and economic questions in most states. Few constitutions did any disfranchising. Florida and Louisiana radicals deserted the Republicans and ran their own slates against the constitution.[8]

How radical the effects of the constitutions would be obviously depended on who administered them. No convention chose a black candidate for governor or Congress. Most gubernatorial nominees had two qualities that might inspire confidence in gentlemen of influence and property, businessmen especially. First, they had a strong interest in broadening the party to include the most respected whites, even if it meant downplaying policies that working-class whites had been counting on. In 1867, for example, Harrison Reed, a Johnson appointee now on the slate for governor of Florida, had proposed a coalition with one of the leading conservatives, former senator David Yulee, against the radicals. Powell Clayton, the Union veteran come south to engage in planting, seemed so moderate that Arkansas conservatives considered running him for governor themselves. Second, Republicans chose men partial to economic development. At least three had independent wealth and standing and an interest in railroad projects. Another was an important planter.

The main issues of the canvass were reunion and racial equality, but Republicans tried to make economic issues the decisive ones for many white voters. That meant railroad construction with state aid in some places and debtor relief in nearly all. Each day the *Atlanta New Era* warned "What Opposition Means": no homestead exemption, no debtor relief, but plenty of desolation, confusion, ignorance, intolerance, and industrial depression. Where the gospel of prosperity was writ large, party advocates spoke small about the Rebellion or race relations. Republican orators deplored "continued strife," perhaps as a euphemism for Ku Kluxing and Confederate loyalties, but it was significant that they preferred using euphemisms. They knew what arguments sold best among white southerners, and they were not those of Union and equal rights. But votes from former Confederates and the less committed conservatives were ones that the new party could not do without. It must broaden, not narrow, its political base, even if that meant putting some distance between the party's first principles and those on which it intended to govern.[9]

Conservatives painted the Republican economic program as the reign of unpropertied savages out for confiscation, the worst enemies that commerce and industry could imagine. That was not their main issue for mobilizing poorer white voters. Race was. Counties would see "nigger sheriffs, nigger judges, nigger assessors, nigger treasurers, nigger collectors and nigger everything," and, Ben Hill warned Georgians, "absolute [black] control and dominion" across almost half the state. Rallying poor white men to defend their wives and daughters from race-mixing and social equality, they warned that Radical rule would let blacks "occupy seats side by side with those most dear to you in theatres—aye, even in the temple of Almighty God." The constitutions were "a plentiful supply of black vomit," the *Iberville South* raged. They had been framed by "the social banditti, domestic bastards, catamites, scalawags, slubberdegullions, cow thieves and jay-hawkers of Louisiana": so the *Bossier Banner* asserted.[10]

Savagery of language reflected savagery of method. Democrats intimidated, whipped, and killed Radicals. The army could do little to protect individuals isolated on their homesteads and alone in the dark of a southern night. State governments did nothing whatsoever. In Alabama and Mississippi, there were complaints that military commanders were using their power to hinder ratification. Elsewhere conservative officials were accused of using their offices to thwart the will of Congress. In Florida, radicals contended that the railroads and mail services were used against them.[11]

Republican victories were more easily won than they might have been, had Democrats put up candidates against them in every case, but they fell below what had been hoped for and with a much smaller white conversion. In Louisiana and South Carolina, Republicans had brought out a solid black vote for their cause. They needed no white votes and ended up winning very few. In Arkansas, conservatives boycotted the election and by letting Radical candidates win by default made the true will of the state's white people impossible to discern.[12] Where many whites did vote for the constitutions, radicals charged that attracting their votes had come at too high a price. Florida Republicans carried a constitution so moderate that many conservatives expressed relief and many radicals vented their fury.

Alabama conservatives knew that they could not vote the constitution down; but by boycotting the polls and by depressing black and white Republican turnout, they could deprive it of the majority of voters essential for passage. Against scalawags the full force of social and economic ostracism was turned. "Let the white dogs stand from under, for they will be crushed," former governor John Winston told a crowd. Acquaintances refused to speak to them or recognize their existence, or that of their wives and children. Those in business could expect to see their clientage fall off sharply. If they attended church, no one would dare offer them a seat, and if they owned a pew, the pews around would vacate at once, the moment they sat down. The blacklist meant that the victims' children were driven out of the Sunday schools, and were not allowed to play with other children during the rest of the week. If a person lay sick or death came to a household, no neighbor would come with sympathy, kindness, or help. Under such pressure, it was a wonder that out of some three hundred or more whites in Montgomery known to favor ratification even forty-two showed up to vote for the constitution. For blacks, the consequences were much direr. Their dependence on white employers and white credit made them vulnerable to intense economic pressure. "Touch not a loyal-leaguer's hand," one newspaper admonished; "taste not of a loyal-leaguer's hospitality; handle not a loyal-leaguer's goods. Oust him, socially, break him, pecuniarily; ignore him, politically; kick him, contagiously; hang him, legally; or lynch him, clandestinely."[13]

The Democratic strategy paid off. Over 70,000 Alabamans voted to ratify the constitution, against 1,000 voting against it. But Reconstruction had needed a turnout of 95,000 votes for any ratification majority to count. Slightly under 19,000 whites had supported the constitutional convention; not quite 8,000 turned out for its ratification.[14]

Mississippi proved much worse. Whites were informed that they could not vote Republican and still count on the tolerance of the community. A clergyman landowner in one county called his hands together just before the election for what he called "good advice." They could "vote as they pleased," he assured them, but he "advised them" not to vote with the Radicals. "If they did they would be killed." In Oxford, Democrats handed out a "negro democratic star" to tell their blacks from Republican ones. Donning one became a form of life insurance. When returns came in, the Democrats had beaten the constitution outright by nearly 8,000 votes. In many places, Republicans stayed home. In others they voted against the constitution because they were forced to do so. Elsewhere, white gunmen guarded every road into town and barred Union voters from approaching. Little violence occurred at the polls. That was saved for later, throughout the summer, with beatings, shootings, and dismissals doled out in generous proportions—the dismissals and evictions timed after the cotton crop could spare them.[15]

So even when the constitutions went through and even after Congress adjusted the Reconstruction law to make Alabama's majority sufficient to continue the process, southern Republicans felt alarm mixing with their elation. And, as in Mississippi and Alabama, the violent work of night riders only picked up its pace after the returns came in and spread wider. "Every hour's delay is wasting away our ranks," the Reverend C. W. Buckley wrote a congressman in pleading for President Johnson's removal. "Every week's delay is atoned for by some loyal man's life."[16]

That removal very nearly happened. By his lights, Johnson had carried out all the Reconstruction Acts in good faith, but he read their provisions as narrowly as he could to disfranchise as few white southerners as possible and limit the military's discretion. Congress had been forced into special session in July to write a third Reconstruction law clarifying the first two. It could not keep him from issuing proclamations widening the amnesty for ex-Confederates. Nor could it keep him from removing the less conservative commanders: Sheridan, Sickles, and Pope. Cries for impeachment may have been mounting, but moderates would not arraign the president as long as he stayed within the law, and as long as the army stayed in trusty Republican hands. With Edwin M. Stanton as secretary of war, the Reconstructionists had that guarantee. Restrained by the Tenure of Office Act from removing cabinet officers appointed during his administration without the Senate's consent, the president suspended Stanton in August, making General Grant secretary of war ad interim. The following January, the Senate refused to confirm the removal. Grant, with no intention of exercising authority in violation of the law, retired from the cabinet and turned the office over to Stanton. The president thereupon took steps to take possession. Appointing General Lorenzo Thomas, he ordered him to take control of the War Department and eject the secretary.[17]

When the news reached the Capitol on February 21, 1868, House and Senate broke into an uproar. Leaning on Ohio congressman John Bingham's arm, Thaddeus Stevens limped from group to group. "Didn't I tell you so?" he kept repeating. "What good did your moderation do you? If you don't kill the beast it will kill you." As knots of excited representatives argued on the floor and in the cloakrooms, and Democrats vainly tried to adjourn the session, Republicans sat at their desks to pen appeals to Stanton to stand firm. Rumors added to the seething, and tension was not eased when, amid the noise, some of the House's glass roof fell and shattered on the floor around members. Members were furious at what seemed to them a flagrant defiance of the law, but they were also fearful. Considering Johnson's utterances, they suspected he might be launching a coup. Taking control of the army, he might be intending to save the Constitution by dispersing or overawing Congress and the Supreme Court. House debate went through Washington's Birthday. Late on Monday, February 24th, as servants lit the gas, the clerk began to call the roll in a scene that one friendly reporter thought "brilliant and impressive beyond description. Everything was as quiet and still as a church meeting, and the answer of each member to the call of his name could be heard distinctly by the vast multitude throughout the great hall." By a strict party vote, an impeachment resolution passed.[18]

By then, the worst fears had begun to dissipate. Army officers rushed to make clear that in any conflict, they would defer to Congress and General Grant. Stanton barricaded himself in his office, with Union veterans guarding him from attack. Before Thomas could make any attempt to employ force, District authorities put him under arrest. The half-hearted effort he made to exercise authority in the War Department ended with no blood spilt and a little bourbon put to good use on both sides. Johnson could not use the army if he would and quickly let it be known that he would not if he could.[19]

Over the next few weeks, the House chose managers to take their case to the Senate and drew up eleven articles of impeachment. The eleventh became something of a catchall, containing not just indictable but unindictable offenses, and the general charge of criminal conspiracy. In March, the trial began, with Chief Justice Salmon P. Chase presiding. Johnson did not choose to appear but chose several prominent Republicans among his counsel, among them the keen New York City lawyer William M. Evarts and former Supreme Court justice Benjamin R. Curtis, whose dissent in the *Dred Scott* decision gave him antislavery credentials that no Republican could question.[20]

At first, most observers expected the overwhelmingly Republican Senate to hold a speedy trial and bring in a swift conviction. Instead, the tribunal insisted on treating the proceedings as a serious juridical matter. Both sides made closely reasoned arguments on the constitutional meaning of high crimes and misdemeanors. A parade of witnesses confirmed the president's intention to mount a court challenge to Stanton's right to the office and fell short on demonstrating any willful violation of the law. In spite of radicals' hopes that "high crimes and misdemeanors" included the violation of trust and abuse of his powers that had done so much to sabotage Reconstruction, most Republican senators clearly believed in a much narrower definition. Johnson could not be removed for "pure cussedness," as Thaddeus Stevens had half-seriously proposed. Nor could it be for his following his usual strategy of looking for ambiguities, silences, or weaknesses in the law and then interpreting them to his best advantage. He had to have broken a law, knowing that he was doing so. As the defense showed, the Tenure of Office Act's provisions were so unclear that they may not have covered Stanton, who was one of Lincoln's appointees. Johnson's counsel also gave plenty of precedents for making an ad interim appointment like Thomas's while Congress was in session; a few of them may even have been applicable.[21]

On legal grounds, almost every senator in both parties found himself unable to accept some of the articles, with the eleventh alone having any chance of the necessary two-thirds vote for conviction, but other considerations also heightened Republican misgivings. Removing the president risked shifting the balance of powers too far in Congress's direction and away from an independent executive. It also would put radical Republican senator Benjamin F. Wade into the White House. As crude, courageous, and blunt as Johnson himself, Wade had economic views worrisome to those who thought the tariff too high and the money supply too loose already. Thanks to Ohio's recent election of a Democratic legislature, he was also a lame duck, soon to be retired. Even a brief stint as president might give him the leverage to put himself on the ticket when the convention met in late May and fill the offices with all his friends. If the election brought General Grant into the presidency, as everybody expected and moderates hoped, he would find a clean sweep of fellow Republicans embarrassing, if not messy.[22]

Even those Republicans inclined to vote for Johnson's acquittal worried that in doing so, they would let him loose to do his worst. That worst grew less terrible all the time, admittedly: by mid-April, the Reconstruction constitutions had carried in seven states. Within a month or two, Congress would readmit them all to Congress. With civil authorities in place, the harm that the president could do with control over military forces as commander in chief would diminish. All the same, senators like James W. Grimes of Iowa and Lyman Trumbull of Illinois needed assurances that the army would be out of his control. Looking for a secretary of war that the Senate would trust enough to confirm as Stanton's successor, the president's lawyers hit on General John G. Schofield, who was then overseeing Virginia's military district. Schofield had conservative leanings. He had disapproved of the disqualifications from office under the Fourteenth Amendment, and his directions postponed any vote on the radical constitution in the Old Dominion, with its disfranchisements. Still, he had obeyed the Reconstruction Acts to the letter, and as a Grant's personal friend, he could be counted on to take the general's advice. Over the dinner table of a third party, the president and senators came to an understanding. Johnson effectively renounced any plan to use the army to overthrow the Reconstruction laws. The senators may also have reflected that Johnson's likeliest opportunity had passed as well. Given a chance to rule the Reconstruction Acts unconstitutional in *ex parte McCardle*, the Supreme Court had given it a pass, perhaps in part because the administration's counsel had not pressed for action. By the time the judges reassembled, new civil governments would be running, recognized by Congress.[23]

By May 12th, the outcome hung in doubt. Every Democrat would vote to acquit, and most Republicans would vote to convict on the eleventh article. A barrage of pleas and threats fell on the few uncommitted senators on whom the verdict now depended. The ugly bullying and accusations of treason and corruption coming from the impeachers' side only revived moderate Republicans' doubts about impeachment itself. If its purpose was to remove Johnson regardless of the legal case, they warned, the process would transform into an engine profoundly subversive of the Founders' intent. It would have become the equivalent of a bill of attainder, the English power allowing punishment of offenders without the need for due process. On May 16th, the Senate voted thirty-five to nineteen for conviction, by the most optimistic reckoning one short of the number required (that is, only if one vote for acquittal had swung the other way). Aware of their slim chances for carrying any other article, Republicans adjourned the court for ten days before taking a vote on the others. When several of the other charges failed then, the Senate dropped the rest. The narrow margin became the stuff of legend, with the seven Republicans who voted for acquittal sacrificing their political future to follow their consciences and perishing under a storm of abuse. In fact, party moderates welcomed most of the "recusants" back and openly expressed relief that the whole adventure had ended. Among those seven at least two, Fessenden and Trumbull, had records of public service too great for any party to dispense with lightly. Insiders knew that Johnson's acquittal had been a surer thing than it seemed. He had allies in reserve; Republican senators pledged to acquit, if their votes were needed. Private correspondence suggested that others, bought to acquit, double-crossed their purchasers.[24]

The stir over impeachment died almost at once, except for an investigation into the president's means of winning senators' votes. It was as ugly as Congressman Benjamin F. Butler could make it and as inconclusive as witnesses' perjury and evasion could allow. By June, nobody cared except Thaddeus Stevens. When he proposed a new impeachment resolution, it came with the half-heartedness of one convinced not only of its futility but of the ultimate failure of Reconstruction. The seven states readmitted that June would send senators and congressmen to Washington again and ratify the Fourteenth Amendment, allowing its adoption into the Constitution. But any promise of Congress mandating a lasting military presence to keep order in the South, the disfranchisement of even the most offensive Confederates, or land redistribution to make the freedpeople into independent farmers, much less a national commitment to fund a universal school system in the former Rebel states, had vanished for good. With civil authority restored, the Freedmen's Bureau sped up a process already under way, to close down its hospitals and clinics, cut costs, and turn over its schools to the new state governments. On July 25th, Congress ordered the commissioner to bring most bureau activities to an end at the start of the new year and relinquish its duties before then in states already fully reconstructed. By 1869, there were no longer Freedmen's Bureau courts, no supervision over laborers' contracts, no relief responsibilities. What was left of the agency handled black Union veterans' claims and ran a few hospitals and orphan asylums until funds ran out. Long before June 1872, when Congress closed the bureau down, it had become more a memory than a reality. Even before the amendment's restrictions on officeholding went into effect, congressmen were offering bills to restore some southerners' full rights. A final Amnesty Proclamation late in the year removed any danger that any onetime Confederate would face legal penalties for wartime action. That August, regretting only that he "had lived so long and so uselessly," Stevens died, buried at his own request in the one graveyard in Lancaster, Pennsylvania, open to white and black alike.[25]

With one exception, there would be no new advances in Radical Reconstruction. From now on, its sponsors' main duty came in maintaining the gains they had made. Their worst challenge, they knew, lay months ahead, in the presidential campaign. Within a week, the Republican convention had nominated General Grant for president, with Speaker of the House Schuyler Colfax of Indiana as his running mate. Endorsing the Reconstruction Acts, the platform declared that black suffrage was a matter best left to each state to decide and committed itself to returning former Confederates to their full rights as quickly as the country's safety allowed. Under pressure, the Alabama and Louisiana legislatures removed their restrictions on white voters that summer. In his acceptance letter, Grant set the watchword for the campaign, very much the antithesis of new crusades and the epitome of the moderate spirit that the party wanted to convey: "Let us have peace."[26]

In making that point, Republicans had indispensable help. Democrats wanted no peace that accepted either a Fourteenth Amendment or impartial suffrage as settled facts. Chief Justice Chase's clear lack of sympathy with impeachment and his evenhanded rulings presiding at the trial had earned him Democratic applause and even some hints that the party might run him for president. An old-line abolitionist, Chase shared eastern Democrats' hard-money views. He was ready to affirm that states had the right to decide on black suffrage for themselves. Beyond that, he would not go. Nominating him would all but commit the party to equal rights and, naturally, to the national banking system that as Treasury secretary he had fathered in wartime. Both views made him anathema to midwestern Democrats. With Johnson's administration calling in and destroying greenbacks to push the country's money supply back to a specie basis, farmers wanted easier credit and more paper money, and thought they could get both by electing former congressman "Gentleman George" F. Pendleton of Ohio, a onetime Copperhead and the 1864 vice presidential candidate. Westerners in both parties wanted the wartime debt paid in greenbacks where the law did not command otherwise. They saw no reason why "the bond-holding, shin-plaster shylocks" should have tax-exempt portfolios; that Pendleton's wartime record would make treason and defeatism the one and only issue in the canvass and drive everyone but a hard-core Democrat away did not trouble them at all. The party's eastern bankers and businessmen in the party had a particular interest in changing the topic to the one on which they and their western critics agreed, the unconstitutionality of Reconstruction and the need to keep America a "white man's country." When former Union general Frank Blair Jr. issued a letter announcing that a Democratic administration would declare the Reconstruction Acts unconstitutional and that the president would use the army to overturn the new governments, he fired many a partisan heart.[27]

When the Democratic convention assembled in New York, Pendleton forces led but could not break the deadlock. Neither Chase nor Johnson could mount more than a forlorn hope. Backroom intrigues brought one favorite son after another to the fore. Then Clement Vallandigham, the Peace Democrat whose accommodation to the new realities had made him one of Chase's most outspoken backers, rose to propose the name of the presiding officer, New York's wartime governor, Horatio Seymour. Genuinely appalled, Seymour tried to refuse; he was hustled weeping out of the hall before delegates could take him at his word. As soon as Pendleton's opponents had carried Seymour through, they looked for a Union war hero from the West to balance the ticket. Blair seemed ready-made for it. The platform fit him better than Seymour. It called for universal amnesty and declared the Reconstruction Acts unconstitutional, null and void.[28]

In what one congressman called "a manifestation of folly well nigh amounting to insanity," Democrats had made themselves effectively the party of revolution and assured that Reconstruction and the Union, not financial issues, would dominate the canvass that followed. They could argue that they were the true party of peace and reconciliation. With three states still unrepresented that summer, restoration remained incomplete. Elsewhere, it was more apparent than real. Any reconstruction, to last, must create two things, Democrats reminded voters: stable, durable, legitimate governments that could earn the people's respect and a restored liberty, in which individual states could exercise all their old authority without oversight from Washington. On any other terms, whatever entity the Congress made would collapse the moment the protective hand was withdrawn. No legitimate government could rest on anything but the consent of its white people. They had most of the property and arms in the South. They paid most of the taxes. How long would they play along with governments elected against their will? And if they did not, what could follow but civil war or a bayonet-backed puppet state? As things stood, John Quincy Adams Jr. cried, Radical rule was "simply this—the rule of the military and nothing else."[29]

A year before, the Democrats could have made a more credible case. By campaign season, Congress had cut back on the army's discretionary powers. With the return of civil government down south, most troops were

THE DEMOCRATIC HELL-BROTH.

Double, double, toil and trouble,
Fire burn and caldron bubble.
Round about the hell-broth go,
In the motley fragments throw:

Hand of Treason, reeking red,
Poison-fang of Copperhead,
Tongue and lip of perjured Lee,
Bitter tear of refugee,
Curse of planter, prayer of slave,
Blossom from a martyr's grave,
Rod of "Moses," which he lost
When he pardoned Pharaoh's host,
Skull of prisoner at Fort Pillow,
Blood of freedman at Camilla,
Hampton's torch, Fred Douglass's fetter,
Booth's revolver, Blair's letter,

Toombs's whip and Forrest's sneer,
And a sigh from Dostie's bier,
Seasoned with guerrilla's oath.

Seymour stirs the horrid broth—
Bound about his head a rag
From the Alabama's flag;
Cloak of canvas that the gale
Wrested from the pirate's sail;
Wand of witchery that bore
Treason's flag in '64.
With a weird and hissing sound
Rocks the caldron round and round,
And he cries, "'Tis very good!
Lo! the cup of Brotherhood!"

W. A. CROFFUT.

"The Democratic Hell-Broth." Thomas Nast, *Harper's Weekly*, October 31, 1868. Frank Blair Jr.,
former Confederate general and future South Carolina governor Wade Hampton, and Horatio
Seymour concoct a brew in a pot symbolizing the Confederacy and the Ku Klux Klan. The
"Moses" referred to in the poem was Andrew Johnson, and Dostie was the Free State leader
killed in the New Orleans riot.

being withdrawn anyhow. In every readmitted state, civil courts were opening; officers appointed by governors were taking over responsibilities handled by military appointees. Democratic claims of widespread disfranchisements depended on fabulous figures. They counted 200,000 white Virginians and 70,000 Texans as supposedly denied the right to vote; the real numbers may have approached 12,000 and 4,000, respectively. Most of the readmitted states opened the ballot box to all adult males. For the proofs of the demoralization of labor and the South's financial ruin, Democrats had to argue against cold figures. A year before, the cotton states had been in desperate shape. Too much rain and army-worm infestations had devastated the crops. Winter had brought hunger, in some places, near famine. White voting may have been all the lower because for so many farmers, the struggle to survive made politics a distraction and made some of them so desperate that even Radical rule seemed a less terrible alternative than what they were undergoing. But the 1868 season was much better. The cotton crop promised to be larger than those of the three years before. Southern newspapers predicted a rice yield big enough to keep imported rice off the domestic market.[30]

Republicans spent little time defending Reconstruction in specific, though there were some exceptions. A few editors frankly hailed the moral uplift that came with an exchange of northern for supposed southern values. "The bowie knife, the rifle, and the mattock will give place to the plow, the loom, and the anvil," said the *Auburn Daily Advertiser*. But they made the most of Frank Blair's threatening letter as proof of a revolutionary purpose. Democratic success in November meant the overturning of three years of progress in bringing the country together and beginning anew. Only a lunatic would think that Republican governments, elected by majority votes, would yield power willingly. Only a madman would expect that those who carried the states for new constitutions would stand idly by as the minority tore them up. And only a Democrat would have the cheek to pretend that a president using the army to compel the Congress to accept his unilateral actions would strengthen republican institutions. Blood would flow, north as well as south. Union men would be slaughtered if they refused to submit, and many of them whether they submitted or not—white and black alike— as former Confederates took hold of the southern states again, armories, militia, and all. What else could the Democratic platform mean but that? If the Reconstruction laws were unconstitutional, revolutionary, and void, Democrats would feel themselves morally bound to set them aside at any price, force included. "This is not a quiet legislative process," one editor commented. "For this there is but one name—it is a counter-revolution in the fullest sense of the term."[31]

For both sides, then, loyalty, reunion, and protection of the Constitution and of the republic itself became intertwined issues. Democrats insisted that most of the Union soldiers were for Seymour's principles, even if they favored Grant more as a person. For Republicans, the leading agency for holding the soldier vote was the newly created Grand Army of the Republic, but every parade had marching legions of Boys in Blue. Democrats, not to be outdone, formed their own soldiers' clubs, the White Boys in Blue, with adjunct Union Clubs for civilians. They could never match the Republican array of top brass, from William Tecumseh Sherman to Philip Sheridan to George H. Thomas, the "Rock of Chickamauga." In the North, every Copperhead effusion told against the Democratic ticket. Republicans claimed to have uncovered a secret society in Connecticut, the Knights of the Cross of St. Wilkes Booth, that chanted hymns lauding Jefferson Davis and Andrew Johnson. Not content to hint that Seymour was about to go mad and that southerners meant to kill him to make Blair the next president, Republicans put the ex-governor's war record in a pitiless and distorting light, turning a critic of Lincoln's constitution-stretching into a Copperhead traitor. During the New York City draft riots in 1863, one speaker charged, Seymour spoke to "the men engaged in this bloody riot, to whose garments still cling the smoke of burning asylums, and whose hands were yet red with the blood of their murdered victims, as his friends!" America was not yet ready for a "grayback candidate on a greenback platform."[32]

Southern Democrats talked with anything but charity. "Elect Seymour and all that the Confederacy fought for will be won," former governor Vance assured North Carolinians—or so Republican editors claimed. The party could not spend its money better than in paying to broadcast reports of Confederates' speeches and their leading soldiers' endorsement of Seymour, one operative advised. He thought that the national committee should make itself a clearinghouse of embarrassing statements, collecting them and then sending party managers the choicest examples in every state.[33]

Virginia, Mississippi, and Texas, still unreconstructed, had no say in making the next president. In Florida, the legislature forestalled violence by declaring that it would choose the presidential electors, rather than leaving it to the voters. A movement in the same direction very nearly carried in Alabama, but the governor vetoed it, apparently after reassurance that federal troops would be on hand to protect loyal voters. Louisiana legislators would have acted as those in Alabama did, but Governor Henry Clay Warmoth discouraged them from doing so. Even so, Alabama had only the most truncated version of a campaign; Governor Smith did not issue a proclamation announcing any election until mid-October, leaving neither side much chance to organize.[34]

Nobody had to guess what southern Democrats would do with a Seymour victory. Every day the wire services hummed with evidence that they had begun doing it already. Some of it was a series of threats to Republicans of what would happen to them if they did not make their peace with the master class. Where black votes were indispensable, Democrats hustled to make converts. They hosted barbecues, open to members of both races, and opened the books for "colored clubs." They tried to find black spokesmen ready to sustain their cause and offered certificates to freedpeople willing to enroll in the party. In some places, they found Republican allies ready to advance themselves at other Republicans' expense, in return for Democratic cooperation or coalition.[35]

But the Democrats' best was not, on the whole, very good. From the first, it had assumed that blacks must accept the role of followers, with white conservatives as leaders. Its promise of all the rights that blacks were entitled to left unclear just what those rights would include. Democratic arguments, as well, had an implausible ring to them. Their speakers insisted that Republicans had never wanted to free the Negro; blacks had freed themselves and owed the party of Lincoln no gratitude. General John B. Gordon solemnly assured South Carolina blacks that land-hungry northerners really wanted to see every one of them dead, because vacant ground was so scarce up north.[36] Masters were the only true friends of black people—always had been. Arguments like these would not have worked even if there had been no Union Leagues, no Republican newspapers, and no two-party system with speakers and handbills to make a reply.

Nor did the white gestures of friendship seem to go very deep. "Stupids, will you never learn anything?" a Georgia paper beseeched the freedpeople. "Will even experience, in the shape of practical kicks and cuffs, fail to teach you on which side your bread is *really* buttered?" Often the overtures came with a very strong "or else" accompanying them. Explaining that whites only wanted peace, General Gordon informed blacks in Charleston that one race "or the other must go down." Spurn the "Southern man," and "these green leaves that now clothe the forest will not grow red with another autumn before they will be drenched with your blood and mine." "I do not think you would find a corporal's guard in any county, of colored men who would vote [Democratic] if they had a free expression," a Georgia lawmaker testified. "Those who did so express themselves were either acting under the degrading influence of pay, or else were driven to it from circumstances of home and family."[37]

Where persuasion did not work, intimidation was tried, and often the two went together from the start. In some areas, whites disarmed the freedpeople, beating or shooting those who resisted having their guns taken from them. They guarded roads into town in one county to keep blacks from attending meetings. Tenants were told that if they cast a Republican ballot, they would lose their livings, if not their lives. Their credit would be cut off at the store. Their families would be turned off the land. In half a dozen Georgia counties, bodies of armed whites halted every black man they met on the roads and threatened to kill him at once unless he signed "An Association of Peace between the Blacks and Whites." The terms required the signer to cast his ballot for Horatio Seymour.[38]

Along with threats came violence. Democrats would insist that they were the peacemakers, that it was Republicans who had the bloody thoughts. Yet no black armies ever appeared by light of day where white people could see them. The planters and their families slept unmolested, however intense the hatreds seething around them. The "streams of blood" flowed from black victims, not white ones. Those Louisiana towns reportedly consigned to the flames remained unsinged, while the *Planter's Banner* successfully provoked its readers to butcher two Union officers. Democrats' fearmongering itself became an incitement to violence, and often probably meant as such, to make the attacks seem defensive rather than aggressive.[39]

None of this needed organizational support. The evidence for the regular, random beatings and killings of black Republicans showed that it took no masks or midnight mobs to do the job. Many of the assaults came from individuals singling out other individuals, usually ones they knew, and there was a constant pattern that wove only indirectly into politics. But much of it was institutional. Starting in 1866 or 1867, the organizations to enforce white supremacy had been growing throughout the Deep South. The most prominent was the Ku Klux Klan.

Founded as a fraternal organization in Pulaski, Tennessee, it attracted its first members with ritual, disguise, and mumbo jumbo. Later accounts would emphasize the prankish nature of its members. Riding and pretending to be Confederate ghosts, pretending to swallow barrels of water at a time, they would scare the freedmen into good behavior. In fact, night riders went beyond pranks soon and into mayhem and threats of violence against supporters of Reconstruction. Visible outside Tennessee only sporadically before the constitutional ratification elections, the Klan grew and spread most as the presidential campaign began, in some states in coordination with Democratic leaders. Handbills with death threats or coffins inscribed appeared on doorsteps. The Klan would fire shots into houses as they rode past. It would call out people from their homes and promise them death or a whipping if they voted Republican. Night riders raided the houses of Republican organizers to confiscate their ballots and make distribution on Election Day impossible. The closer to the election, the more frequent the visits were, reaching a climax on November 2nd. In some places, blacks hid in the woods to sleep safely. Some fled the state.[40]

There were beatings, often by men without disguise. Republican leaders were picked off. The usual "persons unknown" were credited with emptying a double-barreled shotgun into the backs of Congressman James Hinds of Arkansas and Joseph Brooks, the foremost radical Republican in Arkansas, as they headed to a campaign rally. Hinds was killed and Brooks badly wounded. The chief suspect was the secretary of the local Democratic committee, who in addition to declaring that he meant to kill them, was holding the shotgun at the time it was fired. A former chaplain to a black Union regiment, South Carolina Republican chairman Benjamin F. Randolph had earned special unpopularity as the founder not only of black schools soon after the war but of Union Leagues in the period since. He ranked among the state's most able Republican leaders by 1868. Mounted riders shot him in broad daylight on a railroad platform in Abbeville County, fulfilling the promise of one Democratic leader, D. Wyatt Aiken, that if he came into the county he would "get a piece of land *six feet by two*." The killers rode out of town, with nobody prepared to stop them or, as it turned out, to identify them.[41] None of these acts was random. They were part of a process, ever more emboldened.

Louisiana was worse than anywhere. Negro churches and schoolhouses were burned. Two Republican newspapers were smashed. Their editors were beaten or shot to death. In Caddo Parish, the guess was that more than forty-two blacks lost their lives in October alone. In Bossier Parish, an affray resulted in a full-scale "Negro hunt," in which at least 162 blacks were murdered, and over 100 more wounded. In late October, a quarrel between a storekeeper and some blacks in St. Bernard Parish opened four days of massacre, in which more than two dozen blacks were killed. A "reign of terror has been inaugurated by the Democracy throughout this state," Stephen B. Packard, Republican state chairman, wrote from New Orleans. "Hundreds of republicans have been killed. Republican residences, churches, school houses, printing offices are being sacked, flags & fixtures of club rooms destroyed. Registration certificates of republicans taken by armed bands. Democratic secret organizations press & party are in resistance to the laws & advise overthrow of state Government."[42]

Where a robust white Unionist presence allowed, as was the case in some Arkansas counties, authorities could rely on the sheriff to mobilize a posse, but even there, results were mixed. It depended entirely on which side had the most guns, and the process itself meant a rise in violence, at least in the short run. Elsewhere, sheriffs lacked the nerve or the power even to try to summon a posse and found white residents very unwilling to risk themselves by serving. No state militia was called out against them. In most states, one was not even mustered. South Carolina's state constabulary sent officers to the afflicted counties, but they were able neither to catch the Klansmen themselves nor to induce others to join up to help them. The legislature empowered the governor to send out the militia, but Robert K. Scott did no more than issue a proclamation warning that he might, and then just two weeks before the election. In Florida, Governor Harrison Reed went to New York to buy 40,000 rounds of ammunition and 2,000, for a newly authorized militia in September. As the train with the arms on board headed to Tallahassee, Klansmen boarded, broke open the locked freight cars, and heaved the weaponry out. The armaments were gone by the time the train reached its destination, and so were the Klansmen.[43]

Democrats insisted that northern Republicans had "set up a score of extensive . . . establishments, worked by ten thousand dog-power, for the manufacture of Southern murders." Undeniable incidents, like the way-laying of guns for the Arkansas militia, were explained as provocations by Radicals, simply to give them a shocker to stir up the northern electorate. The Ku Klux Klan was "simply a charitable, social institution . . . entirely peaceful and law-abiding in character." All the threatening placards were forgeries, written by "Radical incendiaries" to "endanger the peace and bring odium on the character of our people," said the *Savannah Daily News and Herald*. Talk that Georgia's radical state senator George W. Ashburn had died in white terrorists' hands, while easily proven from eyewitness testimony, was countered by the contention that he was "a most dangerous character, ignorant, energetic, vain and unscrupulous, cruel, malignant and vindictive" and, significantly, that he treated black people "in the most absolute and dictatorial manner." Readers could draw their own conclusions as to who really had been behind his killing. Days before the election, the *New York World* announced: "Terrific Negro Riots in New Orleans and the Adjoining Parishes." The "Negro Riots" apparently deserved the name because blacks appeared there as the victims.[44]

With "innocent lambs of the Democratic flock . . . shooting Negroes almost daily," Governor Scott of South Carolina wrote General E. R. S. Canby, what could any Republican expect if Seymour won? Threats were not merely whispered across the South; they were uttered "so loudly that the air has become vocal with the sound." In Georgia, former Confederate senator Ben Hill's advice that his audience make it "too hot" for any Republican to live in one county set the keynote for the campaign. Intimidation and violence was so bad in Louisiana that the Republican leadership finally decided to urge freedpeople to stay home if they felt themselves at risk. In some parishes, paramilitary bands herded blacks to the polls and made them cast Democratic ballots at pistol-point. Those who so voted were given protection papers signed by the local postmaster, a member of the Knights of the White Camelia. Where there had been no night riding, Republicans brought out a vote about as big as the previous April and ran up margins of comparable size. But in seven Louisiana parishes, good for 4,707 Republican votes for Warmoth, the party now cast no votes at all, and in another eight, the total turnout was 10—over 5,500 short of their previous totals. One black risked his life in Caddo Parish by casting its only Republican vote. He was killed that night.[45]

Northern Republicans wanted to help. But they had no control over the army, and Andrew Johnson's commanders found every excuse to send as few soldiers as they could, as late as possible. The national committee's first priority came with the northern states, particularly the ones with large electoral votes at stake. So the most the South could get was leftovers— leftover speakers and leftover money. The national committee never had enough funds to do much. Altogether, the Reconstructed states got $10,000 less than Pennsylvania or Indiana all by itself. Maine got double the amount allotted to any of them.[46] Still, if Klan violence cost Republicans southern states, it made their case for them up north. Nothing so exposed the revolutionary essence of the Democracy and the unregenerate character of the ex-Confederate South as the civil war unfolding before voters' eyes.

Between the southern horrors and Blair's wild talk, Democratic strategists found themselves thrown on the defensive. Two groups set to work, at cross-purposes. One set plotted to force Seymour out and run Chase after all. The other called for keeping Seymour and dumping Blair. When the *New York World* called for a change in ticket in mid-October, it dealt a last shattering blow to party morale. Nominating the chief justice or sending Blair packing, the Democracy would be disowning its platform, all but admitting it as revolutionary as its critics said. A new ticket would stand as a confession of impending defeat and that Democratic delegates were such dunderheads or traitors that only the national committee, not the convention, could be trusted to choose candidates worth placing before the country. From everywhere, shouts tore the air against the plotters in high places bent on selling out the party's core principles. "Traitor, fool, renegade, tool of a wicked power," Mark M. "Brick" Pomeroy's *New York Democrat* screamed, "uncover your head, take off your shoes, for the place where thou dost stand is holy ground. Your fire will die out, but the bush of Democracy will live for pilgrims to rest under the shade thereof, after turning aside to spit on your graves!"[47]

All that came of the intrigue was that Seymour did what only losing presidential candidates dared attempt: he took to the campaign trail. To his credit, he put a world of distance between Blair's program and his own and linked the nation's economic discomforts to Reconstruction. If the southern economy was underperforming, the candidate argued, Americans everywhere suffered, not even counting the $300 million a year Reconstruction cost to taxpayers (which, *if* true, meant three dollars in every four the government spent). A restoration of the South's natural leadership, politically and economically, would do more for producers in the North and West than cheap money and levying taxes on the bondholders. Taking that line three months earlier might have made some difference. By late October, the conservative merchants and bankers were not about to gamble on a Democratic ascendancy and quibbles about bond redemption. Their donations and support went for Grant and "honest money."[48]

Grant did win 52.75 percent of the vote: a respectable margin, nothing more. The white Republican organization in the upper South still had considerable strength, and some 25,000 whites voted for Grant in North Carolina. The lower South was a rather different story. White conservative turnout was up, and not all due to intimidation. Only West Virginia and Missouri's disfranchisement laws saved the states to Grant. Democratic frauds cost him Georgia, Louisiana, and New York, and a majority of the white vote nationwide went for Seymour; only federal troops gave Republicans their narrow edge in Alabama. Had Florida or Mississippi voted, the Democrats would have won a clean sweep from the Atlantic to the Sabine River. In the end, Republicans owed their edge to the overwhelming black turnout for their side that carried most of the former Confederate states and heavy northern support. They won 214 of the 294 electoral votes and retained a smaller but still commanding lead in the next Congress. Radicals could take comfort that for the first time, voters in a Union state, Minnesota, voted to give blacks the vote. "You should be *kind to Blair*," W. H. Kemble, the Republicans' campaign manager for Pennsylvania wrote Congressman Elihu Washburne, "—he did us a vast service."[49]

Grant had done them a much greater service. Only by running a man above politics were Republicans able to overcome a formidable Democratic challenge. Even against Seymour, a more radical man most likely would have lost. What Grant had promised was not more reconstructing but that tinkering with the southern states was at an end. The new administration meant peace and stability. It was committed to preserve and protect the present order of things, not to make something new, to hold to the full spirit and letter of its promise to those who had lent the nation their credit in wartime. With help from Blair, Republicans had been able to position themselves as centrists, but to do so, they had to mortgage their future. If the Congressional Reconstruction program failed to provide a full measure of equal rights, there would be no new dispensation, no innovation beyond the larger outline of what had been laid down already. As one correspondent reassured a fellow Democrat, the election promised to usher in "a real & true conservative era."[50]

Reconstruction had succeeded; yet 1868 may also be seen as the critical year in which its eventual failure became clear. The message came not in the election returns, nor in the shift toward moderation that the new "carpetbag-scalawag" governments were making already. It came from regular, steady reports, too constant even to rank as news in most northern newspapers, of freedpeople killed. Beyond the killings lay outrages innumerable and incompletely reported, assaults, harassments, arson, vandalism, rape. The attacks were not occasional. They were endemic, with redress inadequate at best. Against such an onslaught of violence and harmfulness, no governments, however large the majorities by which they were elected, no matter how restrained their economic programs, no matter how propitiatory of white entrepreneurs they claimed to be, had a good chance of surviving. Candidates could beg peace; but there would be no peace.

CHAPTER SEVEN

Two Failed Peace Policies

As Andrew Johnson's term entered its waning months, there was a palpable sense that Reconstruction was almost done. The last black-and-tan constitutional convention had closed its work in Austin. In February 1869, the Supreme Court also heard arguments in *Texas v. White*, on the larger constitutional questions of whether states could secede and whether acts committed after secession had any validity. Two months later, Chief Justice Chase handed down a decision upholding "an indestructible Union composed of indestructible States," in effect, quashing any "conquered provinces" theory that declared the states effectively out of the Union. The majority did not invalidate every marriage contract, deed of sale, and corporation charter enacted by Confederate authorities—only acts furthering an illegal insurrection. But that was enough to put southern state governments out of their proper constitutional relations. At the same time, Chase upheld the legality of the Reconstructed governments. The power to guarantee a republican form of government let Congress define the terms on which a seceded state would regain its full privileges. Any hope that a Court that had overturned federal test oaths for lawyers and clergymen would knock Reconstruction down went glimmering at last.[1]

At the same time, Congress itself put a race-blind suffrage beyond repeal by taking up a Fifteenth Amendment to protect black voters. With strong pressure in its favor from the National Convention of Colored Men assembling in Washington that January, it had fallen short of radicals' hopes. Some of them had wanted an outright guarantee of the right to vote and a declaration that Congress, not the states, had the last word about enfranchisement. Instead, the final wording was couched in negatives. The House version forbade denial of the right on three grounds: race, color, or previous condition of servitude. All the other means of disfranchisement—property qualifications, literacy tests, residency, or taxpaying requirements—remained as possible as ever. Senators carried a broader amendment, adding "nativity, property, education, or creed" to the forbidden restrictions and spread the same protection over officeholding. The two chambers deadlocked, but not for long. As the abolitionist leader Wendell Phillips reminded them, without agreement, there would be no amendment at all. The Senate version had no chance of being ratified. Western states would beat any measure opening the polls to the Chinese, and New England lawmakers with their residency and literacy requirements would guard their power to cut the unlettered and unassimilated out of the vote (meaning, in Rhode Island, just about any foreign-born or working-class Democrats). "For the first time in our lives we beseech [radical congressmen] to be a little more *politicians*—and a little less reformers," the *National Anti-Slavery Standard* admonished. It was sound advice. The logjam broke. The amendment carried without the Senate's changes.[2]

Its passage owed something to the quiet pressure of the incoming president to have action completed before his inaugural on March 4th. Quiet but unmistakable: General Grant's intervention was his most conspicuous sign of where he stood that winter. So much the unknown quantity was he as 1869 began that an unusual stir of conjecture rose about whom he would put into his cabinet. Other presidents-elect had begun picking their chief counselors before the first snow flew, but in this case the mystery deepened. Possibilities multiplied, and with one exception, probabilities kept themselves scarce. That exception, the general's mentor in Congress, Elihu B. Washburne of Illinois, seemed destined for the spot fitting his reputation as "watchdog of the Treasury." A few Republican leaders worried that a man so detached from party politics might shake off the regulars entirely and lay the foundations for a personal party, the way the last war hero in the White House, Zachary Taylor, had tried to do.[3]

Among a growing body of reformers, that fear inspired a hope for a president free from partisanship. In the general they sensed independent judgment, the very quality needed to change an administrative system based on self and pelf: the doling out of offices under the spoils system to those who served their party best and would use their positions for those same ends, the pandering to interest groups that wanted government power used on their behalf—shutting out foreign competition with high tariff duties and making every river and harbor in need of dredging flow with the taxpayers' gold. Governance as it was meant licenses to mulct the Indians and customs collectors taking in more in fees than the port took in import revenues. It meant broken-down senators given snug berths in the diplomatic service, clerks coughing up a regular "assessment" to the party machine that gave them their place, an invitation to every officeholder to squeeze every penny from his position he could. Any such system invited ambitious men to see government as a candy store, where everyone on the winning side had unlimited credit. For those who would come to be known as "liberals," the invitation to corruption and malfeasance, to the transformation of public office into a public lust, brought with it the collective selfishness of a thousand interests that profited at consumers' expense. They singled out as examples the unduly high rates in the protective Morrill "War Tariff" and the unreliability of a currency, not yet redeemable in gold, that politicians would tinker with to "move the crops" just before an election. They were also noticing the Republican Party's ready acceptance of crooked, irresponsible state governments—at least, as long as they sent the right kind of representatives to Washington.[4] All this coarsening of public life, the war had stimulated; all of it, a president above politics might remove.

By the time Grant gave his inaugural address, committing himself to the Fifteenth Amendment's adoption and to "honest money"—the eventual resumption of a specie basis, where anyone holding a paper dollar could redeem it for a dollar in silver or gold—no president could have kept all the promises made on his behalf. Then Grant announced his cabinet. "A thunderclap from a clear sky, on a picnic day would not have astonished the people . . . more," one reporter commented—and, he might have added, the nominees, too, most of whom found out that they were under consideration only after their names had been sent in. Washburne's name led all the rest, but for secretary of state, a position given simply to bolster his credentials before sending him as minister to France. Up till that point his total grasp of the world beyond America's shores came from a summer vacation abroad. As one senator grumbled, Washburne could hardly be faulted on knowing no foreign languages: he could barely express himself in his own! One ex-senator, one ex-governor, found places. But the others came from outside politics, old army buddies like John Rawlins, secretary of war, or well-to-do businessmen whose money and whose hospitality to Grant had impressed him. For the Treasury, the notoriously hard-fisted department store owner Alexander T. Stewart proved particularly sensational, not only because he had raised himself from poverty as Grant had to the top ranks of New York City's elite, but also because his appointment violated federal law and forced his retirement within a week. As for the secretary of the navy, an old Philadelphia merchant, Adolph Borie, his only political experience had come in helping found the city's Union League Club. "Borie! Borie! Borie! That's a queer nomination!" a senator exclaimed. Borie thought so too, accepting the job only on the understanding that he be allowed to leave it as soon as he could.[5]

Once reformers caught their breath, they admitted that Grant could have done far worse, even if so many in the "Gift-Enterprise Cabinet" had earned the president's notice for the personal favors they had done him in the past. None of them stood among the pantheon of party statesmen the way Lincoln's cabinet officers did, but Ebenezer Rockwood Hoar, the attorney general, had the rugged integrity calculated to make all the right enemies among officeseekers. Secretary of the Interior Jacob D. Cox would go after spoilsmen and fraudulent land claimants with gusto. Washburne made a surprisingly good minister abroad, hard-working and concerned with American citizens' safety as German troops closed in to starve Paris out during the Franco-Prussian War. As for his successor at the State Department, former senator and governor Hamilton Fish, a New York City banker's sneer that he was "good at a dinner party & that's about all" fell wide of the mark. Able to trace his ancestry back to Nieu Amsterdam days, Fish radiated dignity, tact, levelheadedness, and the shrewdness to pick his battles carefully. That discretion was one reason why he alone of all the cabinet lasted out the following eight years, with Grant meeting every threat to retire with a promise to amend his own behavior—promises never long kept. The Treasury went to radical congressman George S. Boutwell, whose commitment to keeping the money supply stable, reducing taxes, and paying off the public debt helped foster the economic boom that lasted through Grant's first term and into his second.[6]

The new president's reform credentials shone brightest in his first months, though at no time did his cabinet lack some officer that reformers could esteem. Even some of Grant's worse choices, politicos or corruptionists like George M. Robeson, Borie's successor, and William W. Belknap, who took Rawlins's place after tuberculosis claimed his life that fall, came with the glow of good intentions and, in Belknap's case, impressive recommendations. Over the next two years, liberals discovered how promiscuously, even capriciously, the executive made his selections, eagerly accepting the secretary of the Interior's resignation when spoilsmen pressed too hard for the right to shake down department employees for campaign contributions. In Grant they found no hero prepared to battle with the Senate over his right to nominate whom he chose. With some changes, the Tenure of Office Act stayed on the books. So would the protective tariff, and the able commissioner of the revenue, David A. Wells, who did his best to expose the way Americans were overtaxed for special interests' benefits,

"Distribution of Prize-Loaves at the National Bakery." Joseph Keppler, *Leslie's Illustrated Weekly*, March 27, 1875. Politicians retired by the voters besiege President Grant for offices. The same bewildering scramble could have been seen after every election, and not just under Republicans.

found his job eliminated quickly. Grant would not take the trouble to find some other place for him, the way he did the hack congressman from Ohio, Columbus Delano, who, as Jacob Cox's successor, put Indians and the public lands at the mercy of party cormorants. Party fealty and political service continued to define hiring and firing. Great praise met Grant's selection of the cultured historian John Lothrop Motley as minister to England in 1869, but when he was removed in an act of petty spite, Grant replaced him with a lame-duck congressman, Robert Schenck of Ohio, whose most noticed contribution in diplomatic service may have been his pamphlet teaching the British how to play poker.[7]

Perhaps what went unsaid, however, told more about how issues had changed with Andrew Johnson's departure and the submission of the Fifteenth Amendment. The cabinet nominees' fitness, their susceptibility to reform ideas, made grist for no end of editorials. Fewer remarked on the fact that only one of the original cabinet members stood with the radical Republicans. Stewart, Borie, even Fish either had steered clear of politics or had sympathized with Johnson long after his Reconstruction program had lost the party's trust. Cox had marred his usefulness in Ohio politics by proposing that part of the South be set aside for freedpeople, since the two races could not live together successfully on terms of equality. Eventually, Cox would turn against Reconstruction entirely while Fish remained to the end a steady skeptic at the cabinet table about government intervention on freedmen's behalf. The most that could be said on behalf of the president's official councilors was that, now that the amendments had passed, they would support them faithfully. But their stance no longer seemed to matter to Republicans in general. When Boutwell accepted the Treasury portfolio, most observers read it not as representation for a radical but as a much-needed professional politician in a cabinet of amateurs.[8]

Reconstruction from this time forth would need to fight for attention, as matters of political ethics and political economy took front rank, but then, Grant's presidency was premised on the belief that once all the states regained their places in Congress and the still-pending Fifteenth Amendment had been ratified, the national government's program to remake the South would be completed: the chief responsibility would lie with the new state authorities. More than ever before, the administration's task lay in bringing about a full reunion of northerners and white southerners and the effacing of wartime resentments. Within a week of taking office, Grant had given symbolic recognition to the need by nominating former Confederate general James Longstreet for surveyor of the port of New Orleans. That spring the president also welcomed Longstreet's superior officer, Robert E. Lee, to the White House for a friendly chat. The Confederates' chief general invited Grant to visit him, though nothing came of the offer, but the changing temper of northern society showed itself in how little outcry arose about one of the leading figures in the Rebellion figuring on the White House guest list. When Lee died in 1870, obituaries everywhere emphasized his finer qualities, with his treason treated as not much worse than a regrettable flaw in one of nature's noblemen.[9]

With Reconstruction incomplete in four southern states (Georgia's having gone badly awry), the administration threw its influence behind the moderates everywhere and against the disfranchisement of former Confederates. In the Lone Star State, it backed former provisional governor Andrew "Jack" Hamilton's overwhelmingly white faction against the "curl-tails," as the radicals were known, but encouraged harmony on moderate policies, fully committed to equality while showing respect for corporations' vested rights. To the "ab initio" faction's dismay, the new constitution left the railroads chartered since secession in conservative hands; they were even allowed to repay their debts to the school fund in Confederate currency, no better than foolscap. Dreams of carving a rock-solid radical state out of Unionist counties in the Black Belt or German voters in west Texas evaporated. Mississippi and Virginia commanders were given leave to schedule separate votes on the new constitutions and the provisions cutting former Rebels out of the suffrage. These orders may have spared Reconstruction from a defeat at the polls but guaranteed that both states would come back with a heavy white conservative vote for Radicals to overcome.[10]

Moderate Republicans were not out to betray Reconstruction. Their aim was to shore it up, emphasizing its inclusiveness as well as its commitment to full legal equality. Aware of the propensity of critics to see in every general a would-be dictator and committed to an early return to the normal constitutional relationship, where civilians, not soldiers, defined policy, Grant knew his military past limited what he, as president, could afford to do to bail out Republican governments. At the same time, the 1868 election returns had reinforced the message that, based on white unconditional Unionists and freedpeople's votes alone, no political order could long outlast the removal of federal oversight and military protection. Clearly, the winners must broaden their coalition and augment their resources of self-defense, but the good news was that doing so seemed more possible now than before. No longer could white conservatives count on tacit support from the White House. No more could they look ahead to the day when black suffrage would be removed. During the campaign, Democrats down south had made clear that while they believed that white men alone should rule a white man's country, they were not about to draw the color line to keep out converts. Out of grudging acceptance something better might come, as more Democrats grew used to the new order of things, and by early 1869, moderates north and south were readier than ever to believe that at least some ex-Confederates were prepared to cast the politics of race aside, if offered an alternative. A biracial Republican Party with a larger, more propertied, white basis seemed in the offing, with the right kind of nurturing.[11]

The vision of reconciliation caught on, north and south, though its truest believers looked on it differently. In every southern state, white Republicans imagined that with just the right tinkering, always in white conservatives' direction and away from black constituents', they could create a durable political coalition. Some of them saw it as essentially a Republican one. Others, sensing that time lay on the former Confederates' side, projected a party of the middle, accepting the basics of Reconstruction but combining a white Republican minority with all but the most diehard of former Confederates. In such a coalition, freedpeople might not be the biggest gainers, but those who made that deal across party lines would have a chance of modernizing the South and giving it the peace surest to draw investment.

In the North, Republicans hoped to make a lasting southern party, but for many of them, and for many non-Republicans, the policy of reconciliation had purposes entirely beyond Reconstruction itself. They looked to that other aim, a restoration of fellow feeling between the sections—a true Union, not just of soldiers and statutes, but of hands and hearts. Only there could they found a lasting common sense of Americanism. Ending the disfranchisement of white southern voters, they felt, might bring the states closer to republican forms of government, based on the consent of the governed.

The disqualifications from office under the Fourteenth Amendment posed a slightly different challenge. A democratic South certainly was possible without restoring the rights of the small fraction of former Confederates still out in the cold, but as a stigma on society's traditional leaders, northerners recognized it as grounds for resentment. Even most Republicans had bought into the idea not only that the South's best and ablest public servants remained under the ban but that it would be impossible in the former Confederacy to build up a class of the same prestige or skill. Every general could make the same complaint, that in filling local office, they found the most well-educated and professionally trained citizens legally ineligible. Attorney Russell Conwell, journeying through Virginia in late March 1869, saw nothing but outlanders ruling the destinies of the Old Dominion. "For every office, from governor to justice of the peace, seems to be appropriated by Northern men," he wrote. "One would think Boston had depopulated itself in filling the vacant official positions of this State." Experienced administrators able to take the "ironclad oath" were so scarce that commanders had to draw from the army's ranks. Even then, they ran short.

Petersburg's new prosecuting attorney allegedly had "been studying law at most only for a few months."[12] Virginia thus exposed one reason why, for all the radical visions of a long military waiting period in the ex-Confederate states, the reconstructing process had to end, and soon; the restrictions on who could hold office or vote had to be eased and quickly.

Ever since the war's end, the same dilemma had confronted each of the Unionist-held states in the upper South: Maryland, West Virginia, Missouri, and Tennessee especially. How could a minority government keep its legitimacy after the wartime emergency had passed? As the possibility of renewed fighting and of a resurgent Confederacy dwindled to nothing, the argument that the public safety demanded keeping the state in the hands of the undeniably loyal became harder to make. The deeper peace took root, the less easy it was to justify emergency measures. While the Ku Klux levied war on Unionists in Arkansas and Tennessee, Missouri and West Virginia enjoyed a comparative peace. Where was the risk in reopening the vote to all adult males, reconciliationists asked. And what, exactly, was being risked? Increasingly, the disfranchisers had to fall back on the contention that denial of the vote was meant as punishment, and a lifelong punishment at that. That argument had much narrower appeal, ever narrowing further.[13]

Month by month, the unrepublican character of the regimes looked more glaring. Where an oath of past loyalty was required for admission to the bar, Republican attorneys often had worked out partnerships with former Confederates. Did the country's security really depend on them assembling the facts but standing idle outside the courtroom door? critics demanded. What public interest did it serve, barring former Confederates from the pulpit, the classroom, or the county clerk's office? "We cannot afford to keep a large body of our fellow citizens perpetually disaffected," an editor wrote "—if the war is ended, or is ever to come to an end, all these penal statutes must be erased." The politician who would do otherwise once the public safety was assured was as clearly the foe to "peace and social order" as the Rebels themselves.[14]

Disfranchisement was not simply controversial. It was inherently destabilizing. In the long run, if not repealed, its strictures would collapse, burying the party in its wreckage, *New York Tribune* editor Horace Greeley warned. "Every year one thousand of your rebels die, and one thousand more of their sons become of age—you can't disfranchise them. You now have five thousand majority. Six years will convert this into a rebel majority of one thousand. . . . Now you can amnesty the rebels—soon the question will be, shall they amnesty you? Look at Kentucky and Maryland and read your certain fate in theirs."[15]

The danger to Reconstruction governments' majorities came from within as well as without. Every election, Radical turnout in the upper South shrank and conservative numbers grew. Every year, more Unionists drifted away from the party in power or thought that the time had come for restoring full white male suffrage. Those who saw that restoration as inevitable were all the more ready to speed the day of its coming, as an insurance policy on their political lives when it came to pass. By 1870, defections would cost Unionists the state, a West Virginia editor warned, whatever restrictions the ballot laws imposed. Then Democrats would wipe out every last word of them and have a lock on power for generations to come. With "a magnanimous policy," on the other hand, he assumed that Republicans could win over some share of the ex-Confederates when the ballot box had been opened to them.[16]

In the fissure-ridden Republican parties of the South, the disfranchisement issue opened wide breaches with catastrophic results. Within the first months of Grant's administration, Tennessee's Reconstruction government came to grief on the dispute about who should be readmitted to the vote and when. With the retirement of Governor Brownlow to the Senate, a fight erupted over the succession, between his successor, DeWitt Senter, and "the bald eagle of the mountains," Congressman William V. Stokes. When the party convention met, members applied chairs to each others' heads and brandished firearms, with police rushing into the hall to make arrests. The delegates broke up into two bodies, each running a separate ticket. To make matters worse, all at once the state supreme court expanded the "rebel vote" to dangerous proportions by restoring some 30,000 Tennesseans to the rolls, nearly all Democrats. With Republicans evenly split, that group now held the balance of power. It was open for bids; the wherewithal to win them was an even fuller liberalization of the suffrage. Speaking at Nashville before a gathering packed with Stokes supporters and interrupted at one point with the skirl of fifes from an unfriendly brass band, Senter came out for ending all voting restrictions immediately. If elected, he vowed, he would ask the next general assembly to take disfranchisements off every taxpayer in the state.[17]

A month before the election, Governor Senter launched a wholesale purge of the commissioners of registration, to replace them with enemies of proscription. By July 14th, at least fifty-eight new county registrars were administering the law, and by month's end, seventy. Republicans shrugged at first; firing Stokes's loyalists seemed no more than politics as usual. But as Senter men began to be dismissed and former Confederates and Democrats took their place, it became clear that the real issue was not who the new appointees were but what they were prepared to do: not to interpret the suffrage laws liberally, but to flout them. In Knox County, the registrar made more than 1,700 new voters, 1,200 of them in a single day. In many cases he handed out certificates without their even having been applied for. "Politicians got them by the batch," a reporter noted. All registrants needed to take a loyalty oath, but the registrar administered it to none of them, possibly because he had not yet taken it himself. "The suffrage revolution is crushing every thing in its path way," a Democrat concluded. In the August election, Senter won the largest majority in Tennessee history. He took quite a few counties where black voters preponderated—or would have, if they had been allowed to cast a ballot. In some, Stokes got just about no votes at all. As the polls closed in Nashville, crowds thronged the streets and brass bands struck up "Bonnie Blue Flag."[18]

The disfranchisement issue worked slightly differently in Virginia. The delay of a vote on the Underwood constitution had kept its people under a governor, Henry H. Wells, a former Union officer from Michigan who owed his place to military appointment only and could be removed whenever the general in charge saw fit. Diehards swore that if equal suffrage must come, at least they must take no hand in bringing it about; far better that they leave it to radicals and soldiers to force such a distasteful change on the state. "The hotheads, if allowed their way, will ruin all," a journalist wrote. "They have no counter plan save endurance and suffering for some indefinite period. But we need settlement imperatively. . . . A year more of this business & where will our people be?"[19]

Little General William Mahone, now heavily involved in railroad enterprises, could not wait that year. Fearing Wells's opposition to a merger of lines that he needed badly to counter the southward thrust of the Baltimore & Ohio Railroad, he put his energies and exchequer behind efforts to bring moderates in both parties within a winning combination. The conservative Whig elder statesman Alexander H. H. Stuart, of like mind, was urging opponents to draft an alternative to the Underwood constitution, with guarantees for equal rights and no restriction on former Confederates' voting. Universal amnesty, universal suffrage: such a program was sure to find strong support among northern Republicans, for whom it had become the new philosopher's stone, turning southern political conditions into gold.[20]

They were helped by the Virginia Republican convention when it met at the African Methodist church in Petersburg. As usual, the delegates brought along enough ill will to provoke street fights outside the chamber "almost without a parallel," according to one hostile source. The Radicals resolved that they would keep Wells as their candidate and coupled their support for the disability clauses to the state constitution with reasonable flexibility in restoring those Confederates whose change of heart made them deserve it. Wells's platform and the selection of a black former Union army surgeon, Oberlin-educated, for lieutenant governor ("an outrage upon civilization," the *Richmond Dispatch* fulminated) flung away any chance of winning any share of the white conservatives or making a claim for the political center. An "overdose of negro" in a state with a white majority carried near-fatal risks.[21]

Unlike 1867, the moderates had an alternative, Gilbert C. Walker, Yale educated, northern-born, a onetime Douglas Democrat and nominal Republican who had raised a regiment of Illinois volunteers when the war broke out and reached Norfolk in the war's waning days. There he prospered, becoming president of a national bank and an ironworks. It did not hurt him that he was a stockholder in Mahone's railroad enterprises. Most of all, he stood against proscription with far more fervor than he had ever supported black suffrage. Conservatives welcomed the selection and induced their own candidate to drop out of the contest. "As to principles, we know nothing of them," the *Richmond Whig* explained, "—we thought they were all extinct. *Measures and men*—practical expedients for the evils of the day—are all that we are privileged to consider now." To Wells's dismay, President Grant convinced Congress to let him put the disqualifying clauses to a vote separately from the constitution.[22]

Wells campaigned as hard as he could. He reminded black voters that whatever secessionists Virginia had would be working for Walker's success. They had no more come to terms with black suffrage, officeholding, and jury service, or even black testimony in court, than at any time in the past. The "True Republican" slate was "the ticket of the Rebel Conservatives disguised in Union Blue." At the same time, reckoning well how high a white turnout that separate vote on proscription was sure to bring out and pressed hard from northern Republicans, he was forced to declare that he personally would vote against all disqualifications. Indeed, he protested that having a separate vote had been his idea in the first place, and that it had been his persuasion that brought President Grant round.[23]

Wells had no chance and scarcely more cash, at least not on the scale that Mahone's railroad interests did. Businessmen let northern reporters know that if Wells was elected, they would leave the state; merchants would "be sold out by the hundred," while industry came to a standstill. Grant's one-time choice for the Treasury, dry-goods merchant Alexander T. Stewart, may have contributed to the Walker campaign, and Horace Greeley's *New York Tribune* spread the reassuring message that the election's main result would be "the restoration of harmony & good feeling." But as Election Day approached, the conciliatory tone of Walker's Democratic supporters ran alongside the static of irreconcilables grown bolder in their threats against "carpet-baggers" of every kind. The issue at hand, the *Richmond Dispatch* asserted, was "whether the white man shall be subordinated to the negro." Days before the election, black and white partisans came to blows and nearly set off a riot in Petersburg after Democrats tried to mob a Republican speaker.[24] The outcome on July 6th was a virtual rout. Black turnout was heavy, and particularly in the tidewater counties and the largest cities. But white turnout was immense as well. The Underwood constitution sailed through without any serious opposition. The proscriptive clauses lost, though by the far smaller margin of about three to two. With sixty-eight counties and cities to his credit, Walker beat Wells by over 18,000 votes. Walker may have carried no more than one-third of the Republican vote, but that, along with the Democratic surge, was enough to crush the party and put it in a hopeless minority in both houses. "Didn't we give 'em Hell!" a party manager wrote Mahone.[25]

By that time, the disfranchisement question had stirred Hell in Missouri, too. There, as in Tennessee, a Reconstruction government had held firm since wartime, widening its franchise to permit black voting, and trimming ever further back on the white electorate. Early in 1869, opposition to the Radicals led by Senator Charles D. Drake had burst forth in the election of Carl Schurz to the other Senate seat. Firmly committed to impartial suffrage but hostile to the spoilsmen and selfish interests in Washington, Schurz grew less radical the more he saw of the greed and pettiness in Washington. Increasingly, he became the voice of those Republicans questioning how far the North could impose a solution on the South's racial problems. Within the year, he had made common cause with the tariff reformers and liberal Republicans that favored amendments to the Missouri constitution guaranteeing blacks' right to vote and restoring it to former Confederates at the same time. The party's state convention sundered over the issue. Drake's supporters nominated Joseph McClurg for governor, promising nothing more than eventual reenfranchisement, once the danger to the state had passed. Liberals came out for immediate, unconditional reenfranchisement and chose as their gubernatorial nominee former senator B. Gratz Brown, one of the first sponsors of an antislavery amendment and a sure draw among the German voters. The Grant administration threw its support behind McClurg, assessed officeholders to pay for the regulars' campaign, and fired appointees who failed to toe the party line. Democrats turned out en masse for Brown, carrying him into the governor's mansion by over 40,000 votes. A reenfranchisement amendment passed by more than seven to one; even McClurg's supporters went for it. "It is a victory over Federal interference in State elections," the *Missouri Democrat* crowed. "It is a triumph which the people of this State may well be proud of, and many long years will elapse before they will again be called to prove their manhood and patriotism against the combined power of a State and national administration."[26] And so it would, because it would be nearly thirty years before Republicans won another state election.

Missouri, Virginia, and Tennessee all showed the risks of standing by disfranchisement for too long. The results in Texas and Mississippi, though, held out the promise for acting in time. Heartened by their successes in the Border South, leading Democrats looked for a moderate Republican to back against the radicals. In Texas, they gave their support to former provisional governor Andrew J. Hamilton, after the more radical Republicans chose Edmund J. Davis, a staunch wartime Unionist, for governor. Hamilton had sacrificed safety and fortune to fight against the secessionists, but he was perfectly willing to have them help him into office, as long as they committed themselves to the basic Reconstruction settlement that Congress had required. Mississippi Democrats, assuming that Grant could deny his family members nothing, ran Louis Dent, his brother-in-law, for governor. Aware by then that Republican front men had been used and his own trust imposed upon in Virginia and Texas, the president could recognize a stalking horse when he saw one. Dent, a California resident and Washington attorney, paid no tax in Mississippi and did not even have a rented room there that he could call his own—just rented principles. When he came to Washington for backing, he was turned down flat. Grant also turned a deaf ear to Hamilton's request for a free hand filling and emptying out the federal offices. In each case, though, Grant's commitment to the more truly Republican alternative came more easily because disfranchisement was not at issue. Mississippi elected a former Confederate general, James Lusk Alcorn, who himself had needed a special act of Congress removing his disqualifications before he could hold office. Committed though he was to equal rights before the law and, equally important, a comprehensive school system, he quickly showed not only a readiness to consider former Confederates for local office but a reluctance to give them to black Republicans. In the fall of 1869, Texas and Mississippi both ratified the Reconstruction constitutions and elected regular Republican governors and legislatures. Mississippi's disfranchisement provision lost overwhelmingly.[27]

With Arkansas the only holdout, West Virginia found its disfranchisement laws looking more outlandish all the time. No Democrat had to tell party insiders that the governor's appointees had used the registration system whimsically and arbitrarily, discovering all the disloyalty they needed to bring in good Republican majorities, gratifying personal ambitions and paying off private scores with neighbors.[28] A small band of independent Republicans held the balance of power as the legislature assembled in early 1870. Voting with the Democrats, they could dismantle the disfranchisement machinery simply by killing the registration law. To keep it on the books through the next election, the "straight-outs" would need to make a deal to guarantee a wider electorate in the future.[29] With that in mind, William H. H. Flick offered a resolution amending the constitution to open the vote to all adult males, blacks included. But while the test oath was removed for teachers, lawyers, and those seeking court access, it remained applicable to voters until the amendment went through. At the earliest, former Rebels would vote in 1872—or so the planners thought. It seemed, then, that West Virginia's party had escaped the perils that had sundered Republican ranks elsewhere, and that out of their efforts a stable centrist coalition might yet be forged.

How familiar these hopes had been! In July 1869, northerners hailed Gilbert Walker's victory in Virginia as the beginning of a true and solid basis for a lasting Reconstruction. Walker went on record in favor of black education, economic development, equal rights, and ratification of the Fifteenth Amendment. The same might have been said for Schurz and Brown in Missouri, for Dent in Mississippi, and Andrew Jackson Hamilton in Texas. As Virginia's returns came in, the *New York Tribune* crowed that the outcome "probably ends the voting of race against race." This was fantasy; at the very least, the defeat of the disfranchisement provisions guaranteed ten to fifteen thousand more white voters, none of them Republicans. Reconstruction, far from being fulfilled, had suffered a permanent defeat. "We trod last month confidently upon Virginia, and she slipped from under our feet like a row-boat," one supporter wrote ruefully. So did Tennessee, where the new Democratic legislature wasted no time calling a constitutional convention and cutting Senter's gubernatorial term short so that they could elect one of their own. So did Missouri, which immediately sent Democrat Frank Blair Jr. to the Senate, breathing fire against the illegality of the Reconstruction Amendments. So, for all the precautions, did West Virginia. Judges issued decrees effectively wiping out the election officers' power to challenge anyone's vote, and one federal court commissioner threw a county board of supervisors behind bars for trying to scratch suspect names off the registration lists.[30] By September 1870, former Confederates were perjuring themselves wholesale to get on the voting rolls. Registrars, aware that once the amendment passed, their political futures depended on their relations with the disfranchised, were letting them do so. Every means of scaring off black voters or making registrars refuse to place them on the rolls was used. Come November, the Democrats carried everything worth taking. "The result has verified my apprehensions," Senator Waitman Willey wrote in his diary. "The Republican party in West Va. has fallen to rise no more for years to come. The spirit of the late rebellion is in the ascendant; and that spirit is unrelenting."[31]

Andrew J. Hamilton's failed campaign for the Texas governorship in 1869 showed the limits to the centrist gambit. Running against Davis, the old Unionist played himself up as the true moderate, the enemy of disfranchisement, the defender of the "intelligent tax paying citizen." Electing him meant economic development, aid for railroad construction, encouragement to immigration. But whites never missed the underlying message: Davis's faction meant Negro rule and an African party dragooned by George T. Ruby's Union League. Hamilton may have seen his pitch as administering the shock therapy that a Republican Party needed, if it would outlive its infancy. It needed more than white votes. It needed the outright support of respectable propertied classes. "It is idle to talk of negroes standing up against the moral and intellectual weight of the combined force of the white man of the country," he assured one backer. "Mind will control matter." But at least during the campaign, Davis himself hardly sounded any more radical—indeed, much less egalitarian than he proved. The party platform endorsed the Fourteenth and Fifteenth Amendments, but from the candidate's words one might be pardoned for thinking that instead of standing on those planks, he was doing his best to run away from them.[32]

Both men looked to draw a white vote outside Republican ranks, though Hamilton's chances were by far the best, with prominent Democratic politicians giving him their blessing. When voting began at the end of November 1869, however, Davis surged ahead in black counties, just enough to win. His side carried the assembly easily, the senate more narrowly. For freedpeople, that would mean a vital and energetic protection; for the taxpayers, a governor as rigidly honest and as distrustful of giveaways to railroad corporations as any conservative could have wanted. Just about no Republican, white or black, cast a ballot for Hamilton. Somewhat more than half the scalawags stayed home rather than vote for either candidate. The Reconstruction coalition of 1867–68 had crested and was losing support badly. Davis had wasted his time appealing to moderate Democrats. So, to a lesser extent, had Hamilton. The opposition had no interest in any true biracial coalition. Unwilling to swallow a Unionist like Hamilton, they stayed home in droves. With a fuller turnout, Reconstruction would have ended in Texas then and there.[33]

More ominously, the freedpeople's turnout had fallen sharply since the year before, and that with the U.S. military to protect them. The ex-governor's words to the contrary, "mind" did not control "matter" that fall. Muscle did. Across Texas, secret societies sent their agents across the northern counties to threaten blacks thinking about showing up on Election Day. Shotgun blasts tore through black cabins at night, not with any particular target in mind, but as a reminder that "murder & bloodshed would follow" an outpouring for Davis. "We would vote ourselves out of house & home," a former slave remembered being told. Decide wrongly, and his people would "lose their cotton and get shot down in scores."[34]

By 1871, Virginia, Tennessee, West Virginia, and Missouri were in Democratic hands. The pattern should have been clear, and to Grant, at least, it was: any road out of the regular Republican Party led into the Democratic one. No centrist alternative existed. Fresh converts to the Democratic side would find a welcome, as long as they knew their place. Walker's professed Republicanism proved indistinguishable from white conservatism. By the time he won a House seat, he had become an open Democrat. Virginia lawmakers quickly emptied all the judicial offices and gave themselves authority to appoint replacements. They wiped out city governments and chose new municipal rulers. Richmond's Republican mayor was evicted; a white mob besieged his followers in a police station until the army intervened. When voters reelected the mayor, the messenger carrying the returns from the banner Republican ward was waylaid and his ballots taken away. The conservative commissioner of elections then handed the certificate to his adversary. A new election was called, where Democrats imported from Baltimore cast ballots freely and election judges refused the vote to every black they could. Whatever the law allowed, state courts only impaneled white men for their juries. Conservatives disfranchised anyone convicted of petty larceny, a crime almost exclusively committed by the poor, and freedpeople especially. Wherever Democrats controlled state government in the upper South, the legal barriers to black voting rose, and the statute book thickened with laws making offices that blacks might win into appointive ones, which white officials could fill with people of their own color and from their own class.[35]

Moderates had misread the malleability of southern conservatives. For all their talk of creating a new South, friendly to industry and development, for all their professions of a readiness to welcome northern capital and northern immigration, they were determined to set the terms, with the South's traditional rulers defining the pace of change and for whose benefit. Planters objected to freedpeople's schools in their neighborhood, and many white communities showed their unfriendliness with threats, ostracism, and arson. Schoolhouses burned; so did black churches used for holding classes. In Georgia, persons unknown abducted one black schoolteacher and filed his teeth down to the gum-line. Tennessee's "Redeemers" repealed the public school law and hired out black penitentiary convicts to compete with free labor in the coal mines and stevedores at the riverside. They blasted a hole in the law exempting men's teams, wagons, and furniture from foreclosure and made voting conditional on payment of a poll tax that the poor, blacks especially, could not pay. The whipping post reappeared in Virginia, leaving on poor men's backs what a black lawmaker called the "indelible traces of disgrace." Not only did an Atlanta court refuse to respect the Tennessee marriage certificate of a biracial couple; pronouncing their union void; it laid a heavy fine and jail sentence on both parties for fornication. Legislators found money for a portrait of Lee but not of Union general George H. Thomas, and in Tennessee, Democrats insisted on having the latter's picture removed from their sight. Conservatives, then, would accept the most basic results of the postwar amendments but nothing more than that. They had made peace with a lasting, permanent Union, but not with Radical Reconstruction. The more outraged about the horrible tyranny coming out of the North a nonveteran was, the more he could burnish his credentials as southern to the very core. "Their red-hottedness increases in intensity every day," one skeptical journalist wrote, "and they will soon begin to scintillate and emit sparks. The red-hottest of all the red-hot are those fiery spirits who wouldn't submit to abolition tyranny in the late war, and gallantly sold whisky to the bitter end, taking their smells of gunpowder at a range longer than that of any needle-gun."[36]

North of the Ohio River, each party accepted the other as essentially legitimate, deserving obedience if elected by the people's will. But in the South, opponents of the Reconstruction governments refused to go that far. When they referred to "citizens," they meant "white citizens." "Southerners" always meant the white ones exclusively, and not even all of them: only those in residence before the close of the war. "The South" that they eulogized was never the entire South. It was the Confederate South, not the Unionist minority, and certainly not the blacks. For all the talk of reconciliation, those whites who failed to support the Confederacy and had compounded it by not taking an active part against the Republicans were not deemed real southerners. That made it easier for conservatives to depict, if only to themselves, the Reconstruction governments as alien governments set up by intruders and staffed by interlopers. They had been forced on the South by illegal means and depended for their survival on the millions of black inhabitants who had no right to take part in politics at all. Any party supported by black votes was illegitimate because black voting was unnatural and a violation of God's own law.[37]

Against usurpers, none of the customary rules applied. Republican officials, thieves and upstarts, deserved no respect, and the people of the South—meaning always the conservative white people of the South—gave them none. Extremism in the pursuit of white southerners' liberty was no vice. Whites who voted Republican were snubbed, shunned, insulted, their names blackened, their wives degraded, their credit destroyed. Their children faced abuse, their families social isolation. Respectable figures in all parties deplored violence in general and reaffirmed their commitment to the Union, but between Tennessee and the Gulf, deeds made mockery of the words.[38] Attackers, their faces blackened, masked or hooded, took on different names—Palefaces, Men of Justice, or the Black Cavalry. In Louisiana, the Knights of the White Camelia beat and killed as readily as the Knights of the Rising Sun did in Texas, but in most places, the terrorists identified themselves with local chapters of the Ku Klux Klan. Ostensibly directed by former Confederate general Nathan Bedford Forrest, no central organization coordinated their efforts above the state level. Members in one county might lend their services to the like-minded in surrounding areas, and those in one village seem to have taken inspiration from incidents elsewhere. Later legend enrolled almost all the great generals and statesmen of the South in the Klan's ranks, Robert E. Lee included. In fact, for all its evocation of the Lost Cause, the insurgency was mostly home-grown and almost entirely home-run. Leaders in local society, professionals

"Mississippi Ku-Klux in the Disguises in Which They were Captured." *Harper's Weekly*, October 19, 1872. As the varied Klan attire indicates, the organization lacked the centralized planning of its later reincarnation. The inventiveness of display expressed a certain carnival spirit to go with the concealment, possibly the better to distance the perpetrators of atrocities from a sense of the seriousness of what they were doing.

and planters, took part, at least in its first years, but so did small farmers, not always from slaveholding families or with Confederate wartime service. Klan attacks often showed discipline, preparation, and coordination, but the longer the disorders continued, the more they pitched out of the control of the local elites. Forrest's public order disbanding the Klan in 1869 did not slacken the disorders at all. But then, neither he nor any other respected white leader did anything to enforce his decree.[39]

The counterrevolution against Reconstruction was more like an intensification of the disorders that had begun during the war, directed ever more exclusively to the Confederate South's enemies. Mob violence against

Unionists, lynchings and vigilante action against communities' outcasts had marked the South ever since Appomattox. Former slaves had been beaten, whipped, driven from their homes, shot, or burned for plenty of different reasons. Small farmers missing hogs or cotton from the fields and incensed at freedpeople's thieving had made bloody examples of those they suspected.[40]

Nor did it take Radical Reconstruction to set off the savagery. Kentucky rested in Democratic hands from the end of the war on. There was no black militia, no carpetbag governor, no large black vote, no Loyal League worth mentioning. Where Democrats could not win legitimately, they won anyhow. When it came to cheating the adversary out of votes, the Democrats were far more likely to let all scruples go when it was blacks that they were dealing with. For one thing, blacks were much less likely to be armed and able to do anything about it. When the state elections took place in August 1870, the governor asserted later, black Kentuckians voted "with unrestricted freedom." So they did—in some places. All across southern and southwestern Kentucky, freedpeople only voted in the county seats, if anywhere, and in the larger towns where they had safety. No more than four in ten eligible black voters cast a ballot. All the same, the commonwealth had no shortage of night riders in disguise who took on every quality of Klansmen. Residents in all the counties around Magoffin complained that the Ku Klux seemed to be bursting at the seams of that county and spilling into its neighbors. The fact that the county sheriff was one of the night riders had something to do with it. A Confederate veteran from Georgia was hauled out at midnight, whipped, and shot, and he and his younger brother were ordered out of the county. No Republican, he was every bit as bad, a non-Kentuckian. As they explained, "They didn't want no d—d refugees in that neighborhood." A trustee for Berea College was beaten for affiliating with blacks. There were many other whippings for lesser offenses, not to mention sporadic killings. In one case, a gang of sixty men set upon a black family in Fitchburg and tried to kill them all.[41]

Kentucky got off comparatively lightly, and in most states in the Border South, the Klan never had more than a flickering existence. Some counties with heavy black majorities, like the sugar parishes downriver from New Orleans escaped the worst violence. So did those where white Unionists predominated. Even in Alabama, one of the worst-hit states, Klan violence hardly touched half the counties. But in areas where the races were evenly balanced, the outbreaks verged on open warfare. In York County, South Carolina, over some ten months, the Klan had business nearly every night.

Black cabins in one neighborhood would be hit this week, and those in another the next. There were eleven murders and over 600 beatings and assaults, not to mention midnight visitings, warnings, and threats. Klansmen broke into black houses to take their guns, the better to equip themselves, though they also seized guns from a railway station and invaded the probate judge's office to carry off one of the boxes of ammunition stored there.[42]

Everywhere, the terrorism focused on reversing the practical effects of emancipation by reining in the freedom and independence of former slaves. Forcing the Union Leagues to disband, singling their leaders out for attack, crippled black mobilization at election time, but it also wiped out the strongest backing for labor militants, out to get higher wages and better conditions from the planter—or even enforcement of his promises in the contract. Night callers targeted blacks who had spoken out, and those who were most respectable. For talking back to a white man, for supporting social equality, for refusing to take off a cap or make way on the street for whites, for owning a shotgun or disputing an employers' version of what remuneration was due, Ku Kluxing meted out savage punishments. In Noxubee County, Mississippi, the den threatened a whipping to any black failing to work hard enough on a certain plantation. A Lowndes County employer joined another gang that beat one of his workers for having failed to supply stove wood for the kitchen regularly. Planters were able to strengthen their hold over black employees by letting them know that their safety depended on their masters' influence with the violence-minded.[43] Schools and black churches went up in flames, and schoolteachers and preachers from the North were targeted for the Klan's attention. Country stores suspected of dealing in stolen cotton were struck by night.[44]

A black able to take care of himself was a dangerous example to all the others. He did not know his place. Farm laborers had a white employer who was half patron, half master, and that afforded a certain amount of protection. But a freedperson with enough money to rent land for cash, or, even worse, to own land, or, worst of all, to have known freedom even before the war was marked for treatment. Landowners who lent money to blacks to allow them to rent land rather than hiring out became occasional victims. So did freedpeople who had moved into the ranks of skilled labor. Black employees at southern ironworks and skilled miners were threatened or driven out, some 400 in one case, shutting down the mill's operations.[45] Attacking the more well-fixed freedpeople had one other occasional advantage: Klansmen, treating their visits as a paying business, relieved their victims of their money, their watches, and anything else lying handy.

However far the mask of chivalry could cover the hanging of alleged rapists, raiding parties spared neither women nor children in their assault on black communities. Freedwomen across the South were stripped, whipped, assaulted, and sometimes raped. (So were white women accused of sleeping with black men: in South Carolina, a pack of night riders abducted a prostitute and held her down to pour hot tar into her vagina.) Attacks on wives and kin only emphasized the point that freedmen could not fulfill the basic functions of a real head of a family to protect his own, and that black women had no rights that their betters were bound to respect.[46]

Democrats made all kinds of apologies for the spread of terrorism, when they admitted that any attacks had taken place at all, and editors that had publicized the Klan in its early days denied that anything of the kind had ever existed in their communities. They protested that it was only one more secret society, the mirror image of the Loyal Leagues that Republicans had formed to dragoon the freedpeople's votes. They justified it as the protector of white womanhood, threatened by ravening black beasts or as a sort of southern patriotism, understandable even if excessive. They described its victims as the scum of society, from adulterers to rabble-rousers, the "bad Negroes" that misled all the others. Some of the atrocities were exaggerated, they insisted, and others were made out of the whole cloth—or perhaps out of the whole sheet—by Republican propaganda. Fiercely, Democratic congressmen denied any political motive behind the torching of Mississippi schoolhouses. The school system was a "system of robbery," they explained—the schoolteachers spread incendiary notions. Overtaxed white communities (always Democratic) tried to intimidate them (always Republican) into leaving, and when written threats failed to do the job, applied the lash. In any case, apologists contended, force and intimidation, judiciously applied of course, were the only ways of overturning corrupt governments, propped up by bayonets and guaranteed life everlasting by their control over ignorant Negro voters.[47]

Party affiliation: that was the unspoken link between just about all the various night riders' victims—and it was not always unspoken. In any driving off of blacks from their homes, the raiders were driving off Republicans. Party organizers were made special targets. When a Klansman was broken out of jail two weeks before the election, a Republican correspondent guessed that it was because his "services . . . will be needed on or about the 7th of August, and he must be released so as to be ready for party purposes." At least 166 Republicans died in the two-year "Jackson County War" in Florida before Democrats regained power.[48] Local party organizers, black leaders who had given "inflammatory" speeches, stood the surest chance of being attacked.

Only rarely could Republicans muster "regulators" of their own—in the Republican counties along the Appalachian range, say, where the party was well armed and overwhelmingly white. Most blacks did not have the arms with which to protect themselves. Any effort on their part to form a private militia company would have set off race war, and in South Carolina in 1870–71, it did. White supremacy rested on military supremacy. Left on their own, the victims did fight back as best they could. Horse and night rider might pitch down from vines stretched across the roads in the dark, or scatter before the shotguns of those they had thought to catch unawares, and here and there the houses and farms of Klansmen burned down. Grant Clubs were often armed. Before holding rallies, Republicans might throw pickets out around the town as an early-warning system against trouble.[49] But they were outgunned and outmatched. Workers in the sugarcane fields lived close enough together to join for their mutual protection. Away from the cotton planter's big house, living far apart in their isolated cabins, tenant farmers had no defense when four or five dozen well-armed whites showed up after dark. If they survived, they wrote their death sentence by bringing charges against the attackers they recognized. No sheriff would make an arrest; no jury dared bring in a conviction. Those who resisted only bought time. Flight or violent death alone remained to them.[50]

For many blacks and a growing number of whites, Klan violence produced not militancy but a deeper submission, with Unionists withdrawing further into their own communities and away from active politics, except on Election Day—if then—and curbing their pursuit of better conditions from employers. If their family responsibilities were to be met, the children must be fed, and this could happen only by distancing themselves from radicalism. If definitions of manliness had come to encompass the ability to protect and sustain wife and children, black heads of households only risked greater humiliation by challenging those whose guns and numbers could be brought to bear against them. What vestiges of the Union Leagues had survived the terrorism and intimidation before Grant's election dissolved soon after it. Some scalawags quit active involvement in public affairs. Others looked for any excuse to break with the party and reconcile with their conservative neighbors on whatever terms the community would permit. It was such conditions, such recognition of their own powerlessness that brought freedmen to adjourn a political meeting after one disturbance in Georgia and resolve to go home rather than risk a riot by even trying to vote. That evening, they took down their Grant and Colfax banners, though even then they could not escape trouble. A crowd of white men and boys chased the blacks and seized and tore up the banner, the pieces distributed among the attackers as trophies of their victory.[51]

The tumult spreading across the South showed the fragility of Reconstruction's advances and the hollowness of reformers' hopes that freedpeople could be left alone to work out their own destinies. And yet, from the events, those who wanted to drew less obvious conclusions. In 1871, Congress set up a special investigating committee to document terrorism's ravages. More than a dozen volumes of horrific testimony came out of what one Democratic member derided as "the National Coroner's Inquest."[52] On the Klan's behalf, conservative witnesses mixed defamation of the victims' characters with an all-encompassing ignorance of anything related to the lawbreakers, their identities, or their motives. Mendacity, evasion, and contradiction left a bewildering array of charges and countercharges, but no fair-minded reader could miss the essential facts of communities devastated and Unionists forced to sleep in the woods to escape butchery, of official cowardice and the futility of expecting anything from the courts or enlightened public sentiment.

At the same time, from the white South's defenders came a more reassuring message. In no sense did the disorders herald a new rebellion. The terrorists might or might not have defensible motives, but they aimed their guns no farther than offending people in their state or communities. Every outbreak was a local matter, generally arising from distinct individual wrongs: an uppity Negro militia captain who threatened to burn the town, a local Republican notable who uttered indecent taunts at southern ladies. On the contrary, witnesses asserted, nearly every white southerner accepted the war's basic results. They committed their outrages in the South's name, not the Confederacy's. Nobody planned to reinstitute slavery; not even slaveholders longed for its revival. Ex-Confederates swore that the South now accepted the freedpeople's right to marry, hold property, attend school, and even to vote, under proper guidance. Indeed, that readiness to accept the situation dated back to Appomattox, they insisted, and until radicals appeared among them, the two races had basked in mutual good feeling. The South was "very much in need of good men from all parts of the world," former Confederate general James H. Clanton of Alabama protested; "we offer every inducement to get them, and when one comes in we take him by the hand and encourage him—treat him well." Wartime Unionists hastened to vouch for the good character and even better intentions of their Rebel neighbors.[53] This tally of exaggerations and lies could hardly erase the atrocities that so many other witnesses had detailed to the committee. But the point could not be missed that, left to their own resources, white southerners had no quarrel with the Union—only with the carpetbaggers and upstarts in their midst. The way to cement the nation fully would be for the North to trust its fellow Americans better, and the surest sign of that would be to remove the disabilities laid upon the South's so-called natural leaders.

That remedy, as the committee's majority report made clear, would not be enough. It gave ample documentation of a reign of terror, so scathing that readers might overlook how far its authors agreed with the Democratic minority. Denouncing the "general venality" and "utterly indefensible conduct" of some officials, the revenues "shamefully misapplied," the election laws almost calculated to "produce fraud," they blamed conditions on the failure of "business and educated men" to involve themselves in public life. However slowly and with however many setbacks, the South was moving toward a true loyalty, the majority concluded, a movement to encourage by a general removal of disabilities on all but the "great criminals." A Republican subcommittee went further: an amnesty without exceptions would bring an even more complete pacification.[54]

In doing so, the majority exposed the divided mind of Reconstruction's defenders. Committed to equal rights they remained, but that commitment carried them no further than preserving the new birth of freedom as it had been enacted already into law. Always, they fixed their eyes on Reconstruction's other goal: to deepen the foundations for a newly cemented Union and make its permanence secure. But what if the one goal conflicted with the other? Or what if the North came to feel as liberals already did, that the Union stood so firmly rooted that the country could leave wartime memories and wartime issues behind, that the postwar generation's true business lay elsewhere?

CHAPTER EIGHT

Conquered Provinces

T he postwar generation saw the Reconstruction not just of the South but of the trans-Mississippi West. The process was not called that, of course, but a whimsical chronicler might tick off the similarities and the contrasts with what happened in the former Confederate states. Across the plains and deserts, the government really did treat the peoples it vanquished as if their lands were conquered provinces. Their original inhabitants were denied the vote, their lands were subject to confiscation, their villages sacked and burned. There the army had free rein, protecting a flood of newcomers intent on grabbing anything worth having. In the territorial West, not just the South, one might find the mob violence, the midnight terror of fire and murder for the inoffensive and the unprotected; operating out of the Northeast, outside corporations made millions off the public domain in ways that southern railroad promoters could only dream of. Corruption abounded, with the trails leading straight back to Washington. Out of the scramble, the messy tangle of good intentions, base motives, and unrealistic expectations came a myth that would haunt America to the present day.

The reconstructing of the West and of the South occurred at the same time, but clearly they had very different outcomes. The fate of both was bound up in the war and how it had turned out, in lessons learned wrong or learned too well.[1]

The Civil War had not left the trans-Mississippi West alone. Confederate raiders sacked Lawrence, Kansas, and a Texas army sent to seize the gold and silver mines of New Mexico territory had been turned back at Glorieta Pass, its starving remnant reeling back across the parched landscape months later. Partly to secure the Pacific coast for the Union, partly because southern congressmen no longer barred the way, Congress chartered the Union Pacific and Central Pacific Railroads that, in linking up, would provide a railroad connection from Council Bluffs to San Francisco, and gave it generous aid in money and public lands. Nor did the Indian wars cease.

If anything, they worsened, with so many U.S. troops summoned east. In Minnesota, the "great Sioux war" emptied out counties of their white settlers before the Santee Sioux were starved into submission, their leaders sent to the gallows just in time for Christmas. Union forces arriving too late in the Southwest to find any Confederates worth beating threw their energies into attacking the Mescalero Apaches and then the Navajos. Georgians saw no such destruction as Kit Carson's troopers inflicted on the orchards and livestock of the Navajo people, nor knew any deprivation like the starvation that brought the surrender of 6,000 of them. Marched 300 miles to a reservation at Bosque Redondo, they found themselves locked up with their Apache enemies, on land unfit to feed them all, even if insects and droughts had spared the harvest.[2]

In Colorado Territory, occasional raids on ranches and stagecoaches gave the land-grabbers all the excuse they needed to open total war. Dependent on local volunteers, the governor sent Colonel John M. Chivington on the warpath. On November 29, 1864, his forces set upon 500 Cheyennes sleeping in their village by Sand Creek. Thinking themselves covered by a peace treaty, the tribes had turned over their arms to soldiers at Fort Lyon. Now over 150 perished by musket and saber. Chivington's troops paraded Denver waving the scalps and genitals they had collected for souvenirs. Retaliations followed. As a result, by the time Lee had surrendered, ranches were burning all along the South Platte, and the Great Plains were convulsed in conflict, with no settler family spared. Troopers found themselves shifted from one war to another. Not surprisingly, many resented it, with hundreds deserting.[3]

That war weariness may have played its part in putting limits on any full-scale military solution. There never would be volunteers enough in the postwar years. Those that enlisted showed a maddening disinclination to stay. Desertion rates stayed high. But that sliver of the army that had saved the Union also tasted humiliating defeat. The 1865 campaign proved a debacle, and in 1866, the Teton Sioux, angry at the forts guarding the Bozemon Trail, the gold-mining route from Montana, provoked the commander of Fort Phil Kearny, Captain William Fetterman, into sending out a punitive expedition. All of them died in an ambush, their thoroughly mutilated bodies sending a warning to any who would follow after them. The army's retaliatory measures against the Cheyenne and Sioux gained it nothing beyond appreciation that when it came to atrocities, the troopers ranked as amateurs.[4] By 1867, there was no question that the Rebels most soldiers would have preferred to fight were those scattered across the

West, their arms still in their hands. Commanders found a positive relief in being transferred from peacekeeping duties in the South to those in the West, not least because they had a freer hand there and a white population heartily in favor of their using it.

Between treatment of the "red pests of the forests" in the West and blacks in the South there were sharp differences. For one thing, most Indians lived in territories, where federal authority had uncontested jurisdiction and could shape policies as it chose; for another, no pressing apparent necessity to put loyalty on top could bolster a drive to give Indians the vote. But in certain respects, Reconstruction concerns affected attitudes and national action. White southerners used the Indian experience to forecast that, like the tribes on the plains, blacks would all die out by century's end. Democrats and some liberal Republicans equated blacks with Indians and restive urban workers: all lazy spongers that sentimentalists had persuaded that government owed some kind of living. At the same time, policymakers did not have time to concentrate on settling the Indian problem until the southern question had been addressed. "Nobody pays any attention to Indian matters," Nathaniel G. Taylor, Andrew Johnson's commissioner of Indian Affairs wrote, on a tour of the West. "Members of Congress understand the negro question, and talk learnedly of finance, and other problems of political economy, but when the progress of settlement reaches the Indian's home the only question is, 'how best to get his lands.'"[5]

War's end changed the way the government dealt with the so-called Indian problem. No longer were tribes seen as separate nations, with whom formal agreements could be made. There could be no room for nations within the United States. "We might as well hold a 'talk' and make a treaty with the Ku Klux Klan," one editor protested.[6] The last treaty was made in 1871. In 1875 the House explicitly ended the practice and announced that hereafter no tribe should be recognized as an independent sovereignty. That did not mean a war of extermination, however much General William Tecumseh Sherman predicted it and some white settlers hoped for it—and, for that matter, some Indian nations, always in terms of their Indian enemies. President Grant spoke for a general consensus, at least east of the Mississippi River, when he declared, "A system which looks to the extinction of a race is too horrible for a nation to adopt without entailing upon itself the wrath of all Christendom and engendering in the citizens a disregard for human life and the rights of others, dangerous to society." Rather, Indians must become wards of the state, and radicals called for the most active and paternal of states. A few made analogies to the Freedmen's

Bureau in the South. "What is wanted is a Bureau of Civilization, with enough force at its disposal to gather in the remnants of the tribes on the plains and settle them somewhere on farms, and teach them to live by labor," the *Nation* argued. "If they cannot bear civilization, it will at least kill them decently."

Cynical as it sounded, the *Nation's* point was that, as things stood, the Indians were being finished off by policies sometimes unmindful, sometimes genocidal, but always inconsistent, degrading, and inhumane. In 1867, a special joint committee was formed to study the decline of Indians. It laid the blame on disease—smallpox, cholera, measles, and syphilis in particular—on whiskey, and the "irrepressible conflict between a superior and an inferior race when brought into the presence of each other." Informed that the government spent $1 million for every Indian killed and $1 to $2 million a week protecting settlers, Congress passed an act to promote the peace, establishing commissions to parley with western tribes and arrange settlements "such as will most likely insure civilization for Indians and peace and safety for the whites." Treaties on the northern plains removed army posts in Indian country and permitted schoolhouses and missionaries to minister to the Indians.[7] In 1869, a Board of Indian Commissioners was established, staffed by ten men whose expertise and disinterestedness placed them far ahead of the usual political appointments that had administered policy till then. Ely S. Parker, a Seneca and wartime aide to General Grant, was made commissioner of Indian Affairs in the Interior Department, and could count on White House support. Grant's "Peace policy" proposed a comprehensive solution. The tribes would be collected into large reservations that could be given territorial status, including the customary delegate in Congress to represent their interests. They would be encouraged to turn farmers, with private landholdings, and, after an 1875 law allowed it, to file for homesteads, once they had left their tribes. The reservations would be removed from control by Indian agents, chosen for their political connections, and handed over to the missionaries for leading Christian denominations. The government would school the tribespeople and uplift them, as it had the freedpeople. As the only two areas fit for reservations were public lands south of Kansas or north of Nebraska, neither of them in great demand among homesteaders, the program, clearing out the tribes in between, had tentative support from the settlers and the great transcontinental railroad lines. For Kansas in particular it meant that the four million acres in Indian reservations a dozen years later had dwindled to slightly over two hundred thousand.[8]

From the first, though, the Grant administration produced more policy than peace. The Interior Department's Indian Bureau kept the board on a tight rein. The commissioners had to examine over 3,000 accounts every year, but the Interior Department felt free to ignore their findings. In a single year, they rejected $426,909.96 in claims, 98 percent of which ended up being paid anyway. Ten years on, the board had that overwhelming popularity that Congress accorded to any high-minded agency helpless to do any good whatsoever. Parker lasted just two years before unproven corruption charges overthrew him. His replacement, Francis A. Walker, had no hopes for Indian assimilation into white society, not at least in his lifetime. To him, the natives were scarcely better than forward children, to be taught good morals and sound economics, cleansed of their culture, and readied for a citizenship that receded into some dim future. The day when they would be given the ballot extended further off still.[9]

Nor did the policy of removal and concentration long keep much for anything except an ever-shrinking set of Indian enclaves. Protecting tracklayers and emigrants, supplying the railroads with much of its engineer corps and advice about which routes would serve their military purposes, the army sped construction and did its best to fill the vacant lands. Every railroad built inspired calls for branch lines, and tribal lands inevitably stood in the way. As the northern plains opened, white communities saw the great Sioux reservation blocking their railroad-building visions, and when removal meant taking Winnebagos out of Wisconsin to settle them in the Dakotas, the storm of opposition west of the Mississippi was so strong that proponents had to sneak the measure through.[10]

Without constant military pressure, the plains could not be cleared. A roster of generals given the task reads like a more exclusive Grand Review. General William Tecumseh Sherman took charge of the Department of the West. General Phil Sheridan, Oliver O. Howard, John Pope, and E. R. S. Canby all served out west. (Canby not only was killed there; he was shot during a peace conference.) They had seen war and had no romantic notions about the Indians but, for the most part, claimed to admire them as a foe worth their own mettle. If the Indians were brutal, General John Gibbon wondered, were the "civilized" men who seized their land or dug up the bodies of enemy dead at battle sites any better? "If I had been a red man as I was a white man, I should have fought as bitterly," one officer admitted. General Pope, who had blustered about exterminating hostile tribes in 1862, became convinced that the real troublemakers were the white intruders. As head of the Department of Missouri, he spent much of his time trying to forestall war with the Indians by preventive measures, and raised a loud voice against trying to force nations of hunters to put their hand to the plow on land unfit for cultivation.[11]

Most of the officers soon realized that the lessons about war-making that they had learned in the Civil War did not fit Indian war at all. They had nowhere near the manpower at their disposal that they had once enjoyed. With Congress trimming the regular army down to 54,000 enlistees at the war's end, and to 37,000 in 1869, the entire country had to get along on a force half the size that General Meade commanded at Gettysburg. In 1870, the government reduced its army to 30,000 and in 1874 to 25,000. Out of this array, the War Department had to staff coastal forts and federal arsenals, administer the collection of weather reports, police the new national park system, keep order in Chicago after the 1871 fire, pacify the South, run West Point, and occasionally distribute relief supplies when grasshoppers devoured homesteaders' crops. Even then, the official numbers included the dead, deserted, and indisposed. A growing number of new recruits, bereft of battle experience, mustered among the dwindling core of Civil War veterans. Only the desperate enlisted for the $13 a month in pay, and every year, as many as a third of the soldiers deserted. Black veterans were likeliest to stay with the army and reenlist when their service was up. Here, at least, they could get the respect that white communities so rarely gave them—certainly among their adversaries. But for the most part, frontier regulars lacked the training, either at horsemanship or marksmanship, that their wartime equivalents had. Target practice came rarely. The government could not spare the ammunition.[12]

Even with the best troopers, the army found itself outfought and out-maneuvered. With the world all before them, no far-flung sprinkling of forts could keep the peace. The Indians were not likely to hurl themselves against the barricades. Nor did they value heroic stands like the Alamo. Their warfare trained them for attack, not defense, and even then only when they had surprise and superior numbers on their side. So Indians singled out individuals off on their own, homesteaders far from help or small knots of troops not expecting attack. The U.S. Army would have to bring the war to them, but here, the problem was the same as in suppressing the Klan. With luck, at the first word of trouble, they could ride out at the full gallop, reaching the fight hours or days after the nick of time. Military manuals gave no guidance for fighting an enemy that made itself scarce and never gave open battle unless it felt sure of winning. Dependent on their long supply trains for provisioning, the army could never move fast

"Indian Outrages." Thomas Nast, *Harper's Weekly*, August 15, 1874. General William Tecumseh Sherman in his postwar role is preparing to treat the Indian like a naughty child.

enough to catch up with an enemy force. Forced to build a welter of small forts to protect settlement along the newly built railroad lines, they could not easily concentrate their military muscle.[13]

Success took a different strategy, attacking Indians when winter pinned them down. Raiding encampments assured that women and children would number among the slain, even when precautions had been taken. "The confessed aim is to exterminate everyone," Colonel Philippe Régis de Trobriand explained, "for this is the only advantage of making the expedition; if extermination were not achieved, just another burden would be added—prisoners." The government and army's real aim was not to exterminate the Indian peoples, so much as to do away with the tribes as independent dominions and possessors of the soil. For that purpose, they found ready means in the slaughter of the bison that roamed the plains in tens of millions. On the buffalo, Indians relied for food and for most of their commerce. The killing had begun long since; once herds had roamed as far east as the Carolinas. Thanks to the advent of the horse and rifle on the northern plains, Indian tribes themselves were slaughtering bison at an unsustainable pace to suit their own needs as consumers of white society's goods. By 1865, eastern hunters, too, had found a rich market in their hides and in the mere sport of shooting them. With or without official encouragement, the hunters would have come. Between 1872 and 1874, 1.3 million buffalo hides were sent east.[14]

In this mass destruction, the government saw an opportunity to force Indians to give up hunting for farming. As a Texas congressman explained, "So long as there are millions of buffaloes in the West, so long the Indians cannot be controlled, even by the strong army of the Government." General Sherman likened the slaughter to Phil Sheridan's laying waste the Shenandoah Valley in wartime, and other officers proposed it as a punishment that could put a healthy fear into enemies that could not be reached any other way. "Kill every buffalo you can," Colonel Richard Dodge advised. "Every buffalo dead is an Indian gone." Secretary of the Interior Columbus Delano laid his blessing on the private enterprise operating toward just such a result. A bill to outlaw wanton slaughter was vetoed by Kansas governor in 1872; in 1873 General Sheridan induced the Texas lawmakers to drop a similar bill. And in 1874, when a bill to protect the buffalo on Indian territorial grounds from white hunting passed both houses of Congress, Grant vetoed it. In raw military terms, the policy paid off, though soldiers concentrated their own firepower on Indian horses to take the mobility out of their enemies. The Sioux war two years later ended in part because Sitting Bull and his people were starving: the army had driven all the buffalo out of their range. "A cold wind blew across the prairie when the last buffalo fell," the chief would lament, "—a death-wind for my people."[15]

That ability the national government exercised to apply force or uproot communities made all the difference in what settlers would describe as a successful outcome and marks the contrast between Reconstruction West and Reconstruction South. Few of the constraints hedging policy applied on federal domain. National authority could be exercised directly, through territorial governments appointed from Washington. Every officer was a newcomer, and a far larger number of them than in the South came only to go away again, when relieved of office. Most judges, governors, and secretaries served less than four years. Where federal judges elsewhere served a dozen years on average, the norm out west was slightly over three. Occasionally, settlers grumbled about the carpetbaggers they had been inflicted with, but then, most of them met the criteria for being called carpetbaggers themselves.[16]

Federal sway meant that only in the West could the government confiscate and redistribute the land. The idea was not simply proposed, but imposed and, as far as whites judged its final results, worked spectacularly well. Indians lost their land. White emigrants gained it. In most cases, some formal agreement put the gloss of consent on the transaction, but south of Nebraska, the process was rawer. Tribes that had supported the South in the war were required to surrender much of their territory as an indemnity for the wrong they had done the Union. They were, in fact, the only Confederates on whom confiscation was inflicted. A different legal process stripped Hispanics in New Mexico and Arizona Territories of most of their acreage, as land grants issued by the Mexican government were challenged in court, their boundaries redefined, and their titles invalidated. Of 37.5 million acres claimed in New Mexico, the Court of Private Land Claims ended up confirming title to only 2 million by the 1890s.[17]

Natives' losses made newcomers' gains. Population growth rates on the prairies were dramatic: Kansas grew 176 percent in the 1870s, Minnesota 154 percent, Nebraska 310 percent. Here, again, the federal government worked hard to resettle the land. For a mere ten-dollar filing fee, the Homestead Act of 1862 gave 160 acres of land, a quarter section, to anyone willing to settle on it for five years. Sponsors hoped to perpetuate the Jeffersonian ideal of a nation of independent farmers, providing an opportunity for land-poor farmers' sons and unskilled wage earners. As experience showed that an estate princely by eastern standards looked beggarly in drier western conditions, Congress offered new deals. Under the 1873 Timber Culture Act, settlers could earn another quarter section by planting trees on forty acres and maintaining them for ten years longer. With the offer finding no takers, lawmakers cut the requirements to ten acres, and proposed that while a settler had to plant 2,700 seedlings to the acre, only a fourth of them needed to be still growing when he applied for a patent. Under the Desert Act of 1877, emigrants had the chance to buy a square mile of arid land for twenty-five cents an acre down and a dollar an acre later on. The only condition imposed was that the owners be able to conduct water across it within three years' time.[18] Finally, a year later, the Timber and Stone Act opened land "unfit for cultivation" for purchase in quarter-section amounts at $2.50 an acre.

Free land looked like more of a bargain than it was. A family needed money to get to its claim, and funds for farm tools, stock, and fencing. It had to have enough saved to get through until the first crop came in, as well. Tenant farmers and unskilled mill hands had far less chance of taking advantage of the Homestead Act's provisions than midwestern farmers' kin. All the same, many took up the offer, and many of them got by. By 1900, two million homesteads dotted the West.

States counted every newcomer as a capital gain, and most of them founded immigration bureaus to depict their charms. Iowa published handbooks in Danish, Dutch, and Swedish. Kansas boosters swore that the state's "champagne air" contained more oxygen, making its western counties "the paradise of the lungs." The monotony of endless flatland could even be described as one of "topographical equality." The railroads' land departments became the biggest advertisers of the West's attractions. A publicist for the Burlington, who one editor described as "barefooted on top where his brains ought to be," spread the word that Nebraska stood on the "Gulf Stream of Migration," 400 miles wide and stretching west from Illinois to the Rockies, but, he cautioned, its possibilities were so great that it ought better be described as "bounded on the north by the 'Aurora Borealis,' and on the south by the Day of Judgment." Journalists and politicians so touted the fertility and prospects of the Dakotas on the Northern Pacific Railroad's behalf that cynics dubbed it "Jay Cooke's Banana Belt." Equally fantastic, the Santa Fe, running through Kansas, insisted that the "rainbelt" ran through its territory and the "golden mean" between unpleasantly hot and uncomfortably cool. Settlers, with varying levels of skepticism, came to believe that rain followed the plow, turning the arid high plains into a second Ohio. "The rainfall is increasing, and may, at some not very remote day, become excessive," one account of Kansas announced, just a few years before drought scorched the settlers out. Not everybody believed, but tens of thousands came at the railroads' summoning. Within four years, the Burlington's territory in Nebraska went from vacant land to grain belt, shipping out 1,224 carloads' worth of wheat in 1872 and 3,390 a year later. The company sold its holdings at $7.50 an acre and found plenty of takers.[19]

Railroads were more than the settling and, where the Indians were concerned, unsettling force out west. They defined the pace and character of development, for everything depended on them. In 1865, Omaha ran far behind Atchison and Nebraska City catering to the emigrant trade headed to California. Then the Union Pacific set up its machine shops there as the eastern terminus of the transcontinental route. Four years, and Omaha had become the great railroad center of the Missouri River valley, with speculators offering lots at $3,000 an acre. Council Bluffs, across the river, and planning to become the terminus of seven different railroads, benefited, too. It raised 1,300 new buildings in 1868, but Omaha erected twice that number.[20]

Nothing so characterizes the mythical West as the Abilene or Chisholm trail. In 1867, Texas ranchers, finding themselves barred from driving their tick-ridden herds across the uninfected cattle country east of them to St. Louis and without the railroad connections to reach New Orleans, needed a market. They found it when Joseph G. McCoy came up with the idea of shipping livestock east from Kansas. The Missouri Pacific president threw him out as a visionary, but the Hannibal & St. Joe offered him favorable rates to Chicago. All McCoy needed then was a gathering point . . . and cattle. He found the first in Abilene, a "very small, dead place, consisting of about one dozen log huts," with one shingle roof among them. The saloonkeeper augmented his income raising prairie dogs for souvenirs. Then McCoy sent out runners, inviting ranchers to bring their herds north. Jesse Chisholm, a Texas cattleman of Cherokee ancestry, brought the first. Thirty-five thousand head shipped out in 1867, twice that many in 1868, more than 300,000 the next year, and in 1871, 700,000. The trail diverted west to Wichita and then Dodge City, renowned for its violence—at least in legend. In all, over four million cattle made their way north.[21] But none of it would have happened without eastern demand and the railroad and meatpacking companies that filled that demand and met customers' needs. By the end of the 1870s, the trails had wound down. Railroad expansion into Texas played a part; so did the shift to less rangy and better-flavored Shorthorns and Herefords that could be grown close to railheads farther north. A cattle kingdom, much of it sustained on public lands, spread from the Dakotas to the edge of Utah's Great Basin.

The West's destinies therefore rested with investors and directors east of the Mississippi and north of the Ohio. Seeing in cornfields a empire of wealth, the Chicago, Burlington & Quincy ran a network of iron arms through Iowa and Minnesota, and into the Dakotas, but its directors sat in Boston. The Union Pacific boasted some of the biggest names in New England and Philadelphia, including Tom Scott, head of the Pennsylvania

Railroad. Jay Gould won infamy on the Erie Railroad that tapped the Great Lakes commerce for New York City, but he made his most indelible mark on the southern prairies. Controlling the "Katy" (the Missouri, Kansas & Texas Railroad) and the Missouri Pacific Railway, he helped build the wheat and cattle empires of mid-America, and his projects looked toward making their own connections with the western sea.

Just as in the South, so in the West, private capital alone could not have done the job, and congressional sessions turned into a scramble for slices of the public domain. In 1870, one Nebraska senator offered seventeen "land-grab" bills, but every senator from Iowa west claimed paternity to two to five measures. California thought nothing of asking that the government give 10,600 mineral-rich acres to the Sierra Iron Company at $1.25 each, and Senator Samuel S. "Subsidy Pom" Pomeroy of Kansas wanted alternate sections two miles wide on either side of the track given to the Republican Valley Railroad and Telegraph Company. Eastern money came more readily because westerners so willingly taxed themselves. The Katy counted on the national government to muscle the Cherokees into handing over a quarter of a million acres for white settlement. Congress bestowed ten sections of land per mile, and that was on top of the land grant that Kansas gave. The Sunflower State gave every county permission to subscribe to company stock and issue $300,000 in bonds to endow the railroads of their choice. Municipalities committed themselves wholeheartedly. Over eight years, those in Kansas issued $4.3 million in securities for railroad aid, and by 1884, $15.9 million. "We don't care who is governor or who goes to Congress, so [long as] he is sound on the Atchison, Topeka and Santa Fe Railroad," a Topeka paper asserted.[22]

In fact, the securities were risky for whoever held them. Most railroads in their early years could not make the money to survive. Their sponsors underestimated the original start-up costs, or, at any rate, they failed to share their concerns with investors. Far from getting rich off land grants, many companies found that they could not meet the grants' conditions by the time stipulated. Much of the land was impossible to sell, and where railroads competed directly with the Homestead Act, the only way they could unburden themselves was by marketing all but the choicest acres at rock-bottom, competitive prices. In any case, they needed steady customers rather more than one-time buyers. By filling up the surrounding countryside, and that alone, had they any chance of filling up the boxcars rolling east and the passenger cars heading west. Building their tracks too fast and carelessly, forced to replace them within a half-dozen years, lugging the immense fixed costs that overcapitalization burdened their account books with, companies counted on bumper crops and premium prices. West of Iowa, they were lucky to get either one. As crop returns fell, bankruptcies and defaults rose.[23]

The East made the West and the West the East. In 1865, the wheat belt from Ohio up into Iowa and Minnesota produced 148 million bushels—in 1873, 321 million, and most of the growth came at the western end. The wheat belt turned Minneapolis into a flour-mill town, dominated by the Washburns and Pillsburys. Omaha and Kansas City became regional meatpacking centers feeding the plainsfolk. All three cities owed their rise to the railroads flung from there in every direction, but they themselves sped the movement of the frontier westward. Take away Minneapolis and the railroad hub at St. Paul, and it would have taken years longer for the Red River country to turn into a sea of grain.[24] Chicago outdid all rivals. Wharves of lumber, brought from the sawmills of Michigan, Minnesota, and Wisconsin's northern frontiers, built the frame houses for countless settlers on the treeless prairies. From Montgomery Ward and Sears-Roebuck, a mail-order industry supplied westerners with all the amenities of eastern life. So well were they supplied that many a farmer would swear by "God, the Ten Commandments, and Montgomery Ward." Having discovered the cost savings of mass production in slaughtering hogs to feed the Union armies during the war, Gustavus Swift and Philip Armour extended their reach to cattle, creating "Packingtown," which allowed them to sell beef for less in the East than butchers there could manage. But again, they could not have done it without the railroad connections to bring herds in and the refrigerator cars to ship out the "dressed beef." Nor could the farmers hoping to keep the cattle out of their crops have done so without railroads to bring them the barbed-wire fencing that Joseph F. Glidden put on the market in 1874. His Illinois firm did sensationally well. By 1883, the Glidden factory turned out 600 miles of finished barbed wire every ten hours, and the railroad transported nearly all of it.[25]

Western development, then, depended on outside agencies, among them a federal government role far more intrusive, omnipresent, and effectual than the South endured. It also got much more financial support, while paying a much smaller share of the costs of keeping the nation going. On average, the government spent four times as much per person on those in the Mountain West as it did those in the South Atlantic states in 1870. The Homestead Act diminished the flow into the Treasury of money from land sales, the biggest contribution that the territories had made until then.

Only one white American in fifty lived in the territorial West in 1880, but 40 percent of all military spending went there. A denser population east of the Mississippi allowed post offices to turn a profit, but those spread across a sparsely settled West lived off government funding. In all, the average westerner cost the Treasury forty-five dollars more than he or she contributed.[26]

The same forces that stoked so much southern corruption—a government taking on new functions and a crowd of economic interests scrambling for a place at the feast, not to mention a feast of incomparable scope, provided at the national government's expense—gave the West a bumper crop of scandals and tainted the atmosphere of Washington, especially where railroad aid bills were concerned. When Republicans charged that Andrew Johnson had secured acquittal by buying Kansas senator Edmund G. Ross's vote, they missed the mark. His colleague Samuel S. "Subsidy Pom" Pomeroy was the one who invited a bribe and offered to deliver two colleagues in addition. One of them may have been Jim Nye of Nevada, though proofs were lacking. In any case, the president never took up the offer. Nye would have been a natural in a state where senate seats usually went up for auction, silver bonanza kings buying a place, even if the cost included having to leave their comfortable homes in San Francisco to visit Carson City, where legislators waited for bidders. Pomeroy's mixture of pelf and piety earned him literary immortality as oleaginous Senator Abner Dilworthy in Mark Twain and Charles Dudley Warner's *The Gilded Age*, and his downfall became its pièce de résistance. As lawmakers readied for the senatorial election in Topeka, Pomeroy showed up, inviting a state senator, A. M. York, to his hotel room to hand him $7,000 for his support. Soon after that, York rose to throw the packet of cash on the Speaker's table, shouting, "I now redeem that pledge by voting for him to serve a term in the penitentiary not to exceed twenty years." Even as he did so, the public was learning how Ross's successor, Alexander Caldwell, had secured his seat. A banker and railroad man, Caldwell had spent $60,000 to sweeten one rival's withdrawal and win a host of friends on the legislative floor. They came from every corner of the statehouse the moment word got out that "Caldwell was buying." Some later insisted that they had a perfect right to the money, because, having taken it, they voted against him anyway. Caldwell was forced to resign, and Pomeroy went into retirement. His manager, the go-between with Andrew Johnson, Benjamin F. Legate, lasted longer. In 1884, he courted a fat bribe on behalf of the Prohibition candidate for president, who, Legate claimed, would drop out in the Republicans' favor for $50,000. (Legate was lying, but that was not what sent him home empty-handed.

Paying to keep one splinter candidate in the race, the Republican National Committee had nothing left to shove another one out.)[27]

Politicians west of the Missouri had more success raising the wind than farmers did raising crops. The Kansas treasurer deposited state funds in various banks but pocketed the interest on them. His successor quit to escape impeachment. In New Mexico, the "Santa Fe Ring" that Stephen B. Elkins and Thomas B. Catron headed doled out the offices and whatever lands the courts would let them wrest from their Hispanic owners. By 1883, Catron owned nearly a quarter of a million acres in one grant and just under 600,000 acres in another. "Cattle Rings, Public Land Stealing Rings, Mining Rings, Treasury Rings, and Rings of almost every description" ran public affairs to suit themselves, or so a territorial governor later claimed. In Lincoln County, the firm of Murphy, Dolan & Riley dominated everything, and the so-called House could have given the Tweed Ring lessons in thieving. At least New York's grafters did not go into cattle rustling to sell beef to the federal government or Apache reservation officials.[28]

Often the track of crooked gains led straight to Washington, if not further afield. The moral ruin of former House Ways and Means Committee chair Robert C. Schenck came when he became minister to the court of St. James. Unable to afford the upkeep of so prestigious a position, the former Union general joined the board of the Emma Mine, supposedly a western silver lode, and put his official prestige behind advertisements swearing that there were millions in it. There were fat fees for Schenck, to be sure, but the mine went broke. Eventually the diplomat faced a grilling before a congressional committee about the 2,000 shares he sold short on inside knowledge that the price was about to plummet. Expanding postal service across the West, the government paid contractors and looked the other way as they mulcted the Treasury for extra services never provided for. One contract offered to carry the mails across New Mexico for $6,330 and collected $150,592. Holders of the "Star Routes" shared their winnings with an assistant postmaster general and Senator Stephen W. Dorsey of Arkansas, who, having apparently bought a number of legislators back home to further his railroad schemes, may have enjoyed the change of pace in being bought himself.[29]

Contracts to supply the Indians proved a steady source of graft, as everyone knew. Indian agents supplied themselves far better than the tribes that they fobbed off with rotten meats and threadbare blankets. As one expert remarked, traditionally an agent on a $1,500 salary could "retire upon an ample fortune in three years." In July 1875, paleontologist Othniel C.

Marsh exposed the cheating at the Red Cloud agency, with padded freight contracts and repulsive provender. The agent charged the government for feeding 15,000 Indians. At least 7,000 of them lived only in his imagination. The others fed on foul flour ("dark," "wet," and "adhesive"), sugar, tobacco, and coffee, all bought at premium prices. "Wretchedly gaunt and thin" steers staggered onto the agency to be slaughtered, "the poorest lot of Texas cattle I have ever seen during all my experience in the West," Marsh wrote. The pork was so bad that the Indian adults ate only the thin outer rim of fat and tossed the remainder to the ground in disgust. Children who devoured some of it died soon after. Secretary of the Interior Columbus Delano made sure that his son had a share in the refuse passed off to tribes on the reservation, and did his best to discredit those who leveled accusations against him.[30]

An even sadder case involved Grant's secretary of war, William W. Belknap, a florid, genial Civil War soldier from Iowa, who, as it turned out, loved not wisely but too often. Marrying into the Tomlinson family in Kentucky, he gave out an army trading post privilege to one Caleb Marsh, a friend of his wife, Amanda. Marsh showed his gratitude by giving her regular payments out of the profits. When Amanda died, Belknap married her sister Carrie. The payments continued, the same as before. Belknap may have had no idea of what went on, until the House investigation in 1876 brought Marsh to Washington to testify. Or he may have known all the time and had been using his wives as a front while collecting cash for favors done; so Marsh suspected.[31]

Politicians got the largest share of the blame, but just as in the South, the real gainers by corruption were not those bought but those doing the buying. In no other part of the country did wealth confer such power on the few. Where one or two industries predominated, as coal did in West Virginia, silver in Nevada, or railroads in the Great Plains states, no other interest could counter their influence with boodle of its own. Senator Alexander Caldwell had a bottomless purse because the Kansas Pacific Railroad filled it, and Iowa and Nebraska senators drew on Union Pacific funds for their reelection and as a thank-you gift for favors. The corporation made sweetheart land deals with Kansas governor Samuel J. Crawford, who apparently destroyed a bill setting railroad rates before it could go into law. In Nebraska, the Union Pacific and Kansas Pacific battled for dominance, the former controlling politics north of the Platte, the latter south of it. Whenever the legislature met, lawmakers postured while policy was made and bills stifled down the street in the UP's headquarters, the so-called Oil

Room. There liquor and lucre lubricated members' consciences. With some exaggeration, Californians swore that the railroad monopolists Collis Huntington and former governor Leland Stanford of the Central and Southern Pacific lines had a mortgage on both houses and whenever their Republican tools wore down or broke, simply picked up Democratic ones.[32]

The greatest scandal arose out of the greatest venture of its day. On May 10, 1869, two chartered companies, the Union Pacific and Central Pacific, met at Promontory Point, Utah, completing the first transcontinental railroad. Both railroad presidents swung their own hammers to tap the spike joining the tracks. Wires transmitted the blow into the national telegraph system and instantly spread the news worldwide. Cannon and small-arms fire broke out in Omaha. Bells rang in New York, and Chicagoans formed a seven-mile parade. The project had been a heroic undertaking. At its peak, workers laid two to five miles a day across the plains. In the mountains, a crew with pickaxes and handheld iron drills sometimes could advance only eight inches through solid rock in twenty-four hours. The invention of nitroglycerine had proven a godsend. To feed and house employees, the Union Pacific put towns on wheels, boxcars with three tiers of bunks and dining cars able to feed 125 men at a time. Across the prairies, mushroom towns sprang up at the terminus of the moment, complete with all the amenities: saloons, gambling dens, whorehouses, and telegraph offices. Some communities became camp followers themselves, dismantling and following the line of construction to plant themselves on new foundations. Mormons in Brigham Young's commonwealth welcomed an easier connection east, but built the branch lines to the Union Pacific themselves to spare their Deseret pollution from Gentiles' bad habits. (Young only succeeded briefly. Railroad connections made coal mines profitable, and when prospectors discovered silver, they rushed in, no more respectful of Latter-Day Saints than of the Lakota and Cheyenne whose domain was now up for grabs.) Union general Grenville Dodge, the UP's chief engineer, cleared out the Platte Valley so that telegraph lines could run unhindered by Indians— living ones, at least. "Nobody knows where he is," a subordinate wrote General Grant, who wired Omaha to find Dodge's location, "but everybody knows where he has been." Over the next thirty years, 70,000 miles of track would be laid between the Mississippi and the Pacific, and the number of transcontinental lines would increase to five.[33]

Private money had gone into both the Central and Union Pacific, but even more public money: government funding on top of a lavish land grant. Unable to market UP bonds until the railroad's completion, the directors handed them over to its contracting firm, Credit Mobilier, at egregiously high prices. They had no complaints. The directors ran the firm, and the national government would pick up the tab. "Reduced to plain English, the story of Credit Mobilier is simply this," a journalist wrote: "The men entrusted with the management of the Pacific Road made a bargain with themselves to build the road for a sum equal to about twice its actual cost, and pocketed the profits, which have been estimated at about THIRTY MIL-LIONS OF DOLLARS—this immense sum coming out of the pockets of the taxpayers of the United States." As a consequence, shareholders earned immense dividends. One, in June 1868, was 60 percent in cash and 40 percent in Union Pacific Railroad stock. Two weeks later came another dividend, 80 percent in the UP's first mortgage bonds and 100 percent in stock; the next day, there was another dividend, 75 percent in stock and 75 percent in first mortgage bonds, and two months after that, 100 percent in stock and 75 percent in first mortgage bonds. But the December dividend was best of all: 200 percent.[34]

Credit Mobilier would make lurid headlines, but far less attention went to a stealing that went on every day and everywhere. In terms of the number of culprits, land-thieving outdid every other kind of fraud. Amid the genuine homesteaders' claims were lands that speculators had gobbled up, using dummy claimants to take many times the maximum acreage the law allowed. The Timber Culture Act and Desert Act raised the most bountiful crop of cheaters that anyone could have imagined. Claimants stuck twigs of brush and willow spears in the ground, passing them off for groves in the making or "conducted water" by pouring it into a tin cup and riding across their property, or plowing a furrow down a slope that they swore were irrigation ditches. Nineteen acres out of every twenty patented under the Desert Act were gained by fraud. The results of the Timber Culture Act were so embarrassing that Congress repealed it. Buyers had no intention of turning high prairie into farmland; they wanted it for grazing cattle. As for those acres "unfit for cultivation," the stands of virgin forest made them easily worth forty times what the government charged to a timber company. As for those with coal deposits, the profits went beyond calculation, though one company paid $14,000 for 50,000 acres worth $25 million.[35]

If the West served as an example to the South of what railroad development could do and to the nation of the connection between corruption and the powerful economic interests wanting government favors, it also showed how radical the Reconstructed states' advance in racial equality was—while it lasted. Even as black southerners cast their first votes, the Army Medical Museum stepped up its campaign to collect Indian skulls; measuring brain capacity, it assumed, would offer the scientific proof that whites were racially superior. Former Confederate Cherokees not only resented losing their slaves and killed them as readily as white southerners did; they drove them off the land and did their best to refuse them the rights enjoyed by other members of the tribe. Western tribes butchered Chinese miners and farm laborers even more readily than white ones. In one case, Paiutes disarmed some 150 Chinese travelers and then, while they begged for mercy, shot and stabbed them to death; mutilated with miners' picks, the bodies stretched six miles' distance. For San Francisco's black community the Chinese were ideal as a contrast to their own Americanism. Christians like themselves had nothing in common with newcomers "heathen in their worship and naturally licentious."

No matter how lightly they packed, white emigrants across the Missouri found room to carry their prejudices with them. Before the war, many territories and a few states had shut out blacks, slave or free. Those restrictions no longer applied, but that did not make freedpeople welcome. In 1867, voters in Kansas turned down Negro suffrage; Nevada law barred "Negroes, Mongolians, and Indians from white schools" but did nothing to establish any other kind. Toward the Indians, the settlers' views were far more ferocious than those of the army. Even eastern Republicans who spoke with a tried patience of the freedpeople had none for the Indians they saw hanging around the outskirts of western towns: "revolting and degraded; greasy, diseased, naked, and covered with dirt of every imaginable kind, living on entrails and offal meat stolen or begged; their bright red and blue Government blankets worn at will [the] only redeeming or picturesque feature." Indians came in two forms, liberal Republican editor Samuel Bowles commented, the "unmitigated rascal" and the "vagabond."[36]

The Chinese inspired not just contempt but fear. Immigration had begun before the California gold rush (and not even primarily to America: four times as many headed to Java as across the Pacific). It surged in the 1850s, spreading out from California through the Rocky Mountains. Nearly half of the 65,000 who came were sojourners, intending to make money and return home. They were overwhelmingly men, leaving family and culture behind, not the stereotyped dirt-poor "coolies," but immigrants from the more westernized Guangdong Province near the coast. Some paid their passage, others came under contract, bound to their employer for five years at seven dollars a month in wages.[37]

"Pacific Chivalry." Thomas Nast, *Harper's Weekly*, August 7, 1869.

That labor built California and in the postwar period, much of the mountain and desert west, the more so after the Burlingame Treaty in 1868 allowed unrestricted Chinese immigration, a step that found strong support among eastern Republicans, still glowing with the postwar optimism that America could thrive as a nation of nations. Seventeen thousand Chinese worked the mines by 1870. They rode herd on cattle ranches in the great valley and took twenty dollars a month for seasonal labor harvesting the wheat. San Francisco cigars might have a Cuban label, but Chinese hands rolled the tobacco. Gangs of twelve to twenty men toiled to build the transcontinental railroad: 15,000 in all by war's end. Their stone-cutting techniques cut the line's way through the Sierras, and their masonry laid the stone culverts all the way up Donner Pass. Where sheer rock faces gave no ledge for the tracks to run, the Chinese built one 1,400 feet above the Truckee River by lowering their comrades down from above in baskets on ropes, with hammer and chisel. Twelve hundred laborers died before the road was completed and had their bones shipped home.[38]

At no time, though, did white settlers appreciate the intruders in their midst, and western Democrats saw them as even more menacing than their southern allies did the blacks, though for opposite reasons: not that they would amalgamate with white society but that they would create a society all their own. In smearing Republicans as the party of "Chinese, Niggers, and Diggers," Democrats found a winning issue. California Supreme Court decisions before the war ruled that Chinese could not testify against white men in court, because they were Indians and the law forbade Indian testimony, and because they were congenital liars whose word could not be relied on. Agitators everywhere warned laborers that Chinese would take the very bread out of their mouths by working starvation wages. Workingmen's organizations called for boycotts on Chinese cigar-makers and refused to admit them as union members. State laws shut the public schools to Chinese children or made their attendance contingent on white parents' consent, restricted hiring on the public works to white residents, levied prohibitive taxes on Chinese laundries and foreigners engaged in mining or fishing, and required officials to shave off the queues of Chinese under arrest. An 1871 race riot in Los Angeles ended in the sacking of the Chinese community and the massacre of twenty Chinese. By 1876, the apocalyptic rhetoric of the Civil War era had been shifted to this new, apparent threat. "An irrepressible conflict between the Chinese and ours has already been initiated," California's governor warned. Long before then, Republican platforms west of the Mississippi had made clear that whatever commitment to universal suffrage the party had, it did not include Chinamen, any more than it did Indians. In 1875, a Republican Congress passed the Page Act, limiting Chinese immigration. Ostensibly a barrier against contract laborers and prostitutes, it worked in practice against admitting Chinese women, wives included.[39]

The reconstruction of the West, then, had revealing similarities to that in the South. More than that, it may have had crucial importance in undermining Radical Republicans' chances in the Confederate states. For one thing, Grant's "Peace policy" never delivered peace—except for those earning an eternal peace, like Black Kettle or General E. R. S. Canby. The West required a constant military presence, because western settlers, like southern Republicans, found themselves unable to protect themselves. As Congress cut back on the army, resources had to be stretched further, but always the army's first priority carried it where an open war put people in harm's way. Intimidation, threats against potential voters, even floggings and a few shootings by persons unknown in the South had none of the shock value or, after 1874, the headline-producing value of a smoldering homesteader's cabin and a fresh crop of scalps on a Comanche's belt. "During the very last year twenty-seven citizens of this State were butchered, within the State, by savages who had no shadow of right to be upon our soil, but who had roamed from their reservations in defiance of the authority of the Government," Kansas's governor wrote the president in 1875. "Since Kansas became a State considerably more than three hundred thousand dollars has been expended in defending the people against Indian hostilities, an indebtedness of about forty thousand dollars having been incurred during the last year. . . . In Texas the loss of life and property has been vastly greater than in Kansas."[40] Every soldier demanded for the frontier stripped the government of resources that Republican governments in the Gulf states needed desperately; there could never be manpower enough to safeguard the polls outside of the major cities, and military force would fall far short, even there. Without an augmented force, then, the winning of the West meant the losing of the South.[41]

As with manpower, so with money. The West afforded too promising a vista for investors, and always it vied with the South for funds. Southern cotton kept many railroads busy, but its growth in worldwide demand was nowhere near as tremendous as the growth in demand for wheat and corn. In an area developing rapidly, with growing consumer markets and with far more customers able to pay, the West afforded a much better prospect of railroad enterprises turning an early profit. In 1873, New England railroads earned more than a 6 percent return on investment, and those in the middle states nearly as much, but lines on the plains made 2.25 percent. The southern rate was 0.4 percent. As a result, investment pushed western railroads on at a swifter pace and, unlike southern securities, bought western ones at face value. Between 1865 and 1873, the South added nearly 8,000 miles of track. The plains states and territories added nearly 21,000. An infusion of eastern funds of the same magnitude as went west might have given the gospel of prosperity a fighting chance of succeeding and, with it, the kind of diversified economy that eventually might have broken cotton's control.[42]

For a genuine New South of a Republican cast to develop, the Confederate states needed a heavy infusion of newcomers. But immigrants failed to come. Nebraska probably had more "carpetbaggers" than the eleven seceded states put together. For that failure, there were plenty of reasons. People moving to better themselves may have been deterred by the white violence and disorder or the presence of a large black population. They also may have gone where the railroads would take them, and by 1872 nearly every trunk line ran east to west, tying northeastern ports to the prairies. But the West also simply had so much more to offer. The South had nothing to compare with the Comstock Lode, the rich silver and gold deposits on the eastern sides of the Sierras. There was silver to be found at Cripple Creek, Colorado, and copper deposits elsewhere. The West was a bulging storehouse. The timber industry was moving from Wisconsin and Michigan toward the Pacific coast, finding an almost unlimited supply of lumber, inconceivable in size and abundance.

What, by contrast did the South have to offer? No Chicago, Minneapolis, Denver, Omaha, or San Francisco with a wide array of occupations crying out for labor. Thanks to railroad connections, Atlanta, Nashville, and Birmingham throve. The other top cities held their own or stagnated as regional centers, entrepôts for cotton, rice, sugar, and rice to find a foreign market. Upcountry towns became gathering centers for cotton that might have gone to the ports. Texas cattle might not head east by way of St. Louis, but Texas cotton did—to New Orleans' cost.[43] The southern economies remained ones dependent on farming, and the only big money was to be found in large-scale production of cash crops. Start-up costs were far greater than in Iowa or Minnesota. Suitable land was more expensive and less fertile than the West could promise, even if southern landholders were willing to part with it. And with what return? Republican rhetoric had made much of how well free labor would redeem a wasted land. But after the war, the promised returns simply did not come. Southern agriculture recovered. It had only the faintest boom. The promised efficiency that northern travelers foresaw, northern planters now found was mythological.

For those unable to buy, taking employment on a plantation seemed the worst idea of all. It was a plain fact that the western workforce had wider scope than those of the Cotton Kingdom. It was far more mobile, for one thing. A miner, logger, or harvest hand might work for a season and then when the lumber camp closed down or the crops were in would move on for work elsewhere. Employers knew that they could not count on laborers staying. That made wages more competitive. Footloose bindle stiffs had some room to negotiate and a landscape in which to look for other opportunities. For the southern tenant farmer with a family to take care of, no such wide options existed. The escape from a bare subsistence was that much more difficult. Nor did the South have new, virgin, fresh land in abundance. A Southern Homestead Act was a tremendous disappointment, particularly for the freedmen, in large part because the former Confederate states simply did not have prime acreage left free of legal title for homesteaders to file for. That suspicion had underlain the appeal for confiscation: lands worth having the planters owned already.[44]

Separated from all demonstrable fact, the frontier always had assumed a mythological importance. It was the place of promise, of new beginnings, and a place where anyone could strike it rich, where individualism could have its fullest play. That mythology only strengthened in the years after the war. From the West, mass-circulation newspapers published an endless stream of inviting pabulum, the promotional literature of the railroads, the golden perspectives of town boosters, each of whom knew his Gopher Prairie destined to outshine Chicago. From the South, reporters sent back a dispiriting account of trouble, chaos, and corruption, where politics seemed to be the only paying profession. For immigrants, foreign and domestic, then, the South was not the destination of choice; the West was.[45] But that influx of northerners, with Yankee notions, Yankee ideas, and Yankee capital, southern Republicans could not do without, if the South was to be made again. It could not be made by those dwelling there already and living on the margins of failure, white or black. Without that influx, the South would stay as it was, with no reinforcements to a viewpoint that looked to a section freed from the cultural and social preconceptions of its past.

Southern Republican governments tried. They set up bureaus of immigration. They gave tax breaks to companies developing the South. They, like the West, were in the business of promotion. But against the West they could not compete. The West was the land of the future; the South, the land of tradition, of the past. And that past hampered, limited its possibilities, in the way that the new country west of the Missouri did not. Small wonder that southerners, too, bought into that myth of the West. By the 1870s, their ambitions were directed toward a transcontinental line of their own. They would do anything for it. Jay Cooke's Northern Pacific Railroad briefly turned Duluth into a household word and found purchasers for its securities among widows and clergymen, deluded into thinking that the banking house that so successfully marketed U.S. "5–20" bonds in wartime could never touch anything without it turning into gold. Why should not a similar road to Los Angeles or San Diego restore New Orleans to its glory days when cotton had been king? So southern politicians crowded behind General John C. Fremont's rickety Memphis, El Paso & Pacific scheme and then held conventions to lobby for government aid to the Texas & Pacific, the project backed by the most powerful railroad magnate in the middle states, Tom Scott. In 1871, Congress obliged Scott's road with a land grant, the last big giveaway.[46]

In other ways, directly and indirectly, American expansion weakened any argument for Reconstruction based on "the fatherhood of God and the brotherhood of man." For one thing, to most of the new settlers, the problems of North and South felt relatively remote, and on the Pacific coast, almost alien. Reconstruction's travails filtered through their four-page papers was far from the front-page material that Modoc raids or Arizona's great diamond hoax of 1872 was. Editors could not afford the roving correspondents exposing carpetbagger enormities that their eastern counterparts could. Appeals to the outrages and heroics of the Civil War and Negro rule took on a thin, piping, artificial quality in territories without a competitive party system, or even much semblance of organized parties at all. Western politics, to a much more consuming degree, was the politics of economic development. Members might vote the party line in Congress, but they cared more for money to dredge their rivers and funding to build railroad connections. The West lost interest in the South early and was ready to change the topic from 1867 on. Westerners might lean more strongly toward woman suffrage than easterners, but racial equality for nonwhites, unfreighted with the Civil War experience, was a losing cause.

Finally, the West's integration into national markets and its interconnection with the Northeast, financial and political, may have had a long-term effect on Republicans' commitment to maintaining a two-party South. In 1870, a "solid South" would have needed just a few Democratic states up north to command the electoral college. But every new state admitted in the West had a better than even chance of going Republican, and the territories, settled as rapidly as they were by nonsoutherners, promised to put that prospect further out of reach. Republicans' share of the House was sure to grow. What did a single congressman-at-large from Kansas matter? But in 1870 the state delegation increased to three, in 1880 to six, in 1890 to nine. Other areas grew thanks to the western commerce, and they were primarily northern and Republican. Being cheated out of southern states might still rankle party leaders. But more urgency rides on preventing a loss that cannot be made up than one that can. In the backs of their minds, then, it is quite possible that the West drained the East not just of investment capital but of political will. And without that will, Reconstruction could not long prevail.

CHAPTER NINE

Passage to India?

L ooking at the postwar years, expansionism seems like the dog in the Sherlock Holmes story, most noticeable in the barking it failed to do—if not in the bites it failed to take. The Civil War, in fact, worked two ways. Never had American power been so strengthened, nor its apparent potential for expansion been so plain. But because of its costs and sacrifices, never had the constraints against actually doing anything been so compelling: financial, military, and political. Race and Reconstruction played a large part in adding to the distaste Americans felt for new annexations, but they were not the only force, nor indeed the most important.[1]

That the Union came out of the war convinced as never before that the nation was made to last, that it had a destiny in the world, was understandable. The oldest republic on earth, it had emerged, political institutions intact, with the most divisive forces, slavery and state sovereignty, quelled or vanquished for good. Some Confederates took only despair from the outcome. A handful even headed for Brazil, where they proposed to keep on practicing slavery unimpeded, and many others talked of migrating to Central America, though most of them never got around to doing it. A few Confederate leaders skipped the Atlantic and even after the price was taken off their heads, chose not to come back. Judah P. Benjamin made a profitable career for himself as a lawyer in London, and one of the giant soldiers in Lee's army, Johann Heros von Borcke, returned to his native Prussia, though he flew the Rebel flag on his estate for the rest of his life and christened his daughter Virginia.[2] But for most Americans, the war reaffirmed their belief that theirs was a nation of unlimited potential. "The progress of the liberal cause, not in England alone, but all over the world, is, in a measure, in our hands," Charles Francis Adams, minister to the court of St. James, wrote in 1865. America's aim, former general Nathaniel Banks announced in 1866, was "to be the grand disturber of the right divine of kings, the model of struggling nations, the best hope of the independence of states and of national liberty."[3]

So any event in the world that could be associated with freedom, Americans traced back to their own example and their own struggle. Who could doubt that the failure of democracy in America would have thrown an irretrievable damper over efforts to widen it in England? Parliament's passage in 1867 of the Second Reform Act owed some debt to those who gave America its new birth of freedom. Onlookers could hardly help seeing the consolidation of German states into the Second Reich as analogous to their own struggle for Union, and in its new fundamental law, glimpsed similarities deeper than the differences. A centralized government held in check by its component kingdoms—how far did 1871 echo 1787! Historian George Bancroft predicted that the new Germany would be "the most liberal government on the continent of Europe" and credited its creation to the Union's triumph in the Civil War. "Our victory in that strife sowed the seeds of the regeneration of Europe," which made the Second Reich "the child of America."[4] In his defiance of papal authority and war to dismantle Catholics' privileged place in the new nation, Chancellor Otto von Bismarck only reaffirmed America's sense of his as a kindred spirit, and may have inspired Republicans in their own denunciations of the church's power and ambitions here.

Even before the war ended, some nationalists were prepared for the next, if need be: to roust out the French invader from the other side of the Rio Grande. France's emperor, Napoleon III, had taken advantage of Americans fighting Americans to land an army in Mexico, overturn the republic, and place the Hapsburg prince Maximilian on the throne. Americans warned that they would not allow the Monroe Doctrine to be so violated and understood that France's success would embolden European nations to try more of the same. Some patriots rattled the sabers of war. They even suggested that sharing in such a war might be the incentive to make the Confederacy of its own free will rejoin the Union. A robust nationalist foreign policy, Democrats thought, would only add luster and consistency to Andrew Johnson's Unionist credentials in setting southern affairs to rights. For Montgomery Blair, no longer a cabinet member and losing his hopes of going on the Supreme Court, Mexico made the perfect issue for discrediting a less bellicose secretary of state, driving a wedge between him and his president, and maybe forcing him out. He was all for making war to fling Maximilian back across the Atlantic.[5] In the end, no missions bearing ultimatums went into Mexico. But with an American army on the Texas border and with Grant's military reputation at its peak just after the war, nothing more was needed. Aid and arms were shipped across the border. By early

1867, the pressure and the probability of American action had helped convince the French empire to withdraw its soldiery. With its foreign props removed, the puppet regime collapsed, and Maximilian went before a firing squad and into the immortality of a Édouard Manet painting.[6] When, three years later, the French emperor himself took on the German states, Americans had no doubt of the aggressor, cheered the advance of Prussian arms, and welcomed his downfall as a fate long deserved.

America's Mexican success, though, showed not just the nation's strength but the limitations to how it could be applied. There was no serious prospect of the country going to war on Mexico's behalf; even the most aggressive spoke only of restoring the nation's independence, not annexation. Blair himself thought of cutting out a slice along the Rio Grande, into which blacks could be deported, solving the Reconstruction problem, but he found no takers, even in the Confederate South.[7]

Much the same could be said for the two greatest acquisitions of Andrew Johnson's administration. Midway Island became an American possession, not by conquest, but by default. Discovered and claimed just before the war, the uninhabited 2.6-square-mile atoll had nothing anybody could want. A private attempt to dig a harbor for a coaling station ended in fiasco. Even the ship evacuating settlers ran aground. Alaska seemed more promising, more for seals than mineral wealth, but when the Russian government offered it for sale, Secretary of State William Seward found it an irresistible bargain, both to accommodate one of the few European powers supporting the United States in the Civil War and to keep it out of other hands. Congress had deep misgivings about taking Alaska, even as a gift, much less for the $7.2 million price tag. The press quickly dubbed it "Seward's icebox" and "Walrussia," one humorist suggested that the only thing making it an appealing purchase would be if the whole Blair family could be sent there and kept from coming back, and General Sherman snapped, "Give 'em seven millions more to take it back, and be thankful to get off so cheap." Without the support of leading radicals, Charles Sumner in the Senate and Thaddeus Stevens in the House, the secretary would have had no chance at all.[8]

Visions of an American empire withstood even the near collapse of the republic. The same passion for expansion that had spread the flag across a continent by war and treaty had not dimmed much in the late 1850s. It had simply run afoul of the slavery issue. The strongest expansionists came from the South, and their eyes were set toward the Caribbean basin. Filibustering expeditions, armed and manned by proslavery southerners, set

"The Big Thing." Thomas Nast, *Harper's Weekly*, April 20, 1867. Secretary of State William Seward salves the Andy Johnson bump on Uncle Sam's head. The national personification had yet to grow a beard—another contribution (at least in part) from Thomas Nast.

out to overthrow the existing governments in Cuba and Nicaragua. William Walker's foray onto the Mosquito Coast had ended before a firing squad but with a martyr's death, while General John Quitman's political success in Mississippi owed much to his share in adventures to open new lands in the tropics into which slavery might spread. That vision remained among the secessionists, imagining a warm-water destiny for themselves, rich and strange.[9]

Northern Democrats saw the same vistas and more besides: a surge northward into the various provinces united only by their allegiance to the British crown. Had Douglas become president in 1860, talk of America's Manifest Destiny might have been revived, the ideal distraction from the Union's internal broils. Among former Whigs, expansionism took on a more muted form. They had no taste for wars of conquest, and they feared any advance too large for the country's institutions and values to absorb. Many of them in both sections had thought the annexation of Texas and the Mexican cession not so much a step too far as a step too fast, too soon. For the sake of party unity, but also from a recognition of the perils involved, they had urged that the war with Mexico end without acquiring new territory, free or slave. But the robust nationalism, the faith in the good possibilities of a stronger national state, and the belief in the excellence of American values made them just as convinced that what was good for the United States would be good for its neighbors, in or out of the Union. Committed to government programs fostering prosperity at home, they shared a faith that the more markets opened up for American produce abroad, the better for farmers growing more grain and cotton than they could sell at home.

Secretary of State William Seward shared that faith, and then some. Early in 1861, it had been his idea of provoking a war with Spain and perhaps Britain, over the liberation or annexation of Cuba, as a means of rousing the patriotism that he was sure lay dormant in the seceded states back into the Union.[10] With the fighting over, the secretary had his chance to make a shining record in foreign policy. In the age of steam, any world power would need coaling stations across the oceans to make a credible presence, but Seward wanted more than a constellation of friendly ports. His vision may have reached its clearest articulation in Andrew Johnson's last annual message. The president may have declared, "Comprehensive national policy would seem to sanction the acquisition and incorporation into our Federal Union of the several adjacent continental and insular communities," but the words were Seward's. At various times, the secretary had shown an interest in a wide array of acquisitions. At his behest, former secretary of the Treasury Robert J. Walker journeyed to Montreal to feel out Canadians' interest in joining the Union; Walker, who handled the lobby for carrying the Alaska purchase appropriation through the House, had a continental vision with a longer pedigree than Seward's. Always a bargain hunter and something of a compulsive shopper, the secretary talked about bringing the Fiji Islands into the Union (as compensation for three American sailors unfortunately eaten by the king's subjects)—or Samoa—or Hawaii. Seward even toyed with seeking a naval base in Borneo. He negotiated with the Danish government to buy their West Indies possessions. His eyes strayed to Samana Bay, in Santo Domingo, as a good place for a naval base and colonial installation. And always he kept alive the idea of joining the seas with a canal through the narrows of Central America.[11] Put together, all of these ideas seemed to have the comprehensive quality of a man of vision. But Seward never did put them together, and separately they simply looked like the fantasies of a man *with* visions.

Others felt as Seward did, including Nathaniel P. Banks, head of the House Foreign Relations Committee. As a congressman from a factory city with a large Irish constituency, he had mastered the art of twisting the British lion's tail and letting the spread eagle scream. Declaring the country meant "to hold . . . liberty in trust for all mankind," "to enlighten and civilize the rest of the world," he longed to see the United States plant its flag on Hispaniola, in Cuba, and Canada. His eloquence "lifted us out of the passions . . . of the hour, and linked the Great Republic's destiny with the ever-widening progress of humanity," said a labor newspaper admiringly. From Senator Zachariah Chandler of Michigan came crowd pleasers, "a half-and-half of eloquence and gin," to send listeners "soaring on the cheapest calico variety of the American eagle." The same passion could be found stirring Grant's secretary of state, Hamilton Fish, although in a more understated fashion. He, too, believed that by the "inexorable logic of events," some areas, Cuba among them, "ought to belong to the great family of the American republics." Nor did he object to a republic spreading from the Arctic Circle to the Rio Grande, if not farther.[12]

But the expansionists in both parties were a dimming generation and, among Republicans, had always been out of step with most of their colleagues, trained to connect slavery and Manifest Destiny too closely to find any liking for landgrab schemes. Banks, Seward, and Fish had reached the top rank in politics before the war. They had been formed by a party system long since gone and by experiences with Manifest Destiny increasingly strange to a new generation, many millions of whom had come from overseas themselves. Talk as they would, in the end, little expansion was completed even by Seward. Most of his treaties went unratified. For his proposed agreements with Nicaragua and Colombia, permitting American companies to build a transoceanic canal, there was no chance of ratification. A reciprocity treaty with Hawaii "on the most satisfactory terms" and looking toward ultimate annexation failed in the Senate in 1867. A treaty to buy the Danish West Indies met the same fate. Just calling a design "one of Mr. Seward's projects" roused half the world to suspect something wrong with it, an editor complained.[13]

Secretary of State Hamilton Fish did not even do as well as Seward. A treaty to build a Nicaragua canal lost in the Senate in 1870. Another with Colombia did not even come to a vote. Nor did an agreement for a naval base in St. Thomas. Two years later, negotiations to annex Samoa failed. Congress expressed no interest in buying a protuberance of land in the South Pacific, "7,200 miles from anywhere." Former Union general William S. Rosecrans's scheme to have government aid in building railroads from the Gulf into the Mexican interior as the first step in taking over the country met a cool reception from the White House and the reminder that the government had no money to spare, as long as it had so large a war debt to pay off—and that answer came fourteen months after Rosecrans sent his letter.[14] America's bounds were the same when Grant left office as when he came into it.

Manifest Destiny still had its tub-thumpers, of course. The *New York Herald* declared that American trade could not do without sheltered markets in the Caribbean. "It is an undoubted truth that we require a good part of the West Indies," its editors declared. "Our interests are the interests of civilization, and therefore no little revolutionary body of mongrels should be allowed to stand in the way of those interests." For good measure, the *Herald* insisted on taking Panama and Mexico, both of which fate had decreed as part of one civilization. They should be invited to join the Union. And if they refused? "Then—the bayonet." That kind of vaunting triumphalism so common in the 1840s, however, looked increasingly eccentric in Reconstruction America. Part of the reason was a matter of rhetorical style. The blatherskites that had offended a young Charles Dickens and made their way into his novel *Martin Chuzzlewit* no longer barged their way to fore as they had in the 1840s. Dickens himself was cheered by the transformation he found, so much so that he told his publishers to add a permanent note to future editions of the book making amends to America. But the war itself could have played a big part. Heroics on a field against weaker neighbors like Mexico with victory all but guaranteed allowed Americans to exult in combat and to embellish real events with romance. Four years of fighting with an outcome uncertain and the painful rosters of the dead and missing left an entirely different impression. "God avert war!" one New Yorker wrote in a moment of crisis. "I have seen quite enough of war times to last me my life."[15]

Any expansionism, too, was sure to have a deeply sectional cast. If slavery's end made a spread of American institutions southward more thinkable to Republicans, it had much the opposite effect for southerners, white and black. Former slaveholders no longer had an institution needing fresh land to sustain it. A few reformers still talked about colonizing black people abroad, but among Republicans the idea had just about vanished. Those who had seen it as a trade-off, with masters voluntarily setting their slaves free in return for blacks consenting to settle in some tropic clime, no longer had anything to trade off, and the idea sparked no serious interest among former slaves. Never had their prospects for sharing in American life as equals seemed more promising. Those who had despaired that the country would never accept them as more than slaves in all but name now only had to look at the schools and churches they had built, and the plowed acres to which a small but growing fraction of the black southern population held title, to feel a renewed hope. The old idea that blacks naturally would move toward a warmer climate and gradually drain from the tobacco South into Central America, leaving a white man's country, no longer had many believers and had almost as few advocates.[16] In any case, southerners of both races had much too much on their minds in trying to restore a shattered country to pay attention to foreign adventures.

The war also put a tight leash on what any empire-builder could do. The country's real Manifest Destiny was to find the money to pay its national debt, not to contract a heavier debt for new acquisitions. All the government's impulses were toward retrenchment: lower taxes, tighter spending. Just buying new lands would add to the load on taxpayers' shoulders and make the day more distant when that burden could be lifted for good. "What the country now requires is repose," a Boston merchant wrote his congressman, "& a great reduction of taxation. We have no money to waste in acquiring more foreign territory, which would be a calamity to the country to have, even if we could obtain it for nothing."[17]

Retrenchment also meant that the tools so necessary for expansion, a robust army and navy, simply were not at hand. At the beginning of 1865, the United States had the second-largest fleet in the world. In some respects, it was also among the most technologically advanced. For the first time, even the British had to factor American sea power into its calculations. But, just as with the military or with the bureaucracy or taxing power, the navy was meant for the duration of the war, and meant to be dismantled the same way, as soon as the conflict ended. Indeed, as the last Confederate ports fell into Union hands, the dismantling got well under way. There no longer was need for a blockading fleet, and Secretary of the Navy Gideon Welles started recalling it the following winter. By the time Richmond fell, so had the Union's seagoing strength, by nearly half.[18]

The retreat was just begun. Parsimonious and with that old Democratic idea that a rich government was a dangerous one, well aware that the public wanted taxation cut as soon as possible and that the national debt alone was a sacred obligation, Welles retired most of the officers and sent most of the sailors home. He hardly could have done otherwise. Most of them, like most of the enlistees on land, were volunteers for the emergency and eager to return to civilian life. Like soldiers, they would have deserted, if not mustered out officially. With no enemy to fight, there was no need for an endless array of monitors to ply the rivers, nor for frigates to go after Confederate privateers on the oceans of the world. At most, the secretary envisioned a compact, modernized force, in quality the match for any foreign vessel afloat, but small enough for defense purposes.[19]

He could not even get that from the Congress. Every request he made was torn to ribbons in House and Senate. Reconstruction's asperities did Welles no good, and the southern situation meant that if any military force got priority, it would have to be the army. Even after Johnson left office, nothing much changed. It was not to General Grant's credit that his first secretary of the navy, Adolph Borie, had no administrative experience and left policy to Admiral David D. Porter. Wracked with migraines, he retired less than four months later. His successor, George M. Robeson, an obscure lawyer from Camden, New Jersey, knew more about patronage politics than about blue-water policy. For stocking the navy yard with good Republicans and making them pay assessments he could not have been bettered, and his loyalty to Grant was total. But for all his good nature and talent at giving supplicants the soft answer, when it came to getting what he wanted from Congress, he might as well have been Gideon Welles. Quite aware that the navy needed refurbishing and renewal, he made regular requests and was as regularly turned down. Democrats roared at the woeful mismanagement of the navy. They would do anything to change it—except give it money to launch "floating palaces." Between 1864 and 1882, the navy got what it wanted in one single year. Even then, its gains were modest ones indeed.[20]

So year by year, the navy fell into disarray and deepest dishevelment, its monitors soon outmoded, its frigates and sloops the ornament of many a dry dock. None of its ships was any match for passenger liners for speed. Their engines were long out of date, creaking, clanking, smoking things. The rifled guns could barely fire and had no trained gunners to fire them. Other countries' fleets advanced, not just in number but in their quality. In the postwar decade, technological innovation surged, as European designers found how to adapt steam and steel to the demands of a growing arms race between imperial powers. Coal set new requirements that wind-power never had had. All the while, American ships fell further behind. The country's most formidable armor-plated warship, the *Dictator*, had metal one inch thick; the HMS *Inflexible*'s was a foot through. By 1876, the Netherlands had seventeen ironclads, Turkey twenty-four, Brazil seventeen, Austria fourteen, Denmark eight, America none.[21]

With a navy unable to match any of a dozen powers, America found itself wholly unable to project its military force in any conflict that brought the risk of war. Nobody was afraid of the United States. Even some South American countries—Peru and Chile among them—had better, more modern fleets. Spain, the embodiment of backwardness and ineffectiveness, outstripped America, too.

One incident showed how far the constraints that war had set militated against another war. In 1873, a Spanish ship waylaid the *Virginius*, a gunrunner carrying the American flag in its smuggling of arms into the Cuban insurrection. The officer in charge had the crew shot. In America, there was a stir of outrage and some calls for retaliation, even war. Nothing of the kind happened. With an economic panic under way on Wall Street, a foreign broil would only make it worse. But war could not have broken out in any case because neither the army nor the navy was fit. Policymakers knew that there was much more danger of the Spanish fleet bombarding New York or Washington than there was chance of American frigates carrying a landing party ninety miles by water to invade Cuba. A Spanish warship, as it happened, lay within sight of Manhattan: in the Brooklyn navy yard waiting to be fitted with new armored plate. It was no immediate threat, even after completion. A coal barge had been sunk just at the end of the wharf—purely by chance, journalists were assured. But given the right circumstances, the ship could have put the whole shoreline in flames and with no American ship worth the name fit to stand in its way. As businessman

George Templeton Strong remarked, "A squadron of hostile ironclads anchored off the Battery and swarms of black Spanish spiders roaming up and down Broadway demanding your garlic or your life would be annoying."[22]

Besides, Americans already had an empire in its western domain, and it was taking more work to tame it than they had counted on. For those who wanted the glories and passions of armed conflict, there was more than enough of it to be found in the kind of raids that Lieutenant Colonel George Armstrong Custer was making, such as the one he carried out by dividing his forces and descending on unprepared and unwarlike Cheyenne pinned down by winter's blast at Washita Creek in 1868. For those keen to civilize the savage, opportunities enough could be found among the Piute and Piegan. Between needs west and south, there simply was no armed force to spare for more than a punitive expedition, if that, and certainly not enough for occupying a foreign country against its will. As long as that was so, any acquisitions would have to come with the full consent of those dwelling there already.

That narrowed the scope of action down considerably. Much of the talk of taking the various provinces of British North America was based on the idea that the French-speaking Canadians and the British Columbians wanted to be taken. Reportedly, they were almost inviting a seduction. Britain might consent as well, for it was generally understood that the scattered colonies north of the Great Lakes laid a serious financial burden on the mother country.[23] As for Alaska, part of its appeal was that its natives were few, unorganized, and not likely to resent transfer from one inattentive overlord to another.

Events, however, showed that all the American expectations were wrong. The Civil War was not the only force that brought some of the British colonies to join forces and create the Dominion of Canada in 1867. There were plenty of other reasons, just as there would be for plans to build a transcontinental railroad line of their own. But the creation of a more perfect, consolidated Union to their south certainly influenced Canadians. With one of the biggest armies in the world and certainly one better trained than anything inhabitants had fended off before, with American power so close at hand and British military forces so far afield and troubled with distractions on the Continent, safety lay in massing a strength of their own, and dissevered colonies were simply waiting to be picked off, one by one, by American expansionism. The acquisition of Alaska added to that sense of dread, because the Pacific coast, with all its remoteness, seemed the likeliest place where some sort of absorption would happen, and where the cries of "Fifty-four forty or fight" might start to be heard on the British side of the border. From Minnesota, migrants were pushing north into Manitoba and talking about annexation. So a Dominion became necessary, and so did a railroad and the transfer of the Hudson Bay Company's vast interior empire to Canadian control.[24]

If there had been much doubt about how unlikely the Canadian apple was to fall off the imperial tree without being plucked, three events made it clear: the Fenian invasions of 1866 and 1870 and Louis Riel's uprising on the prairies against the new Canadian authority in 1869–70. Organizing "circles" in every factory town and even among Idaho's miners, recruiting their paramilitary core from Union regiments, Fenians pledged themselves to set Ireland free by taking war to the British enemy wherever it was to be found—which meant Canada. They had strong support in the Irish American community in the United States and in the Democratic Party in general. Even Republicans felt sympathy for the troubles of Ireland and had hopes that it might achieve a sort of independence within the United Kingdom that states had within the United States. But the Fenian raids into Canada were crushed; the second was such a fiasco that not a single Canadian soldier was so much as wounded. Riel's uprising among the French-speaking Métis lasted out a winter, long enough to bring the Dominion government to terms on crucial demands like separate schools for Francophones and provincial self-government. The following summer, a British expedition arrived to assert national authority. Riel fled across the border into exile, to rise (and be hanged) another day. In neither case did the rebels find any official American support. On the contrary, the Johnson and Grant administrations put all the hindrance in their way they could.[25]

The likeliest way, then, of taking Canada, since revolution seemed out of the question, was to buy it, and, with the national debt what it was, the best way to buy it would have been with no money down. That, in effect, was Senator Charles Sumner's idea in 1869, when he rose to make a speech about the *Alabama* claims. The Confederate warship the *Alabama* had been built in English dockyards. Its damage to American shipping had been considerable, and its making, in Sumner's view and in those of most Americans, had been a serious breach of international law, a most un-neutral act. This "massive grievance," Sumner insisted, must be paid for. But that compensation need not be in money. Britain, instead, could release Canada instead.[26]

Sumner's address was polished, popular, and, as was often the case, completely out of touch with reality. Americans loved the speech. It also had the quiet approval of President Grant and may even have had more support from his secretary of state, Hamilton Fish, than he later let on. He too had aspirations northward. But in England, it provoked "a great tempest." Even Sumner's friends, and he had many in Britain, were appalled. The idea was unthinkable and insulting. As negotiations proceeded, the idea would be broached over and over, and by Fish among others, and it was rejected every time.[27]

It was significant, too, that Sumner himself had no idea of compelling it by war. He was not particularly disappointed when the final settlement did not include it. On the contrary, he saw in the 1871 Treaty of Washington that submitted the claims to international arbitration a step forward for America's moral power in the world, and for the rule of law. Two great powers had set up as a principle the idea that disagreements could be settled not by bluster or backstairs dealing but by an impartial court at which both could make their case and the results of which both would abide by. That the triumph was one that benefited the Grant administration and ranked as its most impressive foreign achievement may have tempered his enthusiasm a little, but only a little.[28]

The *Alabama* claims controversy had troubled Seward's tenure, too. It was made the harder because wartime resentments could not be forgiven easily. Northerners had stored up more wrath for Britain's course in the conflict and its lack of sympathy with the Union cause than could be dispelled all at once. Conspiracy theorists charged that Britain had spurred southerners to secede in the first place. When former Maryland senator Reverdy Johnson was sent to London to reach an understanding, his terms were dismissed almost before they were known, in part because he had expressed himself publicly in such friendly terms about his hosts.[29]

The Grant administration started off wrong-footedly and continued to blunder its way through. One might almost surmise that luck alone prevented the deadlock from turning into a conflict. There were a number of narrow escapes. Some took place even after the Treaty of Washington, and many were avoidable, particularly the insistence on "constructive damages," which threatened to hold Britain liable for the entire cost of the Civil War from Gettysburg on, an insistence made all the crazier because nobody in the administration dreamed of collecting a penny of it. (The Geneva tribunal of arbitrators dismissed that item on the bill right away and restricted its awards to the harm done by a handful of Confederate cruisers; the administration quickly declared itself wholly vindicated.)[30] That the demands went as far as they did attested to the animus against Britain and the prickly nature of any American acceptance of terms that the British would consider endurable. Far from discrediting Grant's administration, the flare-ups may have been the one way of persuading voters that the president had achieved the most possible and prepared them to accept the final settlement as an American triumph, not just the victory of diplomacy over force.[31]

War, however, was never really all that much of a threat, and not just because the greatest moment of danger came in the midst of an undeclared war down south against the freedmen that stretched military resources to the limit, or because of the pathetic condition of the American navy. Matters aside from diplomacy pushed things toward a peaceful settlement. Most of them had a connection, one way or the other, to the legacies of the Civil War. The national debt needed funding, and those funds must be borrowed from London. The great banker Jay Cooke's role in marketing national bonds depended largely on money markets abroad. Any breach with Britain would cut them off, bringing on a financial crisis, and at the height of the "constructive damages," top financiers of the Northeast—"[Levi] Morton, [Charles] Drexel, [George W.] Childs, [Henry] Clews and all that crowd" descended on Washington to help the Cookes and their "friends" lobby a compromise through. A break in relations would cut off the railroad investment from abroad that so many southern and western lands relied on. It would close the South's best cotton market, not to mention the Midwest's most promising customer for wheat. The cattle boom in Texas, too, owed itself to European demands for its beef, and some of the money invested in western ranching came from the other side of the Atlantic. Even under a protective tariff, the revenue from duties played an essential part in supporting the government, and more than before, now that the Civil War internal taxes were being dismantled; any war was sure to be a war on trade—American trade—for which the U.S. Navy stood woefully unprepared. For Britain, too, a settlement with America was more important than its precise terms because the United States had become a source for so many of its investors to place their money.[32]

An even more revealing case in the limits of American action came in Cuba. In 1868, another of those regular uprisings broke out. Other disturbances had been quelled swiftly, but this one turned into a civil war costing 50,000 Cuban lives (and nearly 150,000 Spanish ones) over the next ten years. Cities survived unscathed, and so did the sugar plantations in the western part of the island, but in the eastern uplands, the fighting was brutal from the first on both sides, and untouched with romance. One rebel general admitted to putting 650 prisoners to death in a single day.[33]

In such a situation, naturally, one might assume that the United States would have used the excuse to pose as liberators. There were from the start some spokesmen for intervention. Spain was, of all the European powers, the least attractive to America. It was doggedly Catholic and superstitious, with a near-absolute monarch tottering on a bankrupt's throne. The imagery of threadbare hidalgos, their temperament composed of half prejudice and half pride, the conjured-up historical memories of the Spanish Inquisition, the Armada, and the Black Legend of rapacious conquistadores, made Spain the object of contumely and contempt. Grant's first choice for secretary of war, John Rawlins, had particularly strong desires to help out Cuba and, with the president's ear, seemed likely to win out over the secretary of state. Congressmen also catered to the demand for "Cuba Libre."[34]

Nothing came of any of it. In the last stages of tuberculosis when he entered the Grant administration, Rawlins died that fall. No successor took up the cause, but the danger of intervention may never have been as strong as others feared, not as long as no peace settlement with Great Britain had been reached; war with one European power would only tempt the other to join in as well. By the time the *Alabama* claims were settled, the prospects of the Cubans being able to impose anything but anarchy on the island by their defeat of Spanish forces had gone glimmering. "Where is their government?" Charles Sumner asked. "Where are their ports? Where are their tribunals of justice? And where are their prize courts?" War was out of the question, and acquiring Cuba could happen no other way. So docile were lawmakers, the president remarked disgustedly, that if Spain sent a fleet to bombard Manhattan, the Senate might pass a resolution of regret that the aggressors had had to go to so much trouble and offering to pay them "for the expense of coming over and doing it." But, then, his secretary of state showed just as little inclination to push Spanish authorities too hard. Furiously, one critic wrote:

Scarcely beneath the stars and stripes
Beats there a heart so lost, so low,
That struggling Freedom's cause will fail
To fire with sympathetic glow.
Alas! could hope itself expect
More than Spain's myrmidons can wish,
When a misguided nation's pulse
Throbs through the cold heart of a Fish?[35]

The only form of expansionism with any chance, either in Congress or with the public, would be one of commercial expansion. Of course sponsors could see reciprocity treaties as a way of laying the groundwork for annexation later on. Countries that found their economies working in tandem would be that much likelier to see other interests in common eventually. So a treaty giving special advantages in Canadian exports could be an augury of things to come. So, too, both administrations thought of closer relations with Hawaii as opening the way to some more permanent arrangement. Some of those defending the treaties spoke in exactly such terms, as if American absorption were only a matter of time.

On the other hand, all those treaties drew widely because for many of their sponsors, they amounted to nothing more than they appeared, an effort to widen the prospects for more trade with the United States. They could not be sold any other way. In fact, most of them could not be sold at all. Hawaiian reciprocity failed over and over, before it found itself making a very hard passage. Had annexation been voiced louder, it would have killed any deal completely. Sarcastically, Mark Twain advised his countrymen to take Hawaii and pen its inhabitants on a reservation, "a sweet Arcadian retreat fenced in with soldiers." Already educated, guileless, and happy, they could be introduced to all the innovations of American civilization, he wrote: thieves "all the way from street-car pickpockets to municipal robbers and Government defaulters," juries filled with "simple and charming leatherheads," railroad corporations that would buy their legislature "like old clothes and run over their best citizens and complain of the corpses for smearing their unpleasant juice on the track." The assimilation of a brown-skinned people, tied neither by language nor orthodox religious practices to the mainland, was more than Democrats were likely to accept, and by 1876, they held the House. Only a fevered imagination could read imperial designs into proposed treaties on the farther shores of the Pacific. Americans came for their goods, not their good.[36] China and Japan stayed as occasional trading partners, while in Korea, a brief punitive expedition only proved the inadequacy of American military muscle beyond our shores.[37]

At least with trade treaties, the government had some direct involvement. Aware of how little support even these efforts had, the State Department counted on private parties to advance American interests. Seward gave verbal support to Western Union's project stringing telegraphic wires across Russia and the Orient. He did his best to interest the ironmonger Peter Cooper and the Vanderbilt clan in building a Panama Canal with private funds. Businessmen hoping for an entrée into foreign markets found in the secretary all the facilitation that some well-chosen words with consuls abroad could allow. Meantime, in Congress, steamship interests pressed for subsidies to establish merchant lines and postal service with Africa and the Antipodes. James Watson Webb, minister to Brazil, tried to win Seward's blessing to open a steamship line to Brazil. Again, though, there were limits in how far Seward would stick his neck out, even for an old friend like Webb. Government protection he would not give "beyond what is due of the strictest obligation."[38]

The reasons that expansionism failed, then, may have been, first, because policymakers never seriously tried; second, because they could not have succeeded, even if they had wanted to; third, because the Civil War, its memory and its consequences, had constrained the ability of America to flex much muscle beyond its shores; and, fourth, because Manifest Destiny had left a legacy, a West so vast that it would take what few resources the new nation could spare to subdue and amalgamate it. At the same time, foreign affairs could not be separated from the tensions arising from Reconstruction itself, and the fears that Reconstruction stirred shaped the way Americans saw foreign adventuring.

The most obvious of these complications was race itself. Nova Scotia might be attractive enough. As one editor explained, "We need their coal, their lumber, their fish, and the steadiness of their population." But Canada excepted, no new territory ripe for the taking had much white settlement, and the farther south it lay, the less likely it would be to attract any. Experience seemed to show that tropical climates were suited for darker-skinned folk and deadly for anyone else. But race was just part of the mix. The residents of Central America and the Caribbean islands, for the most part, could speak no English, had no experience with democratic traditions, and to a deplorable extent were steeped in superstition, which, for many Americans meant not just voodoo but Catholicism. Such a people were rated as unfit for freedom; conceivably, they never might be. Radical Republican though it was, Harper's Weekly had no interest in making citizens of Cubans, "a people wholly alien from us in principles, language, and traditions, a third of whom are barbarously ignorant."[39]

That is how Santo Domingo might be seen. In some ways, it should have been the ideal place for expansion. It was close to American shores; no other colonial power wanted it: President Buenaventura Baez had already tried selling his people out to France and Spain and found no takers. It could be acquired without war; indeed, taking it might well end the war already going on with the neighboring republic of Haiti. For those arguing in favor of uplift, no people could have gained more from an American takeover. Beyond all question the country had been governed with a mixture of stupidity, incompetence, and cruelty almost beyond the reputed capacities of even the Spanish authorities in Cuba. Its natural resources made it attractive in equal measure. If a coaling station or naval port commanding the entry to the Caribbean were wanted, few could find a better. Persuaded that it was "an island of unequaled fertility," covered "with the most valuable timbers known to commerce," with soil so rich that it could produce twice as much per acre as 'the best sugar lands of [Louisiana]" and with far less labor, President Grant imagined it as an Eden, free from the usual tropical diseases that lower-lying islands had. Farmers could raise tobacco, tropical fruits, coffee, and chocolate enough to supply the wants of fifty million consumers. With Santo Domingo in American hands, the sugar and coffee that Americans depended on would cost only half as much; and those goods would be raised by free labor, rather than by the slaves of Cuba and Brazil. The export duties that supported "slavery and Monarchy" could no longer be drawn from buyers in the United States, now that they had an alternative market, and without that revenue, "that hated system of enforced labor" would be wiped from the Western Hemisphere.[40] For Grant, the acquisition promised not just prestige but the chance to succeed where Seward had failed.

Grant did not get his treaty after all. Race certainly played some role in defeating his plans. Democrats and Liberal Republicans troubled by the racial tensions that Reconstruction had aggravated were wary of any annexation that would add still more black people. As Catholics and not speaking English, the new citizens were even more likely to be unassimilable than the ones already in the South allegedly were. All the stereotypes of lazy Negroes, ready for a handout, applied even more intensely to foreigners in the tropics, with their alleged knife-sticking habits, "a population ignorant, treacherous, brutalized and lazy," "incapable of rising above anarchy." In its own sleazy way, Santo Domingo was exotic, and exotic meant a foreignness in culture and habit that went with the climate and stood very little chance of being eradicated. The one image Santo Domingo had conjured up for three generations was that of slave insurrection, bloody and savage, unsparing of white women or children. Black-skinned additions to America as slaves were one thing, as far as white southerners were concerned, but as voters, quite another. With so few white inhabitants, Santo Domingo was surer to elect a solid delegation of nonwhite senators and congressmen than even South Carolina.[41]

All the same, the race question was not the only one involved, and it bolstered both sides of the argument. For Grant, Santo Domingo offered at least the possibility of an outlet for America's blacks, a place more suited to what he assumed was their natural preference for basking tropical warmth. There, too, they might escape the prejudice that clogged their efforts to advance at home. Santo Domingo might serve as a sort of safety valve: as black southerners migrated there to better their condition, southern white landowners, afraid of losing their labor supply, would stop mistreating and exploiting their own tenants. "The key to Southern reconstruction is the annexation of Santo Domingo," one old abolitionist predicted. Senate Foreign Relations chair Charles Sumner, on the other side, saw annexing Santo Domingo as an appetizer. Plant the American flag there, and the country would find excuses to absorb its neighbor Haiti, one of the few independent black states on earth.[42]

What made the Santo Domingo treaty even more controversial, though, were the ways in which it fit in with a growing concern at where Reconstruction was taking the country's institutions and values. The shenanigans of the lobby that Seward had employed to carry through an appropriation for Alaska had left a poisonous residue. It paid for friendly newspaper coverage, and dark rumors spoke of congressmen bought, including leading House members. Five million dollars of the purchase price, one fabulist alleged, had gone into lawmakers' pockets, and Seward himself, who loved a good story untainted by truth, claimed that a sizable packet of cash had been reserved for Thaddeus Stevens, who died before he could collect it.[43] By 1870, rumors talked of a Washington awash in Cuban bonds, issued by the revolutionaries, valueless until the island achieved independence but with a face value of $2 million. Secretary of War Rawlins had owned some. So, reportedly, did Grant's brother-in-law, who took off time from mismanaging the New Orleans customhouse to lobby for Cuban independence in Washington. One senator made so strongly an interventionist speech that reporters joked that he had written it on the backs of Cuban bonds. But he might have replied, as another sympathizer with the rebellion did, "There's a damned sight more Spanish gold than Cuban bonds in this matter" on the other side. Even where no proof existed, critics chose to believe the allegations. As the *Nation* warned, "No great purchase or annexation . . . can be made, in the present state of the art of peculation, without the Ring pocketing enormous profits."[44]

From very early, critics knew that behind the Santo Domingo proposal schemes, seedy or shady, must lie. Far more than in the case of Alaska, they were right. Annexation would prop up the power of a two-bit dictator and burgeon his bank account. Nobody was likely to consult the people of

Santo Domingo about the bartering away of their freedom. They were not likely to share in the purchase price. When, belatedly, Baez called a referendum, the voters, herded to the polls, were as coerced in their choice as any freedperson in the South was by his planter employer. The overwhelming majority for annexation was as trustworthy a measure of public opinion as the tainted returns from Georgia or Louisiana in 1868. Behind Baez lurked more sinister forces, William and Jane Cazneau and Joseph Warren Fabens, as full of schemes for getting rich as Colonel Mulberry Sellers in Twain and Warner's satirical novel *The Gilded Age*. Seemingly, the speculators never saw a gambit that they doubted would pay off. It usually did, too—in beggary and dead bodies. In one of his more harmless ventures, Fabens had imported eighteen camels, and had plans to bring in as many more, for transportation from the mines to settled towns. He had devised another project putting camels from Morocco onto on the Isthmus of Panama to take the place of mules; it had not worked well, or, at any rate the camels—those that did not perish right away—had not, but Fabens was able to take credit for a lively novel about it, which, in fact, Jane Cazneau had written. During the war, the Cazneaus and Fabens joined forces to create the American West India Company, which they hoped would cash in hugely for settling former slaves when Congress raised the funds for colonizing them in the tropics. The settlers came, but they could no more bring prosperity with them than they could fence surrounding strife out. A small band of survivors made it home again. In 1866, Cazneau was awarded a concession to bring immigrants in and settle them along the Haitian frontier, where the Dominican government hoped to make them a buffer against invasion. Between 40 and 200 families, mostly from New York and New England, came to starve, sicken, and die. The survivors ultimately made their way back to the United States on government charity. Cazneau and Fabens had not simply invested their time in Santo Domingo; they had put in their money and, with American help, expected to take still more out. Together, they claimed to own 10 percent of all the land in the country. They were heavily involved in mines and banks and shipping monopolies, largely obtained by sweetheart deals with President Baez.[45] The Cazneaus built wharves and warehouses in Samana Bay for New York merchants and steamship companies and sent letters to the *New York Sun* extolling the benefits of American investment there. They also showed a readiness to know the price of senators and an eagerness to raise the money to meet it. Or did the graft go higher? Wild tales circulated that administration figures shared in the loot, and that large tracts on the island were marked off with Grant and

Babcock's names on them. The harassment of an American businessman who stood in annexation's way and his wrongful imprisonment only confirmed what already was clear: that island of unequaled fertility made the perfect site for holding thieves' carnival.

There was another reason for misgivings about annexation, and it had to do with the domestic repercussions that empire was likely to have. The Constitution had not just been expanded over the past ten years; it had been stretched. Under Lincoln and Johnson, Republicans had seen an overweening executive assuming powers not inherent in the office. Those with a Whig background especially had qualms about presidents setting the agenda, and particularly about unelected figures, the so-called Kitchen Cabinet, making policy. That reason turned the words "my policy" into a shorthanded insult for Andrew Johnson's outlook. As has already been noted, constitutional scholars still emphasized that the country's peacetime direction should be left to Congress, with most initiatives from the executive branch confined to his cabinet officers' recommendations in their annual reports. Grant himself shared some of these reservations about executive leadership. His comparative inactivity as president was meant in contrast to Johnson's persistent interference with matters that Congress considered its own. Any doubts he had about the legislative branch's sense of its own privileges bitter experience erased when the Senate blocked his choice of Alexander T. Stewart for secretary of the Treasury and declined to repeal the Tenure of Office Act entirely. The following winter, the Senate again had shown its uncooperativeness by rejecting his nominee for the Supreme Court, Attorney General Ebenezer Rockwood Hoar.[46]

Under the circumstances, the treaty and the way it was made looked particularly unsettling. It had been negotiated by Orville E. Babcock, the president's secretary, and without any authorization. There had been no consultation about the terms beforehand with the secretary of state. As the struggle for ratification proceeded, the president's direct influence became more marked. In March 1870, he showed up at the Capitol, took over a room, and began summoning senators to give orders and make appeals, a direct use of presidential authority unprecedented. He was ready to make promises to some and relay threats to others, a level of involvement markedly unlike his relative detachment where Reconstruction legislation was concerned. Babcock boasted that Grant's "friends will be provided for at the expense of his enemies (friends). He will strike high and low."[47] So he did—mostly low. For those liberals who had seen in Grant a possible champion of civil service reform, June was the cruelest month. Everywhere there was talk of trades and bargains, of offices handed out and officers removed to carry the votes of a few more senators. The worst shock came when Attorney General Ebenezer Rockwood Hoar, the epitome of probity and the nemesis of spoilsmen, was forced to retire, to make room for an obscure Georgia scalawag, Amos Akerman. Akerman's plain manners and commitment to protecting a full, free vote down south only discredited him with reformers still further. For those hoping to return to the old constitutional means of running the government, this office-brokering was disturbing enough.

But its aftermath was even more worrisome. The treaty may have been dead, but Grant simply would not take Congress's decision as final. On the contrary, he instituted reprisals. Sumner's friend John Lothrop Motley, minister to Britain, may have deserved recall a year before, when he exceeded his instructions, but there was no pretense about his standing in the way of negotiations in the *Alabama* claims to justify his dismissal now. Grant meant it as a slap at Sumner. That winter, the secretary of state chose the president's side aggressively, picking a quarrel with the senator by releasing a misleading version of Motley's humiliation. At the same time, Grant's renewed call for steps that seemed to be leading toward annexation reopened the split between the treaty's opponents and the administration still further. Making public the president's use of the navy to threaten and overawe Haiti, warning that the president's policy invited America into a "dance of blood," Sumner saw a presidential bid for power. In his imagination, Grant transformed into a would-be Caesar, with "political jockeys" like Babcock acting as diplomats without portfolio and styling themselves "aides-de-camp," and with money shoveled out of the Secret Service fund and American gunboats enforcing agreements that the Senate had refused to ratify. Nor did he fail to notice that a president, still so cautious about sending military protection to freedpeople in the South, sent it readily and unlawfully to prop up a dictator who treated his country as a piece of private real estate that he could sell on whatever terms he liked before steaming off to lavish his gains on the allures of Paris.[48]

No event reinforced this sense of a very personal presidency, active, aggressive, and menacing, more disturbingly than the opening of the Forty-Second Congress in March 1871. There, Grant and Fish twisted every arm to do the unthinkable: to depose Sumner as chairman of Foreign Relations. All kinds of specious reasons were offered, of course. Fish let it be known that Sumner had held up a number of vital treaties—none of which were vital and none of which had been held up—and did his best to convince the

Senate that his irresponsible vaporings about the *Alabama* claims risked war with Britain. To the old political manager Thurlow Weed he confided that Sumner had asserted "that no settlement with Great Britain, and no determination on the foreign affairs of the country, shall be made by Grant's Administration." This was quite untrue, as Fish had reason to know. He was not really afraid of Sumner's opposition to peace with England, nor alarmed at the deterioration in their personal relations, to which he had himself contributed so much and with a full awareness of the consequences. But there was another, larger dividend from making war on the senior senator from Massachusetts. In two years of constant struggle with the president, Fish had had to fight to control any aspect of foreign policy. He had been forced to make concessions on Santo Domingo annexation, on diplomatic appointments, and dismissals. But by pressing the war on Sumner, he was taking up Grant's own fight. He could strengthen his influence with the president and his own prospects of having a free hand in diplomacy. The fact that Sumner could be cast as a belligerent figure in the *Alabama* claims controversy would be just what it took to commit Grant to the other side, in favor of peace. It also would make the British negotiators that much more likely to come to terms, aware that if Fish retired, his successor might be nowhere near as friendly. And, finally, as long as Sumner remained "grand Panjandrum, . . . little button and all," as Henry Adams called him, the Senate, not the State Department, would have the final say on foreign affairs.[49]

When the Republican caucus met, the administration had its way, and largely because the southern senators, most dependent on support from Washington, voted as they were told. On the Senate floor, the list of committee assignments set off an angry debate. Sumner's replacement with Simon Cameron only reinforced the feeling among those most disaffected from the administration that the party they had known had changed beyond retrieval, and for the worse. Cameron was a notorious spoilsman and even more notoriously corrupt; one newspaper warned that, given half the chance, he would "steal the whole of Santo Domingo" for himself, "not leaving a single lot to our worthy Executive." His short career as Lincoln's secretary of war had shown him unfit in the most versatile of ways. His Pennsylvania machine had one of the worst reputations anywhere. To elevate him and degrade the greatest of the living Republican leaders from before the war showed plainly an administration fallen into deep waters. Sumner's critics explained that the senator refused to deal with the secretary of state; it turned out that what they meant was that Sumner had broken off social intercourse with Fish, and at a banquet had failed to respond to a question put to him—apparently about whether to try the partridge or the duck. If these were grounds enough for unseating a chairman, a Delaware senator suggested, perhaps the Foreign Relations Committee should change its name to "the Committee of Personal Relations."[50]

Military weakness, financial constraints, shabbiness, corruption, strong-arm tactics, and loose construction of the law: it all seemed so dreadfully familiar. In the administration's assertiveness, its ready use of the armed forces for whatever the president pleased, others leagued on this one issue with Sumner, saw that same disregard for law and tradition that troubled them about Radical Reconstruction. That fear of centralization, clearly, grew out of ground already well prepared. Radicals had seen it in Andrew Johnson, conservatives in the Thirty-Ninth Congress imposing terms on southern states and in its successor forcing impartial suffrage on the North through a constitutional amendment. But Santo Domingo only fastened that image on Grant's presidency.[51] When he was prepared to use gunboats on his brother-in-law Collector of the Port James Casey's behalf in a factional dispute in Louisiana, when he asked for expanded powers to deal with terrorism in the South and lobbied hard to get them in March 1871, that dread of tyranny reawakened. Some of it was manufactured, to be sure. Democrats had become professional alarmists, turning every debate on a Reconstruction issue into a prolonged wake for "the Farmers' republic" and the good old days when every southern white man enjoyed his right to play the despot where his human property was concerned. But that did not make the fears entirely false, and their opposition drove up the political costs of any federal intervention on freedpeople's behalf. Reconstruction, then, did not stop at the water's edge. The Union men of the South would share in the dance of blood.

CHAPTER TEN

On Every Putrid Spot

For many Americans, the Civil War's end promised a second chance not just on the issue of human freedom but on that of fulfilling the highest purposes of the human spirit. For a host of reform causes, bliss was it in that dawn to be alive. "The dispensation is over, the new era begun!" Horace Greeley wrote in the *Tribune*. "A new world is born!" (Ironically, the editorial appeared on April 14, 1865, the morning before Lincoln was assassinated.) The fervent, transformative spirit that had made the age of sectional conflict a great age of reform had been deflected by the slavery issue, and protectors of slavery had done their best to clamp down on every other "-ism" within the South's confines, lest loosening one tradition unsettle the tradition of total control over human property, and challenging one institution undermine the stability of the great "peculiar institution." But with slavery gone, with the issue itself removed, what might not be possible?[1]

That confidence came in part because the war had taught how effective government power could be, and how reliably it could be entrusted to those in charge. After its workout suppressing the Rebellion, the Constitution now looked much less constrictive on national action. "That instrument is not merely a net-work of negatives," a Democratic congressman affirmed. "It clothes the Government in the panoply of national power; it affirms, as well as denies." As for state policy, it always had enjoyed the widest potential scope through the all-encompassing police power. One only had to glance to Deseret, the Mormon domain spreading out from the Great Salt Lake, to see what people expected of their government. Under the paternal gaze of Brigham Young, it had created a host of state-run enterprises. Let the myth of the frontier link its taming to individual initiative: the pony express rider, the army scout, the buffalo hunter, the dead-shot—or all four, in the person of William F. "Buffalo Bill" Cody. The "Great Basin Kingdom" represented just the opposite. Its rulers built foundries, machine shops, and nail factories. The Public Works Department founded sugar refiners and companies to mine iron, coal, and lead. It erected the first important theater west of St. Louis and the vast Mormon Tabernacle that rose on Temple Square just after the war. Heavily subsidized and assigned public functions, the Deseret Agricultural and Manufacturing Society encouraged beekeeping, fruit-growing, and improvements in the breeds of livestock raised. Beyond Deseret's borders, consumers depended on Western Union, a private monopoly, for their telegraph messages, but within it, a tax-supported company that Young headed built and ran all the lines. The commonwealth of the Latter-Day Saints was special, but a new confidence in the use of government power could be found everywhere. Much of it came from the feeling that in an age of rapid economic development, mammoth railroad enterprises, and capital markets on Wall or Broad Street spreading their influence from Maine to Montana, some powerful countervailing force must represent the public interest. "Sir, you will never make me doubt that a government which could put down that mighty Rebellion can regulate the details of a few tariffs of some railroad corporation!" one westerner exclaimed.[2]

In the years following the war, states rewrote their constitutions, stretching the scope of government's responsibilities. They gave more explicit protection to basic civil rights, expanded educational systems, stretched the tax power to raise new sources of revenue and remove the exemptions that church property enjoyed, and legalized local aid for corporations, especially for railroads. Nothing was too small to escape the delegates' attention. In Illinois, a few even tried to add a requirement that doctors' prescriptions stick to English. Just after the war, Republican lawmakers in Albany set up metropolitan boards to run the police and fire departments in New York City and take on responsibility for the public health, expanded state control over local school systems, and funneled downstate money to rural constituencies. Everywhere, legislators found their workloads mounting. In 1859, those in Springfield had passed 359 bills—a decade later, 2,000. Pennsylvania's rose from 753 to over 1,200. Governments not only legislated more. They administered more. In Ohio, the state added a commissioners of railroads and telegraphs and of fisheries. It created state oil inspectors; and it extended permission to cities to create new authorities as well, from fire commissioner to meat inspector.[3]

For Republicans, education always had meant more than learning one's ABC's and three-times-three. Schools must act as the nursery of Protestant American values and the kind of informed citizenry vital to republics' survival. Advocates were sure that ignorance bred Democrats as surely as the whiskey jug did. Schooling made the many into one: Indians, African Americans, Irish immigrants all could find a common sense of Americanism, a patriotism that would bind the republic closer together. Tellingly, the founder of the Carlisle Indian School likened education to full-immersion baptism. Neither he nor Republicans were about to wait for the converts to present themselves. While most northern states had taxpayer-funded common schools open to all, only a few of them had made schooling compulsory. Now the pressure increased. So did funding for "a thorough and efficient system of free schools": from $19.9 million nationwide in 1860 to $81.5 million twenty years later. Twenty-four states set up state boards of education by 1880. Twenty-nine mandated county school superintendents. The Morrill Land Grant College Act of 1862 had extended aid to the founding of state universities, with special attention to agricultural improvement, but the state institutions founded after the war set their sights wider and higher. Those interested in promoting development hoped for a higher education able to train the engineers and specialists an industrial economy would need. Michigan needed chemists, not just farmers, and so governors called for aid to technical programs; the legislature established a school for mines and set up university chairs in dental surgery, as well as architecture and design.[4] When Congress created a Department of Education in 1867, it seemed in perfect keeping with the belief that the state had a vested interest in creating a well-educated citizenry. Senator Charles Sumner's failed proposal to make the establishment of public school systems a requirement for southern states' readmission to Congress was therefore not as outlandish as its paltry support made it seem. His opponents agreed that schooling was a must; but they thought their establishment likely, as soon as the South could afford to build them.[5]

Much legislation went to encourage development, but along with it, states showed a greater willingness to create a lasting public presence on behalf of the public interest. Michigan created an insurance bureau to weed out the fly-by-night fire insurance companies, and Ohio added to the laws to make sure that life insurance firms could deliver on their promised benefits. Other states set up guidelines for the safer manufacture of kerosene and to protect consumers against false weights and measures. It was the state's business to prevent the spread of cattle diseases or to institute quarantines against epidemics.[6]

The activism that applied itself to business promotion and moral reform also worked to encourage railroad construction and to rein in the companies. Aid to railroads was given just about everywhere that state constitutions did not forbid it, and even then lawmakers were generous in extending permission to counties and cities to extend their credit on a project's behalf. They were not always private enterprises: Ohio, for example, allowed Cincinnati to issue $10 million in bonds to build a line connecting with roads tapping the southern trade. New York, Illinois, and Missouri allowed localities to advance more than $70 million to different companies.[7]

A larger public stake demanded a larger public oversight. In 1869, Charles Francis Adams Jr. induced Massachusetts to set up the first efficient railroad regulatory commission. Advisory at first, it found its power expanding as new requirements and needs arose. Other states, too, began to create their own commissions, and some of them took on stronger powers, to compel witnesses to testify before hearings, or to recommend laws for improving the safety of passengers. For many states, commissions began as fact finders and developed into constables. The more developed a state's economy, the more economic interests had reasons to band together against the railroads on which their national markets depended. In the Midwest, the fraternal order of the Grange gave their name to the so-called Granger laws regulating railroad rates, but farmers usually did not dictate legislation. The real forces were often cities angry about how the freight cars bypassed them or levied discriminating charges against their shipments. Iowa's river cities found their river traffic north and south superseded by trunk lines moving east and west. Communities with connections resented potential rivals without. All of them had reasons for beefing against how the railroads did their business. Minnesota lawmakers decided how much companies could charge per mile; Wisconsin's Potter Law gave a commission of experts that power. When the economy slumped after 1873, corporate lobbies had the laws eviscerated or repealed where they could and transferred rate oversight from politicians to professionals elsewhere, but they could not return governance to where it had been in 1869.[8]

Legislative action on labor's behalf occurred much less frequently. Massachusetts set the pace for other states in creating a bureau of labor statistics to compile a yearly survey of industrial conditions. Some states set limits on working hours for women and children. Pennsylvania repealed its Conspiracy Act that made unions criminally liable in the event of a strike and, spurred on by the Avondale mine disaster in 1869, put through the first industrial-safety law anywhere. Elsewhere, the main agitation came over laws mandating an eight-hour day. Right after the war, workers had begun organizing. A federation of trade unions, the National Labor Union, organized in 1866, and within a few years claimed 200,000 to 400,000 members. The eight-hour movement gave them a unifying cause. "Before this movement stops, every child born in America must have an equal chance in life," Wendell Phillips asserted. Congress mandated the eight-hour day for arsenal workers and some 6,000 employees in the navy yards in 1868, only to have Johnson decide that, as their work had been cut by two hours, so should their pay; when Grant came in, he issued an executive order revoking the ruling. He issued it again three years later. Department heads declined to give it practical effect either time. The attorney general ruled that the limits did not apply to government contractors. New York, Missouri, California, and Wisconsin all declared eight hours a legal day's work, usually with killer loopholes, exempting farm labor and any employee who chose to sign a contract agreeing to work longer. In the northeastern states, agitation to make ten hours "a legal day's work" met defeat or ended in symbolic victories and practical defeats. Michigan failed even to restrict child labor, and sawmill owners helped defeat a ten-hour bill when it reached the legislative floor. Worst of all, in terms of future industrial peace, Pennsylvania led the way in allowing mines, banks, and railroads to hire their own paramilitary enforcers.[9]

Sanitary reformers, too, seized on the state's new potential. Epidemics remained a fact of life, or rather, death, in nineteenth-century cities. From its first appearance in 1832, cholera made periodic, fatal sweeps wherever water supplies could be infected. Yellow fever had taken heavy tolls in Federalist Philadelphia in 1793 and made regular visits to New Orleans. General "Yellow Jack" probably killed more Civil War soldiers than any one battle, and in 1878, its toll in the Mississippi River valley cost thousands of lives, including that of General John Bell Hood, survivor of crippling wounds in wartime. Scientific knowledge had not yet identified the pathogens in either disease, but cleaner streets and removal of the puddles at clogged drains where mosquitoes bred could have lowered the human cost. That would have taken government action, state or local, but action came rarely before the war. At most the authorities would set up a board of health when a crisis hit and disband it when the emergency passed. Local agencies acted on their own, not in tandem. The horse manure, piled so high in some Crescent City streets as to block the doors, remained where it was. The householders continued to dump chamber pots into the public thoroughfare, to mingle with the blood pouring out of the slaughterhouses. Military necessity forced the national government into action, for soldiers' sake, not simply to tend the sick but to take preventative measures. The army called in professionals and compelled obedience to public health dictates by military law. General Benjamin Butler, the "Beast of New Orleans," deserved to be renamed "the Blest," in terms of saving Confederates' lives. He put prisoners of war to work scouring the streets, some of them untouched by broom or bucket until now, and empowered the Sanitary Commission to run the effort. Death rates fell sharply; thanks as well to the interruption of foreign commerce, New Orleans had never been as healthy as under Butler—nor would be again in his lifetime.[10]

If government power could do so much in war, why could it not apply the same methods, the same hiring of experts, the same establishment of sanitary rules in peacetime? Reformers hardly needed to look south to find squalor as bad as that with which Butler strove. New York City may have qualified as the filthiest city in the developed world. The death rate in London stood at twenty two per thousand every year; in New York, it approached thirty-three and rose in bad years to forty-one per thousand. Critics guessed the cost in lives needlessly lost at thirteen thousand a year. With waste material choking the streets in the downtown slums, with garbage lingering uncollected on Cherry Street and, for all one could tell, dating back to Pieter Stuyvesant's time on the Bowery, the hogs that roamed the city provided the only waste-disposal system many residents were likely to see. In place of the contractors hired for their services to the party or its campaign war chest, New York needed a board of experts with real power to establish rules. A Republican legislature in 1866 created just that, a metropolitan sanitary district run by a board of health, just in time to meet the latest cholera outbreak. Other states considered the same alternatives; at least four established sanitary boards of their own.[11]

The same energy gave a new logic and system to care for the poor. Instead of many agencies scattering their charities, the old abolitionist Dr. Samuel Gridley Howe, wartime member of the United States Sanitary Commission, persuaded Massachusetts to set up a state board of charity. Nor was it entirely about efficiency. So many of those in need were soldiers crippled in the war or their families, not to mention the widows and orphans of those heroes who had perished for the Union's cause. As a result, in the 1860s, most states doubled their aid to paupers. There was also more money for the deaf and mute and more schools for preparing them to make livings for themselves, more for reform schools, almshouses, and insane asylums. Spending on prisons and efforts to redeem the inmates and prepare them for eventual release picked up momentum as well. The first juvenile reformatories of any consequence made their appearance. Led by Marvin H. Bovee of Wisconsin, a movement spread to end or limit the grounds for capital punishment. Illinois and Iowa joined Michigan and Wisconsin in abolishing it, while New York and Ohio made its implementation more difficult.[12]

The use of state power for Henry Bergh meant quite another humanitarian responsibility. The America coming out of the war gave a brutal inattention to animals in general. Butchers would pluck feathers from living chickens, or drop live pigs into frothing vats, the better to remove their bristles. In any town, those in the know could find a rat pit, where dogs were set to work while a gambling crowd cheered on the fracas, but they could just as easily find a ring with dogs pitted against bulls, or cocks against one another. Cab and omnibus horses, drawing overloaded vehicles, dropped dead in their tracks and were simply cut from the traces and left to putrefy in the summer's heat. Nobody thought much or long about the casual cruelty around them—that is, until Henry Bergh, having witnessed what English law could do and how far its Society for the Prevention of Cruelty to Animals had made it possible, returned to create an SPCA in New York City in 1866. Mobilizing like-minded reformers, he pressured the legislature into enacting laws to protect cattle being shipped to market. Dead-letter laws against cruelty now had unofficial enforcers in Bergh's society. In a single year, the SPCA made 872 arrests and compelled action on horses' behalf simply by the threat of prosecution. What New York did, other states tried as well.[13]

If government could scrub up the streets, moral reformers argued, it had power to clean up the social filth that made unclean souls. Anthony Comstock, burly, impassioned, and palpably aware of the Devil's presence in every intense emotion, dedicated his life to fighting indecency. For all society's public prudery, he never ran out of targets. Anyone in the know could have found material to inflame the imagination, with titles like the *Amorous Sketch-Book* and *The Lascivious London Beauty*. Comstock formed a Society for the Suppression of Vice to close down the smutty literature trade and go after wickedness in music, art, and the theater. In Boston, he helped set up the Watch and Ward Society. Over a decade, the "roundsman of the Lord" boasted that he had suppressed or confiscated fourteen tons of books and over a million and a half circulars, poems, and pictures. Government power helped him do it. A wartime law allowed the government to censor unsealed mail to protect soldiers' morals; in 1865 a new statute allowed officers to bar unsealed obscene material from the mails entirely. Thanks to Comstock, a more comprehensive law suppressing indecent literature passed in 1873, including, among its targets, advertisements for underwear or contraceptives.[14]

Moral action came in other directions as well. Massachusetts and Ohio made prizefighting a penal offense and actually sentenced a few perpetrators. Elsewhere, the law outlawed the sale of contraceptives, while the federal government enacted legislation against lotteries' use of the mails. Seeing Mormonism as the antithesis of free labor, democracy, Christianity, and the secular state, Republicans had already begun legislating to bring the Great Basin Kingdom to heel during the Civil War. An 1862 law disincorporated the church and limited its secular property holdings to $50,000; the Latter-Day Saints got around it by transferring trusteeship over all the church's properties to Brigham Young. Regularly, Congress would debate bills to make Deseret an official federal territory, with a Gentile governor appointed to run it, to abolish trial by jury there or place the selection of juries in outside hands, and to confiscate uncooperative Mormons' property. In 1874, the Poland Act put all territorial cases, criminal, civil, and chancery in federal judges' hands and left them with wide discretion to appoint jurors. A measure to dismember the territory completely and allot its fragments to adjacent territories in ways to make sure that Mormons would not have a voting majority anywhere got serious consideration. None of these steps changed matters while Brigham Young was alive, but they foreshadowed much more effective intervention in the 1880s that included scrubbing Mormon voters off the registration books wholesale and imposing what was, effectively, a carpetbagger occupation government. Branding polygamy and slavery the great twin evils of antebellum America, associating the ease with which Deseret allowed divorce with the threat to the traditional family, Republicans acted on what they felt to be the highest moral grounds, the protection of women against sexual exploitation and, to their view, a lesser enslavement. "The mission which God has called upon me to perform in Utah, is as much above the duties of other courts and judges as the heavens are above the earth," Grant's appointee as territorial chief justice announced. Wherever any laws hindered the Almighty's purposes, "by God's blessing I shall trample them under my feet."[15]

No moral subject, however, commanded as much attention or created so much bother as the struggle against strong drink. The war had had no sobering effect on American life. If anything, more recruits were introduced to the cup that cheered or, in the combined monotony and dread of a soldier's life, the bottle that numbed. They came home to communities as awash with beer and whiskey as when the war began. Official records counted 7,000 licensed saloons in New York City by 1870, enough to line a street thirteen miles long. Reportedly, that city consumed 40,000 kegs of beer daily and lodged 65,000 charges of intoxication a year. That made up a small share of the 140,000 saloons nationwide and the five million customers they served. Temperance advocates blamed the liquor trade for 100,000 prison inmates every year and twice that many children reduced to beggary and want. They inveighed against German immigrants, "who want little but lager here below," and the "rum-ocrats" that parlayed their saloons into political power wherever native-born Americans were scarce. "Here in this land are these legalized assassins," an orator stormed. Three million lives they had cost America since the century's beginning! "The earth is sick of slaughter. The heavens are tired of weeping over the abominations and the desolations of this traffic."[16]

An evil so great required more than moral suasion. Opponents likened the struggle to that against slavery and invoked John Brown's ghost on their side. Some states found the solution in licensing laws that would close down all but the well-heeled proprietors, able to pay five hundred or a thousand dollars a year. Elsewhere, statutes made liquor sellers financially liable for the harm buyers did under the influence. Wives or kin could take a saloon keeper to court for catering to known drunkards. Most places instituted Sunday closing for the Sabbath's sake and because it was the one day in the week when most employees had the free time to frequent a bar in the first place. Opponents who spoke of "German liberty," a minister snorted, deserved as much respect as horse thieves who banded together under the enticing title "Horseflesh liberals." Elsewhere, lawmakers toyed with local option laws, allowing municipalities or counties to abolish the liquor traffic entirely. Finally, a handful of New England states not only kept their antebellum Prohibition laws on the books but set up a state constabulary to strengthen the faltering arms of local enforcers. At least from their public professions, a newspaper joked, Boston had taken intolerance to its furthest point, no doubt forbidding circuses to have "the 'horizontal bar' or a band of 'tumblers' and outlawing trance mediums for calling in the aid of spirits!"[17]

The struggle reached a peak early in 1874 in Cincinnati. Overall, Ohio produced a quarter of a million barrels of whiskey every year, the product of four million bushels of corn and a million of rye. But Cincinnati's brewers and distillers could have doused a nation all by themselves. Allegedly, 30,000 citizens owed their living to the liquor business one way or the other; 800 coopers made barrels for the whiskey trade, while just about half the city councilmen carried on a liquor business.[18] Inspired by a lecturer's address, Protestant women gathered in the streets to kneel in prayer outside saloons and beseech customers to turn away from sin for their families' sake. City officials had made themselves scarce when it came to enforcing the liquor laws, but they found policemen enough to haul the women off for obstructing the streets. Saloon keepers passed out whistles shrill enough to drown out the women's appeals. Arrested, the demonstrators went to jail praying and filled the cells with hymn-singing. Not only did the protests grow; they spread. Cleveland, Chicago, Philadelphia, Pittsburgh, Boston, and some 200 towns across the Midwest saw a Woman's Crusade. Liquor receipts fell off, and police departments found courage enough to crack down on illegal sellers. If the constabulary could not find gin-joints on their own, Crusaders told them where to go. "They drink not, neither do they sin," a Kansas editor joked; "yet Solomon in all his glory was not a raid like one of these." In Springfield, Ohio, a reporter found it took "as much negotiation for a stranger to get a dram" as to buy a horse.[19]

The southern Reconstruction governments could never catch up with northern advances, but they raced ahead of what little had been accomplished before. Gone at last was the whipping post; gone, too, the last few states allowing imprisonment for debt, and a host of capital offenses. Lawmakers created the states' first public hospitals, orphanages, lunatic asylums, and state penitentiaries, none of which came cheaply. South Carolina protected workers' wages from being seized to pay their debts, while other states made workers' dismissal for political reasons illegal and ended the common practice of driving laborers off the plantation before the harvest without compensation for the time they had put in already. States gave workers a lien on their employers' property with priority ahead of those signed away to storekeepers or bankers. Homestead exemption laws went on the books everywhere, and in the cotton states, Republicans made the protection retroactive, voiding old contracts that made owners liable for what they owed. In Georgia, juries could decide just how much of a debt the creditor could collect. (The Supreme Court killed the retroactive provision and voided Georgia's relief laws in the 1870s, but it took ten years before it could make its decree stick.)[20]

Republicans did not, in fact, create the South's public school systems from nothing. Most southern states had made some beginning before the war. North Carolina's had been the fullest and best-financed, with a quarter of a million dollars in state money to complement local resources. One hundred and fifty thousand white children attended. At the opposite extreme, South Carolina stood alone in making no constitutional provision for education. The legislature allowed the counties a niggardly $300 a year per Assembly member. Most places, the South, by northern standards, fell far short of fulfilling basic needs. For a rural South with a dispersed population, getting regular school attendance would be as daunting a challenge as paying for the schools, particularly before harvest season closed. Wartime shuttered what schools there had been, educational funds shifting into Confederate bonds or military spending. The "Johnson constitutions" passed some vague provisions, which conservative governments shrugged aside. With the state's Literary Fund emptied, North Carolina abolished its public school system in 1866. The only schools not underfunded in most of the former slave states were black ones: they were not funded at all. Under the new constitution, Texas lawmakers could have set up a school system for blacks, strictly on black contributions (though nobody seemed concerned that black taxes would help pay for white schools). They did nothing. Florida's legislature did mandate the same separate financing principle. Out of it, twenty-five black schools put in an appearance.[21]

Republicans, then, had the job of creating a comprehensive educational system, as least as far as property and poll taxes could pay for one. State education officials had to make do with far less than northern ones. While they could keep records, make reports, and spread information, they had no big stick to wield on uncooperative districts. County school commissioners did the enforcing and most of the advising of teachers. North Carolina put through one of the best programs, but even there, sixteen counties failed to set up a single school in the first year. Overall, one-third of the money that the state set aside to pay teachers' salaries went unclaimed. Nor could the legislature see its way clear to provide schoolbooks at taxpayer expense or even to give localities the right to extend schooling longer than four months. Angrily, a black assemblyman proposed lowering the flag over the capitol to half-mast. So feeble a bill, he warned, meant "the death of all weak-kneed Republicans." As for institutions higher than a grammar school level, the Reconstruction governments founded very few and, in South Carolina, none for blacks at all, outside of the bigger cities. Only South Carolina required its state university to admit black applicants, and just about all the white students quit. How far those schools had to go, however, was less significant than how far they advanced, and how quickly. Within two years, over three-fifths of all eligible white children and half of all black ones were attending in Arkansas. Within seven years, one black child of school age in two went to school in South Carolina, Florida, and Mississippi, a difference in the Palmetto State between 8,000 in 1869 and 71,000 in 1876. There were more black teachers, as well, nearly all of them southern-born.[22] In 1872 a journalist touring West Virginia noticed that every few miles he would pass a schoolhouse, "each one a monument to Republicanism," built in that party's heyday and now, thanks to its Democratic successor, all unoccupied. The reporter made his living lacerating Reconstruction, but, he admitted, pile up all its blunders, imbecilities, persecutions, and crimes, and the educational system it had left the state offset them all.[23]

Schools north and south separated by race where the counties could afford to operate dual systems, and in the South, they did so regardless. Only a few northern states forbade school segregation at the start of Reconstruction, though at least five more did so postwar, and a scattering of cities (Pittsburgh, New York, and Toledo among them) opened their white schools to black applicants. Even with the law on their side, black families often had to go to court to make the local institutions oblige them. Across most of the North, however, separate schools were, if not mandated, at least allowed, if localities preferred—and they almost always did.[24] In the South, South Carolina's constitution allowed mixed schools, but no community set one up. Only in Louisiana could a visitor have seen black children and white mingling in the classroom, and outside of New Orleans, not all that commonly. Within the city, perhaps one school in three was integrated, but five freedpeople in six were going to all-black schools. Most public universities in the South stayed lily-white. Mississippi founded Alcorn College to forestall black applications to the University of Mississippi. Arkansas taught its black students only after regular hours and once white classes had been dismissed. Black families certainly resented the insult that exclusion implied in these facilities as much as any others, but they put less importance on who their children studied alongside than on guarantees that the doors to education not be shut in their faces entirely. North as well as south, schools of any kind seemed like progress compared to the exclusion so customary before the war. As of 1873, barely one school district in one hundred in Indiana provided any accommodations; not until 1874 did Illinois finally declare black children's right to an education. In the South, the most widespread African American complaints came not at black schools' separateness but in their disparity in funding and advantages.[25]

In other areas, Reconstruction governments took occasional steps to address discrimination in public places. With exclusion the rule until now, just providing facilities for the deaf, mute, and blind or dispensaries and hospitals for indigent freedpeople qualified as an advance, segregated though they might be; South Carolina's admission of blacks to its state-run orphanage made a marked contrast to other states, where only whites had access. The Fourteenth Amendment opened up the witness box to all but said nothing about restaurants or bars, theaters, saloons, or places of public amusement. Railroads and steamboats continued to feel free to refuse first-class service to blacks, whether they could pay first-class fares or not. Republicans denied any intention "to force social equality between the races," or anything beyond the "rights accorded . . . by the laws of our country." For "social equality," they suggested, blacks would find a friendlier welcome among the Democratic planters, at least if the varied color of their offspring indicated anything. "Our race do not demand social equality," William J. Whipper of Beaufort told the South Carolina legislature. "No law can compel me to put myself on an equality with some white men I know." But the term to most blacks meant a forced intermixing in the private realm, not open access to facilities serving a public function or operating under a special charter from public authority. For women in particular, discrimination meant insult as well as injury. The "ladies' car" was barred to them, and they must travel second class, where men, coarse manners, smoke, and tobacco juice were the standard. The propertied minority of blacks who could afford better accommodations and those whose professional or business position entitled them to greater respect resented the discrimination strongly, though they did not insist on integrated facilities—only equal ones. But any African American shoved off a streetcar or refused a place for the night felt the same mixture of humiliation and resentment at the stigma laid on blacks' association with those who, in all their social intercourse, continued to play the role of a superior race.[26]

There, South Carolina lawmakers had some success. One of the first laws passed in 1868 forbade businesses from discriminating "on account of race, color or previous condition." A northern teacher returning to Beaufort late in the year found that black people had the run of the ship. "They were everywhere, choosing the best staterooms and best seats at the table," she wrote. "Two prominent colored members of the State Legislature were on board with their families." But South Carolina—"truly a government of the nigger, and by the nigger, and for the nigger," as one Democratic visitor misleadingly called it—proved exceptional in that respect, as in many others. Republicans in Alabama and North Carolina smothered civil rights bills. Mississippi's conveniently vanished before it could be sent for the governor's signature. Louisiana governor Henry Clay Warmoth vetoed one civil rights bill early in his first term and another two years later. The toothless substitute that became law changed nothing.[27]

Advances in women's rights picked up where they had left off before the war. Thanks to the Morrill Land-Grant Act, states founded liberal arts institutions as well as mechanical and agricultural colleges by the dozens, and many of those in the West started admitting women. Cornell founded a women's branch, Sage College, in 1874. A little over one college in four adopted coeducation; Swarthmore was founded on that basis in 1869. So were Howard, Wilberforce, and Atlanta, the new colleges set up for blacks. But a few of the first real colleges exclusively for women, with curricula beyond those of finishing schools, also opened their doors: Vassar in 1865 and in 1875, within a day of each other, Wellesley and Smith, both of which set the same rigorous entrance requirements that men's colleges demanded. The black Masons formed a women's auxiliary, and black women became preachers in the African Methodist Episcopal Church. A robust press made its appearance. In 1868, Susan B. Anthony founded *The Revolution*, a sixteen-page weekly edited by Elizabeth Cady Stanton with information about every form of women's activity outside the home. Southern Reconstruction helped broaden property rights for women as well. In West Virginia, for example, widows were given the one-third dower right that northern widows already had. The law was strengthened to protect widows from creditors. Wives were allowed to hold their property separately from their husbands, to collect their own wages, to go into business for themselves, and to keep and use those profits as they saw fit. A married woman could deposit money in her own name and vote as a stockholder in any business. No property separately held was open for the husband's creditors to lay claim to or seize for debts.[28]

With so much activity in so many directions, foreign visitors could not help feeling impressed that a people's government could accomplish anything. "A little more attention to Yankee notions would not be thrown away," a visitor reported home. "The great transatlantic workshop possesses models in working order of all our projected reforms." In fact, whenever a change was put forward in Parliament, he commented, members ought to ask at once, "Have they tried it in America? How does it work?"[29] A bewildered onlooker might miss the obvious. Most of the initiative came at the state and local levels, and most of the energy for changes in the political economy on farmers', workers', and consumers' behalf centered there. Whatever the Cassandras of centralized power said, federalism came out of the war alive and well. If anything, the states were taking on new responsibilities faster than the national government did. The message could not be missed: the federal system worked, and the states should be trusted to their own separate spheres of activity.

That faith had reinforcement in two important Supreme Court decisions, one of which proved to have ominous ramifications for Reconstruction. In 1869, Louisiana's Radical government set up a slaughterhouse company with a twenty-five-year monopoly on butchering cattle across the river from New Orleans. Abattoirs were worse than a noisome nuisance. The filth and squalor and the blood poured into the streets presented a threat to public health. Butchers forced to pay the slaughterhouse's rates or go out of business sued. Represented by former Supreme Court justice John A. Campbell, the plaintiffs argued that they were being deprived of property without due process of law. The Fourteenth Amendment was meant to protect the "privileges and immunities" of citizens, and state interference with how they carried on their business violated those rights. Had the Court agreed, just about any business regulation might have been open to challenge at any but the national level, and then only where the constitutional power over interstate commerce came into play. Instead, Justice Samuel Miller issued a majority opinion upholding the Louisiana statute. Americans had two citizenships, one state, one national, he ruled. The Fourteenth Amendment covered only those rights owing "their existence to the Federal Government, its national character, its Constitution, or its laws"—in effect, those related to politics, as well as the writ of habeas corpus, the right to assemble peaceably or to bear arms. All the others stayed where they had been, for the state to regulate; by implication, Miller was accepting that the amendment had incorporated the protections in the Bill of Rights, but he was taking a much narrower view of how far Congress could counter discrimination than the amendment's most radical sponsors had. In the long run, the *Slaughterhouse* decision would mean serious trouble the moment southern Republicans lost control by denying that a whole host of wrongs done to the freedpeople were any of Washington's business. As Congressman Benjamin F. Butler gibed, thanks to cases like these, the government could protect an American's rights anywhere in the world except at home. But Miller's larger point was equally significant, that the state could regulate matters of safety or health under the police power, and that its scope was a broad one. Driving the point home, majority and minority joined to uphold Iowa's statute forbidding liquor sales as no violation of the sellers' national privileges and immunities.[30]

The second case, *Munn v. Illinois*, came in 1877. Railroads wanted to overturn the state's Granger law regulating rates charged at Chicago grain elevators. In effect, they contended, government's deciding what they could charge deprived them of their property (in other words, their profits) without due process. Resting the Court's decision on a long history of states setting interest rates and limiting bridge, road, and ferry tolls, Chief Justice Morrison Waite declared regulation constitutional. He did make two concessions that would turn into weapons against state action in the future: the states' police power *did* have limits, and conceivably it could fall afoul of the due process clause. But any business "affected with a public interest" was fit for public action. Only nine years later did the Court announce that corporations were persons under the Fourteenth Amendment, and covered by its protection for due process; it took the judges twenty years to pluck up their courage to use the due process clause to knock down state regulation of business—and only business. States kept the fullest scope to go after gamblers, drinkers, swearers, and pornographers, or any practice threatening public health or workers' safety.[31]

State activism clearly helped undergird Americans' faith in state's rights. Perhaps for that reason, national forays into new territory had a much harder time of it. The Department of Education stood well below cabinet rank. When Congressman George F. Hoar introduced a bill in 1870 "to compel by national authority the establishment of a thorough and efficient system of public instruction throughout the whole country," he got a respectful hearing but a polite dismissal.[32] Congress put the eight-hour day into effect for some government workers, but the law was a mere signpost, always pointing in a direction without requiring federal employers actually to go there. When sanitary reformers called on Congress to take action against the onset of cholera, by creating a permanent commission able to place a quarantine on ships at any port of entry and to uphold its diktats by imposing martial law, moderate Republicans were appalled. "I would rather have the cholera than such a proposition as that," one senator exclaimed. The bill failed by two votes. Only in 1879 did Congress create a national board of public health, and then only with investigative powers, not coercive ones.[33]

If the federal system's achievements seemed to prove that the states were perfectly capable on their own of fulfilling public needs, the use of government power to advance moral agendas or the radical cause of human equality carried myriad risks for Reconstruction itself. The woman suffrage movement illustrated that point clearly. It had emerged from the war, apparently stronger than ever. Stirrings for the cause in Britain, such as the appearance of John Stuart Mill's *The Subjection of Women* in 1869 and Quaker M. P. John Bright's introduction of a bill in Parliament giving women the vote, added to the feeling that this might be women's moment.

As the American Equal Rights Association argued in 1865, the logic underlying black suffrage applied against gender discrimination with equal force. What exclusive right had men to represent women any more than white ones to represent blacks? Women in the leisure classes might stand on a pedestal, one Ohio trade unionist pointed out, but those "in the bread-and-butter-getting struggle of life" needed the guard that only political rights could give. "Christ came into the world and died upon the cross to give women the ballot," one minister told a suffragist convention.[34]

Some radical Republicans agreed: Charles Sumner, George W. Julian, and Wendell Phillips all gave theoretical or practical support to the cause. The Republican national platforms in 1872 and 1876 made friendly murmurs, depending on the meaning of their endorsement of "additional rights." In Wyoming Territory, legislators ended the 1869 session by giving women the vote. To their surprise, skeptics found that it worked very well. Most women chose not to vote, but the few dozen who did behaved as well as men—according to general report, a great deal better. A New England minister saw rough miners tamed into manners at the approach of a woman voter. In "this new country, supposed at that time to be infested by hordes of cut-throats, gamblers and abandoned characters, I had witnessed a more quiet election than it had been my fortune to see in the quiet towns of Vermont," he wrote. Women sat on juries, and a few were elected to local office. In 1870, Utah Territory followed Wyoming's example, the better to protect Mormons from losing political control to Gentile newcomers. Elsewhere, policymakers allowed women to vote in school board elections, with Kansas enacting it on achieving statehood in 1861 and seventeen other states following suit over the next three decades. When seven women were elected to Boston's school committee in 1874, their right to serve was taken to the state courts and upheld.[35]

Small victories only made the larger setbacks more galling. In the few states that put woman suffrage on the ballot, voters turned it down. Over the next forty years, there were nearly 500 campaigns to have the issue submitted to the voters in thirty-three states. All but seventeen failed to make it that far. Only two ended in women being enfranchised. Efforts to provide taxpaying women a vote in city affairs failed in New York, Rhode Island, and Massachusetts. When Susan B. Anthony led sixteen women to the polls in Rochester in 1872, she found herself arrested, ironically under the provisions of the 1870 Enforcement Act, which was intended to make it easier for southern blacks to cast ballots. The court fined her $100. Anthony swore she would never pay it; she never did, and in 1874 President Grant pardoned her. In 1875, the Supreme Court ruled unanimously in *Minor v. Happersett* that while women were citizens, citizenship conferred no automatic right to vote, and that only a new constitutional amendment could enfranchise women nationwide.[36] But then, two years before, on the same day as the *Slaughterhouse* case, the Court had declared that the right to practice law was not among the privileges and immunities that went with national citizenship. It was a state's business, and in this particular case, Illinois acted within its rights denying women entry into the legal profession. (Women could and did become lawyers elsewhere, and in 1879, after Benjamin Butler carried an enabling bill through Congress, the Court admitted Belva Lockwood as the first woman to practice before it.)[37]

Anthony, Elizabeth Cady Stanton, and other suffragists had worked hard against slavery and for racial equality. For them, the Fourteenth Amendment had an ominous significance, especially amid radical talk of "manhood suffrage." At all events, they were not ready to concentrate on the freedmen's cause at the expense of their own. That, in effect, was what they were being asked to do. "When women, because they are women, are dragged from their homes and hung upon lamp-posts," Frederick Douglass told an audience in 1869, "when their children are torn from their arms and their brains dashed to the pavement; when they are the objects of insult and outrage at every turn; when they are in danger of having their homes burnt down over their heads; when their children are not allowed to enter schools; then they will have an urgency to obtain the ballot." That argument might work with some feminists, Lucy Stone and Julia Ward Howe among them, who felt any step toward equal rights worth making, but it cut no ice with those who felt their own injuries as a gender more keenly than Douglass could imagine.[38] Under such pressures, gatherings of the American Equal Rights Association grew fraught, with men against women, black against white, and feminists against each other.

The Fifteenth Amendment made the divisions permanent and near complete by not including sex among the characteristics forbidden to states in restricting citizens' right to vote. At best, radicals were prepared to submit a separate woman suffrage amendment, which had no chance of passing Congress. Savagely, Stanton denounced giving the vote to "Patrick and Sambo and Hans and Yung Tung" and declared that giving freedmen the vote would only encourage black rapists. When the Equal Rights Association met the following May, it tore apart. Convinced that the male membership had perverted it from its rightful purposes, Stanton and Anthony formed their own organization, the National Woman Suffrage Association, open only to women favoring the cause above all. Within months a rival, the American Woman Suffrage Association, with its own weekly, the *Woman's Journal*, had organized. Open to suffragists, it directed its appeals to professionals, clubwomen, and those for whom enfranchisement held a less momentous importance. "The duties of the family . . . there we shall find our rights," Catherine Beecher told delegates at their first convention; "not in law, not in constitutions, but in that great work, the training of the race." For the next twenty years, the two associations, one slightly more well-heeled and conservative, the other struggling and radical, waged an uneven battle on each other, holding conventions that, as one reporter described them, were "distinguished throughout by . . . dignity, pure English, and the absence of spittoons."[39]

The struggle over woman suffrage showed clearly that not even all radicals were ready to carry their belief in equality one step further. War's emergencies had not changed men's minds. It may have hardened them, as those who came home clutched for stability in a world transformed and cherished it the more in their own households, and as military service became more closely associated with citizenship. A Vermont editor defined women's true rights: "to love her lord with all her heart, and her baby as herself—and to make good bread"—which might explain why, when woman suffrage came up in the state's constitutional convention, it failed by 206 to 1, with one critic warning that letting ladies vote, especially when they outnumbered men, would lead to spinsters legalizing polyandry. The rising cry against politics as a dirty, cynical business only added force to the argument that into such a cesspool the virtuous sex should not be allowed to venture. With husband and wife casting votes on opposite sides, family harmony would be rent, and mothers engaged in politics would leave their offspring untended—that was the argument. Its radicalism fading, E. L. Godkin's *Nation* argued that with American cooking in decline, letting women leave the kitchen for the caucus would simply make it worse. Bring them into public life, another editorial warned, and capitol lobbies would teem with sirens exercising their "female fascinations" to pass charters, land grants, and tariffs! Even the change in wording in the proposed new Ohio constitution to "all *persons* are by nature free and independent, and have certain inalienable rights" alarmed the *Cleveland Plain Dealer* into pronouncing it "a sort of free love document."[40]

Using government on behalf of moral causes stirred the most visceral of feelings. However obvious it might be to Protestant schoolteachers that students would benefit from regular readings of the King James version of the Bible, Catholics wanted no such indoctrination. In 1869, the Cincinnati Board of Education raised a public tempest when it forbade Bible reading as a violation of the state's constitution. Opponents tried to require merger of the parochial and public schools, and gave way gracelessly only after the Ohio Supreme Court upheld the board's decision. The board of education in Long Island City expelled a few Catholic children for refusing to participate in Bible readings; the one in Brattleboro, Vermont, expelled hundreds. In New York, Tammany Hall pushed through a requirement that one-fifth of the funds that the state collected for education go to nonpublic schools—meaning, especially in New York City, the Catholic ones. There and elsewhere, aid for parochial education spurred tumult and efforts to amend the state constitutions to keep any religion from cashing in on the states' largesse.[41]

As enthusiasm for Reconstruction issues slackened, Republicans grew readier to identify themselves with cultural ones. Some thought they had found the new national crusade in a constitutional amendment declaring Christianity the nation's religion or in revealing the pope's designs against the public schoolhouse. A manufactured panic convulsed lawmakers in New York and Ohio when Democrats proposed to allow Catholic prisoners to seek consolation from priests, and not from just Protestant chaplains. In September 1875, while southern Radicals' very lives depended on moral support, if no other kind, President Grant spoke out aggressively—on behalf of the separation of church and state. Seriously disturbed at the violence though he was, his annual message that December had nothing to say about the shotgun strategy that had just carried Mississippi, and no remedies to offer. Instead, it made a bold endorsement of a Sixteenth Amendment, forbidding religious teaching in the public schools or a diversion of school funds to aid parochial education. Just at that time, with news of intimidated white Republicans and murdered black ones, Governor Adelbert Ames received a flier from the Union League of America, once the spearhead of black mobilization across the South. Now the league needed help against "those who seek to sap the foundations of the Republic, and take from you the birthright of an American citizen." The governor's feelings can only be imagined as he read where the true menace to the country lay: "OUR COMMON SCHOOLS ARE IN DANGER."[42]

The school amendment proved a nine-month wonder, but its agitation revealed one of the forces that was weakening support for the wider Republican agenda. By the mid-1870s, the party had identified itself as the foe of what a minister later called "rum, Romanism, and rebellion." It was

"The American River Ganges." Thomas Nast, *Harper's Weekly*, September 30, 1871. Public school children are about to be sacrificed to the crocodiles: Catholic bishops. Over the Capitol fly two banners, one with the Irish harp, the other with the keys and crown of the Vatican.

particularly identified with public schools and uniquely with forcing children to attend them. Woman suffrage found its sincerest advocates in Republican ranks, and desegregation its only sponsors. Before the war, Democrats had linked every "ism" to the opposing party, from prohibitionism to feminism and free-soilism. Invoking Puritanism and witch-burning, they painted Republicans as hypocrites, the kind of saints prone to fanaticism, whether for elevating the Negro into a "man and brother"—or white lady's husband—or for putting the torch to Catholic convents. Well on their way to tagging themselves "the party of moral ideas," Republicans found themselves making an uphill fight against the stereotypes.[43]

Supporting liquor regulation or Protestant values therefore came at a mounting cost as war issues lost their hold. The Woman's Crusade, and all the other efforts to restrict drinking, produced resentment not just in regular customers but especially in German Americans, for whom the *biergarten* was not simply a rendezvous for getting drunk but a pleasant place for a family outing and a valued part of their culture. They did not have to listen long to hear the note behind so many temperance utterances. "I tell you, ladies and gentlemen," one orator shouted, "this country must be Americanized, and if the foreigners don't like that they can go back where they came from." The war against the saloons, as a result, fell far short of accomplishment. Sixty-eight breweries closed down in Ohio after the crusade began and hardly made a drop of difference. Many of them probably failed for the same reason a thousand did nationwide: hard times rather than harsh laws. Beer production did not fall at all. Larger firms simply took up the slack left by the smaller ones. Prohibition remained on the books in most New England states, but anyone could order a glass of "water" over 100 proof in a Boston hotel. Every bar in town was closed—never "the little rooms behind the bar." Forbidden to sell drinks, saloons in Bloomington, Illinois, gave them away, charging customers ten cents for admission. In New York, one citizen explained, Democrats dared not repeal the liquor law and Republicans dared not enforce it.[44]

Win or lose, the moral crusades only confirmed to Catholics and many Germans of all faiths that the Republican conscience, however forgiving it might be of carpetbag thieves and southern ignoramuses, hardened into brass against anybody's conscience but its own. Democrats reminded voters that the same dogmatism that believed in using the law to impose one group's religious views on everybody else fit perfectly with the belief in using the law to impose their own racial views on everybody else. In both cases, they left to law what should be left to individual conscience. It also brought home to many others, native and foreign-born, that a government with power to protect could use it just as easily to oppress, and not just south of the Mason-Dixon Line. If after 1874 the Republicans had to fight for their majorities in every state between the Housatonic and the Mississippi, their use of the state as an agent of moral uplift deserved some of the blame.[45] At the same time, the crusading spirit of many of Reconstruction's strongest supporters had found new outlets as the question of remaking the South seemed to find an answer. They would not return to their earlier commitment when the moment of crisis came. In that respect, Reconstruction would perish not simply because of its failures but because of its apparent success.

CHAPTER ELEVEN

Georgia on Their Minds, 1870–1871

By April 1870, the Reconstruction process should have been complete. Congress had readmitted every state but one. On March 30th, the Fifteenth Amendment was proclaimed the law of the land. Down came the barriers to black voting in the Border South and across the North. With all the compromises made in the amendment's wording, ratification had been touch and go. Senator Oliver Morton bent parliamentary rules to ram it through the Indiana legislature, and President Grant applied pressure to make sure that Nevada and Nebraska voted in its favor.[1]

After nine years' absence from national councils, Mississippi sent a perfect symbol of the regenerated South to represent it in the Senate, Rev. Hiram Rhoades Revels, a black minister and state senator from Natchez who had opened the session with an inspiring prayer. "Ten years ago we should have thought a Feejee president not more absurdly improbable," a New York lawyer marveled. In fact, Revels could hardly have been improved upon as a national representative of the freedpeople. Born free in North Carolina, light-skinned and with some Indian heritage, he was dignified, mannerly, self-effacing, and unobtrusive, so much so that he disappointed those expecting a champion for their cause. Northerners did not miss the symbolism: the new senator held a seat from the state that had once elected former Confederate president Jefferson Davis to the upper chamber. But they did not expect much of him, or of the black congressmen—fourteen in all—that followed. When the subject of white violence or civil rights came up, they won a respectful hearing, sometimes admiration. But whatever their talents, they never joined the inner circle of the powerful. Revels would retire less than a year hence, and the next and last black senator, Blanche K. Bruce, also from Mississippi, would begin his single six-year term in 1875. Black congressmen would follow from most of the Deep southern states, but few of them were allowed to make much of a mark. Most of them were one-termers. House leaders put them on the more obscure committees,

"Time Works Wonders." Thomas Nast, *Harper's Weekly*, April 9, 1870. Jefferson Davis, as Iago, glares balefully at Hiram Revels, the first black senator, surrounded by Republican colleagues Henry Wilson, Oliver P. Morton, Carl Schurz, and Charles Sumner. Nast to the contrary, Revels was not successor to the seat that Davis had once held; his predecessor was Albert G. Brown.

never as chairmen. They proposed bills, which were generally ignored or buried in committee, though they had some success in finding lower-level government jobs for their black constituents. Poorer than most of their colleagues, they found the doors of white Washington society largely shut to them, in an age when those contacts off the floor were among the ways that members gathered influence and gained access.[2]

At no time did any state send as many black congressmen as the freedpeople's share of the population entitled them to, but that made Washington not much different from the Reconstruction state governments. As of 1870, every one of them had a white governor; nor would there be any nonwhite elected to the highest executive post. Most state officers were white, and so were most legislators outside of South Carolina, Mississippi, and Louisiana. They were generally southern-born, too. Fourteen blacks sat in the 100-member Texas House, 18 in North Carolina's, less than 10 in Arkansas', and none at all in Tennessee's. With Louisiana evenly divided between white and black populations, scarcely a third of the first Reconstruction assembly was nonwhite, and in Mississippi, with a narrow black majority, 76 of the 107 assemblymen and 28 of its 33 senators were white. Their preponderant numbers would have entitled the freedpeople to thirty sheriffs in Mississippi, not the dozen they got. Having endowed governors with broad powers of appointment, southern Republicans almost made sure that black majorities at the local level would not always translate into black county officers. Where they did, taxpayers saw resources shifted most sharply toward freedpeople's needs, with tax hikes helping throw landed property on the market, public schoolteachers paid more, and laborers and tenants given a friendlier hearing.[3]

It was no small advance when Republicans sent black men to represent the government in Haiti and Liberia or found postmasterships, federal clerkships, and places in the leading southern customhouses for freedmen. The 600 or so blacks elected to southern legislatures over the whole Reconstruction period amounted to much more than nothing, and in South Carolina, Mississippi, and Louisiana, their share of the elective offices grew as Reconstruction went on. By any antebellum standard, the twenty-five executive offices that blacks won, among them secretary of state, treasurer, superintendent of education, and lieutenant governor, looked revolutionary indeed. On South Carolina's highest court, litigants could see Jonathan J. Wright. He was "no octoroon," one visitor stormed, "no mulatto, but a genuine, low-browed, monkey-eyed, big-lipped negro, clad in his black silk robe, and presiding over the ablest minds of our own race in this State to lay down the law." (In fact, Wright, who had attended college in New York and been the first black admitted to the Pennsylvania bar, had the legal experience to mete out unexceptionable justice, as those "ablest minds" grudgingly allowed.) Black power had its most direct impact on freedpeople's lives at the county level. Over the Reconstruction era, over forty persons of color served as sheriff (nearly all of them in Mississippi and Louisiana) and more than two dozen as deputy sheriff. There were five black mayors and 146 serving on boards of aldermen and city councils. Where county bondholding requirements allowed them to be sworn in—and conservatives strained every muscle to keep black executive officers from obtaining security—African American treasurers, coroners, tax collectors, coroners, constables, members of school boards, and justices of the peace administered the law, made policy. Black patrolmen walking the Charleston streets were like the promise of equal justice made flesh. When a trial justice "as black as a tar bucket" sat on the bench in Orangeburg, South Carolina, he gave visible proof that the old social order had passed away.[4]

Perhaps the most impressive token of Reconstruction's finality was that lawmakers were eager to talk about other things instead. The big legislative initiatives included a transcontinental railroad bill, the first effort at a comprehensive revision of the tariff, tax and revenue cuts, "spigotry," as budget-cutting came to be known, and establishing a Justice Department. Congress shrugged off Grant's request for aid to black education down south, and he had to fight to keep the Bureau of Education alive at all, in spite of the help it afforded freedpeople. For thirty years, Congressman George W. Julian of Indiana had battled slavery. Now as chairman of the Public Lands Committee, he turned his relentless drive to a fight against the corporations pillaging the public lands and depriving settlers of their rights—one reason why Morton's Indiana machine managed to force him into retirement in 1870. Wendell Phillips, reminding his fellow abolitionists that "our work is not done," and that they "probably never shall live to see it done," had more time to support the factory workers and temperance crusaders of Massachusetts; that fall he ran for governor on the Labor Reform ticket. On the fifth anniversary of Robert E. Lee's surrender at Appomattox, the American Anti-Slavery Society disbanded. Its successor, the National Reform League, would agitate against segregated facilities up north and for freedpeople's protection down south. Within two years, it would be gone, too.[5]

For Republicans, it should have been the moment for self-congratulation. The amendment's ratification set off celebration, but the cheering faded fast. Far from completing its work, Reconstruction threatened to go on forever, with each crisis jerking the federal government further off its foundations and with no prospect of peace in sight.

Georgia taught that lesson all too plainly. The Radical coalition of white yeoman farmers and black freedmen had carried a new constitution in April 1868 by promising a fairer, more diverse economy, with public schools, railroads, and relief, as well as equality before the law. No test oaths, no disfranchisement of former Confederates, restricted its suffrage, and ex-Confederate governor Joseph E. Brown became chief justice of the Georgia state supreme court. Electing Rufus W. Bullock, a southern businessman to the governorship, the moderates had shown their eagerness to broaden their elite white support, even if it meant downplaying those policies that attracted poorer whites the most. Even a loose construction of the Fourteenth Amendment would have disqualified as many as forty Democratic assemblymen and eighteen senators, making an evenly balanced legislature securely Republican. But nothing of the kind happened. Based on an understanding made with Democrats that they, in turn, would not raise a question about their own right to serve based on race, black members voted to admit everybody holding a certificate of election. With Democratic help, moderates then elected two senators on the outs with the governor and his "Augusta Ring."

Moderation proved its own reward. Safely seated, the Democrats quickly reneged on their side of the deal and called for blacks' expulsion. The state constitution, they argued, had allowed both races to vote but said nothing about officeholding. "All these rights are enjoyed by prescription—by birthright," one assemblyman argued. "The black man enjoys no rights but by positive enactment." The Speaker ruled that the twenty-five members concerned could not vote on their own eligibility. That left the assembly Democratic by default. Out went black lawmakers, and instead of calling new elections, the legislature filled the vacancies with the Democratic runners-up for the seats, most of them supported by an infinitesimal sliver of the electorate.[6]

Through September the counterrevolution surged ahead. Democrats promised new investigations to find the excuse for turning out carpetbagger members and tossed out a few of their colleagues whose skin was so light that until then they had been mistaken for whites. A clean sweep, the new majority boasted, would produce the votes to impeach Governor Bullock. The assembly took steps to grab the Western & Atlantic Railroad's management—and rich patronage—and put it under a board of

Democratic commissioners. Democrats wrote up an election bill to standardize ballots in ways guaranteeing that illiterate voters would have no symbol at the top of the ticket to tell them how to vote. Exulting at how the expulsions would put "a salutary neglect on negro insolence," the *New York World* insisted that Georgia must go further. The "tranquility of the state requires the suppression of negro voting," the editor argued. (Incensed to the point of insurrection by losing one right, he predicted, blacks would simply shrug about losing the other; that was because, lulled into apathy by not being able to elect one of their own, freedpeople would not care about doing any electing at all.) Briefly, the assembly even mandated that juries be restricted to white people, till northern Democrats reminded them that with a national election pending, the eyes of the North were upon them.[7]

True enough! And the sights that met northerners' gaze outside Atlanta made Democratic posturing seem tame. Already the presidential campaign was descending into chaos across the state. In the mountain counties, violence was "perpetrated almost hourly." Whites there "seem to be born minus the moral attributes of everything manly or good," a Freedmen's Bureau agent wrote. "The great mystery to the many is that a man of my stamp could live in that section of country one year." Disorders broke out in the Black Belt counties. On September 19th, a riot erupted in the village of Camilla. Republican organizers had arranged a rally in town, but when black families from the countryside arrived, they found an armed white posse lining both sides of the main street. A drunk fired a shot into the Republican procession. Instantly the whites opened up in a volley. The attackers were well prepared. They had stacked freshly loaded firearms inside the town's stores. As soon as each had emptied his gun, he stepped inside to seize a replacement. Republicans broke and ran. They were chased down and killed, among them a woman and the child in her arms. At least seven blacks died, and thirty or forty more were wounded, though the full list of casualties may have been much higher. Long after sundown, white vigilantes with buggy-whips flayed every black they could find. They did have their regrets. "If the G-d d-d niggers had only come without arms, as we tried to have them," one white complained, "we could have surrounded them & killed the last d-d one of them."[8]

Violence elsewhere consisted in smaller body counts, blacks killed, beaten, threatened, or driven from their homes in ones and twos, but every day brought a new murder somewhere. "The wrongs these freedmen suffer are unheard of, and I don't see how human nature can stand it without fearful retaliations," a Unionist commented. "Even [U.S.] Major Wilson last night said, 'G-d d-n it, I wish I had a company of cavalry and a roving commission; I'd like to shoot about a hundred." But there was no cavalry, no protection civil or military. Any measure creating a state militia to suppress Klan violence died at once, though the Democratic legislature did pass a resolution inviting the governor to issue a proclamation against unlawful armed assemblages, by which it meant the Union Leagues. In many counties, Republican campaigning stopped more than a month before the polling. Candidates knew that calling a rally only invited disruption or death. On Election Day, Democrats seized Republican ballots before they could be passed out and clubbed ticket distributors near the polls or drove them away. Counting was done creatively, and, in some cases, against all common sense. Columbia County reported one Republican vote, 1,221 fewer than in April, but that put it one ahead of eleven counties where, with 3,559 black voters, Democrats won unanimously.[9]

Georgia gave palpable proof that all Reconstruction's gains could melt in a moment in their holders' hands. Aware of how Democratic majorities had been concocted, the two houses in Congress split over counting its electoral votes for Seymour and over admitting its representatives. In December 1869, President Grant asked for a law authorizing the governor to convene the members originally elected to the legislature, black as well as white, and require them to take the oath prescribed under the Reconstruction Acts. Doing so would not only restore the Republicans. It would eliminate those Democrats that Republicans had allowed to keep their places in spite of the Fourteenth Amendment's provisions. The Georgia Reorganization Act did more. It gave Governor Bullock command of any federal forces necessary to compel its enactments, and it added ratification of the Fifteenth Amendment as a new condition for readmission to Congress. By that time, it seemed quite clear that the amendment, if adopted at all, would need every state it could get and speedily, before a few ratifying states recanted. Georgia's vote assumed critical importance. The same fundamental condition would soon be applied to Virginia, Mississippi, and Texas, and for the same reason. Together, they proved just barely enough. On Christmas Eve, the president put an extremely reluctant General Alfred H. Terry in charge of "the District of Georgia." Civil government would be provisional, with Terry the authoritative power until Reconstruction could be done over.[10]

Lawmakers trooped back to Atlanta to find Governor Bullock's henchmen waiting to institute a purge. Rather than let lawmakers decide on their own membership with a dozen Democrats ready to perjure themselves about their eligibility, Bullock assigned the vetting process to A. L. "Fatty"

Harris, an appointee on the state-owned Western & Atlantic Railroad, with the general as enforcer. Harris gave the broadest reading of the Fourteenth Amendment's disqualifications possible. Notaries, railroad assessors, and public constables all fell under the ban. Many assemblymen had been approached beforehand, with threats of indictments for perjury if they tried and promises that if they applied for pardons, the governor would get Congress to remove their disabilities immediately. To their shock, they learned too late that by filling out an application, they gave Bullock the paper proof he needed to shut them out of the legislature. Taking a page from Democrats' books, the governor filled the vacancies with the losing candidates from 1868. After that, the Fourteenth and Fifteenth Amendments sailed through. Not content with electing two men to replace their already elected senators, the legislators chose three, one for a term beginning more than a year hence. Having passed money bills and a fresh stay law against foreclosures, lawmakers took a three-month recess, to the relief even of Republicans. "The Legislature is nearly quite mad," one wrote. "They ought to be dispersed and abated as a nuisance."[11]

Bullock had just the opposite idea: he wanted to keep them two years extra. By late winter, the governor grasped that the fall elections might well reverse Republican majorities. Reconstruction needed a longer probationary period, and with the state still under military rule and no representation in Congress, Bullock and his allies argued that the general assembly's two-year term should be declared as begun only once Congress had formally readmitted the state. In effect, the next election would be postponed until 1872. For that gambit, though, Bullock would need congressional action. To bring it about, a lobby must work the members assiduously, with newspaper correspondents and editors paid for reporting Georgia events the way the governor wanted them understood. The latter was easy, with John W. Forney's *Washington Chronicle* hungry for advertising and contracts. Forney's golden calf, one observer quipped, proved to be a Georgia Bullock.[12]

The governor could make the case that desperate conditions demanded desperate remedies. Klan violence would make a farce of any election half a year hence. "Murders by the hundred have been committed with perfect impunity," Indiana senator Oliver P. Morton charged, "the murderers going abroad at noonday 'unwhipped of justice,' not arrested, defying the friends and the families of the men who have been murdered." The legislature that the people thought they had elected in 1868 had been "despoiled of its legislative character and just rights" within two months of convening and given no chance to show its mettle over the next year. Two more years could give the Republican program time to be implemented and to work. Then the people could judge its merits fairly.[13]

All the same, Bullock found his case a very hard sell. Having smothered their misgivings in December, moderate Republicans on Capitol Hill could quell them no longer by March. Even before the purge, some of them marked down the governor as one of "the contemptible jack asses whom peculiar circumstances have thrown upon the surface of the South," and, but for the extreme circumstances, might have held off at bailing out the "political fools and knaves" that ran the state. Now they wondered how, in Bullock's rendering, Georgia could be so unruly that an orderly election was impossible but so docile that its people would settle down amicably when deprived of a chance to vote at all. How would giving lawmakers two more years in power suppress the violence, stop murder, or give "some nerve to the judiciary department"? How would a longer term bring "the Executive to a sense of his responsibilities and duties"? And, a Minnesota congressman asked, if conditions in Georgia were so grave, why was the governor lounging on a sofa at the back of the Senate in Washington?[14]

Never wholly easy about "declaring that the Hottentots and cannibals from Africa shall have the right to vote and hold office," Senate Judiciary Committee chairman Lyman Trumbull of Illinois had gone along reluctantly with the re-Reconstruction of Georgia, but the high-handedness of General Terry's purge had appalled him. Now he felt around him the pressure that Governor Bullock had brought to bear on lawmakers. Advocates threaded the House and Senate floor to make their case; seasoned correspondents thought the lobby one of the crassest and most impudent that they had ever seen. The Republican press teemed with dispatches describing the reign of terror for loyalists in Georgia. Many of them were true, but their timing seemed all too convenient. Did "these people think that you and I, sir, are such fools to believe the half of it?" a Nebraska senator demanded. An investigating committee followed money trails right up the Capitol steps: ten thousand dollars in Georgia railroad bonds to buy one senator and a thousand dollars ready the moment another changed his vote.[15]

Bullock's lobby only reinforced a growing feeling up north that the new governments down south were a sorry lot, hardly worth defending. Even sympathetic reporters found the new legislatures shockingly mediocre. A journalist visiting Little Rock was impressed with the acumen of two black senators and the shrewdness of carpetbag governor Powell Clayton and nothing else. The senate consisted of noisy, quarrelsome pettifoggers with "legal talents enough to get them into all sorts of scrapes without common sense enough to get out." The lower house was worse, the black members knowing no more of their duties than "a hog does of theology." Observers sent back the same jaundiced descriptions of legislatures in Texas, Alabama, Florida, and both Carolinas.[16]

Part of the problem, critics declared, was the utter unfitness of black members. A former Confederate in South Carolina saw only "rice field negroes from the low country and cornfield negroes from the upcountry" who "mouthed and made faces at each other on the floor of the House, laboring under the impression that they were engaged in important arguments." Allegedly all illiterate field hands, they naturally voted as their white political bosses directed. "A den of thieves, and ignorant, stupid, bigoted black thieves at that," a journalist wrote of one body.[17] In fact, in South Carolina and Louisiana particularly, freeborn men, some of them professionals or artisans and nearly all property owners, had the best chance of winning office. A heavy majority of the black representatives in every state could read and write. Most of them owned some property, though quite a lot less than the planters and merchants sprinkled through legislative halls before the war. Among those whose occupations are known, there were more barbers than blacksmiths, more lawyers than either, more teachers than all three categories put together, with 243 ministers and over 300 farmers. Yet by antebellum standards, they were most of them poor men, vulnerable to the vagaries of the economy, dependent on patronage once their service ended. They had never held office before Reconstruction and, after a term or two, never stood any chance of serving in so high a position again.[18]

It would take time and experience to give them the professional skills of the old white ruling class, but they could expect neither. Nor, for that matter, could white members. Republicans in most states followed the rule of rotation in office, turning out first- and second-termers to select aspirants fresh from the people. Not one incumbent, white or black, sat in the 1868 Arkansas General Assembly, and from that body just three won a second term in 1870; none of them was reelected two years later, but then, only four of their first-term colleagues got that far, either. Only five of the ninety-six members of the Alabama House and only one of the representatives in the first Reconstruction legislature in Texas had prior experience. Heavy turnover was customary, but at least many of those who served before the war had trained in local offices. Among white Republicans, comparatively fewer enjoyed that advantage.[19] That inexperience helped create chambers where confusion, disorder, incompetence, and perhaps corruption showed themselves more strongly than they would have done otherwise.

Whatever the reasons, by the time Bullock reached Washington, impressions were reaching northern readers that the millennium of equal rights everywhere down south was operating on a cash basis. As Georgia's new capital, Atlanta needed state office buildings, and the governor had used the proceeds from bond sales to advance the cash that speculator Hannibal I. Kimball needed to finish his opera house for use as a capitol. The state treasurer, Nedom Angier, charged the illegal misuse of public funds, though he then had to explain his own unlawful drawing off of over $16,000 to pay for government documents inserted in friendly newspapers. Between Treasury subsidies for party presses and pardons and special railroad charters handed out almost without stint, the Georgia government earned a reputation for financial laxity and favoritism, if not worse. Those familiar with the lobby in Montgomery and Tallahassee disagreed about where legislators' votes could be bought more cheaply. A Floridian claimed that he could "buy able-bodied negro legislators at ten dollars a head," with an Alabama insider boasting "that for small jobs the white scalawags and carpet-baggers at Montgomery can be had for about twenty-five dollars a dozen." An unkindly editor suggested that regular quotations be posted in both capitals, to permit prospective purchasers up-to-date information on the going rates.[20]

Nor had the South's new representatives in Congress raised northerners' estimation of the new governments. Most of them emerged out of political obscurity. In some cases, the more intense the light upon them, the less attractive they looked. They never stopped asking for things. One journalist compared them to tariff protectionists, except in their case, they wanted a "bounty to American loyalists," no matter how much the taxpayer bled for it. "Cease to protect us, and the mills of loyalty will have to suspend," he quoted them in paraphrase. "Our poor operatives, white and colored, must be turned out." Even the upright members, as one editor complained, had no more importance "than a red ant in a meal bag."[21] Ever more forcibly, Republicans had begun to ask not only how far under the Constitution Congress could go to defend readmitted states' governments but whether governments that presented such sorry representatives as these were worth defending at all.

Beyond the sordid means being applied, the Georgia bill raised momentous issues. Long doubtful about the expansive reading of constitutional doctrine to justify just about any use of national authority over the South,

Lyman Trumbull could just barely square his conscience with enacting new conditions on a state twice reconstructed and already once admitted. But now Governor Bullock wanted a bill second-guessing the voters in a state supposedly restored to all its old sovereignty in all but congressional representation. "If this is the panacea for the evils of Georgia," Vermont senator George F. Edmunds challenged his colleagues, "is it not equally a panacea for the evils in Alabama and in Arkansas and in Texas?" Trumbull well remembered how southern Democrats before the war had tried to force Kansas into the Union as a slave state without giving its citizens a chance to vote on their constitution. Now, to his mind, southern Republicans were trying the same thing, canceling a scheduled election and letting a legislature perpetuate itself. It was, a former Tennessee senator commented, "at once subversive of every idea of republicanism."[22]

Republicans who were once ready to go to the ultimate limit on behalf of creating a loyal South had begun to wonder whether Congress held prime responsibility any longer. At what price to constitutional restraint might a successful Reconstruction come? Lawmakers had passed the Reconstruction Acts to put power into the hands of black and white Unionists primarily to protect themselves and as an alternative to long-term military involvement. But the clamor for intervention rose as incessantly as ever. Senator Timothy Howe of Wisconsin stood among the radicals. He had never doubted that Klan outrages were genuine. But even he wondered: how could the presence of a major general in Georgia "turn midnight into day"? For lasting peace, Howe warned, there "must be a public opinion operating, and there must be a civil government there, sustained, to be sure, by physical force adequate to meet whatever organized force resists the action of the government; but it wants to be a civil government" with friends all over the state, ready to help detect and suppress wrongdoing. Even Republicans sympathetic to Bullock's request expected a southern commitment to uphold law and order as firm as that in the North. No secret armed forces could last long in New York once public opinion mobilized against them, one senator asserted. Georgians simply needed the will to do for themselves what was, in any case, the state's responsibility, and not the nation's.[23] The alternative was not simply state governments that chose weakness and dependency on a national power unable to cope. It was also a Reconstruction without end.

Georgia's case illustrated a larger peril. However far senators had tugged the shape of constitutional interpretation to justify Reconstruction measures, they admitted that their readings arose out of an extraordinary situation that allowed them to read the Constitution's requirements more generously than would be the case when America returned to normal conditions. As the crisis faded and particularly as Congressional Reconstruction fulfilled itself by readmitting the last few states and adding the Fifteenth Amendment to fundamental law, the desire intensified among moderates and conservatives to return law to the undisputed constitutional boundaries of the past. But with every new crisis in completing Reconstruction, the voices rose louder from those who put the cause of equal rights foremost, denouncing states' rights in general as outmoded or even as the exclusive doctrine of nullifiers and secessionists, the nursery of treason. The meaning of the constitutional duty to guarantee a republican form of government was changing too, in radical minds. For some, it meant compelling states to erect a public school system, and now, apparently, the right to adjust a sitting state government that failed to meet the latest standard for republicanism. When Missouri senator Charles Drake offered a constitutional amendment letting the president send troops into whatever state he would and declare martial law whenever he thought proper, moderates saw alarming signs of how far the balance had shifted between state and national functions.[24]

National power, indeed, might break free from all limit if Reconstruction's chief defenders had their way. Radicals could find authority in the Declaration of Independence, which, in Sumner's view, had equal importance with the Constitution in defining government's purposes and powers. Whenever anything was necessary, the Massachusetts senator argued, that need itself gave Congress power to act. The Constitution might not say so, Sumner allowed, but the Founders meant Congress to serve as "a High Court of Equity . . . supplying deficiencies in the existing law, . . . and seeing that justice is done." Those who demanded chapter and verse from the Constitution resorted to "technicalities." A future where federal power had no confines beyond the scruples of senators and the predilections of presidents was far from pleasing to moderates. "I thought we lived under a constitutional government," Trumbull protested. "I thought that our ancestors had been struggling for centuries to regulate liberty by law, to put limitations upon those having the exercise of power."[25] But what were those limits worth if rulers could do "whatever necessity requires," and had the right to judge what that necessity was?

Already, necessity seemed to be the mother of endless intervention, and not just in Georgia's case. Virginia and Tennessee delegations had descended on Washington that winter to ask that their new Democratic state governments be overturned. They did not succeed, but Republicans had added new conditions to those in the original Reconstruction Acts, requiring that those states not yet admitted ratify the Fifteenth Amendment. Others called for something more, in effect a national protectorate over former Confederate states, with their permanent readmission contingent on their not backtracking on their guarantee of equal justice under the law. That some southern states would never return to their full original sovereignty, with Congress exercising a permanent oversight, meant a definition of the relationship between federal and state rights far beyond what even most Republicans felt comfortable with. Timothy Howe of Wisconsin proposed a new reading of the Tenth Amendment. The only states with "reserved rights," he argued, were those the Constitution knew at the time of its adoption: the original thirteen, and four of them by secession forfeited that exclusive privilege.[26]

By April, even the more steadily radical Republican press had weighed in against giving Bullock the help he wanted. They hoped that Georgia would vote Republican, but none of them was prepared to make it keep officers that it did not want or to cancel elections likely to go against the party. That, in their view, was just what the lobby had in mind. They did not believe for a moment that Georgia was on the governor's side. It was not white Democrats Bullock feared, they insisted—it was "the people."[27] After three months of confused amendment and substitution, a Georgia bill carried that put the state under a provisional government, subject to military control, but without any specific guidance on whether Bullock had to call elections or not. To the governor's dismay, the Republican legislature forced his hand. To improve the odds in his favor, the governor scheduled the elections over three days at the end of December, carried legislation giving his officers full control over the polling places, abolished the poll tax as a voting requirement, and hoped for the best.[28]

That best, the returns showed, was an unmitigated disaster for Republicans. "Colored men have been shot by scores for simply voting the republican ticket," Rev. Henry M. Turner wrote Sumner, "heads have been smashed, throats cut, limbs broken, etc. etc., thousands arrested illegally packed in the jails and police prisons. United States Marshals have been chased by mobs, and hunted like foxes, election managers arrested, and the ballot boxes taken possession of by the democrats and mad rabble . . . while Democrats repeated their votes three and four times." Democrats carried over four-fifths of either house in the legislature.[29] With its session due to open in November 1871 and Bullock's impeachment certain, the governor fled the state. From a safe distance he announced his resignation. His and Kimball's departure read like a confession of guilt and left Democratic committees to embellish the most appalling charges of malfeasance and embezzlements in lurid rhetoric. Both men would return, Kimball in 1874 and Bullock two years later. All the conservative governor's efforts to find grounds for Kimball's indictment came to nothing, and when Bullock went on trial, witnesses who claimed to have known incriminating facts six years before now denied knowing any such thing. A jury took only two hours to acquit. By then, the stain on Georgia's scalawag government had been set too indelibly for any court decision to erase. Bullock's years would go down in history associated with the song that myth had a handful of black legislators supposedly caroling: "H. I. Kimball's on the floor; / 'tain't gwine to rain no more."[30]

Had Bullock's legislature been wholly blameless, though, he could not have saved the state in 1870. Terrorism and intimidation prevailed in about half the state. That summer it broke out, worse than ever, in Alabama and Mississippi. In Alabama it proved decisive in keeping the Republican vote home and electing a Democratic governor and lower house. The same methods carried the lieutenant governorship for Democrats in Florida, and in both states threatened to undo Reconstruction for good.

Local officers went out of their way to find excuses why nothing could be done, needed to be done, or was any of their business to do. In most incidents, nobody ended up arrested, much less convicted. "We hear of scoundrels going to the houses of peaceable, quiet citizens at the dark hour of the night, taking them from their wives and children, and hanging them upon trees in the adjoining woods," one Republican charged. "We hear of cases of that kind from all over the State; yet we don't hear that the laws have been enforced against these men. Why don't you enforce the laws if you have them? Why not suppress this lawlessness throughout the State? Why not make some effort to do it?"[31]

The one protection on which blacks most depended were the state militias. In white Unionist strongholds, the Klan met armed, organized firepower. There, a white military force could restore the peace in ways that no black forces dared do. Governor William G. Brownlow could call on East Tennessee's Unionists and, having declared martial law in early 1869, brought most of the violence to an end in scarcely a month. Already, facing near insurrection in the southern and eastern plantation district, Arkansas governor Powell Clayton's forces had been outfitted and prepared. When terrorists killed a Republican congressman, the governor proclaimed martial law in a dozen counties. Soldiers arrested, tried, jailed, and in three cases executed accused Klansmen. "If they shoot, we shoot," an Arkansan boasted; "and if they burn, we burn." Having pushed authorization through by arresting Democratic lawmakers so that they could not block legislative business, and having paid ransom to the members holding the bill hostage until their railroad subsidy program could be guaranteed safe passage, Texas governor Edmund G. Davis had considerable success with his state police. Blacks made up four officers in every ten. In two years, the force arrested some 7,000 suspects, including horse thieves and desperadoes. The Texas Klan never recovered.[32]

Elsewhere, the cost of suppressing the Klan was too great politically for governors to bear. For Governor William W. Holden of North Carolina, the potential had always been there for a militia. Yet from the first he dared not depend on black recruits, and did not really trust white ones in the eastern part of the state. So he hesitated as the violence grew in the Piedmont. He tried hiring detectives, with little success in getting indictments. If proclamations and warnings would do the job, so much the better; if the national government would intervene, that would be best of all. Wistfulness protected nobody. In Caswell County, Holden's detective wrote him that law had become a farce; "unless we can get our Co. under Military rule we cannot protect our people." As the violence mounted, the detective wrote even more emphatically. "There is no use of talking about runing a ticket in the next election in this County at all," he assured the governor, "for after the leading republican has bin driven off, the K. K. will have every thing their own way." Five days later the Klan killed him, too. With legislative elections approaching and all other resources failing in the summer of 1870, Holden acted. He decreed martial law. Enlisting western North Carolina Unionists and suspending the courts in some counties where the Klan had justice all its own way, the governor sent out forces to make arrests and try suspects by military commission. It was too late to rebuild Republican strength in the Piedmont counties, and just late enough to make Holden's tactics a rallying issue for white conservatives. The elections swept in a heavily Democratic legislature bent on impeaching Holden the very moment it could unseat enough Republicans to build a majority wide enough to remove him. Not all the volumes of testimony of Klan violence necessitating emergency action could save the governor the following winter. Out he went, the first governor ever removed.[33]

At least Holden had made a serious effort. South Carolina's carpet-bag governor, Robert K. Scott, did authorize a state militia, and used it vigorously in 1870, just before his reelection, but its value seemed to be mostly a means of providing patronage for the governor, and titles for local black leaders, instead of official power, and their appearance set off a virtual civil war upstate, with unarmed blacks providing most of the victims. Far from suppressing the Klan, Scott's move had made it mobilize into a force against which sheriffs, courts, and state troops found themselves helpless. Alabama lawmakers gave the governor the power to set up a militia, but Governor William Smith never used it. Rather, he hoped by his moderation, and still more by his alliance with railroad promoters hoping to build two great trunk lines across the state with government aid, that he could add white conservative support to the Unionists of both colors that made up the core of the party. In Mississippi, Governor James L. Alcorn, no less concerned that so heavily black a majority party needed to attract prominent white backers if it was to endure, was willing to let localities enlist an unarmed, unsalaried militia if they pleased, commissioned ex-Confederate officers to drill recruits in the troubled eastern counties, and waited until violence had reached near-insurrection levels before asking for money to equip the forces. The legislature not only refused it; they defunded his seven-man secret service agency. Georgia's legislature, dependent for its very existence on federal troops, took no action at all.[34]

With disorders worsening, Congress had to step in. Weeks after the adoption of the Fifteenth Amendment, the first in a series of Enforcement Acts was passed to allow government intervention at the polls. Its provisions made any conspiracy against voting rights a federal crime. Most of the laws' provisions, however, applied to cities and were directed at the frauds by which Democrats had rolled up their majorities in New York in 1868. But as soon as the Forty-Second Congress came into session in March 1871, pressure for renewed action on southern states' behalf became irresistible. A riot in Meridian, Mississippi, that began with lynchings and ended with a white judge and over thirty black citizens killed and the mayor driven out of the county exposed the helplessness of state authority. No longer could fair-minded observers dismiss the outbreaks as sporadic or exceptional. Men "banded first under oaths of traitors, now of oaths of traitors, perjurers and assassins," in Congressman Samuel Shellabarger's words, had their knives out and gleaming, "hundreds of thousands, through half of the Republic in the moon-lit air," their victims, exiled or murdered, also numbering in the "hundreds of thousands." What the South showed was not a sprinkling of atrocities but something close to a "second rebellion," so extensive that state authorities either shirked their duty to act or felt helpless to do so.[35]

At first content to appoint a fact-finding commission, lawmakers took some strong and persistent presidential nudging to go further. Responding to the crisis in South Carolina, the president had dispatched troops and arms there. With more needed, Grant felt action indispensable but doubted his constitutional authority. A request for help in putting down an insurrection the national government could meet, but the savagery in South Carolina was not technically an insurrection. Elsewhere he would need to wait for governors' formal request for intervention, which, in Mississippi, was unlikely to come. Well aware of how an ex-general's use of the army could be misread, and with Democrats always ready to raise the specters of Caesar and Napoleon overturning past republics, Grant pushed for explicit legal authorization to act. The Fourth Enforcement Act, branded the "Ku-Klux law," gave the federal courts jurisdiction over violations of Fifteenth Amendment rights and required a particularly stringent "test oath" for jurors. The government could punish conspiracies to hinder witnesses or jurors in federal courts, or state officers in giving equal protection under the law. It could punish the use of intimidation or force against those exercising the right to vote in federal elections. One provision forbade people to appear on the public highways or at a person's residence to deprive anyone of "equal privileges and immunities under the laws." The president was empowered to suspend the writ of habeas corpus and to use the military to enforce the law's provisions. He could send in troops to suppress a rebellion without a formal request from any state authority, and "rebellion" was defined to include "organized and armed" groups able to defy "constituted authorities"—judges, courts, or federal officials among them.[36]

Once more, Democrats formed a funeral cortege for the republic. They declared action wholly unnecessary. They denied that any reign of terror existed, claimed that the disorders were modest, and argued that they had no political bearing and that those who had been attacked had deserved it. Local disorders required local remedies. If national power stepped in, how long would it be before the states withered away entirely and America became another France, that synonym for red tape, where a man could not repair the street before his cottage door without a permit from some bureau in Paris? "The knife of innovation and the dagger of encroachment are still plying their invidious vocation," a Kentucky congressman warned. The bill meant "war upon the Constitution, and the Union, war upon the sovereignty of the States, war upon the liberty of the people, the ballot-box, the poll-book, and the Democratic party." Cries of Caesar and empire rent the air, at least where Democrats could rise to do the rending. The president was "the tyrant of the hour," clothed with "unlimited power," army and navy laid at his feet to use as he would, "without check or limitation." America hurtled toward monarchy, a Maryland congressman asserted.[37]

Liberal Republicans, Trumbull among them, bought into no such fantasies, but they, too, reacted with consternation to the extreme scope of an executive's discretion under the bill. In their view, there had to be some limit on government power, even to protect freedpeople's rights. The Ku-Klux bill breached those limits. They, too, worried about power shifting too far in Washington's direction and toward the executive's unilateral use of power. Along with Democrats, they questioned the whole premise behind federal Enforcement Acts, arguing that the Fourteenth and Fifteenth Amendments provided no authority for any such extension of national power into the maintenance of law and order. Their provisions let Congress intervene against state action, not against individual misdeeds. The new, broader definition of rebellion went far beyond what the Constitution's founders had intended, if it could include any scarred back meted out by a half dozen roughs in the piney woods. What limit beyond presidential caprice could keep an administration from sending out men in arms anywhere, any time, for any incident? (And, indeed, critics found their fears borne out eight months later when federal troops took charge of Chicago after the fire.) "Are we drifting toward a consolidated Military Empire?" former secretary of the Interior Jacob Cox's brother fretted. "It looks very much like it to me."[38]

Uneasy though they were, too, most Republicans in Congress understood that with Americans dying or being terrorized, the guarantees of equal rights would lose all meaning unless Washington acted. "Unexecuted laws are no 'protection,'" Congressman Job Stevenson of Ohio argued. When the state failed to step in, its nonaction was, in effect, a form of action, justifying a federal response. The Constitution's mandate that the United States guarantee to every state "a republican form of government" furnished full authority to intervene unilaterally. To require the formality of a state government's request before acting, Senator John Pool of North Carolina remarked, was to act like the Frenchman who refrained from rescuing a drowning man because they had not been properly introduced.[39]

Aware of how readily Americans saw military men as dictator material, Grant used his new powers selectively. Only in South Carolina did he suspend the writ of habeas corpus. Even there, he left out several of the counties where outrages had occurred. In Yorkville, a northern reporter noticed soldiers everywhere. The "place had the look of a town in war time recently captured by an invading army." Other places never saw a single bluecoat. In most states, soldiers were not needed and in any case in short supply. At most, 328 were detailed for duty in Mississippi. By 1873, the numbers fell to 144, and within the year to 45. The only way most residents saw any of them was by paying them a visit at one of the five posts where they were stationed. In Florida, fourteen cases came into court in 1871, with just one conviction and one acquittal. Eventually, about twenty people were convicted. In Georgia, the government brought only thirty cases and secured just four convictions. By contrast, between 1871 and 1877, South Carolina had 1,387 cases, Mississippi 1,175, and the other thirteen ex-slave states 1,302. Civil officers made the arrests, with troops to back them up. Outside of South Carolina, not even that show of uniforms was necessary after the first few months. There were no military trials; everything was done in federal civil court. Prisoners did complain of unkind handling, but there was very little actual inhumanity or mistreatment. Defendants were put in the county jail, which in one upstate South Carolina community was christened the United States Hotel. In Spartanburg, the cells overflowed with suspects and the government had to requisition the floors above two stores. "It is obvious that the attempt to bring justice, through the forms of law, to even a small portion of the guilty . . . must fail, or the judicial machinery of the United States must be increased," Attorney General Amos Akerman contended. In the end, the prosecution had to distill its cases to the worst offenders and accept plea bargains or permit bail and release of those who made sworn confessions against the others. Those who did confess got off with a stern warning that they would be held to a stricter account if they broke the peace thereafter. Even then, the dockets were loaded past the breaking point. The whole effort was sorely understaffed and underfunded. If Mississippi saw 262 convictions handed down in 1872, that was because the judge and district attorney arranged to trade guilty pleas for suspended sentences.[40]

Indictments did not necessarily lead to arrests, and many of the accused never saw the inside of a courthouse. No death penalties were handed down, because the federal government could not bring murder charges, even when murder had been done. Homicide was a state offense. The most that prosecutors could do was to lodge charges of "a conspiracy to deprive a citizen of his right to vote on account of race or color," even when the deprivation they were referring to left black South Carolina militia captain Jim Williams dead on the ground. Many cases did not come under the Ku-Klux Act at all because they had occurred before its passage. There, prosecutors relied on the 1870 Enforcement Acts. Prison terms went from three months to five years; fines were meted out, some as low as $10 and some as high as $1,000. The more important men in the Klan had the means to quit the state and the strongest motives for doing so. With marshals in short supply, suspects still had days of head start even after federal troops reached York County, South Carolina; there simply were not peace officers enough to arrest everybody all at once. As a result, one judge guessed, 1,500 of his "neighbors" had gone into hiding. Those likeliest to be tried were small-fry, struggling farmers mostly, some of them unpropertied and barely literate. The attorney general was sure that many of those pleading guilty sheltered the men who really "planned and executed" the outrages: the "men of intelligence," the makers of opinion, including "ministers of the Gospel of Christ."[41]

Limited by the lack of administrative machinery and personnel that a full enforcement required, as well as by a military reduced to puny size, the Ku-Klux Act exposed the limits to what the federal government could accomplish. All the same, it fulfilled its main purpose. Where national power exerted itself, the Klan broke up. Night-riding ended in some places and fell off sharply in others. Where Democrats had carried the 1870 elections, terrorism had lost some political value anyhow. A scattered few gentry in North Carolina, Alabama, and Georgia had rediscovered their courage, now that the marauders risked driving away or disrupting the planters' labor force and scaring off northern capital. Even in the Carolina upcountry, violence may have started diminishing weeks before federal forces appeared. But Klansmen's confessions and federal prosecutors' courage put enough risk into brutalizing helpless victims to give potential terrorists second thoughts. Every arrest must have put fear into a score of other men just as guilty, and the Democratic press only heightened that fear by the wildest exaggerations of military brutality and district attorneys' high-handedness under what it termed the "kidnap law." The larger editors inflated the myth of an all-powerful despotism hauling away innocent suspects in their shirt tails without warrant by dead of night, the more guiltier men may have dreaded the knock on the door, the hand clapped on the shoulder. "It is impossible to describe the feelings of consternation and alarm that the action of the court has produced among those hell-deserving wretches and their friends," a black Mississippian wrote in early 1872. "They see the hand-writing on the wall, and like Belshazzar they tremble and fear."[42] By the same token, the public use of national power, even if done sparingly, could only revive morale in the freedpeople's community, the sense that they would not go wholly unprotected in the future. "The courts are going on here," Amos Akerman wrote from Columbia late in 1871. "There is trepidation everywhere." Not, in fact, everywhere, as the attorney general admitted almost at once. Union men and blacks could "sleep at home now—a saying that means a great deal."[43]

A lasting, possibly even a permanent military presence could hold equality's gains. But that, from years before Grant signed the Ku-Klux Act, was politically impossible, fiscally unsustainable. Around him rose an outcry from mainstream Republicans who had reached the limits of what they felt it safe for a republic to do, even for equal rights. They feared damage to the federal system of well-defined state and national spheres of action, worried at military's use in peacetime and the power to declare martial law. Only the safeguards placed on the president's authority and the condition that his extraordinary powers would expire at the end of the next session of Congress let the bill pass at all. Any robust use of that authority would be more than the North could abide. For liberals like Carl Schurz and Lyman Trumbull, the Ku-Klux Act marked a final break, the moment when they lost faith in any kind of national action on the South's behalf, except one: a bill removing the stigma of disqualification from office from southerners still covered by the Fourteenth Amendment. Nor were they alone in that wish. The same House that carried the Ku-Klux bill passed one for widespread amnesty a few days later.

With the collapse of the Klan, then, the administration let up the pressure for prosecutions. Boring other cabinet members with his commitment to aggressive action, Attorney General Akerman offended railroad corporations anxious lest the Justice Department make them do what they had promised when they received their land grants. Early in 1872 he was replaced by George H. Williams, a lackluster former Oregon senator, who dropped all but the most essential prosecutions. Bringing far fewer men to trial after 1873, federal attorneys lacked the means for doing more. Even then, more than nine out of every ten defendants walked free. So did many of those convicted. After the 1872 elections, the administration renewed its peace policy, by handing out batches of pardons to Klansmen behind bars.[44]

Grant may have thought the war on Reconstruction's authority won or gambled that, with generous treatment, white conservatives might respond in kind. Georgia Republicans had made that mistake five years before. If the Klan was demoralized, if, for a time, there was a lull in the violence, the influences that had made it occur were still present, ready to renew the fight the moment the white community gave it sanction. No sooner were the klaverns broken than upcountry Carolinians started organizing white rifle clubs, cloaking their potential menace in the guise of social gatherings. By the summer of 1872, Klan violence had resurfaced in Laurens and Newberry Counties, in South Carolina; the district attorney had had to call on the military for cavalry support as the only means of keeping order. A North Carolinian had warned from the first that until southern authorities found the will to keep order themselves, outside intervention would palliate, not cure. Republicans' faith that the presence of troops could bring lasting peace, he concluded, was a "delusion." With cause, he described "the whole state of things as 'very discouraging—almost hopeless.'"[45]

But was it really so hopeless? The administration had shown that the national government still could exert its authority and that northern voters were still prepared to back it up. The deterrent effect of Grant exercising military power would encourage southern conservatives to look for more peaceful means of regaining power, redoubling their efforts to win black support. More important, the Ku-Klux Act had bought Reconstruction time: time to complete the railroads that might transform the southern economy and break the power of the planters over their black employees and tenants—time for Republicans to shore up their white support—time for the diehards to adjust to the still outlandish sight of black lawyers, landowners, jurors, and voters—time to complete the shift already under way on white southerners' part to accept black schooling as natural and even advantageous—time for more freedpeople to get the learning that might help them rise—and time for white voters to discover how poor an alternative they had to Reconstruction governments. With prosperity and good crop prices, there yet remained a reasonable chance of creating a reasonable South.

CHAPTER TWELVE

Corruption Is the Fashion

T he quickened pace and consolidating force of a restored Union showed itself distinctly in the new Washington. Before the war, Congress met there for six months or so in even-numbered years and four in odd, though members groused their way through cheap-boardinghouse life and could hardly wait to go home again. To a New Englander, Boston remained the true capital, to a westerner, Chicago. A "third rate Southern city," as the correspondent Mary Clemmer Ames recalled, it had no streetcar lines—only "a few straggling omnibuses." Capitol Hill reared out of a virtual desert of "arid hill and sodden plain." Unfinished executive buildings looked best after dark, because Washington was so dimly lighted. The western end of the city lived in "one vast slough of impassable mud" in spring and fall. The length and breadth of its avenues excited admiration; but the hovels and sheds lining them, only dismay. A "nasty stinkin hole," one visitor summed up, and foreign visitors felt the same way.[1]

For northerners, the war turned it into a true national capital, a symbol of the Union worth defending. It also turned into one worth seeing. By 1873, Ames wrote, another city, cosmopolitan and stately, was arising. The mire and poplars that distinguished Pennsylvania Avenue had given way to marble buildings. Broad graveled carriage drives had replaced mud-courses, with concrete paving in place of the clefts and holes that pocked roads in old days. Grassy park succeeded "long vistas of shadeless dust." Fountains marked the crossing of major thoroughfares. Sewer lines carried the waters that once had sat stagnant, green, and malarial.[2]

War alone could not have made such a change. Credit fell, rather, to Alexander R. Shepherd, president of the board of public works under the District governor. Beginning life as a gas fitter and becoming one of the top business figures in the city and one of its canniest real estate speculators, he had none of the polish of antebellum society and no need for it. He was all will and purpose. In 1870, "intelligent citizens" convinced Congress to put the District under a territorial government with its own legislature and much less input from black voters. At its head was Henry D. Cooke, brother of Jay Cooke and partner in his banking enterprises. His money and the high reputation for piety gave him credit with lawmakers—who, if they were a little short, could always depend on getting credit from him. Shepherd showed a more practical bent, ready to spread patronage and contracts to build a capital city worthy of so great a nation. There must be up-to-date sanitation facilities and well-lit streets; horticulturists planted trees by the thousand. Where ten men had taken salaries in the street department, Shepherd needed eighty-six. Those digging up the streets numbered in the thousands. Water mains replaced wells, brick succeeded wooden pavement, black dwellings were torn down and elite residences put in their place, segregated neighborhoods became the norm, and in 1872 over 1,200 new buildings rose.[3]

The new Washington housed a new, sweeping national authority. It did more things than before the war and required more people to do them. In 1863, it started the National Academy of Sciences. A Commissioner of Immigration took up duties in 1864, and in 1866 Congress created a Bureau of Education and a Bureau of Statistics. In 1871, a commissioner of fish and fisheries was chosen. The census became more professional, and under Superintendent Francis A. Walker, the scope of its interests widened. In 1879, the bureau replaced the federal marshals that until then had gathered information and hired enumerators, including 150 census supervisors. Congress found money to begin a survey of the area between the Sierras and the Rocky Mountains under Clarence King, later the first director of the United States Geological Survey. At the direction of the Smithsonian Institution, John Wesley Powell explored and reported on the area around the Grand Canyon; he would succeed King as survey director in 1881 and contribute reams of valuable information and advice about land use and rainfall patterns in the West. Between 1789 and 1865, the attorney general's office prepared ten opinions on matters of government policy; in the sixteen years following, it did forty. Before, each department had hired its own lawyers, with no control by the attorney general, and when arguing cases before the Supreme Court, the attorney general hired private lawyers. With litigation and wartime claims far beyond anything that earlier officers had known, the traditional methods no longer worked. In 1870, Congress created a Justice Department with broadened authority, and a solicitor general to handle court appeals. Other departments' legal help worked for the attorney general. With widened federal jurisdiction over intimidation and fraud in the Reconstruction states, the Justice Department's head earned the nickname "Secretary of State for Southern Affairs."[4]

Relegated to three floors in the Freedman's Savings Bank building, the Justice Department had every right to complain of cramped quarters, not to mention stinky ones: the sewers ran just below the building. But visitors to Washington heard that complaint everywhere. Spanking new marble buildings planned for a century's worth of expansion found themselves housing new responsibilities that outpaced the space provided. The Treasury Building, a reporter wrote, held "a metropolis within its walls." Over 3,000 worked in that "vast human hive." Built on a "truly magnificent scale" to meet "every demand of its own branch of the public service for at least a century," adding a south wing in 1860, a west wing in 1863, and a north wing in 1867, it had already become cramped and crowded by 1873, with planners preparing to erect a new structure.[5]

Founded in 1862, the Agricultural Bureau went without cabinet status, but its functions grew dramatically. The commissioner broadcast packets of new varieties of seeds to whomever asked for them—which included any number of constituents that congressmen hoped to cultivate. In each county, the bureau had at least one correspondent who would send regular reports on how well the crops were doing and how large their yield promised to be. Clerks in Washington compiled the information into monthly and annual reports. Specialists prepared reports on topics of interest. On request, the bureau would tell any land-purchaser just what crops paid best in that location and on that kind of soil; a chemist would analyze the soil or evaluate the fertilizers used. Farmers could even get advice from the bureau's entomologist on how to best rid themselves of every kind of pest.[6]

Few, however remote, could avoid contact with at least one government officer, the local postmaster, and the postmaster general chose more of them than ever before: 27,000 in 1869, 33,000 in 1873, and 77,000 by 1901. The government instituted free mail delivery in major cities in 1863, gradually spreading its reach into the towns; it began special delivery in 1885. But there were more and other officials as well, not seen before the Civil War, among them the internal revenue collectors and a proliferation of deputy marshals. The Land Office had 58 branches in 1862 and 92 a decade later. But then, it had gone from disposing of 1.3 million acres a year to nearly 12 million. The country had needed nine surveyors general before, seventeen now. Federal supervision over the polls expanded in 1870 with the passage of three Enforcement Acts, adding to national oversight of intimidation and fraud in elections for national office. While all of them helped black voters down south, the originators also looked to rein in the ballot box stuffing and manufacturing of naturalization certificates by Democrats up north. Until their repeal in 1894, the Enforcement Acts did some of their most effective work in the metropolises north of the Ohio.[7]

A government that did more things had to spend more doing them. In 1869, its budget amounted to 4.6 percent of the national income, the highest proportion in peacetime at any time until the century's end. Most of it, in fact, was a legacy of the war itself. Direct military costs, including defense, fell sharply, from $1.13 billion in 1865 to $50.1 million in 1871, but the money provided for Union veterans jumped from $9 million to $37.1 million in the same period. In a single year, the eight clerks at the Third Auditor's Office had to pass on over 8,000 claims for horses lost in the war and $5 million worth of state claims for money spent in the war. By 1884, their outlay had passed $44 million. Payments in interest on the debt, nearly all contracted in wartime, went from $126.8 million a year to $181.6 million in 1868 and then declined sharply, falling to $112 million in 1875. All the same, it made quite a dent: the total expenditures of the government before the war had amounted to only $65.8 million, rising to $1.31 billion in 1865, and then hovering slightly below $300 million through the mid-1870s. Altogether, interest and spending on veterans took up more than half of all the funds the government disbursed in the postwar decade. Even so, deducting all of those special needs, the government still spent half as much again on all its other functions as it did on the total outlay before the war, and the Treasury took in five times as much. For river and harbor improvements alone, Congress handed out ten dollars a year for each it had given out in the 1850s.[8]

"It is . . . claimed by the best thinkers that the American Government was never more powerful and influential for good than it is at the present time," a Japanese visitor wrote in 1871.[9] But that power, as the controversy over Santo Domingo annexation or the Ku-Klux Act showed, stirred a fear that the best traditions of republicanism—government selfless, self-denying, and aware of its own limits—were in peril. By the time Grant came to power, critics, especially among the liberal reformers, were in full cry against a pervasive corruption that accompanied government's new ability to tax, spend, favor, and bestow. Faith in public agencies' power to do good rested entirely on faith in their officers' ability to do right.

As government's gorgeous palaces rose in Washington, so did the District's debts: an imperial city cost a king's ransom. Two million dollars a year had gone into improvements by early 1872, and the debt approached

$9.5 million. By 1872, the District carried a debt heavier than thirty states did. By mid-1873, it had collected $3.5 million from Congress and teetered on the edge of bankruptcy. The District's finances were worse than a tangle; they were an incomprehensible mélange, and Jay Cooke grew seriously alarmed that his brother might be risking the banking house's funds as well as its good name. In fact, Cooke was risking the Freedman's Savings Bank's money; when the board found itself out of pocket, it applied for unsecured loans, and Cooke, as one of the directors, helped get them approved. Congress kept appropriating funds, but the drain never stopped. By September 1873, when Henry Cooke had been convinced to step down and the president had put Shepherd in his place, the last money ran out. Hod carriers, clerks, and schoolteachers, even firemen went unpaid for months. Apparently Shepherd assumed all the money would come from Congress, to supply the city's deficits, no matter how high they were—that success was its own reward. A tax revolt burgeoned, with property owners refusing to pay the special assessments. Sewer certificates on which contractors depended for their pay found no buyers.[10]

Congressional investigators uncovered negligence, waste, profiteering, and favoritism in awarding contracts. Shepherd, at least, had kept his hands clean, but around him swarmed influence-peddlers collecting off their ability to steer work contractors' way. No witness had to point out the rotting wooden pavements, no accountant the payroll-padding and jobbery in charges for materials. In all, the Board of Public Works had spent twice the $10 million debt limit that the law had set. Shocked, a House committee persuaded Congress to abolish the District government and appoint commissioners to set things in order. Grant responded by making Shepherd one of the commissioners. The Senate rejected the nomination. For the next century, nationally appointed administrators, not its own voters, ran Washington. White elites, through "citizens committees," had access to the appointees. Less well-off blacks did not.[11]

New York City's Tammany Hall machine earned a special infamy. Bossed in the late 1860s by state senator William M. Tweed, a burly, good-natured rogue with a talent for turning out whopping Democratic majorities, a Democratic ring commanded every city office worth having. In Albany, Tweed's minions, the "Black Horse Cavalry," mulcted every likely interest wanting bills passed or stopped. At home, city patronage filled the offices with partisans so greedy in devouring whatever their places had to offer that they became known as the "Paint-Eaters." Tweed controlled the governor, Mayor A. Oakey Hall, the police, and election officers. On the bench, his judges sucked bankrupt companies dry with lucrative receiverships and opened the jailhouse doors for the pimps, pickpockets, gamblers, Election Day repeaters, "colonizationists" (voters imported from elsewhere), and "resurrectionists" (those voting in the name of dead people still on the registration books). Merchants and saloonkeepers doing a Sunday business paid protection, which, with 10,000 saloons in New York City, amounted to serious money. The Ring contracted with builders, pavers, suppliers, and plumbers at many times what the jobs cost and let them collect $3.3 million on goods never actually delivered. The beneficiaries got rich. So did the ringsters, who took a king-sized share of the rake-off. Doctored account books and padded payrolls made any steal possible. The city courthouse cost almost fifty times its original quarter-million-dollar price tag, set by law. Even then it remained unfinished, with oilcloth carpets and a ceiling near collapse. Repairs began long before its completion. Andrew Garvey, the "prince of plasterers," earned $2,870,464.06 in two years, which, on a building almost entirely made of iron and marble, showed remarkable enterprise. Newspapers closed their eyes to the frauds, consoling themselves with generous dollops of city advertising. To carry the Empire State in 1868, the machine ground out naturalization papers by the bale, 1,600 from one courtroom in a single day. How many illegal votes had been cast? an investigator later asked the boss. "It would need a man higher up in arithmetic than I am to do that," Tweed confessed.[12]

Like Shepherd's Washington, though, Tweed's New York afforded such opportunities because government needed to do so much to keep up with a growing population's demand for a world-class metropolis with services to match. In fact, public facilities could not keep up with demand. At Albany, Tweed sponsored the bill chartering the Metropolitan Museum of Art and arranged for a piece to be cut out of Central Park to put it into. As chairman of the Charitable and Religious Societies Committee, he had the state raise its spending on those in need six times over, funding orphanages, hospitals, "homes for the friendless," and, incidentally, Catholic schools. Tweed kept his popularity by keeping taxes down and issuing bonds to pay for everything, raising city and county debt from $36.3 million to nearly $100 million in two and a half years. None of that would have been possible without the emergence after the war of the international capital markets that the Belmonts and Seligmans had developed, permitting ready sales of securities in Frankfurt and London—the same bond markets that fueled the railroad boom across the West and gave Reconstruction governments the means of financing the expansion of their states' responsibilities.[13]

Activism as ambitious as Shepherd's brought the same payoff. Against Thomas Nast's brilliant cartoons against the Ring and the proofs from the account books that the *Times* printed, Tweed still might have weathered the crisis. But on July 12, 1871, an Orangemen's parade turned into a riot, with stone-throwing Catholics meeting a rattle of musket fire from the city militia sent to protect Protestant marchers. Somewhere between 38 and 105 people died, nearly all of them civilians and most of them Irish. "Dozens of bodies—men, women, and children even—lay upon the ground," a police inspector remembered; "the shrieks and groans of the wounded rang out above the noise of the vast mob, now madly trampling upon the weaker of the fugitives in the wild rush to reach a place of safety." Already terrified by horror stories of the Paris Commune and having watched as striking quarrymen pelted police just two months before, propertied New Yorkers heard echoes in their own streets and counted Tweed's constituents among the mob. Revelations about the misuse of funds made European bondholders skittish. Municipal securities were tossed off the Berlin Stock Exchange's official trading list, and the city credit was ruined. With that, members of the Ring turned tail or state's evidence to save themselves. In the fall elections, Tweed's Ring was crushed, with a clean sweep of aldermen and the defeat of every Tammany assemblyman. Indictments followed. Convicted on over 200 counts, released after an appeal, and slapped with a $6 million civil suit, Tweed could only escape prison by fleeing the country. In Spain he was eventually arrested and identified by a Nast cartoon. An American warship brought him home to Ludlow Street jail. There he made lengthy confessions in return for freedom—a promise never kept. When he died behind bars in 1878, only a few of the poor mourned his passing.[14]

Yet by the 1870s it seemed Americans could hardly look anywhere without finding corruption. Every state had complaints about lawmakers' stupidity, perversity, and crookedness. As the *Chicago Times* grumbled, "The average state legislature did more in a single session than all the atheistic agencies on earth to persuade people that there was no God." So tight a grip had the Camden & Amboy Railroad on the Trenton capitol that one humorist defined the New Jersey government as "a lobby containing a State Legislature." In Harrisburg, critics could have said the same about their commonwealth's relationship to Tom Scott's Pennsylvania Railroad. Wits accused Standard Oil of doing everything to lawmakers except refining them, and when a journalist wanted to refer to bottomless depravity among Kansas politicians, he called it the "Western Pennsylvania." When New York's legislature adjourned in 1873, a diarist wrote that such "a crew of buccaneers has seldom been got together since the days of Captain Kidd."[15]

The saturnalia had opened in Washington well before Grant's inauguration. Even as indignation blazed over the ways that Andrew Johnson was thwarting Reconstruction, Congressman Oakes Ames of Massachusetts, a rough-hewn railroad promoter, was buying friends in the House by selling them stock, for no money down, in Union Pacific's Credit Mobilier contracting company. Top Republicans, including the Speaker, bought in, at least until a lawsuit with unsparing publicity sparked their consciences and made some of them sell their shares back. The next Speaker, James G. Blaine, could be so helpful to the Cookes' banking and railroad interests that they readily obliged him with a loan, while lobbyists for the Memphis, El Paso & Pacific Railroad subsidy bill broadcast stock among a host of senators whose votes could make the stock's value soar.[16]

By 1870, newspapers teemed with tales: the South Carolina congressman with one wife too many, the cluster of southern representatives that sold appointments to West Point (several of whom were expelled, and one of whom, having been reelected, was sent home for good), the lawmakers who used the frank to send their laundry or crates of furniture home. "A congressman is a hog!" one Washington insider told the journalist Henry Adams. He only meant that they were stubborn, stupid, and unsubtle, but the greed and selfishness were there for anyone to see, too. In demanding post offices and tax collectorships for their special friends, the worst members scrambled harder for a place at the trough than a place in history.[17] The biggest, most unapologetic steals, though, seemed to come for the sake of the Republican Party, as customhouse officers showed. Their fees from shaking down merchants helped lard the coffers of Roscoe Conkling's New York machine, just as the hush money that whiskey distillers paid revenue collectors filled the war chests of organizations in the Ohio Valley.

What caused the apparent moral breakdown in politics? Reconstruction's critics blamed it on conditions arising from the war, or out of the war

(opposite) "Puck Wants 'A Strong Man at the Head of Government'—But Not *This* Kind." Joseph Keppler, *Puck*, February 4, 1880. Drawn when Grant's supporters were campaigning to give him a third term, the cartoon emphasizes the administration's scandals: hanging from a Whiskey Ring and a Navy Ring, Grant upholds District boss Alexander Shepherd, New York customhouse collector Thomas Murphy, Secretary of the Navy George M. Robeson, Secretary of War William W. Belknap, Orville Babcock, the president's private secretary implicated in Whiskey Ring kickbacks, and Attorney General George H. Williams.

itself. "The moral law had expired—like the Constitution," Henry Adams wrote several generations later.[18] Of course it had done no such thing: the expansion of churches proved just the contrary. The fact that the postwar generation, Adams included, turned corruption into a searing political issue showed how alert Americans' conscience remained. The war's trauma had simply amputated public memory of the depravity before it. In the 1850s, steamer magnates had bribed through lavish mail subsidies. Street gangs muscled their way to the polls, and party organizers discovered ways of voting the same men twice in two locations (Plaquemining), casting the ballots of the dead (resurrectionists), or hiring laborers from one state to build public works in another and, incidentally, vote there (pipe-laying). If, in Adams's words, "Grant's administration outraged every rule of ordinary decency," it found its match in the so-called Buchaneers and Nebraskals applying public money to proslavery purposes in the 1850s.[19] Not degrading morals, perhaps, the war certainly did not improve them. Military officers got rich smuggling cotton through Union lines. Profiteers with political pull won supply contracts to lay shoddy cloth on soldiers' backs and card-board shoes on their feet. Any civilians in the theater of war knew that if the enemy would commandeer anything from a rail fence to a grandfather clock, their own side was just as likely to take whatever was left.[20]

If the war had not changed Americans' character, it did expand the opportunity to turn a profit. Boom economies generally do. "Everywhere there is dishonesty," one journal reported. "Men are on the make. The air is full of the spirit of peculation." The press teemed with reports of looseness in business and in morals, from bank defalcations to bigamous clerics, adulterous editors, and adulterating grocers sifting chicory into the coffee sacks and marble dust into the sugar barrels.[21]

Certain scoundrels became legendary, like the Wall Street speculator Daniel Drew, whose early career as a cattle dealer supposedly originated the term "watered stock." According to improbable legend, he used to drive his herd close to the market, let them drink to their heart's content, and then collect from buyers for the extra weight the water momentarily put on his animals. Contemporaries knew him as the pious Methodist who prayed to God on Sunday and preyed on unwary investors every other day. His sometime partners Jay Gould and James Fisk improved on the lessons he taught them by ruining him, after he had taken them to the cleaners first. Fisk and Gould could hardly have been less alike. Fisk was an extrovert to the tip of his waxed mustaches, a blustering, showy playboy with a private yacht and a penchant for partying. He raised his own militia company and designed its uniforms. "Jubilee Jim" would die as sensationally as he had lived, gunned down on a hotel staircase by his mistress's other lover, Ned Stokes. Gould was soft-spoken, shy, frail in health, with no pleasures beyond his domestic circle, where he was the doting father and ideal husband. In business, however, Fisk and Gould shared a corsair spirit. They first won notoriety when they took on "Commodore" Cornelius Vanderbilt's New York Central Railroad. The Central controlled the lucrative trade between Buffalo and New York City, at least until Gould and Fisk challenged it by taking control of the rival Erie Railroad. Vanderbilt used front men to buy a controlling interest in the Erie, only to find that the more shares he acquired, the more went on the market. Eight million dollars too late he discovered that Fisk and Gould had ground off 50,000 stock certificates on a printing press in the company basement. Before he could clap them behind bars, they had fled to New Jersey. Swayed by payoffs from both sides, the legislature legalized the stock overissue. The governor readily signed the bill, reportedly after being handed two $10,000 checks.[22] By the time shareholders had ousted Gould from control of the Erie, its debt and deferred maintenance had brought it near bankruptcy.

A year later, Gould and Fisk took an even more daring gamble, by taking advantage of the tight money and shortage of metal currency that came every year at harvest time. Then was the ideal time to corner the gold market, when foreign shipments made exceptional calls on coin and bullion. No lockup could last for long without the government as a partner. With $100 million in gold in its vaults, it could replenish the supply and bring the price down again at short notice. The key to a successful corner, then, was to persuade those in charge to give a freer hand to those bulling the price upward, and, that failing, set up an early warning system, insiders able to tip Gould off ahead of time before the Treasury released gold for sale into the market. Gould bought himself inside information and friends in high places when he took Abel Corbin, the president's new brother-in-law, into the ring and worked out arrangements with the Treasury's man on the spot in New York, Assistant Treasurer Daniel Butterfield. A decorated Union officer, known for having introduced "Taps" to the army's bugle corps in wartime and having helped raise $100,000 as a gift for Grant afterward, Butterfield also had a reputation as a stock plunger who had parlayed his knowledge of how battles were going into money on Wall Street's gold markets.[23] When Grant came to New York, Corbin played host and brought him together with Gould and Fisk. Sitting alongside Fisk in an opera box, enjoying hospitality on his yacht, the president let suggestible minds draw worrisome conclusions about how far he and the speculators were in collusion.

Acting on information in September that the president had ordered that Treasury gold sales be stopped for the next few months, Gould and Fisk began buying all the gold on the private markets. As businesses needing that gold for overseas transactions discovered none to be had, the price leaped. Then came Black Friday, September 24th. Pandemonium broke out on Wall Street, complete with suicides and fainting fits. Realizing belatedly that a crippling panic was under way, the administration reversed course and released $4 million in gold from its vaults for sale. Prices fell instantly. Not as catastrophic as cornering gold might have been, Treasury secretary George Boutwell's intervention action meant ruin enough to those caught in the disarray. By early afternoon, the telegraph wires to brokers' offices had taken such heavy use that they overheated and broke down. Some investment houses were wrecked, with brokers broken. "The spectacle was one such as Dante might have seen in inferno," one onlooker wrote. Even Fisk had been cleaned out, though few people believed it, and reportedly "six or eight revolvers [were] bought" among ill-wishers "for his personal benefit."[24]

A few liberals thought they spied the real culprit: the greenbacks, the government's wartime paper money supply, that a Boutwell could double or halve in value on the gold markets with a well-timed word. The Gold Ring's scheme had depended wholly on a privileged relationship with those wielding powers that would have been inconceivable before the war. The real key to the postwar upsurge in corruption may have lain in the doctrine that the state should do what it could to promote prosperity, with all the favors at its command, from land grants to protective tariff rates. The more the state expanded its scope, the thicker the crowd of supplicants grew, vying for resources that could never satisfy all, and using whatever means worked to sit at the winner's table.[25] Not by coincidence, the greatest scandals came in cities taking on new tasks and vastly expanding their spending on old ones, in the newly settled West, and in a South where Republicanism meant massive investment to create the essentials of the northern nineteenth-century welfare state and the foundations for a diversified political economy.

Those scandals began breaking in the Reconstructed states almost as soon as they came to power. Louisiana took an early bad eminence. At one point, Governor Henry Clay Warmoth, the dashing twenty-eight-year-old Union veteran from Illinois, burst out to a businessmen's delegation, "Why, damn it, everybody is demoralizing down here. Corruption is the fashion." And fashionable he was! Enemies charged him with assigning the state printing to a henchman's newspaper for remuneration twenty times the sum required, issuing $3 million in state bonds to build levees on which barely a million dollars' worth of work ended up being done, and vetoing a paving bill because the $50,000 bribe offered him had been $25,000 less than he thought his services worth. Warmoth denied all the specific charges and issued several ringing vetoes against steals, but anyone could see that he had parlayed the governorship into a fortune.[26]

South Carolina soon matched Louisiana's notoriety, though here the legislature took most of the blame and carpetbagger governor Robert K. Scott was excused as weak and well-intentioned. In fact, he helped cook the state's books to salvage its credit rating. "It is rings within rings, and plunder, plunder all around," wrote reporter Horace Redfield from Columbia in 1874. "You can't reach the bottom; the farther down you go into the dirty transactions of the State officials you find a still lower depth of infamy." One black lawmaker allegedly was asked how he got his money. "I stole it," he snapped. A clergyman elected to office reportedly spurned hundred-dollar bribes: as he explained, he could not honestly demand more than ten. Democrats raged at former field hands feasting on Westphalia hams and guava jelly, or graduating from beds of cornhusks to "sponge mattresses as though they had lived lives of voluptuous ease"—and at taxpayer expense, too! "Do you suppose that if our Saviour would come here with a bill ever so good, and want to get it through, or it was thought best to get up a Committee to investigate him, do you suppose he wouldn't be crucified again if he didn't pay something to prevent it?" Governor Scott asked.[27]

For reporters who ventured south and stuck to white, mostly conservative testimony, corruption became the single test for how Reconstruction had turned out—not land reform, not schools or asylums, and certainly not the incomplete advances toward equal justice under the law. They saw putrefaction where it was and where it was not. Journalism's deadlines ruled out any balanced overview across the whole South. Any such picture would have shown Louisiana and South Carolina's crimes and extravagance as exceptionally bad. In Alabama, Florida, and North Carolina, the corruption came early. By the end of 1870 it had dwindled into barely newsworthy incidents. The third state with a black majority, Mississippi, had few scandals and a succession of honest governors. In Texas, scalawag governor Edmund J. Davis showed a bruising integrity against a bipartisan horde that never saw a railroad subsidy that it did not like.

Black lawmakers were no more greedy or crooked than their white counterparts. Entrusted with less influential positions, they could hardly command top dollar the way governors or committee chairmen did. Some of them later protested that they had taken pay for doing what they would have done anyhow, and only because, with everybody else collecting, there seemed nothing wrong with having a share of it themselves. As South Carolina lawmaker Beverly Nash explained, "I thought I might as well have it and invest it here as for them to carry it off out of the State." Other black leaders raised some of the earliest and most outspoken voices against the rascality; rightly, they saw the thieves as selling out the party's good name. Whoever carried off the swag, they knew, nonwhite members would carry off the lion's share of the blame. "Mr. Cheerman," one black cried, "Judas Iscariot betrayed our Savior for thirty pieces of silver, but dar is men right here on dis floor who can be bought for less dan dat."[28]

Much of the so-called stealing was simply extravagance, lawmakers spending on their own comforts and to shore up a Republican press that without government printing could not subsist to give its side of the story. Stories of bond manipulation and embezzled securities, often enough, turned out nothing more than slipshod record-keeping and confused bookkeeping. The bulk of the tremendous state debts that conservatives counted up proved to be *contingent* debt only: private companies' government-endorsed liabilities that the taxpayers might shoulder only as a last resort. Confronting his accusers, Warmoth reminded them of that every bribe taker had a bribe giver, too. "You charge the Legislature with passing, corruptly, many bills looking to the aggrandizement of individuals and corporations," he exclaimed. "Let me suggest to you that these individuals and corporations are your very best people." In every state, the conservative business interests that crossed lawmakers' palms with silver reaped by far the bigger rewards. Top Democrats shared in the stealing and took the profits, and, indeed, one lobbyist declared the Democratic members "a damned sight cheaper than the niggers."[29]

All those qualifications could not wipe away the two essential facts: corruption plagued the Reconstruction governments beyond anything the South had known in years, and the Republican expansion of government's role made it possible. The gospel of prosperity offered tremendous potential rewards at insupportable cost.

Aware that their governments' survival depended on the good will of the propertied and commercial classes of the South, Reconstruction authorities could not broaden their base among white people by appeals to the Union or equal rights. They had a better chance if they encouraged the section's economic development; that had a universal appeal, and old Whigs in particular agreed that government had a responsibility to foster prosperity. Aid programs to corporations, railroads especially, had respectable precedent from before the war. Southern states and cities had invested taxpayer funds in railroad construction. They even owned a few, like Georgia's Western & Atlantic, from Atlanta to Chattanooga, and the Blue Ridge Railroad from the Carolina coast into the uplands. After the war, conservative governments had expanded aid programs to speed the railroads' building programs. Savannah's city fathers took on prodigious debts not just for railroads but for harbor improvements, a drainage system, and a market house. For Republicans, a commitment to enlarging the railroad aid policy looked like the ideal way to serve the party's political and economic ends at once; planters, merchants, promoters with dreams of tapping the iron and coal in the Alabama hills and forging it into iron in Birmingham all clamored for railroads. "We have heard of so many blessings that are coming at the rate of sixty miles an hour, that we are afraid we are not ripe for them," the *San Antonio Express* protested of one scheme. If all the promises were true, the railroad's president had "enough of the milk of human kindness to start a cheese factory." Citizens would save enough on the flour they bought to build a two-story house and then use the spare change to go to New York in thirty-five minutes and buy goods that the line would pay them to carry home.[30]

Support came in many forms. Charters endowed such generous privileges that a Texas state senator offered an amendment to one letting the promoters "buy, lease, hold, use, sell or operate the whole State of Texas, its Government, and Legislature." Louisiana subscribed $2.5 million in one railroad's stock and promised another $3 million in bonds if it would build a link from New Orleans into Texas. Alabama put $2 million in bonds into the Alabama & Chattanooga, a trunk line intended to connect Meridian, Mississippi, with trunk lines to the north. Legislatures readily lent the state's credit by endorsing the company's bonds or swapping them for state securities; usually they paid in installments, as the track was completed. If the firm defaulted, the taxpayers would take responsibility for paying the interest and, with a mortgage on the road, could recoup some or all of their losses. Mississippi offered as little as $4,000 a mile, North Carolina as much as $20,000, and most states somewhere in between. States also provided public lands, while Georgia exempted rolling stock on certain lines from taxation until after completion. Texas was the only state forbidding land grants—at least until 1872, when the same voters that threw out Republican legislators amended the constitution to throw open the public property. "The donation costs the state nothing," one newspaper explained about the land grant policy, "—it costs the people nothing."[31]

One boon only led to another. States canceled their mortgages or piled aid package on top of aid package. They forgave past debts to the state internal improvement fund and removed limits on the maximum that companies were allowed to borrow. They revived land grants that had expired, after construction fell behind the deadlines that the law assigned. In many cases, the state gave up its stock in railroads or sold it to private parties. Indeed, between 1868 and 1872, nearly every publicly owned railroad property was sold off, at a tremendous loss to the original investors, taxpayers included. The New Orleans, Jackson & Great Northern had public stock worth $1,875,000. Louisiana sold it to Colonel Henry S. McComb for $461,000—and an understanding that he would permit no discrimination between white and black passengers. Florida sold two roads and in payment accepted bonds worth thirty five cents on the dollar. Work proceeded all the faster on South Carolina's Port Royal Railroad using black convict labor, hired out at three dollars a day.[32]

Railroad aid invited intense lobbying. Members wrote themselves into the list of incorporators in railroad charters. Railroads issued free passes to make friends and gave party delegates discounts on excursions to state conventions. In North Carolina, the railroads spent more than a quarter of a million dollars for their lobbyists' efforts. The Alabama & Chattanooga's charter was reputed to have cost $200,000 to carry through the legislature in Montgomery; a bill extending the Spartanburg & Union needed to pay $20,000 in toll to pass the South Carolina Senate. The individual members did not expect to get rich. In South Carolina, they were content with $500 for their votes, or, in one case, $5,000 in scrip, which had a much lower value in hard currency. Some "sold themselves for gold watches," the *Charleston Republican* charged; "one poor member of the house sold himself for the paltry sum of $21; some sold the last remnant of their manhood when the judiciary committee's room was turned into a bar-room, &c."[33]

More powerful politicians prospered far more. In South Carolina, Governor Scott and his allies had the legislature set up a Sinking Fund Commission, empowered to sell the state's interest in the two major trunk lines. Immediately, it sold shares in the Greenville & Columbia, worth $4 a share on the open market, for $2.75—to themselves. Soon after that, carpetbagger "Honest John" J. Patterson bought up the state's interest in the Blue Ridge

Railroad for one-tenth of one percent of what South Carolina had put into it. Georgia governor Rufus Bullock worked out a deal leasing the Western & Atlantic for $25,000 a month to a consortium made up of his Republican allies and prominent Democrats.[34]

Loose allegations, unprovable or preposterous, outnumbered provable cases, and as always, Democrats invented fabulous estimates of the sums stolen and bribes given. But as their investigations showed, the consortium of railroad promoters led by George W. Swepson and Milton Littlefield left little to the imagination in carrying a mob of railroad bills through the North Carolina legislature. Littlefield spread his operations to Florida, where he may even have won votes among Governor Harrison Reed's enemies by forging incriminating letters and signing Reed's name to them: Senator Thomas W. Osborn and his allies wanted the evidence to have the governor impeached. Impeachment foundered, apparently after the governor bought the senator off by approving a large land grant to companies that both of them (and other carpetbag leaders) ran, among them Osborn's Great Southern Railway project. Before the spring was out, Reed had called the legislature into special session to put a $4 million bond issue into Littlefield's hands. In Arkansas, Governor Powell Clayton's authority to issue railroad aid bonds may have helped defeat an impeachment effort in 1871; railroad money came to Scott's rescue in South Carolina when lawmakers thought about starting proceedings to remove him. True or false, the infamous reputation that lobbyists saddled on southern governments discredited the Republicans that put aid through. Later, when the companies failed to build prosperity or went broke before completing their track, it gave enemies the excuse to repeal, revoke, and repudiate the aid program entirely. Among Republicans with very different ideas of where their party should be focusing its energies—lands for the landless, say, or a well-financed school system—the corruption only convinced them that they had been sold out to their worst enemies for a mess of pottage. "We thought that railroad and bank directors would no longer have it all their own way, and fill all the chairs in our Legislatures. But money is ahead of us yet."[35]

Railroad aid, like the whole activist program on which the Reconstruction governments embarked, meant higher taxes and a tremendous leap in most southern states' bonded debt. Critics confused the contingent and real debt figures to make the figures seem even more alarming. Compared to what northerners paid, southern tax rates remained low, but they were much beyond what they had been before the war, and white landowners, still making up for their wartime losses, had much less to spare. All it took for them to feel worse put upon would be to believe that the money spent had been wasted by elected thieves and corporate con men. That was what the corruption issue allowed conservatives to argue from the first. Admittedly, they did not need charges of fraud to make their case. Refusing to admit that any government based on black votes was legitimate, they had challenged bond issues from the first and warned purchasers that when Republicans fell from power, their successors would repudiate them. Anyone not wanting to pay top prices for fistfuls of waste paper had better steer clear of southern bonds. The scare tactics did not drive away all investors, though it may have deflected cautious ones in New York, London, and Amsterdam into putting their funds into safer places, like railroads out west. But it certainly made southern bonds harder to sell at full face value, as purchasers demanded a discount in consideration of the risk they ran. Alabama's sold for eighty cents on the dollar, and South Carolina's dropped to around thirty before it became impossible to market them at all. Since the annual interest remained the same anyhow, the depreciated value meant that far less of the proceeds could be devoted to the purposes that southern governments intended. They had to float even larger bond issues, and the more they placed on the market, the less buyers were willing to pay. As a result, southern debts mounted quickly, adding to property-holders' alarm and requiring even more taxation to pay for servicing the debt. Louisiana added $8 million to its debt in four years, and Governor Robert K. Scott's administration increased South Carolina's obligations by $9.5 million, even after repudiating the fraudulent overissues. North Carolina's debt passed $41 million by 1876, Alabama's, $30 million.

As railroads defaulted and their endorsed bonds became a state responsibility, the fear grew. What if most of the companies went broke? How could taxpayers afford to carry them and state services, too? The Reconstruction governments never had enough money to do all that their black constituents needed done. The drain that railroad aid put on the whole public financing structure was one reason why. In South Carolina, financial jiggery-pokery carried the state to near bankruptcy at the height of the boom. In Alabama, the Alabama & Chattanooga's bond default all but broke the budget. By 1870, North Carolina's legislature was running pell-mell from the obligations that Governor William W. Holden's administration had incurred. Two years later, Georgia's first Democratic government repudiated as much of its railroad debt as it could find an excuse for doing so.[36]

Republicans had enough to fight about among themselves. Blacks grew increasingly distrustful of the good intentions of scalawag leaders in

Mississippi and Alabama; on civil rights issues, they could count on carpetbaggers to show more sympathy with their demands for greater recognition. They had particular suspicions that for Governors James L. Alcorn and William H. Smith, shielding blacks from Klan violence came second to reaching an understanding with development-minded Democrats, and with some grounds: with murder or riot a daily occurrence in Mississippi by the spring of 1871, Alcorn insisted that state forces had the situation entirely under control. With so many second-string party leaders dependent on patronage for their livelihood and frozen out of livings by the surrounding white society, the fighting between those factions trying to hold on to the offices and those wanting into them became fratricidally bitter. Factions centered around federal officers, with access to customhouse, post office, and internal revenue positions, and around governors, with their control over local positions.[37]

All the same, the split between the supporters of railroad aid and its growing array of critics became a constant source of disagreement and a symbol of how the party had fallen into the wrong hands. The corruption issue gave each side a chance to take the high moral ground against the other, not to mention a basis for common action across party lines. Nobody had to take conservative testimony that Republican leaders were thieves or scapegraces. Other Republicans furnished reams of testimony. At the same time, they colluded with Democrats to break their own governors' power or to end it. In Georgia, John E. Bryant did his best to convince authorities in Washington that the governor had sold out to the Democrats, and, when that did not work, joined the Democrats himself. The "Brindletails" in Arkansas, starting as more radical than Governor Powell Clayton, found in the corruption issue the same justification for joining his enemies on the opposite political extreme.

Governments that desperately needed to prove their legitimacy to white propertied southerners fractured so badly that outsiders found it hard taking them seriously as governments at all. When Republican lawmakers started impeachment proceedings against their governors, they gave the clearest kind of testimony that these officials were unfit for office, and still less for protection by national authority. In Florida, the legislature found some excuse to impeach Governor Harrison Reed just about every year. It did not need to convict and remove him; under the state constitution, the governor was suspended the moment proceedings started. That left him powerless to veto legislation or appoint to office. Chicanery like that made it hard to take Florida's government seriously.[38]

Louisiana showed just how dysfunctional a Reconstruction polity could be. Many of its problems stemmed from the same revolutionary methods that Democrats used to undermine Republican regimes elsewhere. Governor Warmoth quickly found that white recruits would not come easily or cheaply. On the contrary, the violence before the 1868 election showed that Democrats would win any way they could. Louisiana Republicanism could not count on the voters to show up, under threat, unless their government made its protective power unmistakable. At Warmoth's behest, the legislature issued a new charter to New Orleans that let the governor to appoint Republicans as its city government. A metropolitan police district run by the governor's board of commissioners put city law enforcement in the governor's grip. He could choose all the patrolmen he needed in an emergency, to enforce his will anywhere in the state. No city in the land had so well-armed and so professional a force. With bayonets, small cannons, Gatling machine guns, and even a steam-powered gunboat, the force could cope with just about anything. It also served as a welfare agency for the destitute, ran soup kitchens and homeless shelters, and cracked down on gamblers and beggars. It was in effect Warmoth's partisan army, and the legislature in 1870 gave him a state militia, all the more professional because about half its membership had seen Confederate service. To lead it, Warmoth chose Robert E. Lee's right-hand man, General James Longstreet. An 1870 law set up a state returning board that not only announced statewide returns but had the power to discard any precinct's results when violence or intimidation poisoned the process. Its authority was so wide that it assured exactly the kind of official majorities that the governor and his associates on the board pleased.[39]

Warmoth's actions were only an extreme version of what other governors had had to do. Arkansas, South Carolina, and Florida created returning boards to cancel out results that Democratic force and fraud had affected, while Governor Scott's militia, expanded after the 1870 election, created disciplined cadres and raised freedmen's morale at a dangerously violent moment. In most places, the governors' wide appointive power let them fill black counties with white officeholders, the kind that white conservatives might accept, at least far enough to stop encouraging terrorism and the armed overthrow of local authorities. But Warmoth carried those powers further, and when it came to dampening black expectations of office, he went far beyond what the rank and file in a state with just about no native white Republican support was willing to tolerate. Creating a white local leadership over an overwhelmingly black constituency, especially when those whites had never shown any sympathy with black desires, meant that in every matter, from the custody of children to disputes over contracts with the planters, the freedpeople would find their lives at the mercy of their enemies. Disturbed at how generously Warmoth rewarded white Confederate supporters and how quickly he removed the disfranchisement clauses from the state constitution, blacks compared it with his coldness toward civil rights legislation. They turned for support to the one man with the patronage to counter the governor's, Collector of the Port James F. Casey. Casey had more than customhouse appointments to distribute. He had the ear of his brother-in-law, President Grant. By 1871, Casey, Senator William P. Kellogg, black Lieutenant Governor Oscar Dunn, and federal marshal Stephen B. Packard had joined forces against the "Ku Klux Governor."[40] Ward club meetings broke up in rows, often with the professional help of New Orleans roughs hired to wallop the opposing faction. The police did their best—to outdo the musclemen at their own game. Patrolmen in civilian garb invaded halls and took over customhouse rallies. When it came to breaking up Republican meetings, Warmoth's forces knew the Democratic playbook by heart.

By the time the Republican convention met in August, bribery and brawling had confused things irretrievably. Most election districts sent double delegations, each swearing that the other was fraudulent. Gatling guns, federal deputy marshals, and U.S. soldiers controlled the convention hall for Casey and Marshal Packard's coterie. Warmoth called a walkout and summoned another convention into existence. He could do it: he had rented all the other vacant halls in town. Both the "Gatling Gun convention" and the "Turner Hall Convention" claimed to be the true Republican assemblage; both chose new central committees. The following winter, the quarrels carried New Orleans to the verge of revolution. Warmoth's enemies could break his power over the state only by impeaching him, but to do that, they needed to elect the right kind of Speaker in the assembly. A mere majority could suspend him from his functions. Casey's allies worked out deals with Democratic members and, having chosen a Speaker, ringed him with a dozen armed men to keep him from being forcibly deposed. Senators fled the city to break a quorum in the upper house and hid on a federal revenue cutter that Marshal Packard put at their disposal. Warmoth assembled his own legislature, with state militia and metropolitan police to guard it. For a while, Democrats thought that the governor would let them raise their own armed force to clean out Casey's followers. Baffled and worried, the president sent in the army to disperse the warring forces, leaving Warmoth in undisputed control of the legislature. "White, black, merchant, lawyer, doctor, preacher, laborer, Christian, Jew & infidel alike unite in cursing him," a Democrat wrote. "Had an attack been made today not one of them tonight would have been left to tell the tale."[41]

Between the corruption and factional feuding, the Reconstruction governments fell short of the basic requirements needed to look legitimate. When they depended on federal intervention, as Warmoth's had, to bail him out, or federal gunboats, as his opposition had, to undo him, those authorities looked all the more artificial and fragile, their own supporters loudest in proclaiming them illegal or an impediment to a true Republican government. Always, opponents swore that if they were in power—if corruption were banished—if a real government worthy of respect were given a chance—the white conversions would come, the respectable white merchants and businessmen, drawn to the gospel of prosperity or to plain, honest, frugal administration would make their move out of the Democratic ranks.[42] It was an illusion. The conversions would not come, then or ever. But Republicans kept believing, and, always, the corruption and self-serving of southern Republicans came in for the largest share of the blame.

The reaction against intervention in the South and government action of any kind built slowly. But by 1870, the problem of corruption had roused a strong response. Democratic platforms, having given ground on the Civil War issues, expressed themselves even more stridently against the whole Republican premise, that a partnership of government with business could promote the public good. The old Jacksonian premise that any government action served one interest at the expense of others fit well with a labor movement discovering that, contrary to Republican free labor doctrine, prosperity's rewards spread unevenly, and the power of privilege to control policymakers was among the reasons why. And everywhere, the independent press latched onto the issue of corruption, at home as well as in Washington and in the South. Regular loud sighs of relief greeted legislative adjournments. "Politically there's millions in getting rid of them early," one Republican wrote Wisconsin's party boss. Critics concentrated not on what the Shepherds accomplished but on what it cost, and they confused extravagance or waste with theft, a blindness that one correspondent dubbed "spigotry." Retrenchment and reform became synonymous. Anyone who saved money, even if it might have been better spent, basked in the glow of an approving press. The problems of the people, the *Chicago Times* raged, came from "too much officialdom, too much board of public works, too much board of health, too much fire department, too much fancy schooling-machine, too much contractors' ring, . . . too much doing and assuming to do what it is outside of the strict functions of a *political agency*; all of which means . . . *too much devouring*." Money and activism went together, as critics knew. The less government did, the less it could spend; the more difficult it became for towns or counties to issue bonds, the less likely they would be to play favorites with those interests able to finance the most seductive lobby.[43]

By the early 1870s, the dimming trust in lawmakers' ability to act honestly or wisely, particularly with corporate lobbyists hammering at the Treasury doors, began to leave marks on the law books. Constitution-writers just after the war had widened public authority to cope with various needs and reinforced the permanency of the Union. Those a decade later put special effort into detailing all the things that legislators, at least, could not do: grant divorces, change people's names, regulate grand juries, lend the state credit to private corporations, hand out land grants, or raise their own pay. Seven mandated general incorporation laws and forbade special legislation where a general law covered a topic. New York's reformers inserted eighteen categories of enactments that were off-limits, Illinois thirty, Pennsylvania forty. Tongue in cheek, a California delegate proposed a provision forbidding any legislature ever to meet again and decreeing that "any person who shall be guilty of suggesting that a Legislature be held, shall be punished as a felon without benefit of clergy." (But then, any easterner reading the state's document, bristling with its restrictions on Chinese immigrants, might have felt the same about anyone proposing a constitutional convention.) The other, less popular branches had their powers enhanced. New provisions lengthened governors' terms or made their vetoes harder to override, and reformers tried to make elective judiciaries appointive instead.[44]

Some liberals had lost faith in democracy. A too-trusting, selfish citizenry, looking no further than the party label, would vote for the wastrels and rapscallions every time, they warned. "Good government is the end," the historian Francis Parkman argued, "and the ballot is worthless except so far as it helps to reach this end." With that in mind, he and like-minded gentlemen urged limiting municipal elections to taxpayers. Their efforts went nowhere; most liberals still trusted that with proper guidance and "campaigns of education," the public would see its duty. Many more found solutions in independent commissions of professionals to handle tasks needing expertise.[45] They favored nonpartisan boards, unbeholden to the patronage brokers, to run parks and libraries, and at the national level, an appointment process dependent on competitive examinations for applicants and security from dismissal without cause. Corruption made them glare less forgivingly on the amateurs mismanaging southern politics.

Corruption in the reconstructed South took on special significance, not because the stealing was worse (or, from the beneficiaries' viewpoint, better) there but because black voters were on trial, and, however unjustly, the whole experiment in black suffrage would get the blame for misbehavior. That the two worst states, South Carolina and Louisiana, had the most African American legislators and state officers and ranked among the three where the black vote was largest only fixed the association firmer. Reporters blamed carpetbagger thieving on the Negro, too, because the freedpeople's unquestioning loyalty to the Republican Party and their overwhelming numbers in the Black Belt counties were as good for scamps of either race as a get-into-the-legislature-free card. South Carolina was "under the heel of the despot," the *Wilmington Morning Star* contended, the legislature's sway "almost as absolute and despotic as that of Abdul Aziz in Turkey," the taxes confiscatory, the judges vile demagogues, and the black voter "the ignorant cause of all these calamities." Government must go into "the hands of the men who own the property of the State," one journalist concluded. "As sure as darkness follows day, thirty thousand negro majority will never reform anything." Those arguments proved particularly effective in Washington. There, white real estate owners, particularly in the West End, made a killing. Territorial government had been the "District Ring's" way of shifting the power to nonelected officials and away from African American voters. Furious at the Ring's obstruction of school desegregation, black activists had even launched an Equal Rights League to challenge Shepherd's machine at the polls. But in the boss's fall, "ignorant black voters" got the blame and the "property-holders" and "citizens"— meaning white ones—the sympathy.[46]

The corruption issue allowed Reconstruction's enemies to pursue their old ends, rule by white conservatives, by new means, but it matters that they had to try new means. By 1871, it was no longer enough to declare the Republican governments illegitimate because blacks voted for them. South Carolina's protesters had to assemble as a "Taxpayer's Convention" and stress the burdens levied on property. Instead of protesting against the expansion of the welfare state, conservatives committed themselves to keeping school systems going. They turned their wrath instead on how black and white alike were being cheated, as wastrels devoured revenues that might have built up the state's resources. And most important, in making their appeal,

Reconstruction's critics were choosing the one issue on which they felt sure of a hearing from northern voters. Far from emphasizing the distinctiveness of the South, conservatives highlighted its similarity to the North. It shared the same problem; it welcomed help in working out the same solution, government by men of independent means and minds. By the mid-1870s, a diminishing number of northerners would see little Rebellions in every white-liner uprising. But they may well have been outnumbered by those who in every southern state capitol saw little Tweeds.

CHAPTER THIRTEEN

Clasping Hands Over the Bloody Chasm

A s 1872 began, Reconstruction seemed settled more firmly than ever before. That year, the last remnant of the Freedmen's Bureau wound up its affairs. General Oliver O. Howard, its longtime commissioner, could head west to make peace with the Apache under Cochise and, five years later, to make war on the Nez Perce of the Pacific Northwest. ("He told me that he thought the Creator had placed him on earth to be the Moses of the Negro," a skeptical General George Crook wrote. "Having accomplished that mission, he felt satisfied his next mission was with the Indian.")[1] The turmoil in the cotton South had lulled. For anyone possessed of the facts, the South, outside of politics, looked better off than at any time since before the war.

By 1868, the share-wage system, where employees worked for part of the crop and then had to struggle to collect it, had begun to shift into a family-based sharecropping system. Tenants would rent land and pay a share of the crop they grew to the landlord in return for rent and supplies furnished. Masters for the most part had taken to the new arrangement reluctantly. It allowed far more freedom from supervision for tenants contracting: the freedom to live apart from the old slave quarters, to set their own hours and pace of work, the right to greater privacy, and the sense of being an independent contractor, rather than having a "master." When landowners grumbled at a system that left them with "no one to cut and haul your family fuel, or go on errands . . . or repair a gate, or hang a fallen door . . . or do anything, except to cultivate the crop," they gave it what, to a tenant, sounded like the highest recommendation. But landowners in return escaped the confrontations and strikes by "turbulent Negroes" that employers of wage labor, like Louisiana's sugar and South Carolina's rice planters, had to cope with. When cotton prices were high, as they were at decade's end, sharecropping also promised the farmers a chance to lay some money by at year's end, in hopes of someday of buying land of their own—a constant hope and dream that former slaves shared with their one-time masters, and as distasteful a token of an irreversible freedom as any master could imagine.[2]

Free labor not only had been tested. It clearly had succeeded. Planters no longer talked of importing Chinese workers to till their fields, the way their counterparts in Cuba and Surinam did, which was just as well: Mississippi ended up drawing only fifty-one "Celestials." Most of the 1,500 that came to Louisiana went into railroad work. "[We] have yet to meet with the first man who would prefer a pig-tail rat-eater to a dusky wooley-head for a laborer," a Carolinian commented. Landowners found, to their disgust, that German and Irish immigrants balked at a fare of bacon and corn meal. Fourteen thousand copies of one immigration commissioner's come-hither pamphlet yielded less than 300 newcomers. On the whole, freedpeople worked best and hardest for the least. A *New York Herald* correspondent came to South Carolina late in 1874 to find the so-called Prostrate State nowhere near the destitution that conservatives pretended. "It is not a ret-rograding State," he wrote. "It makes more cotton and wheat to the acre, has more busy hands, more ships in its docks, more acres under cultivation, and more varieties of products than ever before. It is, to the citizen of the world, a country ahead of its development under slavery." Granting its de-graded politics, the reporter had to conclude that "the political conditions of this State are better settled, better ordered, more durable and nearer a large and long prosperity than elsewhere in the Union."[3]

In Florida all but four counties were taxing themselves to pay for com-mon schools, with 14,000 pupils being taught, in a four-and-a-half-month term. Over the next few years, those numbers rose to 32,000, about one school-age child in two, and several high schools and a normal school for training teachers would be added. Facilities could have been improved, certainly, from a shortage of textbooks to a scarcity of well-trained teach-ers, but at least some beginning had been made. Within a year, northern Methodists would found Cookman Institute, a school in Jacksonville to train black teachers. Georgia had only begun its work, and a Democratic legislature implemented the Radical constitution's mandates to provide the funding necessary to create a statewide school system. But where scarcely one out of five white children and no more than one in twenty black ones had any public schooling in 1871, the numbers would rise to one in three and one in seven, respectively, by 1873. By 1880, 63 percent of all whites of eligible age and 43 percent of black ones were listed as attending.[4] Texas had 1,500 schools, and in South Carolina and Mississippi, one-half the children would be attending school by 1875.

The American Missionary Association continued to foster black education. By 1879, it was estimated that 150,000 black pupils were being taught by graduates from the teaching institutions that the AMA had established, and all the northern missionary societies and churches together sustained over 100 schools, 39 of them seminaries, colleges, and normal schools. If there were 15,000 black teachers by 1888, teaching over 800,000 pupils, 9 out of 10 had come out of schools that the aid societies had funded, with something over half of them owing their education to the AMA. Between 1861 and 1893, almost $31 million flowed out of the North into the South for black education—three dollars in ten of the total amount spent by all sources.[5]

In the courts, a striking difference could be seen in who delivered justice, though not, perhaps, in how it was delivered. Radical rule meant integrated juries and in a few of the Deep South states, a scattering of black trial justices in the petit courts. It also meant a bench much less inclined to reflect planters' interests. Cases involving $100 or less in value often came before black magistrates, and these included nearly all the disputes between landowners and the freedpeople they employed. "To day Warren & I had an arbitration at the mill concerning the rent & fencing he was to pay & to do," a Spartanburg landowner wrote in his diary in 1869. "The arbitrators (as usual) divided the claim & gave me about ½ that I should have had." To his mind, this showed "one can not get justice of a negro." Others recorded just the opposite impression. One reporter dropped in on a case in upstate South Carolina where the black defendant was accused of disturbing a religious meeting. Three blacks shared the jury box with nine whites, but they voted alike for conviction. As the judge later explained, most black jurors "were not disposed to temper justice with mercy, where the criminals were of their own race," and attorneys with black clients understood that so well that they would exhaust their challenges trying to put as many whites on the panel as they could.[6]

Prosperity did not make the freedpeople rich. In a cotton-based economy, where the land stayed in other hands, nothing could have done that. To get along took more than raising a cash crop; wives must tend a garden, market butter and eggs produced by the cow and chickens, if they had them, mend or make the clothing, and, as winter came on, butcher the hogs. On shares, Henry Blake explained years later, his folks made "just overalls and something to eat. . . . A man that didn't know how to count would always lose.

He might lose anyhow. They don't give no itemized statement. No, you just had to take their word." Share-tenants, who provided their own draft animals, might work for two-thirds of the crop, sharecroppers for half or less, and those lucky enough to rent had the best chance of laying something by. All the same, the benefits in material well-being for the poorest tenant still carried him well ahead of his conditions as a slave. Indeed, the gains over the postwar generation in freedpeople's per capita income matched that slowly accumulated over the next seventy years and narrowed the gap between what they made and what small white farmers earned. Instead of the "linsey wolsey, ragged garments, clumsy brogans or bare feet of former times," a traveler saw freedpeople in more substantial material, shoes on boys and girls' feet, "and schoolrooms full of pupils as 'tidily dressed as most of the common schools of the North.'" It was, he declared, "the costume of freedom." Blacks owned more property than before; in one Texas county, selling small allotments to freedpeople was all that kept sugar planters' heads above water. In 1870, only one black family in five had more than $100 in assets, but that number was a tenfold increase over their holdings before the war. In three upper South states there had only been 775 black landowners in 1860; now there were over 6,000. By 1873, freedpeople's savings deposits with the Freedman's Bank amounted to $4 million. Those funds not only helped turn a generation of tenants into landowners but also allowed them to make small withdrawals for improvements and to pay cash for what they needed till year's end. Bank deposits gave merchants, planters, and phosphate miners a fresh source for easy credit.[7]

If the South seemed to be moving toward peace and prosperity, the Democratic decision to drop Reconstruction as an issue helped it happen. Excuse Klan violence how they might, the joint congressional committee's findings turned the murderous white insurgency down south into a liability for Democratic candidates up north. To win power, Democrats were realizing, they must make their peace with the war and its aftermath. That was what Ohio's best-abused politician Clement Vallandigham had in mind when he proposed a "New Departure." With his Copperhead past a particular liability, the onetime congressman had been probing for ways of getting right with the electorate for some while. In 1868, he had pushed Salmon P. Chase for the presidency, universal suffrage and all. After the election, he urged Democrats to make a formal acceptance of the three constitutional amendments as a finality. They might read them as narrowly as possible, restraining state action but not giving the national government any positive accretions of power, but the important thing was to reassure black voters in the South and loyal white ones up north that returning Democrats to power would mean no revolution.[8]

Vallandigham hardly had time to identify himself with the policy before dying on a courtroom floor of a self-inflicted wound, after handling a loaded murder weapon while defending a client, but his advocacy showed how widespread a draw the New Departure had. In the 1868 campaign, southern Democrats already had met the reality that without a share of the black vote, most states and some parts in all of them would remain lost to them. By 1871, even "the bowie-knife, draw-poker, blood-drinking democrats of old chivalry antecedents" had given ground. When the Fifteenth Amendment became part of the Constitution, their northern allies had much less to gain and rather more to lose because those they attacked could pay it back at the ballot box.[9]

The Democratic change in emphasis was more than a cynical ploy. Many Democrats realized how far "rummaging among the dry bones of the past" had given the majority party the power to remake the political economy in ways that distributed prosperity's rewards away from farmers and toilers and toward rich, powerful financial interests, the Jay Cookes and Collis Huntingtons with their subsidized railroads, the national bankers with their exclusive rights to issue paper money. The new economic order founded over the past dozen years was causing their constituency outside the South much more direct and immediate harm than impartial suffrage ever could. Tariffs and bounties, tax exemptions and land grants for corporations all had created a society in which farmers, laborers, consumers in general, were paying for the benefits given to the rich. Free-labor ideology from before the war argued that opportunity stood wide open. Anyone could rise; any laborer might become his own master one day. In an age when a new enterprise relied on the recently grown money markets of Manhattan and corporations of national scope were elbowing their way into businesses where small owners had thriven off a local market, that opportunity had receded. With the rise of a professional, permanent lobby in Washington and at the state level, Democrats saw a partnership of self-interested men fattening off the good things that government had to give and winning advantages that made a mockery of competition. Democratic tradition had predicted just such a result; a generous government was sure to be a corrupt one, with the rich spending thousands to reap millions. The first step would be to drive the money-changers from the Capitol, but till Democrats laid Civil War issues to rest, they could not get voters to take that first step.[10]

The New Departure did not banish the Reconstruction issue, but it changed its tone. Instead of stressing blacks' unfitness, speakers deplored the corruption and incompetence that injured southerners of both parties and all races. In return for accepting the amendments, Democrats insisted that Republicans match their step with one of their own. Let wartime hatreds be abandoned all around! Let Congress restore full political rights to every American by removing the disabilities that the Fourteenth Amendment imposed on Confederate leaders![11]

The amnesty issue had a wide appeal across party lines. With rare exceptions, all of the disqualified southerners could vote already. They no longer stood at risk of prosecution for treason. Nobody knew for sure how many there were. Quite a few had died since the war. Others were so far retired from public life that a restored right would have no practical meaning. But whatever the number, it made up a very small proportion of former Confederates. Supporters argued that passing an amnesty law would touch the better angels of white southerners' nature. Their inability to hold office hurt society more than it did the proscribed men, by depriving the South of its most politically talented and principled white conservatives. Misgovernment in the South had taken place because those fittest to rule were kept from doing so. Good government could only come when the "natural leaders" of society had their full rights restored.[12]

Republicans felt the need for amnesty less urgently. They had restored the rights of those former Confederates likeliest to join their side and did not expect to gain many more. One occasionally heard outbursts: an Ohio congressman's regret that the country did not schedule "a hundred first-class funerals" right after the war or Kansas senator Samuel S. Pomeroy's invocation of "the pleading of ten thousand voices" whose "unavenged blood still cries from the ground" at Arlington. But most opponents of amnesty protested that they were ready to extend forgiveness—just not so promiscuously. Even they admitted that as a security measure, disqualifications had lost their value. The Union was in no peril—at least from the Jefferson Davises and Robert Toombses; their time and their political followings had passed. At best, southerners felt a sentimental, even a nostalgic fondness for them. So every Congress saw comprehensive amnesty bills offered, and individual restoration measures passed by the two-thirds the amendment required. Looking back over five years of statutes, an Indiana senator confessed, "You can scarce count between sunrise and sunset the names of those who have been relieved by special acts." In December 1871, President Grant added his own support to the passage of a broad amnesty bill. The House passed one early in the session, but in the Senate, as one reporter commented, the question looked like it would be debated "until every rebel is dead."[13]

In their call for amnesty and a New Departure, Democrats found especially friendly voices among those Republicans most out of patience with Grant's administration. They had expected so much from the general, as a political outsider, but by 1871, it seemed that his loyalties were to the worst elements in Republican politics. Experience, education, skill all seemed incidental, esteemed in appointees but secondary to party service. The New York customhouse teemed with "commercial barnacles," "quarantine leeches," and "dock monopolists," skilled only at burdening shippers with "enforced bribes and arbitrary annoyances." No such government could be trusted. "Party fealty has destroyed the reason of office-holders," a journalist wrote. "They are intellectual eunuchs."[14]

Sharing much of Democrats' concern about tariffs and subsidies, "liberals" saw more than a drive by the rich to seize the government. They saw a drive by *everybody* to turn government into an instrument working for his own advantage—a grab-bag government in the making. "Politics is not statesmanship, but low attorney-practice," one editor protested. It was "the struggle of rival cupidities, the strife of factions for individual or at most partisan objects." The state had become a Lady Bountiful "who has bread for all mouths, labor for all hands, capital for all enterprises, credit for all projects, oil for all wounds, balm for all sorrows, counsels for all perplexities, solutions for all doubts." No combination of special interests could accumulate itself into a public interest. It could only encourage selfishness and local advantage as a guiding principle, rather than patriotism; it made nonsense of any attempt to create a system.[15]

System, order, and rationality: these were the guiding principles of many so-called liberal reformers. The well-educated urban elite that spoke the purest strain of liberalism believed in economic forces "as things of automatic law," ones in which neither workers seeking higher wages nor industrialists seeking protection should meddle. Experts, not politicians, they believed, should run things. "The mere fact of nomination and selection reduces [a candidate] in their estimation," Senator Roscoe Conkling of New York sneered. "They would have people fill the offices by nothing less than divine selection." If Democrats seemed to be looking for a restoration, liberals saw themselves as modernizers. At the same time, they were genuinely upset at the corruption around them: the speculators touting Santo Domingo's annexation, the swindling handover of public lands to enrich monopolies, the suspicion that Grant had proved himself a man of many gifts, from houses to bull terriers. Yet when they tried to make a case for taking on the tariff or instituting a genuine merit system for choosing public employees, they saw issues related to the war and Reconstruction hogging the spotlight. In politics, a war record counted for more all the time, not just in choosing presidents but in choosing senators, congressmen, and governors. A blue coat covered a multitude of sins. What could one say for John A. Logan of Illinois, working already to displace Senator Lyman Trumbull from the Senate just as his machine had supplanted his followers across the state? Ignorance, bellowing prejudice, unsound financial notions, and a white-hot hatred for professionals in the civil service and West Point all typified Logan. A merit system in government hiring, he roared, was "a monster which will destroy us all." As head of the veterans' organization the Grand Army of the Republic, he had turned Decoration Day into a national holiday, devoted exclusively to the Union dead.[16]

Liberals had not lost their belief that the Union cause had been right, but increasingly, they came to think that that fact was now beside the point. Issues like the finances or "checking the spread of a dry-rot of corruption which is eating away at the heart of the tree of liberty" now ranked as the key issues to address. "We cannot live forever on the dry husks of the antislavery agitation, or upon the animosities of the late war," Charles Francis Adams Jr. lectured. "That long battle is over." Like-minded liberals felt not just indifference but dismay about Reconstruction's results in the South. What they had seen of black voting had disillusioned them or sharpened misgivings they always had held. To some, the freedpeople conjured up nightmarish comparisons closer to home: workers demanding more pay and more say from employers, rowdy Irish just literate enough to mark a ballot and just fool enough to mark it for Boss Tweed. But many more thought of Reconstruction as having succeeded, and the issues that had been at the heart of it settled in practical terms—a reunited nation, a free labor system, and a formal guarantee of equal treatment before the law. They wanted to believe the Democratic New Departure sincere, and the rights of the freedpeople as citizens, even as electors, guaranteed beyond recall; black jurors and officeholders might be another matter, but to liberals, the important thing in government was not that Americans be governed by themselves but that they be governed well and for their own good. The more freedpeople elected "trashy whites and ignorant blacks" to office, the worse the state was administered, and they were among the losers. Added to that, critics like Senators Carl Schurz and Lyman Trumbull, and

E. L. Godkin, the editor of the *Nation*, America's most prestigious journal of opinion, felt a mounting concern at national intervention in southern states' affairs, and nowhere more so than in the Ku-Klux Act and Grant's gunboat support for his brother-in-law in Louisiana. "What between the Force Bill, the Legal Tender Case, San Domingo and Tammany, I see no constitutional government any longer possible," Henry Adams wrote Schurz.[17]

Uncertain whether to create a movement or launch a party, Liberal Republicans soon realized that Grant had too strong a hold to be denied a second nomination. In the end, they called a mass convention for Cincinnati to announce principles and nominate a ticket. Nobody elected the delegates. Some represented states other than their own, others only themselves—especially a coterie of ambitious editors sure they knew what the voters wanted and proud of their power to shape opinion. All the various causes were represented, and among their candidates were none but Republicans, every one of them fearful that Reconstruction had gone too far to allow the real reunion of North and South that everybody claimed to want. By nominating Lincoln's old law partner, Justice David Davis, the delegates could reach out to the Labor Reform Party that had already put him on the ballot and ally with forces deeply critical of the monopolists and banks that seemed to have taken most of the profit in a prospering economy. Selecting Lyman Trumbull of Illinois, first elected senator with Lincoln's help, they would commit themselves to civil service reform. For the selfless refusal to dabble in politics and earnest work in settling England and America's differences, Charles Francis Adams seemed ideal. First making his appearance as vice president on the Free-Soil ticket in 1848, he had done his country great service and had all the charismatic appeal of a killing frost, which to many reformers proved him the kind of irreproachable, unapproachable statesman that America needed. Instead, to the dismay of the convention's managers, the delegates chose Horace Greeley, editor of the *New York Tribune*.[18]

Those who put tariff reform or a purified civil service ahead of every other cause felt betrayed. Many of them sidled back into the Republican Party, Grant and all. Others washed their hands clean of politics for this year, at least. A man who never met an office he wouldn't like, the editor let his wrath over frauds in the New York customhouse kindle into a blaze only after his faction's rogues lost their places to Senator Roscoe Conkling's rascals. No editor had been more protective of the protective tariff, nor freer in trading epithets about "British gold" and "Cobden Club influence" with free-traders. "I personally know no sensible man unconnected with a shade of politics who does not denounce Horace Greeley and deride his nomination," wrote George Templeton Strong, the New York lawyer. Himself no hearty fan of Reconstruction, he was not about to drop Grant for "that very philanthropic old bucolical Scaramouche."[19]

Greeley outpaced his competitors in two respects, however. Gifted with imagination and a facile pen, the "conceited, ignorant, half-cracked, obstinate old creature" had endorsed or pushed for more reforms, covering a wider range of interests, antislavery included, than any man of his day. And he, more than any other candidate named, stood for sectional reconciliation. He had proven it in 1867 by calling on the government to set Jefferson Davis free and helping raise the bail money. Daring so much had cost his paper subscribers by the hundreds and advertising revenue by the thousands. Resentments had cooled since then, and, as everybody admitted, Greeley's paper had made him a power as far as the prairies, which his urge to "Go west, young man" and his promotional reports had done so much to fill. Farmers in Iowa and Vermont subscribed to the weekly edition. Presumably, they knew his views well enough to trust that no editor who once had declared every horse thief a Democrat could really be one himself.[20]

Democrats found themselves tumbling to the bottom of a pit that they had helped dig. With Greeley in the race, they could hardly run a candidate of their own on a platform identical to the Cincinnati platform without splitting the anti-administration vote. Twelve years before, they had made the mistake of fielding two candidates; that was how a Republican president won in the first place. At any rate, Greeley could give the most convincing proof that Democratic attitudes toward war and human rights had changed. All the same, Democrats did not want to acquiesce, but they did just that in July at Baltimore with funereal resignation and much waving of "repulsive, ghastly, flesh-colored fans" fashioned into Greeley's face, with white woolen chin-whiskers attached. One governor guessed he could swallow the Greeley nomination but doubted he could keep it down "any more than the Irishman could the spoiled oyster." A particle of the party, well fed on administration money, called its own straight-out convention in Louisville and nominated the austere constitutional lawyer Charles O'Conor, adjourning hastily before he could decline the honor—which he did, almost immediately.[21]

The only question was, how many Republicans could Greeley carry? There were fantastic estimates, at least at first, plausible enough that many Liberals thought it better to accept the editor than try again, although a gathering at the Fifth Avenue Hotel was called to see whether they could find some way out. The largest accession, in terms of moral weight, was

Senator Charles Sumner, who persuaded himself that his civil rights bill, ending discrimination in public transportation, schools, cemeteries, and accommodations, could expect Greeley's signature; how it could ever pass the Democratic Congress that a Greeley victory would bring in and come to his White House desk, Sumner did not consider. But his endorsement, when it came, seemed like the most powerful argument that the Greeley candidacy was Republican to the marrow.[22]

A few old abolitionists and somewhat more antebellum Republicans joined Sumner. Those likeliest to convert were politicians fallen from power or falling, like Trumbull: easy to dismiss as a "bread-and-butter brigade of soreheads." In the South, those rallying to the Greeley standard were those who had lost control of the party machinery. Joseph Brooks, head of the "Brindletail" faction in Arkansas, needed Democratic votes to win the governorship over Powell Clayton's "Minstrel" Republicans. In Louisiana, Governor Henry Clay Warmoth shouted for reform as best he could, which in practical terms only meant doing his best to bring in a Democratic governor.[23] But no Republicans with much future in their own party swelled Liberal ranks. Most of the old abolitionists grieved at Sumner's defection and put distance between his views and theirs. "We don't want any speeches," one black southerner cried. "Just lift up the shirt of any colored man that ever was a slave and you will find his Democratic history written on his back with a whiplash." African Americans paltering with the enemy always had met insult or worse: they were "white blackbirds" and "sweet-cake sneaks." When North Carolina held its state election in early August, the predicted black defections to the Democratic candidate for governor never took place. Having lost the state two years before, Republicans regained it narrowly. Sumner himself could do nothing more to make Greeley's case. Seriously ill, he took himself off to England for a rest in early September.[24]

Liberals had hoped to make their campaign on the new issues. Greeley's tariff views ruled out an attack on protection, but a Republican Congress had taken the sting out of the revenue reform issue in any case. That May, it carried through a broad tax measure removing most of the internal taxes devised during the Civil War and on which the Treasury still depended for much of its revenue. The income tax was done away with entirely. A "free breakfast table" brought in sugar, coffee, and tea, duty-free, which, popular as it was, cut into the government's revenues so deeply that the protective system had to be left pretty much intact. A 10 percent cut in rates was made across the board, far less than the placing of coal, iron, salt, and lumber on the duty-free list that reformers had been talking about, but more than enough of an apparent down payment to satisfy those consumers paying much attention to the tariff at all.[25]

Congress also passed an amnesty bill that left only some 500 former Confederates out of its provisions. That bill might have passed months before if Sumner had not tacked on his civil rights bill. There was not the least chance of any combined measure winning the two-thirds vote required in the House, as Sumner probably knew. His colleagues, exasperated, embarrassed, but unhappy voting against equal rights, agreed to merge both measures. Most Republicans voted for the bill, but the absentees deprived it of a constitutional margin in mid-February. A second amnesty bill, come from the House, met the same fate in May. Then, while Sumner was out of the chamber, Matthew Carpenter of Wisconsin pushed through a truncated version of the civil rights bill separate and distinct from amnesty. Republicans knew that the House would never take it up before adjournment, but, their duty done, they now could enact the amnesty measure that Grant had asked for. (Stung, perhaps, by the parliamentary fast-shuffle that had doomed his bill and enraged at the whitewashing report about the War Department's sale of arms to French agents during the recent war on the continent, Sumner no longer had a reason to hold himself in, and made a thundering address against Grant as a nepotistic Caesar, which only convinced Grant that the senator really had gone crazy.)[26]

Already, the civil service reform question, first raised eight years before by Sumner and championed in Congress by Trumbull, had found its quietus in the president's endorsement of the principle the winter before and in the creation of a Civil Service Commission able to define rules for promotion and dismissal from public office; at its head, Grant put George William Curtis, editor of *Harper's Weekly* and one of the most respected oracles of reform. A Republican Congress had gone along reluctantly and with an embarrassing background of grumbling, but for those most concerned in the movement, the remedies that the commission offered seemed more palpable and promising than the general promises that the Greeley campaign made to turn the rascals out.[27]

Most of the Liberal issues faded from view early in the campaign, and never put in a reappearance. Democrats had no interest in most of them. Audiences seem to have had even less. For many workers, in fact, a protective tariff looked like one of the few public policies in which they and their employers shared the advantages: guaranteed markets for the one and security from starvation wages for the other. "All last winter the cry went that the people were going to divide on the one issue of revenue reform, and that that discussion was to become the great conduit through which peace, amnesty, and good feeling were to flow in upon us like a spring tide," the *Quincy Herald* jeered. Then the people assembled in party conventions and, lo, cared not at all for "this flimsy sword of lath." They wanted "bread and meat—substantial loaves and honest joints and sounds—and their appetite was not to be fooled away on syllabubs and comfits. They wanted peace, re-union, restoration, resumption, honesty, and it was in vain that the dainty gentlemen and predestinated *doctrinaires* tried to cram down their throats the abstractions and the theorems of political economy."[28]

More than in most campaigns, the contest turned into diatribes about personal character. The corruption issue made it certain that the private lives and moral codes of people on both sides would be fair game; what better way to counter expressions of principles than by exposures of scoundrelry? The most harmless came from an Iowa paper that, having noted that both candidates' names began with the same two letters, analyzed the deeper meaning of the rest. The "-ant" stood for industriousness, prudence, and energy; "-eely" things were wiggling and slippery and could never be found twice in the same place. People could always be found to swear affidavits to any libel, and sometimes it seemed as though ministers had less conscience about it than anybody else. The press teemed with sworn statements that Grant had been drunk at the battle of Shiloh, and that he had been sober, and the *Cincinnati Enquirer* invited volunteers who would take oath that there never had been a battle at Shiloh at all. Greeley's supporters accused the president of taking gifts and awarding offices to his family, though an un-named Bostonian bridled at the idea that Judge Ebenezer Rockwood Hoar would have presented the president with a valuable collection of books: he would as soon think of presenting a eunuch with a harem! In Greeley's case, his past record could be used to defame him as everything that southerners before the war imagined Republicans to be, the enemies of family, church, marriage, country, and property. He was a free lover and a spiritualist, orators announced, an "Anti-Sunday and Bible man," a bigamist, a Know-Nothing, and a potential recruit for any new version of the priest-killing, property-dividing Paris Commune. But there were other campaign speakers who declared as plain fact not only that Greeley had been born and raised in the South but that he had been cruel to his slaves. In Arkansas, an old sup-posed retainer was brought before an audience to confirm that "Massa Gree-ley used to own him; and whipped him awful." Rightly, Greeley would write late in the campaign that he had been so bitterly arraigned "that I hardly know whether I was running for the Presidency or for the penitentiary."[29]

"H. G. [Horace Greeley]: 'Let Us Clasp Hands over the Bloody Chasm.'" Thomas Nast, *Harper's Weekly*, October 19, 1872. Georgia voted for state officers several weeks ahead of the national election. At Savannah, black voters were driven away by Democratic gunfire. Notice that the foremost rioter wears a Confederate uniform as he treads on the American flag.

Yet the transparencies in campaign parades showed that the corruption issue, however strong it had seemed, ranked behind Reconstruction. Even that was seen through the lens of the war itself. "Soldiers still follow their successful leader," Republican banners boasted. "The Enemies of the Union are the Enemies of Grant." Orators and presses alike depicted Greeley as the Confederates' preferred candidate. Every "unrepentant ex-rebel from A to Izzard" backed him, allegedly; what possible reason could they have but the assurance that his win was effectively their own? Why had Confederate bonds worth nothing before the Baltimore convention shot up in value? Soberly, one newspaper came to what it declared the only logical conclusion, that Greeley on taking office would put Jefferson Davis or Robert Toombs into his cabinet; otherwise, it argued, he would not make such a point of insisting on restoring such men to officeholding privileges. The *Milwaukee Sentinel* predicted that the Confederate guerrilla William Quantrill would announce for Greeley, to which the *News* retorted that, like all the other guerrillas, he would side with Grant; having been killed in 1865, Quantrill expressed no opinion.[30]

The biggest issue remained that of reconciliation, and on whose terms. Greeley's slogan, "Let us clasp hands over the bloody chasm," certainly reflected the Reconstruction issue—Reconstruction did stand in the way of full reconciliation—but it was first and most significantly a call for reunion, as much as the Seymour campaign badges with handshakes on them were. It is not surprising, then, that much of Thomas Nast's attack on the image went to the war, and not to Reconstruction itself. Greeley clasping hands with the ghost of John Wilkes Booth over the grave of Lincoln . . . Greeley stretching an arm over Andersonville prison camp . . . Greeley clasping hands with Baltimore rioters over the body of a Union soldier. Even in one of his images reflecting Klan violence, the white southerner in Confederate uniform stood center stage. The *New York Times* reminded women that supporting Greeley would overturn "what was fought for in the war—to confess that the blood of tens of thousands of Union soldiers was poured forth in vain. Surely, no woman who lost a husband, a father, a brother, or son, or even a friend, in the war, can wish such an admission to go forth to the world as this." Sensibly, a Missouri judge predicted that the North would stand by "the man who took Richmond. They are rather shamed of him, but when it comes to the pinch, they will vote for him, rather than endanger the supremacy of *loyalty*."[31]

To make themselves into the exclusive guarantors of the war's results, Republicans had to convince the voters that all the professions of loyalty by Democrats, southern ones especially, were a pose. Loyalty, to them, meant lip service to the flag but not to the causes that the Union had made its own. By reconciliation, the conservative South meant the overthrow of governments democratically elected and the return of the so-called governing class to power. Only a fantasist would think them ready to acquiesce in the Reconstruction Amendments in good faith. "Surely they do not intend to go any further," a Boston correspondent reminded readers. "Surely they are not going to volunteer to pass state laws and town and city ordinances to secure equal rights to the black man or even to the white man. The idea is preposterous. They mean to acquiesce just as far as they are obliged to, and no farther." That may have meant electing Greeley, but, a few Republicans hinted darkly, the old editor need not expect to live much beyond his inauguration; Democrats had got rid of inconvenient presidents before. As one newspaper doggerelist had them confide:

But let us take our dish of dirt
And try to push it through,
And turn our backs upon the past,

When this Old Hat was new,
And when we get old Greeley in,
We'll send him to that shore
Where Harrison and Taylor
And Lincoln's gone before
And then with Gratz and Cousin Frank
And all of the Blair crew,
We'll soon restore the days of yore,
When this Old hat was new.

And, as in every other campaign, stories circulated of Confederate flags used as banners at a "Greeley meeting" and the American flag lowered because it made its audience uncomfortable.[32]

But along with this insistence, Republicans themselves had to profess to favor reconciliation with every former enemy prepared to set wartime differences aside. This meeting could come, not by loyalty giving ground, but by inviting the formerly disloyal to share it. Instead of "going down from the heights we have struggled for forty years to gain, we have gone up nearer God, and tried to carry the world up with us," Senator Henry Wilson explained; "instead of going down, I want to reach down to our Southern brethren and lift them up to the lofty plane on which we stand. I want to breathe into their souls the spirit of patriotism, and of that love of country that sacrifices property and life itself to save. I want to breathe into their hearts the love of liberty—liberty for all classes and conditions of men." Secretary of the Treasury George Boutwell protested the very words "clasping hands cross the bloody chasm made by the war." Rather, let the chasm be filled up! "Produced by injustice, let it be cemented by justice, so that neither we nor our children can find line or seam to mark the ancient divisions between us."

The birds have built nests in the cannon's cold throat;
No longer disfranchised, the rebel can vote,
And we hold out our hands to all men that are true,
Who wear not the grey coat under the blue![33]

Greeley countered the appeal with a personal campaign all his own. Packing his spare clothing in a black carpetbag, he headed west, delivering fifty speeches and a number of brief remarks over ten days. Veterans heckled him. As he crossed Ohio, a fist-sized stone smashed through his train window. It could not shatter his poise or throw him off message. Occasionally he made some gaffes, twisted by Republicans into an admission that he might have been mistaken in his objections to slavery and that he would have let any state secede where a majority of voters favored disunion. Reform, even corruption, hardly earned a walk-on role in his addresses. Instead, what he sought to do was to emphasize the Republican basis of his commitment to sectional reconciliation. Greeley would not appease the South with euphemisms. "The rebellion was a rebellion and nothing else," the *Boston Advertiser* acknowledged. Let no one delude himself: President Greeley would crush out Klan violence as firmly as Grant had. He would hold fast by his lifelong commitment to the protection of equal rights for all. There would be no compensation for slave owners, no payment of the Rebel debt, no pensioning Confederate veterans—and nobody dreamed of such a thing. "I stand this day demanding that there shall be no proscribed class, no disfranchised people, black or white, in this country, but that the genius of universal liberty shall enfold under its mantle the whole American people," he told a Xenia, Ohio, crowd. "That is my platform, and all of it."[34]

Greeley never had any chance to beat Grant. The country was too prosperous to care deeply about scandals yet. The South was quieter and richer than it had been for years. The Treasury was wiping out the public debt; brand new rules had gone into effect to ease government hiring toward the merit system. Greeley had so many odd friends and crazy ideas: "free love and free farms and all that."[35] Was secession really dead? Were the war's results really secure? Once again, Grant seemed the safer choice.

With the October elections, just about all doubt evaporated on either side, and whatever willingness Democrats may have had to stultify themselves vanished; there was no use in casting a paltering ballot in a doomed cause. Southern Democratic newspapers muted the reform issue and brought race issues to the forefront. Aware that the country itself was probably lost, the *Norfolk Virginian* turned all its attention to saving the state and appealing to Confederate sympathies.[36] The Liberal congressional campaign committee quit working and closed its doors. Democrats turned all their attention to saving local candidacies, whatever the fate of the national ticket, and a few made wistful noises about withdrawing Greeley's name from the race entirely.

Greeley lost in a landslide, by three quarters of a million votes. He took just six states, all of them in the former slave South, three of them in the Border South. Their 66 electoral votes paled beside Grant's 286. The North was not simply a unit for the Republicans; Greeley got nearly 200,000 votes less there than Horatio Seymour had four years before. The results did not come from conversions to the Republican side; Grant's absolute numbers did not rise sharply in the North, and owed much of their increase in the South to four states that had not taken part in the 1868 election. In every New England state, the total vote for both nominees was down; the same could be said for New York, while in Pennsylvania some 150,000 voters stayed home. Illinois, Michigan and Wisconsin, and other midwestern states did not have increases to brag about. But the decline in Democratic turnout was what explained most of the fall. As a result, in Pennsylvania, where Democrats had carried thirty-one counties in October, they carried eleven now. Nobody was surprised. The *Springfield Republican* joked that the outcome was like what the Irishman had said about his pig: "It did not weigh as much as he expected, and he never thought it would." The old crusader may have carried some Republicans, but not many. The Liberal rank and file went missing, leaving their would-be chiefs to take the field unsupported. What few did show up on Greeley's behalf scarcely made up for the loss of so many Democrats. Well over 100,000 Democrats who voted for governor in Pennsylvania's election sat out the national contest. Angrily, the *Louisville Courier-Journal* blamed its brethren in the North for failing of their duty—just the way they had in 1861. "If all the Democrats had been true to themselves and the country at the late election," it hazarded, "we should have a very different result." But it could have found defectors much closer to home. Grimly, white southerners took solace in seeing the party punished "for selling itself."[37]

In the general wrack, Democratic and Liberal candidates alike were swept away: Republicans carried the governorships in Illinois and New York. They expanded their lead in the House and held onto their heavy preponderance in the Senate. "May we have better luck next time," wrote William R. Morrison of Illinois (one of the few congressional candidates to extract "crumbs of comfort" that November), "d—d few of us reached dry land this time."[38]

So humiliating a defeat would have been hard for Greeley to bear, but not as hard as losing his wife and his reputation in the course of a few weeks. She had suffered "too deeply and too long" before death took her in the last days of the campaign, and Greeley had been there at the bedside in the final three weeks, not in the campaign. His one regret was that he should long outlive her. With his losses still fresh, his finances a wreck, his health broken, he returned to the *Tribune* to find himself neither welcome nor even heeded. With good reason he felt as though he had lost everything worth living for. On himself he heaped all the blame for the failure of the

Liberal Republican movement. "I stand naked before my God, the most utterly, hopelessly wretched and undone of all who ever lived," he lamented. "I have done more harm and wrong than any man who ever saw the light of day. And yet I take God to witness that I have never intended to injure or harm anyone." His mind, already seriously affected before the returns came in, wholly gave way. When, three weeks later, he died in a sanitarium, he very likely welcomed the release that only death could give him. Those who had scorned the candidate mourned the man. An Iowa paper that had pronounced the candidate to have "no character at all" now hailed his honest convictions and protested that "those who voted against him last loved him most and loved him best."[39]

Perhaps Greeley was mourned the more because he was one more of the many strands that tied postwar Republicanism to the spiritual ferment from which it had come, a ferment that was being lost. Greeley's candidacy itself had sped the process. Many an antebellum figure had come on stage as a Republican for the last time, and many, in politics, would be seen no more. The Greeley campaign had guaranteed that come the following March Lyman Trumbull would leave the Senate forever, and it had erased Charles Sumner's standing in the Republican Party—among white members, at least. There would be no place for Michigan's once-famed war governor Austin Blair (or, for that matter, hard-drinking, hard-swearing Frank Blair Jr., whose brief Senate career Missouri Democrats would not extend), and when Foreign Affairs chairman Nathaniel P. Banks found his way back into the House four years later, it was more as an embodied memory than as a political force for Congress to reckon with. Noted but not so deeply mourned in the closing weeks of the campaign, former secretary of state William Seward, the great world traveler, in one jaundiced diarist's turn of phrase, began his journey into another world. "The decaying carcass of great ideas taints the air," a reporter commented.[40]

Yet time stood with the conservatives. The election had been no endorsement of what went on in the South. It had been a confirmation that Americans wanted, and with Grant in charge, expected, "peace & prosperity as a nation." That may have been a key to the pronounced apathy of so many voters on both sides to the election's outcome. The Union, both sides knew, was no longer in danger. Compared to the war's excitements, what did a political campaign really matter? But that same lack of urgency, in the long run, lessened the force of any argument for federal oversight in the Confederate South. Without the imminence of a new war, the case for upholding Reconstruction governments lay more and more in the merits of those who ran them—merits harder to find all the time. Each day, the arguments from high ideals lost force, until very nearly the whole case for Reconstruction was the one of preserving the gains a war had won. The more Reconstruction was put on that footing, the shakier it became. Every new western state admitted lessened Republicans' need for southern votes. Every year, the Union looked a little safer. As that happened, southern loyalists of both races went from indispensable to insufferable in Republican lawgivers' eyes.

Democrats and Greeley Republicans saw the election as a parting of ways. For Carl Schurz, the results only showed that the Democratic label tainted whatever it touched. The party could not hope to win and must meet critics such as himself on Liberal terms. Democrats read events quite the other way round. They could hardly have done worse on their own than by subsuming their identity; too many of their followers simply were not deliverable, and Liberal leaders had nobody to deliver in the first place. One thing was certain, Ohio senator Allen Thurman predicted: Whatever the Democracy's future, "it will not consent to write, *with its own hand*, the word 'infamy' on its brow."[41]

That feeling had deeper, more fearful meanings in the South than outside of it. Gloating over the "sick set of Greeleyites in this part of the country," a Georgian reported that many of them vowed nevermore to "give up principle for expediency or policy."[42] The principle they were thinking of, very probably, was the preservation of the white man's republic. Even in the North, Democrats briefly spoke of turning their back on the New Departure, though most came to recognize that acceptance would clear the way to run on winning issues next time: free trade, pure government, and a sound currency; their western allies had a different program, but it, too, looked forward, not back. Southern Democrats took a harsher lesson. Greeley's defeat showed that the black vote was beyond winning, and some of them took comfort that they had lost so badly, because it taught their fellows that one lesson. "When the returns came, we thanked God, that the Negroes voted en masse chiefly for Grant," one irreconcilable wrote later. "We do not desire Democrats to be under a shade of political obligation to Sambo; it is degrading to them. They are wasting time that could be better spent on the White Race, than on licking 'black and tan' feet for office."[43] A solid white vote alone afforded any chance for the South's redemption.

Words were cheap in any campaign, and, as the afterthoughts made clear, Democratic words about a New Departure depreciated faster than IOUs on a bankrupt company. But maybe what Republicans had not said gave a clearer signal of coming events. Orators had made much of protecting the Union; less often had they spoken of the need to protect a free ballot and a fair count down south. On the quality of those governments that freedpeople supported, though, campaign speakers and editors expressed their feelings with a silence so penetrating that it ought to have shaken the faith of any black southerner listening for a single supportive word. About the schools, churches, railroad construction, and the abolition of the whipping post . . . stillness. Of former slaves' fulfillment of the hopes promised for them in freedom . . . not a whisper. Most mentions of the "carpetbag-Negro governments" down south came from liberals or Democrats. For the Grant party, the less said about the Scotts, Holdens, Bullocks, and Kimballs, the better; it must have thanked its good fortune that Warmoth hove to the Liberals.

They had good cause: by 1872 in many northern minds, all the South was South Carolina, a state that not even the Ku Klux Klan committee's majority report could steel itself to defend. Nor could Republicans on the spot, who hurled corruption charges at each other and hit the mark just about every time. "Nuthin but tief, tief, tief!" a black attendant at a political meeting grumbled. But then, with the Klan broken, no issue seemed as pressing as the ethical debauch. Black voters were concerned, and some of them alarmed, that the robbery was not just soiling the state but devouring any future that the Republican program would have. Bond issues and giveaways had carried South Carolina to the brink of bankruptcy. At a party barbecue outside Columbia that summer, the largely black audience listened impatiently to State Treasurer Niles G. Parker's defense of the state administration. He pointed out how much further their rights had gone than in Georgia, where blacks could not ride the first-class streetcars in Savannah. Up rose one "level-headed descendant of Ham," in a conservative correspondent's words. "We don't ask you, Mr. Parker, about riding in street cars," he protested. "We wish to know why there is no money in the Treasury; why the Public Schools have been closed; why Penitentiary labor is brought into competition with free labor; and why the Lunatic Asylum is now subsisting on private charity?" A barber, Cap Carroll, mounted the stand. He was as good a Republican as any of them, he cautioned, but he could not glance back over the past four years of party rule without shedding tears at how far short of the ideal their public servants fell. Politicians had warned voters not to make a change, lest it not be for the better, but "before God, we cannot change for the worse."[44]

The question was, who would the party choose for governor? Honest though Robert K. Scott may have been, his weakness, inattention, and bad judgment had left the looters with a free hand, and even in his own party, critics suspected him of banditry as bad as that of any of the men around him. Two other figures showed some interest in the nomination. Both were natives of the state, Franklin J. Moses, Speaker of the State House, and Comptroller General John L. Neagle. "Great God!" a railroad president exclaimed when he heard. "If either of those men should be elected, the whole State will be given over to pillage, like a city taken by storm." Better that South Carolina keep Scott, even if every charge against him held up: no sense "swapping a witch for a devil."[45]

Frank Moses was no devil, but, as future events would confirm, he was a mediocrity in everything but rascality. "Corrupt as Job, and without boils," as a northern journalist put it, he came from the South Carolina elite. In secession days he won a lieutenant's commission in the state infantry. Moving from a Democratic editorial desk into the newly formed Republican Party, Moses made his peace with the new order; his father, somewhat more conservative, became chief justice on the state supreme court. Black voters elected him to the constitutional convention and then to the state House. There Moses impressed the body as "a flashy, open-handed, sporting young native Radical." Open it certainly was, both for grabbing and giving. He was said to have taken $35,000 in bribes for awarding committee assignments the winter before and another $11,000 for blocking Governor Scott's impeachment. Conservatives pointed to the prewar legislature that cost $150,000 per session and compared it to the one that the Speaker presided over. Moses had had authority to issue pay certificates to lawmakers and as of late 1872 was said to have issued between $1.2 and $2 million. Depreciated as they were, and worth a much smaller sum than their face value, they still amounted to a monstrous sum. Those pay certificates, or so it was alleged later, were really drafts on the Treasury to hire supporters for handling the caucuses. From his payments, Moses created a political machine. With about eighteen attendants on the house per county for a single legislative session—561 of them in all—Moses could have organizers all across the state, and could round up the voters with much more ease than any rival.[46]

With other white aspirants for the governorship, Moses still fell short of a majority when the Republican state convention opened. The legislature at its worst "never brought together in the place such a horde of political vultures as are gathered together in the capital to-day," a conservative reporter wrote. Readers could expect "a considerable pulling of wool" when proceedings opened. A pulling of corks would have been more like it. The competing candidates opened up headquarters for entertaining doubtful delegates and reinforcing the faithful. Wild estimates of "hundreds of thousands" of dollars being used to nominate Moses and to defeat him were treated seriously, and, according to some reports, some of the same delegates let both sides buy them—or at any rate, pay them in the hope that they would stay bought. Among the most active influences for Moses were John J. Patterson and the Blue Ridge Railroad ring. A "gentleman of infinite jest and unlimited tact in all things pertaining to the manipulation of legislative bodies with weak morals," as one critic described him, Patterson countered the open threats of the so-called New England Ring to buy the support they needed—or, in their slang, "call in to their assistance 'General Spinner.'" In a game like that, he assured them, he was the best player around. According to the *Beaufort Republican*, he illustrated the point over and over. "From Hardie Solomons and the Carolina national bank came the greenbacks which secured the triumph. At any ticklish moment Patterson's carriage might be seen dashing up to one of the banks and soon after rolling back to the State House."[47]

Shouting fraud and corruption, reform Republicans walked out before Moses could win the nomination. They ran Reuben Tomlinson for governor instead and looked vainly for hearty Democratic support. If anything, their adherents only demonstrated that the party's whole white leadership was rotten clear through. D. T. Corbin had found his conscience quite recently, after years of furthering schemes to make his public position pay. If the *Aiken Tribune* was right, he had carried a general railroad incorporation bill through the Senate in return for a $3,000 "attorney's fee." Timothy Hurley was known more for corrupting others than for taking money himself but was acknowledged to be honest only in the sense that he stood by whatever interest had bought him to start with. Professions of reform sounded queer when they came from Benjamin F. Whittemore, who was expelled from Congress for selling cadetships—or from Christopher C. Bowen, the bigamist and Confederate ex-soldier cashiered for forgery and murder of an officer—or from William J. Whipper. Other prominent black leaders with stained reputations like Samuel Lee and S. A. Swails joined the revolt, too. Even Tomlinson had some explaining to do about his part in one of the phosphate companies that had lobbied for scandalous giveaways of the state's riverbed rights and his double role as state auditor and paid employee of the Greenville & Columbia; the auditor's duties included assessing the railroad's property for tax purposes. With some justice, Thomas J. Mackey allowed that the bolters were "tried Republicans"—"tried and convicted."[48] Moses could not help winning that fall.

Shenanigans like these, or, for that matter, the ones that marred the campaigns in Louisiana, Alabama, and Arkansas, give a skewed impression of Reconstruction's impact down south. That, as noted earlier, could be found in the everyday life of four million black Americans, in the expansion of their communities and institutions, the solidifying foundations of traditional family life, and the gradual, often painfully slow, advance in their economic fortunes—gains dependent on high cotton and sugar prices and the continuation of national prosperity. Scandals, intrigues, and jockeying for power should not have defined how well Reconstruction was working. But they did. By year's end, those aspects, and not the less newsworthy ones, had become the one story northern newspaper readers were likely to see. Even before onetime antislavery correspondent James Shepherd Pike of the *New York Tribune* headed to Columbia to expose the often-exposed "Prostrate State," others had marked the way: journalists, witnesses before the Ku-Klux committee, and southern Republicans themselves. As much as Georgia's absconding governor, they had made the Reconstruction governments, even the cleanest and most capable, morally indefensible before the public. If the Union had just won a great victory with Grant's reelection, the reconstructed South did not share in it, not in full measure. It was as fragile as the language of the New Departure itself.

So the triumph of loyalty over rebellion did not tell the whole story. By the end of the year, the downward lurch had begun. This time, unlike two years before, there would be no reversal in fortunes for southern Reconstruction.

CHAPTER FOURTEEN

Dead Sea Fruits, 1872–1874

S eldom have Dead Sea fruits transmuted so quickly to ashes as did the fruits of Republican victory in 1872. What would follow would be a run of bankruptcies: bankrupted reputations, bankrupted policies, and bankrupted stores of the moral capital on which Reconstruction depended.

The first inkling of trouble came the day Congress returned. Back from Europe, Charles Sumner found scant welcome in Washington, and his actions immediately rendered him even more the outcast. Not only did he again offer his civil rights bill. Within hours, he presented a resolution to wipe the names of Civil War battles from the regimental colors of U.S. regiments and the army register. It was his 1862 motion, with improvements. Having unearthed a copy of the original bill while sifting through the papers piled on his desk, he thought the time ripe for another effort. Indeed, considering his failing health, it might be the last chance he would have.[1] Among veterans, the news stirred a white-hot fury, though one reporter noticed "much more favor among army and navy officers than was anticipated." Critics shouted that Sumner's step would lead to others: the razing of monuments, effacing of memorials, and even the closing of military cemeteries. On such an issue, as the *New York Times* put it, "a man may overdraw the capital of his reputation." In Massachusetts, Grant supporters too timid to attack the senior senator openly until the returns were in now seized their chance to stampede a censure resolution through a cowed legislature. "Sumner is being devoured by his hounds," a gleeful Mississippi journal reported.[2]

Such petty vindictiveness stirred bewilderment and indignation nationwide, and all the more as those reading the bill grasped how limited its scope actually was and how in keeping with worldwide tradition. No country commemorated the victories of one part of its people over another. French banners might honor Valmy, but not the Vendee—British ones Lucknow, but not the Battle of the Boyne. Indeed, as Sumner's defenders noted,

British regimental banners did not even bear inscriptions of encounters in the American Revolution, for, to Britain, the war had been more of a family quarrel than a struggle with some foreign power. Scarcely a score of regiments would be affected at all; most troops had mustered at their states' call and gone out of existence after Appomattox. Ironically, Sumner, the advocate of expanded national power, had given the strongest acknowledgment to the federal principle: what states did about their own banners was their own business, and not Washington's. That regiments hoping in future years to attract recruits from all the states, southern as well, should compel a Georgian to march under a standard celebrating the taking of Atlanta was to impose needless humiliation.[3]

All this Sumner's friends said, and none of this had Sumner been given the chance to say before judgment had been passed on him. It was worse than unfair. The controversy exposed how hollow Republican talk of reconciliation had been. What was amnesty, after all, without forgiveness? The hasty rebuke on one of the last great antislavery leaders still active in politics only reminded those who had quarreled with Sumner of his services to freedom. (Blacks needed no reminding; they sprang to his defense at once.) However far he may have been at fault, no one doubted that he had acted from principle. And of how few of his colleagues in Washington could that now be said! Almost at once, the poet John Greenleaf Whittier launched a petition drive to rescind the censure, and with some of the most illustrious names in the state leading the way: the poets Henry Wadsworth Longfellow and Oliver Wendell Holmes, the industrialist Amos A. Lawrence, Harvard president Charles W. Eliot, and the governor himself. Yet at session's end, the censure still stood. The best the senator's friends could promise was to renew the battle next fall.[4]

Sumner had no need to await vindication. The Forty-Second Congress's closing session did that for him, highlighting the contrast between his qualities and those now defining official Washington. Committees uncovered evidence that Alexander Caldwell had bought his Senate seat in Kansas and that his colleague Samuel "Subsidy Pom" Pomeroy had tried to do so. A Senate investigation could not prove that Powell Clayton had won his place in Arkansas by dispensing railroad aid to companies that could do him the most good, nor indeed that aid had not been administered scrupulously, but lurid stories from all sides painted the state as beset by one pack of scoundrels vying to dislodge another gang, equally bad. Reporters hinted of bribery on behalf of the Pacific Mail Steamship Company, out for a subsidy.[5]

Worse yet was Credit Mobilier, the railroad construction scandal in which Congressman Oakes Ames of Massachusetts had involved himself. During the campaign, various congressmen had denied taking bribes from the retired shovel maker and railroad director; then, at least, members of their party managed to believe them, but that belief did not outlast the autumn. Aware that they had no choice between a carefully controlled inquest and newshounds' broad-ranging exposure, Republicans set up a committee under Congressman Luke Poland of Vermont. All those charged pled on their innocence—until Ames brought out his fatal memorandum book with notes on how much each had received. Among those forced to explain were the leading Republicans of the House: former Speaker Schuyler Colfax, now outgoing vice president, Appropriations chair James A. Garfield of Ohio, Ways and Means Committee chair Henry L. Dawes, and navy chair Glenni W. Scofield, among others. Some of them had been prominent radical Republicans: William D. "Pig Iron" Kelley of Pennsylvania, and vice president elect Henry Wilson. Judiciary Committee chair John A. Bingham, more conservative, had helped design the civil rights section in the Fourteenth Amendment. He too was implicated.[6]

Dishonors were uneven. Some of them had acquired shares, which they paid for out of the first dividend, and, after collecting a few hundred dollars in clear profit, sold out just about the time a lawsuit threatened to make shareholders' names public. All of them insisted nonetheless that, receiving their dividends in Union Pacific Railroad bonds, they had no idea that Credit Mobilier was tied to the Union Pacific in any way. Some, Kelley and Colfax among them, denied receiving a cent, even after canceled checks made out to someone with their initials entered the public record. Colfax belatedly explained that a curious $1,200 deposit that he made right after just such a check had been issued had, in fact, been from funds sent in cash by an admirer, now dead and unable to testify. Republicans took solace in netting a single Democrat, floor leader James Brooks of New York, who, as government director on the Union Pacific, used his position to squeeze special favors from the company. Grimly, the Nation counted the investigation's cost on reputations: "total loss, one Senator; badly damaged, and not serviceable for future political use, two Vice-Presidents and eight Congressmen. The condition of Ames's reputation language is inadequate to describe." So was the House's reputation after it refused to expel anyone and limited its censure to Ames and Brooks. No Massachusetts member ran any risk of sharing Sumner's fate in the state capitol. "Ames and Colfax are received by their constituents with ovations," Garfield wrote unhappily. "My constituents are hunting for ropes to hang me with."[7]

Garfield's offense had nothing to do with the $329 he had collected off his Credit Mobilier holdings. It had to do with one last scandal, in Congress's closing hours, when lawmakers raised government salaries. Members rightly pointed out that they had gone underpaid for years. The president received the same $25,000 a year that the Founders gave George Washington, when a dollar had gone four times as far. Then, the best mutton sold for two cents a pound and the finest cow for ten dollars and the best "woman help" charged seventeen cents a week. Better pay might save lawmakers from the temptation of making money from their influence, as more than one member pointed out. "There's many a rogue saved from the State prison because he has had no need to steal," the *Louisville Courier-Journal* argued. "There's many an honest man been corrupted by his necessities."[8]

With the public so primed to see every spending as a swindle, any pay hike would have set off some grumbling, and at the close of a presidential campaign where Republicans had boasted of their economy and promised to cut back on needless expenses, writing in a big exception for themselves was sure to raise cries of false dealings.[9] But there had been salary increases before, in 1856 and 1866. Each time tempers cooled fast. Not this time: appealing to those lame-duck congressmen never likely to see the inside of the Capitol again, the bill made representatives' pay retroactive to the beginning of the Congress. In effect, the bill handed parting members a $5,000 windfall.

Critics did not see extravagance or waste. Wised up by all the other news stories over the past few years, they saw thieving. Back pay was "not one remove in criminality from absolute larceny." That $5,000 bonus, one midwestern editor calculated, was a farmer's take on 5,000 bushels of wheat, or 20,000 bushels of corn, or 10,000 of oats. Earning a dollar a day in wages, a mechanic would have to work nonstop for more than thirteen years to make as much. Oakes Ames, who voted for the increase, pronounced it a worse outrage than Credit Mobilier, because "the men who had that did pay a little something for it, but this is all steal."[10]

Those voting for the pay raise found their constituents deaf to excuses. Garfield had fought the scheme up to the final roll call. That did not spare him hate mail and a chorus of resolutions from mass meetings demanding his resignation. Those who voted against the "salary grab" but took the pay anyhow left indelible, often fatal scars on their careers. Those like Dawes or Garfield who declined the pay raise and put themselves on record for repealing the "grab" the following December made a slow, painful political recovery. And then there were those like Senators Carl Schurz and Charles Sumner who only burnished their good names by keeping hands off the unclean thing from the first.[11]

Grant could hardly be blamed for Credit Mobilier or the back-pay bill, though he signed it immediately, but as the new year proceeded, reformers found all their hopes dashed that the president, free from worrying about reelection, might carry out his hints of reform. His new cabinet officers did not improve on the old. When Chief Justice Salmon P. Chase died that spring, Grant's first thought was to give it to Senator Roscoe Conkling, arrogant, peevish, and intensely partisan. After Conkling declined the place, the president appalled the legal profession by nominating his attorney general, George Williams. Williams's geniality could not make up for his fumbling the prosecution of Credit Mobilier officers. When revelations about his use of public funds to buy his family a fancy carriage came out, the president was forced to nominate somebody else. Those who could not have imagined a worse choice gasped as Grant sent in the name of onetime doughface Attorney General Caleb Cushing, known as much for his political shiftiness as his legal brilliance. Within days, an embarrassing letter from Cushing to then–Confederate president Jefferson Davis came to light, and Grant had to withdraw his name, too. The Senate finally confirmed the president's last choice, Morrison R. Waite, an Ohio jurist whose reputation had been enhanced when he argued before the *Alabama* arbitrators in Geneva.[12] Where equal rights were concerned, needless to say, neither Waite, Cushing, Conkling, or Williams had the consuming passion of the late chief justice, once famed as the "attorney-general for fugitive negroes."

Instead of pursuing civil service reform, the president allowed it to be modified or overridden by cabinet officers. Embarrassed and humiliated, Civil Service Commission chair George William Curtis resigned. When the Forty-Third Congress assembled in December 1873, it cut off the commission's funding. The administration did not rouse itself to reverse the decision. The civil service experiment perished, at least until the next administration.[13] But already, there had been more than enough evidence that, in appointments, Grant had no interest in affronting his supporters on Capitol Hill. Customhouse scandals continued, with revelations that New York merchants were being regularly shaken down by officers who received a "moiety"—50 percent of any fine that they could get away with levying. In the Treasury, Secretary William A. Richardson allowed one John D.

Sanborn to collect taxes, at a tremendous profit to himself. When, in early 1874, one of Benjamin F. Butler's ablest henchmen, William A. Simmons, was nominated for Collector of the Port in Boston, reformers saw it as the ultimate betrayal, on behalf of the Bay State's most infamous politician.

By mid-1873, then, whatever moral capital at the national level the party favoring Reconstruction may have had, had been almost wholly lost. The reconstructed states had none of their own to spare. Within days of Grant's reelection, southern affairs had barged themselves onto the front page, in the most embarrassing ways. South Carolina's senatorial election turned into an auction, with the carpetbag president of the Blue Ridge Railroad, "Honest John" Patterson, easily tripling the hundred dollars a vote that outgoing Governor Robert Scott reportedly offered. (To their credit, some legislators settled for much less.) Congressman Robert Brown Elliott, who some rated "the ablest negro, intellectually, in the South," had no bankroll and therefore no chance. Whatever help he counted on from governor-elect Frank Moses proved to be an even more depreciated currency than the state's pay certificates. Beverly Nash, one of Elliott's closest low-country allies, turned down a $4,500 offer for him to betray his friend. For $2,000, one of Scott's leading supporters switched before the second ballot, not knowing that after the election "Honest John" would pay him half what he promised. In such an atmosphere, any story seemed believable, especially when the person paid off was black and a Republican. Patterson could afford the $30,000 the seat cost; reportedly, the Pennsylvania Railroad put up the money. "That road elects & owns the Senators from S. C. & will continue to do so until the Texas & Pacific R. R. is finished & a number of branch roads it owns in this section of country," a visitor to Columbia wrote.[14]

In Alabama, both parties claimed a legislative majority, and each organized a legislature of its own. Having raised $29,000 to elect Republicans committed to reelecting him, Senator George Spencer now deepened his investment. A free drinking establishment lubricated legislators' more generous impulses, and money and the promises of offices did the rest. Thirty-eight members and lobbyists for Spencer ended up with federal jobs: postmasters, marshals, mail agents, district attorneys, and even a consul in Canada and a Dakota territorial governor. Guards were posted to make sure that none of the legislators could get out of the body assembled in the courthouse, in case they thought to join the rival concern. With U.S. troops marched into Montgomery to keep the peace between the "courthouse" and "state-house" legislatures, and Republican governor-elect David Lewis recognizing the former, the deadlock ended when Attorney

General Williams brokered a compromise effectively giving Republicans the assembly, which, but for Democratic fraud at the polls, they probably would have had anyhow. In a snap action while several Democrats were absent, Republicans took the senate, too.[15]

Settling Arkansas' disputed election took longer. Governor Powell Clayton's translation into the Senate made no difference in who ran things. "Light-haired, tall, nonchalant," with "a roving, audacious, fighting look in his eye," the governor had been a plucky Union soldier; his loss of a left hand came from a gunshot wound in a hunting accident. Both parties admired him for his coolness and force of will. Fair-minded Democrats admitted that he had done nothing to make himself rich in office—nowhere near as rich as he could have been if he had stuck to planting when both sides invited him into politics in 1867. There was nothing passive or reactive about him. With some exaggeration, a northern reporter likened him to a notorious bandit from the Natchez Trace and to the conquistador Hernando Cortés, prepared to "hang a man at the roadside for a violation of a truce."[16] Espousing the standard Republican policies of Unionism and equal rights, he also championed government programs to hasten economic development. To preserve his influence, he could denounce the former Rebels or become their most ardent defender against proscriptive policies. Clusters of dissidents constantly mingled and separated, left the party or joined the regulars. One thing remained changeless: Clayton's "Minstrels" controlled all the important offices, fending off challenges from the "Brindletails," led by former radical, former minister Joseph Brooks.

Unable to beat Clayton for mastery of the party, Brooks left it in 1872 to run for governor as the Reform candidate. His Brindletails endorsed Greeley for president, and, bidding for Democratic votes, promised a reformed school system, tax and spending cuts, a dismantling of the Clayton patronage machinery, and, most important, full amnesty and universal suffrage, where every former Confederate got back his voting rights—no small concession for Brooks, who until then fought Clayton's every easing of restrictions. Elect him governor, Brooks vowed, and "he would fill the jail so full of [Minstrels] that their legs would stick out of the windows." Still distrusting "Howling Wilderness Joe" Brooks, Democrats endorsed him and his platform all the same and applied their best and worst efforts to carrying the legislature. Embracing moderation, the regular Republican convention nominated a former slaveholder and mild wartime Unionist, Elisha Baxter, for governor on a platform so inoffensive that the worst Brindletails could say of it was that it could not have been meant sincerely.[17]

Baxter may have won the election, though after such an irregular count that nobody on the other side would believe it. As the story went, the secretary of state, whose job it was to receive the returns, sent the reported figures back with instructions to local election officers on how many the Minstrel ticket needed to count itself in. By the time the returns reached the president of the state senate, who made the official announcement of a winner, four counties had fallen out of the count entirely and Baxter had pulled ahead. Brooks petitioned the legislature for the right to contest the election. His request was denied. The state supreme court refused to give the attorney general permission to institute a quo warranto writ requiring Baxter to prove his right to the governorship.[18]

Conservatives felt cheated, but as the new governor proved his sympathy with their ideas, they changed their minds—and so did Republicans. Without Conservative cooperation, Baxter may have calculated, he could not hold power or stave off a challenge to his right to govern. Perhaps he was following the same will-o'-the-wisp that lured party centrists to their ruin in Virginia, Tennessee, Missouri, and West Virginia, that by making advances to the Democracy he could broaden the Republicans' popular base; more likely he meant to sell them out and collect the proceeds for himself. Whatever the reasons, he began dismantling the political machinery that had given the Minstrels their strength. With Democratic backing, he signed an act allowing the people to amend the constitution to restore the last ex-Confederates' voting rights. Republican registrars were dismissed, replaced by officers sure to give every Democratic voter the benefit of the doubt. Finally, he took on the railroad companies linked to the Minstrel machine and beat their efforts to carry relief bills through the legislature that would have saddled taxpayers with $5 million in liabilities in return for canceling another $6 million that past aid laws otherwise might have cost Arkansas. So fierce a struggle did the Baxter faction wage that not even bribery in depreciated railroad securities could sway enough legislators to the corporate viewpoint. Leading Minstrels even tried to buy Baxter. The governor accused Chief Justice John McClure and his cronies of making the offer; the leading Radical organ replied that Baxter's real grievance was that the money, once promised, had not been forthcoming. Amid a hail of charges and countercharges blackening just about every prominent Republican official in the state as a gangster, the bill never reached a final vote.[19] The Minstrel organization lay in shambles, and with it the Reconstruction government's reputation and the cautious and honestly administered economic development program on which Clayton had placed his hopes of remaking Arkansas.

All these incidents should have provided infamy enough, but Louisiana's experience defied comparison. Driven from control of the Republican Party, Governor Henry Clay Warmoth had carried his influence to the Democratic side and against his own party's nominee, Senator William Pitt Kellogg. Democrats promised to give blacks "a 'white man's chance,'" but performance was another matter. "In every Parish of the State that I have visited complaints are made to me by colored men entitled to register who have been refused registration," Lieutenant Governor Pinckney B. S. Pinchback wrote the Republican National Committee. With a fair registration and election, he thought, Republicans would have a 30,000 majority—that is, if Louisiana were not Louisiana.[20] Democrats, or "Fusionists," as they billed themselves this year, used counterfeit tickets with Grant's picture and the American flag on one side but Democratic nominees printed on the other, well aware that the blacks to whom they gave them either would not or could not read the writing and would think that they were voting Republican. With election officials shaping the returns as Warmoth wanted and a returning board that the "bold political Buccaneer" had packed with conservatives just after the votes were in, conservatives could hardly lose. Sure enough, the board found for John McEnery for governor over Kellogg and counted in a conservative legislature. Needing an authority that would rule their way, Republicans had established a returning board of their own and asked the Justice Department to back them up.[21]

On December 3rd, the attorney general sent instructions to U.S. marshal Packard to "enforce the decrees and mandates of the U.S. courts, no matter by whom resisted," and promised all the troops he needed. These were interesting instructions, since no federal court had made a ruling, but Williams seems to have known his man. Ailing and about to retire, federal circuit judge Edward H. Durell had one last service that he might do to the Union. The evening that federal troops reached New Orleans, Durell gave Packard orders to seize the statehouse and throw a cordon around it. Only the authorized members of the legislature could pass through: the ones that Kellogg's board had certified. The city awoke to find cannon and bayonet protecting the Kellogg legislature in session at Mechanics' Hall. Later that day, the judge dismissed all the legal remedies that Democrats had been pursuing in the state courts. Swiftly, the so-called Lynch Board used affidavits, evidence, and intuition to declare Kellogg the winner.[22]

Two legislatures met, each of them seething with the indignation that often goes with a readiness to engage in sharp practice. The Fusionists made a returning board all their own that, not surprisingly, gave them seventy-five seats to the Republicans' thirty-five. All the newly elected senators but four were awarded to the Fusion contestants. The Mechanics' Hall body impeached Warmoth on its opening day, suspended him from office, and made his black lieutenant governor, Pinchback, the acting governor—and, as it proved, the only nonwhite chief executive to serve in any southern state. Now empowered to seek recognition as the one legal government from Washington, Republicans asked for troops to affirm their rights. On December 12, the president did exactly that. The dueling legislatures swore in two new governors, McEnery and Kellogg, and found courts willing to issue injunctions and mete out fines against actors on the opposite side.[23] Over time, federal guns gave Kellogg an edge in claiming legitimacy.

In composer Offenbach's hands, the whole affair might have made wonderful opéra bouffe. Performed in the real world, it guaranteed catastrophe. Within weeks, rival military forces had armed in New Orleans, and in upcountry parishes, there were struggles for control, all stoked by the belief that right and law were exclusively on their side and, among conservatives, at least, the growing conviction that they could make a plausible enough claim of legitimacy to find apologists—even Republican apologists—across the north. In Grant Parish, such a struggle ended in a massacre. Warmoth's returning board had recognized the votes electing a conservative judge and sheriff, but two months into their terms, Kellogg replaced them with appointees of his own. A black militia led by state representative William Ward enforced the governor's decree by seizing the courthouse in Colfax Township, investing it with Enfield rifles, and digging trenches for its defense. Both sides were spoiling for a fight. "The time is past, if it ever existed, when a handful of whites could frighten a regiment of colored men," the *New Orleans Republican* boasted. It was no handful when it came in April, and it came to kill, not to frighten. Ward's defensive force, several hundred strong, had neither the guns nor the discipline to overcome the white posse called in by the ousted sheriff. On Easter Sunday, the posse came into Colfax with warrants for the arrest of certain black leaders, and after a parley broke down, shooting began. Both sides took casualties, and Ward's militia retreated into the courthouse. When it was set afire, the defenders tried to get out. Some burned to death. Others were shot as they fled the flames, and a few managed to escape. Thirty-seven surrendered. That night, the posse took them out and shot them. Only a few managed to live to tell their tale. At least sixty-nine blacks were buried in a common grave, among them a delegate to the black-and-tan convention of 1868. Kellogg's appointee for sheriff was killed, too.[24]

Both sides had discredited themselves long before then, though Kellogg, as the eventual winner, rather more. Taking testimony, a Senate committee found it impossible to decide which side had a legitimate title. The president thought about proposing a new gubernatorial election and then dropped the idea, wrote a special message on the Louisiana mess, and then laid it aside after his cabinet kicked up a fuss.[25] Democrats and most Republicans were appalled, even outraged, at the Grant administration's intervention. At best, his recognition of Kellogg's right to the office came prematurely. At worst, he, Attorney General Williams, and Judge Durell had given an example of the sort of meddling that erected puppet governments and brought constitutional process into contempt. Alabama . . . Louisiana, conservatives protested—how many bayonet-propped state governments could a republic afford?

Grant made no apologies, but the Louisiana imbroglio clearly shook his nerve. It made him warier of intervening and it provided in critics' mind a model by which they would judge every southern election dispute thereafter.

So that winter, when a flare-up put the Texas election returns in question, the specter of another Louisiana hovered over every news dispatch. Republicans in the Lone Star State had done everything they knew how to hold the legislature in 1872. None of it did any good. The party lost the congressional delegation and state House. Over the following year, the Redeemers cut back the school system, gerrymandered legislative districts to add to their advantage, and dismantled the Republican government's military apparatus. In November 1873, their candidate for governor, Richard Coke, won by 50,000 votes, carrying a full state ticket with him.[26]

Edmund G. Davis knew he was licked. He declared his readiness to accept the results, but his supporters went to the state supreme court to void the whole election. The state supreme court agreed in January 1874, which did not surprise anyone: its Republican personnel very likely had scruples about being legislated into private life. Davis felt obliged to hold on and get troops from Washington to keep the peace until the impasse could be settled.

To Democrats and the American reading public in general, the story seemed all too familiar: a power grab by the loser, after an election conceded to have been generally fair. Grant had no intention of burdening himself with two Louisianas. The army could not be sent to restore order. There was no disorder in Texas—not yet, at least. He made quite clear that Davis could expect no support in Washington in resisting "the verdict of the people." The governor indicated that he stood in physical danger, but, as one newspaper jeered, "The President didn't seem to care. The attorney general didn't seem to care. There didn't anybody seem to care. . . . The Administration is so rich in leading statesmen that the peril of a single one, even such a one as Davis, occasions no anxiety." Suspecting his violent overthrow if he did not quit at once, and dependent on a paltry force of black militiamen for protection, Davis resigned three months before his term was supposed to end. From the northern press came no sympathy, and the *New York Tribune*, unaware that Davis had been a Texas Unionist, predicted that he would "pack his carpet-bag and move out of the State."[27]

A few months later, the seething quarrel in Arkansas burst out into open war. Since the summer before, party divisions had only worsened. Baxter gave official printing to the Democratic newspapers and appointed Democrats to officer the state militia. Appointees that the senate refused to confirm were put into office anyway over the legislative recess. The governor was counting on a change of heart from lawmakers, and with good reason: he appointed so many legislators to offices that the general assembly was depopulated and, after a special election that the Minstrels boycotted, fell to Democratic control. Democrats who had stood by Brooks took up Baxter's cause. Minstrel Republicans wavered in their support for the man they had elected and toyed with the idea of proclaiming Brooks the lawfully elected governor. "It is sort of political quadrille, in which the 'gents' have exchanged partners," commented the *Springfield Republican*.[28]

This uneasy peace might have lasted until the next election, but then Baxter stirred up the railroad issue again. Opposed though he was to the new grants of aid, he had not voiced any objection to honoring commitments that the railroad commissioners had already made. On March 16, 1874, he suddenly announced that he would not issue any more subsidy bonds to the Arkansas Central Railroad. Arguing that the referendum that made railroad aid lawful was unconstitutional, Baxter pronounced the law itself void. If new issues were illegal, bonds already issued must be invalid for the same reason. The whole railroad aid policy was virtually overturned. State credit would be destroyed. As directors on many of the subsidized railroads, leading Minstrels had special reason to feel concerned.[29] If the Reconstruction programs—if Republican government itself—were to be saved, something must be done at once.

On April 15, without the governor's lawyers present to contest the decision, a circuit court judge ruled that Brooks had won the election seventeen months before and had legal title to the executive office. With a few dozen armed men behind him, Brooks marched into the statehouse to demand possession. A dumbfounded Baxter was ejected. He marshaled a host of armed desperadoes all his own. For a month the state was in a tumult. Both sides claimed the right to govern and raised their own militias to enforce their wills. In Little Rock, business suspended. Fire engines were piled into barricades. Business houses nailed rough planks over their finer French plate-glass windows. At one governor's direction, a supreme court justice was kidnapped. At another's command, arms from the state armories were distributed to followers. The supreme court opened Treasury vaults to Brooks, while Baxter counted on planters' and merchants' contributions. Meanwhile, Baxter's soldiers sacked shops, paying in vouchers on the state treasurer. To judge from the unsteady stride of newly made major generals, whiskey must have been the biggest item on their requisition list. Most Democrats supported Baxter, most Republicans favored Brooks, but the lines were by now so confused that no allegiance made much sense. Outsiders quite believed that the whole fight came from "the greed and rascality of her ruling politicians," and that while the predominance of black militiamen on one side and white ones on the other brought the state close to "a war of races," race had nothing to do with why either side fielded its forces in the first place. The *New York Tribune* declared the whole affair "an embodied yawn," tiring, tiresome, and not worth figuring out or the federal government bothering about. "Why not let them shoot each other down till *they* get tired of it as well as the President?" it proposed.[30]

The president was not so much tired as guarded. However Republican true believers felt about sustaining Reconstruction governments in black-majority states, nobody had a brief for Arkansas. Assuming that the whole Brooks-Baxter war was a quarrel over the railroad steals, the president could think of no good reason to help Brooks out. On May 15th, deferring to the state legislature's decision, Grant issued a proclamation recognizing Baxter as the lawful governor and ordering Brooks to disperse his forces within ten days. In that paper, Brooks protested, republican government had "received the greatest blow it ever felt since the foundation of the world!" His army melted away; black recruits stole out of town that first night, well aware that they would be the first to be killed if reprisals came.[31]

With Baxter's restoration, the process of dismantling Reconstruction accelerated. A Democratic legislature barred Brooks supporters from taking their seats, impeached the supreme court, vacated the land commissionership, removed Republican sheriffs and county clerks, forced the state treasurer to resign, and appointed former Confederates to the vacant places.

There was no trouble calling a new constitutional convention at the statehouse. Armed guards did sentry duty at the entrance; artillery frowned down crowds from the front. It certainly crossed delegates' minds that a congressional committee was looking into whether Brooks had proper title to the governorship, and whether Arkansas had a republican form of government. The best answer would be a constitution moderate enough to meet northern tastes and ratified by so large a vote before the committee could make its report that any decision in Brooks's favor would look like usurpation of the very government that most Arkansans wanted. In case the thought did not occur to them, the Democratic minority member on the committee jogged their minds.[32]

The convention did behave moderately. Having reimbursed merchants for the Baxter forces' requisition of war materials—including wines, whiskeys, cigars, and ladies' dresses—it suspended the registration law, reduced the government staff and clerks' pay, stripped the executive of his appointive powers, cut his term in half, and restricted the state's power to tax or to contract debts.[33] With Democrats resolved to choose one of their own, former Confederate leader Augustus Garland, Governor Baxter bowed out, never to roil politics again. Garland coasted to easy victory.

Outside Arkansas, the results hardly made the front page, for good reason. With Reconstruction seriously discredited and Republican reputations for honesty deflated to the vanishing point, the administration had clearly lost its mandate to govern before the midsummer of 1873. Then the greatest blow fell. The boom ended.

Prosperity had meant fair prices for wheat, corn, and cotton. It eased the formation of trade unions and added leverage to workers who went on strike for a larger share of their employers' profits. It may well have dulled public sensibilities to public scandal or extravagance in state and national government spending. Relatively easy money and a strong tide of foreign investment capital had encouraged a railroad boom of tremendous proportions, and that, in turn, fostered an iron and steel industry. Not by chance, Andrew Carnegie started his steelmaking plant in 1873 when the demand for steel rails seemed insatiable; also not by chance, his concentration on economies of scale allowed him to cut costs and thrive where other firms foundered. Thanks to the completion of the Atlantic Cable in 1866, capital markets could respond instantly to overseas developments. Savings banks expanded and throve, as workers laid by a financial cushion against harder times. In the first three years of the decade, the nation added as much track as the whole United States could boast fifteen years before. Between 1865 and 1873, the country's rail system had doubled, reaching 70,784 miles. Without a government outlay, that railroad boom would not have burgeoned so large. Between 1862 and 1871, Congress awarded well over 100 million acres to the railroads. By 1880, federal, state, and local authorities together had contributed $700 million for construction and transferred title on over 155 million acres, an expanse larger than France and four times the size of New England.[34]

When George S. Boutwell left the Treasury to become a senator from Massachusetts in March 1873, he left in the glow of an economic boom that, as far as most Americans were concerned, would warm the country for years to come. Boutwell's manipulation of the currency supply to furnish ready credit when money was in high demand, just as the crops were harvested, played its share in bringing about that result. The *New York Herald*'s financial experts declared that panics were a thing of the past as long as the secretary "plays the role of banker for the entire United States." The Treasury's cash balance kept growing through that spring, and come summer, the new secretary, William Richardson, followed the Boutwell policy of selling gold to accumulate $14 million of currency for buying bonds and increasing the money supply to meet "the usual autumn stringency." Preventing that stringency, though, would take a far larger sum than the government felt prepared to give. The national banks were growing less prepared to meet the need every year. Their basic reserves had been falling, and by 1873, banks in many states did not even have the legal minimum that the law required. As Boutwell had warned in his last annual report, "extraordinary events at home or abroad," or ordinary ones due to the harvest reaching the market, would find the financial world helpless to meet a sudden increased demand for money. Those extraordinary events had been under way for some time. As European countries adopted the gold standard, their demands on America's supply increased, while Boutwell's policy of using surplus revenues to retire bonds had forced national banks using them as the basis for issuing banknotes to cut back on circulation. For railroads like Northern Pacific, getting by on a series of fresh loans, tight credit came like an anchor thrown to a drowning man.[35]

There was a far more worrisome trend already under way, connected to Reconstruction. From the first, the great railroad boom had depended on foreign capital. So had the southern states' bond issues. But doubts had been growing that those issues would be paid off, and in Georgia, Democrats' return to power threw many of the securities into serious jeopardy. In Alabama, the Democratic governor Robert B. Lindsay had smudged his own reputation by refusing to pay the interest on bonds guaranteed for the Alabama & Chattanooga. The state had gone into default, one big reason why Republicans had regained the state in 1872. Any slackened taste for American securities in Frankfurt, Vienna, Paris, or London was sure to take away the stimulus from American markets, and that, by 1871, seemed to be happening. The Franco-Prussian War had strained the resources of both Germany and France, and the billion-dollar indemnity expected of the new French republic did still more, and not just there but among London financiers, who served as creditors. Continental investors were finding new destinations for their money: England had placed $200 million in South American railroads by 1869. In late 1871, England raised its money rate from 3 to 5 percent.[36]

By the end of 1872, the more timid investors doubted that the boom could go on. Commodore Vanderbilt, from semiretirement, could see a mania. "Building railroads from nowhere to nowhere at public expense is not a legitimate undertaking," he told reporters. "Men are trying to do four times as much business as they should." Early in September of the following year, it became clear that the banks could not meet seasonal demands. Nor could railroads and construction firms in the South and Southwest repay what they had borrowed. There was a serious near panic. Saturday the 13th brought the collapse of Daniel Drew's firm, and the track of ruin led straight to the Canada Southern Railroad, to which it had made a $1.5 million loan that it turned out was as good as lost.[37] Other railroads announced their default, and then one of the most cautious of the large insurance firms in New York followed suit.

Then on September 17th, a clerk appeared at the doors of Jay Cooke & Company, America's premier banking firm, to announce that it was suspending payments. Its commitment to building the Northern Pacific had dragged it down. A Cooke employee admitted that one could hardly find a rural clergyman, teacher, or farmer in the Midwest "who doesn't have some interest in the Northern Pacific." The Cooke banks closed their doors in New York, Philadelphia, and Washington. With "brute terror" seizing shareholders, the stock exchange dropped like a stone. So did money markets. Some banks refused to accept greenbacks, much less certified checks; they insisted on payment in gold. It was, a broker vowed, "the worst disaster since the Black Death."[38]

Across the country, banks suspended. Brokerage houses closed down, and customers made runs on institutions still open; if Cooke's could fail, what depository could be trusted? Ten days later the stock exchange reopened with a calmer clientele, but share prices, having tumbled so far, did not recover. Rather, they showed a steady decline. Western Union went from 92 to 46, Union Pacific from 26 to 16. That heavy investor in southern bonds and Republican Party success, Henry Clews & Company, failed.[39]

Industry quickly felt the blow. Blast furnaces around Pittsburgh banked their fires. The cotton factories of A. & W. Sprague went bankrupt, carrying with it the junior partner, Senator William Sprague of Rhode Island and wiping out his political influence in the state. The year 1873 would see more than 5,100 bankruptcies, and the numbers stayed high through the decade. They would peak in 1878, when 10,479 firms with assets over a quarter of a billion dollars went under. By late 1874, according to one official, American vessels in New York harbor carried less than half their former tonnage. Taxes rose, real estate lost value. In the Northeast, indeed, property often fell to half of its earlier worth. Even then, property owners could not pay their taxes. The man "who thought himself in comfortable circumstances finds that he is a bankrupt and is obliged in his old age . . . to commence the world anew," a reporter lamented.[40]

Over the next seven years, railroads at best could barely meet operating expenses. By November one-eighth of the total railroad debt of the country stood in default, and as of the fall of 1874 that proportion had risen to one-fourth. There were then 108 companies in default on $47 million worth of bonds, and by 1876, 216 railroads were in the same fix. Most lines either stopped paying dividends or curtailed them sharply. Gross earnings dropped, and the figures were worse because the number of miles in operation was growing, albeit slowly. British investors had kept buying bonds through the first three years of the depression—but stuck to the long-established, completed roads. Now they retreated even from that. Not until 1879 did the United States build as much as one-third the track mileage laid in 1871.[41]

For American workers, the panic ushered in the longest hard times in living memory. No section of the country was exempt, no branch of trade spared—except, perhaps, pawnshops. "You will hear people say that they ought to try their chances somewhere else, and again that they ought to turn their hands to anything and everything," a worker in a Manhattan tenement complained. "Where will they go to? . . . There is nothing for the men to turn their hands to. There is scarce a trade that the winter has not terrors for." Unions slumped or withered away. In 1874 alone, over 9,000 trade union members in New York City fell out: 40 percent of the coopers, 30 percent of the cigar makers, 25 percent of the shoemakers. The Order of

Crispins, 50,000 strong, vanished completely. The Furniture Workers Association of North America amounted to only nine locals when its annual convention met in 1876. None survived a year after.[42]

Rolling-mills, wire mills, chain factories, and woolen mills ran on half-time or quarter-time in Trenton, with the potteries all but closing down, and 2,000 men found themselves without work three years after the panic. In the Lackawanna Valley, ironworks suspended operations during the slow winter months, thrusting anthracite miners into "pinching, pallid poverty," because no furnace needed the coal. There and elsewhere, reduced time meant reduced pay. Those able to keep their jobs full time saw their wages cut, and those on seasonal labor found their services less in demand. Skilled artisans in the coal country who once earned $3.50 a day, took fifty cents for any kind of labor now and gratefully. Rent, clothing, and fuel prices fell slightly in Pennsylvania, but wages fell by half between 1870 and 1876. In Illinois, a special legislative committee found, the cost of skilled labor in 1879 amounted to only 50 percent of what it had in 1872, while that of unskilled had dipped even further, to as little as two-fifths. Lancashire weavers accustomed to twenty cents a cut on print clothes in England left Fall River, Massachusetts' looms when their wages fell to nineteen cents a cut. "Fall River used to have the best help in the country," a reporter wrote. "It will soon have the worst."[43]

The social costs of lingering hard times were incalculable, in starvation, property crime, and suicide. Families lost their homes. Wives were separated from their husbands, children from their parents as the search for employment took breadwinners farther afield. "I have had numbers of married women brought to me charged by the police with soliciting men in the streets," a city judge told a reporter. "I have had parents here in court seeking to reclaim their daughters who made the first plunge into shame." In every case he investigated, poverty had been the cause. "I wish there was a war," a former cigar-packer complained; "anything would be better than parading the streets without a chance of work."[44]

Every city had its charities, soup kitchens, or relief agencies. Churches opened their doors for the destitute, sometimes filling the pews with sleeping men or sending newcomers to the "vermin room" to clean them before they took their meals. In Newark, the Overseers of the Poor passed out 97,000 loaves of bread in two months, and a quarter of a ton of coal per month to each family on their list of 3,000. Even so, charities found their resources strained by the heavy demands put upon them. In ten days, one agency in New York City that doled out free coal found 20,000 people begging assistance. Long lines of coughing adults waited in the January cold from long before sunrise, just on the hope of sharing in the philanthropy's bounty. "Wan faced, hollow-eyed women, with weak looking infants in their arms; stout but crestfallen men, evidently mechanics out of employment and on the verge of starvation; feeble old men, scarcely able to hobble along; weak looking girls and young men well dressed in rags" made up the crowd.[45]

The worse conditions became, the more the respectable classes retreated into denial that matters could be anywhere near as bad as described, and looked with impatience on those "clever, cunning, degraded people" unable to make a quick recovery. The "pretended scientific press and oleaginous parsons" gave moral and statistical backing for those who opposed state intervention, one sympathetic correspondent wrote from New York at the end of the first hard winter. "The tens of thousands of shrunken and haggard wretches who crowded round the soup-houses, station-houses, and charity shops, who hung about the streets and crawled up to every man's doors, were told that they were lazy loafers and swindling frauds, who would not work, but preferred to get a living in these ways." He wondered how they could have overlooked the worst loafers of all, the hardened wretches who "actually had the audacity to lie down and perish of starvation," instead of subsisting long enough to hear themselves "denounced with proper vitreosity by men who believe in free competition, the law of supply and demand, and the devil take the hindmost."[46]

Insecurity bred a new cruelty toward the indigent, especially toward the host of jobless men taking to the roads, perhaps ten for every one just a few years earlier. Thanks to the railroads, country towns that had never seen beggars now found them coming into their midst, and not the habitual sponger, but many who had held steady positions as day laborers or mechanics. A new word entered the language, the "tramp." "Bummer," the nickname of General Sherman's looting soldiers on the march to the sea, became "bum," perhaps because so many vagrants had war records. Mainstream editors turned harshly against the vagrants as members of the "criminal classes," unsightly local nuisances turned public menace, with a penchant for rape, murder, robbery, and the derailing of express trains. In New Jersey, lawmakers proposed bills to arrest any male begging door-to-door and commit them to six months' hard labor on the public highways or an equal term of service to anyone bidding for their service. The *Cincinnati Commercial* urged that those applying for relief be required to produce passes and account for their movements, with policemen acting as relief officers, and that all help be coupled with confinement in the workhouse. Young, able-bodied men should be refused help entirely. "Thus poverty is made a crime and dissipation put on a par with guilt," the *Cincinnati Enquirer* commented sharply.[47]

In fact, the number of undeserving paupers may only have been a fraction of the undemanding poor. Joblessness and want struck deep at laborers' pride. They defined themselves by their ability to provide for their families. Without that, many of them felt that they themselves had failed. Many, even in the greatest need, refused to seek out help from charities except as a last resort, and those in deepest want shunned the workhouse and the shame of admitting their own helplessness. In New York, a reporter saw every kind of man, "from the poor out-at-elbows clerk to the corner bummer," standing before the Washington Market Soup-House, but not one of them lacked "the trace of hunger" on his countenance, and "respectable men," never before dependent on others, stood looking ashamed and shunning the gaze of onlookers. Famished men declared that rather than turn themselves over to the authorities to be fed, they would rather die in the streets, and as for the almshouse, a machinist exclaimed, "No mechanic should do that while he has a breath in him."[48]

If good times had eased public indignation over corruption and extravagance in Washington, hard times only quickened the anger. Already on the prairies the Granger movement had been taking on the railroads for what they claimed were their unfair rate structures. They wanted regulatory agencies or rate-setting done by law. But they also targeted the salary grabbers and revenue eaters, the officeholders paid too much, the fees that local officials charged. Theirs was a revolt as much against government as against the corporations, and the "potato bugs," as critics called the insurgents, made Republican incumbents in the Midwest pay at the polls. With the depression pinching off government revenues, a public clamor grew everywhere for lower taxes, reduced spending, and a trimming of public services. Even Tammany Hall's new boss "Honest John" Kelly, as New York City comptroller, went in for retrenchment. The Empire State's debt fell from $51.8 million just after the Civil War to $9.2 million in 1877. Thanks to general laws and the ban on special legislation, statute books thinned out, with Illinois and Pennsylvania passing barely one-tenth as many laws as they had a decade earlier. Maine lawmakers put through only half, Vermont just one-third as many measures. The surging distrust of government did not reflect a new faith in private enterprise, much less in laissez-faire. On the contrary: one of the great flash points came in the partnership between public and private elites. A searing reaction against land grants and aid to corporations set in, with the House resolving against any future subsidies in December 1875. Disappointed at the results of aid already given, communities barraged the court with appeals to have their past generosity annulled or reversed. The "Great Barbecue" had ended. State railroad regulation halted only briefly; in the next decade, it would strengthen and spread. As for state action on farmers' behalf, the depression quickened the pace. Georgia formed the first state department of agriculture in 1874. By 1889, five other states had followed suit. Virginia set up a state chemist to evaluate fertilizers. And despite the liberal fuss about outdoor relief for the jobless, most cities kept or expanded it.[49]

Another scandal merged the sense of economic and political disillusionment. Since the Civil War, the Freedman's Bank had collected millions of dollars from black depositors. Some of them had believed their money guaranteed from loss by the government, a misimpression that the bank's managers did little to dispel. But around 1870, the directors had changed the rules for keeping deposits secure and had made risky loans, in some cases to themselves. Money had gone into the Cookes' banking houses and into the Northern Pacific Railroad, even into the vast promotional schemes of the Washington Ring in redeveloping and redesigning the capital. Now the vaults lay empty, the real estate loans wastepaper, their collateral presently impossible to realize money on. Frederick Douglass was put in charge, perhaps to work miracles and more likely to stay black depositors' run on local banks. He could do nothing, beyond losing $10,000 of his own, put into the firm in a hopeless attempt to save it from destruction. Hundreds of thousands waited long for partial payment; nearly as many lost everything. Efforts to have the government make good their losses continued for a generation without result.[50] No scandal could better symbolize how those who claimed to wish the freedmen the most good had used him the most carelessly.

To hard times, neither party had good solutions. Liberal reformers declared that recovery depended on business confidence and blamed a paper currency worth less than its face value in gold for America's troubles. Farmers, industrialists, and debtors outside New England looked instead to easier credit, and that, they contended, called for an expanded money supply. Pressured into action, Congress voted to set greenback circulation at $400 million, adding $46 million to the circulation of national banknotes and raising their total numbers to $400 million as well. The inflation bill, so-called, was more of a *re*flation bill, reversing the Treasury's past withdrawal

"Blood Money." Thomas Nast, *Harper's Weekly*, June 17, 1876. Nast's equation of the bank's mulcters with the Klan expressed understandable outrage. In fact, those who brought ruin on the firm were nearly all Republicans in good standing. Incompetence and misguided good intentions shared in the debacle. But by 1876, the assumptions that corruption underlay anything that had gone wrong were near universal.

of paper money from the system. An increase in the money supply that kept pace with an increasing population, Senator Oliver Morton of Indiana argued, was not inflationary at all. As the volume of business increased, so should the volume of currency to handle it. Population had increased sharply in those four years, and business and wealth likewise.[51]

Morton's thinking flew counter to liberal doctrine. Speaking for the country's "intelligence," the *Nation* denounced what it saw as a dishonest dollar, one capable of being manipulated to suit the political fancies and selfish desires of interest groups, rather than having a fixed value dependent on the markets. Favoring an elastic currency, a Cincinnati judge protested, was as crazy as asking for "an elastic yard-stick or an elastic bushel measure." The bill was "a violation of the faith of the United States," and it would prove "a lasting disgrace to the nation," one New Yorker wrote. It would "sacrifice the honor of the govt," a Rochester man argued. A "policy of stupendous wickedness," one minister agreed. Business groups protested any inflationary steps. The Chicago Board of Trade weighed in. So did the Chicago Clearing House and the Merchants' Exchange. The New York Chamber of Commerce sent in a protest, as did mercantile groups in Milwaukee, Cincinnati, and Baltimore. At least one liberal, Charles Francis Adams Jr., noted that the bill's most solid support came from the "political combination of barbarism and corruption" that the North had put on top down south. Even more ominously, others argued that, like the Reconstruction laws, greenbacks arose out of a wartime emergency. Constitutional under those unique circumstances, the government's authority to issue them perished once peace returned the Constitution to its original strict construction. As the bill came to a final vote in the Senate in early April, both sides took on a searing intensity, but in the end, the reflationists' lines held and the bill finally carried by twenty-nine to twenty-three. "We are now at the turning point in our financial system," a commercial reporter wrote. "If inflation is not stopped now, it never will be short of general bankruptcy and ruin."[52]

The bill went to the White House and an uncertain reception. Grant was dead-set against inflating the currency. Now that it had reached his desk, the president had second thoughts. As an old Whig, he may have disliked exercising a veto on anything not clearly unconstitutional. Besides, as written, the bill might mean little, if any, inflation, and perhaps the reverse. On April 22nd, when the president sent a message to a thinly attended Senate, currency expansionists expected it be a presidential acceptance, accompanied by an explanation of his reasons. Only a few minutes into the clerk's reading did senators realize that what they had before them was an outright veto. Writing his reasons for approving the bill, the president had unconvinced himself and prepared another message entirely. Long faces grew short, as one reporter remarked, and short ones long. As one of the bill's opponents put it, "When the log [Grant] ceased rolling they found themselves on top."[53]

"From the West and Northwest there is a general howl," the *Cincinnati Commercial* reporter recorded that evening. "It is a hell of a message," one senator told a reporter the following day; "it is a most wonderful document; more d—d nonsense was probably never condensed into the same space." From the Northeast came strong praise, and it was strongest in the financial centers. Down in Tennessee, a reporter described the veto as falling "like the cold hand of death" on people where money was so hard to come by that banks charged 18 percent on loans.[54]

If the veto restored business confidence, it did so in red ink. The depression deepened. "Those who have money are afraid," a visitor to Evansville reported; "those who have not are desperate." Country storekeepers complained that their customers could afford only the bare necessities. "The *Factory* and the *work shop*, the *forge* and the *furnace* are almost as silent as a grave yard at the midnight hour," a New Yorker wrote. "*Trade* and *Commerce* are fast approaching a point of rest—*absolute* rest. The gloom of real despair is settling around almost all business men very like the heavy pall of night. All—*all* this is owing to the '*veto*' by President Grant of the Bill before referred to."[55]

Propertied men sometimes may have made the analogy between blacks and their own white "dangerous classes," or turned more strongly against democracy and in favor of government by those with the money and education to administer matters in a businesslike manner, but for most Americans, the depression simply created a final breaking point with the importance of Civil War issues. The Forty-Third Congress set about cutting back on government spending and investigating waste. To restore an emptied Treasury, its lame-duck session repealed the 10 percent cut in tariff duties imposed in 1872. By embracing the "war tariff" in all its intricacies again, Republicans found what would eventually prove the winning issue of the future, the one program that had genuine appeal among workers afraid of wage cuts and job losses in the face of competition from "cheap pauper labor." At the same time, because the financial issue had so much divisive impact, Republicans rushed to settle it in a way that would restore business confidence, by carrying the Resumption Act, setting a date after which paper money could be redeemed, dollar for dollar, in gold, though they did not specify how that would come about. An aggressive Treasury quickly answered that question, by retiring paper money as quickly as the law allowed. As a result, the price index fell faster than ever and the hardship of producers worsened.[56]

That sense that the wartime emergency had definitely ended and that other concerns took first place may have explained the slackened commitment to Reconstruction. The tangle of affairs in Alabama, Arkansas, South Carolina, and Louisiana tainted federal involvement still further, while the scandals made suspect any professions that the administration might have of serving the public good.

Other events gave the time a feeling of transition. The first generation of free-soil leaders had been departing fast: George W. Julian and Lyman Trumbull, tossed overboard, Vice President Henry Wilson felled by a series of strokes, Seward, Chase, Greeley, all taken by death in barely a year. Then, just at winter's closing in March 1874, the mightiest voice from the Republican Party's founding was stilled. A virtual outcast among the administration men in Congress, Charles Sumner faced in his ailments an enemy more thorough in silencing him than any senator could have been. He described his angina as "a cold hand feeling about and then compressing my heart." "Sometime," he said, "that hand will close and that will end my life." Yet it was well for him that it delayed as long as it did, until he had seen the dictator Baez driven from Santo Domingo and the Bay State rescind the censure resolutions of a year before. The night after his colleague had made a formal presentation of the declaration that Massachusetts had taken its senior senator to its heart again, Sumner had another attack, worse than before. As news spread the next morning that he was dying, friends came and crowds stood in the anterooms to pay their respects. In his moments of lucidity, one concern stood uppermost in Sumner's mind. "My bill—my civil rights bill—don't let it fail," he begged. Just before the end, he turned to Grant's former attorney general, Ebenezer Rockwood Hoar, who stood at his bedside. "Judge," he pleaded, "tell Emerson how much I love and revere him." "He said of you once, that he never knew so white a soul," his friend replied. Early that afternoon, a convulsion ran through Sumner. His right hand closed on Hoar's, and it was over.[57]

CHAPTER FIFTEEN

Redeemer Nation

U ntil the Panic of 1873, Reconstruction's collapse seemed nowhere near inevitable. Republicans had actually recovered ground in North Carolina, Florida, and Alabama, keeping the governorship in the first two and regaining it in the third. The presidency and federal courts remained firmly Republican; House and Senate had big Republican majorities. Most of the seats in the new apportionment would go to the North and West. Even the ostracism down south lost a little of its edge. "You have but little idea how much my respectability has been increased by the election," a Republican commented after the Greeley debacle of 1872. "I am again recognized as a gentleman by the upper-tendom."[1]

That illusion of Reconstruction's staying power explains the strange stillbirth in Louisiana of the unification movement of 1873. Seeing nothing better than stalemate ahead, alarmed by the violence of the Colfax riot, prominent businessmen in New Orleans reached out to find common ground with the free black elite of the city—or, as one of them put it later, "humbled ourselves into the dirt." Eventually, a biracial Committee of One Hundred, spangled with the names of the civic elite, worked out a program: support for the postwar amendments and all the specific civil and political rights that they guaranteed. Whites offered to end discrimination in hiring, desegregate the school system, and see to it that public accommodations were opened to white and black alike. Black leaders promised to help conservatives cut taxation, adjust the state debt, and restore "honest, economic and patriotic government."[2]

But when the organizers blew their trumpet blasts, the recruits failed to come. Beyond city limits, few in either party raised more than a half-hearted cheer. In New Orleans, spokesmen for the working-class black community demanded deeds, not sugared words, before they would pledge to the cause. They could afford to await a better offer, or so they thought: the Pelican State had a natural Republican majority. With Governor Warmoth and his returning board cast into the outer darkness, the next election could not be as much a close-run thing as the last. From yeoman Democrats upstate, the unificationists earned no thanks. That outstretched hand to nonwhite gentry was quickly withdrawn. "The hope of Louisiana is in the white race, in its increase and in its dominion within her borders," the *Shreveport Times* scolded, "and we hold as folly all political movements that have not that object in view."[3]

Blacks were not simply looking to keep the gains of the past five years. With Grant's reelection, they stepped up their efforts to broaden them. The Reconstruction governments had done much to develop the South, but freedmen's needs remained partially unmet. To judge by the slew of aid bills and proposed charters, white legislators cared more for railroads than social justice. The railroads for which Republican governments had done so much showcased the freedpeople's stinted rights. Blacks had to pay first-class fares for compartments "just as good" as whites obtained, 'though," said one injured party, the cars were "so disgustingly filthy from tobacco smoke and spittle, that a well-trained hog would refuse to enter."[4] White legislators declined to make financial aid conditional on an end to discrimination. Integrated facilities would have ruined the railroads—or so the companies said. Separate first-class cars for either race would have increased railroad operating expenses, too high already.

For five years, it had seemed that one race gave the ruling party most of its support and the other most of its leadership. With all but a handful of congressional seats in white hands, with white officials predominating even in some black counties, the freedpeople in the cotton South felt that they deserved more. Federal patronage never had loaves and fishes enough to feed the multitudes craving them, but it was all too clear that white applicants crowded at the front of the line. When the national government had contracts for deserving publishers down south, it allotted them to white presses. "The white men in the Republican party fill all the paying offices," Mobile's black editor Philip Joseph complained, "and yet if a colored man dare part his lips on the subject he is charged with attempting to raise a black man's party."[5]

Outnumbered but as vital as ever to give the Republican Party whatever legitimacy it could scrape together among white southerners, scalawags clung to every office they could, and not on selfish grounds alone. Accepting blacks' right to vote, they still doubted their capacity to govern. Most disliked and dreaded social equality. Sharing conservatives' belief that southerners should direct the South's fate, they saw northern-led state governments as political suicide. The more freedpeople turned to carpetbaggers for leadership, as opposed to their neighbors, the harder the respectable Republican planters like former governor James Lusk Alcorn would find it to get a fair hearing in the white community. Scalawags and New Departure Democrats wanted railroads, industrial development, relief, schools, levees, or any variety of social and economic legislation. As long as the party would meet such needs, some whites could subdue their racial prejudices and even vote for measures of limited equality. Others, voting Democratic, would feel no need to carry their opposition into open war. As the Reconstruction coalition lost interest in certain reforms and the power to implement others and as the race issue came to the fore again, the scalawags found their fealty sorely tested.[6]

By 1873, then, Republicans faced a serious dilemma. Action and inaction alike carried political risks. Yet gambits like the unification movement may have shown why the party took the risk it did. The Committee of One Hundred had failed. Other such movements might do better. How long could the Republican leadership wave the specter of slave-owner domination and hold blacks in line if the party catered to businessmen and planters while slighting equal rights? And more pertinently, since the party was retreating on railroad aid measures and rescinding many of its riskier commitments, where could the party look for fresh enthusiasm as it dismantled the part of its program with the widest white appeal? In North Carolina, Judge Daniel Russell ruled that one race could not exclude another from a public place. Mississippi and Florida enacted comprehensive civil rights acts, opening public accommodations to all. Louisiana lawmakers strengthened existing statutes. In no case did the law compel integration. Each statute simply declared that no facilities should charge blacks and whites the same rates for unequal services. Defenders of the laws argued that freedmen's rights had not been increased—only the power to enforce rights ensured by common law. Conservatives took another view. To them, the laws meant inevitable "social equality."[7]

Republicans seriously miscalculated. The debates over civil rights legislation brought racial resentments inside the party out into plain view. Democrats responded even more implacably. Universal suffrage was one thing, race-mixing another. Furthermore, this time, the change was not being imposed by outside force against which no recourse existed. The perpetrators were natives whom southern votes had elected but who lacked the power to impose their will. The civil rights laws were not only more in need of resistance than the Reconstruction Acts but more open to resistance. Nor had Democrats really changed their ideals—only their tactics. Upper-class gentry, secure in their status, might hobnob with African Americans and profess solicitude to win their votes, but most whites continued to proclaim their own superiority and stigmatize any Caucasian who "voted against his own race, kindred and friends."[8]

Moderate conservatives' influence in party counsels depended on the salience of the Republicans' economic program. White supremacists would accept a secondary role only as long as concentrating on the issues of corruption and political mismanagement would win Republican votes to the Conservative cause and as long as whites found other issues as inspiring as that of race. While the South prospered, it could be argued that emphasizing the color line would do the section more harm than good.

That was before the Panic of September 1873. Southern roads, the least stable of the lot and the most financially stressed even in the best of times, were special sufferers. Two thousand miles' worth of southern roads were behind on their payment on bond interest as of November 1873; over 4,000 had been foreclosed upon and were managed by the courts three years later. By 1876, more than half the roads in five states had defaulted. For nearly all of them, receivership was inevitable. More than any other section, the South saw a steep drop in new miles built. During the depression years, just 8 percent of all the new construction came in the ex-Confederate South; in 1875 it could point to only fifty new miles completed, with six states not building a single one.[9] For factories, mines, timber companies, and merchants, the New South dream receded into the unforeseeable distance. Credit sources dried up. Tobacco, rice, sugar, and cotton prices fell sharply. If sharecroppers were lucky, their earnings when the crop was sold at year's end barely made enough to cover expenses and goods bought on credit. Others found themselves in debt. So did small property holders for whom cotton provided a supplemental income. Blacks' dependency on planter employers increased—as did their vulnerability to economic pressure at election time. Sharecropping had become a trap and would remain so, affording a life of unyielding destitution, with tenants ill-fed, ill-clad, ill-housed, and fettered to the soil. White yeomen in the cotton South found it, too: by 1880, a third of them were tenant farmers or renters, most of them paying in a share of the crop. For landowners, the Republican governments' taxes, which by prewar standards had seemed onerous, now fell with a crushing burden. Their incomes were falling much faster than their taxes. By early 1874, conservatives were organizing taxpayers' revolts and protest movements.[10]

Among northerners with little or no cash of their own to spare, the outcry among those identifying themselves as taxpayers won a far more sympathetic hearing than similar movements in the prosperous years gone by. Blaming misgovernment and corruption for the South's miseries went over better than an overtly racist appeal would have done, even though the solution proposed was the same: to empty government of Negroes and supposed low-life whites and restore the South's self-proclaimed natural leaders, whites of good family with a large financial stake in society. At the same time, the panic wiped out all the hopes of Republicans embarking on a gospel of prosperity in the South. The money to do so was gone.

In fact, the taxpayers' leagues only acted as the respectable partners of a new, more frankly white supremacist set of "redeemers," as they had begun to call themselves. The rise of "white-liners" might have happened, panic or no. As the unification movement's failure showed, the accommodators' policies had failed utterly to win freedpeople away from the Republican Party. On their side, the color line held. All that moderates had achieved by talking up any issue other than race was to take the heart out of those southerners for whom the section's real problem was a black and white matter. It kept a broad potential white constituency home on Election Day. The state civil rights legislation and the fiscal collapse ended this apathy. When Sumner's civil rights bill carried in the Senate in June, it roused a fury from Indiana to the Gulf of Mexico. "Let me tell you, stranger, a nigger shall never eat at my table, Congress or no Congress," a white farmer swore. "I'm a runnin' this little machine." That bill, he added, had driven the scalawags into Democratic ranks like nothing else. "They have been swallowing nigger, nigger, nigger, for the past seven years, but this last dose is a little too much. They're all a-throwing up."[11]

By mid-1874, the sense of crisis could not be missed. "The time has come to protect their firesides, their wives and daughters," a reporter paraphrased; "to buckle on their arms and continue the fight until the negroes, carpetbaggers and scalawags were driven from power."[12] It became easy to encourage the whites to believe in any dreadful prospect, and polemicists found many. They spread rumors that blacks were arming, that a black militia would be used to suppress white taxpayers, that the so-called Negro governments had begun to arm field hands, and that white women could sleep secure only with the victory of the white man's party and the organization of paramilitary companies, the so-called White Leagues.[13]

Deprivation and newly unaffordable tax rates added to whites' desperate temper. Never particularly fond of Radicalism, they lost their tolerance as they lost their livings and their property went under the sheriff's hammer. That so many of them were idle afforded more time for talking politics. "Words cannot adequately describe the condition of people who have nothing to do or do nothing but drink mint juleps and talk politics," a reporter in New Orleans recorded in 1874. "It would be difficult to convince the men who appeared upon the streets . . . that they were not fighting for their homes, and for the sustenance of their wives and children and for everything which makes life dear," another correspondent remarked.[14]

The Redeemers never spoke with one, harsh voice. Their advocates did not repudiate the Reconstruction Amendments, in their narrowest meaning. Always they had spokesmen in Congress to assure northerners that they waged the fight on thieves and incompetents, not on blacks themselves, and that restoring gentlemen of property and standing to the seats of the mighty would benefit blacks as well as whites. Northern correspondents sent back heartening reports of good government in redeemed states like Georgia, where blacks, having accepted their presumed natural place, had found security, stability, prosperity, and protection for all those rights that they really deserved to enjoy. Everywhere, Redeemers looked for African American supporters that they could showcase as converts to their cause, proofs that the struggles pitted the robbed of every color against the robbers. They formed what black Democratic clubs they could and put on display every northerner come south, Union soldiers particularly, who joined their cause. All those converts gave Redemption that certificate of good character it would need, to show that, as far as Reconstruction's purposes had been to preserve the Union, end slavery, and assure a fundamental equality for all men, those purposes had been met.[15]

Redeemers' actions showed the hollowness of their words. Having boasted that Conservative rule had brought good government and a growing racial understanding, Virginia Democrats mobilized their voters in 1873 by concocting a race issue and playing it up as avidly as if their enemies had been in power all the time. Not one Negro found a place on the Radical state ticket, the *Richmond Whig* screamed—proof that black voters expected "to run riot in the spoil of Virginia" when all the votes were in! Let the Republican candidate for governor talk of building railroads and canals and coaxing in outside capital; his words hid his real aim: "mongrelism." Experience had shown "that the colored men are not true Virginians," orators contended. The Old Dominion had only two alternatives: drive them out or wipe them out.[16] The following year, Alabama white-liners set the tone for the campaign and the pattern for making sure that no scalawag dared give open support to the Republican Party. White Republicans were shunned, denied loans, and threatened. "Let his ship ply without a cargo, or rot unmanned in a breezeless ocean," the *Opelika Times* roared. "Touch him not, nor his goods, nor his cattle, nor anything that he has. . . . The adder that stings should find no warmth in the bosom of the dying victim." A general campaign of intimidation was practiced against blacks who relied for their pay or credit on white patrons. Heavily armed White Leagues and White Men's Associations paraded, marched, and threatened. Night riders beat black organizers. Republican meetings were broken up and a few of their local leaders were killed. "It is thought no more of to kill a negro than a dog," a scalawag wrote, "and hundreds are killed that never are known[,] for our grand juries will not rule against a white man in favor of a negro." The strategy paid off, not so much in keeping freedpeople home as in rousing the white electorate to turn out. Even before the polls closed, voters knew that they were witnessing a Democratic landslide, carrying governor and legislature easily. It did not take the victors long to put through election laws guaranteeing a Democratic count every time and a seriously reduced Republican turnout. The one black judge in the state was legislated out of office. In Republican counties, special laws put the jury-selection process into the hands of commissions sure to bring in all-white panels every time. Half the Republicans elected to county office in 1874 were tossed out by the refusal of white sponsors to post bond for them.[17]

Alabama's killings got less play up north than they might have because so many places had outbreaks of violence that fall. There were shootings in Tennessee and Kentucky, widespread disorders in upstate South Carolina, white paramilitary units drilling in Natchez. Louisiana, with its discredited and paralyzed Republican government, descended into virtual civil war. There the White Leagues mustered in broad daylight, supported with threats (perfectly legal) of economic action, and vague warnings (also perfectly legal) that those firearms on the "Rifle Clubs'" shoulders were not for mere show. "If a single hostile gun is fired between the whites and blacks," the *Shreveport Times* declared, "every carpetbagger and scalawag that can be caught will in twelve hours be hanging from a limb." The White Leagues not only kept blacks in line; they kept them in tow. In some parishes, freedmen were so terrified that they swore public allegiance to the league. Lynchings were reported, usually of "notoriously bad" Negroes, sometimes with the semblance of a trial before self-anointed juries of citizens. These incidents were reported as "executions," and the victims were always black ones.[18]

But officeholders were the main targets. White Leaguers cleaned out the local authorities upstate. In Coushatta, the usual rumors of a Negro uprising brought a white uprising that forced all the local Republican officials to resign, in return for the promise of safe conduct out of the parish. Their armed guard kept its word: they were escorted to the borders, where White Leaguers from the adjoining parish killed them all. Detained by business in New Orleans, state senator Marshall H. Twitchell escaped that fate. When he returned two years later, persons unknown shot off his arms. In Lincoln and Avoyelles Parishes, Republican officers quit while they were still healthy. The governor found that in many places, he had more than enough vacancies to fill, and the nominees most suitable for the job loved staying alive too much to accept. In many places, Republican sheriffs and judges might as well have resigned, for all the good they could do. Fear of White Leaguers had taught them that the tighter they shut their eyes to the intimidators, the more chance they had of serving out their terms.[19]

That September, White Leagues massed in the capital and demanded Governor Kellogg's "abdication." Streetcars, mattresses, and iron gates piled up into street barricades. Detachments commanded by the veterans of gentlemen's clubs seized the city hall and cut the telegraph wires out of town. Routing the state militia and metropolitan police in a brief blaze of gunfire that afternoon in the "Battle of Liberty Place," they proclaimed John McEnery governor. The next day, the White League occupied the statehouse and every police station in New Orleans. They had seized and emptied out the state arsenals. Upstate, Republican parish officers quit without a fight. President Grant was forced to send federal troops to restore Kellogg, but outside the city, he could do nothing. That fall, intimidation, fraud, and the official returning board's tortuous counting brought in an assembly where Democrats had a near majority.[20]

Rousing sympathy for Louisiana's carpetbaggers posed quite as much of a challenge as finding a good word to say about the "Prostrate State" under Governor Frank Moses Jr. But, their respectable apologists' statements to the contrary, the White Leagues were not mobilizing for good government, nor even for a government of white men. Any authority dependent on Negro voters was "Negro rule." Any Republican state, however reformed, required "Redemption."

South Carolina and Mississippi made that perfectly clear. By 1873, in fact, most Reconstruction governments had passed through their gaudiest period. There were no big giveaways and very few scandals. Most of their governors took their jobs seriously and made cutbacks in spending and tax reductions a higher priority than spending programs. In Florida, black voters had kicked the quarreling carpetbaggers and their railroad cronies out of power and chosen a scalawag governor whose conscience was the healthiest thing about him. Mississippi remained perhaps the best governed of any south of the Ohio. Governor Adelbert Ames resisted the corruptionists, pushing spending and tax rates down marginally and using his veto on railroad aid bills implacably. Even in South Carolina, Daniel H. Chamberlain's election as governor in 1874 brought the stealing days to a close.[21]

South Carolina's black majority was too big to be overcome by any surge in white turnout, and a number of prominent Democrats found good reason to make peace with Chamberlain. It was perfectly true that he represented everything bad about the new political order. Born in Massachusetts, bred to abolitionism, an officer over black troops in the war, a frank supporter of woman suffrage,[22] he had shared in the take under Governor Scott. But Democrats came to see him as one of the most upright of the crew of gangsters that had fattened on the state, particularly since after his election he proved his change in faith by substantial works. His inaugural address calling for steps restoring South Carolina's credit and reducing its taxes and assessments set the tone. Lashing out at the malefactors in party ranks, he took on the trial judges and school officials. His black constituents endured regular lectures about their inadequacies and misbehavior. The governor maintained spending for the public schools, but in most things, his administration called for serious reductions: the orphan and lunatic asylums included. The overwhelmingly black state university was to be downscaled drastically and reorganized. In place of professors, it would employ schoolteachers, because, Chamberlain explained, "We only want a good high school." By shipping out "simple, harmless idiots and imbeciles" to county poorhouses, the state asylum could reduce its expenses to the bare minimum, covering the violent and those needing medical treatment exclusively. To save money on the state penitentiary, the governor called for revival of the convict lease system.[23]

To Republican legislators, the cutback in services felt like a betrayal of their constituents. Within the year, many of them had turned implacably against him. From conservative Democrats like those running the *Charleston News and Courier*, Chamberlain won unstinted praise. If in his fight on black politicians he had crossed the Rubicon, as the newspaper headlined one confrontation, the governor may have thought he could glimpse on the farther shore the white conservative hosts, ready to welcome him and the Republicans still following his lead. In fact, Chamberlain spotted the same mirage that had lured governors elsewhere to their political ruin. As always, Democrats were glad to applaud anyone who would wreck the Republican Party. In one member's words, they meant "to keep Chamberlain and some of the carpetbaggers, fighting, till they eat each other up all but the tails," and then "keep the tails jumping at each other, until southern raised gentlemen slide in to office and take the reins of government."[24]

By then, in fact, Chamberlain led the only Reconstruction government not panting for life. Republican governors held on in Louisiana, Florida, and North Carolina, but Democrats ran the legislatures and were slashing spending and taxes, particularly where their actions could starve the patronage-dependent Republican press. An alternative newspaper voice was fading into silence, unable even to make the faintest reply to the roar of allegation and abuse that the well-heeled conservative press sent north to define Reconstruction in voters' minds. Where Democrats had redeemed individual counties, a full, fair turnout of black voters no longer had much chance of happening. But then, South Carolina's governor may have drawn lessons from Mississippi. Possessing a black majority, as South Carolina did, it had proven what so many Louisiana parishes had proven: that without substantial white support, the Republicans' advantage in numbers counted for nothing. For by mid-March 1876, Governor Adelbert Ames had been driven from power—leaving the state, never to return.

Even as Ames had nudged lawmakers toward piecemeal fiscal reforms, the White League infection had spread. Vicksburg showed what muscle could do. Taxes were heavy there, and Treasury warrants had been fiddled with for the profit of local officeholders. By July 1874, armed bodies of men were parading the streets. Browbeaten and helpless, blacks called on the Grant administration for rescue, but none came. On Election Day, the rattle of guns complemented the rustle of ballots, and most of those guns were Democratic ones. So were most of the votes, when the ballot boxes were opened.[25] That December a white mob forced the sheriff, Peter Crosby, to resign. Crosby obeyed to save his life. Unable to find help at the capital, he tried to raise a posse among freedmen in the surrounding countryside to enforce his right to the office. Not clear on the circumstances, but well aware that Crosby was calling them to uphold the law, hundreds of blacks marched toward Vicksburg. Before they could reach the town, they were halted by a white force. Heavily outgunned, they agreed to retire—at which point shooting broke out. The freedpeople fled, their shotguns no match for rifles. The pursuit and the random killings lasted for days. Sixty to eighty of them were killed, perhaps as many as three hundred. The federal government sent a company of troops and restored Crosby, but it could not put the city back into Republican hands, and by the fall of 1875, all Mississippi had caught the Vicksburg virus.[26]

Against White Leagues and the open assertion that Democrats would do whatever it took to carry the election, with the threats to sharecroppers' livelihoods and a relentless campaign against any white still daring to admit to a Republican allegiance, Ames found himself helpless. He held off on summoning a state militia; any forces mustered would have to come almost exclusively from the freedmen, and that would only give the leagues the excuse to open full-scale race war. A riot just outside Jackson finally changed his mind. When gunfire ended in another Negro-hunt, the governor put a few militia units into the field, but timidly and under severe restrictions. "Negro militia has not the courage or nerve—whatever it may be called—to act the part of soldiers," he commented.[27]

His salvation, he thought, lay in Washington, but over the past year, Grant's reluctance to involve himself on behalf of discredited Republican governors had turned into a shyness about stepping in on behalf of any but the most deserving cases, and especially, as now, with a hard-fought gubernatorial campaign under way in Ohio. Northern public opinion may not have turned against Reconstruction's accomplishments, but, egged on by the damning reports in the influential "independent press," it could no longer give any "carpetbag government" the benefit of the doubt. With the military resources Grant had at hand, saving Mississippi looked like a tall order. Doing so almost certainly would cost Republicans Ohio. A Democratic victory there would dim Republicans' already bleak prospects of carrying the White House in 1876, and with a Democratic president, freedpeople could not even expect the shadow of support from Washington.[28]

By now, the president knew how little the public would accept. The year before, Democrats had carried the House. Electing eighty-nine southern members to Republicans' seventeen helped. In thirty-five states holding elections, Democrats carried twenty-three, among them Ohio, Wisconsin, Pennsylvania, and Massachusetts, all, until now, reliably Republican. Scandals cost Republicans their majority; so did objections to the civil rights bill, depressed conditions, and resentment in the countryside over the tight credit that administration monetary policies committed the country to. In vain, party papers played up the assassinations in Louisiana and Alabama. Some voters thought the South's troubles beside the point, considering their own. Others refused to believe the stories true. Reconstruction's enemies branded every outrage as manufactured, to fire northern Republicans' hearts, and they coined a new term for the use of sectional differences for party advantage: "waving the bloody shirt." Folklore traced the metaphor to Sumner's caning: a preposterous myth arose that his shirt, soaked in blood from Congressman Preston Brooks's attack in 1856, had been kept on display or even borne aloft in parades to kindle northern hatred. But Grant's supporters also had to cope with fears of "Caesarism." Playing on traditional American fears for the fragility of the republic, critics accused the president of plotting to win himself a third term. With Grant refusing to squelch the stories, all the anxieties over the national government playing kingmaker at the state level fed into a larger fear that America had slipped far from the constitutional order of restricted, well-defined powers and informal restraints on government action.[29]

That winter, as the Forty-Third Congress met in lame-duck session, the political climate had shifted distinctly. Once again, Louisiana furnished the defining moment. Its general assembly stood almost evenly divided. On opening day, Democrats seized the advantage. Before the roll could be completed, a member leaped to his feet to offer New Orleans mayor Louis Wiltz's name for temporary speaker and to put the question to the body without asking for any roll-call vote. Making up in lungs what they lacked in numbers, Democrats shouted aye. Ignoring Republican objections and fist-waving, Wiltz raced to the podium and seized the gavel out of the hands of the black clerk. A Democratic justice of the peace appeared to swear Wiltz in. Instantly, Wiltz filled all the legislative offices with Democrats, the clerkship included, and chose assistant sergeants at arms to keep order. His three-dozen nominees, many of them captains of New Orleans' White League companies, were not only willing. The moment their names were called, they turned down their lapels to display the blue ribbon badges with gold letters announcing their offices. With their knives and pistols at Democrats' disposal, the five disputed seats were filled on the spot with Democratic claimants. Republican members tried to flee the chamber to break the quorum. Brandishing weapons, the leaguers barred the way. As the uproar spread beyond the legislative chamber, the self-proclaimed Speaker called on Colonel Philippe Régis de Trobriand of the Thirteenth Infantry, commander of the troops stationed around the statehouse, to clear "idlers" from the corridors. De Trobriand did.[30]

An hour later, he was back. Fearful that using the government-run metropolitan police to carry out his instructions would set off a bloody riot like that of 1866 or an insurrection like that of the previous September, and aware that the U.S. Army was the one force that could act without bringing on the widely predicted clash of arms, Governor Kellogg had instructed him to remove the five Democrats that had been illegally seated. The general had to obey his orders but hoped that a request on the Speaker would suffice. Wiltz insisted that if the army wanted it done, it must use force to do it. Not long after, soldiers arrived to escort the five claimants from the chamber. Thereupon, the rest of the Democratic members stalked out of the House in protest. In full sway, Republicans chose a Speaker and filled the five vacancies with their own contestants. It should have been easy, on the merits of it, to figure out which side was in the right, or that neither was, but that was not how the story had been played. As some Democrats admitted, they had sprung "the revolutionary trap" in the legislature not because they expected to get away with it but to provoke military interference.[31] They had got what they wanted. Dispatches flew north describing how a legislature conducting its proceedings in a lawful manner had been purged at bayonet point.

Sent to New Orleans to keep an eye on conditions and take effective command of the Department of the Gulf, peppery General Phil Sheridan only made matters worse. Hearing regular threats to assassinate the governor and regrets that it had not happened already and talk of murdering enough Republican members to guarantee a Democratic majority, aware that one assemblyman had been kidnapped to further the Wiltz plot, he sensed a community on the edge of a new rebellion. Perhaps the efficient methods that he had used in exterminating Indians on the Plains influenced his judgment, or awareness that the White Leagues continued to hold state government arms that they had taken by force in the insurrection and that no police agency could restore them. In either case, he reacted swiftly, and with a regionwide solution. "The 'terrorism now existing in Louisiana, Mississippi, and Arkansas could be entirely removed . . . by the arrest and trial of the ringleaders of the armed White Leagues," he wrote the secretary of war. Congress or the president only need declare the "ringleaders" of the armed White Leagues "banditti." Then soldiers could arrest them and military commissions try them. From Washington, Secretary Belknap quickly wired support for Sheridan's "course" from "the President & all of us."[32]

Sheridan's practicality was of the most terrifying kind. "What you want to do, . . . when you get back to Washington," he told Congressman George Frisbie Hoar, "is to suspend the what-do-you-call it." Hoar thought the general meant the writ of habeas corpus, and got the impression that Sheridan knew nothing about it except that it hindered him getting a necessary job done.[33] The Supreme Court's ban on the use of military courts for trying civilians in peacetime may have slipped his mind entirely. His assumption

"Little Phil's Extinguisher." Thomas Nast, *Harper's Weekly*, February 6, 1875. General Philip Sheridan, celebrated Civil War cavalry leader and postwar Indian fighter, misquoted as saying, "The only good Indian is a dead Indian," suppresses the white resisters as "banditti." The conical hat was the stereotypical headwear for Italian robber bands.

was that the military, being above politics, would remove the issue and the trials' outcome from sordid party warfare. In fact, by early 1875, northerners saw the army not as above politics but as politics in the worst way, the adjunct of a political party that no longer could win through the usual channels of give and take that elections were meant to be.

No advice could have fed better into the wakened fear that free institutions were in danger. Protest resolutions sprang up from the floor of every legislature then in session. Mass meetings assembled to denounce the military for usurpation. A petition was circulated in Boston for use of Faneuil Hall for a demonstration, and the first name fixed to it was that of that old antislavery statesman Charles Francis Adams. The historian Francis Parkman, the celebrated scientist Theodore Lyman, and former governor Alexander H. Bullock signed it, too. When Wendell Phillips spoke, opposing the protest resolutions and warning that "the blood of more than a hundred colored men and a hundred whites would be on their skirts before the first of March," the crowd hissed him long and hard, and the younger John Quincy Adams fled the stage (perhaps confirming the joke that the Adams family was like a potato: the best part lay underground).[34] As the first dispatches in the morning papers reached Washington, Congress broke loose in denunciations, many of them based on the assumption that the ejectment had been Sheridan's work and that Sheridan had the president's full backing. With terrible timing, Benjamin F. Butler brought up the civil rights bill in the House, and at once Democrats stormed. Discussing "a social rights bill" was trifling with the country when the army had invaded the "most important civil rights of the whole nation," Samuel S. "Sunset" Cox of New York protested. "If Caesar attempts to wrap the purple about him," Senator Eli Saulsbury of Delaware thundered, "I say in the name of public liberty let the American people tear the robes from him."[35] Grant had to reassure the Congress that he had no part in either incident, and a compromise settlement in Louisiana left Republicans in undisputed control of the governorship, in return for giving up their legislative majority.

Three weeks later, suspicions reawoke when Grant invited Congress to give him grounds to intervene in Arkansas to reverse Redemption there. In May 1874, he had recognized Baxter as governor; now he asked for authority to recognize Brooks as the real winner of the 1872 election. At the same time, the administration favored a bill strengthening its means for protecting Republican voters down south and giving it new powers to counter the White Leagues.

Southern Republican lawmakers wanted such a measure badly. Especially Alabama Republicans, on their way out of power, hoped to challenge or overturn the new conservative officials and forestall what seemed to be an inevitable constitutional convention that would put the machinery of elections into Democratic hands. Many Republicans saw a crisis well under way, and a danger building of outright political revolution. "The colored men who compose the body of the republican party have been made 'peaceful' by the shot-gun of the raiding white-leaguer, the bowie-knife of the southern desperado, or the whip-lash of an ex-slave master," one Alabama congressman warned. If the party failed to provide southern Republicans with protection before Congress adjourned, "our doom is sealed; liberty of speech will be throttled, and maintenance of liberty in that country will be 'among the things that were.'"[36]

Under the House bill, federal deputy marshals and election supervisors could arrest those accused of intimidation. Other provisions guaranteed full registration of voters. There could be no guns carried "for the purpose of intimidating or injuring" persons at the polls on Election Day or when they registered, and concealed weapons would be presumptive evidence of an intent to intimidate. The third section forbade any Reconstructed state altering its constitution in ways that would keep blacks from voting, and punished election officials refusing to receive black votes; states were kept from fixing the poll tax at any higher per capita rate than it had been when they were readmitted under the Reconstruction Acts. The final section declared that any "unlawful combinations" strong enough to be able to overthrow state authorities or defy them by violence would be deemed a rebellion against the United States, and the president would have the power at his own discretion to suspend the writ of habeas corpus to deal with them; it did not require them to commit any overt act for a federal response to take place.[37]

Put together, the administration's two initiatives looked like a threat to undo Redemption and overturn election results across the cotton South. Well aware that Democrats intended to call new constitutional conventions in North Carolina, Texas, Alabama, and perhaps elsewhere to consolidate their power and roll back Reconstruction's gains, Grant's defenders may have seen a looming crisis in which everything won in the past eight years might be lost. But those defenders were disturbingly few. Critics wondered what proofs had changed the president's mind about Brooks's right to the governorship. Where was the emergency that put Arkansas Unionists at such peril that the government had to act? Grant's solution could not possibly bring tranquility to a state already free of commotion. It would set off disorder of virtually Louisiana proportions, and the chaos might well spread beyond state lines. Governor Augustus Garland may have been a Confederate senator, but no fire-eater; he had all the appearance of the New South, rather than the Old. The new constitution disfranchised nobody, nullified no rights that the freedpeople had. In its second article it recognized the equality of all persons before the law and declared that no citizen should ever be deprived of "any right, privilege, or immunity on account of race, color or previous condition." It declared forever inviolate the freedom of the press and the right to vote without discrimination on the basis of color—a full concession of what Reconstruction had aimed to accomplish. The call for a convention had been approved by about ten to one. And in spite of this, here was the president, apparently telling Congress that a government chosen by four-fifths of those voting was unlawful and that a constitution enacted by a like majority was null and void.[38]

Hints were thrown out that Grant had a fell purpose, to provoke the people of Arkansas into making open war on the U.S. Army. With the excuse that a new rebellion had broken out, the president could put the whole South under military control and suppress it, all "for the double purpose of saving the Republican party and securing himself a third term." From Arkansas, a reporter described the surprise mixed with dread that the presidential message brought. "It is a time for fear," he affirmed. "Wise men who catch glimpses of the course in which we are rapidly drifting as a nation, look at each other in blank dismay, and wonder if the Republic as a Republic, can survive ten years longer."[39] In the wake of the Louisiana crisis just a month before, it seemed like one more grab for power over the South, one more attempt to subject the states to decrees from Washington.

In fact, Grant had no intention of intervening without explicit instruction from Congress. Having to act on his discretion in sustaining the Kellogg government had been embarrassing enough, and the consequences were not good. Uneasy that once Congress adjourned in March he might be forced to do so again without sanction, he clearly wanted a lead—and while Arkansas was a case directly before him, he could foresee others, among them Mississippi. The same desire that impelled him to seek specific legislation empowering him to keep the peace in the South may have pushed him for guidance from Congress on Arkansas. Rightly, a few Republicans guessed that if Congress did not legislate, Grant would take it as a disapproval of his views and a tacit acceptance of Garland's right to the office.[40]

But that sentiment was much less commonly heard than the wish among Republicans that he had held his peace. "I don't mind dying," one growled, "but I don't want to die like a dog in a ditch." On this one issue, at least, the House majority had no intention of giving the president what he wanted, and from the moment the message came out, House members felt free to say so. As head of the House committee sent to investigate affairs in Arkansas, Luke Poland of Vermont summed up the moderates' case convincingly. He granted that all the evidence taken in committee showed that Brooks had received the most votes in the gubernatorial election and been cheated out of the office. But as he reminded his colleagues, the real question was no longer which candidate had won in 1872 but whether national power would interpose now "to wipe out this new constitution." Finally, Poland emphasized what had become clear elsewhere, that, whatever the national government's will, it no longer had the power to create a Republican commonwealth able to stand on its own—ever. Whether the administration enthroned Brooks or Baxter, the regime that resulted would be like Louisiana's, "a government that will be upheld by U.S. bayonets, and just so long as there are enough of them to uphold it it will stand; the moment they are withdrawn it will vanish like dew in the morning."[41] He did not say, perhaps did not need to say, the larger conclusion. Unless Republicans were content to keep southern states as permanent satrapies, the national government would have to loose its grip and let freedpeople take their chances, new state constitutions and all.

With less than a month before final adjournment, the majority would need near unanimity and stern discipline to press the Enforcement bill measure through, ahead of other vital legislation. They had neither. For those glimpsing a Caesar in the White House, such broad authority as this bill gave looked especially terrifying. Its interference with states' rights to administer voting requirements in perpetuity assumed a national oversight over voting that not even most northern states wanted. Four years before, the Ku-Klux law had come only amid a torrent of violence that could be handled no other way; even then its most controversial provisions lapsed after a year. No such crisis loomed in the South now. Republicans, even those acknowledging a serious state of affairs, felt that the government had gone as far as it might. The atrocities and intimidation were real, Congressman Joseph Hawley of Connecticut allowed. But he could not accept further and further terms being imposed "to make that people good, and to control the elections there." There were "wrongs there that we can never reach in this Hall until we have changed the Constitution of the United States." The South needed social, educational, and moral reconstruction. No legislative hall could bring those about—only time and education and the spread of true Christianity. "We cannot put justice, liberty, and equality into the hearts of a people by statutes alone." Severely amended, the bill passed the House. It never reached a third reading in the Senate. Two days before the Congress adjourned, a thinly attended and exhausted House beat the administration's proposition to recognize Brooks as governor. Nearly half the Republicans voted against it. Grant knew when to quit. On March 11, he recognized the Democratic government in Arkansas. Garland called a day of thanksgiving for the state's narrow escape, and for its liberation from the Radicals, giving credit to the "true conservative Republican sentiment in the North."[42]

By Congress's adjournment on March 4th, then, Redemption had become irreversible. The incoming Democratic Party would never pay for an army used aggressively on Republicans' behalf. Whatever inclination toward intervention the White House entertained before, now melted away. Under the circumstances, seven months later, Mississippi governor Adelbert Ames came asking for the near impossible. Grant could not hide his reluctance—nor, to be fair, his regret. As he put it, "The whole public are tired out with these annual, autumnal outbreaks in the South." He did not refuse help outright. If need be, troops would be sent, and, he added, "I shall instruct the Commander of the forces to have no childs play."[43] Changing the emphasis, Attorney General Edwards Pierrepont stressed the governor's need to exhaust every other option before seeking federal aid.

With no time left to muster more than a token force, Ames opened negotiations with Democratic leaders. In return for his halting the deployment of militia, the Democrats promised to keep the peace. Two companies of state troops would be disbanded and disarmed; nothing was said about Democratic rifle clubs laying down their arms—which none of them did. Without an agreement, matters might have been far worse, but they fell far short of the "peace, good order, and a fair election" that the governor predicted. Shootings, threats, and "bulldozing," as the use of intimidating force came to be known, had help from Ames's enemies inside the party, among them former senator Hiram R. Revels and former governor James L. Alcorn, defeated by Ames for governor two years before and ever ready to blame all Mississippi's troubles on the governor's alleged misdeeds. Refugees looking for protection were flocking to the capital. Letters from everywhere called for help. "They have hung six men since the killing of Mr. Fawn," a Republican wrote from Yazoo City. "They won't let the Republicans have [no] ticket. They will not print any at all. For they are going to have war here tomorrow. . . . Send help. They told Mr. Richman if he went to the telegraph office tomorrow they would hang him—help—help—help—soon as you can." The most that the governor could do was to advise voters not to risk their lives by showing up at the polls.[44]

On Election Day, only one side mobilized fully. With Republican organizers intimidated and all but the boldest freedpeople staying home in a scattering of counties, most polling places were "quiet as a funeral." Not in Aberdeen: there, Democrats mounted an old cannon stoked with chains and slugs on a hill overlooking the polling place. The Republican sheriff saved his life by locking himself in his own jail, and at the end of the day, a 648-vote Republican lead from two years before had been changed into a

1,175 Democratic majority. Distributors of Republican ballots in some counties did their work at peril of their lives. Others dared not pass out tickets at all. But as in Alabama the year before, white-line rhetoric brought out an unprecedented turnout among conservative stay-at-homes. The state went heavily Democratic, and as soon as the legislature assembled, it began delving for dirt on Ames. As impeachment proceedings began, the governor knew that his innocence gave him no protection. In return for the charges being dropped, he resigned.[45]

The "Mississippi plan's" success only fired the hearts of those South Carolina Democrats who wanted no accommodation, even with a reformer like Chamberlain. In the whiter upcountry counties, with enough intimidation, Democrats could regain control of local government. There the "Straightout" alternative gathered momentum through the spring of 1876. Refusing to endorse Chamberlain, the Democratic convention nominated former Confederate general Wade Hampton for governor. An incident at Hamburg, across the Savannah River from Augusta in July 1876, settled what debate still existed within the Democracy. A dispute over a right-of-way on the public road between local black militiamen and a carriage of white Democrats ended up in court. On the day the trial opened, Matthew C. Butler, head of the state Democratic executive committee, showed up well prepared: with several hundred whites from the surrounding area and from Augusta, all heavily armed. Fearful for their lives, the militia company barricaded itself in its drill room in a nearby brick warehouse. There was an assault on the building, complete with cannon that Butler had ordered in specially.[46] The blacks surrendered. The leaders died trying to escape—or, rather, at two in the morning they were told to run and were shot in the back doing so. The final count was one white and seven black dead and a number of other freedmen badly wounded.

The massacre drew party lines tight and set the tone for the campaign to follow. Hampton took the high road. He was conciliatory in public utterance, the epitome of gallantry and gentility. But behind the scenes, the organization of the campaign lay with Martin Gary of the upcountry, and his means of victory involved the organization of "rifle clubs," primed for provocation and disruption. Democratic campaigners had their own uniform, too, of dyed red flannel, from which the "Red Shirt" campaign would earn its name. Some 300 or more clubs sprang into existence with 13,000 men under arms, and their guns, rapid-fire rifles, were new and often of the best make. At every Republican rally, clubs showed up to demand equal time for their side. In practice, that meant appearing in battle array where

Republicans spoke, shouting them down, brandishing pistols, and making them realize that every time they spoke, they put their lives in danger, the governor included. The plan stopped so short of violence that it virtually assured its occurrence. "Never threaten a man individually," Gary reminded Democratic organizers. "A dead Radical is very harmless—a threatened Radical . . . often very troublesome, sometimes dangerous, always vindictive."[47]

By September, the killing had begun: an ambush, lynchings, and indiscriminate shooting at blacks working in a cotton field in Aiken County, a race riot in Ellenton that ended with a few whites and over 100 blacks killed, and threats or worse than threats elsewhere. "We write to tell you that our people are being shot down like dogs, and no matter what democrats may say," an Aiken resident wrote Grant, "unless you help us our folks will not dare go to the polls." This time the president did send armed forces to South Carolina, and in the last weeks of the campaign, Republicans got a belated start on organizing their forces. Not that it took much organizing in the heavily black lowland districts. The Red Shirts had done that work for them by reminding freedpeople of why they needed to go to the polls, if their very lives depended upon it. The soothing words of Wade Hampton did not ring half so loudly as the click of Gary's rifles cocking. Those few freedpeople supporting the Redeemers faced ostracism, abuse, and beatings at their neighbors' hands; wives sued husbands for divorce, and women hurled taunts and threats at those who would sell their community to the enemy. In Florida and Louisiana, intimidation and fraud ran unchecked, though the death toll in Louisiana ran far higher. By contrast, Mississippi had one of the most peaceful campaigns in memory—as peaceful as Georgia's or that in Arkansas, and for the same reason. Republicans dared not organize or pass out ballots in most places, and knew that Democratic election officers would count in whatever majority they pleased.[48] A "Solid South" had all but come into being, which, combined with one or two of the largest states in the North, brought Democrats within shooting distance of the presidency—literally.

Consolidating the Redeemers' gains did not happen overnight. Violence in Georgia may have worsened in the months after Republicans' downfall. Tennessee's butcheries won national attention in 1874, and for the next generation, brute force and assassination wiped out one local Republican stronghold after another in the Cotton Kingdom. Texas redeemed was a state where the marauders and night riders carried on as they would. Those teaching in black schools were shot. Freedpeople were robbed. The courts turned into "engines of oppression for the weak and powerless," at least those on the Republican side. Federal officers lacked the courage to execute the laws. With no military authority to back them up, they pleaded that they could do nothing. "Twelve houses burnt up, belonging to colored men," a black correspondent wrote the president from Limestone County. Four hundred armed white men rode through, "running colored men of from their crops and killing Some of us, and whipping Some of us, and hanging Some and burning Some, and Said every one (col man) that did Issue a Republican ticket in that State Should leave or Die. . . . We are not allowed to Sit on grand Jury, or very few of us on Petd. Jury. . . and if we look at white lady very hard as we wish to Say Something to them We are Shot."[49]

For the most part, the victims died unnoticed and, as far as the national press was concerned, unreported. Republican newspapers perished when Reconstruction governments ended, and conservative editors held their tongues. By 1875, in any case, it must have been obvious that the days of federal interference had gone for good, even if the will had been there. The money was not available, nor the manpower. Among white voters in general, the commitment to use national authority to uphold Reconstruction governments down south had weakened decisively. Racism played its part. So did the growing importance of other issues: reining in corruption, restoring the constitutional balance between federal and state powers, and, most of all, coping with an economic crisis. But so, too, did the feeling that the crisis of the Union had passed and with it the need to put none but loyal men on guard down south. Any new civil war was out of the question. If Reconstruction had been to secure freedom and make the reunification of the nation permanent, it had succeeded. The Union stood, rock-bottomed and copper-sheathed, too secure to dislodge. The few surviving Confederate leaders inspired reverent remembrance or wistful nostalgia, but their day for holding power had passed forever, along with that of the original leaders on the Union side.

Clearly, the North as a whole had tired of backing a federal commitment to the Reconstruction governments, but the retreat from Reconstruction's essential purposes was nowhere near as clear, particularly among Republicans. The same lame-duck session that had refused to pass a new "force bill" for the South had carried through Charles Sumner's civil rights law, giving blacks an equal right to public accommodations, schools and cemeteries excepted—"*half* the loaf & that poisoned," Wendell Phillips protested. With no federal enforcement of its provisions, the measure looked like political posturing, and some historians marveled at the government's

"Worse than Slavery." Thomas Nast, *Harper's Weekly*, October 24, 1874. As he did regularly, the cartoonist associates white-line violence with the Confederacy and "the Union as it was," perhaps indicating that attacks on African Americans in themselves were not enough to stir northerners to a proper sense of alarm.

shortsightedness in failing to take action that could have made a difference for Republican voters down south. In fact, no Enforcement Act could work without the police or the soldiers to do the job. As things stood in the West, there was no prospect of either one, especially when a heavy Democratic majority took over the next House. By 1875, it took no second sight to know that opponents would challenge the law in the Supreme Court. The civil rights bill, however, would take far less enforcement; indeed, most of the enforcement would come through the plaintiffs themselves taking their cases to court. A Democratic House could not stymie the law. Nor, with a Republican senate, could it repeal it. Dead letter the bill might be in the South, but it would not be purely symbolic. For black Americans living elsewhere, it offered some avenue of court redress and established a position on which the Republican Party was prepared to stand, in favor of equal rights, at least in the abstract.

Within the year, two Supreme Court decisions showed how treacherous the ground that lay beneath any new bill regulating the political process. *United States vs. Cruikshank* arose out of the Colfax massacre in 1873, *United States vs. Reese* out of a Kentucky election officer rejecting a black's vote for failing to pay his poll tax on time. On technical grounds, a majority declared the 1870 Enforcement Acts insufficient in failing to state that the injury being punished was due to race, color, or previous condition of servitude. The Fifteenth Amendment could punish that, and only that, and then only if the state committed the offense, not private parties. The amendment, Chief Justice Morrison Waite asserted in the *Reese* case, gave nobody a *right* to vote; it simply forbade states to deny it on certain grounds and left them free to limit it any other way they pleased. Building on the *Slaughterhouse* case, he stressed that state and national governments protected distinctly different rights, but he went further in defining just what privileges and immunities national citizenship did not include. As far as the killers interfered with the right of public assembly or the right to bear arms, that was the state's responsibility, not the federal government's, for the Bill of Rights forbade only national interference with either.[50] In 1883, the Civil Rights Act, too, fell afoul of the Supreme Court. A majority decided that while the Fourteenth Amendment forbade state laws denying equal justice, it gave the national government no power to remedy private acts of discrimination, and, again using the *Slaughterhouse* case for its basis, that the rights violated by unfair treatment fell into the scope of state action exclusively.

The chilling effect of the two decisions cannot be underestimated, nor should the extent of retreat. The Court's decision did not gut the Enforcement Acts, much less overturn them. Congress quickly fixed the three sections deemed insufficient by writing in a different justification for intervention. National authorities still could punish intimidation at the polls—if national offices were at stake; they could even go after those breaking up meetings, if those were called to discuss national issues. In an 1879 case, the judges unanimously upheld the acts' constitutionality. Conceivably, an aggressive Justice Department could have persevered in prosecuting, and southern Democrats saw a real danger; otherwise, in 1879, they would not have spent a long special session fruitlessly trying to load army appropriations bills with provisions doing away with federal oversight. All they got for their pains was a provision keeping the army from making arrests in election cases and a North reawakened to how dangerous and unreasonable the Redeemer South was. The Enforcement Acts became dead letter in most of the South, but not because of the court. Bitter experience showed prosecutors that the chances of a white jury bringing in a conviction were practically nil.

As far as black voters were concerned, the Enforcement Acts gave only the illusion of protection; the opposite may have been true of the civil rights law. In the wake of the Court decision, eighteen states enacted civil rights legislation to preserve those rights. Democratic governors in New Jersey, Connecticut, and Ohio called for it as essential. In 1887, the last vestiges of Ohio's antebellum Black Laws, barring black children from white schools and forbidding racial intermarriage, dropped off the books.[51]

In all, the events in Grant's last term show how inadequate the year 1877 was for marking Reconstruction's passing. The retreat from federal intervention had been all but completed two years before; the effort to hold on to the "unfinished revolution's" gains would last another generation.

CHAPTER SIXTEEN

Last Full Measure of Defection

wo months before the nation's hundredth Independence Day, the Philadelphia Exhibition opened to mammoth crowds. A showcase for American progress and unity, it did its best to exclude every reference to the "late unpleasantness." No Union battle flags went on display, and a southern poet, Sidney Lanier, wrote the "Centennial Cantata." Brigades in blue and in grey marched on Independence Day, and crowds cheered them both. The exhibition celebrated the country's material advance, its white inventors and designers especially, with some recognition of the quaint and curious customs of black people and the primitive arts of Indians, now far down their inevitable road to extinction. An enormous Corliss steam engine powered thousands of devices in Machinery Hall. Visitors marveled at hay spreaders and combines, the pyramids of nails and bolts, the column of thirty-eight grindstones, dollar watches out of Waltham, and the seemingly endless array of sewing machines. They left impressed by the latest innovations: a floor covering waterproof and easy to clean called linoleum, arc lights, typewriters, and a squawking device just developed by Alexander Graham Bell that carried the human voice across long distances.[1]

If an exhibit had been made of moral progress, reformers speculated, it would have looked more like a chamber of horrors. That same spring, Grant's secretary of war, William W. Belknap, quit suddenly to cut short an investigation into the kickbacks paid to his wife. Secretary of the Navy George Robeson had to explain how he amassed a fortune on a salary of 8,000 a year. Grant's private secretary, Major Orville Babcock, had already gone on trial for taking bribes from members of the tax-dodging Whiskey Ring and its purchased Internal Revenue Agency accomplices. Whatever roadblocks the president could throw up to prevent a jury from convicting the major, Grant tried. In the end, a presidential affidavit of character was just enough to get Babcock off. From that moment on, his nemesis, Secretary of the Treasury Benjamin Bristow, found his own career marked for death. Within a few months, he had been forced out. Days later, the president fired Postmaster General Marshall Jewell, the only cabinet member left suspected of being a reformer.[2]

House investigators followed other leads from former Speaker James G. Blaine's favors for the Union Pacific Railroad back to a suspicious deal, where the directors bought Little Rock and Fort Smith Railroad construction bonds from Blaine's business clients at far more than their face value. Brought to the stand, the former bookkeeper for the railroad construction company revealed that he had letters showing how Blaine had forced the owners to make him a special deal in recognition of his influence on their behalf. In a bold move, Blaine got hold of the correspondence and strode before the House. "I am not ashamed to show them," he shouted. "Thank God Almighty, I am not ashamed to show them." Whereupon Blaine read them aloud with such panache that his listeners quite overlooked their contents. In cold print, they persuaded anyone ready to be convinced that the most charming, likable man of his day, the man whose supporters so adored him that they were known as "Blainiacs," had the ethics of a riverboat gambler.[3]

Gloomily, James Russell Lowell's 1876 Centennial poem had Brother Jonathan advising Dame Columbia what exhibits would represent America best:

Show your new bleaching process, cheap and brief,
To wit: a jury chosen by the thief.
Show your State Legislatures; show your rings;
And challenge Europe to produce such things
As high officials sitting half in sight
To share the plunder and fix things right;
If that don't fetch her, why, you only need
To show your latest style in martyrs—Tweed:
She'll find it hard to hide her spiteful tears
At such advance on one poor hundred years.[4]

For eight months, partisan investigations unearthed graft and malfeasance in many of the government departments and stirred up mare's nests in all the others that could, at least, give the Democratic Party arguing points.[5] It also had a credible candidate undamaged by any equivocal war record, Governor Samuel J. Tilden of New York.

Cautious, courteous, and cool, Tilden had never married because, as one contemporary suggested, he could not see any advantage in doing so. He had grown grey in the Democracy's service, earning a reputation for political craft and discretion. Flirting with free-soil politics before the war, he threw his energies into practicing corporate law in wartime and fine-tuning the party machinery afterward. As the Tweed Ring fell in 1871, Tilden shared the credit for toppling it, and in the legislature that followed he carried through bills to bring the scoundrels to justice and prevent the scandals' recurrence. Washed into executive office in the "Tidal Wave" election, Tilden took his public duties so seriously that he overspent his strength. Official papers piled up around him at the dinner table, and secretaries hovered at his elbow from the first course to the last. Appointees needed more than political service to receive his consideration. "Sir!" he shouted at one less zealous colleague. "A man who is not a monomaniac is not worth a damn!" His monomania, the public soon found out, was stopping leaks in the Treasury. He won universal acclaim for taking on a second set of Democratic thieves, the upstate grafters and contract-padders in the Canal Ring. "Reform is printed on his underclothes," a critic mocked. "He calls his dog 'reform.' When he asks the cook if she has cooked the mutton, he says, 'have you reformed the sheep?'"[6]

For Tilden, reform went no further than the liberal ideas of honest money, honest men, administrative reorganization, and cheap, uncomplicated government. His vision of an ideal America hearkened back to the frugality and states' rights of Jefferson's day. Legislation on behalf of farmers or laborers found no more sympathy with him than did temperance, feminism, or civil rights laws. Civil service reform, to him, took nothing beyond appointing wisely for fixed terms and dismissing no officeholder without cause.[7] Lacking bold ideas and charisma, however, worked in his favor as a candidate. Admirers could make the case that anyone supporting him would have to do it on his merits and record of accomplishments alone. Democrats could do worse than nominate someone safe, shrewd, and from a state they had to carry to win. Having a fortune, a "barrel," helped, too.

From the first, then, the Democratic race pitted Tilden against the field. Out west, the currency issue set Ohio's two contenders at each other's throats. Reflationists backed former governor "Farmer Bill" Allen, and "honest money" men leaned to Senator Allen G. Thurman, who, visiting politicians grumbled, was "cold as the North Sea, and . . . never asks a fellow to drink." Their rivalry only drove home the message that if the party wanted to hold together till November, it needed to drop the money issue and concentrate on reform. With downstate city bosses against Tilden and his enemies, including the Pennsylvania "Treasury Ring" and railroad baron Tom Scott, the New York governor could turn his executive mansion into a "political factory" and spread his money far and wide, setting up a national organization to sell him like "a recipe for Stomach Bitters," and still come through the St. Louis convention with his reform reputation intact.[8]

He only needed a scandal-besmirched Republican candidate to run against. For all the ruckus about Caesarism in 1874, Grant had no wish for a third term. After long delays he had said so publicly, though editors with nothing better to do speculated about how, if offered, he still might take it and a Democratic House passed a buncombe resolution deploring the very idea. Among the administration's firmest defenders, Senator Oliver P. Morton of Indiana and Roscoe Conkling of New York had aspirations. Each came from a northern state crucial for Republicans to win and nearly unwinnable without a favorite son heading the ticket. Backed, in a Democratic reporter's words, by the "stupid prejudice, North Methodism, Western Reservism, Iowaism and raw-head loyalism generally" that rallied under the bloody shirt, Morton drew from southern Republicans who appreciated his steadfast defense of fair elections. Neither man had the least interest in reform. Both were so closely tied to Grant that the corruption issue would dog their heels throughout the campaign.[9]

The one candidate with strong grassroots support across the North, however, was former Speaker Blaine, soon to be christened the "Plumed Knight." In January, he had turned a debate over an amnesty bill into a free-for-all by insisting that Jefferson Davis be kept in the cold, and by laying at his doorstep the Union dead at the Andersonville prisoner of war camp. Engaging, daring, and known for his "smartness," Blaine had all those flashy qualities that reformers dreaded and none of the gravity that they expected in a statesman. Unlikely to defend the spoils system or carpetbaggers and never on close terms with the Grant administration, Blaine was a bloody-shirt orator; that, too, set reformers' faces against him. Finally, as the revelations that spring showed, there was every good reason to suspect that he was a crook. Reform Republicans, and those Liberals hoping for a good reason to rejoin the party, hunted some candidate of their own. After unsuccessfully trying to market the glacial charm and repelling integrity of Charles Francis Adams, they rallied behind Secretary of the Treasury Benjamin Bristow, nemesis of the Whiskey Ring and, better still, the one candidate that President Grant could not abide. A strong friend of "honest money," he had carried the country closer to specie resumption by retiring all the greenbacks he could. (Considering how many people suffered by that policy and how deeply unpopular it was, that took courage: the only way Republicans could beat the easy-money Democrats in Ohio the fall before was by linking inflation to communism and concocting a Catholic plot to smother the public schools.) He also was known to have serious doubts about federal intervention in the South.[10]

When the convention met in Cincinnati, it deadlocked. Bristow had outside support from what the *Nation* described as the only real gentlemen in the place—and "sadly honest-looking" ones at that. Inside the hall, Blaine opened so long a lead that sage politicians agreed that nobody could stop him, though everybody might: "a conspiracy of minnows against a whale." The minnows working for Grant's closest allies and bitterest critics rallied behind Ohio governor Rutherford B. Hayes, clean, inoffensive, and reassuringly unsensational. Embarking on no big policies, he had avoided making big mistakes. Untied to the scandal-ridden administration, he had made a reform record as mild as his personality, cutting the state debt by nearly $3 million, slashing annual expenditures, and lowering Ohioans' tax rate.[11]

A campaign between two such upright men gave reformers the certainty that the next presidency would do better than the last. Some of them, Adams included, came out for Tilden. Others like Schurz and Bristow embraced Hayes, whose letter of acceptance committed himself to civil service reform principles and a break with the Grant administration's southern policy.[12] With so little to choose from between two hard-money and soft-Reconstruction candidates, Republicans no longer had to defend themselves on the corruption issue. Instead, they could direct their attentions to protecting public schools from Catholics and—just as they always did—to preserving the legacy of the war for the Union. "Our main issue must be, It is not safe to allow the Rebellion to come into power, and next that Tilden is not the man for President," Hayes wrote; and orators and editors made that their watchword.[13]

Reconstruction came into the discussion; it could hardly help doing so, when fresh blood dappled the bloody shirt in South Carolina and Louisiana every week. But Republicans found their southern governments beyond defense, and in more ways than one. The most obvious reason lay on the front page. In early July, headlines screamed that Sioux Indians had wiped out Lieutenant Colonel George Custer and his Seventh Cavalry at Little Big Horn. Trouble had been growing as settlers and gold prospectors invaded Indian lands around the Black Hills. Boomtowns sprang up, raucous and violent, like Deadwood City, where the famed marshal and shootist "Wild Bill" Hickok would die that summer, shot in the back. The government had guaranteed Indians the land under an 1868 treaty. Now it ordered them off large tracts and declared war on those refusing to leave. A self-promoter and speculator with tremendous charisma, Custer had been sent to help suppress the resisting Sioux. Ignoring his Crow scouts' advice and dividing his forces, he rode straight into an Indian host ten times his own and into enduring legend. When a few days later the news came of the affray in Hamburg, only the *Herald* thought to connect the two events. Sitting Bull was said to have been profoundly gratified, it remarked. "It shows that Sioux civilization and Sioux tactics are spreading." Most papers made Custer's Last Stand daily fare for weeks, the metropolitan press sending an army of correspondents west to cover it and the "Great Sioux War." With its modest body count, Hamburg got fleeting coverage. More important, in the fighting that followed, the troops southern Republicans needed for their protection were just not available. They were guarding the frontiers in a *recognized* war— where 12,000 soldiers barely made headway against an evasive enemy.[14]

Nobody, then, spoke about steps to restore a free vote and a fair count in the redeemed states. Republican gubernatorial candidate Stephen Packard had pluck, facing down "disorderly mobs . . . with no other weapon than a small walking-stick," but he found himself helpless to protect his supporters from bullwhip and shotgun, and the Pelican State gave birth to a new term for intimidation through violence: "bull-dozing."[15] Louisiana was "like a doll-baby leaning on props," a journalist wrote. If a national administration pulled out the props or said, "'Hands off—look out for yourselves down there!' . . . it would fall like a block of cards." The same problem held everywhere that Republicans had the votes but Democrats the property and the guns: after eight years, no Reconstructed regime could survive on its own. Until the mid-1870s, intervention may have looked like emergency damage control. Always, Reconstruction's dwindling supporters could tell themselves that the time would come when states with natural Republican majorities would need outside help no longer. Vicksburg, Hamburg, Coushatta: every massacre told a darker story. "You must either let them fall and go under out of sight, and cease to trouble us, or you must use the United States army at every election," the same correspondent concluded. "There is no half-way ground." In a republic where states were meant to handle their own affairs as far as they could, the latter alternative was one that Republicans could not accept—and never could have, not even in Thaddeus Stevens's day.[16]

At the same time, Democrats asserted more unequivocally than ever that they would stand by the Reconstruction legacy that counted: a permanent and fraternal Union of hands and hearts, free labor, and the full civil and political rights that the Fourteenth and Fifteenth Amendments had opened up to all male citizens. Tilden's letter of acceptance flat-out acknowledged the Reconstruction Amendments as the law of the land and promised protection to "all citizens, whatever their former condition, in every political and personal right." Southern campaigners were told plainly to leave their sectional rodomontade at home. Mississippi congressman Lucius Q. C. Lamar, whose eulogy on Sumner two years before had made him the one former Confederate that most northerners treated as fully reconstructed, did his best to show that overthrowing "corruption & misgovernment" down south would change the South "from a discontented & oppressed element of opposition to the national administration into an integral element of support & active co-operator . . . in working out the new order." In some areas, Democratic organizers tried to convince blacks that they, unlike the Republican Party, would not take African American voters for granted.[17] Redeemers' protestations should not be taken too seriously, but it did say something about the acceptable limits of a reaction against Reconstruction that Democrats were reluctant to go further.

Democrats strove to blot out their past, Republicans to highlight it. The bloody shirt waved itself ragged in reminders of what every slave hunter and persecutor of Union prisoners of war had been. Partisans put a wartime speech into vice presidential nominee Thomas Hendricks's mouth, calling Lincoln a smutty tyrant. Hearsay accused Tilden of having once advised Union soldiers that if they stepped onto southern soil, they opened themselves to a lawsuit for trespass. "Samuel J. Tilden is a demurrer filed by the Confederate Congress against the amendments to the Constitution of the United States," Robert G. Ingersoll told audiences.[18] No longer able to make a credible case that a Confederacy would rise again if Democrats won, Republicans had to dwell on the danger of a "Solid South" putting a divided North at its mercy. "The Confederacy is attempting now what the idiots missed doing when they preferred war," editor Murat Halstead wrote Hayes. "And it is the political Gettysburg." Republicans warned that the Solid South would have the $60 million in wartime cotton tax refunded, Confederate soldiers pensioned, and slaveholders compensated for their losses. Dismissing a chorus of denials, party spokesmen predicted that, once Tilden carried the White House, he would pay $2 trillion in southern claims.[19]

Both sides expected a close outcome. On election night, Democrats did not have to wait for the count to be completed before they began celebrating. The tide of their support from 1874 had ebbed, but not enough to keep them from holding the House by nine votes and in making their best presidential showing across the North in twenty years. Tilden's popular majority nationwide had surged ahead of Hayes's. Both candidates went to bed convinced that Hayes had lost—and both awoke to find the game still in play. Republican newspapers proclaimed the results in doubt. A few of them were crowing at a one-vote victory. The decision rested on the last three southern states that Republicans held: Florida, South Carolina, and Louisiana together could carry Hayes through by 185 to 184. There, so overwhelmingly had black voters defied intimidation and turned out for the party (where they could) that the results depended on Republican state returning boards, empowered to decide which votes to count, which precincts to reject, and which candidates to certify as the winners. Democrats cried foul. In their rendering of the event, Republicans had stolen the election.[20]

In fact, Republicans could have argued, they had simply retrieved stolen goods the only way possible—and not even all of those. Intimidation, cheating, partisan election officers, and open fraud characterized the methods making a "Solid South" from Virginia and Tennessee south to the Gulf. Legal enactments had gerrymandered Republicans into hopeless congressional districts and disfranchised blacks by the tens of thousands. Freedmen and scalawags could have mobilized a majority in half a dozen states, given fairness and a free, full count. Then not only would the last three Republican states have given Hayes margins beyond the possibility of manipulation or error; Mississippi, probably Alabama and North Carolina, and perhaps Georgia would have joined them. Without partisan redistricting, Democrats also would have lost the House. If on election night Hayes thought himself beaten, he knew that force and fraud had done the work.[21]

Both sides sent gangs of "visiting statesmen" to observe the returning boards as they came to their final decisions. Republican onlookers saw justice done, and Democrats saw shameless partisanship and clerical astigmatism. No fair-minded observer came away unshaken by the ruthlessness or rottenness on all sides. "It is terrible to see the extent to which all classes go in their determination to win," the future novelist and aspiring Indiana politician Lew Wallace wrote his wife after hearing the Florida returning board quizzing election commissioners about the local returns. "Nothing is so common as the resort to perjury, unless it is violence—in short, I do not know whom to believe." Democrats tried to raise funds to buy returning-board members for their side, and Republican members offered themselves for sale, if the price was right. Plans fell through in Florida only because at the crucial moment, apparently, Tilden's backers gave the green light to one of their two agents in the code used exclusively by the other. In Oregon, a Democratic governor tried to use a legal technicality to invalidate one Republican elector's vote and recognize a Tildenite instead.[22] With Democrats in the House calling witnesses to prove their enemies' depravity, both parties found in the revelations of each other's corrupt intrigues the perfect excuse to feel that right lay on their side, and theirs alone. Insiders knew better. The last thing they really wanted was a full investigation. Both sides had mired themselves too deeply to risk exposure.[23]

Now, if ever, the Union may have faced the test of whether the war had made it permanent. Sixteen years before, an election's results had spurred on the disunionists. Some alarmists saw a like crisis happening again, only worse. Democratic hotheads swore that they would never give in, even if it took force to thrust their candidate into the office. Tilden's campaign manager later asserted that Democrats had organized military forces in fifteen states, "ready once more to take up arms and move on Washington," and Democratic governors had pledged their support. Republicans contended that the Senate president pro tempore had the exclusive right to count the electoral votes; Democrats declared that when the validity of those votes remained in question, the House had the right to have a say in which of two competing sets of returns to consider the right one. If no candidate got a majority of the electoral votes that both chambers could agree upon, then under the Constitution, the House could choose the president, the Senate the vice president. Democrats swore that they were prepared to block any electoral count at all, if it counted Hayes in. On March 4th, let chaos come, or a new presidential election be ordered![24]

But the cry, "Tilden or Blood!" rang hollow. "Why should I fight to put somebody into a post-office?" one Tennessean objected. "That is all there is in this controversy." As one old Confederate told a reporter, he had marched and fought for three years, coming out of the war with an empty belly and a bullet-creased scalp. He "was not yet tired of being home." Senator Francis Cockrell of Missouri, a former Confederate general, swore that if trouble came, he would hunt down the agitators in his own party and thrust them into "the front line of battle, to taste the bloody banquet they were so ready to prepare for others." More militant southern Democrats announced their readiness to go as far as their northern brethren but no further. They had no intention of having treason charges laid against them by being first to take up arms. Editors and correspondents begged Tilden to act. From his mansion in Gramercy Park, only silence came. As the weeks passed, the frumious language that his supporters used all sounded more and more like the outcry of people sure that they would be cheated of their due and ready to strike the hardest blow that a well-turned period would allow.[25]

Business interests, Republican as well as Democratic, pleaded for a peaceful settlement. A perceptible economic recovery seemed as remote as ever. Charities went broke that winter feeding the destitute. As funds ran out, cities and soup kitchens suspended their aid. Political uncertainty made a sterile soil for business confidence to grow in. In some southern cities, gold and silver coinage disappeared, as hoarders stowed it away in case rifles replaced rhetoric. "Give us Hayes or Tilden, it don't make much difference, but somebody quick," a Chattanooga merchant begged. By early December, both parties had members looking for some face-saving way out. A few of Hayes's friends put out feelers to disaffected southerners: in return for help electing a Republican president and, later, a Republican Speaker, patronage, a top cabinet spot, perhaps even aid for Tom Scott's transcontinental Texas & Pacific Railroad might come the South's way. In fact, neither side could deliver. Any Democrat who sold out Tilden would need to collect in the one kind of coin his constituents valued—"home rule."[26]

With both sides open to a face-saving settlement, Congress found it in Vermont's Senator George F. Edmunds's proposal for a special electoral commission of fifteen to determine who had carried any disputed states. Five members would come from the House (three to two Democratic), five from the Senate (three to two Republican), five from the Supreme Court. The fifth jurist would be chosen by the other four; presumably, Republicans and Democrats would have two apiece, and the one name they most likely could agree on would be the portly and independent-minded David Davis. The plan found much more ready favor among Democrats than Republicans. With most of the advantages already—the governor's official certificates for presidential electors, the president, and the army—Republicans were sure that they could compel the inauguration of Hayes. If Tilden "does become President we of the South and Especially the Colored People will occupy a position *which will be worse* than *Slavery*," one freedperson wrote from Arkansas. "Our *Liberty* will be entirely *gone*."[27]

But there seemed no other solution that would allow even the semblance of legitimacy to whoever was inaugurated. If Hayes were inaugurated on the discretionary authority of the president of the Senate, only Republicans would treat his title as valid, and very likely not all of them. Across the North, merchants, chambers of commerce, and boards of trade held mass meetings to endorse the compromise. Both parties found votes enough to pass the bill, though by the time it carried, Democrats realized that Davis, just elected to the Senate, probably would turn them down. Still, even with the more Republican Joseph Bradley as the fifth justice, they thought their chances of winning good.[28]

Sitting in the Supreme Court chamber, formerly the old Senate chamber, the commission was meant to be a judicial tribunal. Both sides hired legal counsel. Behind them were expert assistants, including some of the "visiting statesmen," and the immense library of the Justice Department, in which both sides immersed themselves for "the law case of all history," as Hayes would call it. The issues were clear enough. Did the tribunal have power to look into the evidence beyond what the certificates said, as Democrats insisted (except in Oregon)? Or did it have to accept the governor's certificates as the final word on how the states had voted, as Republicans contended (except in Oregon)? On February 7th, to Democrats' outrage, Bradley came down on the Republican side. By eight to seven, the commission decided not to go behind the official returns. Two days later it gave Florida to the Republicans, and over the next fortnight, Louisiana and South Carolina.[29]

"God damn them, they will beat us and elect Hayes," former attorney general Jeremiah Black raged, "but we shall give them all the trouble we can." How much that was remained anyone's guess. House Democrats mounted a filibuster to delay the formal count of electoral votes. Stalling the count, it was thought, would not simply embarrass the president; it would require a new presidential election, one in which Tilden would coast to power on a tide of popular indignation. More thoughtful Democrats could see quite a different result, with financial upheaval, partisan tumult, violence, and intimidation renewed in the South, and a public, outraged at being put through such an ordeal, taking it out on the Democratic candidate. Tilden knew the game was up. He abandoned any pretense of guiding and began discussing where to take his summer vacation in Europe.[30]

With no prospect of inaugurating Tilden, the filibusterers found their strength surging after each controversial decision by the commission and ebbing once tempers had cooled. A week before the inauguration, the resistance had dwindled into a sputter. Every day, more Democrats concluded that obstruction could win them nothing, not even a salutary and ineffective measure of chaos on Inauguration Day. "If you should meet here and declare Tilden elected, can you put one squadron in the field?" a Virginia congressman taunted the diehards in the Democratic caucus. "Can you do

"Samuel J. Tilden—Died August 4, 1886." Joseph Keppler, *Puck*, August 11, 1886. The verse in the caption reads: "Sagacious, shrewd, and with a heart for Fate, / Once in his life we well may call him great: / When, tricked by knavery and despoiled by Might, / He kept the country's peace—and forfeited his right." Refusing the temptation to stir up civil war, Tilden accepts the judgment of the Electoral Commission.

anything beyond a resistance which from its puerility is madness?" Defections increased steadily, and militants cried ever more loudly that they had been sold out by "crossroads politicians, confederate colonels, 'granger' idiots, partisan mountebanks, and political charlatans of the lowest order."[31]

All that remained in doubt was the fate of those Republican state governments that the returning boards had elected along with Hayes in Louisiana and South Carolina, Florida already having been passed over to the Democrats. By mid-February, their prospects were dimmer than Tilden's. Wade Hampton's administration in South Carolina and Francis Nicholls's in Louisiana had all the money and manpower. In New Orleans, the White Leagues had become official state militia. They manned the artillery and held the state armory. With 3,000 men under arms, Nicholls could force the supreme court to retire and appoint a Democratic bench to apply the law on his side. Outside the capital city, Republican authority in both states had vanished almost completely. Tax collectors dared not raise a penny on their behalf, while voluntary contributions poured into Hampton's coffers and Red Shirts paraded where they would.[32] The only chance either Packard or Chamberlain had of retaining even the empty title of governor depended on active military backing from Washington. Federal troops guarded them to prevent their bloody overthrow and to keep the peace in Columbia and New Orleans. But Grant would not recognize the governments as legitimate or use force to dispel their rivals.[33] Hayes's letter of acceptance had committed him to a friendlier policy toward the white conservative South. His spokesman in the House had promised that henceforth the "flag shall float over States, not provinces; over freemen and not subjects"—a gloss on Reconstruction identical to the Redeemers'. Southern congressmen wanted stronger assurances. Those from Louisiana hoped that if they could persuade Republicans that their support was crucial for ending the filibuster, Hayes and Grant might commit themselves to remove all troops before Inauguration Day. In late February, some of the president-elect's friends gathered in a room at the Wormley Hotel with politicians claiming to speak for the Redeemers in South Carolina and Louisiana. Hayes's emissaries reaffirmed his goodwill, made clear that he had no intention of intervening on behalf of either carpetbag governor. In return they demanded specific assurances that there would be no rollback in freedpeople's rights if Democratic state governments were left alone. Just as important, Hayes wanted a commitment that the Redeemers would sustain black schooling. Within the next two days, Democrats gave those promises. The filibuster ran out of steam, and Speaker Samuel J. Randall, proving to his enemies that he had "a column of mercury in his back instead of a backbone," ruled the obstructionists out of order.[34] A day before Grant's term ended, "Rutherfraud" B. Hayes took the presidential oath in private.

Over the next six weeks, the Hayes administration worked to ease Packard and Chamberlain into retiring. In mid-April, with the Republican legislatures dissolving and all hope of federal intervention gone, the governors submitted. When U.S. troops marched back to their barracks, the last vestiges of Reconstruction government collapsed. The event gave a symbolic closure to the long process of retreat from a national commitment to protecting freedpeople's rights in the South. It amounted to no more than that. The pullback from enforcement of Reconstruction had begun more than two years earlier. Hayes had no real choice. To make Chamberlain or Packard an effective, genuine governor, would have taken intervention on a scale unimaginably vaster than what it had taken to prop up Kellogg four years before. A newspaper publisher needed no second sight to predict what would follow. The president would "have to hold Packard up by bay-onets and gunboats, and put down insurrections about once in 90 days; and we shall be expected to defend and justify such Federal interference in behalf of an odious carpet-bag desperado as the South regards him." The alternative was not Nicholls or Packard, but Nicholls or war. The same may well have been true in South Carolina. And war with what, *for* what? To overturn Democratic governments publicly committed to abide by the Reconstruction Amendments and black civil rights? Fewer than 1,600 sol-diers were stationed for any duty in the South by 1876, and most of them served on coastal defense or in backing up revenue officers. With a Demo-cratic House prepared to cut off civil and military appropriations to the last penny, most of the guns would be massed on the other side, with freed-people hopelessly outmatched. In an encounter, they would do most of the dying—with the most vulnerable the likeliest victims.[35]

Republicans had not abandoned their concern for black southerners' rights entirely. Indeed, Hayes and his supporters could still their consciences only by telling themselves that the rights that mattered the most—those of life, liberty, and property, backed by equal justice under color-blind laws— had become so ingrained that no state would abridge them far. Nor were they quite prepared yet to accept the disfranchisement of black voters. Re-publicans did not hope to trade off government *for* the people for govern-ment *by* the people; they were still hoping for both. Experience had shown them that the federal government fell short in its ability to guarantee the first, and in claiming to protect the second, it had overstepped its ordinary powers in troubling ways. The power to declare which southern state gov-ernment was legitimate only seemed to breed more such cases, with sup-plicants treating the president and army as the final arbiters able to over-ride the voters' decisions. Whatever might be desired in an ideal world, the North simply must get used to the fact that nothing could, in the end, be done by an intermittent show of force or outside pressure. It followed that the only practical way to protect black rights in the South was to encourage southern state governments to do it themselves. If force had not worked, could not goodwill be tried?

Hayes did not mean to leave the South's rehabilitation to chance. To foster a friendly spirit among well-intentioned southern whites and bring as many as possible into the Republican Party, he showered conservatives and Confederates with patronage positions. Touring the South that fall, he brought the message of reconciliation everywhere. The Reconstruction he wanted to see would come not by law but by a new South evolving over time. A new party system, based on economic issues, in which business-minded old Whigs would swell Republican ranks, would provide it with the responsible leadership it needed, if it was to earn the respectability that made the surest safeguard against night riders. Schoolhouses could do more than soldiers ever had to lift the freedpeople out of poverty and free them from the stigma of white prejudice. With property and education, the downtrodden race would find half the objections to impartial suffrage melting away.[36]

The president thought that he was dealing with honorable men—and the assumption that as former Confederate soldiers, Nicholls and Hampton in some sense *were* more honorable than civilians would be may have played into this onetime Union general's faith. Nicholls did not go much further than conciliatory gestures, but Hampton took his promises seriously. More than 100 of his lower-level appointments breached the color line, and the governor made no discrimination in per-pupil spending between black and white children. Still, Hampton could not set the tone for the redeemed South, nor even for his own state, where other leaders sneered at him as the epitome of "conservatism and niggerism." Democrats put on show trials of South Carolina Republicans, and the governor commuted the victims' sentences only in return for Washington dropping charges against Ku-Klux defendants.[37] The last thing even Hampton would have permitted would have been a free ballot and a fair count bringing Republicans back to power at the end of his term. Between the bulldozers and the partisan election officials, Redeemers counted in heavy majorities in Deep South elections in 1878. In Kemper County, Mississippi, a lynch mob gunned down William Chisholm, local Republican leader and defeated candidate for Congress, as well as members of his family. In Louisiana, a white army took over the Natchitoches city streets and sent Republican officeholders running for their lives. A thousand blacks did vote in the following election—every one for the Democratic ticket. They were, one witness lamented, "miserable individuals who hardly dare strike back and are killed like sheep." Red Shirt cavalry did the same work less bloodily to carry South Carolina.[38] Well intended as it might be, then, Hayes's appeasement policy had failed. An observer in quite a different situation would liken the process to a descent down "the stairway which leads to a dark gulf. It is a fine broad stairway at the beginning, but after a bit the carpet ends. A little farther on there are only flagstones, and a little farther on still these break beneath your feet."[39]

By the time Hayes left the White House in 1881, Republicans had lost hope of retrieving much of the South. Yet for those who wanted proofs of

"Death at the Polls and Free from 'Federal Interference.'" Thomas Nast, *Harper's Weekly*, October 18, 1879. Death wears the Red Shirt attire of South Carolina Redeemers. In the background, the cartoonist notes the murder of William Chisholm in Mississippi two years before.

Reconstruction's lasting effect, the continued black turnout, particularly in presidential elections, afforded grounds for reassurance. Here and there a Republican journalistic voice, however faint, survived the party's downfall. Black former Florida lawmaker Henry Harmon managed three such newspapers at one time. As long as Republicans held the White House, postmasterships and minor government jobs could tide over a lucky remnant of the party faithful, a very few prominent freedpeople included. Thanks to gerrymandering that created districts shaped like shoestrings and fishhooks to keep the rest of the state winnable for whites, there would be black congressmen in the Deep South until the century's end. In some states, the number of black legislators rose during Redemption; twelve served in Tennessee in the 1880s. Chattanooga still elected black aldermen until 1911. Cities held onto gains longer than the countryside did. If Republicans had broken the color line on Charleston's and Jacksonville's police force, their successors did not reinstate it. Through the late 1880s, Jacksonville, Florida, had black justices of the peace, circuit and criminal court clerks, and constables.[40]

North of the Cotton Belt, Republicans had more than a mere presence. They elected enough congressmen in a good year to win the House, and as disaffection with the Redeemers stirred with small farmers, they worked out coalitions with the "independents." In some states, opponents of the Redeemers managed to win as much as 48.7 percent of the vote. For all the rough magic practiced by Conservatives, their foes put up a game fight and continued to win local offices. Enraged at how payments on the public debt were swallowing every social service, the school system included, Democrats led by former Confederate general William Mahone made common cause with Republicans in Virginia. Their "Readjuster movement" carried the legislature, governor, and both senate seats. For a brief spell, the Old Dominion had a burst of reform. Taxes shifted from the farmers to railroads and corporations. Out went the whipping post and the poll tax. There would be black jurors, prison guards, and low-level functionaries, till one revenue collector described his own office as looking like Africa. The legislature mandated equal pay for teachers, regardless of race (though not of gender). Black schools doubled in number, black schoolteachers tripled.[41]

Elsewhere, however, that pot of gold at the end of the rainbow never turned up. Even in Virginia, white-line violence helped drive the Readjusters from power by 1884. Their moves toward equal treatment did not long survive them. Intimidation and fraud were only two reasons among many for Republicans' failure to make a comeback. Constant defeat only exasperated the differences within the ranks. The party could not unite in the face of a common enemy. The same factionalism that had helped defeat Reconstruction kept recurring. Providing a more overwhelming share of Republican support than ever, blacks felt entitled to more patronage and more nominations for local offices than whites would allow them. They also proved less than eager about any reshuffling of party lines that would bring in Democratic businessmen and relegate them further to the rear than before. They need not have worried. However far the Republican Party managed to keep its base in the counties of white Appalachia, it could never draw much beyond the black vote anywhere else for long. Northern commentators argued that when the black vote was courted by both parties, the color line would vanish from southern politics. So in theory it might have, if Democrats had wanted nonwhite votes. But outside of localities where black support was a must, the Redeemers had no real interest in appeals to bring the freedmen to the polls, though they took what converts they could get. They found much richer capital in accusing opponents, inside the Democracy and out, of being the black man's party. The charge and the bullying and physical abuse were enough to drive white dissidents back into the regular organization again. As for black voters, they received unmistakable hints that home should be where the heart was on Election Day. Those hints in South Carolina in 1882 included the near-fatal shooting of a black child attending a political rally and the murder of four more freedpeople and then clambering on top of their bodies and imitating roosters, with crowing and wing flapping included. Just before the polls opened, a black was found hanged to a tree, his tongue cut out of his mouth and tossed on the ground. And this was a quiet year.[42]

If the two-party South and black voting persisted for another generation, the opportunities continued to narrow. Redemption was only the first rollback for political democracy; many more would follow. With Democratic election commissioners to count the votes and registration hours cut to a minimum, casting "tissue ballots" with several white votes folded into a thicker one seemed almost superfluous. Polling places in black neighborhoods could be reduced, eliminated entirely, or moved to locations too remote for most registrants to reach before closing hour. In Jacksonville, the legislature made the city council appointive in 1889 and left it to choose the mayor. There would be no Republican Party thereafter. Democrats in Haywood County, Tennessee, later gloated about how in 1888 "the rabbit foot was worked and republican votes became democratic votes"—easy to do, when one party did the counting to please itself. Even heavily black enclaves eventually succumbed to force and fraud. "Yes, boys," a Democrat shouted to his fellows in the "redemption" of one Alabama county, "stuff the ballot boxes, stuff them until they burst, stuff them like you would a fattening goose." Elsewhere, the Republican vote could be trimmed back by well-timed felony convictions—for larceny, say, or minor crimes against property. The courts defined various misdemeanors as fit for disfranchisement. All it took was theft of a one-cent steel pen in Alabama. The 1876 "Pig Law" in Mississippi lowered the definition of grand larceny from twenty-five dollars to ten and defined theft of livestock, even of lesser value (down to a dollar's worth), as grand larceny. By the end of the 1880s, as one conservative paper explained, "nature's own first law of self-defense" had turned South Carolina's elective system into a farce augmented by force.[43]

The same gradual narrowing characterized the "unfinished revolution's" social advances. Every Redemption-era constitution kept certain reforms, including the provisions recognizing married women's property rights. Some parks and most saloons shut out blacks completely, but in most facilities, there was no wholesale return to the exclusion of black people so common before the war. Republicans' welfare institutions remained and in some cases expanded. Only under the Redeemers did Texas, Tennessee, and Georgia set up facilities for the nonwhite deaf, mute, and blind. In 1887, North Carolina opened a Colored Orphan Asylum, and Tennessee ended blacks' exclusion from its industrial school. A biracial longshoremen's union shared work on the New Orleans docks into the 1880s, and white unions called a sympathy strike on behalf of black draymen seeking recognition. Proudly, former senator Blanche K. Bruce declared the lack of a color line "a great feature" of the 1884 New Orleans cotton exposition. Yet outside Queen City limits, separate, if unequal facilities remained the rule, from baseball teams to fairgrounds to houses of prostitution. By the 1890s, custom had hardened into explicit law: first on streetcars and railroads, and later in waiting rooms, circuses, jails, and residential areas.[44]

The South's economic reconstruction stood a better chance than political realignment. There could be no return to the Old South, even if Redeemers had wanted it. Thinned by death or forced into long retirement by disqualification from office, the fire-eaters and secessionists never made a comeback. Their successors dated their renown to service in the Lost Cause, though many emphasized how reluctantly they had chosen to go with their state. Corporation lawyers, railroad directors, and politicians tied to the South's economic developers shared power with planters and farmers. They were quick to call for the new and better South that Henry

W. Grady of the *Atlanta Constitution* agitated for lifelong. They lauded the South's industrial growth, welcomed newcomers and investors, and gloried in the nation's shared destiny. The South needed more factories, foundries, mines, mills, and immigrants, and having solved the race problem, it was on its way to getting them. They needed point no further than the textile mills springing up at the fall-lines of Carolina rivers, or the pillar of smoke by day and fire by night from Birmingham's ironworks, where at war's end nothing but forest and field stood.[45]

A white tide, Redeemers assured the North, lifted all boats, black ones included. This, too, was part of their proof that Reconstruction's most valuable features had been preserved. They pointed to the growth of black schooling, and of black landholding. When it came to education, Henry Grady in 1889 assured a Boston audience, blacks got nearly half a million dollars a year from Georgia for their separate schools, and most of that money came from taxes that whites had paid on their property.[46]

This splendid image was as alluring as a will-o'-the-wisp, and as insubstantial. As of 1890, only 13,623 blacks in Georgia had title to land—though admittedly this was a fourfold increase since 1874, and conditions in the upper South were far better than in the cotton states. However passionately the Gradys supported public education, Democrats from the countryside grumbled at the cost, particularly for future field hands. Over four years, Louisiana cut its education spending in half. Alabama put a cap of $100,000 on school appropriations. There and elsewhere, white district boards could decide how to apportion the funds, a license to shortchange black facilities. As of 1901, forty-seven out of every hundred Georgians was African American—and their schools got one dollar in four. The more heavily black the county, the wider the disparity.

The Redeemers' unwillingness to advance black education assured the South of a large, unskilled labor force, unfit for anything but agricultural work. Laws were rewritten to put all the advantage on the landowner's side and none on the tenant's. Georgia courts ruled that sharecroppers were simply wage earners, with no claim on the crop, beyond what the landlord chose to pay them. Civil law covered the share-tenant, criminal law the sharecropper. Statutes closed off the planters' woods and untilled land to hunters or non-owners' stock. Harsh penalties were meted out against pilfering, arson, and trespass—and against those who might coax one planter's tenants to better their lot elsewhere (which, it should be added, had only middling success; the annual turnover remained high).

Excluded from jury service, blacks could expect no benefit of the doubt as defendants, and only perfunctory attention as plaintiffs. For black women in particular, seeking legal redress for white assaults proved utterly hopeless: white magistrates only protected the virtue of ladies with a reputation to lose—which, in their view, African American women by definition lacked. Across the Deep South, lynch mobs hanged, castrated, and burned blacks accused of crime; authorities shrugged. "They are shooting us down as so many partridges," one Floridian cried in 1887. "Too late to talk about the 'suppressed vote' now," another exclaimed. "We are in the hands of the devil."

The more powerless African Americans became, the more virulent the rhetoric of race hatred grew. It flared up especially whenever the ruling faction felt its tenure of office in danger. Opponents of the New South appealed to prejudice in making any point, even a nonracial one. Novelists and short story writers continued to spread a sweetened version of antebellum society, where everybody knew his (or her) place, and where loyalty defined a laborer, just as leisure defined a lady. The South that orators invoked in their stump speeches was less often the new one than that which perished with the Lost Cause. Even the industrialists and commercial men polished up their wartime credentials for public display. Most conservatives drew strength from the South's distinct heritage. They defined their culture by its distinctiveness from America's in general. To embrace the Lost Cause was to part company with the commercialized, commodified world that industrialism was shaping around them, in favor of ancient values: honor, family, duty, and sacrifice. In Georgia the heartiest diehards even tried to bring back the whipping post and debtors' prison, and to move the capital out of Atlanta. For women forming the Memorial Associations, it was a reaffirmation of their role as preservers of the households and loyal helpmeets, and of the elite women who ran the associations as society's natural leaders.[47]

The Conservative South was more prepared than the antebellum governments to approve of industrial and commercial expansion, but it was less ready than the Republicans to spend much money to achieve it. Doing away with state aid for railroads, it adjusted, "scaled," and repudiated what bond issues it could, voiding $116.3 million worth over a generation. Texas wiped out its Bureau of Immigration. Elsewhere, even tax breaks for new businesses set off fireworks. Taxes and spending were cut to the bone— sometimes to the marrow. Lawmakers were permitted to meet only every other year, sometimes for sixty days at most. Everywhere, the humanitarian strains of the gospel of prosperity—public schools, asylums, poorhouses— were muted as the Redeemers cut back on government expenses, one reason why, sixty years after the war, Georgians had an illiteracy rate almost three times the national average. The convict lease system saved on penitentiary costs, but the turpentine camps and phosphate mines were privately run gulags, where dysentery, malaria, overwork, and the guards' shotguns and whips made life cheaper than the labor itself, and where every woman convict was potentially fair game for rape or assault. The annual death rate in Mississippi rose to a little over one prisoner out of every seven and, among prisoners as a whole, was nine times as high as in northern institutions.[48] The South as of 1900 was only slightly more industrial or diverse in population than it had been before the war. At the end of the century only 6.3 percent of the South's labor force was engaged in manufacturing. Per capita wealth came to $509, a pitiful sum compared to the national average of $1,165; per capita income in the South was $102—the nation's, $203.[49]

Was this, then, the promised end?

Coda

P ut all the facts of Redemption together, and the reconstruction of the South seemed like a flat failure a quarter century
after its demise, and far more so, it needs to be stressed, than
it was or appeared to be in 1880. The course of Redemption ran neither
smooth nor straight. The last twilight of what had seemed once a promising
day of equal rights reached its final darkening only in the 1890s with the
passage of Jim Crow laws formalizing separate facilities from streetcars to
libraries to hotel elevators and legal barriers to the black vote in the cotton
South. Only then were the Enforcement Acts repealed; only after one last
failure to protect their party's voters with a federal elections bill and to foster black education with the Blair aid bill in 1890–91 did Republicans put
away the bloody shirt, though not all of them did so even then, and not all
of those who doffed it gave it up from lack of concern at the travesty on free
government down south.

As far as Reconstruction meant what Wendell Phillips had called for, of
the North making the South over in its own image, or what Charles Sumner, Thaddeus Stevens, and Frederick Douglass had wanted, where no
color line ran its barriers through law, politics, or institutions, it had indeed
been a revolution unfinished at best. From our own perspective, in an age
when the surrender of Lee and Johnston's armies can be seen as having the
finality that only a century and more of a lasting Union could give it and
when the most that the dominant party could give fell woefully short of the
very least that we would find acceptable in a liberal state, no other conclusion would seem possible. In fact, even the radicals can be faulted for having failed to do what might have given the freedpeople a fair chance: land
enough to make an independent living and the administrative apparatus
to guarantee equal justice before the law. But taken at the broader meaning that the word "Reconstruction" had had in 1865, it was not so deep, so
complete a failure after all. In certain respects, in terms of what it had then
meant to do, it ranked as an unqualified success. For it could be argued that

to most white northerners at the war's end, the chief end of Reconstruction was to bring the nation back together and this time for good, to banish the prospect of future war, to break the power of the former slave states to menace or overawe the majority, to end slavery and give that freedom more than a nominal meaning—and all this without sacrificing the basic political framework that had made the Union special, where, under a national government supreme in matters of national import, the states would keep a wide array of powers and responsibilities exclusive to themselves. Quite possibly that assurance allowed potential disunionists to channel their Confederate nationalism into a less dangerous form, devotion to their state within an indissoluble Union, the more dear for keeping such reserves of power.[1] In retrospect, it may not seem so great an achievement to have accomplished reunion with free speech and a free press, a laughably small standing army, and a full amnesty for those on the losing side, saving a handful of ex-Confederates barred from office. But it was far better than many Americans had expected in that first wonderful, terrible spring.

If, as white southerners liked to tell themselves, the North had fought the war to rule the Union as it saw fit, the evidence from century's end could not have reassured them. Not in their lifetime would they see a Senate where the South could dictate or forestall legislation, as before the war. In antebellum days, twenty-four of thirty-six presidents pro tempore came from the South—in the half century postwar, none. Where before secession over half the Supreme Court appointments fell to the slave states, they would scarcely get half a dozen in the fifty years thereafter. Every so often a southerner presided over the House, but with one four-year exception, all of them came from the Union states until December 1931, a year after the last ex-Confederate member of Congress passed away. With six western states admitted to Congress in 1889–90 and the most southerly and Democratic—Arizona, New Mexico, and Oklahoma—reserved for a later generation, with immigration into the Great Plains increasing the imbalance between the South and the rest of the nation, even the House would slip from their grasp, lost for the Democrats by a hopeless majority in 1894 and not regained for the next sixteen years. As for the presidency, it lay beyond the South's control entirely. From 1876 to 1900 every president but one had a Union war record. The only exception, Democrat Grover Cleveland, had sent a substitute to fight in his place. Well into the twentieth century, half or more of the money the government spent went to service or redeem the Union war debt or to pay pensions to Union veterans. That revenue came largely from the protectionist Morrill "War Tariff" and its offspring, the duties of which fell with much more crushing weight on a South with comparatively few items to protect. Between the tariff, the national banking system, and a money supply restrained in its expansion by requiring gold to back it up, the financial advantages that had put the North ahead in industrial growth continued to work against southern development. Textile factories and ironworks the New South could boast of, but most of its industries either processed the agricultural products it made or opened its mines and forests to feed the mills of the North. By 1900, every railroad system of consequence in the Confederate South was run by outsiders.[2]

And if the purpose of the war had been to end slavery? Bleak the story of Redemption was; but the three constitutional amendments endured. Neither the lynch mob's rope nor the landowner's lien could go further than to diminish freedom, often gravely. Given provocation and despair enough, blacks could pick up and head for Kansas, as the Exodusters did in 1879, or go north as many thousands would do in the new century, and no Fugitive Slave Law made the national government an accomplice to bring them back. Few would own land, but the numbers and proportions kept increasing. Ill-schooled or provided with no schools at all, freedpeople would continue to show far higher illiteracy rates than white southerners. But if 40 to 50 percent of them could read by 1900, that was a great advance on the 5 to 10 percent able to do so when slavery ended. In cities like Charleston, the number of illiterates dropped even more dramatically. Some African American colleges founded in Reconstruction endured. Over time, they helped build a small black professional class. From their ranks and from the enduring, independent churches, would come many of the leaders of the civil rights struggle a century hence. Those freedpeople lucky enough to live in town rather than on the plantation were able to build lives with greater freedom and communities with greater resources. Traveling to Greenville, South Carolina, in 1884, a reporter found amid black poverty a richness of culture that in slavery times would have been impossible: temperance organizations and YMCA branches, debate societies, fire companies, private militia companies, amateur theatricals, public suppers, calico hops, and even some minstrel shows. (All of which, the journalist added, just showed how "the negroes imitate the white people.")[3]

Deprivation and denial of equal treatment varied in degree: the countryside worse than the cities, the cotton states worse than those closer to the Ohio, the South more actively oppressive than the North. The Fourteenth and Fifteenth Amendments came closer to their paper promise beyond the former slave states, and in one particular fulfilled promises that the original authors had never made. When the Supreme Court combined its views of substantive due process with the premise that the privileges and immunities that the Fourteenth Amendment protected included those of corporations, not just individual persons, it did lasting damage to the regulatory powers of the states. On the other hand, a half century hence, the Court would come to read the amendment to apply the basic Bill of Rights to states as well as the national government.

Over two generations, the publicists and politicians who hymned a reunited land let the issue of nationhood shove out the others on which South and North could not agree. But it would take time, and even then, those who sang it loudest were those too young to have shared in the costs or taken part in Reconstruction's struggles. Let warriors on both sides meet at Gettysburg, and they indulged in mutual celebration, with honor enough for all. Let them meet separately, and their tone could be much sharper. Reconciliation they welcomed—on their own terms. Old men did not forget their comrades' sacrifices. Nor did they forget so readily what they had sacrificed for. If Confederate veterans' societies lauded the purity of the "Lost Cause," the patriotism of Robert E. Lee, and the Americanness of the values for which they fought against an aggressive North, the Union soldiers strove to keep alive their own version of the war. "We can proudly say, 'There is not a slave in all the broad dominion,'" one of them told his comrades. "Already are the harvests of liberty being gathered from the fields of carnage."[4]

One could end Reconstruction anywhere: with federal soldiers' return to the barracks in New Orleans in 1877; the banquet that Atlanta threw for General William Tecumseh Sherman, the man who, as Henry Grady put it, had been a little careless with fire, in 1879; the return of captured battle flags from the U.S. arsenals in 1905; the passage in 1898 of a final amnesty law removing disabilities from the last Confederate survivors yet covered. Or closure might be found in the capture of Chief Joseph of the Nez Perce and the final victory over an independent Indian nation, or the great railroad strike of 1877, perhaps as a symbol of the moment when Civil War issues gave way more fully than before to those that dominated the quarter century to come, of progress, poverty, vaunting privilege, and lagging opportunity. Or one could say that Reconstruction had no end, as long as the issues that it had raised remained incompletely addressed. But one ceremony might be equally fit. On Lincoln's Birthday, 1878, Congress fulfilled the hope that Sumner had expressed thirteen years before. True to his wishes, the Capitol had put up no paintings commemorating the war itself.

It had failed to adopt his alternative, F. B. Carpenter's picture of Lincoln giving a first reading to the cabinet of his Emancipation Proclamation. Critics pronounced it a "historical idiocy," "done in a leaden, slaty atmosphere, heavy enough to make a dog howl." But its importance could not be missed: it made sure that the president's freeing of the slaves would get the national recognition that countrymen killing countrymen would not. Then in 1877, a benefactor, Elizabeth Thompson, bought the canvas and donated it to Congress. Now in a ceremony, members from both parties made a formal acceptance.[5]

Every inch of space was filled, crowds jamming into the galleries "with the noise and confusion of wild pigeons on a field of corn." They came to hear two orators, a former Union general, James A. Garfield, soon to become president himself, and Congressman Alexander Stephens, once vice president of the Confederacy and now a helpless invalid. In a whispering voice, he spoke of Lincoln's great ability and greater heart, but more than that "the doctrine of forgetfulness and reunion." True, he treated the separation of sections as if all the misunderstanding was the North's fault and expressed his own doubts that emancipation would prove a good thing for freedpeople in the end. But he left no doubt on what terms between the two sides stood beyond negotiation: the Union and universal freedom. Speaking for the South, he declared, "There is not now one who would change the condition of things, resubjugate the colored man, or put him in the condition he was in before." Garfield's address got rather less press attention. Yet he spoke, perhaps, more to generations yet unborn than to his own time; for he implied that as Lincoln had found in the war, justice could not be slowed or stayed, when the life of the republic depended on that justice being done. In the end, the Great Emancipator had "realized that saving truth, that great unsettled questions have no pity for the repose of nations."

Nor had they, over the years since Appomattox. And, perhaps, nor have they to this day.

Notes

Abbreviations

ADAH	Alabama Department of Archives and History, Montgomery
AMA Records	American Missionary Association Records, Amistad Research Center, Tilton Memorial Hall, Tulane University, New Orleans, Louisiana
BDA	*Boston Daily Advertiser*
Bowdoin	Bowdoin College Library, Brunswick, Me.
BRFAL	Registers and Letters Received by the Commissioner of the Bureau of Refugees, Freedmen, and Abandoned Lands, 1865–72
CG	*Congressional Globe*
CR	*Congressional Record*
ChaCou	*Charleston Daily Courier*
ChiTi	*Chicago Times*
ChiTrib	*Chicago Tribune*
CinCom	*Cincinnati Commercial*
CinEnq	*Cincinnati Enquirer*
CinGaz	*Cincinnati Gazette*
ClPD	*Cleveland Plain Dealer*
Duke	Duke University Library, Durham, N.C.
GDAH	Georgia Department of Archives and History, Atlanta
H. Exec. Doc.	House Executive Document
HoL	Hoskins Library, University of Tennessee, Knoxville
H. Rept.	United States House Report
HSP	Historical Society of Pennsylvania, Philadelphia
HU	Houghton Library, Harvard University, Cambridge, Mass.
HuL	Huntington Library, San Marino, California
ISHS	Illinois State Historical Society, Springfield
Ku Klux Test.	Testimony for H. Rept. 22, "Affairs in the Late Insurrectionary States"
LC	Library of Congress, Washington, D.C.
LSU	Hill Library, Louisiana State University, Baton Rouge
MDAH	Mississippi Department of Archives and History, Jackson
MHS	Massachusetts Historical Society, Boston
NHHS	New Hampshire Historical Society, Concord

NNE   *New National Era* (Washington, D.C.)

NYEP   *New York Evening Post*

NYH   *New York Herald*

NYPL   New York Public Library

NYTi   *New York Times*

NYTrib *New York Tribune*

NYW   *New York World*

Oberlin Oberlin College, Oberlin, Ohio

OHS   Ohio Historical Society, Columbus

RBHL   Rutherford B. Hayes Memorial Library, Fremont, Ohio

SCC   South Caroliniana Collection, University of South Carolina, Columbia

S. Exec. Doc. Senate Executive Document

SHC   Southern Historical Collection, University of North Carolina, Chapel Hill

SHSW   State Historical Society of Wisconsin, Madison

SprR   *Springfield (Mass.) Daily Republican*

SprWR *Springfield (Mass.) Weekly Republican*

S. Rept. Senate Report

WVC   West Virginia Collection, West Virginia University Library, Morgantown

Introduction

1. Sumner, *Charles Sumner Complete Works*, 8:361–62, 12:201–3.

2. Bowers, *Tragic Era*; Lears, *Rebirth of a Nation;* Richardson, *West from Appomattox*; Slotkin, *Fatal Environment*; Bensel, *Yankee Leviathan*; Litwack, *Been in the Storm So Long*; Stampp, *Era of Reconstruction*.

3. Foner, *Reconstruction*.

4. A point briefly and well made by Brooks D. Simpson, "Consider the Alternatives: Reassessing Republican Reconstruction," in Gallagher and Shelden, *Political Nation*, 219. Two of the liveliest and most deservedly acclaimed popular accounts of the civil rights struggle during Reconstruction are Dray, *Capitol Men*, and Egerton, *Wars of Reconstruction*.

5. From Matthew Arnold, "Dover Beach."

Chapter One

1. Oakes, *Freedom National*, 431–76; Manning, *What This Cruel War Was Over*, 151–57, 182–95; Vorenberg, *Final Freedom*, 36–71.

2. Vorenberg, *Final Freedom*, 107–12; Montgomery Blair to Andrew Johnson, June 16, 1865, Johnson MSS, LC; Cox and Cox, *Politics, Principle, and Prejudice*, 6–11; *CinEnq*, February 1, 6, 1865; *NYW*, June 17, 30, 1864; *CG*, 38th Cong., 2nd sess., 189 (January 10, 1865), 243 (January 12, 1865), 480, 487 (January 28, 1865); *CG*, 38th Cong., 2nd sess., appendix, 99–101 (February 21, 1865).

3. *BDA*, February 1, 4, 1865; Blaine, *Twenty Years of Congress*, 1:538; "Van," *SprR*, February 4, 1865; "George W. Julian's Journal," 327; *ChiTrib*, February 1, 1865.

4. *Portland (Maine) Eastern Argus*, February 8, 1865; *CinEnq*, February 10, 1865.

5. Oakes, *Freedom National*, 261–66, 434–36; Caleb Mills to his son, February 2, 1865, Mills MSS, Indiana Historical Society, Indianapolis; "Admission of a Colored Lawyer to the Bar of the Supreme Court," *Charles Sumner Complete Works*, 12:97–100; Donald, *Charles Sumner and the Rights of Man*, 153–54, 161, 193.

6. "Modern Minstrelsy," *NYW*, February 18, 1868; *Milwaukee Sentinel*, June 15, 1866; *Christian Recorder*, June 26, July 7, 1866, February 9, 23, 1867; Campney, "'Light is Bursting upon the World!,'" 176–78, 184–88.

7. Kantrowitz, *More than Freedom*, 312–15; Masur, *Example for All the Land*, 91–112; Voegeli, *Free but Not Equal*, 165–67; Paul Finkelman, "Rehearsal for Reconstruction: Antebellum Origins of the Fourteenth Amendment," in Anderson and Moss, *Facts of Reconstruction*, 1–27; *Christian Recorder*, October 21, 1865, April 7, 1866, February 9, 16, 1867; Brown, "Pennsylvania and the Rights of the Negro," 46–51; Aaron H. Cragin to George Fogg, July 2, 1865, Fogg MSS, NHHS. On minstrel shows, see *NNE*, January 30, 1873, January 29, 1874.

8. *BDA*, October 20, 1864; *Kennebec Journal*, February 17, 1865.

9. Marvel, *Tarnished Victory*, 260–324; Harris, *Lincoln's Last Months*, 93–151; George B. Wright to C. G. Ames, February 25, 1865, Wright MSS, Minnesota Historical Society, St. Paul; Leland, "Middleton Correspondence," 100–104.

10. Richardson, *Greatest Nation of the Earth*; Gates, *Agriculture and the Civil War*, 251–323.

11. *Louisville (Ky.) Weekly Journal*, October 4, 1864; *Luzerne (Pa.) Union*, January 18, 1865; *The Age*, April 12, 1865; *Ottawa (Ill.) Free Trader*, November 18, 1865; *Delphi (Ind.) Times*, November 12, 1864, March 4, 1865; *Nation*, October 19, 1865; *Indianapolis Daily Evening Gazette*, May 9, 1865; Summers, *Dangerous Stir*, 23–43.

12. Summers, *Dangerous Stir*, 49–51, 81–85; *ChaCou*, December 29, 1865; Miers, *When the World Ended*, 95, 103; Childs, *Private Journal of Henry William Ravenel*, 228–29, 232.

13. "Are We a Nation?," *Charles Sumner Complete Works*, 16:59–64; *NYW*, March 14, 1864; *NYTi*, November 14, 1865; Elazar, "Preservation of American Federalism," 47–52; Parish, *North and the Nation*, 92–103; *National Anti-Slavery Standard*, May 13, 1865; Benedict, "Preserving the Constitution."

14. This point is most ably advanced in Gallagher, *Union War*, and specifically on pp. 75–92.

15. Trowbridge, *The South*, 25; Salmon P. Chase to "gentlemen" [Rev. George Whipple, J. M. McKim, and Rev. Lyman Abbott], November 20, 1865, McKim MSS, Cornell University Library, Ithaca, N.Y.; *NYEP*, July 7, 1865; *CG*, 38th Cong., 2nd sess., appendix, 80–81 (February 20, 1865).

16. Detroit Post and Tribune, *Zachariah Chandler*, 281–85; Donald, *Lincoln*, 574, 583.

17. *CinGaz*, May 1, 1865; *Delphi (Ind.) Times*, May 15, 1865; Turner, *Beware the People Weeping*, 23–52, 125–37; Varon, *Appomattox*, 189–91, 198–202; Simpson, *Let Us Have Peace*, 105–8.

18. "Is Anybody to Be Punished?," *Nation*, September 28, 1865; *Indianapolis Daily Evening Gazette*, April 28, 1865; *Baltimore Sun*, December 14, 1870; Anna Lee to Oliver O. Howard, February 20, 1866, and Fitzhugh Lee to Howard, March 2, 1866, Howard MSS, Bowdoin; Nicoletti, "Great Question of the War"; Salmon P. Chase to John Sherman, March 3, 1866, Sherman MSS, LC; Burton N. Harrison to James Chesnut, January 11, 1867, Williams-Chesnut-Manning MSS, SCC; Morse, *Diary of Gideon Welles*, 2:335–36 (July 18, 1865), 337–39 (July 21, 1865); *BDA*, May 26, 1865; *SprR*, March 17, 1866; *Christian Recorder*, May 18, 1867.

19. *CinEnq*, April 9, 1862; *CinGaz*, May 11, 1865; Perman, *Reunion without Compromise*, 32–34.

20. For the Democratic case for federal noninterference, see *CG*, 38th Cong., 2nd sess., appendix, 77–80 (February 20, 1864), 88–96 (February 21, 1865). For radicalism, see Bogue, *Earnest Men*, 308–10, and *Pottsville (Pa.) Miners' Journal*, June 24, 1865.

21. Sutherland, *Confederate Carpetbaggers*, 101–10; Buck, *Road to Reunion*, 161; McKitrick, *Andrew Johnson and Reconstruction*, 28–31.

22. *BDA*, June 6, 1865; Frederick Douglass to J. Miller McKim, May 2, 1865, McKim MSS, Cornell University Library, Ithaca, N.Y.

23. Cox, "Negro Suffrage and Republican Politics"; Lex Renda, "'A White Man's State in New England': Race, Party, and Suffrage in Civil War Connecticut," in Cimbala and Miller, *Uncommon Time*, 256–78; McManus, "Wisconsin Republicans and Negro Suffrage," 45–54; Field, "Republicans and Black Suffrage," 141–47; Dykstra and Hahn, "Northern Voters and the Negro Suffrage Question"; Dykstra, "Issue Squarely Met."

24. *Kennebec Journal*, July 14, 1865; *Illinois State Journal*, August 4, 1865; *Galena (Ill.) Weekly Gazette*, August 8, 1865; *Quincy (Ill.) Daily Whig and Republican*, August 18, 26, 1865; *National Anti-Slavery Standard*, May 20, 1865.

25. Richard O. Curry, "Crisis Politics in West Virginia, 1861–1870," in Curry, *Radicalism, Racism and Party Realignment*, 84–90; Williams, "New Dominion and the Old," 323–25, 341–51; Towers, "Strange Bedfellows."

26. Ranney, *In the Wake of Slavery*, 35–36; Harris, *With Charity for All*, 100–103, 161–62.

27. Bergeron, *Andrew Johnson's Civil War and Reconstruction* 23–24; Cimprich, "Military Governor Johnson and Tennessee Blacks"; Hardison, "In the Toils of War," 271, 349.

28. Simpson, *Reconstruction Presidents*, 39–42.

29. Wagandt, *Mighty Revolution*, 223–30; Guy, *Maryland's Persistent Pursuit to End Slavery*, 446–47; Baker, *Politics of Continuity*, 107.

30. Ambler, *Francis H. Pierpont*, 221–22; Lowe, *Republicans and Reconstruction*, 22.

31. McCrary, "Moderation in a Revolutionary World," 284–85, 312–13.

32. Hyman and Wiecek, *Equal Justice under Law*, 269–71; Hyman, *More Perfect Union*, 268; Neal and Kremm, "Loyal Government on Trial," 160–62.

33. Belz, "Henry Winter Davis," 138–43; Hyman, *More Perfect Union*, 276–77; Hyman and Wiecek, *Equal Justice under Law*, 271–75; Vorenberg, "'Deformed Child,'" 242–44.

34. *New Orleans Tribune*, August 9, 1864; McCrary, "Moderation in a Revolutionary World," 271–72, 321.

35. Foner, "Free People of Color in Louisiana and St. Domingue"; Rankin, "Impact of the Civil War," 380–83; Rankin, "Origins of Black Leadership in New Orleans"; Hahn, *Nation under Our Feet*, 104–11.

36. *New Orleans Tribune*, November 11, 1864; Simpson and Baker, "Michael Hahn," 245; McCrary, "Moderation in a Revolutionary World," 375.

37. Simpson, *Reconstruction Presidents*, 60–62; Fredrickson, "A Man but Not a Brother." 58.

38. Baggett, *Scalawags*, 44–80; Browning, "'Little Souled Mercenaries?,'" 337–63; Davis, "White and Black in Blue"; Storey, *Loyalty and Loss*, 102; Current, *Lincoln's Loyalists*, 106, 215–17; Blair, *Virginia's Private War*, 149; Groce, *Mountain Rebels*, 53–61.

39. John C. Inscoe and Gordon B. McKinney, "Highland Households Divided: Family Deceptions, Diversions, and Divisions in Southern Appalachia's Inner Civil War," in Inscoe and Kenzer, *Enemies of the Country*, 64.

40. Blair, *Virginia's Private War*, 138, 143–44; Browning, "Removing the Mask of Nationality."

41. Richard O. Curry, "Crisis Politics in West Virginia, 1861–1870," in Curry, *Radicalism, Racism and Party Realignment*, 91; Talbott, "Some Legislative and Legal Aspects," 14–17; Righi, "'A Power Unknown to Our Laws,'" 198–211; Wennersten, "John W. Crisfield and Civil War Politics," 8–12; Baggett, *Scalawags*, 108–10.

42. Avillo, "Ballots for the Faithful," 165–74; Ranney, *In the Wake of Slavery*, 36–41; Kohl, "Enforcing a Vision of Community," 292; *NYTrib*, October 14, 17, 18, 1864; Baker, *Politics of Continuity*, 130–33; Wagandt, *Mighty Revolution*, 265–70.

43. Curry, *House Divided*, 48–53, 86–89, 100–4, 115–16; Gooden, "Completion of a Revolution," 34–37.

44. Ambler, *Francis H. Pierpont*, 222; Harris, *With Charity for All*, 163–64.

45. *NYW*, June 11, 1864; *Pittsburgh Daily Post*, October 11, 1864; *Dayton (Ohio) Daily Empire*, January 12, 1864; Harris, *With Charity for All*, 101; Ambler, *Francis H. Pierpont*, 216; Moneyhon, *Impact of the Civil War and Reconstruction*, 190–94; Neal and Kremm, "Loyal Government on Trial," 154–57.

46. Perman, *Reunion without Compromise*, 57–60; *CinCom*, June 3, 1865; Breese, "Politics in the Lower South," 71.

47. Varon, *Appomattox*, 163–66; Trowbridge, *The South*, 586; A. J. Ricks to Jacob D. Cox, March 23, 1866, Cox MSS, Oberlin.

48. "D. S.," *CinGaz*, October 20, 1865.

49. Anne E. Marshall, "'The Rebel Spirit in Kentucky': The Politics of Readjustment in a Border State, 1865–1868," in Cimbala and Miller, *Great Task Remaining before Us*, 57–64.

50. Ambler, *Francis H. Pierpont*, 260; *BDA*, May 30, 1865; Lowe, *Republicans and Reconstruction*, 33.

51. Charles Lewis to Waitman T. Willey, April 20, 1866, Willey MSS, WVC.

52. Greenawalt, "Virginians Face Reconstruction," 449; Maddex, *Virginia Conservatives*, 38–39; Ambler, *Francis H. Pierpont*, 282–83; Beverly Fragsen to Waitman T. Willey, March 27, 1866, Willey MSS, WVC.

53. *NYTrib*, October 18, 1864; Baker, *Politics of Continuity*, 145–46.

54. Baker, *Politics of Continuity*, 162–75.

55. Derek W. Frisby, "A Victory Spoiled: West Tennessee Unionists during Reconstruction," in Cimbala and Miller, *Great Task Remaining before Us*, 15–19; "Cedric," *New York Daily News*, May 19, 1866; Gooden, "Completion of a Revolution," 129–37, 343.

56. William B. Lewis to George A. Washington, February 24, 1863, Washington Family MSS, Tennessee State Library and Archives, Nashville.

57. Perman, *Reunion without Compromise*, 32–36; Trowbridge, *The South*, 442; preamble and resolutions, proposing the call of a national convention, March 2, Patton MSS, Governor's Papers, ADAH; Reid, *After the War*, 144–45.

58. T. R. C. Hutton, "UnReconstructed Appalachia: The Persistence of War in Appalachia," in Slap, *Reconstructing Appalachia*, 79–81; Sutherland, *Savage Conflict*, 272–73; Childs, *Private Journal of Henry William Ravenel*, 220, 222, 225, 226, 234.

Chapter Two

1. Nevins, *War for the Union: Organized War to Victory*, 365; Gallagher, *Union War*, 7–28; *NYTrib*, May 24, 25, 1865.

2. *War of the Rebellion*, 5:505–17; Nevins, *War for the Union: Organized War to Victory*, 367; Peterson, "Navy in the Doldrums," 12–40.

3. Thompson, *Thirteenth Regiment*, 605; Rosenblatt, *Hard Marching Every Day*, 327, 330, 342.

4. *Daily Illinois State Journal*, July 25, 1865; *Ottawa (Ill.) Free Trader*, June 24, 1865; *Peoria (Ill.) Weekly Transcript*, July 13, 1865; Thompson, *Thirteenth Regiment*, 628; Sinisi, *Sacred Debts*, 9–40, 171–72; Bremner, *Public Good*, 144–50.

5. Trowbridge, *The South*, 553–56; Andrews, *South Since the War*, 1, 29; Reid, *After the War*, 65, 68.

6. Reid, *After the War*, 138, 205–7; Moneyhon, *Impact of the Civil War and Reconstruction on Arkansas*, 176–77.

7. Trowbridge, *The South*, 143, 484–87; Andrews, *South Since the War*, 30–32; Harris, *Presidential Reconstruction in Mississippi*, 20.

8. Simkins and Woody, *South Carolina during Reconstruction*, 100; Harris, *Presidential Reconstruction in Mississippi*, 21–22; "D. S.," *CinGaz*, September 12, 1865. On the parlous state of rice before emancipation, see Coclanis, "Rise and Fall of the South Carolina Low Country," 153–63.

9. Trowbridge, *The South*, 84, 290; Dennett, *South As It Is*, 34; *Merchants' Magazine & Commercial Review* 55 (November 1866): 361–64; "Affairs of Southern Railroads," 16, 796, 863, 983.

10. Childs, *Private Journal of Henry William Ravenel*, 229, 243–45; Harris, *Presidential Reconstruction in Mississippi*, 26.

11. Fleming, *Civil War and Reconstruction in Alabama*, 277–85; Reid, *After the War*, 211; Trowbridge, *The South*, 69, 455, 462, 563.

12. Andrews, *South Since the War*, 340; Reid, *After the War*, 205–7, 402–3; Lebergott, *Americans*, 243–48; *Baltimore Gazette*, November 21, 1865; *New York Daily News*, December 16, 1865.

13. "Quill," *CinGaz*, May 18, 1865; Coulter, *South during Reconstruction*, 20; Hamilton, *Correspondence of Jonathan Worth*, 2:927–31, 933, 965–67; Andrews, *South Since the War*, 3–4, 34; Reid, *After the War*, 240–41, 371, 382–83; Trowbridge, *The South*, 454; *NYTi*, November 14, 1865.

14. Trowbridge, *The South*, 459; "Affairs of Southern Railroads," 870; Doster, "Were the Southern Railroads Destroyed by the Civil War?"; "Southern Railroads," 3–37; Harris, *Presidential Reconstruction in Mississippi*, 197–204; *NYH*, May 22, June 5, 1865.

15. *NYH*, June 11, 1865; Woodman, *King Cotton and His Retainers*, 246–49; Andrews, *South Since the War*, 6; Thurlow Weed to Oliver O. Howard, Howard MSS, Bowdoin.

16. Woodman, *King Cotton and His Retainers*, 266–67; King, *Great South*, 50–51, 53, 271.

17. Andrews, *South Since the War*, 8; Greene, *Civil War Petersburg*, 263, 271; Sefton, *United States Army and Reconstruction*, 9–12; *NYH*, May 29, 1865; Cooling, *To the Battles of Franklin and Nashville*, 354–67; Bradley, *Bluecoats and Tar Heels*, 36.

18. Trowbridge, *The South*, 426; Gaston, *New South Creed*, 30.

19. *Arkansas Gazette*, August 11, 27, 1867; *NYH*, July 27, 1867; *Merchants' Magazine* 58 (May 1868): 356–58. Yankee peddlers were notoriously accused of selling wooden nutmegs (and hams) to unwary customers.

20. Trowbridge, *The South*, 426; *Tallahassee Floridian*, March 1, 1867; Gaston, *New South Creed*, 27; Henry Wise to William T. Sutherlin, April 8, 1867, Sutherlin MSS, Duke; Moore, *Juhl Letters to the Charleston Courier*, 43, 169, 192.

21. Greenberg, "Civil War and the Redistribution of Land"; McKenzie, "Civil War and Socioeconomic Change," 172–80; Wiener, "Planter Persistence and Social Change"; Coclanis, "Rise and Fall," 157–58; Scarborough, *Masters of the Big House*, 398; obituary and inventory, 1887, Kenner MSS, LSU.

22. *NYH*, May 22, 1865; Myers, *Children of Pride*, 1292.

23. Dennett, *South As It Is*, 26; Rawick, *American Slave*, vol. 13, *Georgia Narratives*, pt. 3, p. 188; supp., ser. 1, vol. 10, *Mississippi Narratives*, pt. 4, p. 1625; pt. 5, pp. 2374, 2397; Rawick, *American Slave*, vol. 2, *South Carolina Narratives*, pts. 1 and 2, p. 211; Rawick, *American Slave*, vol. 8, *Arkansas Narratives*, pt. 1, p. 334, pt. 2, p. 158; supp., ser. 2, vol. 2, *Texas Narratives*, pt. 1, pp. 141, 358.

24. Williamson, *After Slavery*, 34–35; Myers, *Children of Pride*, 1274.

25. Dennett, *South As It Is*, 13–14; Rawick, *American Slave*, ser. 1, vol. 9, *Mississippi Narratives*, pt. 4, pp. 1610, 1612; supp., ser. 2, *Texas Narratives*, pt. 1, pp. 383–84, 403; vol. 2, *South Carolina Narratives*, pts. 1 and 2, pp. 12, 242, 328; vol. 15, *North Carolina Narratives*, pt. 2, p. 190; vol. 13, *Georgia Narratives*, pt. 3, p. 301; vol. 8, *Arkansas Narratives*, pt. 2, p. 14; supp., ser. 2, *Texas Narratives*, pt. 1, pp. 170, 259, 302, 317–18; supp., ser. 1, vol. 10, *Mississippi Narratives*, pt. 5, p. 2374.

26. Reid, *After the War*, 173; Williamson, *After Slavery*, 38–42.

27. Dennett, *South As It Is*, 13–14; Rawick, *American Slave*, supp., ser. 2, *Texas Narratives*, pt. 1, pp. 143, 359; vol. 6, *Alabama and Indiana Narratives*, Alabama, p. 280; Myers, *Children of Pride*, 1302; Samuel P. Richards Diary, March 31, 1870 (typescript), box 1, folder 7, MSS 176, Richards MSS, Atlanta Historical Society.

28. Rawick, *American Slave*, vol. 8, *Arkansas Narratives*, pt. 1, p. 227; pt. 2, p. 164; Smith, Smith, and Childs, *Mason Smith Family Letters*, 226n.; Litwack, *Been in the Storm So Long,* 249; Rawick, *American Slave*, vol. 3, *South Carolina Narratives*, pts. 3 and 4, p. 193; vol. 15, *North Carolina Narratives*, pt. 2, p. 369.

29. Myers, *Children of Pride*, 1308–9; Williamson, *After Slavery*, 47.

30. Avary, *Dixie after the War*, 195; Myers, *Children of Pride*, 1308–9; Litwack, *Been in the Storm So Long*, 224.

31. Dennett, *South As It Is*, 364; Rawick, *American Slave*, supp., ser. 2, *Texas Narratives*, pt. 1, pp. 259, 448; supp., ser. 1, vol. 9, *Mississippi Narratives*, pt. 4, p. 1449; vol. 8, *Arkansas Narratives*, pt. 1, p. 155.

32. Alexander, *North Carolina Faces the Freedmen*, 58–65; Hebert, "Bitter Trial of Defeat and Emancipation," 82–84; Andrew L. Slap, "'No Regular Marriage': African American Veterans and Marriage Practices after Emancipation," in Slap and Smith, *This Distracted and Anarchical People*, 172–83.

33. Andrews, *South Since the War*, 101, 400; Reid, *After the War*, 34, 226; Hamilton, *Correspondence of Jonathan Worth*, 1:570; A. Warren Kelsey to Edward Atkinson, September 4, December 2, 1865, Atkinson MSS, MHS.

34. Scarborough, *Masters of the Big House*, 374; Hamilton, *Papers of Thomas Ruffin*, 40; Eliphalet Whittlesey to Oliver O. Howard, June 24, 1865, Howard MSS, Bowdoin; Dennett, *South As It Is*, 48, 191; Trowbridge, *The South*, 192.

35. Davis Tillson to Oliver O. Howard, December 15, 1865, and Robert K. Scott to Howard, June 30, 1866, Howard MSS, Bowdoin; Williamson, *After Slavery*, 38–39; Egerton, *Wars of Reconstruction*, 93–115; J. W. Sprague to Oliver O. Howard, February 20, March 20, April 10, May 8, 1866, and Samuel Thomas to Howard, March 13, 1866, roll 28: Letters Received, J-M, March–May 1866, BRFAL; R. S. Lacy to Orlando Brown, February 6, 1866, roll 25: Letters Received, V-Y, October 1865–February 1866, BRFAL.

36. *Christian Recorder*, September 14, 1867; Edward Atkinson to M. E. Goddard, December 2, 1865, and A. Warren Kelsey to Atkinson, September 2, 1865, Atkinson MSS, MHS; Schwalm, "'Sweet Dreams of Freedom,'" 18–19; Williamson, *After Slavery*, 44–46.

37. Litwack, *Been in the Storm So Long*, 245; Andrews, *South Since the War*, 100; Trowbridge, *The South*, 138; Farmer-Kaiser, "'Are They Not in Some Sorts Vagrants?,'" 25–27; Jaynes, *Branches without Roots*, 228–32.

38. A. C. Smart to Major General Gillmore, August 26, 1865, roll 64, September 1865, Union Provost Marshal's Files; Rawick, *American Slave,* supp., ser. 2, *Texas Narratives*, pt. 1, 231, 317–18, 403; supp., ser. 1, vol. 9, *Mississippi Narratives,* pt. 4, p. 1436, 1457–58, 1504; pt. 5, pp. 1941, 2374; Hahn, *Nation under Our Feet*, 172–73.

39. Formwalt, "Moving in 'That Strange Land of Shadows,'" 526–30; Ronald L. F. Davis, "Labor Dependency among Freedmen, 1865–1880," in Fraser and Moore, *From the Old South to the New*, 158–61; Ouzts, "Landlords and Tenants," 10.

40. Kelsey to Edward Atkinson, September 15, 1865, Atkinson MSS, MHS. A similar conclusion can be found in Willard Warner to Jacob D. Cox, August 9, 1866, Cox MSS, Oberlin.

41. Ransom and Sutch, *One Kind of Freedom*, 56–64; Jaynes, *Branches without Roots*, 44–49, 111–13.

42. W. F. Eaton to George Whipple, May 26, 1865, AMA Records: Georgia; Palmer Litts to Whipple, July 11, 1865, and Litts to W. E. Whiting, September 8, 1865, AMA Records: Mississippi; S. Straight to Whipple, June 4, 1866, AMA Records: Louisiana; Dennett, *South As It Is*, 206–7; DeForest, *Union Officer in Reconstruction*, 116; Trowbridge, *The South*, 509–10; S. G. Willauer to L. O. Parker, June 29, 1867, roll 47: Letters Received I-Q, BRFAL.

43. Alexander, *North Carolina Faces the Freedmen*, 67; Hoole, "Diary of Dr. Basil Manly," 152; Jenkins, *Seizing the New Day*, 113–32; *Christian Recorder*, January 20, March 31, May 19, September 8, 1866; "Q. P. F.," *CinCom*, November 30, 1865.

44. Alexander, *North Carolina Faces the Freedmen*, 77–78; Williamson, *After Slavery*, 47–48; *Mobile (Ala.) Nationalist*, June 21, July 12, 1866; *Christian Recorder*, October 28, 1865, January 20, July 19, 1866; *Augusta Loyal Georgian*, February 17, 1866; Andrews, *South Since the War*, 120–29.

45. George Whipple to Benjamin F. Butler, February 21, 1866, Butler MSS, LC; Williams, "'Leave the Pulpit,'" 89–98; Hoffert, "Yankee Schoolmarms"; Wakefield, "'Set a Light in a Dark Place,'" 403–14.

46. S. Straight to William C. Whitney, February 5, 1866, AMA Records: Louisiana; Alexander, *North Carolina Faces the Freedmen*, 9–11; Childs, *Private Journal of Henry William Ravenel*, 245–48.

47. Clinton B. Fisk to Oliver O. Howard, May 7, 1866, roll 28: Letters Received, J-M, March–May 1866, BRFAL; William J. Armstrong to Howard, June 18, 1867, Howard MSS, Bowdoin; Cohen, "Black Immobility and Free Labor"; Oakes, "Failure of Vision," 66–69; Rapport, "Freedmen's Bureau as a Legal Agent"; Pearson, "'There Are Many Sick, Feeble, and Suffering Freedmen'"; Savitt, "Politics in Medicine."

48. Samuel Thomas to Oliver O. Howard, March 27, 1866, W. H. Gray to Howard, July 23, 1867, and C. H. Prince to Sidney Perham, March 23, 1866, Howard MSS, Bowdoin; Rufus Saxton to Oliver O. Howard, December 6, 1865, roll 24: Letters Received, S-U, October 1865–February 1866, BRFAL.

49. W. C. Daniell to H. C. Brandt, March 5, 1867, Henry C. Brandt to Edward L. Deane, August 12, 1867, and Stuart Brown to Orlando Brown, February 9, 1866, roll 25: Letters Received, V-Y, October 1865–February 1866; Robert K. Scott to Oliver O. Howard, August 13, December 20, 1867, roll 48: Letters Received, R-Z, June–August 1867, BRFAL; J. W. Alvord to Oliver O. Howard, Howard MSS, Bowdoin; John C. Rodrigue, "The Freedmen's Bureau and Wage Labor in the Louisiana Sugar Region," in Cimbala and Miller, *Freedmen's Bureau and Reconstruction*, 193–213; Pearson, "'There Are Many Sick, Feeble, and Suffering Freedmen,'" 165–70.

50. DeForest, *Union Officer in the Reconstruction*, 32–41; Cimbala, "On the Front Line of Freedom."

51. Samuel Thomas to Oliver O. Howard, March 8, 1866, and S. G. Willauer to L. O. Parker, June 29, 1867, roll 47: Letters Received, I-Q, June–August 1867; C. C. Sibley to Howard, February 7, 1868, roll 53; and Alvan C. Gillem to Howard, March 31, 1868, roll 54: Letters Received, M-R, January–June 1868, BRFAL; *New Orleans*

Tribune, October 21, 28, 1865; Morris, "Equality, 'Extraordinary Law,' and Criminal Justice"; LaWanda Cox, "From Emancipation to Segregation," in Nieman, *Freedom, Racism, and Reconstruction*, 303–4; Shlomowitz, "Planter Combinations and Black Labour in the American South," 72–78.

52. A. Warren Kelsey to Edward Atkinson, September 8, 1865, Atkinson MSS, MHS; Hahn, *Nation under Our Feet*, 146–54.

Chapter Three

1. *CinCom*, October 29, 1866.

2. "Quill," *CinGaz*, May 18, 1865; Trowbridge, *The South*, 188, 585; Reid, *After the War*, 78.

3. Trowbridge, *The South*, 71; George R. Ballou to Oliver O. Howard, November 2, 1868, Bullock MSS, Governor's Papers, GDAH; T. A. Baxter and others to Major General J. J. Reynolds, July 5, 1866, Union Provost Marshal's Files, July–December 1866, National Archives; Andrews, *South Since the War*, 217; *NYTrib*, November 2, 1865. An "Irish hoist" was the colloquialism for a knife in the ribs. On the rarity of white ex-Confederate celebration of July 4th, see *Memphis Daily Post*, July 6, 1869; Stewart, "Journal of James Mallory," 223; and Childs, *Private Journal of Henry William Ravenel*, 287.

4. Trowbridge, *The South*, 577; Buni, "Reconstruction in Orange County, Virginia," 463–64; A. J. Ricks to Jacob D. Cox, November 14, 1867, Cox MSS, Oberlin; Schurz, *Reminiscences*, 3:180.

5. Trowbridge, *The South*, 189, 313; Abbott, "Southerner Views the South, 1865," 478–79; John C. Inscoe and Gordon B. McKinney, "Highland Households Divided: Family Deceptions, Diversions, and Divisions in Southern Appalachia's Inner Civil War," in Inscoe and Kenzer, *Enemies of the Country*, 65.

6. Williams and Williams, "'Women Rising'"; Carlson, "'Loanly Runagee'"; Auman, "Neighbor against Neighbor," 66–67; Moneyhon, "Disloyalty and Class Consciousness," 231; Trowbridge, *The South*, 108.

7. Baggett, "Origins of Early Texas Republican Party Leadership," 447–50; *Mobile (Ala.) Nationalist*, June 16, 1866; Fisher, "'Leniency Shown Them Has Been Unavailing'"; Moneyhon, "Disloyalty and Class Consciousness," 238; Auman, "Neighbor against Neighbor," 78–86; Barnes, "Williams Clan," 286–87, 313–14 ; Joshua Burns Moore Diary, April 24, 1865, Moore MSS, ADAH; Thomas Waters to Joseph Fowler, May 26, 1866, Fowler MSS, SHC.

8. Degler, *Other South*, 129–34; Mobley, "Zebulon B. Vance"; Baker, "Class Conflict and Political Upheaval," 176.

9. B. O. Faxon to Andrew Johnson, September 5, 1865, Case Files of Applications from Former Confederates for Presidential Pardons, National Archives, Record Group 94, reel 49 (Tennessee, Ea–Jo).

10. Degler, *Other South*, 175–87; Steven E. Nash, "'The Other War Was but the Beginning': The Politics of Loyalty in Western North Carolina, 1865–1867," in Slap, *Reconstructing Appalachia*, 105–15; Righi, "'A Power Unknown to Our Laws,'" 194–97; *CG*, 39th Cong., 1st sess., 653 (February 5, 1866); Morgan Hamilton to Elisha M.

Pease, November 9, 1866, Pease MSS, Austin Public Library; McKenzie, "Contesting Secession," 302–6.

11. McKitrick, *Andrew Johnson and Reconstruction*, 85–92; Cutler, "Jackson, Polk, and Johnson," 186–88; Bentley, "Governor Andrew Johnson and Public Education," 10–15.

12. Stampp, *Era of Reconstruction*, 54–61; Foner, *Reconstruction*, 176–77.

13. Speiser, "Ticket's Other Half," 43–63.

14. McKitrick, *Andrew Johnson and Reconstruction*, 53–60.

15. Benedict, *Compromise of Principle*, 73, 105–10; Foner, *Reconstruction*, 178–79; Kelley, "Dangers of the Hour," John Sherman Pamphlet Collection, RBHL; McKitrick, *Andrew Johnson and Reconstruction*, 48–51.

16. Bergeron, *Andrew Johnson's Civil War and Reconstruction*, 80–81, 86–87, 91; McKitrick, *Andrew Johnson and Reconstruction*, 166–69; Foner, *Reconstruction*, 180–81.

17. Andrews, *South Since the War*, 257, 269; Perman, *Reunion without Compromise*, 84–85; McKitrick, *Andrew Johnson and Reconstruction*, 190–92, 196–206; Levi W. Lawler to Lewis E. Parsons, September 11, 1865, and E. S. Dargan to Parsons, August 29, 1865, Parsons MSS, ADAH.

18. Childs, *Private Journal of Henry William Ravenel*, 222, 243; Samuel P. Richards Diary, August 24, 1865 (typescript), box 1, folder 5, MSS 176, Richards MSS, Atlanta Historical Society; *NYTrib*, September 16, 1865.

19. "Andrew," *CinCom*, August 22, 1865; *NYTrib*, September 5, 1865.

20. William G. Brownlow to Andrew Johnson; cover note on William S. Findlay to Andrew Johnson, July 15, 1865; Brownlow cover note on John S. Goforth to Johnson, July [n.d.], 1865; and William Faxon, chief clerk in the Navy Department, to Andrew Johnson, August 28, 1865, Case Files of Applications from Former Confederates for Presidential Pardons, reel 49 (Tennessee, Ea–Jo); "Andrew," *CinCom*, August 22, 1865; Morse, *Diary of Gideon Welles*, 2:358 (August 11, 1865).

21. John A. Winston to Lewis E. Parsons, September 2, 1865, Parsons MSS, ADAH; *NYTrib*, September 11, 1865; Trowbridge, *The South*, 76; *NYW*, October 12, 14, 1865; *CinGaz*, September 19, 1865.

22. Perman, *Reunion without Compromise*, 62–63; "Q. P. F.," *CinCom*, November 9, 1865; "D. S.," *CinGaz*, July 22, September 6, 1865; *NYTrib*, July 3, November 25, 1865; Breese, "Politics in the Lower South," 104–11.

23. Perman, *Reunion without Compromise*, 110–17; Sefton, *United States Army and Reconstruction*, 26–29, 37; McKitrick, *Andrew Johnson and Reconstruction*, 192–95.

24. Harris, *William Woods Holden*, 171; W. A. Champlin to William Sharkey, June 28, 1865, and A. J. Frantz and others to Sharkey, Sharkey MSS, MDAH; Breese, "Politics in the Lower South," 124–25.

25. Perman, *Reunion without Compromise*, 120; Shofner, *Nor Is It Over Yet*, 38–39.

26. "D. S.," *CinGaz*, September 7, 1865; Carter, *When the War Was Over*, 65–67; Breese, "Politics in the Lower South," 160–64; Q. P. F.," *CinCom*, November 14, 1865; Joshua Burns Moore Diary, September 17, 1865, Moore MSS, ADAH.

27. Andrews, *South Since the War*, 80–82; *CinGaz*, September 26, 1865; Breese, "Politics in the Lower South," 184–85; Foner, *Reconstruction*, 194–95.

28. Dennett, *South as It Is*, 168; Andrews, *South Since the War*, 53–54; Carter, *When the War Was Over*, 69.

29. B. F. Moore to William Sharkey, July 28, 1865, Sharkey MSS, MDAH; Kenneth B. Rayner to William A. Graham, September 4, 1865, in Williams, *Papers of William Alexander Graham*, 350; Perman, *Reunion without Compromise*, 73–74; Andrews, *South Since the War*, 60–63, 285.

30. Andrews, *South Since the War*, 61–62, 265, 269, 283–84.

31. Kibler, *Benjamin F. Perry*, 408–9; Shofner, *Nor Is It Over Yet*, 40, 42; Andrews, *South Since the War*, 28, 86–87, 219, 337; Dennett, *South as It Is*, 110–11, 136; Reid, *After the War*, 417.

32. Smith, Smith, and Childs, *Mason Smith Family Letters*, 239; Breese, "Politics in the Lower South," 183–84; Harris, *Presidential Reconstruction in Mississippi*, 57; "D. S.," *CinGaz*, September 6, 1865.

33. "Justice," *CinGaz*, November 21, 1866; Elisha Dyer to Thomas Jenckes, February 2, 1866, Jenckes MSS, LC; Carter, *When the War Was Over*, 94, 228–30; *CinGaz*, November 13, 1865.

34. "Q. P. F.," *CinCom*, November 23, 1865; Perman, *Reunion without Compromise*, 163–64; Andrews, *South Since the War*, 327, 630; Carter, *When the War Was Over*, 228–30; Breese, "Politics in the Lower South," 242–46; Benjamin F. Perry to Andrew Johnson, November 29, 1865, in Bergeron, *Papers of Andrew Johnson*, 9:445; Schott, *Alexander Stephens of Georgia*, 461–62.

35. For how far one of them did go, see J. Mills Thornton, "Alabama's Presidential Reconstruction Legislature," in Gallagher and Shelden, *Political Nation*, 168–73.

36. Perman, *Reunion without Compromise*, 77–78; *NYTi*, December 25, 1865.

37. Moore, *Juhl Letters to the Charleston Courier*, 53; Harris, *Presidential Reconstruction in Mississippi*, 124.

38. Wilson, *Black Codes of the South*, 114; Taylor, *Negro in the Reconstruction of Virginia*, 16–21; Taylor, *Negro in Tennessee*, 5–7, 15–19.

39. Williamson, *After Slavery*, 75; Garner, *Reconstruction in Mississippi*, 114; Conway, *Reconstruction of Georgia*, 56; Carter, *When the War Was Over*, 218; *CinGaz*, December 4, 1865.

40. Alexander, *North Carolina Faces the Freedmen*, 40–43; Shofner, *Nor Is It Over Yet*, 51; Moore, *Juhl Letters to the Charleston Courier*, 82; *Augusta Loyal Georgian*, January 20, 1866.

41. Richardson, "Florida Black Codes," 374–75; DuBose, *Alabama's Tragic Decade*, 56; Litwack, *Been in the Storm So Long*, 367; General Absalom Baird to Oliver O. Howard, February 28, 1866, roll 28: Letters Received, J-M, March–May 1866, BRFAL.

42. Alexander, *North Carolina Faces the Freedmen*, 45; Garner, *Reconstruction in Mississippi*, 113–14; Wharton, *Negro in Mississippi*, 84, 91; Barry A. Crouch, "To Enslave the Rising Generation," in Cimbala and Miller, *Freedmen's Bureau and Reconstruction*, 268–73; *Mobile (Ala.) Nationalist*, March 22, 1866.

43. Flynn, *White Land, Black Labor*, 116–22; Foner, *Nothing but Freedom*, 57–59, 65–66; Steven Hahn, "Hunting, Fishing, and Foraging: Common Rights and Class Relations in the Postbellum South," in Nieman, *Black Southerners and the Law*, 79–86.

44. Simkins and Woody, *South Carolina during Reconstruction*, 49; Harris, *Presidential Reconstruction in Mississippi*, 138; Crouch, "'All the Vile Passions,'" 29; Judge Speed Goodloe to General John Ely, March 12, 1866, roll 28: Letters Received, J-M, March–May 1866, BRFAL; Taylor, *Louisiana Reconstructed*, 100.

45. Hamilton, *Reconstruction in North Carolina*, 153–54; Shofner, *Nor Is It Over Yet*, 54; Richardson, "Florida Black Codes," 374.

46. Dennett, *South As It Is*, 54; Wilson, *Black Codes of the South*, 110; Olson and McGrew, "Prelude to Reconstruction, Part I," 52; Harris, *Presidential Reconstruction in Mississippi*, 132–33; Thomas Bramlette to Speed S. Goodloe, February 2, 1866, Records of the Assistant Commissioner for the State of Tennessee, roll 10: Registered Letters Received, BRFAL.

47. DuBose, *Alabama's Tragic Decade*, 55, 63; Taylor, *Louisiana Reconstructed*, 101; Novak, *Wheel of Servitude*, 3; Trowbridge, *The South*, 573; Crouch, "'All the Vile Passions,'" 21, 32–33; Barry A. Crouch, "To Enslave the Rising Generation," in Cimbala and Miller, *Freedmen's Bureau and Reconstruction*," 264, 177–79; J. B. Kiddoo to Oliver O. Howard, October 2, 1866, Howard MSS, Bowdoin.

48. William Cohen, "Involuntary Servitude in the South, 1865–1940: A Preliminary Analysis," in Nieman, *Black Southerners and the Law*, 37; *Mobile (Ala.) Nationalist*, March 15, 1866; Novak, *Wheel of Servitude*, 5.

49. Richardson, "Florida Black Codes," 375; Shofner, *Nor Is It Over Yet*, 54.

50. *NYTrib*, January 25, 1866; *Augusta Loyal Georgian*, February 3, 1866; *Cincinnati Gazette*, October 25, 1866; "Reports of Assistant Commissioners of the Freedmen's Bureau," S. Exec. Doc. 27, 39th Cong., 1st sess., 6; Alvan C. Gillem to Oliver O. Howard, May 15, 1867, roll 47: Letters Received, I-Q, June–August 1867, BRFAL; L. L. Pinkerton, statement filed February 14, 1866, and Clinton B. Fisk to Oliver O. Howard, March 29, 1866, roll 28: Letters Received, J-M, March–May 1866, BRFAL; Wharton, *Negro in Mississippi*, 91; Evans, *Ballots and Fence Rails*, 74–75. On miscegenation, see C. B. Waldrip, "Sex, Social Equality, and Yankee Values."

51. Reid, *After the War*, 300; Strawbridge, "'Monument Better than Marble,'" 326–30, 333–42.

52. Margaret M. Storey, "The Crucible of Reconstruction: Unionists and the Struggle for Alabama's Postwar Home Front," in Cimbala and Miller, *Great Task Remaining before Us*, 73–74; Trowbridge, *The South*, 176; *CinGaz*, June 13, 1866; D. C. Wright to Benjamin F. Butler, June 25, 1865, Butler MSS, LC; A. J. Ricks to Jacob D. Cox, October 3, 1867, Cox MSS, Oberlin; Dennett, *South As It Is*, 275.

53. Tunnell, *Crucible of Reconstruction*, 95; Taylor, *Louisiana Reconstructed*, 58–59.

54. Tunnell, *Crucible of Reconstruction*, 96; Nathaniel P. Banks to Andrew Johnson, September 8, 1865, Johnson MSS, LC; Don A. Pardee to James A. Garfield, July 15, 1865, Garfield MSS, LC; Reid, *After the War*, 236–37; Thomas W. Conway to Nathaniel P. Banks, March 21, 1865, and A. P. Field to Banks, November 20, 1865, Banks MSS, LC.

55. J. Madison Wells to Andrew Johnson, October 6, 23, 1865, Johnson MSS, LC; Taylor, *Louisiana Reconstructed*, 72. "Evelyn," *NYW*, November 10, 1865; *New Orleans Tribune*, November 11, December 12, 1865; Uzee, "Beginnings of the Louisiana Republican Party," 206–7.

56. Reid, *After the War*, 412; Lionel A. Sheldon to James A. Garfield, December 16, 1865, January 17, 1866, Garfield MSS, LC; E. John Ellis to his father, February 6, March 15, 1866, Ellis Family MSS, LSU.

57. Charles H. Fox to Oliver O. Howard, August 10, 1865, Howard MSS, Bowdoin; Reid, *After the War*, 245; William Fiske to John Whipple, November 20, 1865, January 23, 1866, AMA Records: Louisiana; John Marchais to Nathaniel P. Banks, November 28, 1865, Banks MSS, LC.

58. Dennett, *South As It Is*, 132, 168; Carter, *When the War Was Over*, 222; Baggett, *Scalawags*, 130–36; *Christian Recorder*, February 16, 1867; J. W. Throckmorton to Benjamin H. Epperson, January 21, 1866, Epperson MSS, University of Texas, Austin; William Fiske to Rev. George Whipple, February 5, 1866, AMA Records: Louisiana; S. G. Wright to Whipple, November 11, 18, 1865, AMA Records: Mississippi; "J. Q. T.," *CinCom*, December 4, 1865; E. H. Durell to Nathaniel P. Banks, November 18, 1865, Banks MSS, LC.

Chapter Four

1. McKitrick, *Andrew Johnson and Reconstruction*, 175–86.

2. Benedict, *Compromise of Principle*, 144–45.

3. Trefousse, *Radical Republicans*, 5–20; Foner, *Free Soil, Free Labor, Free Men*, 107–9; Brock, *American Crisis*, 93–94; Paul Finkelman, "The Historical Context of the 14th Amendment," in Reilly, *Infinite Hope and Finite Disappointment*, 39.

4. Cox and Cox, *Politics, Principle, and Prejudice*, 209–11; Trefousse, *Radical Republicans*, 340–45; R. P. L. Baber to James Rood Doolittle, November 20, 1865, Doolittle MSS, SHSW; *National Anti-Slavery Standard*, May 13, 1865.

5. Foner, *Free Soil, Free Labor, Free Men*, 40–72; Benedict, *Compromise of Principle*, 40–41, 48–56; Montgomery, "Radical Republicanism in Pennsylvania," 451–53; Trefousse, *Radical Republicans*, 25–27; "Sumter," *ChaCou*, August 24, 1866; Richard Schell, C. K. Garrison, Henry Hilton memorandum, September 6, 1866, Tilden MSS, NYPL.

6. Cook, *Civil War Senator*, 147–50, 197–204; "Gath," *CinEnq*, October 11, 1879, February 23, 27, 1884; Trefousse, *Benjamin Franklin Wade*, 235.

7. Benedict, *Compromise of Principle*, 140–45.

8. *NYW*, July 18, 21, September 19, 1865; *CinGaz*, July 22, 1865; *Daily Illinois State Journal*, September 7, 1865; Grosvenor, "Law of Conquest"; O. S. Ferry to William M. Grosvenor, January 2, 1865, Grosvenor MSS, Columbia University, New York; Gideon Welles to Mark Howard, December 12, 1865, Howard MSS, Connecticut Historical Society, Hartford.

9. "Our Domestic Relations: Power of Congress Over the Rebel States," *Charles Sumner Complete Works*, 10:167–220; *CinGaz*, June 23, 1864; *National Anti-Slavery Standard*, October 7, 1865; *Boston Evening Transcript*, August 19, 1865; *Daily Illinois State Journal*, August 4, 1865; *Indianapolis Daily Evening Gazette*, September 13, 1865; *Peoria (Ill.) Weekly Transcript*, November 23, 1865.

10. *CinGaz*, June 15, 17, 1865; *NYEP*, September 25, 1865; *Lafayette (La.) Daily Journal*, September 1, 1865; *National Anti-Slavery Standard*, June 3, 1865; *Nation*,

December 7, 1865; Collis P. Huntington to Hugh McCulloch, October 19, 1865, McCulloch MSS, LC.

11. *NYTi*, December 25, 1865; *CG*, 39th Cong., 1st sess., 74 (December 18, 1865), 112 (December 21, 1865), 182 (January 10, 1866); George S. Boutwell to Benjamin F. Butler, December 9, 1865, Butler MSS, LC; Sumner, "One Man Power vs. Congress"; Cox and Cox, *Politics, Principle, and Prejudice*, 129–39; McKitrick, *Andrew Johnson and Reconstruction*, 274–80.

12. Fairman, *Reconstruction and Reunion, Part One*, 1162.

13. "Occasional," *Washington (D.C.) Daily Chronicle*, January 10, 1866; McFeely, *Yankee Stepfather*, 205–8; Halbrook, *Freedmen*, 11–20.

14. Fairman, *Reconstruction and Reunion, Part One*, 1163–73; *CG*, 39th Cong., 1st sess., 499–503 (January 30, 1866); E. Whittlesey to Oliver O. Howard, December 1, 1865, Howard MSS, Bowdoin.

15. Maltz, *Civil Rights, the Constitution, and Congress*, 61–78; Kaczorowski, "To Begin the Nation Anew," 47–62; *CG*, 39th Cong., 1st sess., 211–12 (January 12, 1866), 599 (February 2, 1866).

16. Brock, *American Crisis*, 135–38; Cox and Cox, *Politics, Principle, and Prejudice*, 175–78; McKitrick, *Andrew Johnson and Reconstruction*, 280–87.

17. "Occasional," *Philadelphia Press*, February 20, 1866; Bergeron, *Papers of Andrew Johnson*, 10:120–27.

18. "H. V. N. B.," *CinGaz*, February 23, 1866; James A. Garfield to James M. Comly, February 21, 1866, Comly MSS, OHS; Elisha Whittlesey to Oliver O. Howard, February 27, 1866, Howard MSS, Bowdoin; Oliver O. Howard to Wager Swayne, February 23, 1866, Records of the Assistant Commissioner for the State of Alabama, roll 8, BRFAL; J. Miller McKim to Joseph Simpson, February 28, 1866, Letterbook I:400, McKim MSS, Cornell University Library, Ithaca, N.Y.

19. McKitrick, *Andrew Johnson and Reconstruction*, 294.

20. Cox and Cox, *Politics, Principle, and Prejudice*, 191–94, 213; "Mack," *CinCom*, February 26, 1866; *Albany Evening Journal*, February 21, 1866; Morse, *Diary of Gideon Welles*, 2:436–40 (February 21, 22, 24, 1866); McKitrick, *Andrew Johnson and Reconstruction*, 298–315.

21. Benedict, *Compromise of Principle*, 164–65.

22. *CG*, 39th Cong., 1st sess., 357 (January 22, 1866). .

23. Maltz, *Civil Rights, the Constitution, and Congress*, 124–26, 131–33; Benedict, *Compromise of Principle*, 150–54, 160–61; *ChiTrib*, January 10, 29, 1866; William C. Child to Elihu Washburne, February 1, 1866, Washburne MSS, LC; *CG*, 39th Cong., 1st sess., 355–58 (January 22, 1866).

24. Maltz, *Civil Rights, the Constitution, and Congress*, 79–92.

25. Benedict, *Compromise of Principle*, 169–70, 182–83; "Mack," *CinCom*, April 30, May 10, 11, 13, 14, 1866; *CinGaz*, April 30, 1866; "Dion," *BDA*, May 11, 1866; E. B. Sadler to John Sherman, May 9, 1866, Sherman MSS, LC.

26. Jacob D. Cox to James A. Garfield, May 4, 1866, Garfield MSS, LC.

27. McKitrick, *Andrew Johnson and Reconstruction*, 352–55, 358–61; *CinCom*, May 30, 31, 1866; *Richmond (Va.) Daily Dispatch*, June 15, 1866; "Iota," *Baltimore Sun*, June 1, 2, 4, 6, 9, 19, 1866.

28. *Milwaukee Wisconsin*, July 13, 1866; B. S. Hedrick to Jonathan Worth, June 1, 10, 1866, in Hamilton, *Correspondence of Jonathan Worth*, 1:599, 606; Aaron F. Perry to Jacob D. Cox, June 9, 1866, Cox MSS, Oberlin.

29. Foner, *Reconstruction*, 260–61; Perman, *Reunion without Compromise*, 194–201; James R. Doolittle to Mary Doolittle, July 1, 1866, Doolittle MSS, SHSW; *NYTi*, July 14, 16, 1866; James Dixon to Manton Marble, June 30, 1866, Marble MSS, LC; Thomas Meagher to Samuel L. M. Barlow, October 26, 1866, Barlow MSS, HuL.

30. Perman, *Reunion without Compromise*, 201–21; *CinCom*, July 23, 1866; *Pottsville (Pa.) Miners' Journal*, July 21, 1866; *Philadelphia Press*, July 14, 23, 1866.

31. *NYTi*, July 25, 1866; "Occasional," *Philadelphia Press*, July 27, 1866; *Philadelphia Press*, August 14, 1866; *CinCom*, July 23, 31, 1866.

32. McKitrick, *Andrew Johnson and Reconstruction*, 410–16; Wagstaff, "Arm-in-Arm Convention," 108–19; *Nashville Daily Press and Times*, August 22, 1866.

33. Hollandsworth, *Absolute Massacre*, 34–42; "New Orleans Riot," 23–29; "Fulton," *ChiTrib*, August 4, 1866.

34. Edward H. Durell to his sisters, August 5, 8, 1866, Durell MSS, New-York Historical Society, New York; Vandal, "Origins of the New Orleans Riot," 139–50; Reynolds, "New Orleans Riot of 1866," 21–25.

35. Clinton B. Fisk to Oliver O. Howard, May 3, 10, 1866, roll 28: Letters Received, J-M, March–May 1866, BRFAL; Hollandsworth, *Absolute Massacre*, 61–143; Waller, "Community, Class, and Race"; Shewmaker and Prinz, "Yankee in Louisiana," 293–94; Wetta, "Bloody Monday," 9–11; *ChiTrib*, August 8, 1866; "Virginian," *Christian Recorder*, August 25, 1866.

36. *ChiTrib*, August 3, 1866; *Nashville Daily Press and Times*, August 3, 1866; Charles Nordhoff to Parke Godwin, August 30, 1866, Bryant-Godwin MSS, NYPL.

37. McKitrick, *Andrew Johnson and Reconstruction*, 428–38; Summers, *Dangerous Stir*, 140–43; C. C. Starbuck to Jacob D. Cox, September 10, 1866, Cox MSS, Oberlin; Sylvanus Cadwallader MSS, 786–91, ISHS; James Henderson to William H. Seward, October 8, 1866, Seward MSS, University of Rochester; John W. Forney to William Pitt Fessenden, September 1, 1866, Forney MSS, LC; James R. Doolittle to Orville H. Browning, October 7, 1866, Browning MSS, ISHS.

38. Baggett, *Scalawags*, 137–40; Conklin, "Wiping out 'Andy' Johnson's Moccasin Tracks"; Summers, *Dangerous Stir*, 143–48; Elizabeth Reilly, "The Union as it Wasn't and the Constitution as It Isn't," in Reilly, *Infinite Hope and Finite Disappointment*, 74; Simpson, *Let Us Have Peace*, 153–61.

39. *Boston Post*, November 3, 1866; *NYTi*, September 1, 1866; *ClPD*, September 27, October 6, 1866; *Peoria (Ill.) Daily National Democrat*, October 2, 1866; *Illinois State Register*, November 4, 1866; *The Age*, July 20, 1866; *Albany Argus*, October 23, 1866; *Portland (Maine) Eastern Argus*, October 5, 1866.

40. William Faxon to Mark Howard, October 12, 1866, Howard MSS, Connecticut Historical Society, Hartford.

41. Frederick A. Aiken to Andrew Johnson, November 26, 1866, in Bergeron, *Papers of Andrew Johnson*, 11:486; Summers, *Dangerous Stir*, 152–53; *NYH*, October 20, 1866; *Raleigh (N.C.) Sentinel*, November 16, 1866; *NYW*, October 29, 1866; Perman, *Reunion without Compromise*, 234–65.

42. James L. Orr to Orville H. Browning, October 29, 1866, Browning MSS, ISHS; Carter, *When the War Was Over*, 267; McGee, "North Carolina Conservatives and Reconstruction," 142–44; "Leo," *ChaCou*, January 3, 1867; McGraw, "Texas Constitution of 1866," 225.

43. *CinGaz*, August 15, 1866; *Atlanta Constitution*, October 23, 1868; Egerton, *Wars of Reconstruction*, 154–56, 163–65; S. W. Groesbeck to Oliver O. Howard, March 3, 1868, Howard MSS, Bowdoin; *Nashville Daily Press and Times*, July 26, 1866; Crouch, "Spirit of Lawlessness," 222–26; Smallwood, *Time of Hope, Time of Despair*, 33; *Christian Recorder*, June 16, 23, July 7, August 25, 1866; Zipf, "Reconstructing 'Free Woman,'" 23–26; Oakes, "Failure of Vision," 70–76; Morgan Hamilton to Elisha Pease, November 9, 1866, and Thomas H. Duval to Pease, August 9, 1866, Pease MSS, Austin Public Library.

44. Baggett, *Scalawags*, 150–53, 164–72, 178–81; Edmund J. Davis to Elisha M. Pease, November 24, 1866, and George C. Ruby to Pease, November 13, 1866, Pease MSS, Austin Public Library; *Steubenville (Ohio) Weekly Herald*, December 21, 1866; Samuel Shellabarger to James M. Comly, December 29, 1866, Comly MSS, OHS; Thomas J. Durant to Henry Clay Warmoth, December 9, 1866, Warmoth MSS, SHC; *Mobile (Ala.) Nationalist*, January 10, 1867.

45. Kyle Osborn, "Reconstructing Race: Parson Brownlow and the Rhetoric of Race in Postwar East Tennessee," in Slap, *Reconstructing Appalachia*, 173–79; Benedict, *Compromise of Principle*, 210–16; *CG*, 39th Cong, 2nd sess., 192, 291 (January 5, 1867); Hyman and Wiecek, *Equal Justice under Law*, 381–84.

46. Kincaid, "Legislative Origins of the Military Reconstruction Act," 122; *CG*, 39th Cong., 2nd sess., 250 (January 3, 1867), 559–62 (January 18, 1867); Benedict, *Compromise of Principle*, 216–31.

47. *CG*, 39th Cong., 2nd sess., 1182 (February 12, 1867); *NYW*, February 14, 1867.

48. Benedict, *Compromise of Principle*, 230–33; on the possible impact of the Blaine amendment, see "H. V. N. B.," *CinGaz*, February 19, 1867.

49. *CG*, 39th Cong., 2nd sess., 1364–65, 1368, 1379 (February 15, 1867).

50. William Pitt Fessenden to William Fessenden, February 17, 1867, Fessenden Family MSS, Bowdoin; Lyman Trumbull to William Jayne, February 17, 1867, Jayne MSS, ISHS; *NYTi*, February 18, 1867.

51. Benedict, *Compromise of Principle*, 239–41.

52. John Forsyth to Manton Marble, March 5, 1867, Marble MSS, LC; Childs, *Private Journal of Henry William Ravenel*, 304 (February 15, 1867); *NYW*, February 28, 1867.

53. *Nation*, February 28, March 28, 1867.

54. Perman, *Reunion without Compromise*, 271–72; Halbrook, *Freedmen*, 21, 68–69; William E. Chandler to Richard Baker, February 18, 1867, Chandler MSS, NHHS.

Chapter Five

1. Benedict, *Compromise of Principle*, 240; *CG*, 40th Cong., 1st sess., 50 (March 11, 1867).

2. Alvan C. Gillem to Joseph Fowler, March 17, 1867, Fowler MSS, SHC; *Richmond (Va.) Daily Dispatch*, March 6, 7, 1867; *NYTi*, March 9, 1867; *NYTrib*, March 11, 21, 1867; *CG*, 40th Cong., 1st sess., 97 (March 14, 1867).

3. *CinGaz*, March 21, 1867.

4. "Leo," *ChaCou*, March 16, 1867; *CG*, 40th Cong., 1st sess., 97 (March 14, 1867).

5. *ChiTrib*, March 17, 1867; Oliver P. Morton to Murat Halstead, March 10, 1867, Halstead MSS, Cincinnati Historical Society; *CG*, 40th Cong., 1st sess., 203–8 (March 19, 1867); *Nation*, March 21, November 7, 1867.

6. Harris, *Day of the Carpetbagger*, 5, 11; *NYTrib*, March 30, April 9, May 28, 1867; Cox, "Military Reconstruction in Florida," 224–25; Simon, *Papers of Ulysses S. Grant*, 18:76–78. For horse thieves and other peacekeeping chores, see "Report of the Secretary of War," 288.

7. Simon, *Papers of Ulysses S. Grant*, 17:354; Alvan C. Gillem to Joseph Fowler, March 17, 1867, Fowler MSS, SHC; Richter, "'We Must Rubb Out and Begin Anew,'" 335; McDonough, "John Schofield as Military Director," 240, 255–56.

8. Sefton, *United States Army and Reconstruction*, 113–14; Bradley, *Bluecoats and Tar Heels*, 137–39.

9. "R. J. H.," *BDA*, July 17, 1867; Currie, "Beginnings of Congressional Reconstruction in Mississippi," 268–69; Harris, *Day of the Carpetbagger*, 2, 7; Shofner, *Nor Is It Over Yet*, 162; *CinGaz*, January 17, 1868; Simon, *Papers of Ulysses S. Grant*, 18:76–77.

10. Alvan C. Gillem to Joseph Fowler, March 17, 23, 1867, Fowler MSS, SHC; Dawson, *Army Generals and Reconstruction*, 70; "J. W. M.," *CinCom*, January 30, 1868.

11. Simon, *Papers of Ulysses S. Grant*, 17:354, 18:94.

12. Simkins and Woody, *South Carolina during Reconstruction*, 66; Reynolds, *Reconstruction in South Carolina*, 68; Jonathan Worth to H. J. Harris, April 30, 1867, Worth to N. Kelsey, May 7, 1867, Worth to George Howard, May 11, 1867, Worth to B. S. Gaither, May 16, 1867, and Worth to J. R. Bulla, May 24, 1867, in Hamilton, *Correspondence of Jonathan Worth*, 2:940, 948, 950–51, 954–55, 964–65; Dawson A. Walker to Andrew Johnson, September 23, 1867, Johnson MSS, LC; Simon, *Papers of Ulysses S. Grant*, 17:324–25.

13. "Report of the Secretary of War," 24–25, 322–25, 379–80; Simon, *Papers of Ulysses S. Grant*, 17:185–86n.

14. Shofner, *Nor Is It Over Yet*, 161; Simon, *Papers of Ulysses S. Grant*, 17:186, 18:67; Dawson, *Army Generals and Reconstruction*, 53; Heyman, "'Great Reconstructor,'" 56.

15. Heyman, "'Great Reconstructor,'" 56, 62, 65–66; Cox, "Military Reconstruction in Florida," 219; *Cleveland Daily Leader*, November 14, 1867; *NYW*, July 31, 1867; Harris, *Day of the Carpetbagger*, 51–52; Samuel A. Hale to Henry Wilson, July 9, 1867, and John C. Keffer to Samuel S. Hale, July 26, 1867, Howard MSS, Bowdoin; Report of George Meade, October 31, 1868, in "Report of the Secretary of War," 76; A. A. West to Wager Swayne, May 1, 1867, Swayne MSS, Governor's Papers, ADAH.

16. "Report of the Secretary of War," 336; Drago, "Georgia's First Black Voter Registrars," 764–72; *NYW*, September 19, 1867; Albert Griffin to Wager Swayne, July 25, 1867, Swayne MSS, Governor's Papers, ADAH.

17. Dawson, *Army Generals and Reconstruction*, 65–66; Harris, *Day of the Carpet-bagger*, 10–11.

18. "Report of the Secretary of War," 244; Heyman, "'Great Reconstructor,'" 61–63; Shofner, *Nor Is It Over Yet*, 162; Griffin, "Connecticut Yankee in Texas," 221.

19. Simon, *Papers of Ulysses S. Grant*, 18:6; "Report of the Secretary of War," 349–50; *Jackson (Miss.) Daily Clarion*, June 16, 1867; Harris, *Day of the Carpetbag-ger*, 17–18; Simon, *Papers of Ulysses S. Grant*, 17:324.

20. "Report of the Secretary of War," 325–28; David P. Lewis to Wager Swayne, July 22, 1867, and W. B. Figures to Swayne, July 23, 1867, Swayne MSS, Governor's Papers, ADAH; *Mobile (Ala.) Daily Advertiser and Register*, November 10, 1867; "S. D.," *NYW*, December 26, 1867; entry, August 16, 1867, Knight Diary, GDAH.

21. Clinton B. Fisk to Oliver O. Howard, March 18, 1867, Howard MSS, Bowdoin; G. M. Bascom to Jacob D. Cox, May 31, 1867, Cox MSS, Oberlin.

22. "Report of the Secretary of War," 22, 331–33; Simon, *Papers of Ulysses S. Grant*, 12:169; John Ireland to J. W. Throckmorton, May 4, 1867, and George H. Sweet to Throckmorton, May 9, 1867, Throckmorton MSS, University of Texas Li-brary, Austin; T. M. Peters to Robert M. Patton, August 29, 1867, Patton MSS, ADAH; "R. J. H.," *BDA*, July 17, 1867; McDonough, "John Schofield as Military Director," 243.

23. Jonathan Worth to William Clark, May 25, 1867, and Worth to John H. Wheeler, October 31, 1867, in Hamilton, *Correspondence of Jonathan Worth*, 2:971, 1071; Bancroft, *Speeches, . . . of Carl Schurz*, 437–39.

24. Robinson, "Beyond the Realm of Social Consensus," 288; John Y. Green to James L. Orr, March 9, 1867, Orr MSS, Governor's Papers, South Carolina State Archives, Columbia; John M. Kennedy to Robert M. Patton, March 16, 1867, Patton MSS, ADAH; *Jackson (Miss.) Daily Clarion*, July 4, 1867; *NYW*, March 8, 1867; Wil-liam Henry Trescot to his wife, April 7, 1867, Trescot MSS, SCC; Wade Hampton to Conner, March 24, 1867, Hampton MSS, SCC.

25. Perman, *Reunion without Compromise*, 286–91.

26. *NYW*, March 15, 1867; Kibler, *Benjamin F. Perry*, 449–50; Samuel Matthews to John H. Matthews, September 19, 1867, Matthews MSS, MDAH; William L. Harris to Benjamin G. Humphreys, March 10, 1867, Humphreys MSS, Governor's Papers, MDAH; McGee, "North Carolina Conservatives and Reconstruction," 225–28.

27. Kibler, *Benjamin F. Perry*, 450; William Johnston to William A. Graham, Sep-tember 16, 1867, and Graham to David L. Swain, September 23, 1867, in Williams, *Papers of William Alexander Graham*, 370, 372; Jonathan Worth to D. G. Worth, October 24, 1867, and Worth to James W. Osborn, October 29, 1867, in Hamilton, *Correspondence of Jonathan Worth*, 2:1058; Perman, *Reunion without Compromise*, 307.

28. Perman, *Reunion without Compromise*, 308, 316–17; Kibler, *Benjamin F. Perry*, 451–60; Jonathan Worth to J. M. Coffin, November 6, 1867, in Hamilton, *Correspon-dence of Jonathan Worth*, 2:1074; *Jackson (Miss.) Daily Clarion*, August 24, 1867; Leonard T. Doyal to Andrew Johnson, July 22, 1867, Johnson MSS, LC.

29. Edward G. W. Butler to Andrew Johnson, July 30, 1867, and Ellis Malone to Johnson, August 30, 1867, Johnson MSS, LC; William A. Graham to Messrs Pell and

Gales, October 10, 1867, Jonathan Worth to Graham, October 28, 1867, and William N. H. Smith to Graham, November 22, [1867], in Williams, *Papers of William A. Graham*, 382–88, 397, 405; Perman, *Reunion without Compromise*, 316–30; *Jackson (Miss.) Daily Clarion*, January 8, 1868.

30. William George to Henry Clay Warmoth, May 6, 1867, Warmoth MSS, SHC; Behrend, "Freedpeople's Democracy," 167; *Mobile (Ala.) Nationalist*, January 10, 1867; Holt, *Black over White*, 28.

31. Hahn, *Nation under Our Feet*, 230–35; Rankin, "Origins of Black Leadership in New Orleans"; Baggett, "Origins of Early Texas Republican Party Leadership," 451; Drago, *Black Politicians and the Reconstruction in Georgia*, 26–27.

32. Ku Klux Test., vol. 10 (Alabama, pt. 3), 1417–18, 1687, 1818; Gibson, "Lincoln's League," 16–28; Fitzgerald, *Union League Movement*, 22, 34; Evans, *Ballots and Fence Rails*, 86.

33. William M. Pollan to William Sharkey, July 20, 1865, Sharkey MSS, MDAH; Fitzgerald, *Union League Movement*, 13, 18–23; John Silsby to Wager Swayne, April 1, 1867, Swayne MSS, Governor's Papers, ADAH; Olsen, *Carpetbagger's Crusade*, 83–84.

34. Fitzgerald, *Union League Movement*, 34–35, 58–59, 61; Ku Klux Test., vol. 10 (Alabama, pt. 3), 1687; Saville, *Work of Reconstruction*, 163–66.

35. Fitzgerald, *Union League Movement*, 62–63, 67; Saville, *Work of Reconstruction*, 170–76; Holt, *Black over White*, 31; Towne, *Letters and Diary*, 182–83; Saville, *Work of Reconstruction*, 180–86; Hahn, *Nation under Our Feet*, 177–89; Snay, *Fenians, Freedmen, and Southern Whites*, 26–27.

36. Tunnell, "Creating 'the Propaganda of History.'" The term appeared earlier. In December 1867, a conservative Republican editor in Texas denounced the arrival of "carpet-baggers" in Texas, but the tone of the article made clear that he did not mean Northerners come south to live but those traveling through making speeches, before heading north again. See *Flake's Daily Galveston Bulletin*, December 12, 1867.

37. Olsen, *Carpetbagger's Crusade*, 28; Hume, "Carpetbaggers in the Reconstruction South," 320.

38. Orlando Brown to Oliver O. Howard, March 20, 1868, Howard MSS, Bowdoin; *Little Rock Republican*, October 21, 1868; *NYTrib*, August 3, 1868; *NYH*, June 20, 1871.

39. Olsen, *Carpetbagger's Crusade*, 77–78; Hume, "Carpetbaggers in the Reconstruction South," 325–26.

40. Hirshson, *Grenville M. Dodge*, 159; Olsen, *Carpetbagger's Crusade*, 29–36, 42–46.

41. Harris, "Creed of the Carpetbaggers," 201; Hume, "Carpetbaggers in the Reconstruction South," 325; Hume, "Arkansas Constitutional Convention of 1868," 199.

42. Degler, *Other South*, 192–94, 203–14; Wetta, *Louisiana Scalawags*, 44–60; Olsen, "Reconsidering the Scalawags," 305–24; *Debates and Journals of the Arkansas Constitutional Convention*, January 14, 1868; Ellem, "Who Were the Mississippi Scalawags?"; Baggett, "Origins of Early Texas Republican Party Leadership," 441–50.

43. Degler, *Other South*, 209–12; Baggett, "Origins of Upper South Scalawag Leadership," 59; *NYH*, June 13, 1871.

44. Degler, *Other South*, 220–22; Wetta, *Louisiana Scalawags*, 28–29, 149–54; *ChiTrib*, March 26, 1867; Richter, "James Longstreet," 216–22; James L. Alcorn to Elihu B. Washburne, June 29, 1868, Washburne MSS, LC; Duncan, *Entrepreneur for Equality*, 22–25.

45. Degler, *Other South*, 226–28; Fuke, "Hugh Lennox Bond," 583–84.

46. *New Orleans Republican*, December 24, 28, 1867; Morgan, *Yazoo*, 25; *Little Rock Republican*, October 28, 1867, February 5, 1868; "Wenckar," *National Anti-Slavery Standard*, October 19, 1867; *Vicksburg Republican*, April 28, 1868; Virginia Constitutional Convention *Debates*, 294; *Alabama State Journal*, September 15, 1870.

47. *Augusta (Ga.) National Republican*, April 5, 1868; *Little Rock Republican*, June 24, July 15, September 14, 1867, January 30, May 15, September 11, 1868; *New Orleans Republican*, September 26, October 20, December 5, 1867.

48. *Little Rock Republican*, September 16, November 20, 1867, February 5, June 15, 1868; *New Orleans Republican*, April 10, November 3, 15, December 7, 17, 1867.

49. Herschel V. Johnson to his sister Mary, July 24, 1867, and Johnson to John W. Duncan, July 30, 1867, Johnson MSS, Duke; *NYH*, July 16, September 11, 1867; *Arkansas Gazette*, October 17, 1867; Appell, "Fight for a Constitutional Convention," 52–55.

50. Henry W. McVay to Thaddeus Stevens, March 1, 1867, Stevens MSS, LC; Henry H. Penniman to Elihu Washburne, December 21, 1867, Washburne MSS, LC; Williamson, *After Slavery*, 142–44, 148–49; Ochiai, *Harvesting Freedom,* 142; Appell, "Fight for a Constitutional Convention," 96–98.

51. *Jackson (Miss.) Weekly Clarion*, June 20, 1867; John A. Hedrick to Benjamin S. Hedrick, April 19, 1867, Hedrick MSS, Duke.

52. *Mobile (Ala.) Nationalist*, October 10, 1867; Robert K. Scott to Oliver O. Howard, December 20, 1867, roll 51: Letters Received, S-Z, BRFAL; Plantation Diary, September 27, 1867, Declouet MSS, LSU; entry, September 27, 1867, Erwin Diary, LSU; DeForest, *Union Officer in the Reconstruction*, 126.

53. *Tribune Almanac*, 1868, pp. 62–65; *Mobile (Ala.) Nationalist*, October 10, 24, 1867; Pierce Burton to Wager Swayne, October 7, 1867, Swayne MSS, Governor's Papers, ADAH; Simon, *Papers of Ulysses S. Grant*, 18:6.

Chapter Six

1. "S. D.," *NYW*, January 25, 1868; see also "J. W. M., *CinCom*, January 27, 1868.

2. Hume and Gough, *Blacks, Carpetbaggers, and Scalawags*, 12–13; "S. D.," *NYW*, January 23, 1868; Hume, "Carpetbaggers in the Reconstruction South," 324–27; Hume, "Arkansas Constitutional Convention," 192–206; Hahn, *Nation under Our Feet*, 210–11.

3. *Cleveland Daily Leader*, November 13, 1867; William B. Rodman to David M. Carter, January 23, 1868, Carter MSS, SHC; James H. Clements to Thaddeus Stevens, March 14, 1868, Stevens MSS, LC.

4. Degler, *Other South*, 258–60; Drago, *Black Politicians and Reconstruction in Georgia*, 41, 44; Nathans, *Losing the Peace*, 66; "Stone Mountain," *NYTi*, February 21, 22, 25, March 6, 1868; Palmer, "Miscegenation as an Issue," 100–116.

5. Fitzgerald, *Splendid Failure*, 84–85.

6. *Atlanta Daily New Era*, February 2, 1868; *Little Rock Republican*, February 10, 12, 14, 1868; *South Carolina Constitutional Convention Debates*, 107, 114, 122, 596; Alabama Constitutional Convention, *Journal*, 197–98, 220–21, 269–71; *Augusta (Ga.) National Republican*, March 6, 1868; *Journal of the Proceedings of the Constitutional Convention of the State of Florida*, 10; Olsen, *Carpetbagger's Crusade*, 106; Mississippi Constitutional Convention, *Journal*, 43; Scroggs, "Carpetbagger Influence in the Political Reconstruction," 160–63; Lebsock, "Radical Reconstruction and Property Rights," 195–210.

7. *Constitution of the State of Texas*, 36; Mississippi Constitutional Convention, *Journal*, 739; Louisiana Constitutional Convention, *Journal*, 158; Georgia Constitutional Convention, *Journal*, 144.

8. Entries, December 6, 1867, March 16, 1868, Knight Diary, GDAH; Ware, *Constitutional History of Georgia*, 144–47; *Harper's Weekly*, December 28, 1867; Daniel Hodgin to B. S. Hedrick, April 2, 1868, Hedrick MSS, Duke; *Debates and Journals of the Arkansas Constitutional Convention*, 673–80, 706–7, 726–27; Daniel Richards to Elihu Washburne, February 11, April 14, May 28, 1868, Washburne MSS, LC; F. A. Dockray to Thaddeus Stevens, March 18, 1868, Stevens MSS, LC; Halbrook, *Freedmen*, 88–101.

9. Abbott, "Jason Clarke Swayze," 346–48; *Atlanta Daily New Era*, March 13, 29, 31, 1868; *Raleigh Daily Standard*, April 8, 15, 1868; *Augusta (Ga.) National Republican*, April 17, 19, 23, 1868.

10. *Atlanta Daily New Era*, March 13, 1868; *Arkansas Campaign Gazette*, February 28, 1868; *Iberville (Miss.) Weekly South*, March 28, August 8, 1868; Zipf, "whites Shall Rule the Land or Die,'" 514–25.

11. George Ely to Elihu Washburne, February 9, 1868, and Daniel Richards to Washburne, February 11, April 20, 21, May 6, 1868, Washburne MSS, LC; M. D. Brainard to Benjamin F. Butler, March 23, 1868, Butler MSS, LC.

12. Wetta, *Louisiana Scalawags*, 128–31; Arthur McAllyn to Elihu Washburne, July 13, 1868, Washburne MSS, LC; M. D. Brainard to Benjamin F. Butler, March 23, 1868, Butler MSS, LC; *Little Rock Republican*, May 7, 1868; McGee, "North Carolina Conservatives and Reconstruction," 260–62.

13. "S.," *CinCom*, March 6, 1868; C. W. Buckley to Elihu B. Washburne, January 9, 1868, Washburne MSS, LC; *Montgomery (Ala.) Mail*, February 4, 1868; *Tuscaloosa (Ala.) Independent Monitor*, March 11, 1868.

14. "Report of the Secretary of War," 76–77; "Alabama Election," 2.

15. Powell, "Correcting for Fraud," 637–56; "Condition of Affairs in Mississippi," 53, 58, 142, 144, 150, 205, 255, 270, 272; "Hampden," *CinCom*, July 10, 1868.

16. D. Richards to Elihu Washburne, May 18, 1868, and C. W. Buckley to Washburne, May 1, 1868, Washburne MSS, LC.

17. Stewart, *Impeached*, 96–137; Simpson, *Let Us Have Peace*, 225–36; Morse, *Diary of Gideon Welles*, 3:282–89 (February 19–22, 1868).

18. Clemenceau, *American Reconstruction*, 153; *NYTrib*, February 22, 25, 1868; *ChiTrib*, February 25, 1868; "Dixon," *BDA*, February 25, 1868.

19. *NYTrib*, February 24, 1868; "Supplement to the *Congressional Globe* . . . Impeachment Trial," 56, 140–41 (April 10, 1868); *CinCom*, February 24, 1868.

20. "Gath," *ChiTrib*, November 28, 1874; Milton, *Age of Hate*, 568.

21. Benedict, *Impeachment and Trial of Andrew Johnson*, 143–67.

22. Trefousse, "Ben Wade and the Failure."

23. McDonough and Alderson, "Republican Politics"; *NYH*, October 28, 1868; Fairman, *Reconstruction and Reunion, Part One*, 391–95, 467–78; *Philadelphia Press*, March 30, 1868.

24. Dixon," *BDA*, May 18, 1868; *ChiTi*, May 17, 1868; "J. B. S.," *NYW*, May 18, 1868; *Providence (R.I.) Evening Bulletin*, May 14, 1868; Roske, "Seven Martyrs?"; Cook, *Civil War Senator*, 230–41; White, *Life of Lyman Trumbull*, 321; Benedict, *Impeachment and Trial of Andrew Johnson*, 168–83; Stewart, *Impeached*, 284–99.

25. Bentley, *History of the Freedmen's Bureau*, 199–202; Brodie, *Thaddeus Stevens*, 362–66.   .

26. Simpson, *Let Us Have Peace*, 205–24, 245–47.

27. Sharkey, *Money, Class, and Party*, 98–103; Gambill, *Conservative Ordeal*, 123–36; *Manchester (N.H.) Daily Union*, January 13, 1868; Hugh McCulloch to George O. Glavis, June 16, 1868, McCulloch MSS, Lilly Library, Indiana University, Bloomington; Washington McLean to Manton Marble, March 22, 1868, and George W. Cass to Samuel J. Tilden, June 18, 1868, Marble MSS, LC; Henry D. Cooke to Jay Cooke, March 4, 1868, Cooke MSS, HSP.

28. Gambill, *Conservative Ordeal*, 137–43; Mitchell, *Horatio Seymour of New York*, 423–42.

29. Michael C. Kerr to Manton Marble, November 8, 1868, Marble MSS, LC; *Brooklyn Daily Eagle*, July 11, 1868; Summers, *Dangerous Stir*, 228–31; *Montgomery (Ala.) Mail*, June 23, 1868; *NYW*, September 26, 1868; *Memphis Daily Appeal*, November 1, 1868.

30. *NYTi*, November 4, 1868; *Philadelphia Press*, July 24, September 18, 1868; *ChiTrib*, September 9, 1868.

31. Summers, *Dangerous Stir*, 231–36; *Indianapolis Daily State Journal*, August 3, 1868; *NYW*, June 29, 1868; *Philadelphia Press*, September 29, 1868; *Auburn (Ala.) Daily Advertiser*, July 31, 1868.

32. Richardson, *William E. Chandler*, 108; Joseph Hawley to William C. Claflin, November 19, 1868, Claflin MSS, RBHL; William Bigler to Samuel J. Tilden, September 25, 1868, N. E. Paine to Tilden, August 12, 1868, and Horatio Seymour to Tilden, October 2, 1868, Tilden MSS, NYPL; C. S. Grant to Horatio Seymour, August 12, 1868, Seymour MSS, New York State Library, Albany; *Louisville (Ky.) Courier*, July 14, 1868; *NYH*, July 3, 1868; *ChiTrib*, October 7, 1868.

33. *NYTrib*, August 28, 1868; *Marietta (Ohio) Register*, October 1, 1868; Alfred Barstow to William E. Chandler, July 16, 1868, Chandler MSS, LC.

34. Abbott, *Republican Party and the South*, 190.

35. Eugene Tisdale to Horatio Seymour, September 4, 1868, Seymour MSS, New York State Library, Albany; entry, June 13, 1868, Dixon Diary, LSU; "Louisiana

Contested Elections," pt. 1, pp. 308, 322–24, 342, 549; *Montgomery (Ala.) Mail*, November 17, 1868; Olsen, *Carpetbagger's Crusade*, 117, 124–25.

36. *NYH*, September 15, 1868.

37. Nathans, *Losing the Peace*, 138; *NYH*, September 12, 15, 1868; "Condition of Affairs in Georgia," 9; "Louisiana Contested Elections," pt. 1, p. 532.

38. *Philadelphia Press*, October 2, 1868; Foster Blodgett to William E. Chandler, September 16, 1868, Chandler MSS, LC; George R. Ballou to Oliver O. Howard, August 22, 1868, roll 58: Letters Received, G-H, July–December 1868, BRFAL; "Condition of Affairs in Georgia," 9. On events in Morehouse parish, see "Louisiana Contested Elections," pt. 1, pp. 330–31; *NYTrib*, October 23, 1868.

39. *Memphis Daily Appeal*, September 30, October 2, 20, 1868; "Louisiana Contested Elections," pt. 1, p. 551; *NYH*, September 12, 1868.

40. Trelease, *White Terror*, 115; *NYW*, December 17, 1867; "K. K. K." (August 17, 1868, handbill), Smith MSS, Governor's Papers, ADAH; Rubin, *South Carolina Scalawags*, 49; Ku Klux Test., vol. 6 (Georgia, pt. 1), 10, 239, 244; "Sheafe vs. Tillman," 166; Rawick, *American Slave,* vol. 8, *Arkansas Narratives,* pt. 1, pp. 144–45, 298, 318–19.

41. Trelease, *White Terror*, 115–16; J. R. Lewis to Rufus Bullock, November 10, 1868, Bullock MSS, Governor's Papers, GDAH; *Memphis Daily Appeal*, October 28, 1868; *New York Sun*, October 29, 1868; A. J. Ransier to T. L. Tullock, October 19, 1868, Chandler MSS, LC.

42. Trelease, *White Terror*, 130–33; Hennessy, "To Live and Die in Dixie," 92; Taylor, *Louisiana Reconstructed*, 168; S. B. Packard to William E. Chandler, October 30, 1868, Chandler MSS, LC.

43. Trelease, *White Terror*, 119–20; Singletary, *Negro Militia and Reconstruction*, 27–32, 119–21.

44. *Louisville (Ky.) Daily Journal*, November 4, 1868; *Savannah Daily News and Herald*, April 3, 4, 1868; *Missouri Republican*, July 18, 1868; *Memphis Daily Appeal*, October 28, 1868; "Louisiana Contested Elections," pt. 1, p. 362; *NYW*, November 2, 1868.

45. Robert K. Scott to General E. R. S. Canby, September 8, 1868, Scott MSS, OHS; Joseph McWhorter to Jno. J. Knox, Rufus Bullock MSS, Governor's Papers, GDAH; Trelease, *White Terror*, 130–31; "Louisiana Contested Elections," pt. 1, p. 310.

46. Abbott, *Republican Party and the South*, 195; Thomas L. Tullock to John Eaton, September 19, 1868, Eaton MSS, HoL; Tullock to William E. Chandler, October 13, 1868, Chandler MSS, LC; William E. Chandler to William Sprague, October 16, 1868, Sprague MSS, Columbia University, New York.

47. Coleman, *Election of 1868*, 352–53; Gambill, *Conservative Ordeal*, 150–52.

48. Mitchell, *Horatio Seymour of New York*, 471–74; Richardson, *West from Appomattox*, 89; Trescott, "Federal Government Receipts and Expenditures," 207; Alexander T. Stewart to William E. Chandler, October 20, 1868, Chandler MSS, NHHS; William E. Chandler to Jay Cooke, September 19, 1868, Cooke MSS, HSP; William E. Chandler memorandum of moneys paid, n.d. [1868], Claflin MSS, RBHL.

49. Abbott, *Republican Party and the South*, 201; Gambill, *Conservative Ordeal*, 152; Silbey, *Respectable Minority*, 217–27; Green, *Peculiar Imbalance*, 147–48; W. H. Kemble to Elihu Washburne, November 4, 1868, Washburne MSS, LC.

50. T. J. Barnett to Samuel L. M. Barlow, November 6, 1868, Barlow MSS, HuL.

Chapter Seven

1. Fairman, *Reconstruction and Reunion,* pt. 1, 628–43; Hyman, *Reconstruction Justice*, 143–50.

2. McPherson, *Struggle for Equality*, 424–27; Davis, *"We Will Be Satisfied with Nothing Less,"* 62–66; Gillette, *Right to Vote*, 46–78; "D. W. B.," *Independent*, March 4, 1869.

3. John Russell Young to William E. Chandler, December 22, 1868, Chandler MSS, NHHS; Chandler to William C. Claflin, February 2, 1869, Claflin MSS, RBHL.

4. Lowell, "A Look Before and After," 266–67; Adams, "The Session," 619; *Newark Daily Advertiser*, February 8, 1869; "H. V. B.," *CinGaz*, February 19, September 24, 1869; *NYEP*, February 19, 1872; *Nation*, November 7, 1872. On the liberal Republican movement's long heritage and ideological implications, see Slap, *Doom of Reconstruction*, 25–90, and Cohen, *Reconstruction of American Liberalism*, 45–59, 110–17.

5. McFeely, *Grant*, 290–94; *CinCom*, March 6, 7, 9, 1869; William D. Kelley to Carrie Kelley, March 7, 1869, Kelley MSS, HSP.

6. "The Cabinet," *Harper's Weekly*, March 20, 1869; McFeely, *Grant*, 294–302; Nevins, *Hamilton Fish*, 109–15; *Commercial and Financial Chronicle*, March 13, 1869; Pitt Cooke to Jay Cooke, March 11, 1869, and Jay Cooke to Henry D. Cooke, December 15, 1870, Cooke MSS, HSP.

7. *Nation*, May 6, 20, July 1, 1869; "H. V. B.," *CinGaz*, April 2, 1869; "Gath," *ChiTrib*, January 6, 1870, February 18, 1872; *CinCom*, October 14, 1869; Hesseltine, *Ulysses S. Grant*, 150–56, 192–93, 209–15; Nevins, *Hamilton Fish*, 372–83.

8. Alexander T. Stewart to Samuel J. Tilden, August 27, 1866, Tilden MSS, NYPL; R. Plumb to James A. Garfield, March 10, 1869, Garfield MSS, LC; Nevins, *Hamilton Fish*, 743–58.

9. Hesseltine, *Ulysses S. Grant, Politician*, 153, 181; *NNE*, October 20, 27, November 3, December 1, 1870.

10. Moneyhon, *Republicanism in Reconstruction Texas*, 104–7; *NYTrib*, May 24, July 24, 1869.

11. Ellem, "Overthrow of Reconstruction in Mississippi," 179–86.

12. Conwell, *Magnolia Journey*, 15; *Richmond (Va.) Daily Dispatch*, January 2, March 17, 22, 1869; Jonathan R. Jackson to Waitman T. Willey, March 19, 1869, Willey MSS, WVC; Maddex, *Virginia Conservatives*, 73.

13. Barclay, *Liberal Republican Movement in Missouri*, 183.

14. Gooden, "Completion of a Revolution," 265, 272; Kohl, "Enforcing a Vision of Community," 298.

15. Gooden, "Completion of a Revolution," 267.

16. Granville D. Hall to Charles Sumner, September 14, 1869, Hall MSS, WVC.

17. Parker, "Tennessee Gubernatorial Elections," 39–40; John Williams to Andrew Johnson, May 1869, Johnson MSS, LC; "Y. S.," *CinGaz*, June 7, 1869; *Memphis Daily Post*, May 22, June 2, 1869; L. B. Eaton to John Eaton, June 2, 1869, and W. H. Stilwell to John Eaton, June 10, 11, 16, July 8, 1869, Eaton MSS, HoL.

18. W. H. Stilwell to John Eaton, June 11, July 8, 1869, Eaton MSS, HoL; John Williams to Andrew Johnson, July 6, 1869, Johnson MSS, LC; *CinGaz*, August 3, 6, 7, 1869; "Y. S.," *CinGaz*, July 17, 28, 1869; "Myron," *CinGaz*, August 2, 5, 1869; Parker, "Tennessee Gubernatorial Elections," 34–48.

19. Maddex, *Virginia Conservatives*, 73.

20. *Richmond (Va.) Daily Dispatch*, January 4, 6, 7, 1869; Maddex, *Virginia Conservatives*, 69–70.

21. Lowe, *Republicans and Reconstruction*, 166–67; "Y. S.," *CinGaz*, June 30, 1869; *CinEnq*, July 3, 1869; *Richmond (Va.) Daily Dispatch*, March 10, 11, 12, 13, 15, 16, 20, May 30, 31, 1869.

22. *NYTrib*, May 22, July 8, 14, 1869; Maddex, *Virginia Conservatives*, 76; Lowe, *Republicans and Reconstruction*, 170; Ulysses S. Grant message, in Simon, *Papers of Ulysses S. Grant*, 19:163–64; Hamilton Fish Diary, April 5, 1869, Fish MSS, LC.

23. Lowe, *Republicans and Reconstruction*, 173; *Richmond (Va.) Daily Dispatch*, April 12, 19, May 5, 15, 1869; *NYTrib*, May 3, 17, June 29, 1869.

24. *NYH*, July 6, 1869; Alexander H. H. Stuart to Horace Greeley, June 25, 1869, Greeley MSS, NYPL; *Richmond (Va.) Daily Dispatch*, June 10, 12, 1869; "R. J. H.," *CinGaz*, June 23, 1869; *NYTrib*, July 5, 1869; *CinEnq*, July 5, 1869.

25. *NYTrib*, July 14, 27, 1869; Blake, *William Mahone*, 108.

26. Downey, "Rebirth of Reform," 280; *Missouri Republican*, August 25, 1870; *ChiTrib*, October 4, 1870; *SprR*, July 1, 1870; B. Gratz Brown to James Rood Doolittle, October 17, 1870, Doolittle MSS, SHSW; *St. Louis (Mo.) Daily Democrat*, November 9, 10, 1870.

27. Harris, *Day of the Carpetbagger*, 238–61; *NYH*, August 12, 13, 1869; *NYTi*, October 23, 1869; Moneyhon, *Republicanism in Reconstruction Texas*, 113–26; *CinCom*, July 26, November 24, 1869.

28. Granville D. Hall to Carl Schurz, October 5, 1869, Schurz to Hall, October 8, 1869, and Hall to Charles Sumner, September 14, 1869, Hall MSS, WVC.

29. John Marshall Hagans to Waitman T. Willey, January 1, 1870, Willey MSS, WVC.

30. *NYTrib*, July 8, 9, 1869; *NYH*, July 8, 1869; "W. J. A.," *CinCom*, August 20, 1869; Gooden, "Completion of a Revolution," 293.

31. T. A. Bradford, A. G. Russell, and others to Jonathan M. Bennett, October 7, 1870, Bennett MSS, WVC; Granville D. Hall to Horace Greeley, October 3, 1870, Hall MSS, WVC; Gooden, "Completion of a Revolution," 299.

32. Moneyhon, *Republicanism in Reconstruction Texas*, 117–18; Carrier, "Political History of Texas," 377–82; Andrew J. Hamilton to W. W. Mills, June 1, 1869, Mills MSS, University of Texas, Austin.

33. Baum, *Shattering of Texas Unionism*, 189–226; William H. Fleming to Elisha Pease, July 8, 1869, A. J. Bryant to Pease, September 25, 1869, and E. M. Wheelock to Pease, April 11, 1869, Pease MSS, Austin Public Library.

34. Moneyhon, *Texas after the Civil War*, 110; Smallwood, *Time of Hope, Time of Despair*, 135–36.

35. *New Era* (Washington, D.C.), March 24, 1870; Naragon, "From Chattel to Citizen," 107–111; George M. Arnold to Charles Sumner, December 26, 1871, Sumner MSS, HU; Jones, "James L. Kemper," 402–12.

36. Grant, *The Way It Was in the South*, 228–29; *NNE*, January 26, March 16, 1871; *New Orleans Semi-Weekly Louisianian*, August 27, 1871; "Boanerges," *ChiTi*, September 1, 1870.

37. Murphy, *L. Q. C. Lamar, Pragmatic Patriot*, 114; William B. Figures to William H. Smith, July 26, 1870, Smith MSS, Governor's Papers, ADAH; *NYTrib*, May 31, June 14, 1871; Hamilton, *Reconstruction in North Carolina*, 453–54; *CG*, 42nd Cong., 1st sess., appendix, 171 (April 5, 1871).

38. Fairclough, "'Scalawags,' Southern Honor, and the Lost Cause"; Zuczek, *State of Rebellion*, 56–60; Trelease, *White Terror*; Rable, "But There Was No Peace."

39. Fitzgerald, "Ku Klux Klan," 186, 194–206; Poole, *Never Surrender*, 111; *NYTrib*, June 14, 1871; "Traveller," *Philadelphia Press*, March 17, 1868; Gorman, "'This Man Felker,'" 902–11.

40. Margaret M. Storey, "The Crucible of Reconstruction: Unionists and the Struggle for Alabama's Postwar Home Front," in Cimbala and Miller, *Great Task Remaining before Us*, 81–87; T. R. C. Hutton, "UnReconstructed Appalachia: The Persistence of War in Appalachia," in Slap, *Reconstructing Appalachia*, 71–90; "Report of Outrages Committed Upon Citizens of the State of Georgia from Jan. 1st to Nov. 15th, 1868," and Frank Watkins to W. H. Harrison and Barnes, April 25, 1870, Bullock MSS, Governor's Papers, GDAH.

41. *Louisville (Ky.) Daily Commercial*, January 7, 10, 12, July 9, 1871.

42. Trelease, *White Terror*, 354–66; James Martin et al. to William H. Smith, May 25, 1869, "Colored citizens of Tuscaloosa" to Smith, April 22, 1869, John H. Wager to Smith, July 3, 1869, and William B. Figures to Smith, July 26, 1869, Smith MSS, Governor's Papers, ADAH; *NYTrib*, May 2, 1871; Joseph Surratt to Governor Robert K. Scott, November 19, 1870, R. L. M. Camden to Scott, January 23, 1871, Scott MSS, Governor's Papers, South Carolina State Archives, Columbia.

43. Ku Klux Test., vol. 6 (Georgia, pt. 1), 12–13, 125, 405, 463; "Sheafe vs. Tillman," 46, 165; *Tuscaloosa (Ala.) Independent Monitor*, April 18, 1868; Gorman, "'This Man Felker,'" 906.

44. Ku Klux Test., vol. 6 (Georgia, pt. 1), 10, 93–94; vol. 10 (Alabama, pt. 3), 1548, 1739; Thomas C. Cass to Rufus Bullock, January 12, 1870, Bullock MSS, Governor's Papers, GDAH; Rawick, *American Slave*, supp., vol. 9, *Mississippi Narratives*, pt. 4, p. 1493; W. P. Carlin to Oliver O. Howard, September 28, 1868, roll 61: Letters Received, T-Y, July–December 1868, BRFAL.

45. W. P. Carlin to Oliver O. Howard, September 28, 1868, roll 61: Letters Received, T-Y, July–December 1868, BRFAL; Ku Klux Test., vol. 6 (Georgia, pt. 1), 2–13; Rawick, supp., ser. 2, *American Slave*, vol. 6, *Alabama and Indiana Narratives*, pp. 153, 218; Rawick, *American Slave*, supp., ser. 2, vol. 10, *Mississippi Narratives*, pt. 5, p. 2114; ser. 1, vol. 15, *North Carolina Narratives*, pt. 2, p. 334; supp., ser. 2,

Texas Narratives, pt. 1, pp. 144, 349, 394; Stagg, "Problem of Klan Violence"; *NYTi*, January 2, 1872; *Louisville (Ky.) Daily Commercial*, January 27, July 9, 1871.

46. James Elder affidavit, January 20, 1870, Bullock MSS, Governor's Papers, GDAH; "Report of Outrages Committed Upon Citizens of the State of Georgia, November 15, 1868, ibid.; Ku Klux Test., vol. 10 (Alabama, pt. 3), 1723; vol. 6 (Georgia, pt. 1), 40, 172; "Sheafe vs. Tillman," 214; Rawick, *American Slave*, supp., ser. 2, vol. 10, *Mississippi Narratives*, pt. 5, p. 2060; *Louisville (Ky.) Daily Commercial*, January 21, July 9, 25, 1871; Edwards, *Gendered Strife and Confusion*, 197–98; Poole, *Never Surrender*, 112; Clinton, "Bloody Terrain."

47. *Atlanta Constitution*, September 10, 1868; *Savannah Daily News and Herald*, January 11, 1868; *NYTrib*, May 2, 29, 1871; Parsons, "Klan Skepticism and Denial"; Coulter, *Civil War and Readjustment in Kentucky*, 360–61; Thompson, *Reconstruction in Georgia*, 365–70; Trelease, *White Terror*, 396.

48. *Louisville (Ky.) Daily Commercial*, July 14, 1871; *CinGaz*, March 27, 1869; *NYTi*, January 31, 1871, August 15, 1874; Weinfeld, "'More Courage than Discretion,'" 501–2.

49. Hahn, *Nation under Our Feet*, 281–83; Smith, "'Southern Violence' Reconsidered," 428, 563; O'Donovan, "Transforming Work," 418–19; Rawick, *American Slave*, supp., ser. 2, vol. 9, *Mississippi Narratives*, pt. 4, pp. 1355–56, 1563; vol. 8, *Arkansas Narratives*, pt. 1, p. 314.

50. W. P. Carlin to Oliver O. Howard, September 28, 1868, roll 61: Letters Received, T-Y, July–December 1868, BRFAL; *NYTrib*, May 8, 1871; Ku Klux Test., vol. 10 (Alabama, pt. 3), 1600, 1763; Jon W. Cheek to R. H. Atkinson, May 22, 1870, Bullock MSS, Governor's Papers, GDAH.

51. O'Donovan, "Transforming Work," 421–22; J. Murray Hoag to Colonel J. R. Lewis, November 9, 1868, Bullock MSS, Governor's Papers, GDAH.

52. *CinCom*, August 7, 1871.

53. "Affairs in the Late Insurrectionary States," minority report, 296, 308; majority report, 52–53; Ku Klux Test., vol. 10 (Alabama, pt. 3), 1642–43, 1859–60; Ku Klux Test., vol. 12 (Mississippi, pt. 2), 630–31, 869–72, 883, 1049.

54. "Affairs in the Late Insurrectionary States," majority report, 86–93, 99–100; subcommittee report, 285–87.

Chapter Eight

1. That recasting of westward expansion as part of a "Greater Reconstruction" finds an able expression in West, *Last Indian War*, xx–xxii, 95–97, 101–5, and West, "Reconstructing Race," 7–26.

2. Stanley, *Civil War in New Mexico*, 211–51; Utley, *Indian Frontier*, 72–86; Thompson, *Army and the Navajo*, 10–67.

3. Utley, *Indian Frontier*, 86–93.

4. Ibid., 93–105; McDermott, *Red Cloud's War*, 219–37.

5. *Pittsburgh Gazette*, July 30, 1868; Dippie, *Vanishing American*, 122–32; McFeely, *Grant*, 307–8.

6. *Nation*, October 31, 1867; *Newark Daily Advertiser*, December 30, 1868.

7. McFeely, *Grant*, 313; Oman, "Beginning of the End."

8. McFeely, *Grant*, 309–12; Priest, *Uncle Sam's Stepchildren*, 5–7; Genetin-Pilawa, "Ely Parker and the Contentious Peace Policy."

9. Priest, *Uncle Sam's Stepchildren*, 47–50; H. Craig Miner, "Francis A. Walker," in Kvasnicka and Viola, *Commissioners of Indian Affairs*, 135–39; Walker, "Indian Question," 337–50.

10. Angevine, *Railroad and the State*, 174–83; Priest, *Uncle Sam's Stepchildren*, 9.

11. Wooster, *Military and United States Indian Policy*, 47–51, 56–57; Smith, *View from Officers' Row*, 15–24; Leonard, "Red, White and the Army Blue"; Skelton, "Army Officers' Attitudes towards Indians"; Ellis, "Humanitarian Generals."

12. Wooster, *Military and United States Indian Policy*, 14–16; "Reduction of the Military Establishment," 9–13; Fowler, *Black Infantry in the West*, 114–39.

13. Angevine, *Railroad and the State*, 191–92; Wooster, *Military and United States Indian Policy*, 37–38.

14. Wooster, *Military and United States Indian Policy*, 127–33; Clark, *Then Came the Railroads*, 101–2; Dobak, "Killing the Canadian Buffalo"; Isenberg, "Toward a Policy of Destruction," 236.

15. Richardson, *Wounded Knee*, 47–48; Smit, "Frontier Army and Destruction of the Buffalo"; Dobak, "Army and the Buffalo"; Retzinger, "Framing the Tourist Gaze," 220; Isenberg, "Toward a Policy of Destruction," 236.

16. Limbaugh, *Rocky Mountain Carpetbaggers*, 86–92; Spence, *Territorial Politics and Government in Montana*, 80–87.

17. Milner, O'Connor, and Sandweiss, *Oxford History of the American West*, 292–93; "Gath," *ChiTrib*, February 26, 1871; Deutsch, *No Separate Refuge*, 17–20.

18. Shannon, *Farmer's Last Frontier*, 51–59; Athearn, *High Country Empire*, 185–86. On the Desert and Timber Culture Acts, see Webb, *Great Plains*, 412–13.

19. Overton, *Burlington West*, 284–85, 317, 352–57; De Bres, "Come to the 'Champagne Air,'" 120–22; Retzinger, "Framing the Tourist Gaze," 223; Wrobel, *Promised Lands*, 38–45; Brockett, *Our Western Empire*, 865; Miner, *West of Wichita*, 47–49.

20. Bowles, *Our New West*, 46–49; "Acorn," *Philadelphia Press*, July 24, 1868; *Pittsburgh Gazette*, July 30, 1868.

21. Webb, *Great Plains*, 207, 219–23; Milner, O'Connor, and Sandweiss, *Oxford History of the American West*, 255.

22. *CinEnq*, April 11, 1870; W. S. Banning to Jay Cooke, February 28, March 29, 1870, Cooke MSS, HSP; Zornow, *Kansas*, 124; Quastler, "Charting a Course," 26–28.

23. Mercer, "Taxpayers and Investors," 279–94; Mercer, "Land Grants to American Railroads"; Miner, *West of Wichita*, 33–34.

24. Gates, *Agriculture and the Civil War*, 375; Morton Rothstein, "America in the International Rivalry for the British Wheat Market, 1860–1914," in Scheiber, *United States Economic History*, 290–308.

25. Milner, O'Connor, and Sandweiss, *Oxford History of the American West*, 255–59; Webb, *Great Plains*, 298–309; *ChiTrib*, January 9, 1869; Williamson, *Growth of the American Economy*, 434–36.

26. Davis and Legler, "Government in the America Economy."

27. Jay Cooke to Henry D. Cooke, February 1, 1870, Cooke MSS, HSP; Green, "Diehard or Swing Man"; "Dixon," *BDA*, May 18, 1868; LaForte, "Gilded Age Senator"; "Pomeroy Investigation," 1–34, 40–45; McCabe, *Behind the Scenes in Washington*, 174–88; Summers, *Rum, Romanism, and Rebellion*, 232–35.

28. *SprWR*, September 6, 1872; T. W. Davenport to William Henry Smith, July 10, 1876, Smith MSS, OHS; Lamar, "Carpetbaggers Full of Dreams," 189–92; *NYTrib*, May 26, 1874; Larson, *New Mexico's Quest for Statehood*, 137–44; Jacobsen, "Excess of Law in Lincoln County," 134–51.

29. *Washington (D.C.) Capital*, December 10, 1871; H. Rept. 579, 44th Cong., 1st sess., i–xiii; Samuel Wilkeson to Jay Cooke, November 25, 1871, Cooke MSS, HSP; Reeves, *Gentleman Boss*, 216, 228–29.

30. Rosen, "Pueblo Indians and Citizenship," 13–18; Simon, *Papers of Ulysses S. Grant*, 26:208–15n., 329–32n.

31. "Gath," *New York Graphic*, March 4, 7, April 26, 1876; "Management of the War Department," 219–26, 237–50; William W. Belknap to Hugh Belknap, March 21, 1876, and Belknap to Anna, July 13, August 3, 1876, Belknap MSS, Princeton University Library.

32. Plummer, *Frontier Governor*, 95–98; McCabe, *Behind the Scenes in Washington*, 187; White, *Railroaded*, 114–18; *Dubuque (Iowa) Herald*, April 17, 1870; Summers, *Party Games*, 161–74.

33. Bain, *Empire Express*, 227–31, 272–75, 296–300, 606–7, 654–72; *Railway Times*, August 1, 1868, p. 241; Arrington, *Great Basin Kingdom*, 258–70.

34. White, *Railroaded*, 32–36; McCabe, *Behind the Scenes in Washington*, 258–59; but in Ames's defense, see Ames, *Pioneering the Union Pacific*, 454–59.

35. Athearn, *High Country Empire*, 187; Hawgood, *America's Western Frontiers*, 356; Charles S. Sargent, "The Protection of the Forests," *North American Review* 311 (October 1882): 400–401; Dick, *Lure of the Land*, 195–97, 228.

36. West, "Reconstructing Race," 18–21; Reese, "Cherokee Freedwomen," 285–87; Liestman, "Horizontal Inter-Ethnic Relations," 335–43; Paddison, *American Heathens*, 21; Green, *Peculiar Imbalance*, 171–72; Rusco, "Good Time Coming?," 80–89; Dippie, *Vanishing American*, 134; "Acorn," *Philadelphia Press*, July 24, 1868; *SprWR*, September 27, 1872.

37. Tong, *Chinese of America*, 21–23; Chen, "Internal Origins of Chinese Emigration"; Chen, *Chinese San Francisco*, 12–13.

38. Bowles, *Our New West*, 400–401; Chen, *Chinese of America*, 51–53, 67–71, 84, 109; Randall E. Rohe, "After the Gold Rush: Chinese Mining in the Far West, 1850–1890," in Dirlik, *Chinese on the American Frontier*, 10–13.

39. Wunder, "Chinese in Trouble," 36–40; Minturn, *Travels West*, 339; Paddison, *American Heathens*, 20–22, 83–86, 124–31; Chen, *Chinese of America*, 137–39; Peffer, "Forbidden Families."

40. Simon, *Papers of Ulysses S. Grant*, 26:161–62.

41. Wooster, *Military and United States Indian Policy*, 14.

42. Poor, *Manual of the Railroads of the United States, 1874–1875*, xliii.

43. Ransom and Sutch, *One Kind of Freedom*, 116–17; Doyle, *New Men, New Cities, New South*, 37–86.

44. Richardson, *West from Appomattox*, 79–81, 83; Robbins, *Colony and Empire*, 151.

45. Richardson, *West from Appomattox*, 117–20.

46. *New York Sun*, February 13, 1875; *Alabama State Journal*, March 27, 1869; John W. Forney to Justin Smith Morrill, May 27, 1870, Morrill MSS, LC; Woodward, *Reunion and Reaction*, 73–101.

Chapter Nine

1. Sexton, "Toward a Synthesis of Foreign Relations in the Civil War Era"; Mark M. Smith, "The Past as a Foreign Country: Reconstruction Inside and Out," in Brown, *Reconstruction*, 117–40.

2. Roark, *Masters without Slaves*, 124–30; Evans, *Judah P. Benjamin*, 372–83; Joseph D. Shields to Mary J. Conway, September 23, 1865, and Shields to his wife, April 23, 1866, Shields MSS, LSU; James Purviance to James A. Gillespie, March 18, 1866, Gillespie MSS, LSU; Clark, *Gettysburg*, 17. Most expatriates came home eventually, and as Congressman Job Stevenson of Ohio noted in 1872, some of them came at the U.S. government's expense. "Thus, while other nations banish men for rebellion, the United States brings the self-banished home," he remarked. See *New Era* (Washington, D.C.), July 28, 1870; "Affairs in the Late Insurrectionary States," subcommittee report, 248.

3. Keller, *Affairs of State*, 85–86.

4. Ibid., 86.

5. Schoonover, *Mexican Lobby*, 95–99.

6. *NYTi*, October 16, 1865, January 8, 1866; Schoonover, *Dollars over Dominion*; Summers, *Dangerous Stir*, 161–68; Simpson, *Let Us Have Peace*, 152–60; Ibsen, *Maximilian, Mexico, and the Invention of Empire*, 51–81.

7. Montgomery Blair to Samuel L. M. Barlow, July 16, 1865, Barlow MSS, HuL; F. L. Claiborne to William N. Whitehurst, June 24, 1865, Whitehurst MSS, MDAH.

8. Dulles, *America in the Pacific*, 85–86; Van Deusen, *William Henry Seward*, 537–49; Locke, *Nasby Letters*, 78–82; *CinGaz*, July 24, 1867; Donald, *Charles Sumner and the Rights of Man*, 304–10.

9. May, *Manifest Destiny's Underworld*, 71–74, 178–82, 215–48; May, *Southern Dream of a Caribbean Empire*.

10. Nevins, *War for the Union: Improvised War*, 57–64.

11. Keller, *Affairs of State*, 91; *SprWR*, January 4, 18, 1868; Van Deusen, *William Henry Seward*, 528–36; Shippee, *Canadian-American Relations*, 200; Tansill, *Purchase of the Danish West Indies*, 150–79. The best case for Seward as a coherent expansionist can be found in Paolino, *Foundations of the American Empire*.

12. Harrington, *Fighting Politician*, 176–77; Smith, *Republican Expansionists*; "Gath," *ChiTrib*, June 7, 1870; *Pomeroy's Democrat*, February 21, 1875; Keller, *Affairs of State*, 91, 94; see also U. S. Department of State, *Papers Relating to the Foreign Relations of the United States*, 859–63.

13. Van Deusen, *William Henry Seward*, 527–28; *Independent*, July 18, 1867; *Nation*, April 21, 1870; *BDA*, January 2, 1868.

14. Dulles, *America in the Pacific*, 98–107; Chapin, "Hamilton Fish and American Expansionism," 314–18; *Portland (Maine) Eastern Argus*, May 25, 1874; Simon, *Papers of Ulysses S. Grant*, 20:160–61. Nothing can replace Allan Nevins's superb (if occasionally superbly misleading) biography, *Hamilton Fish*, but Fish's expansionist inclinations and their frustration get their best coverage in Chapin's "Hamilton Fish and American Expansionism."

15. *NYH*, January 12, 1869; Mecker, *Innocent Abroad*, 238–39; Wilkins, *Charles Dickens in America*, 263–68; *NNE*, January 12, 1871; Nevins and Thomas, *Diary of George Templeton Strong*, 4:502 (November 21, 1873).

16. *New Era* (Washington, D.C.), February 3, 1870; *NNE*, February 5, 1874; For an exception, see W. Ulhf to Ulysses S. Grant, July 25, 1869, in Simon, *Papers of Ulysses S. Grant*, 19:492–93. On lingering colonizationist efforts, see *NNE*, January 19, 1871, December 19, 1872, February 13, 27, March 13, 1873.

17. William F. Weld to Benjamin F. Butler, April 2, 1870, Butler MSS, LC.

18. Peterson, "Navy in the Doldrums," 12–15.

19. Ibid., 37–40.

20. Bartlett, "Not Merely for Defense," 31; Peterson, "Navy in the Doldrums," 50–67. On Borie and Robeson, see "Gath," *CinEnq*, February 21, 1877, September 7, 9, 1888; *NYH*, January 10, 1871.

21. *NYTi*, April 23, September 18, 20, 1870; Bartlett, "Not Merely for Defense," 24–29; Peterson, "Navy in the Doldrums," 83–93, 96. For the figures in late 1873, see *NYTi*, November 15, December 7, 1873. On the *Inflexible*, with full description of this iron "armored castle," see *NYTi*, August 22, 1875.

22. Bradford, *Virginius Crisis*; Peterson, "Navy in the Doldrums," 70–71; *NYTi*, November 23, 25, 26, December 9, 15, 1873; Nevins and Thomas, *Diary of George Templeton Strong*, 4:502 (November 22, 1873). On the size of the Spanish navy, which by 1875 ranked fifth in the world, see *NYTi*, March 8, 1875.

23. *SprWR*, December 18, 1869; *NYW*, January 14, 1870; *CinGaz*, November 30, December 1, 1870; *NYTrib*, January 6, 1871.

24. Warner, *Idea of Continental Union*, 46–59, 65–71, 87–95; Kaufman, *Origins of Canadian and American Political Differences*, 220–28; Irwin, *Pacific Railways and Nationalism*, 61–100.

25. Shippee, *Canadian-American Relations*, 213–39; Snay, *Fenians, Freedmen, and Southern Whites*, 55–57, 62–67, 171; Chapin, "Hamilton Fish and American Expansionism," 397–401; Warner, *Idea of Continental Union*, 104–25.

26. Donald, *Charles Sumner and the Rights of Man*, 374–78.

27. Eugene V. Smalley to James A. Garfield, May 22, 1869, Garfield MSS, LC; "H. V. B.," *CinGaz*, April 19, 1869; *NYH*, January 18, 1870; Chapin, "Hamilton Fish and American Expansionism," 401–12.

28. *SprWR*, September 25, 1869; Cook, *Alabama Claims*, 194–205.

29. Nevins, *Hamilton Fish*, 143–49.

30. *NYTrib*, February 6, 7, 8, 9, 13, 14, 17, 27, 1872; entry, February 6, 23, 1872, Fish Diary, Fish MSS, LC.

31. It had political advantages in one other particular. In February 1872, Sumner called for an investigation of the War Department's arms sales to parties who were

sending them to France during the Franco-Prussian War. If the department had acted knowledgeably, it would have committed a violation of neutrality equivalent to that which the British had committed in letting the *Alabama* be built. In addition, Sumner and Republicans, out of sympathy with Grant's administration, suspected payoffs to administration hangers-on and a cavalier disregard for a law that Congress had passed to restrict the department's arms sales—neither of which they could prove. With negotiations over the *Alabama* claims in crisis, administration supporters could accuse Sumner and his allies of being unpatriotic and handing the British an argument that could free them from all liability. Moreover, they warned, the revelations were sure to anger Germany, and the Germans supplied one of the arbiters at Geneva. In the end, administration senators stacked an investigating committee to find as little as possible and excuse what little turned up. Sumner got no place on it. See *CG*, 42nd Cong., 2nd sess., February 12th through March 1st, particularly pp. 1286–88 (February 29, 1872). See also "The Sale of Arms Debate," *Harper's Weekly*, March 16, 1872, p. 202.

32. Sexton, *Debtor Diplomacy*; Chapin, "Hamilton Fish and American Expansionism," 425–26; Henry D. Cooke to Jay Cooke, February 9, 10, May 8, 9, 13, 14, 1872, and Pitt Cooke to Jay Cooke, May 14, 1872, Cooke MSS, HSP; *ChiTrib*, February 19, 1872. On the recognition that America's navy was no match for Britain's in a crisis, see an exhaustive article on our vessels in *CinEnq*, February 6, 1872.

33. Schwartz, *Lawless Liberators*, 41–44; *NYTrib*, June 17, 1870.

34. "A.," *SprWR*, October 2, 23, 1869; Nevins, *Hamilton Fish*, 231–48.

35. *SprWR*, September 25, 1869; Chapin, "Hamilton Fish and American Expansionism," 249–90; Foner, *History of Cuba*, 2:246; *Washington (D.C.) Capital*, March 16, 1873.

36. *NYH*, January 27, 1873; *NYTrib*, January 6, 9, 1873; Chapin, "Hamilton Fish and American Expansionism," 512–38.

37. *Nation*, July 6, 20, 1871; Change, "Whose 'Barbarism'? Whose 'Treachery'?"

38. Keller, *Affairs of State*, 92.

39. *SprWR*, December 18, 1869; Keller, *Affairs of State*, 94.

40. *NNE*, March 10, 1870, February 2, March 2, 1871; Simon, *Papers of Ulysses S. Grant*, 20:74–75, 155–56.

41. Nevins, *Hamilton Fish*, 250–52; *NYTi*, February 8, 1869; see also *Hartford Daily Courant*, December 13, 1872; and Love, *Race over Empire*, 27–72.

42. *NNE*, January 12, 1871; A stimulating study of the egalitarian case for annexation can be found in Guyatt, "America's Conservatory." See also Samuel Gridley Howe's "Justice for Santo Domingo," *Independent*, September 21, 1871, p. 4.

43. Holbo, *Tarnished Expansion*, 27–29, 48–71; "Gath," *ChiTrib*, February 25, 1869; H. Rept. 35, "Alaska," 19–20; on the Stevens story, which was balderdash, see Korngold, *Thaddeus Stevens*, 430–33.

44. *NYTi*, February 4, 1870 (speech); *NYTrib*, June 10, 17, 1870; *SprR*, June 10, 17, 1870; *ChiTrib*, June 16, 1870; *Nation*, January 7, 1869. On the persistence of Cuban bonds, see *Portland (Maine) Eastern Argus*, May 16, 1874; *CinEnq*, August 22, 1877.

45. *NYTi*, February 11, 1869; "Gath," *ChiTrib*, January 17, 1871. The book was called *The Camel Hunt*. William Cazneau appeared as Tom Eddington, Jane Cazneau as Jane Eddington, with Fabens as Joseph Warrener. On Cazneau's

authorship of this and other books credited to Fabens, see Hudson. "Jane McManus Storm Cazneau," 181–83, 295–97; Donald, *Charles Sumner and the Rights of Man*, 439–40. Two revealing interviews with Fabens appear in "Gath," *ChiTrib*, January 16, 17, 1871.

46. Nevins, *Hamilton Fish*, 303–5; *Louisville (Ky.) Courier-Journal*, February 9, 17, 1870.

47. Nevins, *Hamilton Fish*, 264–70; *NYW*, March 10, 1870; *NYTrib*, March 18, 22, 23, 1870; Simon, *Papers of Ulysses S. Grant*, 20:164.

48. Nevins, *Hamilton Fish*, 372–83; Donald, *Charles Sumner and the Rights of Man*, 477–80; *CinGaz*, December 22, 1870.

49. Hamilton Fish to Richard Smith, March 25, 1871, Fish MSS, LC; Donald, *Charles Sumner and the Rights of Man*, 484–86, 493–96; Cook, *Alabama Claims*, 192–93; Henry Adams to Charles Milnes Gaskell, April 19, 1869, Adams, *Letters*, 25.

50. "Gath," *ChiTrib*, March 30, 1871; *NYW*, March 8, 10, 1871; *NYH*, March 13, 1871; Donald, *Charles Sumner and the Rights of Man*, 491–92; "Gath," *ChiTrib*, March 21, 1871.

51. Steiner, "'To Save the Constitution,'" 306–7.

Chapter Ten

1. Keller, *Affairs of State*, 46.

2. Hyman, *More Perfect Union*, 136–40; Arrington, *Great Basin Kingdom*, 108–30, 216–31; Keller, *Affairs of State*, 177.

3. Keller, *Affairs of State*, 111–12; Thompson, "Illinois Constitutions," 197; Mohr, *Radical Republicans and Reform*; Morton, "Ohio's Gallant Fight," 6.

4. West, *Last Indian War*, 103–4; Fishlow, "Levels of Nineteenth-Century American Investment"; Morton, "Ohio's Gallant Fight," 9; Keller, *Affairs of State*, 133–34; Mohr, "Free School Law of 1867," 248; Blackburn, "Michigan," 133. Spending for schools, private as well as public, rose from $34.7 million to $106.4 million.

5. "H. V. N. B.," *CinGaz*, June 14, 22, 1866; *NYTrib*, June 9, 20, 1866, February 27, 1867; McAfee, "Reconstruction Revisited," 133–42.

6. Hyman, *More Perfect Union*, 358; Blackburn, "Michigan," 133.

7. Clark, *Then Came the Railroads*, 77–78; Keller, *Affairs of State*,165–67; Kirkland, *Men, Cities, and Transportation*, 387–432, 454–55.

8. Kirkland, *Industry Comes of Age*, 117–20; Woodman, "Chicago Businessmen"; McAfee, "Local Interests and Railroad Regulation"; *Kankakee Gazette*, March 20, 1873; Ridge, *Ignatius Donnelly*, 158–64; *Milwaukee News*, March 3, 1874; Miller, *Railroads and the Granger Laws*, 93–95, 116, 129–34, 156–60.

9. Hyman, *More Perfect Union*, 341–42, 356–57; Jentz and Schneirov, *Chicago in the Age of Capital*, 81–109; Kingsbury, *Labor Laws and Their Enforcement*, 93–125; Keller, *Affairs of State*, 169–70; Montgomery, *Beyond Equality*, 176–96, 296–320; Blackburn, "Michigan," 135.

10. Hyman, *More Perfect Union*, 315–23; Carrigan, "Yankees versus Yellow Jack in New Orleans"; Jackson, *New Orleans in the Gilded Age*, 145, 153–56.

11. Mohr, *Radical Republicans and Reform*, 61–114; Hyman, *More Perfect Union*, 330–36.

12. Bremner, *Public Good*, 152–85.

13. Hyman, *More Perfect Union*, 336–38; *NYW*, August 17, 1867; *NYH*, February 12, 1866, January 1, 13, 1877; *BDA*, January 16, 1873; *New Hampshire Patriot* (Concord), May 14, 1873; *ChiTrib*, January 6, 7, 1872.

14. Broun and Leech, *Anthony Comstock*, 16–35, 128–69; Boyer, *Purity in Print,* 2–15; Hyman, *More Perfect Union*, 339–40, 392–93.

15. Arrington, *Great Basin Kingdom*, 356–58; Gordon, *Mormon Question*, 58–68, 111–16, 172–81.

16. *Milwaukee Wisconsin*, June 15, 1866; *Independent*, March 5, 1874; *CinCom*, February 16, 1874; *CinEnq*, September 25, 1871.

17. *Appleton's Annual Cyclopedia and Register* (1875), 398, 475–76; *Independent*, February 19, 1874; *SprWR*, August 9, 1872; *CinEnq*, September 25, 27, 1871; *CinCom*, February 27, 1874; *Arkansas Gazette*, May 19, 1867.

18. *CinCom*, March 29, 1874; Ohio Constitutional Convention, *Debates*, 2921 (April 21, 1874); Dannenbaum, *Drink and Disorder*, 216–17.

19. Dannenbaum, *Drink and Disorder*, 223–27; *Des Moines Iowa State Register*, April 1, 1874; *CinCom*, February 24, March 11, 13, 1874; Garner, "'Prayerful Public Protest.'"

20. Foner, *Reconstruction*, 364–65, 372–74.

21. Ranney, *In the Wake of Slavery*, 94–97; Vaughn, *Schools for All*, 51–54; McGraw, "Texas Constitution of 1866," 175–78; Bell, "Samuel S. Ashley," 476.

22. Bell, "Samuel S. Ashley," 477–79; Balanoff, "Negro Legislators," 35; Williamson, *After Slavery*, 229; Vaughn, *Schools for All*, 59; Wakefield, "'Set a Light in a Dark Place,'" 416–17.

23. *CinCom*, April 8, 1872.

24. The five states ending segregation postwar were Connecticut, Minnesota, Iowa, Kansas, and Rhode Island. See Davis, *"We Will Be Satisfied with Nothing Less,"* 107–8, 118–24; McPherson, "Abolitionists and the Civil Rights Act of 1875," 498–99; Vaughn, *Schools for All*, 55–56.

25. Harlan, "Desegregation in the New Orleans Public Schools," 663–75; Vaughn, *Schools for All*, 89–90; Williamson, *After Slavery*, 233.

26. *Alabama State Journal*, May 29, 1874; Rabinowitz, "From Exclusion to Segregation," 328–32; Masur, *Example for All the Land*, 127–31, 160–63; McPherson, "Abolitionists and the Civil Rights Act of 1875," 495–98; *New Era* (Washington, D.C.), January 13, May 5, 1870; "P. H. C.," *NNE*, February 23, 1871, "Civis," ibid., January 18, 1872; *New Orleans Semi-Weekly Louisianian*, January 19, April 6, May 25, 1871; Williamson, *After Slavery*, 176, 284.

27. Williamson, *After Slavery*, 277–78, 283; Botume, *First Days among the Contrabands*, 267–69; "S. D.," *NYW*, April 28, 1871; *New Era* (Washington, D.C.), June 2, 16, 1870; "Civis," *NNE*, April 4, 25, 1871; Vincent, *Black Legislators in Louisiana*, 92–97; *New Orleans Semi-Weekly Louisianian*, March 2, 1871.

28. Flexner, *Century of Struggle*, 122–27, 151; Butcher, *Education for Equality*, 33–44; Kantrowitz, *More than Freedom*, 334–35; Lebsock, "Radical Reconstruction and the Property Rights"; Bercaw, *Gendered Freedoms*, 173–75; Ray, "Impact of Statehood and Republican Politics," 93.

29. Hyman, *More Perfect Union,* 309–10, 325.

30. *New Orleans Semi-Weekly Louisianian*, February 23, 26, 1871; Fairman, *Mr. Justice Miller*, 180–86; Hyman and Wiecek, *Equal Justice under Law*, 473–80, 492; Maltz, *Fourteenth Amendment*, 90–105; Ross, "Justice Miller's Reconstruction." On Miller's strong support for the Fourteenth Amendment's power to protect black civil rights, see Ross, *Justice of Shattered Dreams*, 202–10, 246–50.

31. Fairman, *Reconstruction and Reunion, 1864–1888, Part Two*, 327–71; Beth, *Development of the American Constitution*, 169–83.

32. Keller, *Affairs of State*, 133; Hyman, *More Perfect Union*, 387–90. For arguments against such a measure, see *CR*, 43rd Cong., 1st sess., appendix, 70–74 (February 28, 1874).

33. Hyman, *More Perfect Union*, 381–85, 402–5. On cholera, see ibid., 393–97.

34. Martin Foran, in Ohio Constitutional Convention, *Debates*, 1866–67; *NYW*, January 29, 1870.

35. Flexner, *Century of Struggle*, 160–63; "Suffrage in Utah," 1; *ChiTrib*, October 1, 1867.

36. McKenna, "'With the Help of God and Lucy Stone,'" 13–26; "Susan B. Anthony," 1–8; Flexner, *Century of Struggle*, 143, 165–70.

37. Norgren, *Belva Lockwood*, 43–45, 73–83.

38. Flexner, *Century of Struggle*, 144–45; Dudden, *Fighting Chance*, 61–87, 89–102.

39. Dudden, *Fighting Chance*, 162–82; Riegel, "Split of the Feminist Movement in 1869"; Masur, *Example for All the Land*, 179–84; *Charleston (S.C.) Daily Republican*, January 25, 1870; *Republican Standard*, October 30, 1869; *NYW*, May 13, 1870, January 12, 1871.

40. *Bangor (Maine) Whig and Courier* July 20, 1866; *NYW*, July 1, 1865, June 17, 1870; *CG*, 39th Cong., 2nd sess., pt. 1, p. 79 (December 12, 1866); *Nation*, November 25, 1869, April 28, 1870, April 21, 1871; "Raconteur," *New Orleans Times*, December 19, 1866; *ClPD*, July 24, 1874.

41. Paddison, *American Heathens*, 80–83; Kleppner, *Third Electoral System*, 219–34.

42. Kleppner, *Third Electoral System*, 215–17, 232–34; National Council of the Union League of America, November 18, 1875, Adelbert Ames, Governor's Papers, MDAH.

43. Foner, *Free Soil, Free Labor, Free Men*, 227–42.

44. Kleppner, *Third Electoral System*, 211–17; Keller, *Affairs of State*, 139; McAfee, "Reconstruction Revisited," 137–39; *CinCom*, March 11, 1874; *Nation*, August 12, 1869; *NYTrib*, February 5, 1874; *Milwaukee News*, July 27, 1874; *Des Moines Iowa State Register*, April 1, 1874.

45. Kleppner, *Third Electoral System*, 128–42; Jentz and Schneirov, *Chicago in the Age of Capital*, 145–54; Green, "National Reform Association," 82–91; McAfee, "Reconstruction Revisited," 145–47.

Chapter Eleven

1. Simpson, *Reconstruction Presidents*, 143–44.

2. Harris, *Day of the Carpetbagger*, 264–66; Dray, *Capitol Men*, 60–61, 70–76, 172–78; Napton Diary, February 25, 1870, Missouri Historical Society, Columbia;

Nevins and Thomas, *Diary of George Templeton Strong*, 4:278 (March 17, 1870); *NNE*, February 16, 23, November 30, 1871, January 2, 1873.

3. Vincent, *Black Legislators in Louisiana*, 71, 82; Wharton, *Negro in Mississippi*, 168–72; Barr, "Black Legislators of Reconstruction Texas," 342; Moneyhon, *Republicanism in Reconstruction Texas*, 277; Balanoff, "Negro Legislators," 23; Holt, "Negro State Legislators in South Carolina," 329; Hahn, *Nation under Our Feet*, 239–45.

4. Foner, *Freedom's Lawmakers*, xiii–xviii; "S. D.," *NYW*, April 28, 1871; "H. V. R.," *CinCom*, July 31, 1874; Williamson, *After Slavery*, 330; Oldfield, "On the Beat," 154–58.

5. Simpson, *Reconstruction Presidents*, 144; Adams, "The Session" (1870), 29–62; *Daily Davenport (Iowa) Democrat*, September 15, October 6, 1870; McPherson, *Struggle for Equality*, 427–30.

6. Nathans, *Losing the Peace*, 102–14, 122–26; *NYTrib*, September 9, 12, 15, 1868; *NYW*, September 8, 9, 10, 1868; H. Misc. Doc. 6, "Memorial of the Members of the Legislature of Georgia and Others," 1; "Condition of Affairs in Georgia," 6.

7. *NYTi*, September 9, October 6, 1868; *NYW*, September 9, 10, 1868; *NYTrib*, September 9, 17, 21, 1868.

8. Formwalt, "Camilla Massacre of 1868"; John Davis affidavit, September 26, 1868, Lewis Smith affidavit, September 24, 1868, and Davis Sneed affidavit, September 25, 1868, roll 58: Letters Received, G-H, July–December 1868, BRFAL; Foster Blodgett to William E. Chandler, September 13, 1868, Chandler MSS, LC.

9. W. C. Morrill to "dear General," November 2, 1868, Bullock MSS, Governor's Papers, GDAH; Nathans, *Losing the Peace*, 144–46; "Condition of Affairs in Georgia," 12, 63–67. 80–81; "Affairs in the Late Insurrectionary States," pt. 6, pp. 454–59; Jaset Jackson memo, n. d. [but relating to the 1868 Randolph County election], Bullock MSS, Governor's Papers, GDAH.

10. "Reconstruction of Georgia," 3–4; *CG*, 41st Cong., 2nd sess., 208–9 (December 17, 1869), 276, 279, 281, 284 (December 21, 1869); Jesse H. Moore to Richard J. Oglesby, January 2, 1870, Oglesby MSS, ISHS.

11. Nathans, *Losing the Peace*, 172–79; Rufus Bullock order, January 19, 1870, Bullock MSS, Governor's Papers, GDAH; "Reconstruction of Georgia," 5–28; entry, April 28, 1870, Knight Diary, GDAH.

12. "Georgia Investigation," 5–8.

13. *CG*, 41st Cong., 2nd sess., 1994 (March 16, 1870), 2423–24 (April 5, 1870).

14. Jesse H. Moore to Richard J. Oglesby, January 2, 1870, Oglesby MSS, ISHS; *ChiTrib*, April 16, 1870; *CG*, 41st Cong., 2nd sess., 2609 (April 12, 1870), 2641 (April 13, 1870), 2673 (April 14, 1870).

15. *NYW*, March 15, 1870; *CG*, 40th Cong., 3rd sess., 1036 (February 9, 1869); 41st Cong., 2nd sess., 2608–9 (April 12, 1870); "Gath," *ChiTrib*, March 25, 1870; *CinGaz*, April 19, 20, 1870; "Georgia Investigation," 1–8.

16. *Little Rock Republican*, March 16, 20, 1871; Pike, *Prostrate State*, 15, 33, 34. One can find regular denunciations of the legislature in the *San Antonio Express* of November 1871, the *Alabama State Journal* of February 1871 and April 1873, the *Port Royal (S.C.) Commercial* of late 1873 and early 1874, and the *Beaufort (S.C.) Republican* of late 1871. Democratic papers were still less guarded.

17. *NYW*, September 17, 1868; J. Rollins to James S. Rollins, December 26, 1872, Rollins MSS, Missouri Historical Society, Columbia; "H. V. R.," *CinCom*, July 27, 1874; *Tuscaloosa (Ala.) Independent Monitor*, July 28, 1868; Morgan, *Recollections of a Rebel Reefer*, 341.

18. Vincent, *Black Legislators in Louisiana*, 72; Holt, "Negro State Legislators in South Carolina," 232; King, *Great South*, 314–15; Hine, "Black Politicians in Reconstruction Charleston," 560–71; "H. V. R.," *CinCom*, July 29, 1874; Barr, "Black Legislators of Reconstruction Texas," 344–45.

19. Holt, "Negro State Legislators in South Carolina," 234.

20. Duncan, *Entrepreneur for Equality*, 111–15; Rufus Bullock to Benjamin F. Conley, February 21, 1872, Conley MSS, GDAH; "Mack," *Savannah Morning News*, October 11, 1870; *CinEnq*, March 19, 1870.

21. Seip, *South Returns to Congress*, 114–20, 220–37; Amos Akerman to James W. Patterson, January 12, 1870, Bryant MSS, Duke; "Gath," *ChiTrib*, February 18, 1869, June 27, 1870; *Louisville (Ky.) Courier-Journal*, March 10, 1870; "XL," *Louisville (Ky.) Courier-Journal*, February 27, March 2, 4, 12, 1870; Summers, "Radical Reconstruction and the Gospel of Prosperity," 412.

22. Krug, *Lyman Trumbull*, 285–86; *CG*, 41st Cong., 2nd sess., 2674 (April 14, 1870), 1926, 1928 (March 14, 1870).

23. Ibid., 2617 (April 12, 1870), 2674 (April 14, 1870).

24. Ibid., 2423 (April 5, 1870); "A Republican Form of Government," *Nation*, April 28, 1870.

25. Ibid., 391–93 (January 12, 1870), 2423–25 (April 5, 1870), 2612 (April 12, 1870), 2749, 2752–53 (April 18, 1870), appendix, 291–92 (April 19, 1870).

26. Ibid., 2612 (April 12, 1870), 2752 (April 18, 1870); W. H. Stilwell to John Eaton, March 15, April 6, 1870, and A. T. Bradley to —, January 31, 1870, Eaton MSS, HoL.

27. *ChiTrib*, April 5, 16, 1870.

28. *NYW*, June 24, 25, 1870; *Nation*, June 30, July 7, 14, 1870; *CG*, 41st Cong., 2nd sess., 5581 (July 14, 1870); Amos T. Akerman to William W. Belknap, August 6, 1870, Belknap MSS, Duke; entry, August 1, 1870, Knight Diary, GDAH; *NYTrib*, August 13, 1870; Nathans, *Losing the Peace*, 190–95.

29. *NNE*, December 29, 1870, January 26, 1871; Angell, "Black Minister Befriends the 'Unquestioned Father of Civil Rights'," 36–37; Rogers, "'Not Reconstructed by a Long Ways Yet,'" 272–77.

30. Conway, *Reconstruction of Georgia*, 212–14; Duncan, *Entrepreneur for Equality*, 36–44; Rufus B. Bullock to Benjamin F. Conley, October 26, 1871, Conley MSS, GDAH; Bowers, *Tragic Era*, 300–302.

31. Gorman, "'This Man Felker,'" 911–12; *Louisville (Ky.) Daily Commercial*, July 6, 1871.

32. Singletary, *Negro Militia and Reconstruction*, 39–41; Nunn, *Texas under the Carpetbaggers*, 43–45, 74; *NNE*, March 16, 1871; "Pulaski," *NNE*, March 23, 1871; Moneyhon, *Republicanism in Reconstruction Texas*, 139, 142–43.

33. Evans, *Ballots and Fence Rails*, 133–48; Massengell, "Detectives of William W. Holden"; "Phil," *NNE*, February 16, 1871; Brisson, "'Civil Government Was Crumbling Around Me.'"

34. Rubin, *South Carolina Scalawags*, 54–55; Singletary, *Negro Militia and Reconstruction*, 11–15; Blain, "Challenge to the Lawless," 119–32; Harris, *Day of the Carpetbagger*, 392–95.

35. Hennessey, "To Live and Die in Dixie," 165–81; *CG*, 42nd Cong., 1st sess., 518 (April 11, 1871), 820, 829 (April 19, 1871).

36. Swinney, "Suppressing the Ku Klux Klan," 160–63.

37. *CG*, 42nd Cong., 1st sess., 364, 367, 372 (March 31, 1871), 827–28 (April 19, 1871).

38. Krug, *Lyman Trumbull*, 297–99; *Nation*, April 13, 1871; James A. Garfield to Samuel Bowles, March 31, 1871, Garfield MSS, LC; *CG*, 42nd Cong., 1st sess., 575–79 (April 11, 1871); Theodore Cox to Jacob D. Cox, April 8, 1871, Cox MSS, Oberlin; Slap, "'Strong Arm of the Military Power,'" 146–63.

39. Swinney, "Suppressing the Ku Klux Klan," 165–66; *CG*, 42nd Cong., 1st sess., 368 (March 31, 1871), 389 (April 1, 1871), 477 (April 5, 1871).

40. Swinney, "Suppressing the Ku Klux Klan," 269; Shofner, *Nor Is It Over Yet*, 234; Trelease, *White Terror*, 404–10; Harris, *Day of the Carpetbagger*, 401–2; Zuczek, *State of Rebellion*, 101; S. Exec. Doc. 32, 42nd Cong., 3rd sess., 11.

41. Zuczek, *State of Rebellion*, 100–102; Zuczek, "Federal Government's Attack on the Ku Klux Klan"; Trelease, *White Terror*, 407–8; Harris, *Day of the Carpetbagger*, 400–404; Kaczorowski, *Politics of Judicial Interpretation*, 57–72.

42. Trelease, *White Terror*, 399; Stewart, "'When Darkness Reigns,'" 473–74; Fitzgerald, "Ku Klux Klan," 194–206; Michael W. Fitzgerald, "Extralegal Violence and the Planter Class: The Ku Klux Klan in the Alabama Black Belt during Reconstruction," in Waldrep and Nieman, *Local Matters*, 160–68; Kaczorowski, *Politics of Judicial Interpretation*, 82–87; Harris, *Day of the Carpetbagger*, 399, 405.

43. J. G. Tracy to William E. Chandler, March 14, 1872, Chandler MSS, LC; Webb, *Benjamin Helm Bristow*, 93.

44. Swinney, "Suppressing the Ku Klux Klan," 234–35, 317; Kaczorowski, *Politics of Judicial Interpretation*, 101–13; Williams, *Great South Carolina Ku Klux Klan Trials*, 122–27. The reasons for Akerman's fall remain unclear. See Nevins, *Hamilton Fish*, 591; Amos Akerman to Benjamin F. Conley, December 2, 28, 1871, Conley MSS, GDAH; Amos Akerman to J. R. Parrott, December 6, 1871, Amos Akerman Letter-Books, University of Virginia, Charlottesville; and *NYTrib*, December 16, 1871.

45. Poole, *Never Surrender*, 113–14; Simon, *Papers of Ulysses S. Grant*, 20:68n., 72n., 269n.; *Nation*, June 29, 1871.

Chapter Twelve

1. Ames, *Ten Years in Washington*, 67–69; J. B. Turner to Richard Yates, May 31, 1868, Yates MSS, ISHS; Blaine, *Twenty Years of Congress*, 2:548.

2. Ames, *Ten Years in Washington*, 72–75; *CR*, 43rd Cong., 1st sess., appendix, 121 (February 28, 1874).

3. "H. V. B.," *CinGaz*, October 15, 1870, June 26, 1871; Masur, *Example for All the Land*, 194–207, 215–17, 232–37; Green, *Washington*, 338–55.

4. Keller, *Affairs of State*, 101–5; Elazar, "Civil War and the Preservation of American Federalism," 44–47; Thompson, "Corruption—Or Confusion?," 172–78; Cummings, *Federal Justice*, 224–28.

5. Ames, *Ten Years in Washington*, 305, 307.

6. Ibid., 545–46.

7. Ibid., 412; White, *Republican Era*, 259.

8. Trescott, "Federal Government Receipts and Expenditures"; Sinisi, *Sacred Debts*, 174–75; Keller, *Affairs of State*, 102, 167.

9. Keller, *Affairs of State*, 101.

10. Green, *Washington*, 347–58; "Government of the District of Columbia," 2–28.

11. Masur, *Example for All the Land*, 250–61; S. Rept. 453, "Affairs in the District of Columbia," 43nd Cong., 1st sess., Shellabarger argument, 18–37; "Report of the Committee," 28–29.

12. Callow, *Tweed Ring*, 8–13, 28–29, 40–44, 123–24, 136–40, 166–71, 190–93, 199–205, 211–17; Ackerman, *Boss Tweed*, 169–70.

13. Callow, *Tweed Ring*, 155–57, 168; Ackerman, *Boss Tweed*, 66, 175; Burrows and Wallace, *Gotham*, 931.

14. Paine, *Th. Nast*, 137–205, 335–37; Ackerman, *Boss Tweed*, 157, 176; Callow, *Tweed Ring*, 276–78, 291–98; Burrows and Wallace, *Gotham*, 1011.

15. *New York Graphic*, May 10, 1876; "The New Jersey Monopolies," *North American Review* 104 (April 1867): 428–76; *ChiTrib*, March 12, 1873; *Philadelphia Inquirer*, March 28, 1870; "Gath," *ChiTrib*, February 26, 1870; *Kansas City Times*, August 23, 1876; Nevins and Thomas, *Diary of George Templeton Strong*, 4:481 (May 31, 1873); "Pickaway," *CinEnq*, February 15, 1875.

16. Summers, *Era of Good Stealings*, 48–59; Henry D. Cooke to Jay Cooke, February 3, 1872, and Jay Cooke to Henry D. Cooke, April 1, 1870, February 5, 1872, Cooke MSS; Ames, *Pioneering the Union Pacific*, 198–213.

17. *CG*, 41st Cong. 2nd sess., 1522–33 (February 23, 1870), 1616–18 (March 1, 1870); *Nation*, March 3, 10, 24, 1870; Adams, *Education of Henry Adams*, 261.

18. *NYEP*, February 19, 1872; Adams, *Education of Henry Adams*, 280.

19. Adams, *Education of Henry Adams*, 280. For a fuller antebellum account, see Summers, *Plundering Generation*.

20. Summers, *Era of Good Stealings*, 16–21.

21. *NYW*, January 1, 2, 28, 30, 1869; *New York Graphic*, March 3, 1876; *ChiTrib*, February 11, 1869, March 5, 1875.

22. Myers, *History of the Great American Fortunes*, 407–21; Adams, "A Chapter of Erie," 30–106. On the checks, see *Nation*, March 18, 1869. For a less sensational reading of the governor's motives, see Mohr, *Radical Republicans and Reform*, 276.

23. *CinCom*, October 20, 21, 1869. On the necessity for gold, see Wimmer, "Gold Crisis of 1869," 106–7.

24. Ackerman, *Gold Ring*; Klein, *Life and Legend of Jay Gould*, 87–109.

25. Thompson, "Corruption—Or Confusion?," 179–89; Summers, *Era of Good Stealings*, 108.

26. *SprR*, April 5, 1871; Current, *Those Terrible Carpetbaggers*, 243–45; John Ellis to Tom Ellis, March 6, 1869, Ellis Family MSS, LSU; Henry Clay Warmoth to John

Q. A. Fellows, May 9, 11, 1872, Fellows to Warmoth, May 11, 1872, and C. J. Jones to Warmoth, December 27, 1869, Warmoth MSS, SHC; *New Orleans Semi-Weekly Louisianian*, April 9, 1871.

27. Current, *Those Terrible Carpetbaggers*, 217–25; Pike, *Prostrate State*, 28; Democratic Party National Committee, *Campaign Text Book*, 427–34; "H. V. R.," *CinCom*, April 6, 1871, July 29, 31, 1874.

28. "H. V. R.," *CinCom*, April 6, 1871; Summers, *Era of Good Stealings*, 155; South Carolina Reports and Resolutions, *Fraud Report*, 1630–31, 1639–45; *ChaCou*, February 19, 1870; *NNE*, January 11, 1872; Wallace, *Carpet-Bag Rule in Florida*, 103–4; Evans, *Ballots and Fence Rails*, 162.

29. Current, *Those Terrible Carpetbaggers*, 243; Fitzgerald, "Railroad Subsidies and Black Aspirations," 250–53; *Raleigh (N.C.) Sentinel*, January 5, 1876; W. W. Howe to Henry Clay Warmoth, July 21, 1870, Warmoth MSS, SHC; *NNE*, March 14, 1872; *New Orleans Semi-Weekly Louisianian*, February 22, 25, 1872; R. Hutchinson to Alexander Long, May 27, 1871, Long MSS, Cincinnati Historical Society.

30. Price, "Railroads and Reconstruction in North Carolina," 22–27, 358–61; Fitzgerald, "Railroad Subsidies and Black Aspirations," 241–44; Bond, *Negro Education in Alabama*, 38–47; Summers, *Railroads, Reconstruction, and the Gospel of Prosperity*, 9, 32–39; Denmark, "'At the Midnight Hour.'"

31. H. Rept. 771, "Affairs in Arkansas," 149–51; Conway, *Reconstruction of Georgia*, 203–9; Price, "Railroads and Reconstruction in North Carolina," 361–69; Summers, *Railroads, Reconstruction, and the Gospel of Prosperity*, 40–45.

32. H. S. McComb to Henry Clay Warmoth, April 2, June 22, 1870, Warmoth MSS, SHC; *New Orleans Semi-Weekly Louisianian*, June 25, July 6, 9, 1871; Davis, "'Black an' Dusty, Goin' to Agusty,'" 207; Summers, *Railroads, Reconstruction, and the Gospel of Prosperity*, 47–58.

33. Summers, *Railroads, Reconstruction, and the Gospel of Prosperity*, 101–15, 121–25, 214–17; Price, "Railroads and Reconstruction in North Carolina," 407–14; Edwin Hill to Adelbert Ames, May 9, 1871, Ames Family MSS, Smith College Library, Northampton, Mass.; Oscar F. Hunsacker to Henry Clay Warmoth, March 22, 1872, Warmoth MSS, SHC; *Charleston (S.C.) Daily Republican*, February 25, March 10, 1871; South Carolina Reports and Resolutions, *Fraud Report*, 569–71, 1582–83.

34. *Charleston (S.C.) Daily Republican*, March 4, 6, 8, 1871; Current, *Those Terrible Carpetbaggers*, 217–21, 227–28.

35. Price, "Railroads and Reconstruction in North Carolina," 397–491; "Allegations against Senator Powell Clayton," 220–21, 225–27, 235–42; *Charleston (S.C.) Daily Republican*, March 19, 1870; Brown, "Carpetbagger Intrigues," 278–81. Osborn's railroad intrigues are further discussed in Weinfeld, "'More Courage than Discretion,'" 504–11.

36. Hollman and Murrey, "Alabama's State Debt History," 309–15; Price, "Railroads and Reconstruction in North Carolina," 552–68; Summers, *Railroads, Reconstruction, and the Gospel of Prosperity*, 196–207.

37. Degler, *Other South*, 256–60; Fitzgerald, "Republican Factionalism and Black Empowerment," 474–90; Pereyra, *James Lusk Alcorn*, 128–33, 135–44; Ellem, "Overthrow of Reconstruction in Mississippi," 186–87.

38. John E. Bryant to J. M. Edmunds, September 12, 1871, Bryant MSS, Duke; Brown, "Carpetbagger Intrigues," 277–92; for other impeachments, see Current, *Those Terrible Carpetbaggers*, 232–35, 240–42, 257–60.

39. Nystrom, *New Orleans after the Civil War*, 88; Warmoth, *War, Politics, and Reconstruction*, 165; Taylor, *Louisiana Reconstructed*, 180–82; Tunnell, *Crucible of Reconstruction*, 159–61; Powell, "Centralization and Its Discontents."

40. John Scollard to Thomas W. Conway, June 6, 1871, and J. R. West to Henry Clay Warmoth, March 6, 24, 30, April 2, 1871, Warmoth MSS, SHC; Warmoth, *War, Politics, and Reconstruction*, 112–18; Tunnell, *Crucible of Reconstruction*, 164–65.

41. Lonn, *Reconstruction in Louisiana after 1868*, 96–104; Singletary, *Negro Militia and Reconstruction*, 69–71; Warmoth, *War, Politics, and Reconstruction*, 118–49; E. John Ellis to Tom Ellis, January 22, 1872, Ellis Family MSS, LSU.

42. See, for example, Charles S. Evans to John E. Bryant, May 11, 1870, and Bryant to Horace Porter, May 21, 28, 1870, Bryant MSS, Duke; Isaac Seely to William E. Chandler, March 25, 1872, Chandler MSS, LC.

43. James Bintliff to Elisha W. Keyes, February 6, 1877, Keyes MSS, SHSW; *Philadelphia Inquirer*, April 8, 1870; "A Third Stage of Constitution-Making," *Nation*, April 17, 1873, p. 265.

44. Bridges, "Managing the Periphery in the Gilded Age"; Keller, *Affairs of State*, 112, 114; Chausovsky, "State Regulation of Corporations," 40–42; James, *Growth of Chicago Banks*, 400–401; Thompson, "Illinois Constitutions," 197–200; "A Third Stage of Constitution-Making," *Nation*, April 17, 1873, p. 265; Howard, *Illinois*, 333.

45. Cohen, *Reconstruction of American Liberalism*, 133–37; *Peoria (Ill.) Daily National Democrat*, February 8, 1872; *New York Graphic*, February 23, 1874.

46. *Wilmington (N.C.) Morning Star*, January 5, 1876; "H. V. R.," *CinCom*, July 29, 1874; Masur, *Example for All the Land*, 239–54.

Chapter Thirteen

1. Utley, "Oliver Otis Howard," 59–63.

2. Reid, "Sharecropping as an Understandable Market Response"; Ransom and Sutch, *One Kind of Freedom*, 87–90, 94–103; Foner, *Nothing but Freedom*, 82–94.

3. Absalom Baird to Oliver O. Howard, December 29, 1865, Howard MSS, Bowdoin; Loewenberg, "Efforts of the South to Encourage Immigration"; Moran, "Chinese Labor for the New South"; Ouzts, "Landlords and Tenants," 7–8; *NYH*, October 19, 1874.

4. Shofner, *Nor Is It Over Yet*, 151–52; Foster and Foster, "Last Shall be First," 277–78; Jones, *Soldiers of Light and Love*, 198–99.

5. McPherson, *Struggle for Equality*, 406–7.

6. Durrill, "Political Legitimacy and Local Courts." 587–96; Williamson, *After Slavery*, 114; *NYTrib*, May 10, 1871; see also "Finch," *SprR*, January 4, 1871.

7. Loren Schweninger, "Black Economic Reconstruction in the South," in Anderson and Moss, *Facts of Reconstruction*, 179–87; Edwards, *Gendered Strife and Confusion*, 148–51; Angelo, "Wage Labour Deferred," 594–95; *New Era* (Washington, D.C.), January 13, March 10, May 12, June 9, June 23, July 7, 14, 28, 1870; Rawick, *American*

Slave, vol. 8, *Arkansas Narratives*, pt. 1, p. 178; *NYTrib*, May 10, 1871; Ng and Virts, "Value of Freedom"; Kelley, "Texas Peasantry," 196–203; Davis, "Bankless in Beaufort," 38–40. Free black women may have been the exception. Their reported holdings from before the war plummeted, though much of the reason may be a statistical illusion, as legalized marriage with former slaves put the property in their husbands' name. Schweninger, "Property-Owning Free African American Women," 26–29.

8. *CinGaz*, April 21, May 24, June 19, 1871; Vallandigham, *Clement L. Vallandigham*, 436–51.

9. Vallandigham, *Clement L. Vallandigham*, 520–32; *NYH*, July 12, 21, 1871; *NYTrib*, December 2, 1870, May 17, 1871; *Dubuque (Iowa) Herald*, April 5, 1870.

10. Merrill, *Bourbon Democracy of the Middle West*, 63–70; Polakoff, "Disorganized Democracy," 15–18; Democratic platforms, *Appleton's Annual Cyclopedia* (1871), 393, 406, 416, 482, 493, 547, 556, 571, 621, 775–76; *Dubuque (Iowa) Herald*, September 27, 1870.

11. *ChiTi*, April 24, 1870.

12. *CinEnq*, February 12, 1872.

13. *Baltimore Sun*, December 20, 1870; "Lee's Perjury and Treason," *Independent*, January 21, 1871; *Nation*, July 14, 1870; D. Heaton to D. M. Barringer, February 20, 1870, Barringer MSS, SHC; George M. Arnold to Charles Sumner, December 26, 1871, Sumner MSS, HU; *NNE*, December 22, 1870, January 5, February 2, 1871, February 15, 1872, *CG*, 42nd Cong., 2nd sess., 3252 (May 9, 1872); *CinCom*, February 2, 1872.

14. Gerber, "Liberal Republican Alliance"; William E. Chandler to William Claflin, February 22, 1872, Claflin MSS, RBHL; *NYEP*, March 7, 1872; "Gath," *ChiTrib*, December 21, 1870.

15. *Nation*, January 21, 1869; *NYEP*, January 6, 26, February 14, 19, 27, 1872. On liberalism, see Sproat, *"The Best Men,"* and in the most recent of many positive correctives, Slap, *Doom of Reconstruction*, and with far greater sophistication and much more emphasis on economic ideology, Cohen, *Reconstruction of American Liberalism*, 23–140. Cohen makes a reaction against labor's rising force the decisive one in shaping liberal republican ideology after 1868. Slap traces a coherent liberal republican mind-set back to before the war and does not notice labor at all. The best accounts of the Liberal Republican movement itself—that is, versions that participants in the movement would have recognized—remain Downey, "Rebirth of Reform," and Gerber, "Liberal Republican Alliance."

16. Benedict, "Reform Republicans and the Retreat from Reconstruction"; Cohen, *Reconstruction of American Liberalism*, 113–20; *SprR*, July 1, 1876; *NYH*, November 9, 1877; J. M. Forbes to Edward Atkinson, December 23, 1872, Atkinson MSS, MHS; *Indianapolis News*, October 8, 1870; A. P. Lathrop to James A. Garfield, December 20, 1871, Garfield MSS, LC; W. E. Rowe to Carl Schurz, February 16, 1872, Schurz MSS, LC; Gerber, "Liberal Republican Alliance," 230; *CG*, 40th Cong., 3rd sess., 265 (January 8, 1869).

17. Benedict, "Reform Republicans and the Retreat from Reconstruction," 75–76; Richardson, *Death of Reconstruction*, 94–101; *ChiTi*, October 2, 1872; "Finch," *SprWR*, November 25, 1870, January 19, 1876; Charles Francis Adams to Henry Adams,

January 20, 1870, Adams Family MSS, MHS; *Nation*, January 28, June 10, 1869; Jacob D. Cox to Carl Schurz, February 14, 1872, Schurz MSS, LC; *NYEP*, July 29, 1872; Adams, *Letters*, 108.

18. *CinEnq*, April 30, May 1, 1872; Krug, *Lyman Trumbull*, 399–26; Unger, *Greenback Era*, 186–89; Gerber, "Liberal Republican Alliance," 436–45.

19. Downey, "Rebirth of Reform," 569–74; William S. Grosvenor to Edward Atkinson, May 12, 1872, and Mahlon Sands to Atkinson, May 10, 22, 1872, Atkinson MSS, MHS; *NYH*, May 5, June 18, 1872; Hoogenboom, *Outlawing the Spoils*, 115–17; Nevins and Thomas, *Diary of George Templeton Strong*, 4:433 (August 6, 1872).

20. Edwin L. Godkin to Carl Schurz, May 19, 1872, Schurz MSS, LC; Van Deusen, *Horace Greeley*, 319–24, 353–56, 381–87.

21. *CinCom*, June 21, 22, July 8, 9, 10, 1872; *NYTi*, July 10, 1872; Horatio Seymour to Samuel J. Tilden, October 3, 1872, Tilden MSS, NYPL; Richardson, *William E. Chandler, Republican*, 142–43.

22. "Interest and Duty of Colored Citizens in the Presidential Election," *Charles Sumner Complete Works*, 20:173–95; "Mr. Sumner's Letter," *Harper's Weekly*, August 17, 1872.

23. *NNE*, April 25, 1872; Warmoth, *War, Politics, and Reconstruction*, 161–98; Stephen B. Packard to William E. Chandler, April 9, 28, 1872, Chandler MSS, LC; Thomas W. Conway to William M. Grosvenor, April 2, 1872, Grosvenor MSS, Columbia University, New York.

24. J. G. Frisbie to Charles Sumner, August 3, 1872, Edward Belcher to Sumner, August 5, 1872, and Sambo Estelle to Sumner, August 5, 1872, Sumner MSS, HU; William Lloyd Garrison to Sumner, August 3, 1872, in Merrill and Ruchames, *Letters of William Lloyd Garrison*, 238–47; "William Lloyd Garrison" and "Frederick Douglass Upon Mr. Sumner's Letter," *Harper's Weekly*, August 24, 1872; *NNE*, November 3, 1870, April 11, October 31, 1872; "Warrington," *SprWR*, September 13, 1872.

25. Taussig, *Tariff History of the United States*, 179–90.

26. Rawley, "General Amnesty Act of 1872"; *NYH*, February 8, 9, 1872; *NNE*, January 18, February 15, May 16, 1872; *CG*, 42nd Cong., 2nd sess., 3728–40 (May 21, 1872); "Republicanism vs. Grantism," *Charles Sumner Complete Works*, 20:83–172.

27. Hoogenboom, *Outlawing the Spoils*, 90–96; *Nation*, December 21, 1871.

28. *Daily Quincy (Ill.) Herald*, July 23, 1872.

29. *ChiTrib*, September 12, 1872; *SprWR*, September 13, 1872; *Nation*, August 8, 1872; Horace Greeley to Mason W. Tappan, November 8, 1872, Greeley MSS, LC. This letter was made public soon after Greeley's death. See *SprWR*, December 6, 1872.

30. *Minneapolis Daily Tribune*, October 10, November 5, 1872; *Milwaukee News*, May 15, 1872.

31. Paine, *Th. Nast*, 246–61; *NYTi*, November 5, 1872; Phillips and Pendleton, *Union on Trial*, 451 (July 24, 1872).

32. "Warrington," *SprWR*, September 13, 1872; *NNE*, April 25, September 12, 1872; *Knoxville (Tenn.) Daily Chronicle*, August 25, 1872; *Minneapolis Daily Tribune*, October 31, 1872.

33. *Keokuk (Iowa) Daily Gate City*, October 13, 1872; *NYTrib*, July 18, 1872; *CinGaz*, October 26, 1872; *Minneapolis Daily Tribune*, October 13, 1872.

34. *CinGaz*, September 20, 21, 1872; *Lynchburg Daily Virginian*, September 25, 1872; *NYH*, September 25, 29, 1872; *SprWR*, September 27, 1872; *ChiTrib*, September 27, 1872; *CinEnq*, September 21, 30, 1872; Gillette, *Retreat from Reconstruction*, 67.

35. "A Singing Campaign," *Nation*, October 10, 1872.

36. *Norfolk Virginian*, October 11, 12, 19, 20, 1872.

37. *Missouri Republican*, November 7, 8, 1872; Phillips and Pendleton, *Union on Trial*, 458 (November 6, 1872); *Cleveland Daily Leader*, November 19, 1872; *Louisville (Ky.) Courier-Journal*, November 7, 11, 1872; Paul H. Hayne to Alexander H. Stephens, November 11, 1872, Stephens MSS, LC.

38. *Tribune Almanac, 1873*, pp. 47–83; *Nation*, November 14, 1872; William R. Morrison to John F. Snyder, November 14, 1872, Snyder MSS, ISHS.

39. Van Deusen, *Horace Greeley*, 420–24; *Keokuk (Iowa) Daily Gate City*, August 23, December 1, 1872.

40. Krug, *Lyman Trumbull*, 337–41; G. L. Fort to Richard Oglesby, November 9, 1872, Oglesby MSS, ISHS; *NYTi*, November 7, 1872; *NYH*, November 2, 1872.

41. R. F. Laurence to Nathaniel P. Banks, November 7, 1872, Banks MSS, LC; *Missouri Republican*, November 7, 1872; Allen G. Thurman to J. J. Faran, November 21, 1872, Thurman MSS, OHS.

42. Benjamin F. Perry to his son, November 8, 1872, Perry MSS, SCC; F. W. Alfreund to Alexander H. Stephens, November 10, 1872, Stephens MSS, LC.

43. Merrill, *Bourbon Democracy of the Middle West*, 77–80; Grossman, *Democratic Party and the Negro*, 43–44.

44. *ChaCou*, July 31, August 1, 1872.

45. Current, *Those Terrible Carpetbaggers*, 268–69; James W. Grace to Robert K. Scott, February 24, 1872, and Thomas J. Mackey to Scott, March 21, 1872, Scott MSS, OHS.

46. Ginsberg, *Moses of South Carolina*, 127, 133–34; *NYH*, September 16, 1872; *NYW*, August 22, 1872; "Gath," *ChiTrib*, October 4, 1872; *NYEP*, November 1, 1872.

47. Ginsberg, *Moses of South Carolina*, 150–51; *NYH*, September 16, 1872; *NYW*, September 13, 1872; "Nemo," *ChaCou*, August 22, 23, 1872; *Beaufort (S.C.) Republican*, August 29, 1872.

48. *Nation*, October 10, 1872; Ku Klux Test., vol. 4 (South Carolina, pt. 2), 729, 740; *Aiken (S.C.) Tribune*, August 31, 1872.

Chapter Fourteen

1. Donald, *Charles Sumner and the Rights of Man*, 563–64; "Greeley or Grant?," *Charles Sumner Complete Works*, 20:229–40; "No Names of Battles with Fellow-Citizens on the Army-Register or the Regimental Colors of the United States," *Charles Sumner Complete Works*, 20:255; *Nation*, December 27, 1872.

2. *SprWR*, December 27, 1872; *BDA*, December 18, 19, 1872; *NYTi*, December 20, 1872; *Jackson (Miss.) Weekly Clarion*, December 26, 1872.

3. Elihu Burritt to Charles Sumner, December 27, 1872, Sumner MSS, HU; *Boston Commonwealth*, February 7, July 25, 1874; *BDA*, March 11, 1873.

4. Donald, *Charles Sumner and the Rights of Man*, 569–71; *SprWR*, December 27, 1872; Willard P. Phillips to Charles Sumner, March 4, 16, 1873, Sumner MSS, HU; *BDA*, March 6, 7, 11, 1873; *Boston Commonwealth*, August 1, 1874.

5. "Pacific Mail Steamship Service," ii–xix; "Pomeroy Investigation," i–x; "Allegations against Senator Powell Clayton," 4–21, 235–42.

6. "Credit Mobilier Investigation," v–xiv; McCabe, *Behind the Scenes in Washington*, 260–79.

7. "Credit Mobilier Investigation," 81–84, 128–31, 197–204, 243–61; McCabe, *Behind the Scenes in Washington*, 268–301; Peskin, *Garfield*, 366–67; *Nation*, January 30, 1873. For a more sympathetic reading of Ames's guilt, see Ames, *Pioneering the Union Pacific*, 459–89.

8. *CG*, 42nd Cong., 3rd sess., 1675 (February 24, 1873); *Louisville (Ky.) Courier-Journal*, March 3, 12, 1873.

9. *CG*, 42nd Cong., 3rd sess., 2103 (March 3, 1873).

10. Alston, Jenkins, and Nonnenmacher, "Who Should Govern Congress?"; *ChiTrib*, March 5, 1873; *Milwaukee News*, April 11, 1873 ; "H. M. B.," *CinGaz*, March 18, 1873.

11. *SprR*, April 29, May 5, 15, 1873.

12. Nevins, *Hamilton Fish*, 659–66; Fairman, *Mr. Justice Miller*, 260–77; "D. W. B.," *Independent*, January 22, 1874; *Washington (D.C.) Daily Chronicle*, January 12, 1874.

13. Hoogenboom, *Outlawing the Spoils*, 119–34.

14. Lamson, *Glorious Failure*, 165–66; "H. V. R.," *CinCom*, January 1, 2, 1873; J. Rollins to J. S. Rollins, December 26, 1872, Rollins MSS, Missouri Historical Society, Columbia.

15. *Report of the Joint Committee of the General Assembly of Alabama*, 23–29.

16. "Gath," *ChiTrib*, October 4, 15, 1872; "Troy," *ChiTrib*, August 20, 1872.

17. Clayton, *Aftermath of Civil War*, 347; Staples, *Reconstruction in Arkansas*, 391; George H. Thompson, "Leadership in Arkansas Reconstruction," 162–75; *Little Rock Republican*, August 17, September 16, 1871, August 23, 26, 1872.

18. Thompson, "Leadership in Arkansas Reconstruction," 182–94; "A. R. K.," *CinGaz*, September 7, 1874; H. Rept. 771, "Affairs in Arkansas," 47–53; minority report, "Condition of Affairs in the State of Arkansas," H. Rept. 127, 43rd Cong., 2nd sess., 22.

19. H. Rept. 771, "Affairs in Arkansas," 18–20, 98–103, 154–56, 161; *Little Rock Republican*, April 11, May 21, July 8, August 1, 1873; "A. R. K.," *CinGaz*, September 7, 1874; "H. V. R.," *CinCom*, May 23, 1874.

20. *Daily Shreveport Times*, September 19, 1872; P. B. S. Pinchback to William E. Chandler, October 15, 1872, Chandler MSS, LC.

21. *New Orleans Daily Picayune*, November 5, 1872; H. C. Hobart to Benjamin F. Flanders, December 13, 1872, Flanders MSS, LSU; Thomas Ellis to E. J. Ellis, November 16, 1872, Ellis Family MSS, LSU; Frank Morey to Henry Clay Warmoth, December 4, 1872, Warmoth MSS, SHC.

22. Dawson, *Army Generals and Reconstruction*, 134–36. A House committee unanimously found Durell's action illegal and unwarranted, and with one

exception, recommended impeachment. H. Rept. 732, "Judge E. H. Durell," 43rd Cong., 1st sess., 8–13.

23. Taylor, *Louisiana Reconstructed*, 246.

24. Ibid., 268–71; "Condition of the South," 847–65; Lane, *Day Freedom Died*, 78–109.

25. Gillette, *Retreat from Reconstruction*, 116–17.

26. Carrier, "Political History of Texas," 505–6; Williams, *Beyond Redemption*, 17–33.

27. Moneyhon, *Republicanism in Reconstruction Texas*, 191–94; Singletary, *Negro Militia and Reconstruction*, 38–39; "Modus," *NNE*, February 18, 1873; *NYTrib*, January 13, 17, 20, 1874; Simon, *Papers of Ulysses S. Grant*, 25:9–11.

28. H. Rept. 771, "Affairs in Arkansas," 18–20; "A. R. K.," *CinGaz*, September 7, 1874; *Little Rock Republican*, August 8, 26, 28, 1873; *SprR*, April 24, 1874.

29. Thompson, "Leadership in Arkansas Reconstruction," 262–65.

30. Singletary, *Negro Militia and Reconstruction*, 53–65; "H. V. R.," *CinCom*, May 14, 18, 1874; *CinEnq*, April 22, 1874; *NYTi*, April 17, 1874; *Newark Daily Advertiser*, May 14, 16, 1874; *NYH*, April 16, May 16, 1874; *NYTrib*, May 9, 1874.

31. Gillette, *Retreat from Reconstruction*, 138–44; Singletary, *Negro Militia and Reconstruction*, 64–65; "H. V. R.," *CinCom*, May 18, 19, 1874.

32. A. R. C. Rogers to Benjamin F. Butler, May 25, 1874, Butler MSS, LC; "A. R. K.," *CinGaz*, September 11, 1874; Thompson, "Leadership in Arkansas Reconstruction," 284–88.

33. *NYH*, August 22, 23, 1874; H. Exec. Doc. 25, "Affairs in Arkansas," 20–21, 24–39, 108–46.

34. Wall, *Andrew Carnegie*, 307–19; Hoag, "Atlantic Telegraph Cable"; Kirkland, *Industry Comes of Age*, 57–67; Fraser, *Every Man a Speculator*, 119.

35. Sobel, *Panic on Wall Street*, 173; White, *Railroaded*, 78–79; Timberlake, *Monetary Policy in the United States*, 104.

36. Mixon, "Crisis of 1873"; Sobel, *Big Board*, 93.

37. Warshaw, *Story of Wall Street*, 192; Sobel, *Panic on Wall Street*, 174–77.

38. *NYH*, September 19. 1873; Osthaus, *Freedmen, Philanthropy, and Fraud*, 150–99; Simkins and Woody, *South Carolina during Reconstruction*, 271; Warshaw, *Story of Wall Street*, 191; Fraser, *Every Man a Speculator*, 123; Sobel, *Panic on Wall Street*, 184.

39. Warshaw, *Story of Wall Street*, 192; Kirkland, *Industry Comes of Age*, 4; Sobel, *Panic on Wall Street*, 188–92.

40. Sobel, *Panic on Wall Street*, 92; Davis, "Improved Annual Chronology of U.S. Business Cycles," 104–7; *NYH*, October 28, 1874; *Nation*, August 5, 1875; *Alabama State Journal*, February 17, 1874.

41. Kirkland, *Industry Comes of Age*, 6; Stover, *Railroads of the South*, 122–23; Adler, *British Investment in American Railways*, 75–83, 89–93.

42. *NYH*, December 6, 1876; Bernstein, "American Labor in the Long Depression," 67–68.

43. Bernstein, "American Labor in the Long Depression," 68–69; *NYTrib*, December 10, 1874; *NYH*, September 27, December 16, 21, 1876.

44. *NYH*, September 1, 2, 1875, December 12, 14, 1876.

45. *NYH*, January 16, February 5, 7, 1877.

46. *NYTrib*, May 23, 1874; "Broadway," *CinCom*, May 29, 1874.

47. Cresswell, *Tramp in America*, 52–55, 92–93; Kusmer, *Down & Out*, 35–56; *NYH*, August 13, 23, 24, 1875, February 9, August 24, 1876, March 2, 1877; *CinEnq*, November 22, 1875.

48. *NYH*, December 14, 20, 21, 1876, February 5, 1877.

49. Keller, *Affairs of State*, 114, 184–87; *St. Paul Pioneer*, October 25, 31, 1873; Ratchford, *American State Debts*, 249, 256; Clark, *Then Came the Railroads*, 78; Shannon, *Farmer's Last Frontier*, 269; Kusmer, *Down & Out*, 52.

50. *New Orleans Semi-Weekly Louisianian*, June 1, 1871; *NNE*, December 29, 1870, May 21, 28, 1874; D. L. Eaton to William C. Claflin, March 17, 1870, Claflin MSS; Osthaus, *Freedmen, Philanthropy, and Fraud*, 152–200.

51. Gramm and Gramm, "Free Silver Movement in America," 1108–27; *CinGaz*, April 14, 1874; *CinEnq*, April 4, 15, 1874; Simon, *Papers of Ulysses S. Grant*, 25:68–69n.

52. *Independent*, April 9, 23, 1874; *NYTi*, April 7, 1874; *CinCom*, April 15, 1874; Simon, *Papers of Ulysses S. Grant*, 25:70–71n.; Adams, "Currency Debate of 1873–74," 117; *CinGaz*, April 7, 12, 15, 1874.

53. Simon, *Papers of Ulysses S. Grant*, 25:71n.; *CinGaz*, April 23, 1874; *CinCom*, April 18, 23, 1874.

54. Nevins and Thomas, *Diary of George Templeton Strong*, 4:523 (April 23, 1874); Isaac N. Morris to Richard J. Oglesby, April 28, 1874, A. M. Jones to Oglesby, April 25, 1874, H. A. Mills to Oglesby, May 1, 1874, and M. M. Bane to Oglesby, May 5, 1874, Oglesby MSS, ISHS; "H. V. R.," *CinCom*, April 24, 30, 1874.

55. *CinCom*, May 24, 1874; Marcus Norton to Benjamin F. Butler, May 26, 1874, Butler MSS, LC.

56. *Ravenna (Ohio) Democratic Press*, October 7, 1875; Jentz and Schneirov, *Chicago in the Age of Capital*, 95–97; Frieden, "Monetary Populism in Nineteenth-Century America," 367–69.

57. "M. C. A.," *Independent*, March 26, 1874; Storey and Emerson, *Ebenezer Rockwood Hoar*, 239–40; "Recollections of Charles Sumner"; Donald, *Charles Sumner and the Rights of Man*, 584–87.

Chapter Fifteen

1. Fitzgerald, *Splendid Failure*, 165.

2. J. Stockton Brown to Manton Marble, July 2, 1874, Marble MSS, LC; "Condition of Affairs in the South," 1037–38.

3. Taylor, *Louisiana Reconstructed*, 277–79; Fischer, *Segregation Struggle in Louisiana*, 75–78; Robinson, "Beyond the Realm of Social Consensus," 293–95.

4. Schweninger, "Black Citizenship and the Republican Party," 90–92; Woolfolk, "Role of the Scalawag," 136–43; see also *Alabama State Journal*, July 9, September 6, 1873, April 9, May 9, 1874; *Little Rock Republican*, December 25, 1868; *Charleston (S.C.) Daily Republican*, December 9, 13, 1869, February 1, 1870. For more on the railroad segregation issue, see Pereyra, *James Lusk Alcorn*, 115–16; and *Acts of Louisiana*, 1869, p. 37.

5. "Phil," *NNE*, February 16, 1871; Fitzgerald, "Republican Factionalism and Black Empowerment," 490–92; Fitzgerald, *Splendid Failure*, 166–67.

6. Ellem, "Overthrow of Reconstruction in Mississippi," 186–95.

7. "Civil Rights," 1–3; "National Civil-Rights Bill," 1; Crow and Durden, *Maverick Republican in the Old North State*, 26–28; *NNE*, January 23, March 13, May 29, 1873; *Alabama State Journal*, February 25, March 1, 5, 7, 13, 14, 19, 20, 26, 1873; Ginsberg, *Moses of South Carolina*, 159–63.

8. *Alabama State Journal*, August 21, December 15, 28, 1870, July 30, August 9, September 13, 1873; *Aiken (S.C.) Tribune*, November 12, 1872; Charles E. Kennon to Thomas Ellis, June 27, 1870, June 13, 1874, Ellis MSS, LSU; *Jacksonville (Fla.) New South*, October 21, 1874.

9. Denmark, "'At the Midnight Hour,'" 374–89; Stover, *Railroads of the South*, 123–25.

10. "Condition of the South," pt. 1, pp. 6–7; pt. 2, pp. 279–81.

11. *CR*, 43rd Cong., 1st sess., appendix, 4–5 (January 7, 1874), 240–44 (May 4, 1874); "H. V. R.," *CinCom*, September 28, 1874.

12. *Alabama State Journal*, October 1, 1874; *NYH*, May 18, August 12, 25, 28, September 3, 4, 26, 1874.

13. Lonn, *Reconstruction in Louisiana after 1868*, 255–56; *NYH*, September 11, October 19, 1874; Lestage, "White League in Louisiana," 681–82; "Alabama," xiv; "Condition of Affairs in the South," 248–52; Fairclough, "Alfred Raford Blunt," 299–301; Rosenbaum, "Incendiary Negro," 514–15.

14. *NYH*, September 26, 1874.

15. "Mississippi in 1875," 1053, 1192.

16. *Washington (D.C.) National Republican*, August 26, 28, October 10, 1873; *Richmond (Va.) Whig*, October 3, 17, 1873; *NYH*, October 23, 1873.

17. Michael Perman, "Counter Reconstruction: The Role of Violence in Southern Redemption," in Anderson and Moss, *Facts of Reconstruction*, 132–35; "Affairs in Alabama," iii, 291–92, 373–76, 396–99; Herbert Posey to Benjamin F. Butler, October 19, 1874, Butler MSS, LC; Rogers et al., *Alabama*, 264; "Alabama," ii, 131, 134–37, 373–76, 396–99.

18. "Condition of Affairs in the South," 279–90, 752–72, 1004–11.

19. Taylor, *Louisiana Reconstructed*, 285–86; "Condition of Affairs in the South," 773–94, 884–88, 1003–4; Fairclough, "Alfred Raford Blunt," 290–92; Dawson, *Army Generals and Reconstruction*, 158–61.

20. Dawson, *Army Generals and Reconstruction*, 164–80; "Condition of the South," 5–6; "Condition of Affairs in the South," 798–840, 1022–30; Powell, "Reinventing Tradition," 129–31.

21. "Alabama," 347–48; Brown, "Carpetbagger Intrigues," 293–301; Harris, *Day of the Carpetbagger*, 608–10, 630–32; Current, *Those Terrible Carpetbaggers*, 311–12, 328–34.

22. See letter from Chamberlain, *Charleston (S.C.) Daily Republican*, March 3, 1870.

23. Holt, *Black over White*, 181; Foner, *Reconstruction*, 543–45.

24. Holt, *Black over White*, 186–97.

25. Rable, *But There Was No Peace*, 146; Simon, *Papers of Ulysses S. Grant*, 25:157.

26. Ellem, "Overthrow of Reconstruction in Mississippi," 176–77; Gillette, *Retreat from Reconstruction*, 150–53; Foner, *Reconstruction*, 558–59.

27. "Mississippi in 1875," 1021–26, 1036–37; Gillette, *Retreat from Reconstruction*, 154–55; Singletary, *Negro Militia and Reconstruction*, 86–97; Fitzgerald, *Splendid Failure*, 192.

28. Simpson, *Reconstruction Presidents*, 184–87.

29. Summers, *Era of Good Stealings*, 249–54; *NYH*, May 31, 1875. On Sumner's alleged "bloody shirt," see *Memphis Daily Appeal*, March 13, 1871; *NYTi*, July 19, 1874. The term itself, used only very occasionally before 1874 and with varying applications, may originally have come from a parade of the widows of a massacre at Glenfuin in Scotland in the sixteenth century; they were said to have borne the shirts of their murdered husbands to Stirling Castle in protest. See *NYTi*, October 25, 1885. For early uses, see *NYW*, February 13, 1867, September 15, 1868.

30. Dawson, *Army Generals and Reconstruction*, 201–5; *NYH*, January 10, 1875. On the legal intricacies, see letter of E. Stoughton, *NYTi*, January 14, 1875.

31. *NYH*, January 5, 14, 1875; Chauncey — to his father, January 15, 1875, Anonymous Reconstruction Letters, LSU; Simon, *Papers of Ulysses S. Grant*, 26:18n.; *CinGaz*, January 6, 1875; "Condition of the South," 10–12; pt. 2, pp. 288–307.

32. Dawson, *Army Generals and Reconstruction*, 200–202, 206–7; *NYH*, January 10, 1875; *CinGaz*, January 6, 1875.

33. Hoar, *Autobiography*, 1:208–9.

34. Simon, *Papers of Ulysses S. Grant*, 26:21n; *NYH*, January 13, 16, 1875. Another account says that the response was "loud laughter." See *CinGaz*, January 19, 1875.

35. *CR*, 43rd Cong., 2nd sess., 309–13 (January 7, 1875), 329–35, 336–44 (January 8, 1875), 365–74 (January 11, 1875); Dawson, *Army Generals and Reconstruction*, 208–10; *NYH*, January 6, 1875.

36. *CR*, 43rd Cong., 2nd sess., 1852 (February 26, 1875).

37. Gillette, *Retreat from Reconstruction*, 280–85; *CinCom*, February 13, 1875; *CinGaz*, February 13, 1875.

38. Gillette, *Retreat from Reconstruction*, 146–48; H. Exec. Doc. 25, "Affairs in Arkansas," 79–96, 109–12; John Bigelow to Samuel J. Tilden, February 10, 1875, Bigelow MSS, NYPL; Thomas Allen to Henry L. Dawes, January 6, 1875, Dawes MSS, LC.

39. *NYH*, February 16, 1875; *CinEnq*, February 9, 13, 1875; *CinCom*, February 11, 1875; "H. V. R.," *CinCom*, February 15, 19, 1875; "Mississippi in 1875," 1078.

40. *NYTrib*, February 6, 1875; *CinGaz*, February 20, 1875; *NYH*, February 11, 1875.

41. Edward Stoughton to Benjamin H. Bristow, February 11, 1875, and John M. Harlan to Bristow, February 17, 1875, Bristow MSS, LC; *NYH*, February 15, 16, 1875; *CinCom*, February 10, 1875; *CR*, 43rd Cong., 2nd sess., 2108 (March 2, 1875).

42. Gillette, *Retreat from Reconstruction*, 148–49, 286–90; *CR*, 43rd Cong., 2nd sess., 1853 (February 26, 1875).

43. Edwards Pierrepont to Ulysses S. Grant, September 12, 1875, and Grant to Pierrepont, September 13, 1875, in Simon, *Papers of Ulysses S. Grant*, 26:311–12; Gillette, *Retreat from Reconstruction*, 157–60. On Grant's sincere wish to act in freedpeople's defense the winter before, see Brooks D. Simpson, "Consider the

Alternatives: Reassessing Republican Reconstruction," in Gallagher and Shelden, *Political Nation*, 224–26.

44. Houston Burris to Adelbert Ames, November 1, 1875, J. B. Allgood to Ames, October 30, 1875, and C. H. Green to Ames, November 22, 1875, Ames MSS, Governor's Papers, MDAH; Gillette, *Retreat from Reconstruction*, 160–62; "Mississippi in 1875," 1081–84, 1191, 1216–18.

45. Hiram Johnson to Adelbert Ames, November 3, 1875, W. W. Chisholm to Ames, November 3, 1875, and Thomas W. Stinson to Ames, November 3, 1875, Ames MSS, Governor's Papers, MDAH; Wharton, *Negro in Mississippi*, 196; "Mississippi in 1875," 1028–34, 1052, 1171–82; Harris, *Day of the Carpetbagger*, 696–97.

46. "South Carolina in 1876," 1:603–18, 703; Zuczek, *State of Rebellion*, 164.

47. "South Carolina in 1876," 2:7–10, 18–19, 173–74, 186, 233–35, 542–44; 3: 499–509, 828; Zuczek, "Last Campaign of the Civil War," 24.

48. Rable, *But There Was No Peace*, 175–76; "South Carolina in 1876," 2:203, 395–98, 529–34, 539–42, 549–56; Zuczek, "Last Campaign of the Civil War," 22–27; Poole, *Never Surrender*, 132–33; Hahn, *Nation under Our Feet*, 307–9.

49. Simon, *Papers of Ulysses S. Grant*, 25:14–15.

50. Halbrook, *Freedmen*, 168–75; Scaturro, *Supreme Court's Retreat from Reconstruction*, 52–57.

51. McPherson, "Abolitionists and the Civil Rights Act of 1875," 507–10; Wendell Phillips to Benjamin F. Butler, January 6, 1875, Butler MSS, LC; Brown, "Pennsylvania and the Rights of the Negro," 54–57; Schwalm, *Emancipation's Diaspora*, 207; Middleton, *Black Laws*, 254–59.

Chapter Sixteen

1. Hicks, "United States Centennial Exhibition of 1876," 11, 19, 137–47; Gold, "Imaging Memory," 24–35; *CinGaz*, May 21, 1876.

2. *Nation*, December 16, 23, 1875; Webb, *Benjamin Helm Bristow*, 189–201; Nevins, *Hamilton Fish*, 821–25.

3. Muzzey, *James G. Blaine*, 83–96; Summers, *Era of Good Stealings*, 54–58; "Laertes," *New York Graphic*, June 8, 1876.

4. *Nation*, August 5, 1875.

5. "Pickaway," *CinEnq*, April 17, 1876; Samuel L. M. Barlow to Thomas F. Bayard, May 3, 1876, Bayard MSS, LC.

6. Mushkat, *Reconstruction of New York Democracy*, 189–90, 237–41; Murphy, "Samuel J. Tilden and the Civil War"; Flick, *Samuel Jones Tilden*, 82–86, 260–61, 264–75.

7. Kelley, "Thought and Character of Samuel J. Tilden," 176–205; "D. P.," *CinEnq*, January 25, 1877.

8. Merrill, *Bourbon Democracy of the Middle West*, 105–9; *CinEnq*, June 21, 22, 1876; Flick, *Samuel Jones Tilden*, 282–92; William L. Grant to Samuel L. M. Barlow, June 20, 1876, Barlow MSS, HuL.

9. Polakoff, *Politics of Inertia*, 18–21; "A. C. B.," *CinEnq*, March 6, 1876; *ChiTi*, March 28, 1876.

10. Polakoff, *Politics of Inertia*, 21–25, 39–40; DeCanio, "State Autonomy and American Political Development," 125–33; *Waseou (Ohio) Democratic Expositor*, October 8, 1875; George W. Morgan to William Allen, October 16, 1875, Allen MSS, LC.

11. Polakoff, *Politics of Inertia*, 30–37; 59–67; "Buckeye," *ChiTi*, May 5, 1876; *CinEnq*, June 16, 1876; *SprR*, October 3, 1876.

12. Hoogenboom, *Outlawing the Spoils*, 141–45.

13. Polakoff, *Politics of Inertia*, 115. See also Rutherford B. Hayes to Edwards Pierrepont, September 16, 1876, and Hayes to Murat Halstead, September 18, 1876, Hayes MSS, RBHL. On the school issue, see McAfee, "Reconstruction Revisited," 147–48.

14. Slotkin, *Fatal Environment*, 419–74.

15. The term, one reporter explained, originated in "bull-dosing," as the heavy use of a whip to move stubborn cattle was known.

16. Dawson, *Army Generals and Reconstruction*, 222–34; "H. V. R.," *CinCom*, September 4, 9, 1876, March 3, 1877.

17. Lucius Q. C. Lamar to William H. Trescot, October 6, 16, 1876, Trescot MSS, SCC.

18. *NYTi*, July 24, 1876; *ChiTrib*, September 23, 1876; *SprR*, October 4, 1876; *Bangor (Maine) Whig and Courier*, August 26, 1876; *CinEnq*, September 18, 1876.

19. Gillette, *Retreat from Reconstruction*, 309–10; *ChiTrib*, September 26, 28, 1876; Murat Halstead to Rutherford B. Hayes, September 19, 1876, Hayes MSS, RBHL; *Bangor (Maine) Whig and Courier*, August 19, October 26, 1876; Eugene Casserly to Thomas F. Bayard, November 6, 1876, Bayard MSS, LC.

20. Polakoff, *Politics of Inertia*, 201–6; Sternstein, "Sickles Memorandum"; Hahn, *Nation under Our Feet*, 309–10.

21. Polakoff, *Politics of Inertia*, 242–43; McKinney, "Zebulon Vance and His Reconstruction," 81–83; S. Rept. 704, "Alabama," viii–xiii; Shofner, "Fraud and Intimidation"; King, "Counting the Votes"; King, "Most Corrupt Election"; "H. V. R.," *CinCom*, September 4, 1876.

22. Polakoff, *Politics of Inertia*, 208–20; Guenther, "Potter Committee Investigation"; Clark, "Fox Goes to France"; Kennedy, "Oregon and the Disputed Election of 1876," 135–38.

23. *NYH*, February 22, 1877.

24. Polakoff, *Politics of Inertia*, 206–7; Flick, *Samuel Jones Tilden*, 400.

25. Polakoff, *Politics of Inertia*, 234–42; Rable, "Southern Interests and the Election of 1876," 348–52; "H. V. R.," *CinCom*, January 1, 1877; "H. V. R.," *CinCom*, January 9, February 1, 1877; *New Orleans Daily Picayune*, January 6, 1877; *NYEP*, April 16, 1877.

26. Polakoff, *Politics of Inertia*, 244–69; Rable, "Southern Interests and the Election of 1876," 352–57; "H. V. R.," *CinCom*, January 1, 9, 1877. The deal that wasn't gets full play in Woodward, *Reunion and Reaction*, so well-written that it deserves to be right. For serious doubts, see Peskin, "Was There a Compromise of 1877?"; Woodward, "Yes, There Was a Compromise of 1877"; and Benedict, "Southern Democrats in the Crisis of 1876–1877."

27. Calhoun, *Conceiving a New Republic*, 114–16; Northrup, "Grave Crisis in American History," 924; Polakoff, *Politics of Inertia*, 269–79.

28. Polakoff, *Politics of Inertia*, 279–84; *CinCom*, January 23, 24, 25, 29, 1877.

29. Polakoff, *Politics of Inertia*, 285–91.

30. *ChiTrib*, February 17, 18, 1877; George M. Dallas to Samuel J. Randall, February 25, 1877, Randall MSS, Rare Book and Manuscript Library, University of Pennsylvania, Philadelphia; Flick, *Samuel Jones Tilden*, 417–18. For similar fears, see C. Ingersoll to Randall, February 27, 1877, Randall MSS, Rare Book and Manuscript Library, University of Pennsylvania, Philadelphia.

31. *ChiTrib*, February 17, 18, 1877; *NYEP*, February 19, 20, 1877; *NYH*, February 22, 23, 24, 1877; *CinCom*, February 24, 1877.

32. Zuczek, "Last Campaign of the Civil War," 28–30; *New Orleans Daily Picayune*, January 4, 10, 1877; "H. V. R.," *CinCom*, March 2, 3, 1877.

33. Dawson, *Army Generals and Reconstruction*, 243–52; *New Orleans Daily Picayune*, January 9, 1877; "H. V. R.," *CinCom*, March 2, 3, 1877.

34. Gillette, *Retreat from Reconstruction*, 328–31; *NYH*, February 21, 22, 1877; *Charleston (S.C.) News and Courier*; February 26, 1877; *NYEP*, February 28, 1877; "H. V. R.," *CinCom*, March 3, 1877; Mary Clemmer, in *CinCom*, March 8, 1877.

35. Polakoff, *Politics of Inertia*, 298–300; "H. V. R.," *CinCom*, April 2, 1877; *NYEP*, April 21, 22, 1877; Clendenin, "President Hayes' 'Withdrawal' of the Troops."

36. On the significance of education to Hayes's vision, see McAfee, "Reconstruction Revisited," 149–51.

37. Andrew, *Wade Hampton*, 422–31; William A. Courtenay to William H. Trescot, January 18, 1877, and Wade Hampton to Trescot, October 6, 13, 1879, Trescot MSS, SCC; Ellis G. Graydon to Martin W. Gary, August 19, 1878, Gary MSS, SCC; J. D. Kennedy to Charles S. McCall, August 23, 1878, McCall MSS, SCC.

38. Sledge, "Chisholm Massacre"; Fairclough, "Alfred Raford Blunt," 284–87; Bauer, "Trial of the Natchitoches 48."

39. James, *Churchill*, 354.

40. Young, "Henry S. Harmon," 194–95; Potts, "Unfilled Expectations"; Taylor, "Crime and Race Relations," 26–27; for a less positive picture, see Oldfield, "On the Beat," 159–62.

41. Olsen, *Carpetbagger's Crusade*, 208; Kousser, *Shaping of Southern Politics*, 12–15, 18–19, 28; Blake, *William Mahone of Virginia*, 176–95; Morsman, *Big House after Slavery*, 146–52; Moore, "Black Militancy in Readjuster Virginia," 167–84.

42. Morsman, *Big House after Slavery*, 152–56; *Mobile (Ala.) Daily Register*, October 31, November 4, 1875; *Alabama State Journal*, October 12, 1875; Schweninger, "Black Citizenship and the Republican Party," 100–102; Francis W. Dawson to Matthew Ransom, August 13, 1884, Ransom MSS, SHC; William P. Snyder to William E. Chandler, February 20, 21, 1883, Chandler MSS, LC. For a similar career of division and pressure for a lily-white organization, see Shadgett, *Republican Party in Georgia*, 80–81, 84–87.

43. "Alabama," 401; L. M. Pleasant to William E. Chandler, July 19, 1890, Chandler MSS, LC; Granberry, "When the Rabbit Foot Was Worked," 38–46; Taylor, "Crime and Race Relations," 27–28; Ortiz, *Emancipation Betrayed*, 37–46; Jeffries,

Bloody Lowndes, 16; Holloway, "'Chicken-Stealer Shall Lose His Vote'"; *Arkansas Gazette*, January 9, 1889. The "Pig Law's" twenty-five-dollar definition was restored in 1888. See *Jackson (Miss.) Clarion-Ledger*, February 16, 1888.

44. Ranney, *In the Wake of Slavery*, 99–101; Woodward, *Strange Career of Jim Crow*, 19–25, 81–94; Somers, "Black and White in New Orleans," 27–42; Rabinowitz, "From Exclusion to Segregation," 336–50.

45. Woodward, *Origins of the New South*, 7–18; Parks, *Joseph E. Brown*, 531–32, 563–64; *Republic*, October 1875, pp. 209, 213; Maddex, *Virginia Conservatives*, 290; *Mobile (Ala.) Daily Register*, April 5, 1873; *Arkansas Gazette*, March 30, April 4, 1873; *Galveston (Tex.) Tri-Weekly News*, August 6, 11, 1873; *Atlanta Constitution*, June 26, 1877.

46. Wynne, *Continuity of Cotton*, 92.

47. *Report of the Commissioner of Education*, xxxiv, xxxvii, 233; Ortiz, *Emancipation Betrayed*, 54–55, 61–64; Maddex, *Virginia Conservatives*, 291; *Atlanta Constitution*, September 12, 1877; Woodward, *Origins of the New South*, 20–21; Perman, *Road to Redemption*, 202, 210, 242–58; Grant, *The Way It Was in the South*, 141–43, 231–36; Bond, *Negro Education in Alabama*, 148–63; Angelo, "Wage Labour Deferred," 590–97; Hair, *Bourbonism and Agrarian Protest*, 24–26, 76–81; Poole, *Never Surrender*, 67–71, 81–84; Edwards, *Gendered Strife and Confusion*, 200–17; Anderson, "Down Memory Lane."

48. Perman, *Road to Redemption*, 212–16; Cooper, *Conservative Regime*, 116–21; Going, *Bourbon Democracy in Alabama*, 111–21; Williams, *Beyond Redemption*, 125–32, 162–64; Brackett, "Cutting Costs by Cutting Lives," 69–76; Griffiths, "State of Servitude Worse than Slavery," 9–15; Curtin, *Black Prisoners and Their World*, 62–78, 119–29.

49. Woodward, *Origins of the New South*, 139–40, 318–19.

Coda

1. Elazar, "Civil War and the Preservation of American Federalism," 55–56.

2. McPherson, *Abraham Lincoln*, 12–13; Bensel, *Political Economy*, 132, 344–47, 462–67, 484–88.

3. Jenkins, *Seizing the New Day*, 89–91, 162–63; Bensel, *Political Economy*, 34–36; McPherson, *Abraham Lincoln*, 16–19; *NYEP*, January 5, 1884.

4. Harris, "Across the Bloody Chasm," 162–65; Blight, "Fifty Years of Freedom," 121–26.

5. "Gath," *ChiTrib*, December 3, 1870; *CinEnq*, February 13, 1878; "D. P.," *CinEnq*, February 22, 1878; *NYTrib*, February 13, 1878.

Bibliography

Manuscript Collections

Albany, New York
  New York State Library
    Horatio Seymour MSS
Atlanta, Georgia
  Atlanta Historical Society
    Samuel P. Richards MSS
  Georgia Department of Archives and History
    Governor's Papers
      Rufus W. Bullock MSS
      Benjamin F. Conley MSS
    Noel Burton Knight Diary
Austin, Texas
  Austin Public Library
    Elisha M. Pease MSS
  University of Texas Library
    Benjamin H. Epperson MSS
    W. W. Mills MSS
    James W. Throckmorton MSS
Baton Rouge, Louisiana
  Hill Library, Louisiana State University
    Anonymous Reconstruction Letters
    Alexander DeClouet MSS
    William Y. Dixon Diary
    Ellis Family MSS
    Isaac Erwin Diary
    Benjamin F. Flanders MSS
    James A. Gillespie MSS
    Duncan F. Kenner MSS
    Joseph D. Shields MSS
Bloomington, Indiana
  Lilly Library, Indiana University
    Hugh McCulloch MSS

Boston, Massachusetts
  Massachusetts Historical Society
  Adams Family MSS
    Edward Atkinson MSS
Brunswick, Maine
  Bowdoin College Library
    Fessenden Family MSS
    Oliver Otis Howard MSS
Cambridge, Massachusetts
  Houghton Library, Harvard University
    Charles Sumner MSS
Chapel Hill, North Carolina
  Southern Historical Collection, University of North Carolina
    Daniel M. Barringer MSS
    David M. Carter MSS
    Joseph Smith Fowler MSS
    William A. Graham MSS
    Matthew W. Ransom MSS
    Henry Clay Warmoth MSS
Charlottesville, Virginia
  University of Virginia
    Amos Akerman Letter-Books
Cincinnati, Ohio
  Cincinnati Historical Society
    Murat Halstead MSS
    Alexander Long MSS
Columbia, Missouri
  Missouri Historical Society
    William B. Napton Diary
    James S. Rollins MSS
Columbia, South Carolina
  South Carolina State Archives
    Governor's Papers
      James L. Orr MSS
      Robert K. Scott MSS
  South Caroliniana Collection, University of South Carolina
    Martin W. Gary MSS
    Wade Hampton MSS
    Charles Spencer McCall MSS
    Benjamin Franklin Perry MSS
    William Henry Trescot MSS
    Williams-Chesnut-Manning MSS
Columbus, Ohio
  Ohio Historical Society
    James M. Comly MSS

Robert K. Scott MSS
Allen W. Thurman MSS
Concord, New Hampshire
New Hampshire Historical Society
William E. Chandler MSS
George Fogg MSS
Durham, North Carolina
Duke University Library
William Worth Belknap MSS
John E. Bryant MSS
Benjamin S. Hedrick MSS
Herschel V. Johnson MSS
William T. Sutherlin MSS
Fremont, Ohio
Rutherford B. Hayes Memorial Library
William C. Claflin MSS
Rutherford B. Hayes MSS
John Sherman Pamphlet Collection
Hartford, Connecticut
Connecticut Historical Society
Mark Howard MSS
Indianapolis, Indiana
Indiana Historical Society
Caleb Mills MSS
Ithaca, New York
Cornell University Library
J. Miller McKim MSS
Jackson, Mississippi
Mississippi Department of Archives and History
Governor's Papers
Adelbert Ames MSS
Benjamin G. Humphreys MSS
William G. Sharkey MSS
James E. and Samuel Matthews MSS
William N. Whitehurst MSS
Knoxville, Tennessee
Hoskins Library, University of Tennessee
John Eaton MSS
Madison, Wisconsin
State Historical Society of Wisconsin
James Rood Doolittle MSS
Elisha W. Keyes MSS
Montgomery, Alabama
Alabama Department of Archives and History
Governor's Papers

Lewis E. Parsons MSS
Robert M. Patton MSS
William H. Smith MSS
Wager Swayne MSS
Joshua Burns Moore MSS
Morgantown, West Virginia
West Virginia Collection, West Virginia University Library
Jonathan M. Bennett MSS
Granville D. Hall MSS
Waitman T. Willey MSS
Nashville, Tennessee
Tennessee State Library and Archives
Washington Family MSS
New Orleans, Louisiana
Tilton Memorial Hall, Tulane University
Amistad Research Collection
American Missionary Association Records
New York, New York
Columbia University
William M. Grosvenor MSS
William A. Sprague MSS
New-York Historical Society
Edward Durell MSS
New York Public Library
John Bigelow MSS
Bryant-Godwin MSS
Horace Greeley MSS
Samuel J. Tilden MSS
Northampton, Massachusetts
Smith College Library
Ames Family MSS
Oberlin, Ohio
Oberlin College
Jacob Dolson Cox MSS
Philadelphia, Pennsylvania
Historical Society of Pennsylvania
Jay Cooke MSS
William D. Kelley MSS
Rare Book and Manuscript Library, University of Pennsylvania
Samuel J. Randall MSS
Princeton, New Jersey
Princeton University Library
William Worth Belknap MSS
Rochester, New York
University of Rochester

William Henry Seward MSS
St. Paul, Minnesota
   Minnesota Historical Society
      George D. and Serena Ames Wright MSS
San Marino, California
   Huntington Library
      Samuel L. M. Barlow MSS
Springfield, Illinois
   Illinois State Historical Society
      Orville H. Browning MSS
      Sylvanus Cadwallader MSS
      William Jayne MSS
      Richard J. Oglesby MSS
      John F. Snyder MSS
      Richard Yates MSS
Washington, D.C.
   Library of Congress
      William Allen MSS
      Nathaniel P. Banks MSS
      Thomas F. Bayard MSS
      Benjamin Helm Bristow MSS
      Benjamin F. Butler MSS
      William E. Chandler MSS
      Henry Laurens Dawes MSS
      Hamilton Fish MSS
      John Wien Forney MSS
      James A. Garfield MSS
      Horace Greeley MSS
      Thomas Jenckes MSS
      Andrew Johnson MSS
      Manton Marble MSS
      Hugh McCulloch MSS
      Justin Smith Morrill MSS
      Carl Schurz MSS
      John Sherman MSS
      Alexander Stephens MSS
      Thaddeus Stevens MSS
      Elihu Washburne MSS

Newspapers

The Age (Philadelphia)
Aiken (S.C.) Tribune
Alabama State Journal (Montgomery)
Albany Argus
Albany Evening Journal
Arkansas Campaign Gazette (Little Rock) (1868)
Arkansas Gazette (Little Rock)

Atlanta Constitution
Atlanta Daily New Era
Auburn (Ala.) Daily Advertiser
Augusta Loyal Georgian
Augusta (Ga.) National Republican
Baltimore Gazette
Baltimore Sun
Bangor (Maine) Whig and Courier
Beaufort (S.C.) Republican
Boston Commonwealth
Boston Daily Advertiser
Boston Evening Transcript
Boston Post
Brooklyn Daily Eagle
Charleston (S.C.) Daily Courier
Charleston (S.C.) Daily Republican
Charleston (S.C.) News and Courier
Chicago Times
Chicago Tribune
Christian Recorder
Cincinnati Commercial
Cincinnati Enquirer
Cincinnati Gazette
Cleveland Daily Leader
Cleveland Plain Dealer
Commercial and Financial Chronicle
    (New York)
Daily Davenport (Iowa) Democrat
Daily Illinois State Journal (Springfield)
Daily Quincy (Ill.) Herald
Dayton (Ohio) Daily Empire
Delphi (Ind.) Times
Des Moines Iowa State Register
Dubuque (Iowa) Herald
Galena (Ill.) Weekly Gazette
Galveston (Tex.) Tri-Weekly News
Harper's Weekly
Iberville (Miss.) Weekly South
Illinois State Register (Springfield)
Independent
Indianapolis Daily Herald
Indianapolis Daily Evening Gazette
Indianapolis Daily State Journal
Indianapolis News
Jackson (Miss.) Clarion-Ledger

Jackson (Miss.) Daily Clarion
Jackson (Miss.) Pilot
Jackson (Miss.) Weekly Clarion
Jacksonville (Fla.) New South
Jamestown (N.Y.) Journal
Kansas City Times
Kennebec Journal (Augusta, Me.)
Keokuk (Iowa) Daily Gate City
Knoxville (Tenn.) Daily Chronicle
Lafayette (La.) Daily Journal
Little Rock Republican
Louisville (Ky.) Daily Commercial
Louisville (Ky.) Courier
Louisville (Ky.) Courier-Journal
Louisville (Ky.) Daily Journal
Louisville (Ky.) Weekly Journal
Luzerne (Pa.) Union
Lynchburg Daily Virginian
Manchester (N.H.) Daily Union
Marietta (Ohio) Register
Memphis Daily Appeal
Memphis Daily Post
Merchants' Magazine
Milwaukee News
Milwaukee Sentinel
Milwaukee Wisconsin
Minneapolis Daily Tribune
Missouri Republican (St. Louis)
Mobile (Ala.) Daily Register
Mobile (Ala.) Nationalist
Montgomery (Ala.) Mail
Nashville Daily Press and Times
Nation
National Anti-Slavery Standard
Newark Daily Advertiser
New Era (Washington, D.C.)
New National Era (Washington, D.C.)
New Orleans Daily Picayune
New Orleans Republican
New Orleans Semi-Weekly Louisianian
New Orleans Times
New Orleans Tribune
New York Daily News
New York Evening Post
New York Graphic

New York Herald
New York Sun
New York Times
New York Tribune
New York World
Norfolk Virginian
North American Review
Ottawa (Ill.) Free Trader
Peoria (Ill.) Daily National Democrat
Peoria (Ill.) Weekly Transcript
Philadelphia Age
Philadelphia Inquirer
Philadelphia Press
Pittsburgh Daily Post
Pittsburgh Gazette
Pomeroy's Democrat (New York)
Portland (Maine) Eastern Argus
Port Royal (S.C.) Commercial
Pottsville (Pa.) Miner's Journal
Providence (R.I.) Evening Bulletin
Quincy (Ill.) Daily Whig and Republican
Raleigh (N.C.) Sentinel
Raleigh (N.C.) Daily Standard
Ravenna (Ohio) Democratic Press

The Republic
Richmond (Va.) Daily Dispatch
Richmond (Va.) Whig
Rutland (Vt.) Weekly Herald
St. Louis (Mo.) Daily Democrat
San Antonio Express
Savannah Daily News and Herald
Savannah Morning News
Springfield (Mass.) Daily Republican
Springfield (Mass.) Weekly Republican
Steubenville (Ohio) Weekly Herald
Tallahassee Floridian
Tuscaloosa (Ala.) Independent Monitor
Vicksburg Republican
Waseou (Ohio) Democratic Expositor
Washington (D.C.) Capital
Washington County News (Marietta, Ohio)
Washington (D.C.) Daily Chronicle
Washington (D.C.) National Republican
Wilmington (N.C.) Morning Star
Worcester Spy (Massachusetts)

U.S. Government Documents

Congressional

"Affairs in Alabama." House Report 262, 43rd Cong., 2nd sess.
"Affairs in Arkansas." House Report 771, 43rd Cong., 1st sess.
"Affairs in Arkansas." House Executive Document 25, 43rd Cong., 2nd sess.
"Affairs of Southern Railroads." House Report 34, 39th Cong., 2nd sess.
"Affairs in the Late Insurrectionary States." House Report 22, 42nd Cong., 2nd sess.
"Alabama." Senate Report 704, 44th Cong., 2nd sess.
"Alabama Election." House Executive Document 238, 40th Cong., 2nd sess.
"Alaska." House Report 35, 40th Cong., 3rd sess.
"Allegations against Senator Powell Clayton." Senate Report 512, 42nd Cong., 3rd sess.
Case Files of Applications from Former Confederates for Presidential Pardons. National Archives, Record Group 94.
"Civil Rights." House Miscellaneous Document 58, 42nd Cong., 3rd sess.
"Condition of Affairs in Georgia." House Miscellaneous Document 52, 40th Cong., 3rd sess.
"Condition of Affairs in Mississippi." House Miscellaneous Document 53, 40th Cong., 3rd sess.
"Condition of Affairs in the South." House Report 261, 43rd Cong., 2nd sess.

"Condition of the South." House Report 101, 43rd Cong., 2nd sess.

Congressional Globe.

Congressional Record.

"Credit Mobilier Investigation." House Report 77, 42nd Cong., 3rd sess.

"Georgia Investigation." Senate Report 175, 41st Cong., 2nd sess.

"Government of the District of Columbia." House Report 647, 43rd Cong., 1st sess.

"Louisiana Contested Elections." House Miscellaneous Document 154, 41st Cong., 2nd sess.

"Management of the War Department." House Report 799, 44th Cong., 1st sess.

"Memorial of the Members of the Legislature of Georgia and Others, Relative to the Illegal Organization of that Body under the Reconstruction Acts." House Miscellaneous Document 6, 40th Cong., 3rd sess.

"Mississippi in 1875." Senate Report 527, 44th Cong., 1st sess.

"National Civil-Rights Bill." House Miscellaneous Document 79, 42nd Cong., 3rd sess.

"New Orleans Riot." House Report 16, 39th Cong., 2nd sess.

"Pacific Mail Steamship Service." House Report 268, 43rd Cong., 2nd sess.

"Pomeroy Investigation." Senate Report 523, 42nd Cong., 3rd sess.

"Reconstruction of Georgia." Senate Executive Document 41, 41st Cong., 2nd sess.

"Reduction of the Military Establishment." House Report 384, 43rd Cong., 1st sess.

Report of the Commissioner of Education, 1877. Washington, D.C.: Government Printing Office, 1879.

"Report of the Secretary of War, Part 1." House Executive Document 1, 40th Cong., 3rd sess.

"Sheafe vs. Tillman." House Miscellaneous Document 53, 41st Cong., 2nd sess.

"South Carolina in 1876." Senate Miscellaneous Document 48, 44th Cong., 2nd sess.

"Southern Railroads." House Executive Document 73, 40th Cong., 2nd sess.

"Suffrage in Utah." House Miscellaneous Document 95, 42nd Cong., 3rd sess.

"Supplement to the *Congressional Globe* . . . Impeachment Trial." 40th Cong., 2nd sess.

"Susan B. Anthony." House Report 648, 43rd Cong., 1st sess.

"Vicksburg Troubles." House Report 265, 43rd Cong., 2nd sess.

Military

Registers and Letters Received by the Commissioner of the Bureau of Refugees, Freedmen, and Abandoned Lands, National Archives. Microfilm edition.

Union Provost Marshal's Files of Papers Relating to Two or More Civilians. National Archives. Microfilm edition.

War of the Rebellion: A Compilation of the Official Records. Series 3. Washington, D.C.: Government Printing Office, 1900.

Other Government Documents

Acts of Alabama. 1866–1875.

Acts of Louisiana. 1868–1876.

Alabama Constitutional Convention. *Journal*. 1867–68.

Constitution of the State of Texas, Adopted by the Constitutional Convention Convened under the Reconstruction Acts of Congress Passed March 2, 1867, and the Acts Supplementary Thereto. Austin, 1869.

Debates and Journals of the Arkansas Constitutional Convention. 1868.

Georgia Constitutional Convention. Journal. 1868.

Journal of the Proceedings of the Constitutional Convention of the State of Florida, Begun and Held at the Capitol, at Tallahassee, on Monday, January 20th, 1868. Tallahassee, 1868.

Louisiana Constitutional Convention. Journal. 1868.

Mississippi Constitutional Convention. Journal. 1868.

Ohio Constitutional Convention. Debates. 1873–74.

Report of the Joint Committee of the General Assembly of Alabama in Regard to the Alleged Election of Geo. A. Spencer as U.S. Senator, Together with Memorial and Evidence. Montgomery, 1875.

South Carolina Constitutional Convention Debates. 1868.

South Carolina Reports and Resolutions. Fraud Report. 1878.

Tribune Almanac. New York: New York Tribune, 1865–77.

U.S. Bureau of the Census. Historical Statistics of the United States: Colonial Times to 1970. Washington, D.C.: Government Printing Office, 1975.

U. S. Department of State. Papers Relating to the Foreign Relations of the United States. Washington, D.C.: Government Printing Office, 1874.

Virginia Constitutional Convention. Debates. 1868.

Contemporary Accounts, Polemics, and Memoirs

Abbott, Martin, ed. "A Southerner Views the South, 1865: Letters of Harvey M. Watterson." Virginia Magazine of History and Biography 68 (October 1960): 478–89.

Adams, Charles Francis, Jr. "A Chapter of Erie." North American Review 109 (July 1869): 30–106.

———. "The Currency Debate of 1873–74." North American Review 119 (July 1874): 111–65.

Adams, Henry. The Education of Henry Adams. Boston: Houghton Mifflin, Riverside Press, 1918.

———. The Letters of Henry Adams. Edited by J. C. Leverson, Ernest Samuels, Charles Vandersee, and Viola H. Winner. Vol 2. Cambridge: Harvard University Press, 1982.

———. "The Session." North American Review 108 (April 1869): 610–40.

———. "The Session." North American Review 111 (July 1870): 29–62.

"Address of the Hon. Richard Yates." Jacksonville, Ill.: Journal Steam Power Press Print, 1866.

Ames, Mary Clemmer. Ten Years in Washington: Life and Scenes in the National Capital, as a Woman Sees Them. Hartford, Conn.: A. D. Worthington, 1874.

Andrews, Sidney. The South Since the War, as Shown by Fourteen Weeks of Travel and Observations in Georgia and the Carolinas. Boston: Ticknor and Fields, 1866.

Appleton's Annual Cyclopedia and Register. 1865–78.

Avary, Myrta Lockett. *Dixie after the War: An Exposition of Social Conditions Existing in the South, during the Twelve Years Succeeding the Fall of Richmond.* New York: Doubleday, Page, 1906.

Bancroft, Frederic, sel. and ed. *Speeches, Correspondence and Political Papers of Carl Schurz.* Vol. 1. New York: G. P. Putnam's Sons, 1913.

Bergeron, Paul H., ed. *Papers of Andrew Johnson.* 16 vols. Knoxville: University of Tennessee Press, 1991.

Blaine, James G. *Twenty Years of Congress.* 2 vols. Norwich: Henry Bill, 1884–86.

Botume, Elizabeth Hyde. *First Days among the Contrabands.* Boston: Lee and Shepard, 1893.

Bowles, Samuel. *Our New West.* Hartford, Conn.: Hartford Publishing Company, 1869.

Brockett, L. P. *Our Western Empire: Or, the New West Beyond the Mississippi.* Philadelphia: Bradley, Garretson, 1882.

Buni, Andrew, ed. "Reconstruction in Orange County, Virginia: A Letter from Hannah Garlick Rawlings to Her Sister, Clarissa Lawrence Rawlings, August 9, 1865." *Virginia Magazine of History and Biography* 75 (October 1967): 459–65.

Childs, Arney Robinson, ed. *The Private Journal of Henry William Ravenel, 1856–1887.* Columbia: University of South Carolina Press, 1947.

Clayton, Powell. *The Aftermath of Civil War.* New York: Neale, 1915.

Clemenceau, Georges. *American Reconstruction, 1865–1870, and the Impeachment of President Johnson.* New York: Dial Press, 1928.

Conwell, Russell. *Magnolia Journey: A Union Veteran Revisits the Former Confederate States.* Arranged and edited by Joseph C. Carter. Southern Historical Publications No. 17. University: University of Alabama Press, 1974.

DeForest, John William. *A Union Officer in the Reconstruction.* Edited by James H. Croushore and David M. Potter. New Haven, Conn.: Yale University Press, 1948.

Democratic Party National Committee. *Campaign Text Book. Why the People Want a Change.* New York: National Democratic Committee, 1880.

Dennett, John Richard. *The South as It Is, 1865–1866.* Edited by Henry M. Christman. Athens: University of Georgia Press, 1965.

Detroit Post and Tribune. *Zachariah Chandler: An Outline Sketch of His Life and Public Services.* Detroit: Post and Tribune, 1880.

"George W. Julian's Journal—the Assassination of Lincoln." *Indiana Magazine of History* 11 (December 1915): 324–37.

Greenawalt, Bruce S., ed. "Virginians Face Reconstruction: Correspondence from James Dorman Davidson Papers, 1865–1880." *Virginia Magazine of History and Biography* 78 (October 1970): 447–63.

Grosvenor, William M. "The Law of Conquest the True Basis of Reconstruction." *New Englander* 24 (January 1865): 111–35.

Hamilton, J. G. de Roulhac, ed. *Correspondence of Jonathan Worth.* 2 vols. Raleigh: Edwards and Broughton, 1909.

————. *The Papers of Thomas Ruffin*. Vol. 4. Raleigh: Edwards and Broughton, 1920.

Hoar, George Frisbie. *Autobiography of Seventy Years*. 2 vols. New York: C. Scribner's and Sons, 1903.

Hoole, W. Stanley, ed. "Diary of Dr. Basil Manly, 1858–1867." *Alabama Review* 5 (April 1952): 142–55.

Julian, George W. *Political Recollections, 1840–1872*. Chicago: Jansen, McClurg, 1884.

Kelley, William Darrah. "The Dangers of the Hour: An Address Delivered at Concert Hall, Philadelphia, March 15, 1866, by Hon. William D. Kelley." Washington, D.C.: Chronicle Book and Job Print, 1866.

King, Edward. *The Great South*. Hartford, Conn.: American Publishing, 1875.

Leland, Isabella Middleton. "Middleton Correspondence, 1861–1865." *South Carolina Historical Magazine* 65 (April 1964): 98–109.

Locke, David Ross. *The Nasby Letters*. Toledo: Toledo Blade, 1893.

Lowell, James Russell. "A Look Before and After." *North American Review* 108 (January 1869): 255–73.McCabe, James Dabney. *Behind the Scenes in Washington*. New York: Continental, 1873.

McDonough, James L., and William T. Alderson, eds. "Republican Politics and the Impeachment Andrew Johnson." *Tennessee Historical Quarterly* 26 (Summer 1967): 177–83.

Merrill, Walter M., and Louis Ruchames. *The Letters of William Lloyd Garrison*. Vol. 6. Cambridge, Mass.: Harvard University Press, 1974.

Miers, Earl Schenck, ed. *When the World Ended: The Diary of Emma LeConte*. New York: Oxford University Press, 1957.

Minturn, William. *Travels West*. London: Samuel Tinsley, 1877.

Moore, John Hammond, ed. *The Juhl Letters to the Charleston Courier: A View of the South, 1865–1871*. Athens: University of Georgia Press, 1974.

Morgan, Albert T. *Yazoo: On the Picket-Line of Freedom*. Washington, D.C., 1884.

Morgan, James Morris. *Recollections of a Rebel Reefer*. New York: Houghton Mifflin, 1917.

Morse, John T., Jr., ed. *Diary of Gideon Welles*. 3 vols. Boston: Houghton Mifflin, Riverside Press, 1911.

Myers, Robert Manson, ed. *The Children of Pride: A True Story of Georgia and the Civil War*. New Haven, Conn.: Yale University Press, 1972.

Nevins, Allan, and Milton Halsey Thomas, eds. *The Diary of George Templeton Strong*. 4 vols. New York: Macmillan, 1952.

"The New Jersey Monopolies." *North American Review* 104 (April 1867): 428–76.

Northrup, Milton Harlow. "A Grave Crisis in American History: The Inner History of the Origin and Formation of the Electoral Commission of 1877." *Century Magazine* 62 (October 1901).

Olson, Otto H., and Ellen Z. McGrew. "Prelude to Reconstruction: The Correspondence of State Senator Leander Sams Gash, 1866–67, Part I." *North Carolina Historical Review* 60 (January 1983): 37–88.

Palmer, Beverly Wilson, ed. *The Selected Letters of Charles Sumner*. 2 vols. Boston: Northeastern University Press, 1990.

Phillips, Christopher, and Jason L. Pendleton, eds. *The Union on Trial: The Political Journals of Judge William Barclay Napton, 1829–1883*. Columbia: University of Missouri Press, 2005.

Pike, James Shepherd. *The Prostrate State*. New York: D. Appleton, 1874.

Poor, Henry V. *Manual of the Railroads of the United States, 1874–1875*. New York: H. V. and H. W. Poor, 1875.

Rawick, George P., ed. *The American Slave: A Composite Autobiography*. Westport, Conn.: Greenwood Press, 1972.

"Recollections of Charles Sumner." *Scribner's Monthly* 8 (August 1874).

Reid, Whitelaw. *After the War: A Southern Tour*. London: Moore, Wilstach & Baldwin, 1866.

Rosenblatt, Emil and Ruth, eds. *Hard Marching Every Day: The Civil War Letters of Private Wilbur Fisk, 1861–1865*. Lawrence: University Press of Kansas, 1983.

Schoonover, Thomas D., ed. *Mexican Lobby: Matias Romero in Washington, 1861–1867*. Lexington: University Press of Kentucky, 1986.

Schurz, Carl. *Reminiscences of Carl Schurz*. 3 vols. New York: McClure, 1908.

Shewmaker, Kenneth E., and Andrew K. Prinz. "A Yankee in Louisiana: Selections from the Diary and Correspondence of Henry R. Gardner, 1862–1866." *Louisiana History* 5 (Summer 1964): 271–95.

Simon, John Y., ed. *Papers of Ulysses S. Grant*. 28 vols. Carbondale: Southern Illinois University Press, 1967–.

Smith, Daniel E. Huger, Alice R. Huger Smith, and Arny R. Childs, eds. *Mason Smith Family Letters*. Columbia: University of South Carolina Press, 1950.

Stewart, Edgar A., ed. "The Journal of James Mallory, 1834–1877." *Alabama Review* 14 (July 1961): 219–32.

Sumner, Charles. *Charles Sumner; His Complete Works*. 20 vols. Boston: Lee and Shepard, 1900.

———. "The One Man Power vs. Congress! Address of Hon. Charles Sumner, at the Music Hall, Boston, October 2, 1866." Boston: Wright and Potter, 1866.

Thompson, S. Millett. *Thirteenth Regiment of New Hampshire Volunteer Infantry in the War of the Rebellion, 1861–1865: A Diary Covering Three Years and a Day*. Boston: Houghton Mifflin, 1888.

Towne, Laura M. *Letters and Diary of Laura M. Towne; Written from the Sea Islands of South Carolina, 1862–1884*. Edited by Rupert Sargent Holland. Cambridge, Mass.: Riverside Press, 1912.

Trowbridge, John T. *The South: A Tour of Its Battle-Fields and Ruined Cities, a Journey through the Desolated States, and Talks with the People*. Hartford, Conn.: L. Stebbins, 1866.

Walker, Francis A. "The Indian Question." *North American Review* 116 (April 1873): 329–88.

Wallace, John. *Carpet-Bag Rule in Florida*. Jacksonville, Fla.: DaCosta, 1988.

Warmoth, Henry Clay. *War, Politics, and Reconstruction: Stormy Days in Louisiana*. New York: Macmillan, 1930.

Wilkins, William Glyde, comp. and ed. *Charles Dickens in America*. New York: Haskell House, 1970.

Williams, Max R., ed. *The Papers of William Alexander Graham*. Vol. 6. Raleigh: North Carolina Department of Cultural Resources, 1976.

Secondary Sources

Books

Abbott, Richard H. *The Republican Party and the South, 1855–1877: The First Southern Strategy*. Chapel Hill: University of North Carolina Press, 1986.

Ackerman, Kenneth D. *Boss Tweed: The Rise and Fall of the Corrupt Pol who Conceived the Soul of Modern New York*. New York: Carroll & Graf, 2005.

———. *The Gold Ring: Jim Fisk, Jay Gould, and Black Friday, 1869*. New York: Harper Business, 1988.

Adler, Dorothy R. *British Investment in American Railways, 1834–1898*. Charlottesville; University Press of Virginia, 1970.

Alexander, Roberta Sue. *North Carolina Faces the Freedmen: Race Relations during Presidential Reconstruction, 1865–1867*. Durham, N.C.: Duke University Press, 1985.

Ambler, Charles H. *Francis H. Pierpont: Union War Governor of Virginia and Father of West Virginia*. Chapel Hill: University of North Carolina Press, 1937.

Ames, Charles Edgar. *Pioneering the Union Pacific: A Reappraisal of the Builders of the Railroad*. New York: Appleton-Century-Crofts, 1969.

Anderson, Eric, and Alfred A. Moss Jr., ed. *The Facts of Reconstruction: Essays in Honor of John Hope Franklin*. Baton Rouge: Louisiana State University Press, 1991.

Andrew, Rod, Jr. *Wade Hampton: Confederate Warrior to Southern Redeemer*. Chapel Hill: University of North Carolina Press, 2008.

Angevine. Robert G. *The Railroad and the State: War, Politics, and Technology in Nineteenth-Century America*. Stanford: Stanford University Press, 2004.

Arrington, Leonard J. *Great Basin Kingdom: An Economic History of the Latter-Day Saints, 1830–1900*. Lincoln: University of Nebraska Press, 1958.

Athearn, Robert G. *High Country Empire: The High Plains and Rockies*. New York: McGraw-Hill, 1960.

Baggett, James Alex. *The Scalawags: Southern Dissenters in the Civil War and Reconstruction*. Baton Rouge: Louisiana State University Press, 2003.

Bain, David Haward. *Empire Express: Building the First Transcontinental Railroad*. New York: Viking, 1999.

Baker, Jean H. *The Politics of Continuity: Maryland Political Parties from 1858 to 1870*. Baltimore: Johns Hopkins University Press, 1973.

Barclay, Thomas S. *The Liberal Republican Movement in Missouri*. Columbia: State Historical Society of Missouri, 1926.

Barr, Alwyn. *Reconstruction to Reform: Texas Politics, 1876–1906*. Austin: University of Texas Press, 1976.

Baum, Dale. *The Shattering of Texas Unionism: Politics in the Lone Star State during the Civil War Era*. Baton Rouge: Louisiana State University Press, 1998.

Belz, Herman. *Reconstructing the Union: Theory and Policy during the Civil War*. Ithaca, N.Y.: Cornell University Press, 1969.

Benedict, Michael Les. *A Compromise of Principle: Congressional Republicans and Reconstruction, 1863–1869*. New York: Norton, 1974.

————. *The Impeachment and Trial of Andrew Johnson*. New York: Norton, 1973.

Bensel, Richard Franklin. *The Political Economy of American Industrialization, 1877–1900*. Cambridge: Cambridge University Press, 2000.

————. *Yankee Leviathan: The Origins of Central State Authority in America, 1859–1877*. Cambridge: Cambridge University Press, 1990.

Bentley, George R. *A History of the Freedmen's Bureau*. Philadelphia: University of Pennsylvania Press, 1955.

Bercaw, Nancy. *Gendered Freedoms: Race, Rights, and the Politics of Household in the Delta, 1861–1875*. Gainesville: University Press of Florida, 2003.

Bergeron, Paul H. *Andrew Johnson's Civil War and Reconstruction*. Knoxville: University of Tennessee Press, 2011.

Beth, Loren P. *The Development of the American Constitution*. New York: Harper and Row, 1971.

Blair, William. *Virginia's Private War: Feeding Body and Soul in the Confederacy*. New York: Oxford University Press, 1998.

Blake, Nelson M. *William Mahone of Virginia: Soldier and Politician*. Richmond: Garrett and Massie, 1935.

Blight, David W. *Race and Reunion: The Civil War in American Memory*. Cambridge, Mass.: Belknap Press of Harvard University Press, 2001.

Bogue, Allan. *The Earnest Men: Republicans of the Civil War Senate*. Ithaca, N.Y.: Cornell University Press, 1981.

Bond, Horace Mann. *Negro Education in Alabama: A Study in Cotton and Steel*. New York: Atheneum, 1969.

Bowen, David Warren. *Andrew Johnson and the Negro*. Knoxville: University of Tennessee Press, 1981.

Bowers, Claude G. *The Tragic Era: The Revolution after Lincoln*. Cambridge, Mass.: Riverside Press, 1929.

Boyer, Paul S. *Purity in Print: Book Censorship in America from the Gilded Age to the Computer Age*. 2nd ed. Madison: University of Wisconsin Press, 2002.

Bradford, Richard H. *The Virginius Affair*. Boulder: Colorado Associated University Press, 1980.

Bradley, Mark L. *Bluecoats and Tar Heels: Soldiers and Civilians in Reconstruction North Carolina*. Lexington: University Press of Kentucky, 2009.

Bremner, Robert H. *The Public Good: Philanthropy and Welfare in the Civil War Era*. New York: Knopf, 1980.

Brock, W. R. *An American Crisis: Congress and Reconstruction, 1865–1867*. New York: St. Martin's Press, 1963.

Brodie, Fawn. *Thaddeus Stevens: Scourge of the South*. New York: Norton, 1959.

Broun, Heywood, and Margaret Leech. *Anthony Comstock: Roundsman of the Lord*. New York: Literary Guild of America, 1927.

Brown, Thomas J., ed. *Reconstructions: New Perspectives on the Postbellum United States*. New York: Oxford University Press, 2006.

Buck, Paul Herman. *The Road to Reunion, 1865–1900*. Boston: Little, Brown, 1937.

Burrows, Edwin G., and Mike Wallace. *Gotham: A History of New York City to 1898*. New York: Oxford University Press, 1999.

Butcher, Patricia Smith. *Education for Equality: Women's Rights Periodicals and Women's Higher Education, 1849–1920*. Westport, Conn.: Greenwood Press, 1989.

Calhoun, Charles W. *Conceiving a New Republic: The Republican Party and the Southern Question, 1869–1900*. Lawrence: University Press of Kansas, 2006.

Callow, Alexander B., Jr. *The Tweed Ring*. New York: Oxford University Press, 1966.

Carter, Dan T. *When the War Was Over: The Failure of Self-Reconstruction in the South, 1865–1867*. Baton Rouge: Louisiana State University Press, 1985.

Cartwright, Joseph H. *The Triumph of Jim Crow: Tennessee Race Relations in the 1880s*. Knoxville: University of Tennessee Press, 1976.

Chen, Jack. *The Chinese of America*. San Francisco: Harper and Row, 1980.

Chen, Yong. *Chinese San Francisco, 1850–1943: A Trans-Pacific Community*. Stanford: Stanford University Press, 2000.

Cimbala, Paul A., and Randall Miller, eds. *The Freedmen's Bureau and Reconstruction: Reconsiderations*. New York: Fordham University Press, 1999.

———. *The Great Task Remaining before Us: Reconstruction as America's Continuing Civil War*. New York: Fordham University Press, 2010.

———. *An Uncommon Time: The Civil War and the Northern Home Front*. New York: Fordham University Press, 2002.

Clark, Champ. *Gettysburg*. Alexandria, Va.: Time-Life Books, 1985.

Clark, Ira G. *Then Came the Railroads: The Century from Steam to Diesel in the Southwest*. Norman: University of Oklahoma Press, 1958.

Cohen, Nancy. *The Reconstruction of American Liberalism, 1865–1914*. Chapel Hill: University of North Carolina Press, 2002.

Coleman, Charles H. *The Election of 1868: The Democratic Effort to Regain Control*. Studies in History, Economics, and Public Law. New York: Columbia University Press, 1933.

Conway, Alan. *The Reconstruction of Georgia*. Minneapolis: University of Minnesota Press, 1967.

Cook, Adrian. *The Alabama Claims: American Politics and Anglo-American Relations, 1865–1872*. Ithaca, N.Y.: Cornell University Press, 1975.

Cook, Robert J. *Civil War Senator: William Pitt Fessenden and the Fight to Save the American Republic*. Baton Rouge: Louisiana State University Press, 2011.

Cooling, Benjamin Franklin. *To the Battles of Franklin and Nashville and Beyond: Stabilization and Reconstruction in Tennessee and Kentucky*. Knoxville: University of Tennessee Press, 2011.

Cooper, William J., Jr. *The Conservative Regime: South Carolina, 1877–1890*. Baltimore: Johns Hopkins University Press, 1968.

Coulter, E. Merton. *The Civil War and Readjustment in Kentucky*. Chapel Hill: University of North Carolina Press, 1926.

———. *The South during Reconstruction*. Baton Rouge: Louisiana State University Press, 1947.

Cox, LaWanda, and John H. Cox. *Politics, Principle, and Prejudice, 1865–1866: Dilemma of Reconstruction America*. New York: Macmillan, 1963.

Cresswell, Tim. *The Tramp in America*. London: Reaktion Books, 2001.

Crow, Jeffrey J., and Robert F. Durden. *Maverick Republican in the Old North State: A Political Biography of Daniel L. Russell*. Baton Rouge: Louisiana State University Press, 1977.

Cummings, Homer. *Federal Justice: Chapters in the History of Justice and the Federal Executive*. New York: Macmillan, 1937.

Current, Richard. *Lincoln's Loyalists: Union Soldiers from the Confederacy*. Boston: Northeastern University Press, 1992.

———. *Those Terrible Carpetbaggers*. New York: Oxford University Press, 1988.

Curry, Richard O., ed. *Radicalism, Racism, and Party Realignment*. Baltimore: Johns Hopkins University Press, 1969.

———. *House Divided: A Study of Statehood Politics and the Copperhead Movement in West Virginia*. Pittsburgh: University of Pittsburgh Press, 1964.

Curtin, Mary Ellen. *Black Prisoners and Their World, Alabama, 1865–1900*. Charlottesville: University Press of Virginia, 2000.

Dannenbaum, Jed. *Drink and Disorder: Temperance Reform in Cincinnati from the Washington Revival to the WCTU*. Urbana: University of Illinois Press, 1984.

Davis, Hugh. *"We Will Be Satisfied with Nothing Less": The African American Struggle for Equal Rights in the North during Reconstruction*. Ithaca, N.Y.: Cornell University Press, 2011.

Dawson, Joseph G., III. *Army Generals and Reconstruction: Louisiana, 1862–1877*. Baton Rouge: Louisiana State University Press, 1982.

Dearing, Mary R. *Veterans in Politics: The Story of the G.A.R.* Baton Rouge: Louisiana State University Press, 1952.

Degler, Carl. *The Other South: Southern Dissenters in the Nineteenth Century*. New York: Harper and Row, 1974.

Deutsch, Sarah. *No Separate Refuge: Culture, Class, and Gender on an Anglo-Hispanic Frontier in the American Southwest, 1880–1940*. New York: Oxford University Press, 1987.

Dick, Everett. *The Lure of the Land: A Social History of the Public Lands from the Articles of Confederation to the New Deal*. Lincoln: University of Nebraska Press, 1970.

Dippie, Brian W. *The Vanishing American: White Attitudes and U.S. Indian Policy*. Middletown, Conn.: Wesleyan University Press, 1982.

Dirlik, Arik, ed. *Chinese on the American Frontier*. Boulder: Rowman and Littlefield, 2001.

Donald, David. *Charles Sumner and the Rights of Man*. New York: Knopf, 1970.

———. *Lincoln*. New York: Simon and Schuster, 1995.

Dorris, Jonathan T. *Pardon and Amnesty under Lincoln and Johnson: The Restoration of the Confederates to Their Rights and Privileges, 1860–1898*. Chapel Hill: University of North Carolina Press, 1953.

Doyle, Don H. *New Men, New Cities, New South: Atlanta, Nashville, Charleston, Mobile, 1860–1910*. Chapel Hill: University of North Carolina Press, 1990.

Drago, Edmund Lee. *Black Politicians and Reconstruction in Georgia*. Baton Rouge: Louisiana State University Press, 1982.

Dray, Philip. *Capitol Men: The Epic Story of Reconstruction through the Lives of the First Black Congressmen*. Boston: Houghton Mifflin, 2008.

DuBose, John Witherspoon. *Alabama's Tragic Decade: Ten Years of Alabama, 1865–1874*. Birmingham: Webb Book Co., 1940.

Dudden, Faye E. *Fighting Chance: The Struggle over Woman Suffrage and Black Suffrage in Reconstruction America*. New York: Oxford University Press, 2011.

Dulles, Foster Rhea. *America in the Pacific: A Century of Expansion*. Boston: Houghton Mifflin, 1938.

Duncan, Russell. *Entrepreneur for Equality: Governor Rufus Bullock, Commerce, and Race in Post–Civil War Georgia*. Athens: University of Georgia Press, 1994.

Edwards, Laura F. *Gendered Strife and Confusion: The Political Culture of Reconstruction*. Urbana: University of Illinois Press, 1997.

Egerton, Douglas R. *The Wars of Reconstruction: The Brief, Violent History of America's Most Progressive Era*. New York: Bloomsbury Press, 2014.

Evans, Eli W. *Judah P. Benjamin: The Jewish Confederate*. New York: Free Press, 1988.

Evans, W. McKee. *Ballots and Fence Rails: Reconstruction on the Lower Cape Fear*. Chapel Hill: University of North Carolina Press, 1966.

Fairman, Charles. *Mr. Justice Miller and the Supreme Court, 1862–1890*. Cambridge, Mass.: Harvard University Press, 1939.

———. *Reconstruction and Reunion, 1864–1868, Part One*. New York: Macmillan, 1971.

———. *Reconstruction and Reunion, 1864–1868, Part Two*. New York: Macmillan, 1987–88.

Fischer, Roger A. *The Segregation Struggle in Louisiana, 1862–1877*. Urbana: University of Illinois Press, 1974.

Fitzgerald, Michael W. *Splendid Failure: Postwar Reconstruction in the American South*. Chicago: Ivan R. Dee, 2007.

———. *The Union League Movement in the Deep South: Politics and Agricultural Change during Reconstruction*. Baton Rouge: Louisiana State University Press, 1989.

———. *Urban Emancipation: Popular Politics in Reconstruction Mobile, 1860–1890*. Baton Rouge: Louisiana State University Press, 2002.

Fleming, Walter. *The Civil War and Reconstruction in Alabama*. Gloucester, Mass.: P. Smith, 1949.

Flexner, Eleanor. *Century of Struggle: The Woman's Rights Movement in the United States*. New York: Atheneum, 1968.

Flick, Alexander C. *Samuel Jones Tilden: A Study in Political Sagacity*. New York: Dodd, Mead, 1939.

Flynn, Charles L. *White Land, Black Labor: Caste and Class in Late Nineteenth-Century America*. Baton Rouge: Louisiana State University Press, 1983.

Foner, Eric. *Freedom's Lawmakers: A Directory of Black Officeholders during Reconstruction*. Baton Rouge: Louisiana State University Press, 1996.

———. *Free Soil, Free Labor, Free Men: The Ideology of the Republican Party Before the Civil War*. New York: Oxford University Press, 1970.

———. *Nothing but Freedom: Emancipation and Its Legacy*. Baton Rouge: Louisiana State University Press, 1983.

———. *Reconstruction: America's Unfinished Revolution, 1863–1877*. New York: Harper and Row, 1988.

Foner, Philip S. *A History of Cuba and Its Relations with the United States*. New York: International Publishers, 1962.

———. *History of the Labor Movement in the United States*. Vol. 1. New York: International Publishers, 1955.

Fowler, Arlen L. *The Black Infantry in the West, 1869–1891*. Westport, Conn.: Greenwood, 1971.

Fraser, Steve. *Every Man a Speculator: A History of Wall Street in American Life*. New York: HarperCollins, 2005.

Fraser, Walter J., Jr., and Winfred B. Moore Jr., eds. *From the Old South to the New: Essays on the Transitional South*. Westport, Conn.: Greenwood Press, 1981.

Gallagher, Gary W. *The Union War*. Cambridge, Mass.: Harvard University Press, 2011.

Gallagher, Gary W., and Rachel W. Shelden, eds. *A Political Nation: New Directions in Mid-Nineteenth-Century American Political History*. Charlottesville: University of Virginia Press, 2012.

Gambill, Edward L. *Conservative Ordeal: Northern Democrats and Reconstruction, 1865–1868*. Ames: Iowa State University Press, 1981.

Garner, James W. *Reconstruction in Mississippi*. Baton Rouge: Louisiana State University Press, 1968.

Gaston, Paul M. *The New South Creed: A Study in Southern Mythmaking*. New York: Vintage, 1970.

Gates, Paul W. *Agriculture and the Civil War*. New York: Knopf, 1965.

Gillette, William, *Retreat from Reconstruction, 1869–1879*. Baton Rouge: Louisiana State University Press, 1979.

———. *The Right to Vote: Politics and the Passage of the Fifteenth Amendment*. Baltimore: Johns Hopkins University Press, 1965.

Ginsberg, Benjamin. *Moses of South Carolina: A Jewish Scalawag during Radical Reconstruction*. Baltimore: Johns Hopkins University Press, 2010.

Going, Allen J. *Bourbon Democracy in Alabama, 1874–1890*. University: University of Alabama Press, 1951.

Gordon, Sarah Barringer. *The Mormon Question: Polygamy and Constitutional Conflict in Nineteenth-Century America*. Chapel Hill: University of North Carolina Press, 2002.

Grant, Donald L. *The Way It Was in the South: The Black Experience in Georgia*. New York: Birch Lane, 1993.

Green, Constance McLaughlin. *Washington: Village and Capital, 1800–1878*. Princeton: Princeton University Press, 1962.

Green, William D. *A Peculiar Imbalance: The Fall and Rise of Racial Equality in Early Minnesota*. St. Paul: Minnesota Historical Society Press, 2007.

Greenberg, Dolores. *Financiers and Railroads, 1869–1889: A Study of Morton, Bliss, and Company*. Newark: University of Delaware Press, 1980.

Greene, A. Wilson. *Civil War Petersburg: Confederate City in the Crucible of War*. Charlottesville: University of Virginia Press, 2006.

Groce, W. Todd. *Mountain Rebels: East Tennessee Confederates and the Civil War, 1860–1870*. Knoxville: University of Tennessee Press, 1999.

Grossman, Lawrence. *The Democratic Party and the Negro: Northern and National Politics, 1868–1892*. Urbana: University of Illinois Press, 1976.

Guy, Anita Aidt. *Maryland's Persistent Pursuit to End Slavery, 1850–1864*. New York: Garland, 1997.

Hahn, Steven. *A Nation under Our Feet: Black Political Struggles in the Rural South from Slavery to the Great Migration*. Cambridge, Mass.: Belknap Press of Harvard University Press, 2003.

Hair, William Ivy. *Bourbonism and Agrarian Protest: Louisiana Politics, 1877–1900*. Baton Rouge: Louisiana State University Press, 1969.

Halbrook, Stephen P. *Freedmen, the Fourteenth Amendment, and the Right to Bear Arms, 1866–1876*. Westport, Conn: Praeger, 1998.

Hamilton, J. de Roulhac. *Reconstruction in North Carolina*. Studies in History, Economics and Public Law. New York: Columbia University, 1914.

Harrington, Fred H. *Fighting Politician, Major General N. P. Banks*. Philadelphia: University of Pennsylvania Press, 1948.

Harris, William C. *The Day of the Carpetbagger: Republican Reconstruction in Mississippi*. Baton Rouge: Louisiana State University Press, 1979.

———. *Lincoln's Last Months*. Cambridge, Mass.: Belknap Press of Harvard University Press, 2011.

———. *Presidential Reconstruction in Mississippi*. Baton Rouge: Louisiana State University Press, 1967.

———. *William Woods Holden: Firebrand of North Carolina Politics*. Baton Rouge: Louisiana State University Press, 1987.

———. *With Charity for All: Lincoln and the Restoration of the Union*. Lexington: University Press of Kentucky, 1997.

Hart, Roger L. *Redeemers, Bourbons, and Populists: Tennessee, 1870–1896*. Baton Rouge: Louisiana State University Press, 1975.

Hawgood, John A. *America's Western Frontiers: The Exploration and Settlement of the Trans-Mississippi West*. New York: Knopf, 1967.

Hesseltine, William B. *Ulysses S. Grant, Politician*. New York: Dodd, Mead, 1935.

Hirshson, Stanley P. *Grenville M. Dodge, Soldier, Politician, Railroad Pioneer*. Bloomington: Indiana University Press, 1967.

Holbo, Paul S. *Tarnished Expansion: The Alaska Scandal, the Press, and Congress, 1867–1871*. Knoxville: University of Tennessee Press, 1983.

Hollandsworth, James G. *An Absolute Massacre: The New Orleans Race Riot of July 30, 1866*. Baton Rouge: Louisiana State University Press, 2001.

Holt, Thomas. *Black over White: Negro Political Leadership in South Carolina during Reconstruction*. Urbana: University of Illinois Press, 1977.

Hoogenboom, Ari. *Outlawing the Spoils: A History of the Civil Service Reform Movement, 1865–1883*. Urbana: University of Illinois Press, 1968.

Howard, Robert P. *Illinois: A History of the Prairie State*. Grand Rapids: William B. Eerdmans, 1972.

Hume, Richard L., and Jerry B. Gough. *Blacks, Carpetbaggers, and Scalawags: The Constitutional Conventions of Radical Reconstruction*. Baton Rouge: Louisiana State University Press, 2008.

Hyde, Samuel C., Jr. *Pistols and Politics: The Dilemma of Democracy in Louisiana's Florida Parishes, 1810–1899*. Baton Rouge: Louisiana State University Press, 1996.

Hyman, Harold M. *A More Perfect Union: The Impact of the Civil War and Reconstruction on the Constitution*. Boston: Houghton Mifflin, 1975.

———. *The Reconstruction Justice of Salmon P. Chase: In Re Turner and Texas v. White*. Lawrence: University Press of Kansas, 1997.

Hyman, Harold M., and William M. Wiecek. *Equal Justice Under Law: Constitutional Development, 1835–1875*. New York: Harper and Row, 1982.

Ibsen, Kristine. *Maximilian, Mexico, and the Invention of Empire*. Nashville: Vanderbilt University Press, 2010.

Inscoe, John C., and Robert C. Kenzer, eds. *Enemies of the Country: New Perspectives on Unionists in the Civil War South*. Athens: University of Georgia Press, 2001.

Irwin, Leonard Bertram. *Pacific Railways and Nationalism in the Canadian-American Northwest, 1845–1873*. New York: Greenwood, 1968.

Jackson, Joy F. *New Orleans in the Gilded Age: Politics and Urban Progress, 1880–1896*. Baton Rouge: Louisiana State University Press, 1969.

James, F. Cyril. *The Growth of Chicago Banks*. Vol. 1, *The Formative Years, 1816–1896*. New York: Harper and Brothers, 1938.

James, Robert R. *Churchill: A Study in Failure, 1900-1939*. New York: World, 1970.

Janney, Caroline E. *Remembering the Civil War: Reunion and the Limits of Reconciliation*. Chapel Hill: University of North Carolina Press, 2013.

Jaynes, Gerald David. *Branches without Roots: Genesis of the Black Working Class in the American South, 1862–1882*. New York: Oxford University Press, 1986.

Jeffries, Hasan Kwame. *Bloody Lowndes: Civil Rights and Black Power in Alabama's Black Belt*. New York: New York University Press, 2009.

Jenkins, Wilbert L. *Seizing the New Day: African Americans in Post–Civil War Charleston*. Bloomington: Indiana University Press, 1998.

Jentz, John B., and Richard Schneirov. *Chicago in the Age of Capital: Class, Politics, and Democracy during the Civil War and Reconstruction*: Urbana: University of Illinois Press, 2012.

Jones, Jacqueline. *Soldiers of Light and Love: Northern Teachers and Georgia Blacks, 1865–1873*. Chapel Hill: University of North Carolina Press, 1980.

Kaczorowski, Robert J. *The Politics of Judicial Interpretation: The Federal Courts, Department of Justice, and Civil Rights, 1866–1876*. New York: Oceana, 1985.

Kantrowitz, Stephen David. *More than Freedom: Fighting for Black Citizenship in a White Republic, 1829–1889*. New York: Penguin, 2012.

Kaufman, Jason. *The Origins of Canadian and American Political Differences*. Cambridge, Mass.: Harvard University Press, 2009.

Keith, LeeAnna. *The Colfax Massacre: The Untold Story of Black Power, White Terror, and the Death of Reconstruction*. New York: Oxford University Press, 2008.

Keller, Morton. *Affairs of State: Public Life in Late-Nineteenth-Century America*. Cambridge, Mass.: Harvard University Press, 1977.

Kibler, Lillian Adele. *Benjamin F. Perry: South Carolina Unionist*. Durham, N.C.: Duke University Press, 1946.

Kingsbury, Susan M., ed. *Labor Laws and Their Enforcement*. New York: Longmans, Green, 1911.

Kirkland, Edward C. *Industry Comes of Age, 1860–1897: Business, Labor, and Public Policy, 1860–1897*. New York: Holt, Rinehart, and Winston, 1961.

———. *Men, Cities, and Transportation*. Vol. 1. Cambridge, Mass.: Harvard University Press, 1948.

Kirwan, Albert D. *Revolt of the Rednecks: Mississippi Politics, 1876–1925*. Lexington: University Press of Kentucky, 1951.

Klein, Maury. *The Life and Legend of Jay Gould*. Baltimore: Johns Hopkins University Press, 1986.

Kleppner, Paul. *The Third Electoral System, 1853–1892: Parties, Voters, and Political Culture*. Chapel Hill: University of North Carolina Press, 1979.

Korngold, Ralph. *Thaddeus Stevens: A Being Darkly Wise and Rudely Great*. New York: Harcourt, Brace, 1955.

Kousser, J. Morgan. *The Shaping of Southern Politics: Suffrage Restriction and the Establishment of the One-Party South, 1880–1910*. New Haven, Conn.: Yale University Press, 1974.

Kusmer, Kenneth L. *Down & Out, and on the Road: The Homeless in American History*. New York: Oxford University Press, 2002.

Kvasnicka, Robert M., and Herman J. Viola, eds. *The Commissioners of Indian Affairs, 1824–1877*. Lincoln: University of Nebraska Press, 1979.

Lamson, Peggy. *The Glorious Failure: Black Congressman Robert Brown Elliott and the Reconstruction in South Carolina*. New York: Norton, 1974.

Lane, Charles. *The Day Freedom Died: The Colfax Massacre, the Supreme Court, and the Betrayal of Reconstruction*. New York: Henry Holt, 2008.

Larson, Robert W. *New Mexico's Quest for Statehood, 1846–1912*. Albuquerque: University of New Mexico Press, 1968.

Lawson, Melinda. *Patriot Fires: Forging a New American Nationalism in the Civil War North*. Lawrence: University Press of Kansas, 2002.

Lears, Jackson. *Rebirth of a Nation: The Making of Modern America, 1877–1920*. New York: HarperCollins, 2009.

Lebergott, S. *The Americans: An Economic Record*. New York: Norton, 1984.

Limbaugh, Ronald H. *Rocky Mountain Carpetbaggers: Idaho's Territorial Governors, 1863–1890*. Moscow: University Press of Idaho, 1982.

Litwack, Leon F. *Been in the Storm So Long: The Aftermath of Slavery*. New York: Vintage Books, 1979.

Lonn, Ella. *Reconstruction in Louisiana after 1868*. New York: G. P. Putnam's Sons, 1918.

Love, Eric T. L. *Race over Empire: Racism and U.S. Imperialism, 1865–1900*. Chapel Hill: University of North Carolina Press, 2004.

Lowe, Richard. *Republicans and Reconstruction in Virginia, 1856–1870*. Charlottesville: University Press of Virginia, 1991.

Maddex, Jack P. *The Virginia Conservatives, 1867–1879: A Study in Reconstruction Politics*. Chapel Hill: University of North Carolina Press, 1970.

Maltz, Earl M. *Civil Rights, the Constitution, and Congress, 1863–1869*. Lawrence: University Press of Kansas, 1990.

———. *The Fourteenth Amendment and the Law of the Constitution*. Durham: Carolina Academic Press, 2003.

Manning, Chandra. *What This Cruel War Was Over: Soldiers, Slavery, and the Civil War*. New York: Random House, 2007.

Marvel, William. *Tarnished Victory: Finishing Lincoln's War*. Boston: Houghton Mifflin Harcourt, 2011.

Masur, Kate. *An Example for All the Land: Emancipation and the Struggle over Equality in Washington, D.C.* Chapel Hill: University of North Carolina Press, 2010.

May, Robert E. *Manifest Destiny's Underworld: Filibustering in Antebellum America*. Chapel Hill: University of North Carolina Press, 2002.

———. *The Southern Dream of a Caribbean Empire, 1854–1861*. Baton Rouge: Louisiana State University Press, 1973.

McDermott, John D. *Red Cloud's War: The Bozeman Trail, 1866–1868*. Norman: Arthur H. Clark, 2010.

McFeely, William S. *Grant: A Biography*. New York: Knopf, 1982.

———. *Yankee Stepfather: General O. O. Howard and the Freedmen*. New Haven, Conn.: Yale University Press, 1968.

McKinney, Gordon B. *Southern Mountain Republicans, 1865–1900: Politics and the Appalachian Community*. Chapel Hill: University of North Carolina Press, 1978.

McKitrick, Eric L. *Andrew Johnson and Reconstruction*. New York: Oxford University Press, 1960.

McPherson, James M. *Abraham Lincoln and the Second American Revolution*. New York: Oxford University Press, 1990.

———. *The Struggle for Equality: Abolitionists and the Negro in the Civil War and Reconstruction*. Princeton: Princeton University Press, 1965.

Mecker, Jerome. *Innocent Abroad: Charles Dickens's American Engagements*. Lexington: University Press of Kentucky, 1990.

Merrill, Horace Samuel. *Bourbon Democracy of the Middle West, 1865–1896*. Baton Rouge: Louisiana State University Press, 1953.

Middleton, Stephen. *The Black Laws: Race and Legal Process in Early Ohio*. Athens: Ohio University Press, 2005.

Miller, Edward A. *Gullah Statesman: Robert Smalls from Slavery to Congress, 1839–1915*. Columbia: University of South Carolina Press, 1995.

Miller, George H. *Railroads and the Granger Laws*. Milwaukee: University of Wisconsin Press, 1971.

Milner, Clyde A., II, Carol A. O'Connor, and Martha A. Sandweiss, eds. *The Oxford History of the American West*. New York: Oxford University Press, 1994.

Milton, George Fort. *The Age of Hate: Andrew Johnson and the Radicals*. New York: Coward-McCann, 1930.

Miner, Craig. *West of Wichita: Settling the High Plains of Kansas, 1865–1890*. Lawrence: University Press of Kansas, 1986.

Mitchell, Stewart. *Horatio Seymour of New York*. Cambridge, Mass.: Harvard University Press, 1938.

Mohr, James C. *The Radical Republicans and Reform in New York during Reconstruction*. Ithaca, N.Y.: Cornell University Press, 1973.

———, ed. *Radical Republicans in the North: State Politics during Reconstruction*. Baltimore: Johns Hopkins University Press, 1976.

Moneyhon, Carl. *The Impact of the Civil War and Reconstruction on Arkansas: Persistence in the Midst of Ruin*. Baton Rouge: Louisiana State University Press, 1994.

———. *Republicanism in Reconstruction Texas*. Austin: University of Texas Press, 1980.

———. *Texas after the Civil War: The Struggle of Reconstruction*. College Station: Texas A&M University Press, 2004.

Montgomery, David. *Beyond Equality: Labor and the Radical Republicans, 1862–1872*. New York: Vintage, 1967.

Morsman, Amy Feely. *The Big House after Slavery: Virginia Plantation Families and Their Postbellum Domestic Experiment*. Charlottesville: University of Virginia Press, 2010.

Murphy, James B. *L. Q. C. Lamar, Pragmatic Patriot*. Baton Rouge: Louisiana State University Press, 1973.

Mushkat, Jerome. *The Reconstruction of the New York Democracy, 1861–1874*. Rutherford, N.J.: Fairleigh Dickinson University Press, 1981.

Muzzey, David Saville. *James G. Blaine: A Political Idol of Other Days*. New York: Dodd, Mead, 1934.

Myers, Gustavus. *History of the Great American Fortunes*. New York: Modern Library, 1936.

Nathans, Elizabeth Studley. *Losing the Peace: Georgia Republicans and Reconstruction, 1865–1871*. Baton Rouge: Louisiana State University Press, 1968.

Nevins, Allan. *Hamilton Fish: The Inner History of the Grant Administration*. New York: Dodd, Mead, 1936.

———. *The War for the Union: The Improvised War, 1861–1862*. New York: Charles Scribner's Sons, 1959.

———. *The War for the Union: The Organized War to Victory, 1864–1865*. New York: Charles Scribner's Sons, 1971.

Nieman, Donald G., ed. *Black Southerners and the Law, 1865–1900*. New York: Garland, 1994.

———. *Freedom, Racism, and Reconstruction: Collected Writings of La Wanda Cox*. Athens: University of Georgia Press, 1997.

Norgren, Jill. *Belva Lockwood: The Woman Who Would Be President*. New York: New York University Press, 2007.

Novak, Daniel A. *The Wheel of Servitude: Black Forced Labor after Slavery*. Lexington: University Press of Kentucky, 1978.

Nunn, W. C. *Texas under the Carpetbaggers*. Austin: University of Texas Press, 1962.

Nystrom, Justin A. *New Orleans after the Civil War: Race, Politics, and a New Birth of Freedom*. Baltimore: Johns Hopkins University Press, 2010.

Oakes, James. *Freedom National: The Destruction of Slavery in the United States, 1861–1865*. New York: Norton, 2013.

Ochiai, Akiko. *Harvesting Freedom: African American Agrarianism in Civil War Era South Carolina*. Westport, Conn.: Praeger, 2004.

Olsen, Otto H. *Carpetbagger's Crusade: The Life of Albion Winegar Tourgee*. Baltimore: Johns Hopkins University Press, 1965.

Ortiz, Paul. *Emancipation Betrayed: The Hidden History of Black Organizing and White Violence in Florida from Reconstruction to the Bloody Election of 1920*. Berkeley: University of California Press, 1965.

Osthaus, Carl R. *Freedmen, Philanthropy, and Fraud: A History of the Freedman's Savings Bank*. Chicago: University of Chicago Press, 1976.

Overton, Richard C. *Burlington West: A Colonization History of the Burlington Railroad*. Cambridge, Mass.: Harvard University Press, 1941.

Paddison, Joshua. *American Heathens: Religion, Race, and Reconstruction in California*. San Marino: Huntington Library, 2012.

Paine, Albert Bigelow. *Th. Nast: His Period and His Pictures*. New York: Harper and Brothers, 1904.

Paolino, Ernest N. *The Foundations of the American Empire: William Henry Seward and U.S. Foreign Policy*. Ithaca, N.Y.: Cornell University Press, 1973.

Parish, Peter J. *The North and the Nation in the Era of the Civil War*. Edited by Adam I. P. Smith and Susan-Mary Grant. New York: Fordham University Press, 2003.

Parks, Joseph H. *Joseph E. Brown of Georgia*. Baton Rouge: Louisiana State University Press, 1976.

Parrish, William E. *Missouri under Radical Rule, 1865–1870*. Columbia: University of Missouri Press, 1965.

Pereyra, Lillian A. *James Lusk Alcorn, Persistent Whig*. Baton Rouge: Louisiana State University Press, 1966.

Perman, Michael. *Reunion Without Compromise: The South and Reconstruction, 1865–1868*. Cambridge: Cambridge University Press, 1973.

———. *The Road to Redemption: Southern Politics, 1869–1879*. Chapel Hill: University of North Carolina Press, 1984.

Peskin, Allan. *Garfield: A Biography*. Kent, Ohio: Kent State University Press, 1978.

Plummer, Mark A. *Frontier Governor: Samuel J. Crawford of Kansas*. Lawrence: University Press of Kansas, 1971.

Polakoff, Keith Ian. *The Politics of Inertia: The Election of 1876 and the End of Reconstruction*. Baton Rouge: Louisiana State University Press, 1973.

Poole, N. Scott. *Never Surrender: Confederate Memory and Conservatism in the South Carolina Upcountry*. Athens: University of Georgia Press, 2004.

Priest, Loring Benson. *Uncle Sam's Stepchildren: The Reformation of United States Indian Policy, 1865–1887*. Lincoln: University of Nebraska Press, 1942.

Rabinowitz, Howard N., ed. *Southern Black Leaders of the Reconstruction Era*. Urbana: University of Illinois Press, 1982.

Rable, George C. *But There Was No Peace: The Role of Violence in the Politics of Reconstruction*. Athens: University of Georgia Press, 1984.

Ranney, Joseph A. *In the Wake of Slavery: Civil War, Civil Rights, and the Reconstruction of Southern Law*. Westport, Conn.: Praeger, 2006.

Ransom, Roger L., and Richard Sutch. *One Kind of Freedom: The Economic Consequences of Emancipation*. New York: Cambridge University Press, 1977.

Ratchford, B. U. *American State Debts*. Durham, N.C.: Duke University Press, 1941.

Reeves, Thomas C. *Gentleman Boss: The Life of Chester Alan Arthur*. New York: Knopf, 1975.

Reilly, Elizabeth, ed. *Infinite Hope and Finite Disappointment: The Story of the First Interpreters of the Fourteenth Amendment*. Akron: University of Akron Press, 2011.

Reynolds, John S. *Reconstruction in South Carolina*. Columbia: State Company, 1905.

Richardson, Heather Cox. *The Death of Reconstruction: Race, Labor, and Politics in the Post–Civil War North, 1865–1901*. Cambridge, Mass.: Harvard University Press, 2002.

———. *The Greatest Nation of the Earth: Republican Economic Policies during the Civil War*. Cambridge, Mass.: Harvard University Press, 1997.

———. *West from Appomattox: The Reconstruction of America after the Civil War*. New Haven, Conn.: Yale University Press, 2007.

———. *Wounded Knee: Party Politics and the Road to an American Massacre*. New York: Basic Books, 2010.

Richardson, Leon B. *William E. Chandler, Republican*. New York: Dodd, Mead, 1940.

Ridge, Martin. *Ignatius Donnelly: The Portrait of a Politician*. Chicago: University of Chicago Press, 1963.

Roark, James L. *Masters without Slaves: Southern Planters in the Civil War and Reconstruction*. New York: Norton, 1977.

Robbins, William G. *Colony and Empire: The Capitalist Transformation of the American West*. Lawrence: University Press of Kansas, 1994.

Rodrigue, John C. *Reconstruction in the Cane Fields: From Slavery to Free Labor in Louisiana's Sugar Parishes, 1862–1880*. Baton Rouge: Louisiana State University Press, 2001.

Rogers, William Warren, Jr. *Black Belt Scalawag: Charles Hays and the Southern Republicans in the Era of Reconstruction*. Athens: University of Georgia Press, 1993.

Rogers, William Warren, Robert David Ward, Leah Rawls Atkins, and Wayne Flynt. *Alabama: The History of a Deep South State*. Tuscaloosa: University of Alabama Press, 1994.

Ross, Michael A. *Justice of Shattered Dreams: Samuel Freeman Miller and the Supreme Court during the Civil War Era*. Baton Rouge: Louisiana State University Press, 2003.

Rubin, Anne Sarah. *A Shattered Nation: The Rise and Fall of the Confederacy, 1861–1868*. Chapel Hill: University of North Carolina Press, 2005.

Rubin, Hyman. *South Carolina Scalawags*. Columbia: University of South Carolina Press, 2006.

Rusco, Elmer R. *"Good Time Coming?" Black Nevadans in the Nineteenth Century.* Westport, Conn.: Greenwood Press, 1975.

Salter, William. *The Life of James W. Grimes, Governor of Iowa, 1854–1858; a Senator of the United States, 1859–1869.* New York: D. Appleton, 1876.

Saville, Julie. *The Work of Reconstruction: From Slave to Wage Laborer in South Carolina, 1860–l870.* New York: Cambridge University Press, 1994.

Scarborough, William Kauffman. *Masters of the Big House: Elite Slaveholders of the Mid-Nineteenth-Century South.* Baton Rouge: Louisiana State University Press, 2003.

Scaturro, Frank J. *The Supreme Court's Retreat from Reconstruction: A Distortion of Constitutional Jurisprudence.* Westport, Conn.: Greenwood Press, 2001.

Scheiber, Harry, ed. *United States Economic History.* New York: Knopf, 1964.

Schoonover, Thomas D. *Dollars over Dominion: The Triumph of Liberalism in Mexican–United States Relations, 1861–1867.* Baton Rouge: Louisiana State University Press, 1978.

Schott, Thomas E. *Alexander Stephens of Georgia: A Biography.* Baton Rouge: Louisiana State University Press, 1988.

Schwalm, Leslie A. *Emancipation's Diaspora: Race and Reconstruction in the Upper Midwest.* Chapel Hill: University of North Carolina Press, 2009.

Schwartz, Rosalie. *Lawless Liberators: Political Banditry and Cuban Independence.* Durham, N.C.: Duke University Press, 1989.

Sefton, James E. *The United States Army and Reconstruction, 1865–1877.* Baton Rouge: Louisiana State University Press, 1967.

Seip, Terry L. *The South Returns to Congress: Men, Economic Measures, and Intersectional Relationships, 1868–1879.* Baton Rouge: Louisiana State University Press, 1983.

Sexton, Jay. *Debtor Diplomacy: Finance and American Foreign Relations in the Civil War Era, 1837–1873.* Oxford: Oxford University Press, 2005.

Shadgett, Olive Hall. *The Republican Party in Georgia: From Reconstruction through 1900.* Athens: University of Georgia Press, 1964.

Shannon, Fred A. *The Farmer's Last Frontier, Agriculture, 1860–1897.* New York: Farrar & Rinehart, 1945.

Sharkey, Robert P. *Money, Class, and Party: An Economic Study of the Civil War and Reconstruction.* Baltimore: Johns Hopkins University Press, 1939.

Shippee, Lester Burrell. *Canadian-American Relations, 1849–1874.* New Haven, Conn.: Yale University Press, 1939.

Shofner, Jerrell M. *Nor Is It Over Yet: Florida in the Era of Reconstruction, 1863–1877.* Gainesville: University of Florida Press, 1974.

Silbey, Joel H. *A Respectable Minority: The Democratic Party in the Civil War Era, 1860–1868.* New York: Norton, 1977.

Simkins, Francis B., and Robert Hilliard Woody. *South Carolina during Reconstruction.* Chapel Hill: University of North Carolina Press, 1932.

Simpson, Brooks D. *Let Us Have Peace: Ulysses S. Grant and the Politics of War and Reconstruction, 1861–1868.* Chapel Hill: University of North Carolina Press, 1991.

———. *The Reconstruction Presidents.* Lawrence: University Press of Kansas, 1998.

Singletary, Otis. *Negro Militia and Reconstruction*. Austin: University of Texas Press, 1957.

Sinisi, Kyle S. *Sacred Debts: State Civil War Claims and American Federalism, 1861–1880*. New York: Fordham University Press, 2003.

Slap, Andrew L. *The Doom of Reconstruction: The Liberal Republicans in the Civil War Era*. New York: Fordham University Press, 2007.

———, ed. *Reconstructing Appalachia: The Civil War's Aftermath*. Lexington: University Press of Kentucky, 2010.

Slap, Andrew L., and Michael Thomas Smith, eds. *This Distracted and Anarchical People: New Answers for Old Questions about the Civil War–Era North*. New York: Fordham University Press, 2013.

Slotkin, Richard. *The Fatal Environment: The Myth of the Frontier in the Age of Industrialization, 1800–1890*. Middletown, Conn.: Wesleyan University Press, 1985.

Smallwood, James M. *Time of Hope, Time of Despair: Black Texans during Reconstruction*. Port Washington, N.Y.: National University Publications, 1981.

Smith, Joseph P. *The Republican Expansionists of the Early Reconstruction Era*. Chicago: University of Chicago Libraries, 1933.

Smith, Sherry L. *The View from Officers' Row: Army Perceptions of Western Indians*. Tucson: University of Arizona Press, 1990.

Snay, Mitchell. *Fenians, Freedmen, and Southern Whites: Race and Nationality in the Era of Reconstruction*. Baton Rouge: Louisiana State University Press, 2007.

Sobel, Robert. *The Big Board: A History of the New York Stock Market*. New York: Free Press, 1965.

———. *Panic on Wall Street: A History of America's Financial Disasters*. New York: Macmillan, 1968.

Spence, Clark C. *Territorial Politics and Government in Montana, 1864–1880*. Urbana: University of Illinois Press, 1975.

Sproat, John G. *"The Best Men": Liberal Reformers in the Gilded Age*. New York: Oxford University Press, 1968.

Stampp, Kenneth M. *The Era of Reconstruction, 1865–1877*. New York: Knopf, 1965.

Stanley, F. *The Civil War in New Mexico*. Denver: World Press, 1960.

Staples, Thomas S. *Reconstruction in Arkansas, 1862–1874*. New York: Columbia University, 1923.

Stewart, David O. *Impeached: The Trial of President Andrew Johnson and the Fight for Lincoln's Legacy*. New York: Simon and Schuster, 2009.

Stewart, James Brewer. *Wendell Phillips: Liberty's Hero*. Baton Rouge: Louisiana State University Press, 1986.

Storey, Margaret M. *Loyalty and Loss: Alabama's Unionists in the Civil War and Reconstruction*. Baton Rouge: Louisiana State University Press, 2004.

Storey, Moorfield, and Edward W. Emerson. *Ebenezer Rockwood Hoar: A Memoir*. Boston: Houghton Mifflin, 1911.

Stover, John F. *American Railroads*. Chicago: University of Chicago Press, 1961.

———. *The Railroads of the South, 1865–1900*. Chapel Hill: University of North Carolina Press, 1955.

Summers, Mark Wahlgren. *A Dangerous Stir: Fear, Paranoia, and the Making of Reconstruction*. Chapel Hill: University of North Carolina Press, 2009.

———. *The Era of Good Stealings*. New York: Oxford University Press, 1993.

———. *Party Games: Getting, Keeping, and Using Power in Gilded Age Politics*. Chapel Hill: University of North Carolina Press, 2004.

———. *The Plundering Generation: Corruption and the Crisis of the Union, 1849–1861*. New York: Oxford University Press, 1988.

———. *Railroads, Reconstruction, and the Gospel of Prosperity: Aid under the Radical Republicans, 1865–1877*. Princeton, N.J.: Princeton University Press, 1984.

———. *Rum, Romanism, and Rebellion: The Making of a President, 1884*. Chapel Hill: University of North Carolina Press, 2000.

Sutherland, Daniel E. *The Confederate Carpetbaggers*. Baton Rouge: Louisiana State University Press, 1988.

———. *A Savage Conflict: The Decisive Role of Guerrillas in the American Civil War*. Chapel Hill: University of North Carolina Press, 2009.

Tansill, Charles C. *The Purchase of the Danish West Indies*. Baltimore: Johns Hopkins University Press, 1932.

Taussig, F. W. *The Tariff History of the United States*. 8th rev. ed. New York: G. P. Putnam's Sons, 1931.

Taylor, Alrutheus Ambush. *The Negro in Tennessee, 1865–1880*. Washington, D.C.: Associated Publishers, 1941.

———. *The Negro in the Reconstruction of Virginia*. Washington, D.C.: Association for the Study of Negro Life and History, 1926.

Taylor, Joe Gray. *Louisiana Reconstructed, 1863–1877*. Baton Rouge: Louisiana State University Press, 1974.

Thompson, C. Mildred. *Reconstruction in Georgia: Economic, Social, Political, 1865–1872*. Studies in History, Economics and Public Law. New York: Columbia University, 1915.

Thompson, Gerald. *The Army and the Navajo*. Tucson: University of Arizona Press, 1976.

Thompson, William Y. *Robert Toombs of Georgia*. Baton Rouge: Louisiana State University Press, 1966.

Timberlake, Richard H. *Monetary Policy in the United States: An Intellectual and Institutional History*. Chicago: University of Chicago Press, 1993.

Tong, Benson. *The Chinese Americans*. Westport, Conn.: Greenwood Press, 2000.

Trefousse, Hans L. *Andrew Johnson*. New York: Norton, 1989.

———. *Benjamin Franklin Wade, Radical Republican from Ohio*. New York: Twayne, 1963.

———. *The Radical Republicans: Lincoln's Vanguard for Racial Justice*. New York: Knopf, 1969.

Trelease, Allen W. *White Terror: The Ku Klux Klan Conspiracy and Southern Reconstruction*. Baton Rouge: Louisiana State University Press, 1971.

Tunnell, Ted. *Crucible of Reconstruction: War, Radicalism, and Race in Louisiana, 1862–1877*. Baton Rouge: Louisiana State University Press, 1984.

Turner, Thomas Reed. *Beware the People Weeping: Public Opinion and the Assassination of Abraham Lincoln*. Baton Rouge: Louisiana State University Press, 1982.

Unger, Irwin. *The Greenback Era: A Social and Political History of American Finance, 1865–1879*. Princeton: Princeton University Press, 1964.

Utley, Robert M. *The Indian Frontier of the American West, 1846–1890*. Albuquerque: University of New Mexico Press, 1984.

Vallandigham, James L. *A Life of Clement L. Vallandigham*. Baltimore: Turnbull Brothers, 1872.

Van Deusen, Glyndon. *Horace Greeley, Nineteenth-Century Crusader*. New York: Hill & Wang, 1953.

———. *William Henry Seward*. New York: Oxford University Press, 1967.

Varon, Elizabeth R. *Appomattox: Victory, Defeat, and Freedom at the End of the Civil War*. New York: Oxford University Press, 2013.

Vaughn, William P. *Schools for All: The Blacks and Public Education in the South, 1865–1877*. Lexington: University Press of Kentucky, 1977.

Vincent, Charles. *Black Legislators in Louisiana during Reconstruction*. Baton Rouge: Louisiana State University Press, 1976.

Voegeli, V. Jacque. *Free but Not Equal: The Midwest and the Negro during the Civil War*. Chicago: University of Chicago Press, 1967.

Vorenberg, Michael. *Final Freedom: The Civil War, the Abolition of Slavery, and the Thirteenth Amendment*. Cambridge: Cambridge University Press, 2001.

Wagandt, Charles Lewis. *The Mighty Revolution: Negro Emancipation in Maryland, 1862–1864*. Baltimore: Johns Hopkins University Press, 1964.

Waldrep, Christopher, and Donald G. Nieman, eds. *Local Matters: Race, Crime, and Justice in the Nineteenth-Century South*. Athens: University of Georgia Press, 2001.

Wall, Joseph Frazier. *Andrew Carnegie*. New York: Oxford University Press, 1970.

Ware, Ethel K. *A Constitutional History of Georgia*. New York: Columbia University Press, 1947.

Warner, Donald F. *The Idea of Continental Union: Agitation for the Annexation of Canada to the United States, 1849–1893*. Lexington: University Press of Kentucky, 1960.

Warshaw, Robert Irving. *The Story of Wall Street*. New York: Greenberg, 1929.

Webb, Ross A. *Benjamin Helm Bristow: Border State Politician*. Lexington: University Press of Kentucky, 1969.

Webb, Walter Prescott. *The Great Plains*. Boston: Ginn, 1931.

West, Elliott. *The Last Indian War; The Nez Perce Story*. New York: Oxford University Press, 2009.

Wetta, Frank J. *The Louisiana Scalawags: Politics, Race, and Terrorism during the Civil War and Reconstruction*. Baton Rouge: Louisiana State University Press, 2012.

Wharton, Vernon Lane. *The Negro in Mississippi, 1865–1890*. Chapel Hill: University of North Carolina Press, 1947.

White, Leonard D. *The Republican Era: A Study in Administrative History*. New York: Macmillan, 1958.

White, Horace. *The Life of Lyman Trumbull*. Boston: Houghton Mifflin, 1913.

White, Richard. *Railroaded: The Transcontinentals and the Making of Modern America*. New York: Norton, 2011.

Williams, Lou Falkner. *The Great South Carolina Ku Klux Klan Trials, 1871–1872*. Athens: University of Georgia Press, 1996.

Williams, Patrick G. *Beyond Redemption: Texas Democrats after Reconstruction*. College Station: Texas A&M University Press, 2007.

Williamson, Harold F., ed. *The Growth of the American Economy*. 2nd ed. New York: Prentice-Hall, 1951.

Williamson, Joel. *After Slavery: The Negro in South Carolina during Reconstruction, 1861–1877*. Chapel Hill: University of North Carolina Press, 1965.

Wilson, Theodore B. *The Black Codes of the South*. University: University of Alabama Press, 1965.

Wood, Forrest G. *Black Scare: The Racist Response to Emancipation and Reconstruction*. Berkeley: University of California Press, 1970.

Woodman, Harold D. *King Cotton and His Retainers: Financing and Marketing the Cotton Crop of the South, 1800–1925*. Lexington: University of Kentucky Press, 1968.

Woodward, C. Vann. *Origins of the New South, 1877–1913*. Baton Rouge: Louisiana State University Press, 1951.

———. *Reunion and Reaction: The Compromise of 1877 and the End of Reconstruction*. Boston: Little, Brown, 1951.

———. *The Strange Career of Jim Crow*. Rev. ed. New York: Oxford University Press, 1957.

Wooster, Robert. *The Military and United States Indian Policy, 1865–1903*. New Haven, Conn.: Yale University Press, 1988.

Wrobel, David M. *Promised Lands: Promotion, Memory, and the Creation of the American West*. Lawrence: University Press of Kansas, 2002.

Wynne, Lewis Nicholas. *The Continuity of Cotton: Planter Politics in Georgia, 1865–1892*. Macon, Ga.: Mercer University Press, 1986.

Zornow, William Frank. *Kansas: A History of the Jayhawk State*. Norman: University of Oklahoma Press, 1957.

Zuczek, Richard. *State of Rebellion: Reconstruction in South Carolina*. Columbia: University of South Carolina Press, 1996.

Scholarly Articles

Abbott, Richard H. "Jason Clarke Swayze, Republican Editor in Reconstruction Georgia, 1867–1873." *Georgia Historical Quarterly* 79 (Summer 1995): 337–66.

Alston, Lee J., Jeffery A. Jenkins, and Tomas Nonnenmacher. "Who Should Govern Congress? Access to Power and the Salary Grab of 1873." *Journal of Economic History* 66 (September 2006): 676–701.

Anderson, David. "Down Memory Lane: Nostalgia for the Old South in Post–Civil War Plantation Reminiscences." *Journal of Southern History* 71 (February 2005): 105–36.

Angell, Stephen W. "A Black Minister Befriends the 'Unquestioned Father of Civil Rights': Henry McNeal Turner, Charles Sumner, and the African-American Quest for Freedom." *Georgia Historical Quarterly* 85 (Spring 2001): 27–58.

Angelo, Larian. "Wage Labour Deferred: The Recreation of Unfree Labour in the U.S. South." *Journal of Peasant Studies* 22 (July 1995).

Auman, William T. "Neighbor against Neighbor: The Inner Civil War in the Randolph County Area of Confederate North Carolina." *North Carolina Historical Review* 61 (January 1984): 59–92.

Avillo, Philip J. "Ballots for the Faithful: The Oath and the Emergence of Slave State Republican Congressmen, 1861–1867." *Civil War History* 22 (June 1976): 164–74.

Baggett, James A. "Origins of Early Texas Republican Party Leadership." *Journal of Southern History* 40 (August 1974): 441–54.

———. "Origins of Upper South Scalawag Leadership." *Civil War History* 29 (March 1983): 53–73.

Baker, Robin E. "Class Conflict and Political Upheaval: The Transformation of North Carolina Politics during the Civil War." *North Carolina Historical Review* 69 (April 1992): 148–78.

Balanoff, Elizabeth. "Negro Leaders in the North Carolina General Assembly, July 1868-February 1872." *North Carolina Historical Review* 49 (Winter 1972): 22–55.

Barnes, Kenneth C. "The Williams Clan: Mountain Farmers and Union Fighters in North Central Arkansas." *Arkansas Historical Quarterly* 52 (Autumn 1993): 286–317.

Barr, Alwyn. "Black Legislators of Reconstruction Texas." *Civil War History* 32 (December 1986): 340–52.

Bauer, Penelope H. "The Trial of the Natchitoches 48." *Louisiana History* 5 (Fall 2001): 421–39.

Brackett, John M. "Cutting Costs by Cutting Lives: Prisoner Health and the Abolishment of Florida's Convict-Lease System." *Southern Studies* 14 (Fall/Winter 2007): 69–84.

Bell, John L. "Samuel S. Ashley, Carpetbagger and Education." *North Carolina Historical Review* 72 (October 1995): 456–83.

Belz, Herman. "Henry Winter Davis and the Origins of Congressional Reconstruction." *Maryland Historical Magazine* 67 (Summer 1972): 129–43.

Benedict, Michael Les. "Preserving the Constitution: The Conservative Basis of Radical Reconstruction." *Journal of American History* 61 (June 1974): 67–74.

———. "Reform Republicans and the Retreat from Reconstruction." In *The Facts of Reconstruction: Essays in Honor of John Hope Franklin*. edited by Eric Anderson and Alfred A. Moss Jr., 53–76. Baton Rouge: Louisiana State University Press, 1991.

———. "Southern Democrats in the Crisis of 1876–1877: A Reconsideration of *Reunion and Reaction*." *Journal of Southern History* 46 (1980): 489–524.

Bentley, H. Blair. "Governor Andrew Johnson and Public Education in Tennessee." *Tennessee Historical Quarterly* 47 (Spring 1988): 10–16.

Bernstein, Samuel. "American Labor in the Long Depression." *Science and Society* 20 (Winter 1956): 59–83.

Blackburn, George M. "Michigan: Quickening Government in a Developing State." In *Radical Republicans in the North: State Politics during Reconstruction*, edited by James C. Mohr, 119–43. Baltimore: Johns Hopkins University Press, 1976.

Blain, William T. "Challenge to the Lawless: The Mississippi Secret Service, 1870–1871." *Journal of Mississippi History* 40 (May 1978): 119–32.

Blight, David. "Fifty Years of Freedom: The Memory of Emancipation at the Civil War Semicentennial, 1911–1915." *Slavery and Abolition* 21 (August 2000): 117–34.

Bridges, Amy. "Managing the Periphery in the Gilded Age: Writing Constitutions for the Western States." *Studies in American Political Development* 22 (Spring 2008): 32–58.

Brisson, Jim D. "'Civil Government Was Crumbling Around Me': The Kirk-Holden War of 1870." *North Carolina Historical Review* 88 (April 2011): 132–63.

Brown, Canter, Jr. "Carpetbagger Intrigues, Black Leadership, and a Southern Loyalist Triumph: Florida's Gubernatorial Election of 1872." *Florida Historical Quarterly* 72 (January 1994): 275–301.

Brown, Ira V. "Pennsylvania and the Rights of the Negro." *Pennsylvania History* 28 (January 1961): 45–57.

———. "William D. Kelley and Radical Reconstruction." *Pennsylvania Magazine of History and Biography* 85 (July 1961): 316–29.

Browning, Judkin Jay. "'Little Souled Mercenaries?' The Buffaloes of Eastern North Carolina during the Civil War." *North Carolina Historical Review* 77 (July 2000): 337–63.

———. "Removing the Mask of Nationality: Unionism, Racism, and Federal Military Occupation in North Carolina, 1862–1865." *Journal of Southern History* 71 (August 2005): 587–620.

Campney, Brent M. S. "'Light Is Bursting upon the World!' White Supremacy and Racist Violence against Blacks in Reconstruction Kansas." *Western Historical Quarterly* 41 (Summer 2010): 171–94.

Carlson, David. "The 'Loanly Runagee': Draft Evaders in Confederate South Georgia." *Georgia Historical Quarterly* 84 (Winter 2000): 589–615.

Carrigan, Jo Ann. "Yankees versus Yellow Jack in New Orleans, 1862–1866." *Civil War History* 9 (September 1963): 248–60.

Change, Gordon H. "Whose 'Barbarism'? Whose 'Treachery'? Race and Civilization in the Unknown United States–Korean War of 1871." *Journal of American History* 89 (March 2003): 131–65.

Chausovsky, Jonathan. "State Regulation of Corporations in the Late Nineteenth Century: A Critique of the New Jersey Thesis." *Studies in American Political Development* 21 (Spring 2007): 30–65.

Chen, Yong. "The Internal Origins of Chinese Emigration to California Reconsidered." *Western Historical Quarterly* 28 (Winter 1997): 520–46.

Cimbala, Paul A. "On the Front Line of Freedom: Freedmen's Bureau Officers and Agents in Reconstruction Georgia." *Georgia Historical Quarterly* 76 (Fall 1992): 587–606.

Cimprich, John. "Military Governor Johnson and Tennessee Blacks, 1862–1865." *Tennessee Historical Quarterly* 39 (Winter 1980): 459–70.

Clark, James C. "The Fox Goes to France: Florida Secret Codes and the Election of 1876." *Florida Historical Quarterly* 69 (April 1991): 436–56.

Clendenin, Clarence C. "President Hayes' 'Withdrawal' of the Troops—an Enduring Myth." *South Carolina Historical Magazine* 70 (October 1969): 243–50.

Clinton, Catherine. "Bloody Terrain: Freedwomen, Sexuality and Violence during Reconstruction." *Georgia Historical Quarterly* 76 (Summer 1992): 313–32.

Coben, Stanley. "Northeastern Business and Radical Reconstruction: A Re-examination." *Mississippi Valley Historical Review* 46 (June 1959): 67–90.

Coclanis, Peter A. "The Rise and Fall of the South Carolina Low Country: An Essay in Economic Interpretation." *Southern Studies* 24 (Summer 1985): 143–66.

Cohen, William. "Black Immobility and Free Labor: The Freedmen's Bureau and the Relocation of Black Labor, 1865–1868." *Civil War History* 30 (September 1984): 221–34.

Conklin, Forrest. "Wiping Out 'Andy' Johnson's Moccasin Tracks: The Canvass of Northern States by Southern Radicals, 1866." *Tennessee Historical Quarterly* 52 (Summer 1993): 122–33.

Cox, John H. and LaWanda. "Negro Suffrage and Republican Politics: The Problem of Motivation in Reconstruction Historiography." *Journal of Southern History* 33 (1967): 303–30.

Cox, Merlin G. "Military Reconstruction in Florida." *Florida Historical Quarterly* 46 (January 1968): 219–33.

Coxe, Eckley B. "Mining Legislation." *Journal of Social Science* 4 (1871).

Crouch, Barry. "'All the Vile Passions': The Texas Black Code of 1866." *Southwestern Historical Quarterly* 97 (July 1993): 12–34.

———. "A Spirit of Lawlessness: White Violence, Texas Blacks, 1865–1868." *Journal of Social History* 18 (Winter 1984): 217–32.

Currie, James T. "The Beginnings of Congressional Reconstruction in Mississippi." *Journal of Mississippi History* 35 (August 1973).

Cutler, Wayne. "Jackson, Polk, and Johnson: Defenders of the Moral Economy." *Tennessee Historical Quarterly* 54 (Fall 1995): 178–89.

Davis, John Martin, Jr. "Bankless in Beaufort: A Reexamination of the 1873 Failure of the Freedman's Savings Branch at Beaufort, South Carolina." *South Carolina Historical Magazine* 104 (January 2003): 25–55.

———. "Black an' Dusty, Goin' to Agusty': A History of the Port Royal Railroad." *South Carolina Historical Magazine* 105 (July 2004): 198–226.

Davis, Joseph H. "An Improved Annual Chronology of U.S. Business Cycles since the 1790s." *Journal of Economic History* 66 (March 2006): 103–21.

Davis, Lance E., and John Legler. "The Government in the American Economy, 1815–1902: A Quantitative Study." *Journal of Economic History* 26 (December 1966): 514–52.

Davis, Robert S., Jr. "White and Black in Blue: The Recruitment of Federal Units in Civil War North Georgia." *Georgia Historical Quarterly* 85 (Fall 2001): 347–74.

De Bres, Karen. "Come to the 'Champagne Air': Changing Promotional Images of the Kansas Climate, 1854–1900." *Great Plains Quarterly* 23 (Spring 2003): 111–26.

DeCanio, Samuel. "State Autonomy and American Political Development: How Mass Democracy Promoted State Power." *Studies in American Political Development* 19 (Fall 2005): 117–36.

Denmark, Lisa L. "'At the Midnight Hour': Economic Dilemmas and Harsh Realities in Post–Civil War Savannah." *Georgia Historical Quarterly* 90 (Fall 2006): 350–90.

Dobak, William A. "The Army and the Buffalo: A Demur. A Response to David D. Smit's 'The Frontier Army and the Destruction of the Buffalo: 1865–1883.'" *Western Historical Quarterly* 26 (Summer 1995): 197–202.

———. "Killing the Canadian Buffalo, 1821–1881." *Western Historical Quarterly* 27 (Spring 1996): 33–52.

Doster, James F. "Were the Southern Railroads Destroyed by the Civil War?" *Civil War History* 7 (September 1961): 310–20.

Drago, Edmund Lee. "Georgia's First Black Voter Registrars during Reconstruction." *Georgia Historical Quarterly* 78 (Winter 1994): 760–93.

Durrill, Wayne K. "Political Legitimacy and Local Courts: 'Politicks at Such a Rage' in a Southern Community during Reconstruction." *Journal of Southern History* 70 (August 2004): 577–602.

Dykstra, Robert. "The Issue Squarely Met: Toward an Explanation of Iowans' Racial Attitudes, 1865–1868." *Annals of Iowa* 47 (Summer 1984): 430–50.

Dykstra, Robert H., and Harlan Hahn. "Northern Voters and the Negro Suffrage Question: The Case of Iowa, 1868." *Public Opinion Quarterly* 32 (Summer 1968): 202–15.

Elazar, Daniel J. "Civil War and the Preservation of American Federalism." *Publius* 1 (1971): 39–58.

Ellem, Warren A. "The Overthrow of Reconstruction in Mississippi." *Journal of Mississippi History* 54 (May 1992): 175–201.

———. "Who Were the Mississippi Scalawags?" *Journal of Southern History* 38 (1972): 217–40.

Ellis, Richard N. "The Humanitarian Generals." *Western Historical Quarterly* 3 (April 1972): 169–82.

Fairclough, Adam. "Alfred Raford Blunt and the Reconstruction Struggle in Natchitoches, 1866–1879." *Louisiana History* 51 (Summer 2010): 284–305.

———. "'Scalawags,' Southern Honor, and the Lost Cause: Explaining the Fatal Encounter of James H. Cosgrove and Edward L. Pierson." *Journal of Southern History* 77 (November 2011): 799–826.

Farmer-Kaiser, Mary. "'Are They Not in Some Sorts Vagrants?' Gender and the Efforts of the Freedmen's Bureau to Combat Vagrancy in the Reconstruction South." *Georgia Historical Quarterly* 88 (Spring 2004): 25–49.

Field, Phyllis F. "Republicans and Black Suffrage in New York State: The Grass Roots Response." *Civil War History* 21 (June 1975): 136–47.

Fisher, Noel. "'The Leniency Shown Them Has Been Unavailing': The Confederate Occupation of East Tennessee." *Civil War History* 40 (December 1994): 275–91.

Fishlow, Albert. "Levels of Nineteenth-Century American Investment in Education." *Journal of Economic History* 26 (1966): 418–36.

Fitzgerald, Michael W. "The Ku Klux Klan: Property Crime and the Plantation System in Reconstruction Alabama." *Agricultural History* 71 (Spring 1997): 186–206.

————. "Railroad Subsidies and Black Aspirations: The Politics of Economic Development in Reconstruction Mobile, 1865–1879." *Civil War History* 39 (September 1993): 240–56.

————. "Republican Factionalism and Black Empowerment: The Spencer-Warner Controversy and Alabama Reconstruction, 1868–1880." *Journal of Southern History* 64 (August 1998): 473–94.

Foner, Laura. "The Free People of Color in Louisiana and St. Domingue." *Journal of Social History* 3 (Summer 1970): 406–30.

Formwalt, Lee W. "The Camilla Massacre of 1868: Racial Violence as Political Propaganda." *Georgia Historical Quarterly* 71 (Fall 1987): 402–25.

————. "Moving in 'That Strange Land of Shadows': African-American Mobility and Persistence in Post–Civil War Southwest Georgia." *Georgia Historical Quarterly* 82 (Fall 1998): 507–32.

Foster, John T., Jr., and Sarah Whitmer Foster. "The Last Shall Be First: Northern Methodists in Reconstruction Jacksonville." *Florida Historical Quarterly* 70 (January 1992): 265–80.

Fredrickson, George M. "A Man but Not a Brother: Abraham Lincoln and Racial Equality." *Journal of Southern History* 41 (February 1975): 39–58.

Frieden, Jeffrey A. "Monetary Populism in Nineteenth-Century America: An Open Economy Interpretation." *Journal of Economic History* 57 (June 1997): 367–95.

Fuke, Richard Paul. "Hugh Lennox Bond and Radical Republican Ideology." *Journal of Southern History* 45 (November 1979): 569–86.

Garner, Nancy G. "'A Prayerful Public Protest': The Significance of Gender in the Kansas Woman's Crusade of 1874." *Kansas History* 20 (Winter 1997–98): 213–29.

Genetin-Pilawa, C. Joseph. "Ely Parker and the Contentious Peace Policy." *Western Historical Quarterly* 41 (Summer 2010): 197–217.

Gorman, Kathleen. "'This Man Felker Is a Man of Pretty Good Standing': A Reconstruction Klansman in Walton County." *Georgia Historical Quarterly* 81 (Winter 1997): 897–914.

Gramm, Marshall, and Phil Gramm. "The Free Silver Movement in America: A Reinterpretation." *Journal of Economic History* 64 (December 2004): 1108–29.

Granberry, Dorothy. "When the Rabbit Foot Was Worked and Republican Votes Became Democratic Votes: Black Disfranchisement in Haywood County, Tennessee." *Tennessee Historical Quarterly* 63 (Spring 2004): 34–47.

Green, Michael. "Diehard or Swing Man: Senator James W. Nye and Andrew Johnson's Impeachment and Trial." *Nevada Historical Society Quarterly* 29 (Fall 1986): 175–91.

Greenberg, Kenneth. "The Civil War and the Redistribution of Land: Adams County, Mississippi, 1860–1870." *Agricultural History* 52 (April 1978): 297–307.

Griffiths, John D. M. "A State of Servitude Worse than Slavery: The Politics of Penal Administration in Mississippi, 1865–1900." *Journal of Mississippi History* 55 (February 1993): 1–18.

Guenther, Karen. "Potter Committee Investigation of the Disputed Election of 1876." *Florida Historical Quarterly* 61 (January 1983): 286–93.

Guyatt, Nicholas. "America's Conservatory: Race, Reconstruction, and the Santo Domingo Debate." *Journal of American History* 97 (March 2011): 974–1000.

Harlan, Louis R. "Desegregation in the New Orleans Public Schools during Reconstruction." *American Historical Review* 67 (April 1962).

Harris, William C. "The Creed of the Carpetbagger: The Case of Mississippi." *Journal of Southern History* 40 (May 1974): 199–224.

Hebert, Keith S. "The Bitter Trial of Defeat and Emancipation: Reconstruction in Bartow County, Georgia, 1865–1872." *Georgia Historical Quarterly* 92 (Spring 2008): 65–92.

Heyman, Max L., Jr. "'The Great Reconstructor': General E. R. S. Canby and the Second Military District." *North Carolina Historical Review* 31 (January 1955): 52–81.

Hine, William C. "Black Politicians in Reconstruction Charleston, South Carolina: A Collective Study." *Journal of Southern History* 39 (November 1983): 555–84.

Hoag, Christopher. "The Atlantic Telegraph Cable and Capital Market Information Flows." *Journal of Economic History* 66 (June 2006): 342–52.

Hoffert, Sylvia D. "Yankee Schoolmarms and the Domestication of the South." *Southern Studies* 24 (Summer 1985): 188–200.

Hollman, Kenneth W., and Joe H. Murrey Jr. "Alabama's State Debt History, 1865–1921." *Southern Studies* 24 (Fall 1985): 306–25.

Holloway, Pippa. "'A Chicken-Stealer Shall Lose His Vote': Disfranchisement for Larceny in the South, 1874–1890." *Journal of Southern History* 75 (November 2009): 931–62.

Thomas C. Holt, "Negro State Legislators in South Carolina during Reconstruction." In *Southern Black Leaders of the Reconstruction Era*, edited by Howard N. Rabinowitz, 223–46. Urbana: University of Illinois Press, 1982.

Hume, Richard L. "The Arkansas Constitutional Convention of 1868: A Case Study in the Politics of Reconstruction." *Journal of Southern History* 39 (May 1973): 192–206.

———. "Carpetbaggers in the Reconstruction South: A Group Portrait of Outside Whites in the 'Black and Tan' Constitutional Conventions." *Journal of American History* 64 (September 1977): 313–30.

Isenberg, Andrew. "Toward a Policy of Destruction: Buffaloes, Law, and the Market, 1803–1883." *Great Plains Quarterly* 12 (Fall 1992): 227–41.

Jacobsen, Joel K. "An Excess of Law in Lincoln County: Thomas Catron, Samuel Axtell, and the Lincoln County War." *New Mexico Historical Review* 68 (April 1993): 132–51.

Jones, Robert R. "James L. Kemper and the Virginia Redeemers Face the Race Question: A Reconsideration." *Journal of Southern History* 38 (August 1972): 393–414.

Kaczorowski, Robert J. "To Begin the Nation Anew: Congress, Citizenship, and Civil Rights after the Civil War." *American Historical Review* 92 (February 1987): 45–68.

Kelley, Robert. "The Thought and Character of Samuel J. Tilden: The Democrat as Inheritor." *Historian* 26 (February 1964): 174–205.

Kelley, Sean. "A Texas Peasantry? Black Smallholders in the Texas Sugar Bowl, 1865–1890." *Slavery and Abolition* 28 (August 2007): 193–209.

Kennedy, Philip W. "Oregon and the Disputed Election of 1876." *Pacific Northwest Quarterly* 60 (July 1969): 135–44.

King, Ronald F. "Counting the Votes: South Carolina's Stolen Election of 1876." *Journal of Interdisciplinary History* 32 (Autumn 2001): 169–91.

———. "A Most Corrupt Election: Louisiana in 1876." *Studies in American Political Development* 15 (October 2001): 123–37.

Kohl, Martha. "Enforcing a Vision of Community: The Role of the Test Oath in Missouri's Reconstruction." *Civil War History* 40 (December 1994): 292–307.

LaForte, Robert S. "Gilded Age Senator: The Election, Investigation, and Resignation of Alexander Caldwell, 1871–1873." *Kansas History* 21 (Winter 1998–99): 240–55.

Lamar, Howard R. "Carpetbaggers Full of Dreams: A Functional View of the Arizona Pioneer Politician." *Arizona and the West* 7 (Autumn 1965): 187–206.

Lebsock, Suzanne. "Radical Reconstruction and the Property Rights of Southern Women." *Journal of Southern History* 43 (May 1977): 195–216.

Leonard, Thomas. C. "Red, White and the Army Blue: Empathy and Anger in the American West." *American Quarterly* 26 (May 1974): 176–90.

Lestage, Oscar. "The White League in Louisiana and Its Participation in Reconstruction Riots." *Louisiana Historical Quarterly* 18 (July 1935): 617–95.

Liestman, Daniel. "Horizontal Inter-Ethnic Relations: Chinese and American Indians in the Nineteenth-Century American West." *Western Historical Quarterly* 30 (Autumn 1999): 327–49.

Loewenberg, Bert J. "Efforts of the South to Encourage Immigration, 1865–1900." *South Atlantic Quarterly* 33 (October 1934): 363–85.

Massengell, Stephen E. "The Detectives of William W. Holden." *North Carolina Historical Review* 62 (October 1985): 448–87.

McAfee, Ward. "Local Interests and Railroad Regulation in California during the Granger Decade." *Pacific Historical Review* 37 (February 1968): 51–66.

———. "Reconstruction Revisited: The Republican Public Education Crusade of the 1870s." *Civil War History* 42 (June 1996): 133–53.

McDonough, James L. "John Schofield as Military Director of Reconstruction in Virginia." *Civil War History* 15 (September 1969): 237–56.

McKenna, Jeanne. "With the Help of God and Lucy Stone." *Kansas History* 36 (Spring 1970): 13–26.

McKenzie, Robert Tracy. "Civil War and Socioeconomic Change in the Upper South: The Survival of Local Agricultural Elites in Tennessee, 1850–1870." *Tennessee Historical Quarterly* 52 (Fall 1993): 170–84.

———. "Contesting Secession: Parson Brownlow and the Rhetoric of Proslavery Unionism, 1860–1861." *Civil War History* 48 (December 2002): 294–312.

McKinney, Gordon B. "Zebulon Vance and His Reconstruction of the Civil War in North Carolina." *North Carolina Historical Review* 75 (January 1998): 69–85.

McManus, Michael J. "Wisconsin Republicans and Negro Suffrage: Attitudes and Behavior, 1857." *Civil War History* 25 (March 1979): 36–54.

McPherson, James M. "Abolitionists and the Civil Rights Act of 1875." *Journal of American History* 52 (December 1965): 493–510.

Mercer, Lloyd J. "Land Grants to American Railroads: Social Cost or Social Benefit?" *Business History Review* 43 (Summer 1969): 134–51.

Mixon, Scott. "The Crisis of 1873: Perspectives from Multiple Asset Classes." *Journal of Economic History* 68 (September 2008): 724–55.

Mobley, Joe A. "Zebulon B. Vance: A Confederate Nationalist in the North Carolina Gubernatorial Election of 1864." *North Carolina Historical Review* 77 (October 2000): 434–54.

Mohr, James C. "The Free School Law of 1867." *New-York Historical Society Quarterly* 53 (1969).

Moneyhon, Carl H. "Disloyalty and Class Consciousness in Southwestern Arkansas, 1862–1865." *Arkansas Historical Quarterly* 52 (Autumn 1993): 223–43.

Montgomery, David. "Radical Republicanism in Pennsylvania, 1866–1873." *Pennsylvania Magazine of History and Biography* 85 (October 1961): 439–57.

Moore, James T. "Black Militancy in Readjuster Virginia, 1879–1883." *Journal of Southern History* 41 (May 1975): 167–86.

Moran, Jeffrey. "Chinese Labor for the New South." *Southern Studies* 3 (Winter 1992): 277–95.

Morris, Thomas D. "Equality, 'Extraordinary Law,' and Criminal Justice: The South Carolina Experience, 1865–1866." *South Carolina Historical Magazine* 83 (January 1982): 15–33.

Murphy, Charles B. "Samuel J. Tilden and the Civil War." *South Atlantic Quarterly* 33 (July 1934): 261–71.

Naragon, Michael. "From Chattel to Citizen: The Transition from Slavery to Freedom in Richmond, Virginia." *Slavery and Abolition* 21 (August 2000): 93–116.

Neal, Diane, and Thomas W. Kremm, "Loyal Government on Trial: The Union versus Arkansas." *Southern Studies* 25 (Summer 1986): 148–62.

Ng, Kenneth, and Nancy Virts. "The Value of Freedom." *Journal of Economic History* 49 (December 1989): 958–65.

Oakes, James. "A Failure of Vision: The Collapse of the Freedmen's Bureau Courts." *Civil War History* 25 (March 1979): 66–76.

Oldfield, John. "On the Beat: Black Policemen in Charleston, 1869–1921." *South Carolina Historical Magazine* 102 (April 2001): 153–68.

Olsen, Otto H. "Reconsidering the Scalawags." *Civil War History* 12 (December 1966): 304–24.

Oman, Kerry R. "The Beginning of the End: The Indian Peace Commission of 1867–1868." *Great Plains Quarterly* 22 (Winter 2002): 35–51.

Ouzts, Clay. "Landlords and Tenants: Sharecropping and the Cotton Culture in Leon County, Florida, 1865–1885." *Florida Historical Quarterly* 75 (Summer 1996): 1–23.

Palmer, Paul C. "Miscegenation as an Issue in the Arkansas Constitutional Convention of 1868." *Arkansas Historical Quarterly* 24 (Summer 1965): 99–119.

Parker, James C. "Tennessee Gubernatorial Elections: I: 1869—The Victory of the Conservatives." *Tennessee Historical Quarterly* 33 (Spring 1974): 34–48.

Parsons, Elaine Frantz. "Klan Skepticism and Denial in Reconstruction-Era Public Discourse." *Journal of Southern History* 77 (February 2011): 60–84.

Pearson, Reggie L. "'There Are Many Sick, Feeble, and Suffering Freedmen': The Freedmen's Bureau's Health-Care Activities during Reconstruction in North Carolina, 1865–1868." *North Carolina Historical Review* 79 (Spring 2002): 141–81.

Peffer, George Anthony. "Forbidden Families: Emigration Experiences of Chinese Women under the Page Law, 1875–1882." *Journal of American Ethnic History* 6 (Fall 1986): 28–46.

Peskin, Allan. "Was There a Compromise of 1877?" *Journal of American History* 60 (June 1973): 63–75.

Phifer, Gregg. "Andrew Johnson Takes a Trip." *Tennessee Historical Quarterly* 11 (March 1952): 3–22.

Potts, Nancy J. "Unfilled Expectations: The Erosion of Black Political Power in Chattanooga, 1865–1911." *Tennessee Historical Quarterly* 49 (Summer 1990): 112–28.

Powell, Lawrence N. "Centralization and Its Discontents in Reconstruction Florida." *Studies in American Political Development* 20 (Fall 2006): 105–31.

———. "Correcting for Fraud: A Quantitative Reassessment of the Mississippi Ratification Election of 1868." *Journal of Southern History* 55 (November 1989): 633–58.

———. "Reinventing Tradition: Liberty Place, Historical Memory, and Silk-Stocking Vigilantism in New Orleans Politics." *Slavery and Abolition* 20 (April 1999): 127–49.

Quastler, I. E. "Charting a Course: Lawrence, Kansas, and Its Railroad Strategy, 1854–1872." *Kansas History* 18 (Spring 1995): 18–34.

Rabinowitz, Howard N. "From Exclusion to Segregation: Southern Race Relations, 1865–1890." *Journal of American History* 63 (September 1976): 325–50.

Rable, George C. "Southern Interests and the Election of 1876: A Reappraisal." *Civil War History* 26 (December 1980): 347–61.

Rankin, David C. "The Impact of the Civil War on the Free Colored Community of New Orleans." *Perspectives in American History* 11 (1977–78): 379–418.

———. "The Origins of Black Leadership in New Orleans during Reconstruction." *Journal of Southern History* 40 (August 1974): 417–40.

Rapport, Sarah. "The Freedmen's Bureau as a Legal Agent for Black Men and Women in Georgia, 1865–1868." *Georgia Historical Quarterly* 73 (Spring 1989): 26–53.

Rawley, James A. "The General Amnesty Act of 1872." *Mississippi Valley Historical Review* 47 (December 1960): 480–84.

Reese, Linda W. "Cherokee Freedwomen in Indian Territory, 1863–1890." *Western Historical Quarterly* 33 (Autumn 2002): 273–96.

Reid, Joseph D., Jr. "Sharecropping as an Understandable Market Response—The Postbellum South." *Journal of Economic History* 33 (March 1973): 106–30.

Retzinger, Jean P. "Framing the Tourist Gaze: Railway Journeys across Nebraska, 1866–1906." *Great Plains Quarterly* 18 (Summer 1998): 213–26.

Reynolds, Donald E. "The New Orleans Riot of 1866 Reconsidered." *Louisiana History* 5 (Winter 1964): 5–28.

Richardson, Joe M. "Florida Black Codes." *Florida Historical Quarterly* 47 (April 1969): 365–79.

Richter, William L. "James Longstreet: From Rebel to Scalawag." *Louisiana History* 11 (Summer 1970): 215–30.

———. "'We Must Rubb Out and Begin Anew': The Army and Republican Party in Texas Reconstruction, 1867–1870." *Civil War History* 19 (December 1973): 334–52.

Riegel, Robert E. "The Split of the Feminist Movement in 1869." *Mississippi Valley Historical Review* 49 (December 1962): 487–96.

Righi, Brandon P. "'A Power Unknown to Our Laws': Unionism in Kent County, Maryland, 1861–1865." *Maryland Historical Magazine* 103 (Summer 2008): 186–223.

Robinson, Armstead L. "Beyond the Realm of Social Consensus: New Meanings of Reconstruction for American History." *Journal of American History* 68 (September 1981): 276–97.

Rogers, William Warren, Jr. "'Not Reconstructed by a Long Ways Yet': Southwest Georgia's Disputed Congressional Election of 1870." *Georgia Historical Quarterly* 82 (Summer 1998): 257–82.

Rosen, Deborah A. "Pueblo Indians and Citizenship in Territorial New Mexico." *New Mexico Historical Review* 78 (Winter 2003): 1–28.

Rosenbaum, Ephraim Samuel. "Incendiary Negro: The Life and Times of the Honorable Jefferson Franklin Long." *Georgia Historical Quarterly* 95 (Winter 2011): 498–530.

Roske, Ralph J. "The Seven Martyrs?" *American Historical Review* 64 (January 1959): 323–30.

Ross, Michael A. "Justice Miller's Reconstruction: The *Slaughter-House Cases*, Health Codes, and Civil Rights in New Orleans, 1861–1873." *Journal of Southern History* 64 (November 1998): 649–76.

Savitt, Todd L. "Politics in Medicine: The Georgia Freedmen's Bureau and the Organization of Health Care." *Civil War History* 28 (March 1982): 45–64.

Schwalm, Leslie A. "'Sweet Dreams of Freedom': Freedwomen's Reconstruction of Life and Labor in Lowcountry South Carolina." *Journal of Women's History* 9 (Spring 1997): 9–38.

Schweninger, Loren. "Black Citizenship and the Republican Party in Reconstruction Alabama." *Alabama Review* 29 (April 1976): 83–103.

———. "Property-Owning Free African American Women in the South, 1800–1870." *Journal of Women's History* 1 (January 1990): 13–44.

Shlomowitz, Ralph. "Planter Combinations and Black Labour in the American South, 1865–1880." *Slavery and Abolition* 9 (May 1988): 72–84.

Sexton, Jay. "Toward a Synthesis of Foreign Relations in the Civil War Era, 1848–1877." *American Nineteenth Century History* 5 (Fall 2004): 50–73.

Shofner, Jerrell H. "Fraud and Intimidation in the Florida Election of 1876." *Florida Historical Quarterly* 42 (April 1964): 321–30.

Simpson, Amos E., and Vaughn B. Baker. "Michael Hahn: Steady Patriot." *Louisiana History* 13 (Summer 1972): 229–52.

Skelton, William B. "Army Officers' Attitudes towards Indians, 1830–1860." *Pacific Northwest Quarterly* 67 (July 1976): 113–24.

Slap, Andrew L. "'The Strong Arm of the Military Power of the United States': The Chicago Fire, the Constitution, and Reconstruction." *Civil War History* 47 (June 2001): 146–64.

Sledge, James L., III. "The Chisholm Massacre: Politics and Violence in East Mississippi." *Journal of Mississippi History* 55 (August 1993): 203–15.

Smit, David D. "The Frontier Army and the Destruction of the Buffalo, 1865–1883." *Western Historical Quarterly* 25 (Autumn 1994): 313–38.

Smith, Albert C. "'Southern Violence' Reconsidered: Arson as Protest in Black-Belt Georgia." *Journal of Southern History* 69 (November 1985): 527–64.

Somers, Dale A. "Black and White in New Orleans: A Study in Urban Race Relations, 1865–1900." *Journal of Southern History* 40 (February 1974): 19–42.

Speiser, Matt. "The Ticket's Other Half: How and Why Andrew Johnson Received the 1864 Vice Presidential Nomination." *Tennessee Historical Quarterly* 65 (Spring 2006): 43–64.

Stagg, J. C. A. "The Problem of Klan Violence: The South Carolina Up-Country, 1868–1871." *Journal of American Studies* 8 (December 1974): 303–18.

Sternstein, Jerome L., ed. "The Sickles Memorandum: Another Look at the Hayes-Tilden Election." *Journal of Southern History* 32 (August 1966): 342–57.

Stewart, Bruce E. "'When Darkness Reigns Then Is the Hour to Strike': Moonshining, Federal Liquor Taxation, and Klan Violence in Western North Carolina, 1868–1872." *North Carolina Historical Review* 80 (October 2003): 453–74.

Strawbridge, Wilm K. "'A Monument Better than Marble': Jefferson Davis and the New South." *Journal of Mississippi History* 69 (Winter 2007): 325–47.

Talbott, Forrest. "Some Legislative and Legal Aspects of the Negro Question in West Virginia during the Civil War and Reconstruction, Part I." *West Virginia History* 24 (October 1962): 1–31.

Taylor, Robert A. "Crime and Race Relations in Jacksonville, 1884–1892." *Southern Studies* 2 (Spring 1991): 17–38.

Thompson, Margaret Susan. "Corruption—or Confusion? Lobbying and Congressional Government in the Early Gilded Age." *Congress and the Presidency* 10 (Autumn 1983): 169–93.

Towers, Frank. "Strange Bedfellows: The Union Party and the Federal Government in Civil War Baltimore." *Maryland Historical Magazine* 106 (Spring 2011): 7–30.

Trefousse, Hans L. "Ben Wade and the Failure of the Impeachment of Andrew Johnson." *Bulletin of the Historical and Philosophical Society of Ohio* 18 (October 1960): 241–52.

Trelease, Allen W. "Who Were the Scalawags?" *Journal of Southern History* 29 (November 1963): 445–68.

Trescott, Paul B. "Federal Government Receipts and Expenditures, 1861–1875." *Journal of Economic History* 26 (1966): 206–22.

Tunnell, Ted. "Creating 'the Propaganda of History': Southern Editors and the Origins of *Carpetbagger* and *Scalawag.*" *Journal of Southern History* 72 (November 2006): 789–822.

Utley, Robert M. "Oliver Otis Howard." *New Mexico Historical Review* 62 (January 1987): 55–63.

Uzee, Philip D. "The Beginnings of the Louisiana Republican Party." *Louisiana History* 12 (Summer 1971): 197–212.

Vandal, Gilles. "The Origins of the New Orleans Riot of 1866, Revisited." *Louisiana History* 22 (Spring 1981): 135–66.

Vorenberg, Michael. "'The Deformed Child': Slavery and the Election of 1864." *Civil War History* 47 (September 2001): 240–57.

Wagstaff, Thomas. "The Arm-in-Arm Convention." *Civil War History* 14 (June 1968): 101–19.

Wakefield, Laura Wallis. "'Set a Light in a Dark Place': Teachers of Freedmen in Florida, 1864–1874." *Florida Historical Quarterly* 81 (Spring 2003): 401–17.

Waldrip, C. B. "Sex, Social Equality, and Yankee Values: White Men's Attitudes towards Miscegenation during Mississippi's Reconstruction." *Journal of Mississippi History* 54 (Summer 2002): 125–45.

Waller, Altina L. "Community, Class, and Race in the Memphis Riot of 1866." *Journal of Social History* 18 (1984): 233–46.

Weinfeld, Daniel R. "'More Courage than Discretion': Charles M. Hamilton in Reconstruction-Era Florida." *Florida Historical Quarterly* 84 (Spring 2006): 479–516.

Wennersten, John R. "John W. Crisfield and Civil War Politics on Maryland's Eastern Shore, 1860–1864." *Maryland Historical Magazine* 99 (Spring 2004): 5–16.

West, Elliott. "Reconstructing Race." *Western Historical Quarterly* 34 (Spring 2003): 6–26.

Wetta, Frank. "Bloody Monday: The Louisiana Scalawags and the New Orleans Riot of 1866." *Southern Studies* 2 (Spring 1991): 5–16.

Wiener, Jonathan M. "Planter Persistence and Social Change: Alabama, 1850–1870." *Journal of Interdisciplinary History* 7 (Autumn 1976): 235–60.

Williams, John A. "The New Dominion and the Old: Ante-Bellum and Statehood Politics as the Background of West Virginia's 'Bourbon Democracy.'" *West Virginia History* 33 (July 1972): 317–407.

Williams, Learotha. "'Leave the Pulpit and Go into the School Room': Jonathan Clarkson Gibbs and the Board of Missions for Freedmen in North and South Carolina, 1865–1866." *Southern Studies* 13 (Spring/Summer 2006): 89–104.

Williams, T. Harry. "The Louisiana Unification Movement of 1873." *Journal of Southern History* 11 (August 1945): 349–69.

Williams, Teresa Crisp, and David Williams. "'The Women Rising': Cotton, Class, and Confederate Georgia's Rioting Women." *Georgia Historical Quarterly* 86 (Spring 2002): 49–83.

Wimmer, Larry T. "The Gold Crisis of 1869: Stabilizing or Destabilizing Speculation under Floating Exchange Rates?" *Explorations in Economic History* 12 (April 1975): 105–22.

Woodman, Harold D. "Chicago Businessmen and the 'Granger' Laws." *Agricultural History* 36 (January 1962): 16–24.

Woodward, C. Vann. "Yes, There Was a Compromise of 1877." *Journal of American History* 60 (March 1973): 63–75.

Wunder, John R. "Chinese in Trouble: Criminal Law and Race on the Trans-Mississippi West Frontier." *Western Historical Quarterly* 17 (January 1986): 25–41.

Young, Darius J. "Henry S. Harmon: Pioneer African American Attorney in Reconstruction-Era Florida." *Florida Historical Quarterly* 85 (Fall 2006): 177–96.

Zipf, Karin L. "Reconstructing 'Free Woman': African-American Women, Apprenticeship, and Custody Rights during Reconstruction." *Journal of Women's History* 12 (Spring 2000): 8–31.

———. "'The WHITES Shall Rule the Land or Die': Gender, Race, and Class in North Carolina Reconstruction Politics." *Journal of Southern History* 65 (August 1999): 499–534.

Zuczek, Richard. "The Federal Government's Attack on the Ku Klux Klan: A Reassessment." *South Carolina Historical Magazine* 97 (January 1996): 47–64.

———. "The Last Campaign of the Civil War: South Carolina and the Revolution of 1876." *Civil War History* 42 (March 1996): 18–31.

Unpublished Dissertations

Appell, Stephen M. "The Fight for a Constitutional Convention: The Development of Political Parties in North Carolina during 1867." M.A. thesis, University of North Carolina, 1969.

Bartlett, Laurence Wood. "Not Merely for Defense: The Creation of the New American Navy, 1865–1914." Ph.D. dissertation, Texas Christian University, 2011.

Behrend, Justin J. "Freedpeople's Democracy: African-American Politics and Community in Post-Emancipation Natchez District." Ph.D. dissertation, Northwestern University, 2006.

Breese, Donald H. "Politics in the Lower South during Presidential Reconstruction." Ph.D. dissertation, University of California at Los Angeles, 1964.

Carrier, John Pressley. "A Political History of Texas during the Reconstruction, 1865–1874." Ph.D. dissertation, Vanderbilt University, 1971.

Chapin, James Burke. "Hamilton Fish and American Expansionism." Ph.D. dissertation, Cornell University, 1971.

Downey, Matthew T. "The Rebirth of Reform: A Study of Liberal Reform Movements, 1865–1872." Ph.D. dissertation, Princeton University, 1963.

Gerber, Richard Allan. "The Liberal Republican Alliance of 1872." Ph.D. dissertation, University of Michigan, 1967.

Gibson, Guy James. "Lincoln's League: The Union League Movement during the Civil War." Ph.D. dissertation, University of Illinois, 1957.

Gold, Susanna W. "Imaging Memory: Re-presentations of the Civil War at the 1876 Centennial Exhibition." Ph.D. dissertation, University of Pennsylvania, 2004.

Gooden, Randall Scott. "The Completion of a Revolution: West Virginia from Statehood through Reconstruction." Ph.D. dissertation, West Virginia University, 1995.

Green, Stephen Keith. "The National Reform Association and the Religious Amendments to the Constitution, 1864–1876." M.A. thesis, University of North Carolina at Chapel Hill, 1987.

Griffin, Roger Allen. "Connecticut Yankee in Texas: A Biography of Elisha Marshall Pease." Ph.D. dissertation, University of Texas, 1973.

Hardison, Edwin T. "In the Toils of War: Andrew Johnson and the Federal Occupation of Tennessee, 1862–1865." Ph.D. dissertation, University of Tennessee, 1981.

Harris, Michael Keith. "Across the Bloody Chasm: Reconciliation in the Wake of Civil War." Ph.D. dissertation, University of Virginia, 2004.

Hennessy, Melinda Meek. "To Live and Die in Dixie: Reconstruction Race Riots in the South." Ph.D. dissertation, Kent State University, 1978.

Hicks, John Henry. "The United States Centennial Exhibition of 1876." Ph.D. dissertation, University of Georgia, 1972.

Hudson, Linda Sybert. "Jane McManus Storm Cazneau (1807–1878): A Biography." Ph.D. dissertation, University of North Texas, 1999.

Hume, Richard. "The 'Black and Tan' Constitutional Conventions of 1867–1869 in Ten Former Confederate States: A Study of their Membership." Ph.D. dissertation, University of Washington, 1969.

Kincaid, Larry George. "The Legislative Origins of the Military Reconstruction Act, 1865–1867." Ph.D. dissertation, Johns Hopkins University, 1968.

McCrary, James Peyton. "Moderation in a Revolutionary World: Lincoln and the Failure of Reconstruction in Louisiana." Ph.D. dissertation, Princeton University, 1972.

McGee, E. "North Carolina Conservatives and Reconstruction." Ph.D. dissertation, University of North Carolina at Chapel Hill, 1959.

McGraw, John Conger. "The Texas Constitution of 1866." Ph.D. dissertation, Texas Tech, 1980.

Morton, Jack Devon. "Ohio's Gallant Fight: Northern State Politics during the Reconstruction Era, 1865–1878." Ph.D. dissertation, University of Virginia, 2005.

Nicoletti, Cynthia. "The Great Question of the War: The Legal Status of Secession in the Aftermath of the American Civil War." Ph.D. dissertation, University of Virginia, 2010.

O'Donovan, Susan E. "Transforming Work: Slavery, Free Labor, and the Household in Southwest Georgia, 1850–1880." Ph.D. dissertation, University of California at San Diego.

Peterson, William Scott. "The Navy in the Doldrums: The Influence of Politics and Technology on the Decline and Rejuvenation of the American Fleet, 1866–1886." Ph.D. dissertation, University of Illinois, 1986.

Polakoff, Keith Ian. "The Disorganized Democracy: An Institutional Study of the Democratic Party, 1872–1880." Ph.D. dissertation, Northwestern University, 1968.

Price, Charles Lewis. "Railroads and Reconstruction in North Carolina, 1865–1871."
Ph.D. dissertation, University of North Carolina at Chapel Hill, 1959.

Rable, George. "But There Was No Peace: Violence and Reconstruction Politics."
Ph.D. dissertation, Louisiana State University, 1978.

Ray, Amanda J. "The Impact of Statehood and Republican Politics on Women's
Legal Rights in West Virginia, 1863–1872." M.A. thesis, West Virginia University,
2001.

Scroggs, Jack B. "Carpetbagger Influence in the Political Reconstruction of the
South Atlantic States, 1865–1876." Ph.D. dissertation, University of North
Carolina at Chapel Hill, 1951.

Silvestro, Clement Mario. "None but Patriots: The Union Leagues in Civil War and
Reconstruction." Ph.D. dissertation, University of Wisconsin, 1959.

Steiner, Dale Roger. "'To Save the Constitution': The Political Manipulation of
Foreign Affairs during Reconstruction." Ph.D. dissertation, University of
Virginia, 1973.

Summers, Mark Wahlgren. "Radical Reconstruction and the Gospel of Prosperity."
Ph.D. dissertation, University of California at Berkeley, 1980.

Swinney, Everette. "Suppressing the Ku Klux Klan: The Enforcement of the
Reconstruction Amendments, 1870–1874." Ph.D. dissertation, University of
Texas, 1966.

Thompson, George H. "Leadership in Arkansas Reconstruction." Ph.D. dissertation,
Columbia University, 1968.

Thompson, William Robert. "Illinois Constitutions." Ph.D. dissertation, University
of Illinois, 1960.

Woolfolk, Sarah. "The Role of the Scalawag in Alabama Reconstruction." Ph.D.
dissertation, Louisiana State University, 1965.

Index

Catholicism: hostility to, 62, 205, 218, 220, 246–48; and public schools, 229–30, 247, 375

Catron, Thomas B., 193

Cazneau, Jane and William, 223

Central Pacific Railroad, 10, 179, 195–96; Chinese labor builds, 198

Chamberlain, Daniel, 355–56, 366–67, 383–85

Chandler, Zachariah, 14, 209; caricatured, 157

Chase, Salmon P., 25, 137, 153; appointed chief justice, 9; and reconciliation, 14; and black suffrage, 141; presidential candidacy, 141–42, 150–51, 301; upholds Reconstruction, 153; death, 326, 346

Chicago Board of Trade, 344

Chicago, Burlington and Quincy Railroad, 189

Chicago Clearing House, 344

Chicago fire, 184, 268

Childs, George W., 217

Chinese, Indian attacks on, 197

Chinese immigration, 154, 197–99, 299; laws restricting, 199, 295

Chisholm, Jesse, 189

Chisholm, William, 386

Chisholm trail. See Abilene trail

Chivington, John M., 180

Christmas uprising, 57, 70

Churches. See Religion

Churchill, Winston S., 386

Cincinnati Convention, 306. See also Liberal Republican movement

Civil rights, 229, 292–23; and antebellum northern law, 9; and emancipation, 47–49; in black convention movement, 54; and Freedmen's Bureau, 55–57, 86–87, 100; and 1865 elections, 81; federal action on behalf of, 86–91; and Fourteenth Amendment, 90–93; Unionist attitudes toward, 101; protections in Reconstruction Acts, 103–4, 115–16; in constitutional conventions, 130–31; officeholding right, 131, 234; and segregation, 131, 239–41, 253; and Fifteenth Amendment provisions, 153–54; and Chinese immigration, 154, 197–99; and women's rights, 241, 243–46; court enforcement of, 242, 370; and 1872 election, 307–8, 309, 312; Supreme Court decisions about, 370–71. See also Civil Rights bill

Civil rights bill: 1866, 86–90, 115; 1875, 309, 322, 346, 351, 357, 361, 368–71

Civil rights cases, 370–71

Civil Service Commission, 309, 326

Civil service reform, 156, 157; liberals support, 154, 295–96, 304–6; Grant implements, 309; Grant abandons, 326; Tilden's view of, 374; Hayes endorses, 376

Civil War: purpose of, 1, 3–4, 11, 13–14, 16–18; impact on slavery, 7–9; end of, 10, 12–16, 31, 253, 395; economic legislation of, 11; and political suppression, 12; antiwar Democrats and, 12, 101, 145; and southern Unionists, 27–30, 33–34, 59–62; demobilization, 36–37, 211–13, 323; devastation of the South, 37–40; fear of war's renewal, 86, 97–98, 316–17, 368, 380–81; as a campaign issue, 98, 145, 311–13, 376, 378; demoralizing effect of, 155, 280–82; in West, 179–80; effect on expansionism, 205–6, 220; *Alabama* claims from, 215–18; Britain blamed for, 216; Cameron as war secretary, 226; activism encouraged by, 228; and health regulation, 232–33; and nostalgia, 305, 392, 396, 398

Clanton, James H., 177

Clayton, Powell, 258, 289, 291; elected governor, 133; defeats Klan, 264–65; and factional fights, 308, 323, 328–29

Cleveland, Grover, 396

Clews, Henry, 217, 228

Cochise, 298

Cockrell, Francis, 380

Cody, William F. "Buffalo Bill," 228

Colfax, Schuyler, 90, 141; and Credit Mobilier, 280, 324

Colfax massacre, 331, 370

"Colonizationist" (vote fraud), 278

Colonization schemes, 206, 211, 221–22, 432 (n. 16)

Colorado, 180, 201

Committee of One Hundred (New Orleans), 347–49

Comstock, Anthony, 234

Confiscation of property, 140; fears of, 12; property restored, 16, 43, 50, 80, 89; radical support for, 18, 83, 85–86, 109; Andrew Johnson and, 50, 64, 65, 66; black interest in, 50, 127–28; moderate rejection of, 128, 132; and constitutional conventions, 132; from Native Americans, 179, 187

Congressional Reconstruction: Fourteenth Amendment as peace settlement, 90–93, 97–99, 101; First Military Reconstruction Act, 102–6; Supplementary Reconstruction Act, 107–9; northern aid to party building, 118, 121, 129; legality challenged, 119, 139, 142; and Republican Party formation, 120–28; and constitutional conventions, 130–33; opposition to constitutions, 134–36, 142–45; constitutionality upheld, 153

Conkling, Roscoe, 304, 306, 326, 375

Connecticut, 145, 371; defeats equal suffrage, 20, 81

Conquered provinces theory, ix, 6, 17, 85 153

Constitution, U.S.: and Reconstruction, 6, 17, 84–86, 101, 103, 109, 153, 259–63; Democratic views of, 7–8, 17, 84–85, 94, 97–98, 104, 116, 142–45, 227, 228; and presidential power, 12, 24–25, 81–82, 85; Radical Republican view of, 17, 98; and federalism, 84–85, 91–92, 99, 105–6, 228, 241–43, 253–54, 267–68, 363–64; and Freedmen's Bureau, 86–89; and civil rights laws, 87–89, 91; and suffrage, 91–92, 364; and monetary expansion, 141–42, 344; and secession, 153; and inherent potential, 228; and Enforcement Acts, 267–72. See also Thirteenth Amendment; Fourteenth Amendment, Fifteenth Amendment; individual court decisions

Constitutional conventions, southern (1863–67), 22–26, 28–29, 34–35, 65–72, 79, 84, 95–97, 104

Constitutional conventions, southern (1867–69), 102–5, 107, 130–33; blacks' role in, 130; personnel, 130, 331; on disfranchisement provisions, 130–31, 133; on civil rights, 131, 133; on schooling, 131, 133; on debtor relief, 131–32; on homestead exemptions, 132; on internal improvements, 132–33; ratification of, 133–36

Constructive damages. See Alabama claims

Convict labor, 288, 394

Conwell, Russell, 160–61

Cooke, Henry D., 274, 280; and Freedman's Savings Bank, 217, 277

Cooke, Jay, 274, 277; and bond marketing, 11, 202, 217; Northern Pacific Railroad project and, 188, 202, 280, 302; and Alabama claims, 217; lobbying efforts of, 217, 280; and 1873 Panic, 337, 342

Cookman Institute, 299

Cooper, Peter, 219

Corbin, Abel. See Gold corner

Cornell University, 241

Corruption, 192–96, 279–96, 323–26; election fraud, 151, 256, 263, 276, 278, 292, 328–31, 379–80, 386, 389–90; in Indian contracts, 154, 158, 193–94; in the West, 154, 179, 183, 192–96; in customhouses, 154, 280–81, 304, 326; in Grant administration, 158, 193–94, 222–24, 280–81, 304, 325–27, 359, 372–73; in South, 175, 259–60, 284–91, 293–94, 296–97, 299, 318–21, 327–28, 329, 330, 354; railroads and, 194–96, 280, 288–89, 324–25; and expansionism, 222–25; wartime, 226, 282, 283; District Ring, 276–77, 296; Tammany Ring, 277–79, 374; antebellum, 282; blacks' response to, 285–86, 296, 318; and taxation, 289–90; and retrenchment, 294–95; and civil service reform, 295–96; northern response to, 296, 318, 321, 368; as issue in 1872, 304–6, 310, 314; as issue in 1874, 357; in disputed election, 379–80

Cotton, 200; war's devastation of, 38–39; northern interest in restoring, 40–41; and postwar recovery, 41–42, 144, 298–99; northern planters and, 122–23, 127; and British markets, 217; sharecropping in, 298–99, 300–301. See also Agriculture, southern

Couch, Darius, 95

Coushatta massacre, 353–54, 377

Cox, Jacob D., 156–57

Cox, Samuel S. "Sunset," 361

Cragin, Aaron H., 10

Crawford, Samuel J., 194

Credit Mobilier, 195–96, 280; investigated, 324–25, 326

Crook, George, 298

Crosby, Peter, 356–57

Cuban insurrection (1868–78), 213–14, 217–18, 222

Cuban bonds, 222

Currency. See Money

apportionment, 90–91; Owen's proposal, 91; black suffrage under, 91–93; and Confederate officeholding, 92–93, 104, 109, 112–13, 130, 140, 254, 256–57, 271, 303–4, 309; Tennessee ratification of, 93, 101; passage of, 93–94; southern rejection of, 99–100, 102; Johnson opposition to, 102; and segregation, 239–40; Supreme Court and, 242, 245, 370, 398; applied to corporations, 243, 398; and women's rights, 245; and federal intervention, 268, 271, 370; New Departure accepts, 301–2, 312, 378; under conservative governments, 397–98

Franco-Prussian War (1870–71), 156, 205, 206

Free labor ideology, 83, 235, 294, 302

Freedman's Savings Bank, 55, 275, 277, 301, 342

Freedmen's Bureau, 41, 54–57, 71, 97, 99, 100, 101, 109, 114; and Freedman's Savings Bank, 55; attitudes toward blacks, 47, 50–51; and education, 55; and Freedman's Savings Bank, 55; discipline of freed-people by, 55, 57, 76; and black testimony, 55, 100; white hostility to, 56, 65, 68, 80; renewed, 86–89; and Johnson veto, 89–90; provides Republican leadership, 120, 123; winding down, 140, 298; application to Indians, 181–82

Freedmen's Bureau bill, 86–90

Fremont, John C., 202

Furay, W. S., 127

Garfield, James A., 89, 383, 399; and Credit Mobilier, 324–25

Garland, Augustus, 335, 361–64

Garvey, Andrew, 278

Gary, Matthew, 366–67

Gens de couleur, 25–26

Georgia, 27, 31, 60, 99, 151, 170, 223, 225, 237, 266, 270–71, 291, 311, 317, 323, 336, 342, 398–99; physical reconstruction of, 38, 39, 40–42; emancipation in, 50, 51; Presidential Reconstruction in, 66, 68–69, 75, 80; Radical Reconstruction in, 119, 120, 126; constitutional conven-tion in, 131, 133; and ratification, 133–34; terrorism in, 149, 255–56, 257–58, 261, 263; Bullock administration, 254–64;

remanded to territorial status, 256–57; corruption in, 260, 264; railroads and, 287, 288–89, 290; conservative rule in, 367, 390–93

Georgia Reorganization Act, 256

Gilded Age (Twain and Warner), 192, 223. See also Pomeroy, Samuel S.

Gillem, Alvan C., 110, 111, 114

Glidden, Joseph F., 191

Godkin, Edwin L., 246; and liberal reform movement, 306. See also Nation

Gold corner, 283–84

Gordon, John B., 146–47

Gospel of prosperity, 125–28

Gould, Jay, 190; in Erie Ring, 283; and gold corner, 283–84

Grady, Henry, 390–91, 398

Grand Army of the Republic, 98, 145; and Decoration Day, 305

Grand Review, 36

Granger Laws, 231, 242–43; scaled back, 341

Grant, Ulysses S., 16, 83, 112, 232, 235, 244–45, 247, 253, 303–6; wartime career, 10, 14; in Swing around the Circle, 97; military role under Johnson, 98, 111–12, 136, 137, 139; and Mexico intervention, 98, 205; in 1868 campaign, 141, 145; elected president, 151–52; and Fifteenth Amendment, 154, 158; and civil service reform, 154–55, 156–57, 304, 309, 326; chooses cabinet, 154–59; caricatured, 157, 280–81; administration corruption and, 193–94, 222–24, 280–81, 304, 326, 372–73; and Alabama claims, 215–17; and Santo Domingo annexation, 220–27, 306; and Louisiana tangle, 227, 293–94, 330–32, 359–61; Mississippi interven-tion, 247, 356–57, 365; suppressing the Klan, 267–72; and District Ring, 277; and Gold Ring, 283–84; and amnesty bill, 303–4, 309; and 1872 campaign, 306–15; and Arkansas troubles, 334, 361–64; and Inflation bill, 344–45; and Redemption, 348, 367

Greeley, Horace, 165, 228; and Davis pardon, 16, 307; on removing dis-franchisements, 161–62; presidential campaign, 306–15, 347; caricatured, 311; death, 315–16, 346